"A stimulating source of ideas, and a conspectus of how broadly and deeply many archaeologists are thinking about the way their discipline relates to the modern world"
Times Higher Education Supplement

"This book is clearly organized and the material presented in a fair and often innovative manner."
Bryn Mawr Classical Review

"This volume presents a refreshingly wide set of topics, covered by an impressive and authoritative array of authors. This is archaeology understood in its broadest terms. Theory and method, ethics and practice, distant ages and recent moments, links to other disciplines, are all explored in this impressive and accessible collection."
Ian Hodder, *Stanford University*

"Bintliff has assembled a broad array of talented archaeologists, who present us with a rich portrait of contemporary archaeology. Technical yet easily accessible, this important book offers a thought-provoking analysis of many of archaeology's most pressing controversies. Both students and interested laypeople will find this a satisfying journey though the complexities of a rapidly changing, increasingly multidisciplinary archaeological world."
Brian Fagan, *University of California Santa Barbara*

John Bintliff is Professor of Classical and Mediterranean Archaeology at Leiden University. His previous publications include: *Natural Environment and Human Settlement in Prehistoric Greece* (1977); *Palaeoclimates, Palaeoenvironments and Human Communities in the Eastern Mediterranean in Later Prehistory* (with W. van Zeist, 1982); *European Social Evolution: Archaeological Perspectives* (1984); *Archaeology at the Interface: Studies in Archaeology's Relationships with History, Geography, Biology and Physical Science* (with C.F. Gaffney, 1986); *Conceptual Issues in Environmental Archaeology* (with D.Davidson and E. Grant, 1988); *Extracting Meaning from the Past* (1988); *The Annales School and Archaeology* (1991); *Europe Between Late Antiquity and the Middle Ages* (with H. Hamerow, 1995); *Recent Developments in the History and Archaeology of Central Greece* (1997); *Structure and Contingency in the Evolution of Life, Human Evolution and Human History* (1999); and *Reconstructing Past Population Trends in Mediterranean Europe* (with K. Sbonias, 2000).

A Companion to Archaeology

Edited by

John Bintliff

Advisory Editors
Timothy Earle and Christopher S. Peebles

© 2004, 2006 by Blackwell Publishing Ltd

BLACKWELL PUBLISHING
350 Main Street, Malden, MA 02148-5020, USA
9600 Garsington Road, Oxford OX4 2DQ, UK
550 Swanston Street, Carlton, Victoria 3053, Australia

First published 2004 by Blackwell Publishing Ltd
First published in paperback 2006 by Blackwell Publishing Ltd

1 2006

Library of Congress Cataloging-in-Publication Data

A companion to archaeology / edited by John L. Bintliff.
p. cm. – (Blackwell companion to archaeology)
Includes bibliographical references.
ISBN 0-631-21302-3 (alk. paper)
1. Archaeology. I. Bintliff, J. L. (John L.) II. Series.
CC173.C65 2003
930.1–dc21
2003009296

ISBN-13: 978-0-631-21302-4 (alk. paper)
ISBN-13: 978-1-4051-4979-2 (paperback)
ISBN-10: 1-4051-4979-5 (paperback)

A catalogue record for this title is available from the British Library.

Set in 9.5 on 11pt Sabon
by Kolam Information Services Pvt. Ltd, Pondicherry, India

For further information on
Blackwell Publishing, visit our website:
www.blackwellpublishing.com

This book is dedicated to my dear wife Elizabeth, and to our equally dear children, David, Esther, and Aileen, who all had to cope with my lengthy periods of preoccupation and absence when I was toiling at its creation.

Contents

List of Figures   x

List of Contributors   xiv

Acknowledgments   xvi

Introduction   xvii
    John Bintliff

Part I   Thinking About Archaeology   **1**

  1 Analytical Archaeology   3
      Stephen Shennan

  2 The Great Dark Book: Archaeology, Experience, and
     Interpretation   21
      Julian Thomas

Part II   Current Themes and Novel Departures   **37**

  3 Archaeology and the Genetic Revolution   39
      Martin Jones

  4 Archaeology and Language: Methods and Issues   52
      Roger Blench

  5 The Archaeology of Gender   75
      M. L. S. Sørensen

  6 Archaeology and Social Theory   92
      Matthew Johnson

  7 Materiality, Space, Time, and Outcome   110
      Roland Fletcher

  8 Archaeological Perspectives on Local Communities 141
      Fokke Gerritsen

9   Archaeology and Technology   155
    Kevin Greene

10 Time, Structure, and Agency: The Annales, Emergent
    Complexity, and Archaeology   174
    John Bintliff

Part III   Major Traditions in Archaeology in Contemporary Perspective   195

11 Archaeological Dating   197
    J. A. J. Gowlett

12 Chronology and the Human Narrative   206
    J. A. J. Gowlett

13 Archaeology and Indigenous Peoples: Attitudes Towards
    Power in Ancient Oaxaca   235
    Maarten Jansen

14 Classical Archaeology   253
    Ian Morris

15 The Archaeologies of Recent History: Historical,
    Post-Medieval, and Modern-World   272
    Charles E. Orser, Jr.

16 Animal Bones and Plant Remains   291
    Peter Rowley-Conwy

17 Ecology in Archaeology: From Cognition to Action   311
    Fekri A. Hassan

18 The Archaeology of Landscape   334
    T. J. Wilkinson

19 Archaeology and Art   357
    Raymond Corbey, Robert Layton, and Jeremy Tanner

20 Putting Infinity Up On Trial: A Consideration of the Role of
    Scientific Thinking in Future Archaeologies   380
    A. M. Pollard

21 Experiencing Archaeological Fieldwork   397
    John Bintliff

Part IV   Archaeology and the Public   407

22 Public Archaeology: A European Perspective   409
    Timothy Darvill

23 Persistent Dilemmas in American Cultural Resource
    Management   435
    Joseph A. Tainter

24 Museum Studies   454
    Linda Ellis

25 Relating Anthropology and Archaeology   473
    Michael Rowlands

26 Archaeology and Politics   490
    Michael Shanks

27 Archaeology and Green Issues   509
    Martin Bell

Index   532

Figures

6.1	Conway Castle, ca. 1300: a royal castle of Edward I.	101
6.2	Bolton Castle, late fourteenth century.	102
6.3	Hardwick Hall, later sixteenth century.	103
7.1 (a)	San camps, southern Africa, 1960s AD.	113
7.1 (b)	Djeitun assemblage settlement plans, central Asia, fifth millennium BC.	113
7.2 (a)	Gorilla lying on nest.	117
7.2 (b)	Plans of camps of mountain gorillas.	117
7.2 (c)	Spatial patterning in camps of mountain gorillas (*Gorilla gorilla*) in the Virunga Mountains, Uganda and Rwanda.	117
7.3 (a)	Plan and reconstruction view of a latte, the elevated houses indigenous to Guam.	119
7.3 (b)	Spatial patterning in the dimensions of latte in village sites in Guam.	119
7.4 (a)	Plan of Munyimba (Ghana), a village of the Konkomba, in the early 1970s.	121
7.4 (b)	Complex spatial signature of Munyimba.	122
7.5 (a)	The Bororo village, Amazonia, 1950s AD: schematized ideal of the variety of clan divisions and the material/social non-correspondence.	123
7.5 (b)	Bororo village.	123
7.6 (a)	The Wang Cheng ideal.	124
7.6 (b)	Da-du, the Mongol Yuan Dynasty capital in north China where modern Beijing now stands (thirteenth to fourteenth centuries AD).	124
7.7	The operational ceiling on the duration of compact urban settlements from circa 400 BC to the mid-nineteenth century AD.	127
7.8 (a)	The growth and decline of the areal extent of Abbasid Baghdad, Mesopotamia.	128

7.8 (b)	The growth and decline of the population of Abbasid Baghdad.	128
7.9	The extent of Angkor (Cambodia), late twelfth century to circa sixteenth century AD.	130
7.10	The growth and decline of Rome and Constantinople and the Roman and Byzantine empires.	132
7.11	The outcome triad.	134
10.1	Monumental equestrian statue in Durham marketplace, northeast England.	178
10.2	Location of Montaillou, Ariège, southwestern France.	179
10.3	Settlement evolution in the territory of Lunel Viel, Languedoc.	180
10.4	Rise of the royal Capetian dynasty in France during the Middle Ages.	183
10.5	Territorial competition in the later Middle Ages between the kingdoms of England and France in the territory of modern France.	184
10.6	Population cycles in Provence, fourteenth to eighteenth centuries AD.	184
11.1	Radiometric dating techniques available through the Pleistocene, showing the approximate time ranges of their application.	198
12.1	The lead aerosol record of Arctic ice cores gives a dated index to production of lead and silver through the last 5,000 years.	221
13.1	Codex Tonindeye (Nuttall), p. 36: the landscape of Yuta Tnoho (Apoala).	243
13.2	Monte Albán, South Platform, Stela 1: the ruler seated on the mat and the throne, with his staff and nahual attributes.	245
13.3	Yucu Ndaa Yee (Tequixtepec), Carved Stone 19: Lord "Roaring Jaguar" climbs the throne in the year 6 L.	246
13.4	Ceramic urn from Tomb 5, Cerro de las Minas, Ñuu Dzai (Huajuapan): the transformation of a ruler into a fire serpent.	246
13.5	Codex Borgia, p. 29: the preparation of a hallucinogenic ointment in the Temple of the Death Goddess Cihuacoatl.	248
14.1	Archaeological theory in 1988 (cartoon by Simon James).	254
14.2	Archaeological theory in 1998 (cartoon by Matthew Johnson).	255
16.1	Diagrammatic views of a cereal ear and spikelet (top) and an animal skeleton (bottom), showing nomenclature used in the chapter.	292
16.2	Frequency of animal skeletal parts, comparing the goat bones collected by C. K. Brain from modern herders' villages at Kuiseb River with frequencies of antelope and other animal bones from the hominid site of Makapansgat.	296
16.3	Seasonality of hunting and gathering at Abu Hurayra 1, Syria.	299
16.4	Lengths of pig second molar from a population of modern wild boar from Turkey compared to those from Neolithic Gomolava in Serbia.	301
16.5	Animal husbandry from Bronze Age Grimes Graves, Norfolk.	302

16.6	Pie charts showing plant frequencies at two Bronze Age settlements in Denmark: Lindebjerg and Voldtofte.	303
18.1	Diagram showing the nature and preservation of archaeological sites along a transect through the rainfed, marginal, and desert zones.	342
18.2	The hinterland of Sohar Oman showing landscape features in the desert, zone of survival, and zone of destruction.	343
18.3	Prehistoric field systems near Daulatabad, southeast Iran.	344
18.4	Field scatters and infilled canals near Mashkan Shapir, Iraq.	346
18.5	Landscape zones in the area of Lake Assad, Tabqa Dam, Syria, showing shifts in the locations of major Uruk (fourth millennium BC), Early Bronze Age, and Late Bronze Age centers.	348
18.6	Dhamar, highlands of Yemen.	350
19.1	Attic black-figure amphora signed by Exekias, with scene combat between Achilles and Penthesilea, ca. 530 BC.	358
19.2	Bison bull in the Lascaux cave, Montignac, southern France.	360
19.3	An Aurignacian lion-human statuette from the Hohlenstein-Stadel cave, Germany.	360
19.4	Very regular Middle Palaeolithic handaxe, Lailly, Vanne river valley, France.	365
19.5	Cycladic marble figurine, ca. 2500 BC.	372
19.6	Bronze ritual vessel, *hu*. Shang Dynasty, 1300–1100 BC.	372
19.7	Olmec head, from La Venta Archaeological Park, originally San Lorenzo, Veracruz, Mexico.	374
20.1	Simple model of relationship between complexity of society and rates of environmental change.	388
22.1	Schematic representation of the archaeological management cycle.	416
22.2	Comparison of principal attributes identified in archaeological value systems.	423
22.3	Bar chart showing the number of field evaluations carried out each year in England between 1990 and 1998.	425
23.1	Exploring the ruins of the American southwest.	437
23.2	Discussions of how to practice cultural resource management in *American Antiquity*, 1969–98.	443
23.3	Discussions of archaeological significance, 1973–93.	443
23.4	Implicit criteria for the National Register evaluation of archaeological sites in northern New Mexico.	444
27.1	The bog at Ravensmose, Jutland, Denmark: at the spot marked by the stone the Iron Age Gundestrup Cauldron was found.	517
27.2	Archaeology and nature conservation around Newbury, UK: the route of the Newbury bypass A34T, and associated archaeology and Holocene sediments.	518

27.3   The Gwent Levels Wetland Reserve, Goldcliff, South Wales.   522
27.4   View of the saline lagoons after completion.   523
27.5   Holme-next-the-Sea, Norfolk: (a) "Seahenge" wooden circle on the
        foreshore; (b) another tidal wooden feature; (c) reconstruction
        of the "Seahenge"; (d) a peat block thrown up on the beach near
        the "Seahenge."   524

Contributors

Martin Bell is Senior Lecturer in the Department of Archaeology, Reading University.

John Bintliff is Chair of Classical Archaeology in the Faculty of Archaeology, Leiden University.

Roger Blench, formerly of the Overseas Development Institute, is a self-employed consultant specializing in development anthropology based in Cambridge, at CISPAL.

Raymond Corbey is a Lecturer in Philosophy at Tilburg University and Professor in the Epistemology of Archaeology in the Faculty of Archaeology, Leiden University.

Timothy Darvill holds a Chair in Archaeology and the Historic Environment in the School of Conservation Sciences, Bournemouth University.

Linda Ellis is Professor and Director of the Museum Studies Program, San Francisco State University.

Roland Fletcher is Associate Professor in the Department of Archaeology, University of Sydney.

Fokke Gerritsen is Lecturer in Archaeology in the Department of Archaeology and Prehistory, the Free University of Amsterdam.

J. A. J. Gowlett holds a Chair in the School of Archaeology, Classics and Oriental Studies, Liverpool University.

Kevin Greene is a Senior Lecturer in the Department of Archaeology, University of Newcastle upon Tyne.

Fekri A. Hassan is Petrie Professor of Archaeology at the Institute of Archaeology, University College, London University.

Maarten Jansen is Dean of the Archaeology Faculty and holds a Chair in Indian American Archaeology at Leiden University.

Matthew Johnson is Professor of Archaeology at the University of Southampton.

Martin Jones is George Pitt-Rivers Professor of Archaeological Science in the Department of Archaeology, Cambridge University.

Robert Layton holds a Chair in the Department of Anthropology, Durham University.

Ian Morris is Jean and Rebecca Willard Professor of Classics and Professor of History in the Department of Classics, Stanford University.

Charles E. Orser, Jr. is Distinguished Professor in the Department of Sociology and Anthropology, Illinois State University.

A. M. Pollard holds the Chair of Archaeological Science in the Department of Archaeological Sciences, Bradford University.

Michael Rowlands holds a Chair in Material Culture in the Department of Anthropology, University College, London University.

Peter Rowley-Conwy is Reader in Environmental Archaeology in the Department of Archaeology, Durham University.

Michael Shanks holds a Chair in Classics in the Department of Classics, Stanford University.

Stephen Shennan is Chair of Theoretical Archaeology at the Institute of Archaeology, University College, London University.

M. L. S. Sørensen is Senior Lecturer in the Department of Archaeology, Cambridge University.

Joseph A. Tainter is Project Director of Cultural Heritage Research at the Rocky Mountain Research Station, Albuquerque.

Jeremy Tanner is Lecturer in Greek and Roman Art and Archaeology at the Institute of Archaeology, University College, London University.

Julian Thomas holds a Chair in Archaeology in the Department of Art History and Archaeology, University of Manchester.

T. J. Wilkinson is Lecturer in Near Eastern Archaeology in the Department of Archaeology, Edinburgh University.

Acknowledgments

The chapters in this volume were submitted between 1999 and early 2002. In late 2002 and again in 2005 all authors had the opportunity to update text and references. However, this large volume would not have come and remained together, as a coherent platform for presenting the rich variety of contemporary archaeology and archaeologists, had I not had the constant and enthusiastic support of my production and commissioning editors at Blackwell – Jane Huber and Annie Lenth – who deserve very great thanks.

Introduction

As someone who has been teaching archaeology for many years, at all levels, I have been struck particularly over the last ten years by the difficulty of finding a single volume which portrays the richness of the modern discipline in the ways archaeologists try to understand the human past. That is not to say that there are no excellent textbooks which systematically present key topics suitable for students or interested laypersons starting up in the discipline: Kevin Greene's *Archaeology: An Introduction* and Renfrew and Bahn's *Introduction to Archaeology*, regularly revised, present all the main facets of the subject. Yet for the next stage, the more advanced student or amateur, the field instantly fragments. There are very good single volumes on specialized aspects of the archaeologist's craft, such as geoprospection (Clark, *Seeing Beneath the Soil*), and there are encyclopedias and compendia of key topics (Fagan, *The Oxford Companion to Archaeology*; Barker, *The Companion Encyclopedia of Archaeology*). Either these are explicitly specialist reviews of subdisciplines within archaeology, as with the former class, or with the latter group, we are presented with summaries of subtopics within the discipline offered in something of a "shopping list" of discrete essays retaining the character of an encyclopedia entry. Finally, there are books which aim to cover the ways archaeologists think about the past (such as Hodder, *The Archaeological Process*, or Johnson's *Archaeological Theory: An Introduction*). In reality these are written by enthusiastic proponents of one particular school – the postprocessual (inspired by postmodernist thought) – and fail to represent the true range of intellectual approaches and ways of seeing that exist in the current discipline.

What, it seemed to me, was missing and needed, was a single and necessarily large volume in which I invited a cross-section of that great variety of archaeologists to do one thing above all: talk about their field with enthusiasm and personal commitment. In this way I hope to provide the reader with a real feel for the breadth of our modern subject. These are then very personal essays, reflecting what the contributors love and loathe, and they were asked specifically to avoid worthy "laundry-list" summaries of their field in favor of expressing their own priorities and the things that are most important and exciting in the area of interpreting the past that they are international experts in.

In one, however fat, volume, it has not been possible to include chapters covering every subdiscipline or approach within contemporary archaeology, and indeed you will now see that such encyclopedic coverage was far from the aim of the book. Moreover, of the large number of scholars canvassed for possible participation, several were unable in the end to find the time to compose an essay. Nonetheless, in the existing 27 contributions, the reader is in a position to touch the pulse of archaeological approaches to the past, and it seems the pulse is running fast in the highly personalized essays presented in this volume.

I would also like to mention that the stimulus to edit such a book arose from my experience in teaching a course in comparative theory: Archaeology and twentieth-century thought. Whereas archaeology seemed to focus its textbooks on encyclopedic summaries, its introductions to specialisms within the discipline, and its theory books on the promotion of a particular intellectual position, other disciplines were producing more inclusive volumes which covered the entire range of ways of looking at their discipline. My initial inspiration was in geography, where a series of books and edited volumes by Ron Johnston (e.g., *The Future of Geography, Geography and Geographers, Philosophy and Human Geography,* and many others) explicitly address the need to offer balanced combinations of the often contradictory and even warring intellectual factions which have become common in most humanities subjects since World War II. Another good example is Terry Eagleton's *Introduction to Literary Theory,* which wonderfully gives the reader an understanding of the varied ways scholars have "read" and do "read" and interpret literature, while at the same time telling us what he considers the strengths and weaknesses of each approach, and equally importantly where he stands himself; but in the end he wants his book to bridge intellectual divides rather than reinforce them.

The current volume also rests on the editor's own conviction that a healthy discipline needs endless variety of opinions and methods and should avoid doctrinaire ideologies, yet at the same time in practical terms the student and interested layperson

will gain little from seeing merely fragmentation and polarized attitudes. Much better if we encourage the understanding and then application of a wide spectrum of approaches. This is surely a plea for eclecticism, since I am opposed to the limitations which instantly arise when one adopts a particular perspective – whether it is an animal bone specialist who shows no interest in how culture affects what we eat, or a "high theorist" who insists we have to read the past through the dark glasses of Marxism. Of course, eclecticism is in its own way a biased perspective, as it privileges integration over factionalism and champions a non-political, non-ideological stance. Put simply, it says: "We don't know what happened in the past: we need all the tools, mental and practical, at the archaeologist's disposal, to find out and comprehend past societies."

Is this in effect a version of postmodern relativism? Are all approaches equal? If so, why does this volume lack chapters by astro-archaeologists, ley-line advocates, and treasure hunters? I have elsewhere outlined my views on how diverse approaches can be combined, without sacrificing the special value of each constituent part of the eclectic battery of methods and ways of thinking. In this I have been inspired by one of the greatest of modern thinkers – the philosopher Ludwig Wittgenstein – and his peculiar way of seeing human intellectual endeavors (Bintliff 1995, 2000). Famously, Wittgenstein suggested that different methodologies and approaches are best seen as complementary rather than oppositional, most strikingly in the case of traditional friction between the humanities and the sciences. Not only do we need such varied approaches to understand a multifaceted world, but also they are not commensurable: a useful contribution in one methodology is best evaluated in terms of that method, not by the standards and doctrines of another. In archaeology, then, there should be a political approach, and it cannot be judged by the empirical and statistical measures of archaeophysicists trying to determine the source of a copper object through laboratory analysis. But neither is it necessary to insist that metal analyses be subordinated to studies of power and gender in the past, or even in the present. Wittgenstein argued that there are standards of good practice and judgment which have to be applied within professional communities of scholars, but these differ widely according to the "language game" or body of rules and procedures which have developed within each approach – and all disciplines comprise a spectrum of such approaches. A good way to see the eclectic archaeologist faced with the current variety of ways of seeing the past is Wittgenstein's image of the craftsman going out on a job with a large bag full of tools – each ideally suited to a particular application within the remit of the profession.

Finally, I shall offer some introductory comments on the 27 chapters before you in this volume, emphasizing my own reaction to each contribution.

In chapter 1, "Analytical Archaeology," Stephen Shennan turns to an older source of ideas in our discipline, the late David Clarke. Shennan argues that archaeology needs to focus more on its own specific data – material culture – and believes that the study of patterning in past objects and structures – "Archaeology is Archaeology" – is more than the sum of intended actions by past human actors. It is only archaeologists who can finally see in perspective how the material past was formed, and we must be wary of limiting ourselves to what we think past peoples thought about their world – especially of wanting to explore the past in terms of our modern concerns.

In chapter 2, "The Great Dark Book: Archaeology, Experience, and Interpretation," by Julian Thomas, we are led into a very different worldview, the archaeologist first and foremost needing to be a philosopher, and a very particular kind of philosopher – one focusing on the experience of being in the world. We cannot in a way escape our own embeddedness as modern researchers, so that encounters with past so-

cieties must be and should be translations into our own ways of life; past data serve to feed our own concepts of value or meaning.

In chapter 3, "Archaeology and the Genetic Revolution," a more global perspective from Martin Jones conveys the excitement of the fast-developing field of archaeogenetics. Sensitive to the murky history of racist models of biological purity and the tendentious use of migrationism to bolster imperialist ambitions during the later nineteenth and early twentieth centuries, modern studies utilizing the high-technology techniques of genetic research are nonetheless beginning to establish on a firmer basis the pathways of human origins and expansion over the world, the different areas of discovery and diffusion of the key plant and animal domesticates involved with the shift from hunter-gatherer to agricultural and pastoral economies, and finally the more recent migrations and invasions of human groups. Jones' belief that critical application of scientific analyses can ward off the misuse of results by politically motivated groups is a clear provocation to other scholars who adopt a postmodernist perspective in which value-free research is an impossibility, and allows us all to think more deeply about the issues involved.

Chapter 4, "Archaeology and Language," by Roger Blench, likewise deals with a topic that has had its past share of overspeculation and murky associations with racist or nationalist politics. Blench shows us how the subject of the origin and spread, as well as modification, of the world's multitudinous languages, is finally emerging into a more analytical, politically sensitive field, in which archaeology – rather than being an often-abused prop – is becoming a vital tool for calibration and testing of linguistic theories. Links to genetic research are promising, but we find that no simple correlation between biology and languages should be expected. Indeed, the many and varied ways in which spoken communication systems can disperse and change require a new sophistication in understanding both demography and social processes well beyond the traditional culture = people concept which archaeologists also till recently took for granted.

In chapter 5, "The Archaeology of Gender," by Marie Louise Sørensen, a rather different way of linking past experience and modern concerns is revealed. Here we clearly see that contemporary changes in Western society regarding gender roles have had a strong effect on everyday research into past societies. We want to know now whether traditional gender stereotypes have relevance to past societies in general, and if so how did they arise and decay – if not, then perhaps the revelation of past variety can help us comprehend the rapid social changes going on around us. Sørensen admits, however, how difficult gender research can be, working with material culture, unless historic sources are abundant.

In chapter 6, "Archaeology and Social Theory," Matthew Johnson deals with the importance of social theory for archaeologists. This is something we can all relate to from our daily experience, and thus understand why it should rank highly in archaeological aims. For Johnson, human agents and their power to change their world are central in social life.

In chapter 7, "Materiality, Space, Time, and Outcome," Roland Fletcher seems to me to combine the material "neutrality" of Stephen Shennan with the intentional human actors of Thomas and Johnson. Material culture – here, settlements – shows trajectories and repeated norms. These are both affected by the aims of conscious societies and also by their own inbuilt pressures of structural consistency and directional change. The creations of human culture may be more than the sum of their constituent parts.

Chapter 8, Fokke Gerritsen's "Archaeological Perspectives on Local Communities," shows the renewed importance of studying social groups at small spatial scales in current research work. Perhaps owing to the considerable transformations in Western social life since the later twentieth century, we are questioning older assumptions about how social relations are formed, maintained, and reorganized. This chapter finely demonstrates how this exciting field is built around fine-detailed excavation sequences in areas such as the Netherlands. I find it significant in the context of the underlying program of this edited volume that Gerritsen challenges the assumption which has become too common in archaeological thinking since the 1960s: that older work is of little relevance to the research one does today. In the case of social change, he shows that internal cultural factors may be balanced by external political or environmental factors, when small-scale local groups undergo important transformations, thus finding it valid to combine earlier "processual" and modern "postprocessual" approaches in making sense of the Dutch social sequences he describes for us in his case study.

In Chapter 9, "Archaeology and Technology," Kevin Greene both excites us with the neglected importance of this facet of material culture change, and challenges our preconceptions about the development of human technologies. Just as he finds fault with those who underplay the real significance of improved or effective means of production, he also reminds us that effectiveness may be defined socially or in terms of the number of people benefiting, rather than through our modern, elitist, Western, and high-tech viewpoint. The history of technology from an archaeological perspective is certainly infinitely less interesting as a thinly disguised narrative of Western triumphalism, than as an investigation into the varied ways cultures in time and space have perceived their methods of producing and transforming material culture, and those of others they are brought into contact with.

In chapter 10, "Time, Structure, and Agency: The Annales, Emergent Complexity, and Archaeology," John Bintliff explores further some of those themes of complex meshing of past individuals and elaborate social and cultural structures raised in Fletcher's contribution (chapter 7). Moving between human agency – conscious or otherwise –

and complex institutions such as small and very large political groups, between individual events and tendencies only revealed at time spans well beyond human lives – requires well-adapted methods and approaches. In this chapter a number of these are introduced and their integration attempted.

In chapters 11 and 12, "Archaeological Dating" and "Chronology and the Human Narrative," John Gowlett shows us how vital diverse approaches can be, to allow archaeologists to make interpretations of the past. In his case the role of dating methods for past events and processes both constrains and enables us in our readings of the past. Putting human actions into sequences, and calculating rates of change, proves to be fundamental to all our understanding of how and why things may have happened – at all timescales. In demonstrating these theoretical principles, Gowlett also takes us on a roller-coaster tour through the current versions of the human narrative – from our beginnings as undistinguished higher apes among other species, to the foundations of urban civilization.

Chapter 13, "Archaeology and Indigenous Peoples," by Maarten Jansen, is a powerful and committed essay on the need for archaeologists to engage in entirely new ways with native peoples, when there is strong ethnic and cultural continuity from the past societies under investigation. This is all the more pressing as a moral obligation when, as so often, these peoples remain marginalized economically and politically in their own countries, deprived even of genuine respect for their ancestral achievements and self-awareness. A second theme raised very clearly in this chapter is the fashion in which native history and prehistory has been molded into preconceived ideas of the positive evolution of such societies into modern state structures, despite evidence to the contrary in terms of their contemporary plight. Nonetheless, as indicated here for Mexico, and in other chapters in this volume (e.g., chapters 23 and 24), the rights of native

peoples have become formalized in a growing mass of formal legislation and initiatives by academics and government organizations, although much archaeological research remains "outsider," with objectives and concepts which need to be carefully unpacked for inbuilt biases, not least through direct engagement with the ideas, language, and memories of modern-day representatives of past communities. As well as the intrusive obsession with state formation, Jansen tellingly criticizes our contemporary Western overconcern with projecting "power" into past societies where alternative social concepts may have been more influential.

In chapter 14, "Classical Archaeology," Ian Morris takes us into a field of archaeology with a traditionally strongly defined (or even patrolled) border of interest – one of the first such to emerge in the discipline. For Morris, a distinctive feature of current ideas in this field is the challenge to the founding charter of classical archaeology, whose origins are intimately linked to a rather supremacist view of Western civilization and its classical roots. As classical archaeology forges closer links to other historical archaeologies, and the boundaries to associated civilizations in time and space appear more permeable, Morris draws a parallel with the deconstruction of Orientalism as a biased, Western mode of packaging and neutralizing Islamic societies.

In chapter 15, "The Archaeologies of Recent History: Historical, Post-Medieval, and Modern World," Charles Orser gives to the study of early modern historical archaeology a specific goal and overall purposeful dynamic, focused on the stages and effects of global capitalism and globalization. This means directing attention to themes such as colonialism, ethnocentrism, capitalism, and modernization. Archaeology has a particular value even here, despite the dense textual sources available, as it offers easier and more accurate access to groups underrepresented even in recent historical documents – the poor, exploited, illiterate communities, especially slaves and peasants. The evidence revealed is moving and indeed shocking, while the crusade is inspiring.

In chapter 16, "Animal Bones and Plant Remains," Peter Rowley-Conwy, in a brief compass, offers us a global and long-time-span vision of how he and other specialists analyzing "ecofacts" from the human past can painstakingly bring out central aspects of human community life. Lifestyles and economies, social and ethnic differences, all can be comprehended from the at-first unpromising debris of broken bones and burnt plants and other "rubbish" revealed in excavation. One aspect clearly brought out in this chapter is the progressive refinement of methodology since the first studies in this field, and deepening of questions that can successfully be asked of the material. The reader will be struck by the complementarity between such empirical and scientific "middle-range" approaches and the more humanistic, ideological, and philosophical chapters found elsewhere in this Companion.

In chapter 17, "Ecology in Archaeology: From Cognition to Action," Fekri Hassan challenges us to cut the Gordion knot of deciding whether the environmental setting of past human communities is the product of nature or culture. Both human perception and action, and ecological processes in which humans are unwitting or knowing participants, are essential. Hassan warns us that extreme culturalism, which gives no scope to natural forces, such as some current forms of phenomenology in archaeological approaches to the environment, fails to deal with the long-term realities of human ecology as a form of mutual survival of habitats and their varied species of occupants.

In chapter 18, "The Archaeology of Landscape," Tony Wilkinson likewise sees the humanly occupied landscape as a unity, in which we cannot sacrifice considerations of ecological balance and survival, nor the pragmatic study of technology and forms of land use, nor the role of human perception, in any thorough appreciation of how a particular stretch of countryside was lived in and utilized by a past society. On a more practical level, his treatment of how we can extrapolate from fragments or windows of palaeoenvironments is a striking insight into how landscape archaeology is carried out in practice.

In chapter 19, "Archaeology and Art," Raymond Corbey, Robert Layton, and Jeremy Tanner offer a balanced comparison of ways of approaching art for archaeologists, arguing that we can and should combine previously polarized viewpoints which stressed either individualistic, particularizing interpretations, or generalizing cross-cultural readings. Particular case studies of past art can then fruitfully be placed in the ways they illustrate compatibility with, or divergence from, wider understandings of artistic production and visual meaning, with the expectation that both are likely to be relevant. There are exciting prospects for future studies in this field.

In chapter 20, "Putting Infinity Up On Trial," Mark Pollard takes on those current archaeological theorists who reject "scientism" in archaeology and the strong position that hard science professionals have carved out as specialist collaborators on archaeological projects. Pollard argues that science with a capital S has and will continue to play a vital role in achieving recognizable landmark insights from the past of relevance to the future. Yet, at the same time, he demonstrates that technical science in archaeology has come more and more to depend on data and refinements emerging from archaeological insights, thus making a dialectical model of the relationship between archaeological chemists, physicists, and biologists, etc. and archaeologists the most realistic model. On the other hand, by stressing the importance of clear and testable procedures, Pollard – to my mind – reminds us of the complementary way that parts of the archaeological process gravitate towards "scientism" in judging successful operations, while others feel that their kinds of work – perhaps in artistic, emotional, symbolic, political readings and researches into the past – succeed better with more humanistically oriented, hermeneutic and empathetic skills. As noted elsewhere in this introduction, such a Wittgensteinian view of subdisciplinary variety is for me a source of strength rather than conflict. Another aim, however, of Pollard's contribution is to challenge the postmodernist concern with uniqueness: tautologically all archaeological sites are unique, even each trench or bone, but not only does privileging each item or locality run against financial realities for modern-day professional archaeology, but also it fails to meet the requirement to evaluate the wider significance archaeological research should try to achieve to justify itself as a source of general knowledge beyond meaningless description. This is a point well expressed that demands all our attention.

In chapter 21, "Experiencing Archaeological Fieldwork," John Bintliff challenges most accepted versions of the *raison d'être* for archaeological activity. Undermining claims that archaeology primarily serves the nation or the public, this essay claims instead that delving obsessively into the relics of past societies is an inherited biological propensity closely related to grassroots scientific research, a human drive to take apart the world that has had survival value for our species. Thinking about archaeology (i.e., theory) is most useful when it helps us locate new sources of data, but generally merely reflects passing intellectual fashions that will not survive in the longer-term knowledge-base of the discipline, and – provocatively – this kind of activity is rather poor in skill-level compared to practical archaeology. Real progress in archaeology can be measured in the rising mountain of structured knowledge of what happened in the past, continually constraining or even eliminating weaker models, while strengthening better models, of the key processes involved in its trajectory and character.

In chapter 22, "Public Archaeology: A European Perspective," Timothy Darvill exposes the conflict, past and present, over our archaeological heritage and its use for modern purposes. Both manipulation for political ends and attempts at neutral research and presentation can be shown. Today, the ever-increasing role of public archaeology as opposed to academic university and museum-based research calls for careful attention not only to the interpretive goals sought by the latter, but also to the day-to-day realities of public interest and financial responsibility in which the former are deeply embedded.

In chapter 23, "Persistent Dilemmas in American Cultural Resource Management," Joseph Tainter gives us an American viewpoint on the same topic of heritage archaeology. This contribution is a passionate plea to reopen the debate on the nature of public archaeology, particularly the imbalance between financial goals and academic value. Since the latter constantly gets updated, old lists of what sites can tell us – such as condition the amount of money and attention they are allocated by public archaeology – fail to help us gain better insights into the past.

In chapter 24, "Museum Studies," Linda Ellis takes us into another prime sector of archaeology with which the public or public institutions are closely involved. The remarkable and accelerating processes of questioning within the last generation as to what museums are for and what they do or should do are well exposed, and placed in the historical contexts of how museums have evolved. A strong set of opinions is given on issues of education, repatriation of objects, and the place of museums in contemporary society.

In chapter 25, "Relating Anthropology and Archaeology," Michael Rowlands shows a masterful understanding of the tortuous relations between these two disciplines. He takes a strongly political reading of the dominance of Western origin myths and colonial–imperial worldviews in the ways in which both archaeology and anthropology have striven to write the story of the development of human social forms. The challenge of globalization is not so much the further spread of such Western ideologies, but the possibility of backward flows from other cultures in terms of alternative ways of conceiving society and social change. Another theme is the current convergence between the two disciplines through a common interest in the active roles material culture can play in both reproducing and aiding the transformation of human societies.

In chapter 26, "Archaeology and Politics," Michael Shanks offers us a (characteristically) strong argument for the conscious politicization of archaeology and archaeologists. He makes a powerful case for the history of our discipline as dominated by political ideologies and manipulations, claiming that the modern situation is no different from earlier versions of our subject. Archaeology has never been a "value-free" empirical subject, nor can it be; indeed, Shanks sees little role for it unless it is an active force in contemporary debates about the nature of human society now and for the future. Archaeology is less a mode of scientific discovery than a mode of cultural production firmly locked into modern issues.

In chapter 27, "Archaeology and Green Issues," Martin Bell also confronts us with debates very much of the moment, surrounding a discipline of relatively recent emergence but with major political influence: ecology. Many of the themes of this contribution are revelatory. If we care about nature conservation there is a problem as to what is a natural environment. What are the vital arguments for identifying which fragments of our past environmental context mean something important to us today? Can environmental history be deployed to help us predict and influence global environmental futures? Many other important issues in human engagement with the physical world – past, present, and future – are skillfully set forth in this passionately argued contribution.

References

Bintliff, John 1995. "'Whither archaeology?' revisited." In M. Kuna and N. Venclova, *Whither Archaeology?*, pp. 24–35. Prague.

Bintliff, John 2000. "Archaeology and the philosophy of Wittgenstein." In C. Holtorf and H. Karlsson, *Philosophy and Archaeological Practice*, pp. 152–72. Göteborg.

Part I
Thinking About Archaeology

1

Analytical Archaeology

Stephen Shennan

The mere recognition and definition of an activity by the production of a concomitant set of artefacts constitutes the transmission of information or a message . . . A child brought up amongst motor-cars and skyscrapers is differently informed to another child born amongst stone axes and pig-hunts.

Clarke (1968: 86)

Introduction

Archaeology today is subject to the tyranny of the present. Its ideas are reduced to their sources in contemporary or recent society and subject to retrospective disapproval. That the origins of culture history go back to dubiously motivated nationalism, or that "New Archaeology" can be seen as an aspect of 1960s American imperialism, encourages the assumption that the approaches have no intrinsic value, rather as if the origin of some of Darwin's ideas in nineteenth-century capitalist economics should justify discarding the theory of evolution by natural selection (cf. Klejn 1998). With the rise of the cultural heritage movement more interest is devoted to the ownership of archaeological material and its political and economic implications, than what the material tells us about the past. Furthermore, the focus of interpretation now places archaeologists in the role of ethnographers of a lost "ethnographic present," struggling hopelessly against the

fact that the people we need to talk to are long dead and most of the residues of their lives long decayed. One example is the current preoccupation with how prehistoric people perceived past landscapes, where studies leave it willfully unclear whether the perceptions proposed are those of the investigator or of the past people being studied. Finally, our desire to see people in the past as the active, knowledgeable agents we believe ourselves to be, means requiring all material culture variation to result from self-conscious identity signaling and all change to be the outcome of the conscious choices of individuals with existentialist mentalities who walk clear-sightedly into the future.

In contrast, this chapter assumes that the aim of archaeology is to obtain valid knowledge about the past. It tries to show that archaeologists do not need to be failed ethnographers. It argues that there are diachronic patterns in the past which we can discern retrospectively but of which people at the time would have been totally unaware, or only perceived from a limited perspective, and which can only be explained from the point of view of the present-day archaeologist. This does not mean that we are condemned to producing teleological accounts of "progress" leading to the present, but that we should investigate the past in a way that plays to archaeologists' strengths, which undoubtedly lie in the characterization of long-term patterning in past societies. Furthermore, such investigations should provide a basis for supporting their claims, which goes beyond mere assertions on the part of the investigator appealing to some undefined notion of plausibility. Accordingly, this chapter is an argument for *Analytical Archaeology* in both the senses intended by Clarke: the characterization of diachronic patterns and processes through the application of analytical methodologies.

Diachronic Patterns and Culture History

Within the American or European traditions, the only archaeological approach which has ever studied diachronic patterning in the archaeological record seriously is culture history, originating with Kossinna and Childe in Europe and with Kroeber and Kidder in North America. Its aims involved the characterization of cultural traditions, including spatial extent and changes through time. These two versions differed significantly.

In Europe "cultures" were characterized by distinctive artefact types associated chronologically, geographically, and contextually. They were represented by static distribution maps of particular periods, leading to change being seen as the comparison of successive "snapshot" maps. Partly this was because European cultural descriptions were qualitative rather than quantitative; for example, cultures might be defined by the presence of a particular kind of painted pottery.

In North America, in contrast, the approach developed by culture history was quantitative, with the construction of so-called "battleship curves": chronologically ordered sequences showing the frequency of different stylistically defined ceramic types in successive assemblages (see Lyman et al. 1997). Through time these types showed a characteristic pattern of origin, followed by increasing popularity to a peak, in turn succeeded by decline and disappearance. The resulting double-lenticular curve had the shape of a battleship hull. By looking at patterns in these curves for particular sites or regions it was possible to see that at certain points in time there were major breaks in such sequences, where several types came to an end and others started; more commonly, there was a more gradual pattern of different types coming into fashion and going out again.

What both European and American versions of culture history shared, was an interest in explaining cultural change and a set of assumptions making this possible. The central assumption was that the spatial or chronological entities identified represented human group traditions. It followed from this that major changes occurred through the replacement of one tradition by another and therefore of one people by another, at least where material culture production was domestic rather than in the hands of specialists. Within the European tradition, this idea suited the relatively short timescales available for change, and the nationalistic view of peoples as historical actors having pasts and destinies. Lesser changes were seen as resulting from diffusion. Both migration and diffusion were considered unproblematic concepts.

When the New Archaeology emerged in the 1960s, there was some interest in developing the culture historical ideas (e.g., Deetz 1965), but the dominant Binfordian strand rejected norms and traditions. It took the view that the key to understanding culture change was to see the artefacts produced by human communities as a means of adaptation, rather than as reflections of population replacement or cultural influence. In detail though, its protagonists appreciated that material culture was multi-dimensional, affected by a variety of factors, and explored the implications of this. For example, changes in the size of ceramic serving vessels might signal changing sizes of the groups which ate together, rather than an incursion of a new population which preferred vessels of a different size, while new vessel forms might indicate new food consumption practices, perhaps associated with the emergence of new patterns of social interaction or differentiation.

Lyman et al. (1997: 224) suggest that North American culture history failed because it used the *archaeological* units it had created, which were largely stylistic and defined by the archaeologist, as *anthropologically meaningful*, supposing them to correspond to the cultural classifications of the people who used the artefacts, or to produce useful information about function and adaptation. Indeed, a key argument of the New Archaeology was that classifications of the data could not be taken as somehow natural. Rather, classifications are developed for specific purposes and, depending on the purpose, one might use completely different sets of attributes of a group of artefacts as the basis of a classification.

The implication of this perspective was that cultural complexes defined by culture historians either didn't exist or didn't matter. What was left of the issues which they raised was subsumed under "style," which was regarded as a residue, that variation in artefacts which didn't seem to have any obvious functional explanation (cf. Binford 1962).

Analytical Archaeology

The only large-scale systematic attempt to transform this culture historical tradition in the light of the early stirrings of the New Archaeology and parallel developments in other disciplines, such as geography, was David Clarke's *Analytical Archaeology* (strongly criticized by Binford 1972).

Clarke (1968: 20) presented archaeology as a discipline in its own right, arguing that the data it studies are so unlike those of other disciplines that archaeology has to develop its own systematic approach. This involved three main objectives: the definition of fundamental entities, a search for repeated regularities within and between them, and what he called "the development of higher category knowledge" (Clarke 1968: 21). He defined a hierarchical set of fundamental entities, from the *attribute* (the "atomic" level), through *artefact*, *assemblage*, and *culture*, up to what he called a *technocomplex*, a broad response to specific environmental and/or technological conditions. A single set of processes operated on these different entities, albeit differently at different levels of the hierarchy, including invention, diffusion, and cultural selection. In specific circumstances, the combined operation of these processes, in varying combinations, could lead to other processes, such as cultural growth, decay, and disintegration (Clarke 1968: 22). In contrast to the culture historians, these differing levels of cultural entities were conceived not as lists of traits but as dynamic systems characterized by such systemic processes as negative and positive feedback.

At all levels beyond the "atomic" one of the attribute itself, *key attributes* could be identified whose continued joint covariation expressed the survival of a particular inner pattern or structure (Clarke 1968: 71). These covarying sets were characterized by strong negative feedback processes, which ensured that they stayed in the same relation to one another over time. Cultural entities, whether artefact types or cultures, ceased to exist when a specific set of through-time correlations between attributes disintegrated, and new cultural entities came into existence when new relatively fixed constellations of attributes emerged. Outside the core set of attributes others were more free to vary. Because cultural entities are not capable of immediate and complete transformation they can be regarded as (semi-) Markovian systems: systems in which the transition probabilities from one state to the next depend on previous system states (Clarke 1968: 63).

In fact, cultural systems are essentially systems for transmitting acquired information; even the recognition and definition of an activity by a concomitant set of artefacts constitutes information transmission (Clarke 1968: 86). New information will not be accepted if the dislocation introduced cannot be reduced to vanishing point (Clarke 1968: 97). Nevertheless, since the pooled innovation rate of groups of cultures is correspondingly greater than the innovation rate of a single culture, it follows that the integration and modification of innovations derived from diffusion will provide most of the variety within a given system (Clarke 1968: 122; cf. Neiman 1995).

For Clarke then, it was diachronic trajectories that were central – the patterns of correlation between different attributes through time at any given level of the hierarchy. It follows that the primary aim in classifying data is to identify different vertical traditions (Clarke 1968: 148), and only secondarily to ascribe things to phases, which are more artificial entities than vertical traditions, given the problematical nature of contemporaneity in most archaeological situations. Within this framework an artefact type is not simply something arbitrarily defined by a specific analyst's artefact classification system, but has a reality as a highly correlated core of attributes accompanied by an outer cloud of attributes which have decreasing levels of correlation with the core (Clarke 1968: 196). The resultant types are real but fuzzy.

Through time such types change and new types emerge which are *transform types*, linked by descent to earlier types, and distinct from *independent types*, "not connected or derived from one another although they may be used within a single cultural assemblage" (Clarke 1968: 211). Change represented by transform types linked by descent is very different from change characterized by replacement of a set of types by new independent types.

At the level of the cultural assemblage, change works in a similar way. Diachronic cultural entities have formative phases in which much variety is generated from multiple sources and gradually integrated into a pattern, which then remains relatively stable (Clarke 1968: 279). One way in which this often occurs is through the occupation of new ecological and/or social environments, resulting in rapid rates of change: "As this cumulative change progresses, the possible developmental trajectories or formats become increasingly restricted as the traits are highly integrated within a functional whole" (Clarke 1968: 253). However, at levels of the hierarchy higher than the society or culture – the culture group or technocomplex – the entities are less tightly integrated (Clarke 1968: 287).

Clarke summarized his approach by suggesting that archaeology has a small number of regularities useful in archaeological interpretation (Clarke 1968: 435–6).

- *The inherent space-time population regularities of archaeological entities.* These include the battleship curve pattern in which attribute and type states increase then decrease in popularity through time, and the patterned intercorrelation through time of attributes forming particular types at low levels of the hierarchy of entities, or of types forming particular cultural assemblages at a higher level.

- *The inherent system regularities of archaeological entities as related kinds of special system.* These include his general model of archaeological systems as semi-Markovian systems linked to contextual systems, with historically generated transition probabilities from one state to another, and a capacity for dramatic system changes when the introduction of new features reaches a particular threshold.

- *The inherent system regularities of archaeological entities as parts of sociocul-*

tural information systems, in particular the "continuity hypothesis," the idea that sociocultural systems change so as to minimize short-term disruption of the system.

- *The inherent distribution and diffusion regularities of archaeological entities as parts of sociocultural population networks.* For example, since the internal integration defining a culture depends on a set of key artefact types, any area which is claimed as the origin of such a cultural entity must show a set of sources from which these key elements developed and then became integrated with one another.

This final systematization of the culture historical tradition by Clarke was never followed up; it remained moribund for over twenty years in Anglo-American archaeology (cf. Shennan 1989a) and indeed has no descendants. As noted already, processual archaeology was dominated by synchronic studies of function and adaptation, while postprocessual archaeology has been concerned with political critique and studies of past meaning. Clarke's scheme sketched out in abstract terms a way in which Binford's devastating critique of culture history could be transcended and the study of culture change addressed, but no one was interested and indeed it is perhaps difficult to see how the approach could have been carried forward at the time, despite Clarke's presentation of an array of modern analytical techniques in the second part of his book.

Darwinian Archaeologies

Since the end of the 1980s, however, the issues raised by culture history have attracted renewed interest from a source with very different theoretical antecedents, through the emergence of various "evolutionary" or "Darwinian" archaeologies. Like most such labels, this one covers an enormous range of often mutually antagonistic views (see Boone and Smith 1998; Lyman and O'Brien 1998).

The unifying element is that all of them draw on aspects of the modern neo-Darwinian evolutionary synthesis in biology in attempting to explain culture change (examples may be found in Teltser 1995; Maschner 1996; Steele and Shennan 1996; O'Brien 1996; Shennan 2002). It is impossible here to describe the different strands in any detail, but we may distinguish two poles of the approach.

One of them derives from the assumption that in evolutionary terms humans are like any other animal. Accordingly, as a result of natural selection, humans have a propensity to take decisions, consciously or otherwise, in the light of the costs and benefits of the consequences for their reproductive success or inclusive fitness. Culture makes little difference to this process because cultural behavior which leads to deviation from this cost-benefit calculus will not last very long. The best-known substantive approach based on these assumptions is optimal foraging theory (e.g., Kaplan and Hill 1992), which generates predictions about the subsistence strategies which will best meet these criteria in a given set of circumstances and compares them with actual subsistence strategies or their material residues (e.g., Mithen 1990; Broughton 1997). Although this end of the spectrum of evolutionary approaches is interesting and important, it is the cultural end of the continuum, and its relevance to the *Analytical Archaeology* agenda, which will be explored further here.

This argues that cultural variation cannot be explained solely in terms of criteria linked to the reproductive success of humans as "culture bearers," but that culture can be considered as a distinct kind of inheritance system, since cultural traditions are handed down from one generation, and indeed from one day, to the next, by specifically cultural mechanisms. Accordingly, we can explore the analogies between the operation of the cultural inheritance system and the biological inheritance system of the genes. The attraction is that the processes of biological evolution and genetic transmission, and the factors affecting them from one generation to the next, are much better understood than cultural transmission, so we can learn from exploring both positive and negative analogies between the two systems and the way they operate. This process may lead to the development of useful theory helping us to understand particular cases of cultural stability and change.

The best-known version of the analogy between cultural and genetic transmission is Richard Dawkins' concept of the meme (Dawkins 1976; 1982: 109–12; see also Blackmore 1999 for a more extended analysis):

A unit of particulate inheritance, hypothesized as analogous to the particulate gene, and as naturally selected by virtue of its "phenotypic" consequences on its own survival and replication in the cultural environment.

Despite the fact that there are serious problems with the meme concept (for a summary, see Shennan, 2002), and that an adequate understanding of the manner in which culture operates as an inheritance system is far from achieved, there is considerable evidence that it does operate in this way.

Boyd and Richerson (1985: 46–55) reviewed extensive psychometric and sociological evidence supporting the view that social learning acts as an inheritance mechanism by producing significant similarities between learners and those they learn from, which cannot be accounted for by genetic transmission or correlated environments. They concluded: "The calculated heritabilities for human behavioral traits are as high as or higher than measurements for behavioral and other phenotypic characters in natural populations of non-cultural organisms . . . Thus it may be that [social learning] is as accurate and stable a mechanism of inheritance as genes" (Boyd and Richerson 1985: 55).

Ethnographic studies suggest that the ways of carrying out many human practices exhibit a strong element of social learning, including many practices which create social institutions (e.g., Toren 1990) and those involved in craft production (Shennan and Steele 1999). In other words, they are phenomena subject to inheritance. Archaeological evidence adds support. Some specific practices acquired by social learning show considerable similarity over time even in the absence of strong functional constraints; ceramic decoration practices defining regional traditions provide one obvious example.

This returns us to the agenda of culture history, at least in descriptive terms: we need to reconstruct cultural phylogenies, histories of specific traditions, because we cannot understand cultural variation in time or space without them, just as we cannot understand organic evolution without reconstructing biological phylogenies. Whether such phylogenies will have the relatively straightforward branching structure of most biological trees or whether the branches will be completely intertwined with one another is something still to be resolved (cf. Moore 1994; Mace and Pagel 1994; Collard and Shennan 2000).

Acknowledging cultural inheritance then has important consequences for the kinds of archaeology we should be carrying out, since we have to revisit the concerns of culture history. But this is not the only such consequence. It also follows that we cannot define a set of functional attributes or types resulting from adaptive processes and a different set of stylistic features which simply reflect learning and interaction histories. Every practice which is socially learned, whether it is a way to hunt or a way to decorate a pot, in other words whether obviously functional or not, will have a history of descent. Furthermore, in any given case we cannot establish whether or not the presence of a particular feature in several different nearby cultural contexts arises from a common convergent adaptation without first carrying out a phylogenetic analysis: adaptation can only be understood through a diachronic approach which recognizes descent. Equally, style is more than a residue after the function has been taken out. Style is simply a "way of doing." Some "ways of doing" are designed with immediate practical consequences, but they can possess a historical signature as well.

The Coherence of Cultural Traditions

As Clarke pointed out (see above), the through-time reality of cultural traditions, whether at the level of individual artefacts and artefact types, or at the level of "cultures," depends on continued patterns of correlation between the elements of the entity concerned. Clearly, there will be different factors leading to the maintenance or disintegration of these diachronic patterns of correlation between sets of attributes characterizing a particular artefact type, or between practices in different areas of life. There will be external limiting constraints, such as functional requirements; there will be the mutual compatibilities required in different aspects of a single process, such as pottery-making, or of different processes which are carried out together, for example, the embedding of lithic procurement in a mobility pattern conditioned by the requirements of hunting expeditions; and there will be the extent to which the different activities or elements are transmitted from one person to another in similar ways, not to mention variations in the pattern and strength of social sanctions concerning appropriate ways of doing things.

The nature of archaeological cultures is much better addressed from this vertical diachronic perspective than by looking at synchronic cultural distributions, as is usually done, since, by focusing on the latter, we get little further than pointing out that distributions of particular features never coincide with one another, so that it is implausible to think of cultures as real entities in any sense (Shennan 1978, 1989b).

In descent and diachronic continuity terms we can think of a continuum of possibilities

as regards cultural coherence (Boyd et al. 1997). At one extreme, whole cultures may be transmitted between generations, hermetically sealed from others, each characterized by its own worldview. This possibility, favored by ethnic nationalists and others who regard cultures as unique constellations of meaning, understandable solely in their own terms, seems unlikely given that diffusion certainly occurs, and that in synchronic distributional terms it is impossible to identify such perfectly coherent blocks, as we have seen. At the other end of the spectrum we have a situation where there is no spatial or temporal coherence: people always make their own decisions about how to carry out any specific activity on the basis of their own trial and error experience and the alternatives to which they are exposed. The temporal coherence we see in the archaeological record, together with the importance of social learning, suggests that this extreme is as unlikely as the first.

A more likely possibility than either of the two extremes is that there are core traditions (cf. Clarke's "key attributes") whose components stick together over time and provide a basic cultural framework, which has a major influence on social life but does not organize everything, so that there also exist "peripheral" cultural elements not closely tied to the core (Boyd et al. 1997: 371). The latter authors cite a number of anthropological cases where such core traditions are maintained over long periods. One example is a study by Rushforth and Chisholm (1991) on linguistic groups of the Athabaskan language family, whose social behavior was linked to the language spoken because they were related historically by culture birth. They concluded that the cultural values of these groups were "genetically related" to one another, since they "originated in and developed from a common ancestral cultural tradition that existed among Proto-Athabaskan . . . peoples . . . this cultural framework originated once . . . and has persisted (perhaps with some modifications) in different groups after migrations separated them from one another" (Rushforth and Chisholm 1991: 78; quoted in Boyd et al. 1997: 374). Similar conclusions are reached by Vansina (1990; quoted in Boyd et al. 1997: 375) in his study of African political traditions: despite extensive outside influence, internal factors determined development and meant that traditions remained recognizably continuous even though they changed and branched in different directions. As we have seen already, the key to understanding in such cases is the identification of cultural homologies (similarities arising from common descent).

Similar ideas are discussed by Rosenberg (1994), who also favors the idea that cultural cores exist; what he calls, following Gould and Lewontin (1979), the cultural *Bauplan*, "the central ideational component of its superstructure system" (Rosenberg 1994: 320). A culture remains itself, "as long as the systemic integrity of its *Bauplan* is maintained" (Rosenberg 1994: 320). On this view though, in contrast to that of processual archaeology, a culture is not an adaptive system but a self-replicating reservoir of information which is differentially used by real actors in the world, whether individuals, families, or larger entities such as communities. Because the elements of the *Bauplan* are tightly linked, not only are they not easily changed, but also they can themselves constrain innovation and lead to cultural stasis.

Such a view can accommodate the well-rehearsed argument from structuration and *habitus* theory (Giddens 1984; Bourdieu 1977) that individuals are not robots mechanically reproducing their culture, but are constantly using and modifying cultural resources to achieve their own ends. However, mere agency is insufficient as an account of the process of change because we have quite clear archaeological evidence of periods of stasis and of others when change occurs rapidly. In other words, saying that in one period the outcome of myriad actions based on individual agency is that people continue doing the same thing, while in another it leads to people engaging in new forms of action, only pushes the problem back a step.

Rosenberg (1994: 326) suggests that innovations/novelty which have the potential to break up an existing *Bauplan* are most likely to be extensively adopted when they are essential to individual/family survival; more often than not in the context of "infrastructural stress" or new economic/ecological challenges. In particular, such processes of cultural disintegration and the formation of new cultural *Baupläne* are likely to occur in new circumstances which will produce an increase in the rate of innovative behavior, in small groups physically separated from their larger parent population, because the social sanctions maintaining the existing *Bauplan* are likely to be weaker (Rosenberg 1994: 330). The new core which emerges will have a strong stochastic element: founder effects, in terms of those elements of the cultural repertoire which exist within the small sub-population; chance effects of transmission in the small population, relating for example to the number of children particular families have; and the compatibility of specific elements of the old cultural *Bauplan* with the new practices. Such situations arise particularly in the context of migration processes, which have consistently produced punctuated change.

But the cultural core or *Bauplan* phenomenon is not the only plausible point on the continuum of cultural coherence outlined above. Towards the other extreme we have the case where there is no cultural core but rather a series of distinct groups of elements, each with its own distinct pattern of descent. Boyd et al. (1997: 377) suggest that in general smaller coherent units are more likely than large ones in the case of cultural attributes, because different elements of people's cultural repertory will be acquired at different times from different people for different reasons. Furthermore, the rates of change in different areas of cultural practice may be very different. In some cases, such as the rituals of the Mountain Ok of New Guinea, famously described by Barth (1987), they change extremely quickly, so similarities due to common descent rapidly become dissipated. However, we need not consider that either the "cultural core" view or the "multiple packages" view is right or wrong. It seems plausible to suggest that in some cases there are genuine, powerful, "cultural cores" and in others there are not. The point is not to decide the issue *a priori* in principle, but to find out which is relevant in any particular case and then try to explain why.

There is every reason to assume that these issues can be approached archaeologically; for example, by looking at patterns of correlation between different types through time in different assemblages, or by comparing the descent relationships between sites with regard to different types of material. The pattern of cultural descent relationships between sites for pottery decoration, for example, may be very different from that for house form.

These diachronic material culture patterns are real and are not an epiphenomenon of anything else. They have their own internal logic, since the way they change depends on their own state at a given time: this is the essence of an evolutionary process. Change can only operate on the forms or practices inherited from previous generations. New social conditions, for example, may lead to changes in pottery-making, but those changes will be responses to the existing practices and organization of pottery-making. Moreover, the sort of knowledge we acquire from describing and explaining these patterns is in no sense an inferior kind of knowledge to that obtained by talking to people or reading written sources. As Clarke (1968: 86) says, people's activities and the material environment around them play a key role in creating their consciousness.

This diachronic approach clearly represents a move away from "presentist" archaeological ethnography. It is not trying to provide an inevitably inadequate account of what it felt like to be living, for example, in the region of Stonehenge in the late Neolithic. The patterns it deals with are only recognizable to the global retrospective view of the archaeologist and are only com-

prehensible through archaeological analysis. Not only would the perspectives of the social actors concerned have been almost entirely limited to the specific time and place in which they were living (cf. again the Mountain Ok, Barth 1987, for a discussion of this issue), but also the kinds of practices whose outcome we study would not most of the time have been the object of conscious thought. Accordingly, while we can happily accord people their capacity for conscious agency, doubtless submerged most of the time in their daily routines, and while the explanations we come up with must not contradict what we know about people and the way they act, a desire to write an intuitively accessible "people's prehistory" – a tabloid human interest story – should not blind us to the fact that many important patterns and processes would not have been immediately visible. This may even be the case in the present-day context of global scientific research; for example, despite the spending of enormous amounts of money and a global perspective, it is still not clear how much impact human activity has been having on climatic patterns and it is likely to become so only in retrospect.

Explaining Stability and Change

So far I have been arguing for the importance of describing diachronic patterns as an archaeological enterprise. In some respects, the culture historians achieved this with considerable success. Their failure lay in assuming that "cultures" were always real entities at the high coherence end of the spectrum, which has just been described. The degree of coherence has to be established, not assumed, and the multidimensionality of the variation in the archaeological record which the New Archaeologists established suggests that high coherence is less likely rather than more.

Under a different guise, this issue of coherence has also been an implicit concern in some structuralist approaches. The premise behind these studies is that there are symbolic structures generating social action which lead to similar patterns and symbolic relationships in different spheres of activity; for example, the organization of burial space and domestic space (e.g., Hodder 1982). Most such studies are purely synchronic, of course, examining symbolic relationships in a notional present, but essentially they are based on a claimed pattern of coherent correlation between different material culture phenomena. Whether such patterns of coherent correlation really are based on some generative structure which, for example, leads to common patterning in domestic and burial space, or whether they simply represent our rationalizations and explanations of the observed correlations, is another matter. Of course, such synchronic studies never have to face up to the question of the mechanisms which create or maintain the patterns. In fact, failure to do this is one of the most important weaknesses in one of the few such studies which have attempted to take a diachronic view, Hodder's (1990) study of symbolic structures in the European Neolithic. As Sperber (1985) has pointed out, "structures" are abstractions which do not as such have causal power. Ideas and practices can only spread through time and space by taking some public form which is passed on from one person to another.

At this point then we need to outline a framework for understanding the processes responsible for the patterns of stability and change we observe. Our object of study is not past people but the traditions they were involved in perpetuating and changing. Archaeologically, as we have seen, it is the history of these practices, as represented in their residues, that we observe in the record from our privileged position. However, this is not the most important reason for adopting such a perspective, which is simply that traditions and social institutions are always prior to any individual: norms and social contracts are not invented anew each day but depend on those prevailing the day before. Individuals are born into this flow of

traditions and with propensities derived from a long biological heritage. Accordingly, our aim must be to understand how people's actions, consciously and unconsciously, alter those traditions and practices. The ways in which it can occur are many and various.

One of them is copying error. People can alter the way they do things quite unwittingly. In many circumstances this will not matter. If one person unwittingly decorates a pot in a slightly different way from the norm, this will not make any difference at all if there are many potters, unless some at least begin to deliberately copy the innovation. In other circumstances though, copying error can make a difference. For example, if a small number of elders carry out an initiation ceremony at relatively rare intervals then, as their memories fade, with relatively few people to check against, change can be quite rapid through this process alone. This seems to be the process responsible for the rapid divergent evolution of ritual reported by Barth (1987) for the Mountain Ok. The result over time is a cultural drift process which has no other cause than successive erroneous copying among small numbers of people who are not in a position to keep it in check.

Other processes can also produce such drift. For example, if pottery-making is transmitted from mothers to daughters and a particular mother has more surviving daughters than others, who in turn have more reproductively successful daughters themselves, then the result will be that the variations in pottery-making which characterized the mother who started the sequence will become more prevalent in the population. This latter sort of founder effect is of particular significance in small, often pioneer colonizing, populations. The initial members of a small group separating from a larger population are most unlikely to be culturally representative. If the pioneering group is successful in expanding and producing its own increasingly large group of descendants, their cultural repertoire will be based on the particular variants which characterized the founders, and it may well look very different culturally from the descendants of the main population from which its founders initially separated (cf. the discussion of *Baupläne*, above).

In fact, such demographic issues are more widely relevant. If a particular population is expanding, then much of its cultural repertoire will expand with it because of the importance of parent–offspring cultural transmission, even if that repertoire has nothing to do with the reasons why the population is expanding. Similarly, if it goes extinct, then those aspects of its cultural repertoire which have a strong element of vertical transmission will go extinct too, even if they were not the reason for the decline. If past demographic patterns had been relatively unchanged, representing a slowly rising growth trend as often assumed, these demographic phenomena would not make much difference. However, it has become increasingly clear that past populations have been much more dynamic than we appreciated until the advent of modern genetic studies, which have enabled the identification of bottlenecks and expansions.

Other processes of potential change to cultural trajectories may be more conscious. Just because someone has learned from their parents a particular way to make an arrowhead, for example, or the best time to plant a crop, it does not mean they will always follow it. They may experiment with alternatives, especially if their current way of doing things does not seem very successful. If they permanently adopt their new variation, it is likely to be copied by their children. If it appears to be more successful than what other people are doing, it may be copied by them as well. From the "tradition-centered" perspective which is being advocated here, we may imagine some sort of competitive process between different practices, where the selective environment for that competition is the human population, or certain elements of it. To give a slightly more extended example, we can imagine two different ways of hafting an ax blade present

within a human population (cf. Pétrequin 1993), one of long standing and widely prevalent, the other relatively novel and little used. These methods of ax hafting can themselves be considered in population terms and their population trajectories traced through time as the two types compete with one another. The selective environment in which the competition takes place is the human population of ax makers and users. Decisions will be made about which form of ax haft to make in the light of a number of factors; for example, the size of trees to be cut down (which may change as clearance proceeds and primary gives way to secondary forest); the raw material sources available (which may affect the form and the size of the ax blade); the ways in which axes are held and used; within a broad least-effort framework which assumes that, other things being equal, people would rather spend less effort cutting down a tree, rather than more.

This sort of relatively conscious selection process need not just operate in very practical domains. Another case might be competition between existing and novel methods of enhancing sexual attractiveness. Furthermore, if people decide to switch to new modes of enhancing perceived sexual attractiveness, they may also go a step further and start copying attributes of a sexually attractive or prestigious person which are not actually anything to do with the reasons why they are sexually attractive or prestigious, perhaps their style of speech. Finally, people may change what they do or the way that they do it simply to conform to the majority; for example, if what they have learned from their parents is ridiculed by their peers (Boyd and Richerson 1985).

Of course, in some areas of life, whether the consequences of a particular action are good or bad may not be at all obvious until long after the event, which adds a considerable element of uncertainty to the generation of novelty and argues in favor of adopting existing modes of behavior whose consequences in older individuals can be observed, or simply accepting what one first learned from a member of the older generation. The result is that such practices may be largely insulated from competition and continue undisturbed.

In fact, it seems likely that what people learn as children in their natal household, in addition to their evolved psychological propensities, provides a foundation which considerably affects their susceptibility to novelty to which they are subsequently exposed, especially if this cannot be judged against obvious standards of instrumental rationality. The fact that initial learning from close relatives of the older generation creates an important filter against the subsequent acquisition of incompatible cultural practices is a main reason for the existence of specific "cultural logics," and for some of the regularities in the patterns of change in cultural systems which Clarke discussed. Moreover, such filters are often enhanced by the existence of sanctions against behavior not corresponding to traditional practices, where the severity of sanctions and the strictness of adherence required are themselves norms which can vary through time in response to selective pressures, such as those relating to "grid" and "group" in Douglas' (1978) well-known scheme.

One more aspect of the relatively conscious decision-making processes which have a selective effect on continuity and change in cultural practices must be mentioned: the fact that decision-making powers are not evenly distributed through populations. Some people, such as political leaders, may be in a position to make decisions in certain areas of life on behalf of a large number of others who have much less autonomy. This has important consequences. First, even if the overall population is very large, if the population of decision-makers is very small then major changes can potentially occur as a result of the sort of chance processes discussed above in relation to copying error. Second, selection of such practices will be in terms of criteria which benefit the decision-makers. It seems possible that the Japanese rejection of guns and the eventual

Chinese rejection of ocean-going navigation should be seen in this light (cf. Diamond 1998).

It remains to mention briefly two more or less conscious processes which have a bearing on issues of cultural stability, or at least processes where conscious actions have unintended dynamic outcomes of which people are likely to be unaware. The first concerns game theory.

When people interact to achieve some end which each has in mind, the strategy to adopt cannot be decided in advance and then applied to obtain the end in view, because the best approach to adopt will depend on what the other person does. Moreover, it is quite easy for the outcome to be sub-optimal for both of them even though both could have done better if they had adopted different strategies. Game theorists have explored a variety of different theoretical games and examined the payoffs to the individuals concerned when different strategies interact repeatedly. In some cases one strategy takes over, since this always gives the best return to both players. In other cases the equilibrium best outcome may involve a mix of two different strategies within the population, at a specific proportion. Such optimal equilibrium outcomes can be established by mathematical modeling or computer simulation. In some cases it turns out that when different strategies are played against each other in this way an equilibrium can emerge in which strategies continue to be maintained in the population even though they do not show *modular rationality* – they are not a rational choice in terms of the payoffs obtained in specific situations (Skyrms 1996: ch. 2).

The significance of game theory from our point of view is that, as with all the other practices we have been discussing, we can imagine populations of social strategies evolving over time and changing in relative frequency as they compete with one another in terms of the payoffs that they give to the individuals using them. Given enough time an equilibrium will emerge, but the precise equilibrium reached may be dependent on the specific history of the interactions. As an example, we might imagine a hypothetical case where one strategy to obtain social advantage is to hold a major funeral feast when a group member dies, involving the deposition of large amounts of grave goods, while an alternative is to pass on the wealth to the next generation to use as "capital" to build up a social position. It is hard to imagine having the information to explore the payoffs and dynamics in a real past situation, at least in prehistory. Nevertheless, it may still be useful to think in game theory terms and it brings social strategies into the same diachronic framework of looking at the trajectories of past populations of cultural practices that we have seen in the other areas discussed.

In a similar vein are models derived from complexity theory involving "self-organized criticality" (e.g., Bentley and Maschner 2000). These have been used to explain the distributions of species lifespans and extinctions in the fossil record. They hypothesize that patterns in such events – for example, the scale of extinction events in terms of the number of species that go extinct at the same time – result from the interactions between "agents" which are competing to survive within a limited space. Such interconnected agents, whose success depends on one another, could include artefact styles (Bentley and Maschner 2000). In other words, complex interactions produce specific types of dynamics simply as a result of their interconnectedness and complexity. It remains to be seen how the consequences of such ideas will be worked out in archaeology (see, for example, Bentley and Maschner 2001), but the existence of the phenomenon of self-organized criticality makes the important point that, even though the starting point for the processes may be patterns of decision-making, the resulting dynamics of change through time can be both complex and counter-intuitive.

Given the complexity and abstraction of the ideas which have been presented in this chapter, it seems appropriate to finish by looking briefly at two examples which attempt to understand precisely the kind of Markovian diachronic patterns which Clarke argued were the concern of analytical archaeology and which are also at the heart of evolutionary approaches to culture.

Stylistic change in the Woodland period of Illinois

Neiman's (1995) analysis of Illinois Woodland ceramic assemblage variation focused on diachronic variation in exterior rim decoration, and explored the implications of assuming that the decoration system represented a tradition maintained by social learning, in which the only relevant evolutionary forces accounting for change through time in the form and frequency of decorative attributes in a given ceramic assemblage are mutation and drift, because stylistic variation is regarded as adaptively neutral and therefore not subject to selection. As we have seen above, drift represents the chance element affecting the prevalence of practices: even if we assume that all potters and/or all decorative motifs are equally likely to be taken as models in an episode of social learning and subsequent ceramic production, in any finite population not all potters or motifs will be copied the same number of times. For smaller populations, the chances of such random variation are particularly great. By the time a few "generations" of ceramic decoration copying/production have gone by, some of the motifs will have disappeared altogether, while others will be present at high frequency. Eventually, only one will prevail and the time taken for this to happen will depend on the population size.

Mutation refers to the introduction of novelty into the decorative repertoire of a particular group. This can come from local innovation or from the adoption of new motifs from other groups. To the extent that groups are in contact with one another, the drift-driven changes in the different groups should go in step with one another.

Neiman (1995) carried out a simulation to demonstrate that, for a given population size, higher levels of intergroup transmission produce lower equilibrium values of intergroup divergence. It follows from the theory and its mathematical specification that when drift and neutral innovation are the only forces operating, then, if we examine the relationship between the variation within an assemblage and the differences between different assemblages, as one decreases the other will increase (Neiman 1995: 27).

An analysis of the differences between a number of Woodland ceramic assemblages from different sites, for a series of seven successive phases, showed a trend of decreasing then increasing difference between them. It also showed the pattern of inverse correlation between intra- and intergroup variation just mentioned: as inter-assemblage differences went down, the variation within assemblages increased. Neiman (1995: 27) therefore concluded that the trends through time in inter-assemblage distance were indeed a function of changing levels of intergroup transmission, which started low, reached their highest level in Middle Woodland times, and sank to new low levels in the Late Woodland period. The Middle Woodland was also the time of the "Hopewell Interaction Sphere," evidenced by the widespread appearance of exotic trade goods.

Neiman went on to suggest that since the attribute being studied was decoration on cooking pots, and since ethnoarchaeological work suggests that successful transmission of ceramic traditions requires a long-lasting relationship between teacher and learner (cf. Shennan and Steele 1999), then the changes in level of intergroup transmission must relate to changes in the level of long-term residential movement of potters between groups. He also pointed out that his conclusions about the patterns of interaction through time in this period and area correspond to those of the culture historians who had studied the phenomenon, rather than with those of subsequent analyses undertaken within a New Archaeology frame-

work. These had suggested that the end of the Middle Woodland and the cessation of exotic goods exchange represented the replacement of gift exchange relations by more frequent, routine, everyday forms of contact. This does not appear to be the case.

Diachronic variation in LBK ceramic decoration patterns in the Merzbachtal, Germany

The second example is very similar to the first, in that it involves accounting for changing patterns in the frequency of ceramic decorative patterns; in this case decorative bands on the bodies of ceramic vessels from two settlements of the early Neolithic *Linienbandkeramik* in western Germany. However, the conclusions reached in this case are different from those of Neiman (Shennan and Wilkinson 2001).

The two settlements are located within a small early Neolithic settlement cluster along the shallow valley of a stream, the Merzbach, which was totally excavated in advance of mining. A quantitative analysis of the decorative motif frequency data was undertaken in the same way as Neiman had done. In this case the analysis of the changing diversity of the decorative assemblage through time, established that the diversity values derived from the neutral model of stylistic change and those based on the band type frequencies in the LBK data were completely different from one another. More specifically, it appeared that in the early phases the diversity of the ceramic assemblage in terms of its decoration was less than would be expected under the neutral model, while in the later phases it was greater. This indicated the existence of some directional selective forces acting on ceramic production decision-making, thus leading to the departure from neutrality: to the rejection of novelty (or conformist transmission) in the early phases and a much more positive attitude towards it in the later ones.

In fact, the increased decorative diversity within each of the two sites analyzed is chronologically associated with the founding of separate but adjacent settlements within the Merzbach valley. There appear to have been strict norms regarding band type choice in the early phases, followed by an assertion of distinctiveness at both the intra- and inter-site level in the later ones. This argument is supported by a recent cladistic analysis of the ceramic assemblages from all the Merzbach settlements (Collard and Shennan 2000), which suggested that the ceramic assemblages from the newly founded settlements arose as a result of processes of branching differentiation from ancestral assemblages, despite the fact that all the sites concerned are extremely close together.

Conclusion

Analytical Archaeology argued for the centrality of describing and explaining diachronic patterns in the archaeological record at a series of different hierarchical levels and suggested that there were general processes operating which produced regularities in how such patterns developed over time. As the quotation at the head of this chapter indicates, it also insisted on the importance of people's interactions with the humanly constructed material world around them in creating their identities. Nevertheless, although that world has an enormous influence on creating the sorts of people who grow up and lead their lives within it, its simple presence does not provide sufficient information to reproduce it for the future, in just the same way that looking at and tasting a cake does not provide sufficient information to make one. For that you need the passing on of instructions from someone who knows how to do it.

This point has become particularly central for those archaeologists who have suggested that the cultural lineages created by social learning can be regarded as analogous in certain respects to genetic lineages, and who have begun to explore the implications of this in terms of the impact of analogues of mutation, selection, and drift on diachronic patterns in cultural practices.

A key area of concern to both Clarke's agenda and that of the evolutionary archaeologists (*sensu lato*) is the identification and characterization of coherent patterns of diachronic correlation at the different levels of the hierarchy identified by Clarke, between attributes characterizing types or between elements of assemblages relating to different cultural practices. The extent of cultural coherence is likely to be very variable and must be an object of investigation rather than being assumed at the outset. Nettle (1999) has recently made a similar point in relation to language, pointing out that it is mistaken to talk of the history of "a language," but that we need to look at the separate histories of its various elements. In an archaeological context differential patterns of correlation among the attributes characterizing arrowheads have been used to infer different processes in the introduction of arrowheads in different regions (Bettinger and Eerkens 1999).

This approach puts the diachronic patterns in material culture (in the widest possible sense) and the cultural practices associated with them at the center of archaeological investigation, not people. Moreover, these are patterns recognized by the archaeologist after the event. Nevertheless, human action isn't written out of the picture. In the various complex ways outlined above, it modifies the diachronic patterns. Much of that modification occurs as a result of processes which people are unaware of or don't intend; for example, some of the drift processes described or the interactions whose implications are being explored by complexity theory. Some of it appears to be more deliberate, such as the switch from suppressing novelty to embracing it in LBK pottery decoration. But it is important to note that this inference is a conclusion, based on the rejection of a null hypothesis of stylistic neutrality, not an untested starting assumption about the ubiquitous centrality of self-conscious identity signaling. Indeed,

Neiman's Illinois Woodland results show that the latter is not always the case.

Paradoxically, however, given what was said at the beginning of this chapter, the focus on documenting diachronic lineages of cultural practices and the factors affecting them may also ultimately tell us a lot more about the links between the past and the present.

References

Barth, F. 1987. *Cosmologies in the Making: A Generative Approach to Cultural Variation in Inner New Guinea.* Cambridge: Cambridge University Press.

Bentley, R. A. and H. D. G. Maschner 2000. "Subtle nonlinearity in popular album charts." *Advances in Complex Systems* 2: 1–10.

Bentley, R. A. and H. D. G. Maschner 2001. "Stylistic change as a self-organised critical phenomenon." *Journal of Archaeological Method and Theory* 8: 35–66.

Bettinger, R. L. and J. Eerkens 1999. "Point typologies, cultural transmission, and the spread of bow-and-arrow technology in the prehistoric Great Basin." *American Antiquity* 64: 231–42.

Binford, L. R. 1962. "Archaeology as anthropology." *American Antiquity* 28: 217–25.

Binford, L. R. 1972. "Contemporary model building: paradigms and the current state of Palaeolithic research." In D. L. Clarke (ed.), *Models in Archaeology*, pp. 109–66. London: Methuen.

Blackmore, S. 1999. *The Meme Machine.* Oxford: Oxford University Press.

Boone, J. L. and E. A. Smith 1998. "Is it evolution yet?" *Current Anthropology* 39: 141–73.

Bourdieu, P. 1977. *Outline of a Theory of Practice.* Cambridge: Cambridge University Press.

Boyd, R. and P. Richerson 1985. *Culture and the Evolutionary Process.* Chicago: University of Chicago Press.

Boyd, R., M. Borgerhoff-Mulder, W. H. Durham, and P. J. Richerson 1997. "Are cultural phylogenies possible?" In P. Weingart, S. D. Mitchell, P. J. Richerson, and S. Maasen (eds.), *Human By Nature*, pp. 355–86. Mahwah, NJ: Lawrence Erlbaum.

Broughton, J. 1997. "Widening diet breadth, declining foraging efficiency and prehistoric harvest pressure: Ichthyofaunal evidence from the Emeryville shellmound, California." *Antiquity* 71: 845–62.

Clarke, D. L. 1968. *Analytical Archaeology.* London: Methuen.

Collard, M. and S. J. Shennan 2000. "Processes of culture change in prehistory: a case study from the European Neolithic." In C. Renfrew and K. Boyle (eds.), *Archaeogenetics: DNA and the Population Prehistory of Europe*, pp. 89–97. Cambridge: MacDonald Institute of Archaeological Research.

Dawkins, R. 1976. *The Selfish Gene.* Oxford: Oxford University Press.

Dawkins, R. 1982. *The Extended Phenotype.* Oxford: Oxford University Press.

Deetz, J. 1965. *The Dynamics of Stylistic Change in Arikara Ceramics* (Illinois Studies in Anthropology No. 4). Urbana: University of Illinois Press.

Diamond, J. 1998. *Guns, Germs and Steel: A Short History of Everybody for the Last 13,000 Years.* London: Jonathan Cape.

Douglas, M. 1978. *Cultural Bias.* London: Royal Anthropological Institute.

Giddens, A. 1984. *The Constitution of Society.* Cambridge: Polity Press.

Gould, S. J. and R. C. Lewontin 1979. "The spandrels of San Marco and the Panglossian paradigm: A critique of the adaptationist programme." *Proceedings of the Royal Society of London*, Series B, 205: 581–98.

Hodder, I. 1982. *Symbols in Action.* Cambridge: Cambridge University Press.

Hodder, I. 1990. *The Domestication of Europe.* Oxford: Blackwell.

Kaplan, H. and K. Hill 1992. "The evolutionary ecology of food acquisition." In E. A. Smith and B. Winterhalder (eds.), *Evolutionary Ecology and Human Social Behavior,* pp. 167–202. New York: Aldine de Gruyter.

Klejn, L. 1998. "Comment on 'Archaeologists and migrations: a question of attitude', by H. Haerke." *Current Anthropology* 39: 30–1.

Lyman, R. L. and M. J. O'Brien 1998. "The goals of evolutionary archaeology." *Current Anthropology* 39: 615–52.

Lyman, R. L., M. J. O'Brien, and R. C. Dunnell 1997. *The Rise and Fall of Culture History.* New York: Plenum.

Mace, R. and M. D. Pagel 1994. "The comparative method in anthropology." *Current Anthropology* 35: 549–64.

Maschner, H. (ed.) 1996. *Darwinian Archaeologies.* New York: Plenum Press.

Mithen, S. 1990. *Thoughtful Foragers: A Study of Human Decision-Making.* Cambridge: Cambridge University Press.

Moore, J. H. 1994. "Putting anthropology back together again: the ethnogenetic critique of cladistic theory." *American Anthropologist* 96: 925–48.

Neiman, F. D. 1995. "Stylistic variation in evolutionary perspective: inferences from decorative diversity and interassemblage distance in Illinois Woodland ceramic assemblages." *American Antiquity* 60: 7–36.

Nettle, D. 1999. *Linguistic Diversity.* Oxford: Oxford University Press.

O'Brien, M. J. (ed.) 1996. *Evolutionary Archaeology: Theory and Application.* Salt Lake City: University of Utah Press.

Pétrequin, P. 1993. "North wind, south wind: Neolithic technological choices in the Jura Mountains, 3700–2400 BC." In P. Lemonnier (ed.), *Technological Choices,* pp. 36–76. London: Routledge.

Rosenberg, M. 1994. "Pattern, process and hierarchy in the evolution of culture." *Journal of Anthropological Archaeology* 13: 307–40.

Rushforth, S. and J. S. Chisholm 1991. *Cultural Persistence: Continuity in Meaning and Moral Responsibility among Bearlake Athabascans.* Tucson: University of Arizona Press.

Shennan, S. J. 1978. "Archaeological 'cultures': an empirical investigation." In I. Hodder (ed.), *The Spatial Organization of Culture,* pp. 113–39. London: Duckworth.

Shennan, S. J. 1989a. "Archaeology as archaeology or anthropology? Clarke's Analytical Archaeology and the Binfords' New Perspectives in Archaeology 21 years on." *Antiquity* 63: 831–5.

Shennan, S. J. 1989b. "Introduction: archaeological approaches to cultural identity." In S. J. Shennan (ed.), *Archaeological Approaches to Cultural Identity,* 1–32. London: Unwin Hyman.

Shennan, S. J. 2002. *Genes, Memes and Human History: Darwinian Archaeology and Cultural Evolution.* London: Thames and Hudson.

Shennan, S. J. and J. Steele 1999. "Cultural learning in hominids: a behavioral ecological approach." In H. Box and K. Gibson (eds.), *Mammalian Social Learning: Comparative and Ecological Perspectives,* pp. 367–88 (Symposia of the Zoological Society of London 72). Cambridge: Cambridge University Press.

Shennan, S. J. and J. R. Wilkinson 2001. "Ceramic style change and neutral evolution: A case study from Neolithic Europe." *American Antiquity* 66: 577–93.

Skyrms, B. 1996. *Evolution of the Social Contract.* Cambridge: Cambridge University Press.

Sperber, D. 1985. "Anthropology and psychology: towards an epidemiology of representations." *Man* 20: 73–89.

Steele, J. and S. J. Shennan (eds.) 1996. *The Archaeology of Human Ancestry: Power, Sex and Tradition*. London: Routledge.

Teltser, P. (ed.) 1995. *Evolutionary Archaeology: Methodological Issues*. Tucson: University of Arizona Press.

Toren, C. 1990. *Making Sense of Hierarchy: Cognition as Social Process in Fiji*. London: Athlone Press.

Vansina, J. 1990. *Paths in the Rainforests: Towards a History of Political Tradition in Equatorial Africa*. Madison: University of Wisconsin Press.

2

The Great Dark Book: Archaeology, Experience, and Interpretation

Julian Thomas

History is, as it were, the great dark book, the collected works of the human spirit, written in the languages of the past, the text of which we have to understand.

Gadamer (1975: 156)

Archaeology's Interpretive Turn

Over the past decade archaeology has embraced what Rabinow and Sullivan (1987) would describe as the "interpretive social sciences": hermeneutics and phenomenology. The early critiques of processual archaeology (e.g., Miller 1982) were principally inspired by structuralism, Marxism, and structuration theory, and sought to replace explanations that emphasized ecological, demographic, and technological factors with a consideration of internal social dynamics, structuring principles, and agency. More recent work has questioned the appropriateness of an *explanatory* framework within archaeology, preferring *understanding* as the criterion of a satisfactory investigation of the past (Johnson and Olsen 1992: 419). Consequently, it has been suggested that "postprocessual archaeology" could be redefined as "interpretive archaeology" (Shanks and Hodder 1995: 5). This concern with interpretation has been explicitly linked with the investigation of human experience, both in the past and in the present (Shanks 1992), a connection which echoes the historical convergence of the hermeneutic and phenomenological traditions.

As a number of authors have pointed out, the redefinition of archaeology as a hermeneutic enterprise immediately raises a series of new questions: What does it mean to interpret material culture? Are material things in any sense analogous to written texts? To what extent can we "recover" past meanings? What is the character of the relationship between the past and the present? (Johnson and Olsen 1992: 428). These are issues that I will address in this chapter, yet my intention is to present a distinctive point of view on interpretation and experience, rather than simply a review.

It is broadly accepted that an interpretive archaeology involves a new way of working: interpretation is something that we *do*,

21

practically. However, this activity is composed of a number of different elements. To interpret is to make sense of something, but this can involve developing an understanding, or clarification, or searching for a hidden or encrypted meaning beneath the apparent surface of things (Ricoeur 1974: 13; Taylor 1985: 15). For the most part, accounts of interpretation in the archaeological literature have concentrated on the last of these alternatives. In one of the most extensive and sophisticated discussions of the topic, Tilley (1993) argues that interpretation begins when we are confused or ignorant about something. For as long as we are happy to accept the nature of something as given, we do not interpret; only those phenomena which are not transparent require interpretation. As Tilley puts it, "when it is obvious to me that a figurine is a frog, I do not interpret it *as* a frog" (Tilley 1993: 2). Hodder (1999: 66) concurs with Tilley in making a distinction between description and interpretation, arguing that only a portion of archaeological activity involves the latter. Counting potsherds, for example, is cited as a non-interpretive undertaking. However, Hodder makes the important qualification that most description actually depends upon interpretation: being able to count potsherds relies upon an act of interpretation at some time in the past, whereby certain objects were identified as fragments derived from pottery vessels.

If interpretation is a practice, it can be argued that it forms a fundamental element of what all archaeologists do. Archaeologists engage with their evidence in an interpretive labor, which produces archaeological knowledge (Shanks and McGuire 1996: 79). This archaeological knowledge is constructed in the present, and involves judgments regarding what is and is not important, omissions, classifications, and a recognition that the evidence itself is radically incomplete (Shanks and Hodder 1995: 5; Tilley 1993: 1). So although archaeological interpretation is concerned with meaning, this may be a contemporary meaning that is read into the

evidence, rather than a past meaning that is discovered intact. However, while these arguments cast interpretation as a form of knowledge production, it is as well to remember that some authorities have questioned the whole interpretive enterprise. For Susan Sontag (1967: 5–6), it represents a pathological attempt to burrow destructively beneath the surface of things, searching for deeper and deeper truths. This is characteristic of a modern era in which hidden depths are opposed to surfaces, the former associated with profundity and the latter, by implication, with superficiality. In place of a depth hermeneutics, Sontag advocates an "erotics" in which we explore the sensuous productivity of the world that surrounds us. Sontag's point is well taken, but depends upon a limited conception of what interpretation is and what it does: that is, the search for deep meaning.

The Interpretive Tradition

In their helpful account of the development of hermeneutics, Johnson and Olsen (1992: 429) draw a distinction between "earlier" and "later" manifestations of the tradition, the earlier being historical and Romantic in outlook, while the latter was more explicitly philosophical. The early hermeneutics of Schleiermacher, Droysen, and Dilthey maintained that as creatures who are ourselves subject to the conditions of history, we are able to appreciate the significance of texts written in the past. In order to do this, we should free ourselves from the assumptions and prejudices of our own era, and enter into the mental life of a person who lived in the past, and who wrote the document that we study. This framework was radically challenged by Hans-Georg Gadamer (1975), who denied emphatically that such a break with one's own historical context was either possible or desirable. On the contrary, the prejudices and fore-knowings that we bring to any analysis are precisely what make understanding possible. It is because we are the product of a particular time and a particular set of traditions that we are motivated to investigate the past in the first place. A being who had achieved context-freedom and objectivity could not be expected to have any concern with human history. Indeed, it is our worldly engagement with others that enables us to *care*. Moreover, the temporal distance that severs us from the past is less an unbridgeable gulf than a productive space which enables us to enter into a creative dialogue with another historical or cultural horizon (Gadamer 1975: 264). So rather than attempting to enter into the mental space of another, we engage in a conversation with the cultural Other. The distance between the present and the past, or between two cultures, may never finally be overcome in a "fusion of horizons," but the continual movement between the two in the attempt to apprehend alterity produces the most important effect of hermeneutics: a deepening of our self-understanding.

Gadamer's positive embrace of prejudice (in the sense of "pre-judgment") is a superficially shocking aspect of his project. More subtle, perhaps, is his recognition that hermeneutics should be concerned as much with pre-understanding as with interpretation *per se*. In this respect his work drew upon the phenomenology of Martin Heidegger, and represents an important link between the two forms of inquiry. Phenomenology, in the more restricted contemporary sense of the word, emerged from a perceived "crisis of science" in the early part of the twentieth century (Jay 1973: 61). Like both logical positivism and the critical theory of the Frankfurt School, phenomenology represented an attempt to refound scientific knowledge. However, rather than asserting the absolute objectivity of the scientist or revealing the political interests embedded in scientific practice, Edmund Husserl sought to clarify the process of experience through which we gain our knowledge of the world. Husserl's project reveals something of the ambivalence of the category of experience: it is at once a cornerstone of the Romantic appeal to subjective sensibility and the foundation of the experimental method in natural science. Talk of human experience within archaeology is sometimes derided as unscientific (e.g., Jones 1998: 7), and yet positivism dictates that only those facts that are demonstrated by sensory experience can be recognized as "true" (Scott 1992).

While positivism in one form or another came to dominate Western academia in the period after World War II, both hermeneutics and phenomenology, alongside critical theory, gained a renewed impetus from a growing crisis in *social* science from the 1960s onwards (Rabinow and Sullivan 1987: 5). One way of explaining this is to say that while positivism represents a restatement (and hardening) of the Enlightenment project of knowledge, the interpretive social sciences have always embodied a critique of the Enlightenment in particular and modernity in general. The later twentieth century saw an unprecedented skepticism regarding triumphalist readings of history: what Jean-François Lyotard refers to as an "incredulity toward metanarratives" (Lyotard 1984: xxiv). At the end of a century which had seen the Battle of the Somme, the Holocaust, the atomic bomb, and near-universal environmental degradation the notion that we might be headed toward "the best of all possible worlds" could seem no more than a bad joke. Under these circumstances, the Enlightenment project that is embedded in our liberal political systems and our humanist moral order is undergoing an increasingly critical evaluation from both ends of the political spectrum.

While the aspirations of the Enlightenment were probably more diverse than is commonly recognized, the core idea of the movement involved the replacement of religion and superstition by a morality that could be independently grounded (Gray 1995: 147). This grounding was to be found in reason, which was identified as a universal aspect of human nature. If human reason were freed from superstition, ethical traditions, and hierarchical controls, it was considered that people would automatically act for the good (Carroll 1993: 122). Locating "Man" at the center of the moral order placed a new emphasis on human autonomy, and can be seen as implicated in the emergence of a characteristically modern form of "individuality," most clearly identifiable in "contract" theories of society. In this way of thinking, human beings emerge into the world as fully formed and self-contained agents, who later enter into relationships with one another in pursuit of their personal benefit. Ultimately, the Enlightenment vision of humanity as dynamic and cultural, gaining control over and giving meaning and value to a passive nature, is responsible for the worldview of contemporary globalized capitalism (Gray 1995: 158). While much of the Romantic reaction to Enlightenment rationalism was cast within the terms of humanist individualism, stressing personal creativity and sensibility, the interpretive tradition has been responsible for more powerful criticisms. Gadamer, for instance, argued that in its "year zero" rejection of tradition the Enlightenment demonstrated a prejudice against prejudice, robbing us of the ability to evaluate our own motivations (Gadamer 1975: 239–40). Moreover, Gadamer traces the single-minded faith in rationality to Descartes, who held that a thorough and disciplined application of reason can in all cases remove the threat of error (Gadamer 1975: 246). Only where our use of reason is incomplete, or is compromised by the influence of superstition or authority, do we act incorrectly. Of course, this implies that knowledge can be separated from human interests in general and power in particular, a proposition which has more recently been contested by Foucault (1980).

Humans as Interpreting Beings

We have already noted Gadamer's argument that in interpreting the Other, we come to reflect on ourselves. Paul Ricoeur takes this line of reasoning further, suggesting that

through self-reflection we come to recognize our "placement in Being." By this he means the way in which we are always already in a world and amidst other beings before we come to identify ourselves as distinct persons (Ricoeur 1974: 11). From Dilthey onwards, the claim has been made that it is our ability to interpret which sets human beings apart, and that for this reason hermeneutics should form the basis for a methodology which is specific to the human sciences. This argument bears with it the implication that interpretation is far more than an operation that historians perform on written texts. It is what human beings do and what they are: *interpreting Being* (Gadamer 1975: 235). This realization transforms the interpretive sciences from a pursuit of methodology into an ontology of the social world (Gadamer 1975: 230). Indeed, for Heidegger, interpretation and understanding are the only things that define humanity at all. Being human (or to use his language, *Dasein*) is something that one does, rather than the essential characteristic of a particular kind of biological entity. "Human being is interpretation all the way down" as Dreyfus (1991: 37) puts it, yet the outcome of this process is that human beings interpret themselves *as if* there were some stable substance beneath the layers of understanding. Resisting the unsettling conclusion that what they are is a *doing* rather than a thing, humans persist in identifying themselves as a material body, containing a mind and an immortal soul (Heidegger 1993: 228).

As interpreting beings, humans have no essential nature. Thus Heidegger (1962: 68) prioritizes existence over essence, implying that whatever is most important about humans will not be found deep inside them (or for that matter encoded in their DNA). On the contrary, the significant role that humans play can be found in the world, in the way that they "ground presence." This is a notion that requires some discussion, and perhaps the best place to begin is by returning to the concept of experience. As we have seen, Husserl proposed a phenomenology that clarified the way in which we encounter worldly things, by reducing our sensory engagements to a series of primordial mental experiences, or "phenomena." By encapsulating the experience of things within the inner world of the mind, Husserl reaffirmed the notion of a human subject whose characteristics were given and transcendental. Putting it bluntly, for Husserl, the human being is an apparatus for experiencing phenomena. In contrast to such a view, we might wish to argue that experience is not simply consumed by a subject with fixed attributes, but actually represents some part of the process through which the subject is brought into being (Scott 1992: 28). It was in this spirit that Heidegger was able to reframe the phenomenological question. Rather than asking what happened in our heads when we experience things, he enquired how things reveal themselves to us (Heidegger 1962: 58).

Necessarily, this change of emphasis requires that we consider precisely *who* does the experiencing. Husserl's subject is much the same as Descartes's *cogito*. For Descartes, thought is the guarantee of existence and identity, so that *I am* is the location where my thought takes place. Thinking happens in an inner realm, and our inner life precedes any action in the outer world. Thought is consequentially understood as an internal reflection or representation of the external world (Gray 1995: 152). This kind of a subject is *self-present*: known to itself in a way that others cannot be (Glendinning 1998: 23). Such a "monological," encapsulated thinking self, a source of all meaning and awareness, is of course the modern "individual" whose universality we have already questioned. As soon as we accept that we are what we do, this separation between an inner world of subjectivity and an outer public world can no longer be sustained.

Breaking down a division between human interiority and exteriority (or mind and body) has implications for the way in which we conceive our world. The world ceases to be a set of surroundings to which we have discontinuous access, and which we periodically enter before withdrawing again into our private mental space. Nor is it adequate to imagine the world as a vast geometrical space within which we are contained, as one object within another. This would only compound our mistaken sense of our own "thinghood." Rather than any kind of entity, the world in which we operate as human beings is a context, or a "within-which" (Glendinning 1998: 55). Here, of course, we are using the word "world" in a rather specialized way, although I will argue that it is the one which is appropriate to understanding human existence. By "world," Heidegger means neither the planet earth, nor the totality of all material things, nor a specialized subset of human endeavor ("the world of sport," "the world of pets," "the world of computing"). Instead, the world is the network of relational involvements within which we find ourselves, and which provides a horizon of intelligibility for any object or utterance. Just as classical hermeneutics argued that we can understand any cultural fragment (a document or a potsherd) by placing it in the context of the cultural whole from which it derives, Heidegger argues that the things that we encounter are rendered comprehensible by the background of habituated practices and traditions in which both we and they are embedded. As Gadamer suggests, whatever is "given" or presented to us occurs within a world, and hence brings a horizon of worldhood with it (Gadamer 1975: 217).

Such a world is not composed of objects, but of relationships. Getting on with the world requires a set of ingrained coping skills that enable us to deal with our network of involvements (Dreyfus 1991: 116). When we say that human beings are "in" the world, what we mean is that we always find ourselves imbricated in such a set of relationships. Indeed, it is unthinkable that we could be human without traditions of meaning to sustain us, and other humans to exist alongside. Being-in-the-world is therefore not exclusively a matter of spatial location, although it is equally impossible to imagine a human being who exists without existing *somewhere*. We are not beings of pure spirit who latterly find themselves transported into a world of materiality (Heidegger 1962: 83). Being-in-the-world is an indissoluble structure of involvement which enables "experience" to take place, in that it is the condition under which things can be recognized as such. Things are "revealed" to humans, but they require a relational "background" in order to make sense. Similarly, in the absence of people, trees and rocks and streams might have a material existence of sorts, but they would never be comprehended *as* such. In this sense "world" is even less like a thing and more like a process, in that it is continually brought into being by the *working* of the relationships between people and things. As Heidegger (1971: 44) puts it, world *worlds*.

We can render anything that we experience comprehensible because it "stands out from a background." This background, our world, is composed of things which we always already understand intuitively, without having to think about it thematically or grasp it in its entirety. Although we "know" our world, and to a greater or lesser extent are at home in it, we would find it impossible to give a full verbal account of it. So we inhabit a context of intelligibility that we understand in an inchoate way, not as "bits" or gobbets of fully digested information but as a familiar life-world (Taylor 1993). What this means is that even before we focus on something and interpret it in an analytical fashion, some kind of understanding of it already exists, as a result of its being placed in a context of involvement (Heidegger 1962: 203). Paradoxically, although the aim of interpretation is understanding, we already have an understanding before we begin to interpret. This kind of understanding (which we might call "pre-interpretive") is characteristic of our everyday dealings with things. Most of the time we can cope in a skillful way with the material tasks that present themselves to us: walking

along a pavement, turning a door handle, chopping vegetables with a knife. It is generally only when the things involved fail in their task (the pavement trips us, the door handle comes loose, the knife is blunt) that we need to reflect on them, and figure the problem out (Dreyfus 1991: 195). Attempting to grasp the problem presented by a failing piece of equipment is a good example of interpretation, in the sense suggested by Tilley and Hodder. But the claim that I want to make is that the pre-understanding that constitutes our ordinary everyday experience of the world is also to some degree interpretive, in that it involves *understanding-as*.

Grounding Presence

Any interpretation that we undertake rests upon the background of what we already understand. But in addition we will also always have a "fore-sight," a particular position from which to interpret, and a "fore-conception," a set of expectations concerning what we are going to uncover through interpreting (Dreyfus 1991: 199). Interpretation makes sense of something, but in so doing we differentiate the thing from its context: we make it stand clear from the background. Putting it another way, things are "made present" through interpretation, so that experiencing something and interpreting it are one and the same process. It is not the case that we first identify something as an entity and then proceed to interpret it: it is in the process of interpretation that things come to reveal themselves, or "come into focus." This way in which things become identifiable or intelligible as distinct entities we can refer to as *disclosure*. Disclosure is not something that goes on inside our minds. It depends upon an understanding of the world which is culturally constructed and inherited, and on the interactions and discourse that we share with others. Beyond this, what is disclosed to us depends upon the mood in which we find ourselves, a particular relationship with the world in which we may be, for example, fearful or assured (Heidegger 1962: 175). These moods are cultural attunements that reveal the world to us in particular ways, and we should not imagine that past people experienced the same moods as we do today.

Disclosure is a relational happening, which occurs through understanding and showing and telling. Moreover, the intelligibility of things is articulated through language, which is the prerogative of a community rather than a single being (Taylor 1992: 264). We might argue, then, that human beings can "ground presence," in the sense of making things comprehensibly "there," because they are linguistic beings. The world is revealed to us because we can grasp things conceptually, and because a "space of expression" exists between people, and between people and things (Taylor 1992: 258). This leads to another paradox, in that we always experience the world from the perspective of a single embodied person. What Heidegger somewhat poetically refers to as "the clearing" describes the way in which the things of which we are most aware are those to which we are closest, as if we were stood in a clearing in a forest with our surroundings shading off into darkness. By "closeness," though, he does not necessarily mean spatial proximity, so much as concern and attachment. Yet while the clearing is experienced from a bodily center, it is made possible by a more extensive relationality within which we are positioned.

Heidegger's account of the disclosure of worldly things is in some ways comparable with Judith Butler's more recent discussion of *materialization*. For Butler, materiality is the ultimate given of the Western philosophical tradition, something which appears to be so fundamental as to require no explanation. But as she points out, this gives the impression that culture is no more than a skin of superficial interpretation spread over the surface of a material world whose nature is always directly accessible to us (Butler 1993: 2). Or to paraphrase Dr. Johnson, if I kick

something and it hurts, then it's real. In the case of the human body, the implication of the conventional argument is that "gender" is a cultural interpretation which is imposed on the surface of a biological entity whose "sex" can be definitively identified by medical science (Butler 1993: 2). On this basis, anthropologists have frequently argued that while the human body is a universal, it is understood in different ways by different peoples, so that they may have very different gender orders. However, Butler insists that sex is no more than another interpretation of the body. Medicine and biological science are disciplinary mechanisms that make statements about human anatomy; they are discourses that have emerged under particular historical and political conditions (see Foucault 1973). The knowledge that they produce is specific and contingent rather than universal.

Butler suggests that rather than human bodies "having" a particular sex, they have to perform in a certain culturally sanctioned way, continually reiterating a set of norms, in order to sustain their materialization (Butler 1993: 32). Putting this in the terms that we have been using, gender performance secures the cultural intelligibility of the body; it makes the body present. To be part of our world, to escape abjection, human bodies have to *matter* in a particular way, and I will argue that this is the case with all material things. To register with us as comprehensible at all, things have to show up *as* something.

The As-Structure

This brings us to a critically important point. If anything is to be intelligible to us, it will be subject to what Heidegger (1962: 189) calls the "as-structure." We can never evade the pre-understanding that enables any phenomenon to be recognized. So, for instance, we are able to hear because we have already understood:

What we "first" hear is never noises or complexes of sounds, but the creaking wagon, the motorcycle . . . It requires a very artificial and complicated frame of mind to "hear" a "pure noise." (Heidegger 1962: 207)

Human beings operate in a world of significance, not one of pure uninterpreted sense data. There are no "bald" or naked experiences of things taken in abstraction from our pre-understanding and expectation. Indeed, to be able to recognize the sound of the motorcycle as a pattern of sound waves requires us to carry out an "unworlding," stripping away its significance in order to hear the "pure noise." So everything that we encounter is experienced-as-something, everything has already been interpreted.

This has profound implications for the way in which we understand the material traces of the human past. For instance, Ian Hodder grounds his argument for the "partial objectivity" of the archaeological record on the premise that some part of the material that we study lies beyond interpretation:

We are not just interpreting interpretations but dealing with objects that had practical effects in a non-cultural world – an ecological world organized by exchanges of matter and energy. (Hodder 1991: 12)

On the face of it this would seem to be an appeal to some level of reality which exists independently of the cultural world, and which can be accessed in a non-interpretive way by the natural sciences (e.g., Rabinow and Sullivan 1987: 9). Similarly, it should by now be clear that Tilley's claim that when I can readily identify the frog figurine I do not interpret it *as* a frog, needs to be reassessed. I may not need to actively ponder what the figurine represents, but in the moment of identification I understand it *as* a frog, and this identification is already interpretive at some level. The as-structure is fundamental to all experience.

Language and Signification

We have already mentioned that language has a distinctive role to play in revealing material things to us. It is worth returning to this point, as a very particular view of language is implied in this argument. Broadly speaking, there are two distinct perspectives on signification at work in archaeology and in the humanities in general. In the first, it is proposed that ideas exist inside our minds in a non-linguistic state, as images or patterns of neural energy. These ideas are then transformed into language, which enables them to traverse the public space between persons before entering into another mind (Glendinning 1998: 94). It follows from this that material things in the world are separate from their representation in the mind, but that our access to worldly things is unproblematic: they are simply "there." Of course, this conception of language is Cartesian, in distinguishing an internal world of meaning from an exterior space of pure substance: language is meaning made substantial. The second view adopts the position that thinking does not take place in a secluded interior world, and that language is not restricted to an outer, public sphere. In other words, it rejects the mind-body dichotomy. Language is not simply a vehicle that allows thoughts to be transmitted from person to person; it is the means through which ideas are constituted, formulated, and articulated (Taylor 1992: 248). Thoughts are iterable linguistic events, and they are brought into being in the public world (Glendinning 1998: 120). Language is interpretive, in that it allows entities to be understood-as-something, and in this sense it also enables things to show up as culturally intelligible (Taylor 1992: 256). This is what I take Butler to mean when she writes that any human body that is posited as existing prior to its signification is always signified as such. Language does not simply refer to things, it provides the conditions under which those things appear to us (Butler 1993: 30–1).

These points underscore the sense in which we inhabit a world of significance or meaning. We do not encounter things in isolation or in a raw materiality that precedes culture and interpretation. Instead, it is through their meaningfulness and through their place in our world that they are revealed to us. Anything which is comprehensible to us is already in language: signification is not a metaphysical add-on to a material world which we can fully apprehend through our senses. This should cause us to reflect on the way in which the issue of meaning has been discussed in archaeology. Hodder, for instance, has at various times employed a distinction between practical and representational meanings (Hodder 1999: 135), or functional and symbolic meanings (Hodder 1986: 121). In either case the implication is that those forms of meaning which are concerned with the function or material presence of a thing can be more readily approached, while those that are more hidden require abstraction from the object. This appears to give a kind of self-evident primacy to the practical meaning, which is closer to the thing itself, while the symbolic meaning is a secondary addition. But meaning is not a label that is added to an object: it is what the thing *is* to a particular group of people.

To give an example: Pierre Bourdieu (1970) describes the rifle that stands beside the weaving loom in a Berber house in North Africa. Its functional meaning is that it is a weapon, but it is symbolically associated with female virtue, of which it is the guarantor. Whoever shames the women of the house is likely to be shot. Entering the house, a member of the community would not first identify the offensive role of the rifle, and then subsequently reflect on the purity of the female inhabitants of the dwelling. The two are thoroughly bound up with one another: they are "co-disclosed" in the way in which the object reveals itself. Both are equally fundamental within the Berber cultural world. Hodder's hierarchy of kinds of meaning is perhaps better understood as a description of the perspective of the interpreting archaeologist. The functional meaning of a prehistoric artefact appears more accessible to us in the present because we can identify it as an object of a particular kind, which forms part of *our own* world horizon.

Digression: Interpretive Field Practice

So far, the argument that I have outlined has been largely abstract and philosophical. Yet I suggest that an interpretive archaeology has the most fundamental implications for our practice in the field. For the most part, the discipline of archaeology is still dominated by the model of explanation, whether by induction or deduction. Explanation involves the definition of a series of variables, and the construction of statements considered to account for the interactions between these entities. In its most rigorous form, explanation demands that these statements should be law-like, or at least probabilistic, enabling the relations between variables to be expressed as mathematical formulae and even simulated in a computer. The immediate and obvious drawback of such an approach is that it necessarily privileges entities over relationships, promoting a way of thinking that is overwhelmingly monadic. This presents a view of the world as composed of freestanding objects, or of naturally bounded "subsystems." As both philosophy and ethnography have demonstrated, such a perspective is highly specific to the modern West (Heidegger 1971; Strathern 1988).

A more subtle problem with the explanatory framework is that analysis takes place at a remove from the acquisition of evidence. Under the hypothetico-deductive approach approved by the New Archaeology, hypotheses are constructed in advance, and "tested" on results obtained in the field, while the inductive procedure that still characterizes much fieldwork involves the composition of explanatory relations between observed phenomena on a post-hoc basis. While it is often recognized that archaeological evidence is to some degree "theory laden," the bulk of observations made in the field are treated as if they were neutral and objective. Indeed, the methodologies that we use to excavate and record archaeological sites strive to minimize "human error" and to produce an objective description of features, structures, and deposits (e.g., Barker 1977). It is held that the dissection and description of the archaeological record should not be allowed to become "infected" by personal opinion or aesthetic judgment. Context sheets, Harris matrices, Munsell charts, and scale drawings make up an apparatus that serves to present archaeological sites as composed of distinct and equivalent entities, each of which can be adequately described in a formal and standardized manner. I submit that this is because the archaeological profession continues to maintain an absolute distinction between data collection and explanation. Explanation may involve the generation of hypotheses before fieldwork begins, or the evaluation of results after it finishes. But in either case, the effect is that excavation and survey take on a structure that is deeply hierarchical.

In practice, the explanation of archaeological sites generally begins only when the last turf has been replaced, the last sherd has been counted, and the last specialist report has been gathered in. This means that it becomes the prerogative of the person who will synthesize the results of excavation and write the site report, usually the site director. Under these conditions, the role of the excavator, and to some extent that of the specialist, is reduced to that of the technician (or the data-collecting robot). They perform a series of tasks by rote, according to the strictures of a disciplinary code. In contemporary Britain this situation has been exacerbated by the doctrine of "preservation by record," a legacy of the "rescue" era. Where sites and monuments have been threatened with destruction, they have often been excavated and described in an admirably thorough manner, but with little regard to "making sense" of the evidence that is collected.

In recent years some of the drawbacks of an overly formulaic and dispassionate field method have been recognized. Increasingly, fieldworkers have come to resent the way in which they have been marginalized in the representation of projects that they have been actively involved in (Lesley McFadyen, pers. comm.). It has been proposed that the use of new information technologies will allow excavators and specialists to share information among themselves and with a wider public as an excavation progresses, and that the use of online diaries and the like will introduce a subjective element to complement the objective, scientific description of sites (Hodder 1999). I suggest that an altogether more radical approach is required. If we wish to thoroughly transform archaeological field practice, it will not be by introducing new technologies but by changing the social relations within which fieldwork is conducted. Similarly, it is insufficient to incorporate a "subjective" element into the description of excavation. Instead, we need to transcend the modernist dichotomy between subject and object altogether.

This can be achieved through an interpretive archaeology. As we have seen, interpretation does not begin once an excavation or survey has been completed. Archaeological fieldwork is interpretive in all of its stages: from deciding where to work and what kinds of traces are significant to our understanding of the past, through to sampling and recovery strategies. At each level, prejudices, assumptions, and preunderstandings are mobilized in the decisions that we make. Moreover, when a field walker stoops to pick up a potsherd, or when an excavator scrapes to the edge of a pit with their trowel, fills in a context form, or draws a section, they are making use of interpretive skills. To be intelligible, archaeological evidence must be interpreted-as-something. What this means is that the site director is not the only person in the project who is involved in interpretation. All fieldworkers are interpreting beings, by virtue of their Being-in-the-world. It follows that if explanation tends to promote a hierarchical division of labor, the shift to interpretation can potentially facilitate a way of working in the field that is more democratic. Each series of actions that we pursue on an archaeological site promotes a particular understanding of the place and of what has taken place there. Far from being the outcome of a piecing together of the evidence by a single gifted individual, what is written in a site report is the product of a prolonged negotiation over the meaning of a place and its history, conducted by a community of skilled interpreters who occupy that location, experience it, and live through it over a period of weeks or months.

Archaeologies of Experience and Perception

In the past few years there has been a growing acceptance that it is worthwhile to address the ways in which past people experienced their worlds. However, in many cases this is conceived as a subsidiary form of inquiry, in which we investigate how "they" (in the past) perceived a material reality whose contours are already fully known to us (in the present) through dietary reconstruction, GIS, catchment analysis, population modeling, and the like. Similarly, there has been a call for a more rigorous approach to past people's perceptions (Jones 1998: 7), involving the foundation of a testable methodology. This seems to require that the investigative procedures of one framework of inquiry (phenomenology) be rendered accountable to the criteria of adequacy of another (positivism). Revealingly, the heuristic by which Jones proposes to establish his science of past perception is what he calls the "perceptual framework," a structure which is generated in "the interaction between the individual and the environment" (Jones 1998: 10). According to Jones,

> Stimuli are received by the individual through the perceptual framework and con-

versely . . . people act on the world through the perceptual framework. (Jones 1998: 8)

In other words, information that exists in a raw and uninterpreted form in the outside world is internalized through a kind of cultural filter, which distorts or overlays these data with meaning, creating a particular mental image of the world. This mental image amounts to a kind of "false consciousness" when juxtaposed with scientific reality. I focus on Jones' account here because I believe that it is characteristic of much work currently being undertaken in archaeology, in that it is concerned with the perceptions of individuals, who represent atomized information-processing entities. As Charles Taylor has remarked, computers have increasingly become a model of what human minds do (Taylor 1985: 20). The mind-as-computer image chimes with Enlightenment conceptions of the individual, in which each person is hardwired to operate in the external world, and where intelligibility is reduced to the ability to be processed by the mind (Taylor 1993: 324). In this view, perception is not merely a secondary impression superimposed on the material reality of things; it is a distorted picture that results from an imperfect processing of environmental stimuli.

More productive has been the idea of an archaeological phenomenology, conceived not simply as a description of past people's experience, but as an investigation of how different experiences have been possible, in both the past and the present (Shanks 1992: 154). This has most characteristically taken the form of a series of analyses of monumental and domestic architecture (e.g., Barrett 1994; Richards 1993; Tilley 1994). Although these studies are often informed by quite different theoretical perspectives, each contrasts lived, three-dimensional space with the abstraction of archaeological plan views and distribution plots. Each maintains that movement through space generates particular understandings of place, but that architecture does not contain intrinsic meaning.

Most of these approaches have been concerned with the implication of the human body in power relations, so that the experience of space is never innocent, and almost all have stressed the way that a range of different understandings of place will have been produced by people who brought different resources of knowledge with them, and who gained differential access to particular locations (Richards 1993: 176).

In Tilley's case, the project of imagining how past people would have moved through constructed spaces was taken a stage further, in the suggestion that archaeologists should themselves walk across the landscapes which still contain the traces of prehistoric monuments. Tilley (1994: 73–5) argues that we can distinguish between the "skin" and the "bones" of the landscape: the superficial changes which have overtaken the topography with the passing of the years, and the more fundamental changelessness of landforms. It is the enduring structure of the land which encourages Tilley to walk the course of the Dorset Cursus, and the megalith-strewn Welsh uplands of the Black Mountains and Pembrokeshire, in such a way that his own embodied experiences become analogies for those of past people. For Tilley, it is the way that space is experienced through the body, "a privileged vantage point from which the world is apprehended" (Tilley 1994: 13), which is the key element of his "phenomenology of landscape." Such an approach finds support in Heidegger's conception of the clearing as a moving field of disclosure centered on the body. Moreover, our embodied engagement with things in working and using equipment is the principal means by which our background understanding of the world is continually recreated (Dreyfus 1991: 164; Taylor 1993: 319).

With hindsight, some of the incompleteness of these approaches has started to come into focus. Karlsson (1998: 192), for instance, has suggested that much of the application of phenomenology to archaeology has been excessively consciousness-centered, following the "humanistic geography" of

the 1970s in stressing "how it feels" subjectively at the expense of investigating the construction of that subjectivity. Similarly, Brück (1998: 28) argues that Tilley's account of the experience of moving along the Dorset Cursus is written from a single perspective. How would it seem to a pregnant woman, a small child, or a disabled person, she asks. The problem here is that all of these categories of personhood – "pregnant," "woman," "small," "child," "disabled" – are modern Western cultural understandings. None of these need have been the criteria upon which difference was constructed in the Neolithic. Moreover, if we resort to the "self-evident" differences among prehistoric bodies (pregnant people *simply are* encumbered in a certain way; very young people *simply are* smaller than fully grown ones) this concedes to biology the status of a universal and grounding truth. We can be sure that people in the Neolithic were different from one another, and that those differences afforded them different experiences of the world, but we do not yet know what those differences were.

Related criticisms have been raised by Meskell (1996) and Hodder (1999). Both authors argue that investigations of the physical experience of monuments and landscapes have employed "universal bodies" (Hodder 1999: 136) "without any corporeal, lived or individual identity" (Meskell 1996: 6). I would suggest that precisely the opposite is the case: there is no universal body, and the bodies involved in these studies (whether in reality or imaginatively) are those of white, male, middle-class, mostly heterosexual, late twentieth-century academics. These are the only bodies that those concerned have at their disposal, or at least the only ones that they have lived through. I do not imagine that any of them believed their own experiences to be definitive, but as I have already suggested, the use of one's own body as a medium for experience is a means of "reworking" the relationality of a past world, producing an analogy for past experience. As Gadamer might argue, our own movement through a building or across a hillside is a way of opening a dialogue with a past cultural horizon, rather than imagining that we have entered into that horizon.

For this reason, any phenomenology of past experience must be distinguished from empathy, or the attempt to enter into past minds and think past thoughts. Hodder rejects such reasoning:

> The claim is frequently made . . . that archaeologists can avoid meaning and empathy and engage in the description of practices . . . The implication is that archaeologists can study the practices and the mechanisms for creating and recreating meanings without the need to know what the meanings were. (Hodder 1999: 133)

Two different claims are being made here, and I believe that it is important to distinguish between them. The first is that some archaeologists have proposed that we can comprehend the past in a way that is shorn of all meaning. Hodder is perhaps entitled to argue this on the basis of Barrett's (1987: 471) suggestion that past cultural meanings would have been too fleeting and unstable to be apprehended through the material evidence, and that we would do better to concern ourselves with the "material conditions" which underpinned social relationships and facilitated the emergence of meaning. It should be clear from what I have argued so far that human beings exist in worlds of meaning and significance, and that they can have no access to material conditions which is not interpretive. However, our interpretation of the mechanisms and conditions that surrounded the creation of meaning in the past is a contemporary one, which need not coincide with the understandings of past people.

Hodder's second assertion is that any archaeology of meaning must be empathetic, or at the least an attempt to enter into the heads of ancient people. This need not be so: the notion (and the very locution) of "getting inside" past minds relies upon the mind-body split, and identifies meaning as a subjective ascription which is locked away in the mental sphere. I suggest that meaning, as *significance*, is the way in which things are understood by people: not as a surface comprehension underlain by a hidden meaning, but just the way that things *are*. In this sense meaning is not a cognitive phenomenon, but something that happens in the world, created in the relations between people and between people and things, and drawing on traditions of interpretation. Meaning is produced in interaction, negotiated in the public world. Furthermore, the possibility of creating a bond of empathy with another cultural horizon requires that something essential must be held in common between the two. Implicitly, this suggests the existence of a "universal grammar" (Hodder 1986: 123–4), whose very universality indicates its embedding in human nature. I suggest that simply assuming the existence of such universals would commit us to a metaphysical perspective, which is generally recognized as the grounding of liberal humanism.

Brück's criticisms of Tilley are pertinent, raising the question of *who* is involved in the experience of landscape. However, I would argue that prehistoric monuments were not encountered by a series of pregiven subjects, however diverse. Instead, the experience of these places represented one part of the way in which the distinctive identities of these people were generated. People were *positioned* by the architecture, afforded different possibilities for seeing, walking, hearing, and giving voice. It is interesting that Hodder approvingly cites Paul Treherne, who suggests that my own work on monuments has been less concerned with personal experience than with "an *external* process of subjectification" (Treherne 1995: 125; my emphasis). What this indicates is that both Hodder and Treherne are content to distinguish between an external, public world of power in which subjectification takes place, and an inner world of subjectivity in which sensations are experienced. Following Butler (1997), I would argue on the contrary that there is no private space that escapes power, and that our subjectivity is both initiated and sustained *by* power. Experience happens in the world, and is made possible as well as constrained by power relationships. Power is not simply an external force that bears down upon us; it is the set of possibilities immanent in the social and material relationships in which we are engaged.

Both Hodder and Meskell argue that what is missing from contemporary "archaeologies of practice" is a concern with individual agency, lived in a specific time and place (e.g., Hodder 1999: 136). This reflects Hodder's long-established concern with the active individual, originally developed in reaction to the New Archaeology's disdain for cultural belief and creative action (Hodder 1986: 6). In consequence, Hodder advocated a consideration of the relationship between the individual and the social whole, their ability to renegotiate and transform social structures, and their role in producing material culture (Hodder 1986: 7–8, 149). As an indication of the way in which explicitly addressing individuals can enrich the writing of prehistory, Hodder presents the example of the "Ice Man" from the Ötzal Alps of the Austrian–Italian border (Hodder 1999: 138). This person's body and his material possessions, according to Hodder, serve as a "window on the deep past," giving us access to how long-term processes like the Secondary Products Revolution were lived through at a personal level. The problem with this vignette of prehistoric life is that the category of the individual that it employs is not evaluated. While Hodder is quite right to emphasize the human scale and the lived experience of historical processes, what appears to be missing from his account is a theory of the subject. The Ice Man's status as an individual is taken as given, and I argue

that by implication it is assumed that he was a modern individual "just like us."

Conclusion: Without Fixed Points

Interpretation is a circle that we cannot escape (Gadamer 1975: 235). Before we start to interpret in any explicit way, we have already understood our world, which provides the context for our interpretation. Any act of interpretation feeds back into our background understanding. The modern era has been characterized by the attempt to find "a place to stand," a solid foundation which lies beyond interpretation (Carroll 1993: 25). Human nature, or moral universals, have been presumed as the ground for political systems and social order. But there is no such Archimedean point; there is no outside to the circle. The abiding problem for an interpretive archaeology is one of where to enter into the hermeneutic circle, if we have no fixed point of departure. We cannot assume that the human body is biologically fixed and ahistorical, or that the human mind has a set of hardwired capabilities, which create a stable bridge into the past. The most that we can do is to experience and interpret prehistoric artefacts and ancient landscapes through our own embodiment and our own prejudices, knowing that what we create is a modern product, enabled and limited by our own positioning in the contemporary world. But at the same time, the contingent position from where we take a stand on ourselves *does* provide a point from which we can engage with the past. What remains unresolved is how we can appreciate the *diversity* of ways in which any past world must have been understood, with only our own location to speak from.

Acknowledgments

Thanks to John Bintliff and two anonymous reviewers for their comments on an earlier draft of this chapter. Thanks also to Lesley McFadyen, Maggie Ronayne, Ange Brennan,

Colin Richards, and Randy McGuire, who have all discussed fieldwork with me at various times.

References

Barker, P. 1977. *Techniques of Archaeological Excavation*. London: Batsford.

Barrett, J. C. 1987. "Contextual archaeology." *Antiquity* 61: 468–73.

Barrett, J. C. 1994. *Fragments from Antiquity*. Oxford: Blackwell.

Bourdieu, P. 1970. "The Berber house or the world reversed." *Social Science Information* 9: 151–70.

Brück, J. 1998. "In the footsteps of the ancestors: a review of Christopher Tilley's 'A Phenomenology of Landscape: Places, Paths and Monuments.' " *Archaeological Review from Cambridge* 15: 23–36.

Butler, J. 1993. *Bodies that Matter: On the Discursive Limits of "Sex."* London: Routledge.

Butler, J. 1997. *The Psychic Life of Power: Theories in Subjection*. Stanford, CA: Stanford University Press.

Carroll, J. 1993. *Humanism: The Wreck of Western Culture*. London: Fontana.

Dreyfus, H. 1991. *Being-in-the-World: A Commentary on Heidegger's "Being and Time," Division 1*. Cambridge, MA: MIT Press.

Foucault, M. 1973. *The Birth of the Clinic: An Archaeology of Medical Perception*. London: Tavistock.

Foucault, M. 1980. "Truth and power." In: C. Gordon (ed.), *Power/Knowledge*, pp. 109–33. Brighton: Harvester.

Gadamer, H.-G. 1975. *Truth and Method*. London: Sheed and Ward.

Glendinning, S. 1998. *On Being with Others: Heidegger, Derrida, Wittgenstein*. London: Routledge.

Gray, J. 1995. *Enlightenment's Wake: Politics and Culture at the Close of the Modern Age*. London: Routledge.

Heidegger, M. 1962. *Being and Time*, translated by J. Macquarrie and E. Robinson. Oxford: Blackwell.

Heidegger, M. 1971. "The origin of the work of art." In M. Heidegger, *Poetry, Language, Thought*, pp. 15–88. New York: Harper and Row.

Heidegger, M. 1993. "Letter on humanism." In: D. F. Krell (ed.), *Martin Heidegger: Basic Writings* 2nd edn., pp. 213–65. London: Routledge.

Hodder, I. R. 1986. *Reading the Past: Current Approaches to Interpretation in Archaeology*. Cambridge: Cambridge University Press.

Hodder, I. R. 1991. "Interpretive archaeology and its role." *American Antiquity* 56: 7–18.

Hodder, I. R. 1999. *The Archaeological Process: An Introduction*. Oxford: Blackwell.

Jay, M. 1973. *The Dialectical Imagination: A History of the Frankfurt School and the Institute of Social Research 1923–50*. London: Heinemann.

Johnson, H. and B. Olsen 1992. "Hermeneutics and archaeology: on the philosophy of contextual archaeology." *American Antiquity* 57: 419–36.

Jones, C. 1998. "Interpreting the perceptions of past people." *Archaeological Review from Cambridge* 15: 7–22.

Karlsson, H. 1998. *Re-Thinking Archaeology*. Göteborg: Göteborg University Department of Archaeology.

Lyotard, J. F. 1984. *The Postmodern Condition: A Report on Knowledge*. Manchester: Manchester University Press.

Meskell, L. 1996. "The somatisation of archaeology: institutions, discourses, corporeality." *Norwegian Archaeological Review* 29: 1–16.

Miller, D. 1982. "Explanation and social theory in archaeological practice." In C. Renfrew, M. Rowlands, and B. Seagraves (eds.), *Theory and Explanation in Archaeology: The Southampton Conference*, pp. 83–95. Cambridge: Cambridge University Press.

Rabinow, P. and W. M. Sullivan 1987. "The interpretive turn: a second look." In P. Rabinow and W. M. Sullivan (eds.), *Interpretive Social Science: A Second Look*, pp. 1–30. Berkeley: University of California Press.

Richards, C. C. 1993. "Monumental choreography: architecture and spatial representation in late Neolithic Orkney." In C. Y. Tilley (ed.), *Interpretative Archaeology*, pp. 143–78. London: Berg.

Ricoeur, P. 1974. *The Conflict of Interpretations: Essays in Hermeneutics*. Evanston, IL: Northwestern University Press.

Scott, J. W. 1992. "Experience". In J. Butler and J. W. Scott (eds.), *Feminists Theorize the Political*, pp. 22–40. London: Routledge.

Shanks, M. 1992. *Experiencing the Past: On the Character of Archaeology*. London: Routledge.

Shanks, M. and I. Hodder 1995. "Processual, post-processual and interpretive archaeologies." In I. Hodder, M. Shanks, A. Alexandri, V. Buchli, J. Carman, J. Last, and G. Lucas (eds.), *Interpreting Archaeology: Finding Meaning in the Past*, pp. 3–29. London: Routledge.

Shanks, M. and R. McGuire 1996. "The craft of archaeology." *American Antiquity* 61: 75–88.

Sontag, S. 1967. *Against Interpretation*. London: Eyre and Spottiswode.

Strathern, M. 1988. *The Gender of the Gift*. Berkeley: University of California Press.

Taylor, C. 1985. *Philosophy and the Human Sciences: Philosophical Papers* 2. Cambridge: Cambridge University Press.

Taylor, C. 1992. "Heidegger, language, and ecology." In H. Dreyfus and H. Hall (eds.), *Heidegger: A Critical Reader*, pp. 247–69. Oxford: Blackwell.

Taylor, C. 1993. "Engaged agency and background in Heidegger." In C. Guignon (ed.), *The Cambridge Companion to Heidegger*, pp. 317–36. Cambridge: Cambridge University Press.

Tilley, C. Y. 1993. "Interpretation and a poetics of the past." In C. Tilley (ed.), *Interpretative Archaeology*, pp. 1–27. London: Berg.

Tilley, C. Y. 1994. *A Phenomenology of Landscape: Places, Paths and Monuments*. London: Berg.

Treherne, P. 1995. "The warrior's beauty: the masculine body and self-identity in Bronze-Age Europe." *Journal of European Archaeology* 105–44.

Part II
Current Themes and Novel Departures

3

Archaeology and the Genetic Revolution

Martin Jones

Introduction

"Discourse on beginnings" and "pertaining to origins" are the literal meanings of the two keywords in the title to this chapter, "archaeology" and "genetic." It is little surprise that the two disciplines carrying those names have remained intimately intertwined, though the actual form of their coupling has been subject to continuous transformation in response to a diverse range of stimuli. These include the turbulent twentieth-century history of racial politics, the discovery of the structure of DNA, a growing skepticism to the philosophy of the Enlightenment, and most recently the rapid completion of the Human Genome Project, lying at the heart of the genetic revolution referred to in the title. In the course of those many transformations, the questions archaeologists and geneticists ask have evolved as much as the manners in which they can be answered. This is especially true of the last decade, in which the growth of the science of genetics has been dramatic.

When archaeology emerged out of antiquarianism in the nineteenth century, it drew a clear evolutionary agenda from the optimism of the Enlightenment, and the concept of universal progress from simple to complex forms. Nineteenth-century archaeology became closely allied to Darwin's

evolutionary paradigm. They came together in the study of our own species' origins, and of our relationships with those other hominid bones that had been recognized from not long before Darwin's seminal publications on the issue. Modern genetics was not yet in place, and did not come into being until the following century, when Darwin's evolutionary insights were finally brought together with Mendel's observations on the logic and pattern of inheritance. Ideas from the new genetics were almost immediately drawn upon to explore further critical themes of the distant human past. One such theme was the movement of early human groups around the world, in some cases negotiating sizable expanses of sea, desert, or ice. Linked to that was another theme, the beginnings of farming, and how that novel ecology enabled and encouraged episodes of population movement. These have been the central issues addressed through a twentieth-century interplay between archaeology and genetics.

Most recently of all, a revolution in the technological possibilities of DNA analysis has both transformed the precision and detail with which these issues can be explored, and opened up the possibility of addressing new questions, on a variety of scales, about human society and human ecology in the past. In this chapter I look briefly at the history of this highly productive inter-action, move on to highlight some of the advances of recent years, and end by looking forward to how the two disciplines might continue to engage.

Background

Throughout, the most prominent interaction between archaeology and genetics has in-volved our own species, its origins and spread across the world. It has also been very productive in relation to the species we eat, notably our domesticated plants and animals. More recently it is also yielding results in relation to the species that consume us, our "micropredators," the organisms as-sociated with disease. The origins and geo-graphical movement of all three trophic levels are intimately interlinked, and come together within the emerging subdiscipline of archaeogenetics (Renfrew and Boyle 2000).

Early in the twentieth century, the discip-lines had begun to interact at the first two trophic levels. Soon after World War I, Hirschfeld and Hirschfeld (1919) gathered human blood group information, and at-tempted to find patterns relating to racial ancestry. Later, Boyd and Boyd (1933) ap-plied immunological techniques for deter-mining blood groups to Old World and New World mummies. By that time, Nikolai Vavilov (1992) was charting genetic vari-ation among the world's crop plants. His global maps of "centers of diversity" still serve as preliminary signposts for archaeolo-gists seeking to find the earliest farming sites around the world (Harris 1990).

Genetics at that stage was very much de-pendent on "expressed genes," in other words, genes that actually generate some fea-ture that may be easily observed in the living organism. When it came to looking into the past and seeking origins, the use of expressed genes was sometimes unreliable, and some-times politically highly sensitive. In Russia, Vavilov was imprisoned for subscribing

to the Western "doctrine" of Darwinism. In the West, observations of human genetics extended from blood groups to racial groups, and to such attributes as physical fitness and intelligence, the foci of eugenics.

The occasional unreliability of expressed genes became clear with the growth of molecular genetics. Many of the characters that do appear to be inherited are controlled, not by one gene, but indirectly by a wide array of different genes, their expression in turn mediated by growth and environment. The characters may reflect ancestry, but in a manner that is indirect and complex. By the second half of the twentieth century, the focus moved towards "discrete polymorph-isms" like the ABO blood group, that could only exist in a small number of states, sug-gesting control by a small number of genes. Ideally, these characters also displayed a rather limited functionality, such that growth and environment did not overly confuse the ancestral signal. This emphasis on non-functionality had the added advantage of dis-tancing postwar genetics from the eugenics that had been so conspicuously discredited in the context of wartime Nazi atrocities.

Within domestication, a whole series of world crops was studied through charting discrete protein polymorphisms, for which the molecular technology had grown fast. These studies formed the basis of a wide range of arguments about the origins of plant cultivation (Zohary and Hopf 1993). Within human studies, protein polymorph-isms provided the basis for the seminal syn-thesis of Cavalli-Sforza et al. (1994) on human genetic diversity, and its relationship to history and prehistory. That work pro-vided a clear illustration of the considerable impact genetics could have on the models we construct for the human past.

The synthesis was based upon global patterning in the expression of a wide range of polymorphisms, largely relating to blood group systems, and from which a series of maps was generated through principal components analysis. Placing these in the context of a detailed résumé of world prehistory, the authors suggested that human genetic diversity in the present could be accounted for in terms of a series of human migrations, in which movements of pioneer hunter-gatherers and of early farmers predominate. These patterns have had considerable ramifications upon our archaeological studies of the origins and spread of *Homo sapiens*, and of farming and language. In relation to the distancing of postwar human genetics from eugenics, it was of interest to note that, within their model, the physical characters associated with race, such as skin color, had a phylogenetic depth that was shallow in comparison with human origins.

By the time the synthesis had appeared in print, another trajectory in genetics had reached a point where the synthesis could be challenged. Its conclusions from the most intensively studied continent of all, Europe, did not seem to fit with evidence coming, not from proteins, but from mitochondrial DNA (Richards et al. 1996).

The DNA Era

The way in which DNA worked as an encoded replicator was established in 1953 (Watson and Crick 1953). However, it was not for another two decades that the chemical toolkit of the genetic engineer was sufficiently advanced for DNA phylogenetics to be developed on a par with the better-established protein studies. Its impact on archaeology and the human past has tended to move forward significantly each time that a major project of DNA sequencing has drawn to completion. The first of these was the complete sequencing of the human mitochondrial genome, the continuous loop of DNA at the heart of each of the sub-cellular "powerhouses" that drive each cell in our body (Anderson et al. 1981).

Within a few years of its publication, researchers at Allan Wilson's Berkeley laboratory had charted enough variation in a small part of that sequence to generate a phylogeny with a single woman (mitochondria are maternally inherited) at its ancestral base (Cann et al. 1987). She acquired the name Mitochondrial Eve, and her phylogeny has had a profound impact on discussions of the Out-of-Africa model, and our understanding of the short timescale on which it occurred. The mitochondrial genome continues to be one of the major genetic sequences from which hypotheses have been generated about the human past, and the wild and domestic animals associated with our expansion across the world. Indeed, it is one small part of the mitochondrial sequence that is common to many such studies. That sequence is the first hypervariable segment of the control region (a section of the genome from which much "gene-reading" or transcription is initiated). This segment within the control region comprises just a few hundred of the 16,000 or so base pairs making up the mitochondrial genome. Its virtue is that it evolves rapidly. The tiny evolutionary steps that interest archaeologists may show up here, when most of the remaining genome remains virtually unchanged, charting instead much slower evolutionary processes. There are two further hypervariable segments within the control region. These other fast-evolving sequences have also been exploited to a lesser extent, as have some adjacent, slower-evolving regions that chart longer-term evolutionary trajectories.

From the mid 1990s the Y chromosome became sufficiently well charted to allow parallel analyses of the fast-evolving "microsatellites" along this chromosome's length (e.g., Underhill et al. 1996). Just as mitochondrial phylogenies reflect the female line, Y phylogenies reflect the male line. We can anticipate that other chromosomes, once well enough understood, could elaborate the composite phylogenetic picture yet further.

Owing to the relative similarity of all mammalian mitochondrial and Y sequences, the human sequence paved the way for similar studies of domesticated animals. Cattle have been studied in greatest detail, but DNA sequence data also exist for all the principal domesticated animals worldwide

(MacHugh and Bradley 2001). In plants, other categories of DNA "hotspot" are studied, and analyzed in a parallel manner to explore agricultural origins (Jones and Brown 2000). Mitochondrial DNA has also illuminated the phylogeny of certain members of the Pleistocene megafauna, but this has involved the parallel development of ancient DNA science.

Ancient DNA

Between the mid-1980s and mid-1990s the groundwork was being laid for the detection and study of ancient DNA (Jones 2001). In the short period of time since Allan Wilson's student Russell Higuchi (Higuchi et al. 1984) successfully cloned DNA from an extinct quagga, shortly after Wang and Lu (1981) had done something similar with a mummified human liver, ancient DNA science has gone through three distinct episodes. The first of these could be described as a kind of "molecular antiquarianism" in which the new technology was tested on some rather unusual curiosities, from the quagga skin, and mummified liver, to some shrunken human brains from a Florida bog. The second episode was a short interval of excessive optimism about what DNA science might achieve, from an ultra-fine analysis of archaeological sites, to a probe into the geological world of dinosaurs and insects in amber (Austin et al. 1998). This second episode was propelled by the discovery of the Polymerase Chain Reaction (PCR) that could endlessly amplify tiny quantities of DNA *in vitro* (Mullis and Faloona 1987). It was brought to an end with the sober realization of how much PCR could also amplify tiny traces of contaminant DNA, together with a more sophisticated understanding of the chemical diagenesis of DNA. The third episode has been more modest and skeptical, confining attention to the most recent 100,000 years, in the context of a clearer understanding of both DNA chemical kinetics and of how contamination operates.

Another feature of the third episode has been the realization that, within the shorter timescale, ancient DNA is retained within some far more ordinary archaeological materials than the oddities of the molecular antiquarian phase. Indeed, if it persists at all, it is likely to do so in such commonplace archaeological finds as seeds, teeth, and bones.

The current state of play is that there are a large number of archaeological research questions waiting to be addressed through modern DNA, ancient DNA, or some combination of the two. As there are only a relatively small number of laboratories fully equipped for such analyses, the field is currently in the position that modern DNA and ancient DNA projects tend to compete for research group time and attention. At present, the road to interesting results from the former is so much faster and more straightforward to follow than the latter, so that many potential ancient DNA projects remain "on hold" while the prolific vein of information from modern DNA is being intensively tapped. However, there already exist a number of key examples of how the two can be combined to address archaeological questions to a very fruitful effect. The examples chosen here also illustrate the range of scales in space and time, to which archaeogenetics can be applied.

Global Patterns: Human Origins

Molecular genetics has had a significant role in human evolutionary studies since the work of Vincent Sarich and Allan Wilson (1967) on primate albumins. They used chemical variation in albumin structure between primate species to build a phylogeny, or "family tree." They then used molecular clock arguments to argue that the common ancestor of all primates was around six times as ancient as the common ancestor of humans and our closest living relatives, the chimps and gorillas. Collation with the fossil record placed this latter ancestor around

6 million years ago. Two decades later, Wilson's students, Rebecca Cann and Mark Stoneking (Cann et al. 1987), embarked on a complementary project involving human placentas and mitochondrial DNA. From their phylogeny they inferred that a considerable part of human genetic diversity is to be found within one particular continent, Africa, and that a common ancestor of all anatomically modern humans lived around 200,000 years ago. Both the chronology and the geography of the molecular genetic results were seen as lending support to what came to be known as the Out-of-Africa model, in which anatomically modern humans evolved relatively recently in Africa, and earlier forms of *Homo* constituted separate, now extinct, species. The mitochondrial tree has been actively refined by many researchers across the world, and continues to provide rich detail to that model, and on the fate of the various branches and subbranches of human dispersal.

The alternative model of multi-regionalism remained alive, in part through the difficulty of saying anything definitive about those earlier forms of *Homo*. This situation has changed with a series of ancient DNA analyses of Neanderthal remains. The first of these was conducted on the bones of the very first Neanderthal to be recognized as a distinct form of *Homo*, the specimen unearthed from the Prussian cave at Feldhof in the mid-nineteenth century. As with so many mammalian studies, it was the first hypervariable segment of the mitochondrial control region that was initially amplified. This was sufficiently distinct from the range among modern humans to argue that Neanderthals did constitute a separate line, as envisaged in the Out-of-Africa model.

By the time Krings et al. (1997) published their first results on Neanderthal DNA, ancient DNA science had reached a level of sophistication evident in their publication. While earlier ancient DNA publications had passed over the nature of molecular preservation in the specimen, Krings' paper pays considerable attention to the molecular state

of the assayed material, through assessment of the condition of associated proteins. The amplification was independently performed in a separate lab, and due consideration was given to the problems of contamination. The DNA of two further Neanderthal specimens has since been successfully amplified (Ovchinnikov et al. 2000; Krings et al. 2000), as has the second hypervariable segment of the control region within the original Neanderthal (Krings et al. 1999). All these support the original conclusions that Neanderthals form a distinct genetic line of which no trace survives today. In addition, advances in our understanding of DNA kinetics allow us to predict where early hominid DNA might be found. While this turns our attention to the world's colder regions, where chemical breakdown is conveniently slow, a further ancient DNA result, from a decidedly warm region, has been held by some to challenge the Out-of-Africa model.

By the time Collins et al. (1999) had sufficiently developed their thermal model to predict patterns of ancient DNA persistence, one of the last places they would anticipate the survival of the ancient form was the hot Australian desert. Yet this was the source specified in the next critical aDNA publication in the debate over human origins. Adcock et al. (2001) report the amplification of mitochondrial sequences from ten hominid specimens, including a 60,000-year-old "anatomically modern" skull from Lake Mungo, subsequently dubbed Mungo Man. A human mitochondrial tree incorporating these Australian amplifications has its deepest root outside Africa, apparently challenging the original foundation of the Mitochondrial Eve hypothesis. Adcock's paper suffers from not addressing the issue of thermal history head-on. While we by no means understand everything about how DNA persists in ancient skeletal tissue, enough had been published about DNA diagenesis and contamination by the time of publication of this paper for a discussion to be appropriate. There has been subsequent published discussion of the Australian findings, and the possibility raised that amplifications arise from nuclear pseudogenes originating from modern, contaminant human DNA (Trueman 2001).

Global Patterns: Domestication

The above example illustrates a pattern of analysis that has recurred in archaeogenetics. A phylogeny is developed through extensive survey of contemporary DNA of two sorts: hypervariable segments of the mitochondrial control region, and microsatellites within the Y chromosome. From these, together with projections of the mitochondrial clock, global models are built of patterns of origin and dispersal. In the context of this analysis, ancient DNA allows lost genetic diversity to be recovered and incorporated, either to refine or to test the model. Such a pattern of analysis has also been applied successfully to animal domestication, where the lost genetic diversity in a number of instances relates to the wild progenitor.

One of the best-studied domesticates is the cow, in which phylogenetic analyses of modern breeds suggest at least three, and possibly five or more, geographically separated paths into domestication (Bradley et al. 1998; Hanotte et al. 2002). Ancient DNA from wild cattle (aurochsen) has only been amplified in Europe, but here, its mitochondrial proximity to modern European "taurine" cattle supports the multicenter model. In essence, the constructed phylogeny of cattle coalesces at too deep a point in time for that coalescence to be explained by the relatively recent phenomenon of domestication. Furthermore, the different branches of that coalescence have very distinct biogeographies. A rather similar line of argument has been used to argue for multiple domestications of several other animal species, in each case spread quite broadly across the putative range of the wild progenitor (MacHugh and Bradley 2001).

In contrast to this, Heun et al. (1997) and Badr et al. (2000) have used DNA data to argue for unitary domestications of einkorn and barley, respectively. It is important to note that the form of DNA analysis employed here is different to that used above. Rather than targeting a single sequence, a "fingerprint" is developed by systematically fragmenting the DNA sequences in their entirety. Not for the first time in genetic analyses, a pattern drawn from across the entire genetic range appears to be in conflict with a pattern derived from a particular sequence (cf. Cavalli-Sforza and Richards, above). Once again, it is important to recognize that these seemingly contrasting patterns may coexist on different scales of analysis. In the case of crop domesticates, the fingerprint analyses may indicate that the full domestic range incorporates only a small portion of the potential wild progenitor range. The DNA sequence may indicate that within that small portion, actual pathways to domestication are multiple, and geographically dispersed (Jones and Brown 2000).

Local Patterns: Kinship

In both humans and domesticates, that issue of scale has been followed down from global to regional patterns through to local patterns of animal breeds, crop varieties, and human family lineages. An instructive example of the level of precision that may be attempted is the study by Gerstenberger et al. (1999) of the earls of Konigsberg. In this, she examined a combination of mitochondrial, Y, and autosomal sequences to establish the family relationships between eight bodies buried within a chapel. That family structure could then be compared, and in some cases matched up, with seven memorial plaques on the walls of the ruined chapel. It transpired that the mismatches were as interesting as the matches, indicating an occasional conflict between how the earls actually lived and how their descendants chose to remember them. A great number of archaeological funerary groups, and all those from prehistory, will lack a parallel series of names and dates. A number of projects, however, have begun to explore patterns of kinship, exogamy, and residence from detailed DNA studies of this kind.

The Third Trophic Level

It was suggested earlier that archaeology and genetics could potentially interact at three trophic levels in the human food chain. However, most of the actual interaction has related to the lower two levels, humans and their own food species. Exploration of the level above has been constrained by the difficulty of connecting expressed gene data with the very patchy archaeological evidence for our micropredators (disease organisms). That evidence has been limited to skeletal deformations resulting from slow-acting bacteria. Over the past ten years, several publications have reported amplifications of ancient pathogens, and in addition, comprehensive gene maps have been published for living pathogens.

Of particular interest is the complete gene map for the plague bacterium *Yersinia pestis* (Parkhill et al. 2001). The profound demographic impact of *Y.pestis* on European populations in the mid-second millennium AD is well attested, and there is a strong argument for a similar or even greater impact in the mid-first millennium AD. Taking these pandemics together, this single micropredator would appear to have had an abating effect on the human population on a scale comparable to the exponential growth in evidence of intervening periods from the first millennium BC onwards. It has not been possible to determine whether these millennial predator–prey cycles were just a feature of the last two millennia, or whether, like other disease patterns, they were triggered by some earlier ecological shift, such as the beginnings of permanent settlement and agriculture. One interesting feature of the *Y.pestis* gene map has been a range of attributes associated with a "youthful"

genome. It has been inferred that the plague bacterium may have evolved from a relatively mild gastric complaint as recently as 20,000–15, 000 years ago. To place this evolutionary episode in its historical context, its chronology needs tighter resolution, something that is less than straightforward.

Timescales

One of the main difficulties facing archaeologists when tackling some of the principal questions about population movement, language spread, food production, or disease, is that answering those questions entails distinguishing at least three separate cultural horizons within the last 50,000 years. To be more specific, there are three distinct types of episode in our species' past that it has been suggested could have a radical impact on each of these patterns.

1 The first spread of anatomically modern humans across the globe.
2 The transition from foraging to farming, and subsequent expansion of farmers.
3 The migration of later "complex" culture groups, often with an urban and/or military dimension.

The most commonly employed timescale in archaeogenetics has been the molecular clock (Zuckerkandl and Pauling 1965). The principle behind that clock is that certain molecular sequences, particularly in the non-coding regions of DNA, mutate randomly and thus related lineages accumulate within those regions differences that collectively serve as a measure of the passage of the time period that separates them from their common ancestor. Different forms of the molecular clock were used by Sarich and Wilson (1967) to date the divergence of hominids and chimpanzees, by Cann et al. (1987) to date Mitochondrial Eve, and many subsequent researchers to date yet more finescale changes within the human past. In archaeological terms the molecular clock is never a precise instrument. Some critiques questioned whether the 200,000-year estimate for Mitochondrial Eve was pushing the clock beyond its capacity for precision. Nonetheless, subsequent publications have used the principle to derive dates that are a mere fraction of this, often published without any reference to an error term.

The molecular clock has proven invaluable within the wider evolutionary field, distinguishing events that are millions of years apart. There remains significant doubt about whether the conventional use of the molecular clock confidently allows discrimination between three distinct time horizons within the last 50,000 years. There are two routes to addressing this problem. The first involves refining the molecular clock, and finding ways to measure its error term (cf., Saillard et al. 2000). The second involves calibration by ancient DNA. Refinement of the clock involves two things: first, the assessment of an error term, and second, an improved understanding of factors affecting sequence mutation. Both these are proceeding, but are in their early stages. The principles of calibration by ancient DNA are more straightforward, and entail connecting a fragment of DNA sequence with a well-dated archaeological context.

The principal use of ancient DNA science in published studies to date has been to recover genetic diversity lost through shrinkage or extinction. While its potential to calibrate the clock has been self-evident, that potential has rarely been explored. One rare example of such a project is the work of Goloubonoff et al. (1993) on maize, which had the specific goal of testing whether the rate of molecular clocks was affected by domestication. More recently, Lambert et al. (2002) brought ancient DNA analysis of a stratigraphic sequence of Antarctic penguin remains, together with detailed radiocarbon dating, to question the accuracy of the molecular clock. How soon the potential for such calibration approaches will be explored probably depends on the success or otherwise of refining the molecular clock in its

own right. However, it seems likely at some stage that resolution to specific archaeological questions will require the tight chronological and contextual information that can only be derived from ancient stratified genetic data.

The Current State of Play

The detailed charting and phylogenetic analysis of modern DNA sequence variation is currently proving highly productive for models of origin and geographical movement directly relating to the human past. Such momentum shows no signs of abating. Within human sequence diversity, striking patterns have been emerging on two distinct scales, the broadly global and the very local.

The broadly global patterns published by Cavalli-Sforza et al. (1994), and since elaborated in a range of DNA sequence projects, would not have emerged from any data set. There is no intrinsic reason why so much of the genetic variation need have so clearcut a geographic structure, and global gene maps could theoretically have been far more confused. The fact that they are not highlights the importance of a relatively small number of principal drivers for human colonization of the world. Discussion of these drivers has revolved around the three episodes outlined above.

The very local patterns are steadily emerging from detailed sequence analyses, particularly of mitochondrial DNA. They suggest that once modern humans had reached a certain area, much of subsequent human movement was highly localized, such that certain identifiable lineages or "haplotypes" retain much the same epicenter, with a few hundred kilometers at least, for several thousand years (Forster et al. 2002).

In fact, the two trends are not in conflict, and need not be segregated to different episodes in time. If we were to surmise that for most of the human past, many individuals have remained geographically close to their recognized kin, from this would emerge the latter, local pattern. Against this background, if we were also to surmise that those individuals moving beyond this "familiar" zone have always been able to move a considerable distance within their lifetime, then from a relatively modest "leakage" of this kind could emerge the former pattern. There is much unspecified in this dual model that is, in principle, open to inquiry. For example, the simplicity of the global patterns could either come from the episodic nature of the "leakage" as has been surmised in many archaeogenetic studies to date, or from the constraint along geographical corridors of a more sustained leakage, or from some combination of the two. Well within reach is a more detailed commentary on the different mobilities of men and women, as reflected by Y and mitochondrial patterns, respectively. As our understanding of these patterns improves, so archaeologists and geneticists alike may be expected to shift from such unspecific concepts as "migration" to more specific consideration of such concepts as "emigration" (the wholesale movement of domestic units) and "exogamy" (the transfer of marriage partners between existing communities).

Interposed between these two scales, the broadly global and the very local, are a series of intermediate categories that tend to conflate lineage, ecology, and the constitution of society in an often complex manner. They have, however, had a powerful influence over how the interaction between archaeology and genetics has been articulated. The categories include "race," "population," and "ethnic group." For much of the twentieth century, those categories were regarded as more or less coterminous. Their primacy in archaeological and genetic discourse seemed unproblematic. Developments in both science and politics have changed that. On the one hand, the usage of each has had its own trajectory. On the other, the relationship of each to archaeogenetics has been different.

It could be argued that "race" has often involved a classification of encounter, with considerable attention drawn to features of the face, the head, and bodily posture, and in second place to categories less evident when coming face to face with another individual. Some of the component elements, such as skin color (Jablonski and Chaplin 2000), are proving to have an interesting evolutionary ecology in their own right. It is generally agreed that the attributes traditionally associated with race have an evolutionary timescale that is relatively short in comparison with the species as a whole (Cavalli-Sforza et al. 1994).

The term *population* has been used to indicate a group within which gene flow is relatively unimpeded, and has a boundary that constitutes a complete or partial barrier to gene flow. The human species as a whole could be regarded as a population, as could subsections separated by some unnavigated ocean, mountain range, or stretch of ice. The term has also been commonly used on a far more local scale, in which the barriers to gene flow are far more open to question. In this sense, the term is typically conflated with ethnic group.

Ethnic group is primarily a socially constructed entity. It refers to the group as actually recognized by its members, and who may incorporate biological ancestry into their sense of collective identity in a variety of ways. While post-World War II archaeogenetics has taken great care with its usage of "race," the common identity of "ethnic group" and "population" has often been taken as a premise, with the concomitant danger of circular argument. In some cases that association may be strong, in others weak, and in others it may mask the real geographic pattern within the data. If premise and inference are duly separated, then archaeogenetics has considerable potential to investigate the dynamics of ethnicity as a changing cultural construct.

This potential relates to the different kinds of genetic pattern open to detection. On the one hand, there are *qualitative* differences between individuals (for example, the Sub-Saharan marker sequences, or the Pacific 9 base-pair deletion), which may only be explained by common ancestry or parallel evolution. On the other hand, there are *quantitative* differences in lineage frequencies between populations, which may also be generated by sustained reproductive isolation. Separate analyses of these should allow distinctions to be drawn between such scenarios as the following:

1 Ethnic categories whose roots are in biological ancestry.
2 Ethnic categories whose origins and iteration through time are culturally constructed.
3 Ethnic categories whose roots are in sociopolitics and allegiance, but in which avoidance of intermarriage has generated a quantitative genetic signature, through founder effects and drift.

Much archaeology grew out of nineteenth-century episodes of nation building, in which the conflation of the terms discussed above was close to the central goals of the discipline. We are now at a more critical stage of using archaeology to explore how notions of societal identity come about, and which involves disaggregating those concepts and exploring their historical and evolutionary interrelationships.

Some Future Prospects

The global geographical pattern of genetic diversity is rapidly unfolding a range of taxa in the human food web, not least humans themselves. In some cases, this is being enhanced by the lost genetic diversity revealed in ancient DNA, and a number of approaches are being brought together to provide a timescale for their inferred phylogenies. As has been discussed above, the precision of that timescale is itself a key target for future research. Beyond this, we may also anticipate a greater resolution of the ecological and social dimensions of the processes behind these genetic patterns, within a more critical treatment of scale.

The improved ecological picture may be expected to come from two paths: the integrated study of coexisting species, and interaction with Quaternary science. One illuminating example of the meeting of these two paths is found in the passage of human communities across Beringia. Humans were not alone in facing the ecological challenge of colonizing the most northerly latitudes and then spreading into a new continent, and much can be learnt from genetic studies of other mammals, birds, and micropredators. To this end, modern and ancient DNA studies have each been brought together to study the late Quaternary movement from the Old World to the New, in relation to bears (Leonard et al. 2000), dogs (Leonard 2000, 2002), and the TB bacillus (Arriaza et al. 1995). As with humans, these studies are now situated within a detailed understanding of Quaternary climate change and its implications for ice cover, coastal change, and biomass.

An improved understanding of the social dimension of gene movement may also be expected to come from two paths: first, from the detailed analysis of kinship, exogamy, and residence patterns (cf. Oota et al. 2001); second, from historical sociolinguistics. What genetic and linguistic diversity have in common is that many of the global patterns are rather simpler than we might have imagined. We know enough about how people move, interact, and learn language, to envisage considerable potential complexity in the resulting patterns of diversity. Sometimes that complexity is encountered, yet in many cases there are simple, global patterns to be observed. It is the recurrent simplicity of pattern that has proven so stimulating for archaeology in recent years. The migration models thus far proposed to account for such patterns have not taken full account of the ecological and social structures of past human communities, and the importance of scale in linking local and global patterns. It is in these areas that we may anticipate the next episode of refinement and interaction between the disciplines.

A Productive Engagement

Disciplinary interaction can be as difficult as it is stimulating. It is frequently initiated from the hope of one discipline to gather up the "results" produced by the other, in order to answer its own internally generated questions. Archaeologists might ask geneticists to clarify the beginnings of agriculture, the "origins" of the Polynesians, or the ethnic composition of Anglo-Saxon England, for example. Geneticists might seek a discrete and uncontroversial sequence of migration episodes to match with, and thereby explain, a series of maps, trees, and networks generated from their genetic data. Sooner or later, researchers in each discipline discover the uncertainties, disagreements, and evolving perceptions in each other's community. At this point they move on from the straightforward consumption of each other's results to the more challenging exploration of shared problems. The core problem shared by archaeology and genetics (and indeed language history) today is how to relate multiscalar patterns of contemporary human diversity with the multiscalar processes of human history.

My emphasis on multiple scale highlights one of the key challenges to a productive engagement. There has been a reasonable hope that genetic maps of one kind or another might guide archaeologists in their search for excavated data. Indeed, the search for agricultural origins is testimony to how productive such an approach can be. The data being matched, however, exist on very different scales. While the genetic patterns have emerged from hundreds of human generations, an excavated site often reflects just a few generations of one community, and any excavated feature and its contents an individual episode within a single human biography. There is no inherent reason why the patterns experienced within that one biographical episode need correspond to any structure emerging from hundreds of generations. The models that once reduced pattern to a single scale, in which community, population, ethnic group, language, material culture, and genetic signature were treated as coterminous, are no longer viable. Future analyses will need to adopt a kind of *Braudelian*, step-wise approach, which moves from individuals to their immediate familiar community, through the difficult and elusive level of "population" and on to the global patterns of the human community as a whole. Each scale has its own recoverable genetic and archaeological manifestations, involving such things as agency and kinship at one extreme, and gene flow, clines, and bottlenecks at the other. The great challenge is to understand how patterns at these different scales interconnect. The great potential, which lies at the core of the genetic revolution itself, is the newly emerged potential to explore and chart these relationships on so many different scales and levels.

References

Adcock, G. J. et al. 2001. "Mitochondrial DNA sequences in ancient Australians: implications for modern human origins." *Proceedings of the National Academy of Sciences* 98: 537–42.

Anderson, S. et al. 1981. "Sequence organization of the human mitochondrial genome." *Nature* 290: 457–64.

Arriaza, B. T., W. Salo, A. Aufderheide, and T. Holcomb 1995. "Pre-Columbian tuberculosis in northern Chile: molecular and skeletal evidence." *American Journal of Physical Anthropology* 98 (1): 37–45.

Austin, J. J. et al. 1998. "Ancient DNA from amber inclusions: a review of the evidence." *Ancient Biomolecules* 2 (2): 167–76.

Badr, A. et al. 2000. "On the origin and domestication history of barley (*Hordeum vulgare*)." *Molecular Biology and Evolution* 17: 499–510.

Boyd, W. C. and L. G. Boyd 1933. "Blood grouping by means of preserved muscle." *Science* 78 (2034): 578.

Bradley, D. G., R. T. Loftus, E. P. Cunningham, and D. E. MacHugh 1998. "Genetics and domestic cattle origins." *Evolutionary Anthropology* 6 (3): 79–86.

Cann, R. L., M. Stoneking, and A. C. Wilson 1987. "Mitochondrial DNA and human evolution." *Nature* 325: 31–6.

Cavalli-Sforza, L. L., P. Menozzi, and A. Piazza 1994. *The History and Geography of Human Genes*. Princeton, NJ: Princeton University Press.

Collins, M. J., E. R. Waite, and A. C. T. Van Duin 1999. "Predicting protein decomposition: the case of aspartic-acid racemization kinetics." *Philosophical Transactions of the Royal Society, Series B* 354: 51–64.

Forster, P. et al. 2002. "Continental and subcontinental distributions of mtDNA control region types." *International Journal of Legal Medicine* 116: 99–108.

Gerstenberger, J. et al. 1999. "Reconstruction of a historical genealogy by means of STR analysis and Y-haplotyping of ancient DNA." *European Journal of Human Genetics* 7 (4): 469–77.

Goloubonoff, P., S. Paabo, and A. C. Wilson 1993. "Evolution of maize inferred from sequence diversity of an Adh2 gene segment from archaeological specimens." *Proceedings of the National Academy of Sciences* 90: 1997–2001.

Hanotte, O. et al. 2002. "African pastoralism: genetic imprints of origins and migrations." *Science* 296: 336–9.

Harris, D. R. 1990. "Vavilov's concept of centres of origin of cultivated plants: its genesis and its influence on the study of agricultural origins." *Biological Journal of the Linnean Society* 39: 7–16.

Heun, M. et al. 1997. "Site of einkorn wheat domestication identified by DNA fingerprinting." *Science* 278: 1312–14.

Higuchi, R. G. et al. 1984. "DNA sequences from the quagga, an extinct member of the horse family." *Nature* 312: 282–4.

Hirschfeld, L. and H. Hirschfeld 1919. "Serological differences between the blood of different races." *Lancet* 2: 675–8.

Jablonski, N. G. and G. Chaplin 2000. "The evolution of human skin coloration." *Journal of Human Evolution* 39: 57–106.

Jones, M. K. 2001. *The Molecule Hunt: Archaeology and the Search for Ancient DNA*. London: Allen Lane.

Jones, M. K. and T. A. Brown 2000. "Agricultural origins: the evidence of modern and ancient DNA." *Holocene* 10 (6): 775–82.

Krings, M. et al. 1997. "Neandertal DNA sequences and the origin of modern humans." *Cell* 90: 19–30.

Krings, M. et al. 1999. "DNA sequence of the mitochondrial hypervariable region II from the Neandertal type specimen." *Proceedings of the National Academy of Sciences* 96: 5581–5.

Krings, M. et al. 2000. "A view of Neandertal genetic diversity." *Nature Genetics* 26: 144–6.

Lambert, D. M. et al. 2002. "Rates of evolution in ancient DNA from Adélie penguins." *Science* 295: 2270–3.

Leonard, J. A. 2000. "Origin of American dogs, a separate domestication?" Presentation to the 5th International Ancient DNA Conference, UMIST, Manchester.

Leonard, J. A., R. K. Wayne, and A. Cooper 2000. "From the cover: population genetics of Ice Age brown bears." *Proceedings of the National Academy of Sciences* 97: 1651–4.

Leonard, J. A. et al. 2002. "Ancient DNA evidence for Old World origin of New World dogs. *Science* 298 (November 22): 1613–16.

MacHugh, D. E., and D. G. Bradley 2001. "Livestock genetic origins: goats buck the trend." *Proceedings of the National Academy of Sciences* 98: 5382.

Mullis, K. B. and F. A. Faloona 1987. "Specific synthesis of DNA in vitro via a polymerase catalysed chain reaction." *Methods in Enzymology* 155: 335–50.

Oota, H. W. et al. 2001. "Human mtDNA and Y-chromosome variation is correlated with matrilocal vs. patrilocal residence." *Nature Genetics* 29: 20–1.

Ovchinnikov, I. V. et al. 2000. "Molecular analysis of Neanderthal DNA from the northern Caucasus." *Nature* 404: 490–3.

Parkhill, J. et al. 2001. "Genome sequence of Yersinia pestis, the causative agent of plague." *Nature* 413: 523–7.

Renfrew, A. C. and K. Boyle 2000. *Archaeogenetics: DNA and the Population Prehistory of Europe*. Cambridge: McDonald Institute Monographs.

Richards, M. et al. 1996. "Paleolithic and Neolithic lineages in the European mitochondrial gene pool." *American Journal of Human Genetics* 59 (1): 185–203.

Saillard, J. et al. 2000. "mtDNA variation among Greenland Eskimos: the edge of Beringian expansion." *American Journal of Human Genetics* 67: 718–26.

Sarich, V. M. and A. C. Wilson 1967. "Immunological timescale for hominid evolution." *Science* 158: 1200–3.

Trueman, J. W. H. 2001. "Does the Lake Mungo 3 mtDNA evidence stand up to analysis?" *Archaeologia Oceania* 36: 163–5.

Underhill, A. et al. 1996. "A pre-Columbian Y chromosome-specific transition and its implications for human evolutionary history." *Proceedings of the National Academy of Sciences* 93 (1): 196–200.

Vavilov, N. 1992. *The Origin and Geography of Cultivated Plants*. Cambridge: Cambridge University Press.

Vilà, C., J. E. Maldonado, and R. K. Wayne 1999. "Phylogenetic relationships, evolution, and genetic diversity of the domestic dog." *Journal of Heredity* 90 (1): 71–7.

Wang, G. H. and C. L. Lu 1981. "Isolation and identification of nucleic acids of the liver from a corpse from the Changssha Han tomb." *Shen Wu Hua Hsueh Yu Sheng Wu Li Chin Chan* 17: 70–5.

Watson, J. D. and F. C. Crick 1953. "Molecular structure of nucleic acids: a structure for deoxyribose nucleic acids." *Nature* 171: 737–8.

Zohary, D. and H. Hopf 1993. *Domestication of Plants in the Old World: The Origin and Spread of Cultivated Plants in West Asia, Europe and the Nile Valley*. Oxford: Oxford University Press.

Zuckerkandl, E. and L. Pauling 1965. "Evolutionary divergence and convergence in proteins." In V. Bryson and H. J. Vogel (eds.), *Evolving Genes and Proteins*, pp. 97–166. New York: Academic Press.

4

Archaeology and Language: Methods and Issues

Roger Blench

Introduction

The relationship between linguistics and archaeology reflects both the internal dynamic of the disciplines themselves and external political and social trends. Many archaeologists have asserted that archaeology and linguistics do not share much common ground; some for reasons internal to archaeology, while other reasons may be traced to the sometimes startling misuse of the conjunction of disciplines by earlier scholars. Linguistics is in many ways more internally diverse than archaeology; a much greater proportion of its practitioners are engaged in high theory, and fieldwork is often perceived as a low-prestige activity. The great majority of linguists are engaged in an enterprise that really does have no relevance for archaeology, while the reverse is not true. However, among the subset of linguists interested in historical topics, few have not at least glanced at archaeology, in the light of its potential to provide interpretive tools for their findings.

The argument from the linguists' point of view is simply put: languages were spoken by real people in the past and indeed form striking patterns in the present. This must have been the consequence of distinct strategies of movement and diversification of peoples and somehow reflects their changing social and economic conditions. Historical linguistics appears to tell us that we can plot the development of language families, and reconstruct particular lexical items of economic significance, such as hunting gear or food crops. It therefore seems that we should be able to map archaeological findings against these. Although dating algorithms, notably glottochronology, have been developed by historical linguists, few now subscribe to them, and a radiocarbon date for the first settlement of a Polynesian island is on the whole much more satisfying than a calculation from an equation developed for Indo-European.

Things are much different on the other side of the divide. Most archaeologists spend their entire careers without giving any thought to comparative linguistics. There are two distinct reasons for this: either because it is evident what language was spoken by the people who occupied the sites they excavate, or because they have actively rejected linguistics. In the case of medieval, classical, Egyptian, or Mayan archaeology, such questions do not usually arise; although epigraphy may play an active role in the interpretation of their data, archaeologists do not engage with the findings of historical linguistics. The rejection of the opportunity to identify speech communities is more interesting but also more problematic, as it seems to arise from a barely articulated background ideology. Glyn Daniel, for example, wrote:

> We must alas, for the most part, keep the builders and bearers of our prehistoric cultures speechless and physically neutral. This may seem to you an unsatisfying conclusion. And so it is but then much of our prehistory is unsatisfying and difficult, tantalizingly meager and sketchy. We can appreciate this and accept the limitations of prehistory along with its excitements. (Daniel 1962: 114–15)

There are two things going on here: on the one hand, a fear of being identified with the sort of nationalist archaeology characteristic of Nazi Germany and Soviet Russia; on the other hand, a fear of being identified with the crackpot theorizing that has blurred the serious study of prehistory from the seventeenth century onwards (Blench and Spriggs 1999). In more recent times, with the growth of the nation-state, a more diffuse and less threatening nationalist archaeology has developed. The past is hauled in to underwrite the present, most notably in countries where a major tourist income derives from that past, such as Mexico or Egypt. Although avoiding any engagement with this more recent agenda may also be an implicit strategy, there is a more general feeling that archaeology is a discipline with its own highly positivist and empiricist traditions and that speculation about "peoples" and "cultures" is simply irrelevant to, say, the classification of lithics. Trigger (1989: 356) comments:

> Yet there is little general awareness of the value of combining the study of archaeological data with that of historical linguistics, oral traditions, historical ethnography and historical records, although it is clear that many archaeological problems can be resolved in this way . . . the resistance seems to come from the view, widely held by processual archaeologists, that their dis-

cipline must be based as exclusively as possible on the study of material culture.

For very different reasons, then, only 10 percent of archaeologists engage with a similar proportion of linguists. Nonetheless, the engagement has been largely fruitful and continues to be so. The rest of this chapter[1] looks at the major issues in this engagement, both methodologically and practically, and considers some particular topics that have been the recent focus of debate.

The Genesis of an Idea

Historical linguistics, like many another discipline, has a slightly disreputable past. Some of its early practitioners developed models of world prehistory by arguing for links between geographically remote languages in the context of biblical references, such as the location of the lost tribes of Israel (Wauchope 1962). This type of scholarship is often broadly referred to as Voltairean linguistics, from a famous apothegm attributed by Max Müller (1871: 238) to Voltaire: "Etymology is a science in which the vowels count for nothing and the consonants for very little."[2]

Historical linguistics in the modern sense began as a comparison of written languages and textbooks. Sir William Jones' famous lecture in 1786 is typically cited as demonstrating the links between Sanskrit and the classical languages of Europe. Precursors to historical linguistics existed, both among the Sanskrit grammarians and in the works of rabbinical scholars. For example, Yehuda Ibn Quraysh, who lived in Fez, Morocco in the tenth century, was the first to compare the phonology and morphology of Hebrew, Aramaic, and Arabic in his book 'Risāla (Téné 1980). However, Van Driem (2001: 1039 ff.) has shown that the conventional accounts (Bonfante 1953; Muller 1986) of the predecessors of Jones, notably Marcus van Boxhorn, are highly inaccurate.[3] Boxhorn's (1647) study of "Scythian" (comparative Indo-European) represents the first discussion of the methodological issues in assigning languages to genetic groups. He observed that to use lexical cognates, loanwords must be first eliminated, and he placed great emphasis on common morphological systems and on irregularity, *anomalien*, as an indicator of relationship. Even the expression *ex eadem origine*, "from a common source," first appears in a book by Johann Elichmann (1640: iii), who served as a doctor at the Persian court, and which uses morphology to relate European languages to Indo-Iranian. Indeed, these earlier accounts were significantly more accurate than Jones, who erroneously believed that Egyptian, Japanese, and Chinese were part of Indo-European while Hindi was not, which suggests that his method was seriously flawed.

The concept of reconstructing an Indo-European proto-language appears as early as 1713 in the works of the English divine William Wotton:

> My argument does not depend on the difference of Words, but upon the Difference of Grammar between any two languages; from whence it proceeds, that when any Words are derived from one Language into another, the derived Words are then turned and changed according to the particular Genius of the Language into which they are transplanted . . . I can easily suppose that they might both be derived from one common Mother, which is, and perhaps has for many Ages been entirely lost. (Wotton 1730 [1713]: 57)

Wotton showed that Icelandic ("Teutonic"), the Romance languages, and Greek were related, which is certainly as convincing a demonstration of Indo-European affinities as Jones' links between classical languages and Sanskrit.

Although earlier scholars worked principally with written languages, most historical linguistics today is used to illuminate the evolution of unwritten or recently written languages, and it is this which has been of

greatest interest to archaeologists. The recognition of the major language families is often surprisingly early. The outlines of the Austronesian family were first recognized in the early eighteenth century by the Dutch scholar Adriaan van Reeland, who compared Malay, Malagasy, and Polynesian (Relandus 1708). Remarkably, the earliest sketch of an entirely unwritten language phylum appears to be Arawakan, the languages spoken in the pre-Columbian Caribbean, but stretching into today's southeast Colombia, which dates from 1782 (Gilij 1780–4). Gilij's insights were remarkable for their time; he recognized sound-correspondences as a key tool in classifying languages, focused on the importance of word order patterns, and discussed the diffusion of loanwords.

The earliest phase of historical linguistics was then essentially classificatory, as linguists discovered the tools that were available to assign individual languages to specific groups. If there was any interpretation of these findings it was in terms of a vague migrationism, unanchored in specific historical events. However, by the nineteenth century, scholars had begun to turn to the analysis of language to establish historical results. Donaldson (1839: 12) observed in the 1830s:

> There is in fact no sure way of tracing the history and migrations of the early inhabitants of the world except by means of their languages; any other mode of enquiry must rest on the merest conjecture and hypothesis. It may seem strange that anything so vague and arbitrary as language should survive all other testimonies, and speak with more definiteness, even in its changed and modern state, than all other monuments, however grand and durable.

At the same time, both the analogy with biological speciation and the identity of language with supposed human race began to be developed. Darwin (1859: 405) commented:

> If we possessed a perfect pedigree of mankind, a genealogical arrangement of the

races of man would afford the best classification of the various languages now spoken throughout the world; and if all the extinct languages, and all intermediate and slowly changing dialects had to be included, such an arrangement would, I think, be the only possible one . . . this would be strictly natural, as it would connect together all languages extinct and modern, by the closest affinities, and would give the filiation and origin of each tongue.

Almost simultaneously, Pictet (1859–63) had begun to develop the notion of "linguistic palaeontology," the idea that prehistory can be reconstructed from specific evidence drawn from modern spoken languages and the transformation of individual words. That he used the data to evolve convoluted and highly suspect theories of the migrations of the Aryan race should not distract attention from the significance of the enterprise.

Another development in the same era was lexicostatistics, the counting of cognate words between two or more languages in a standardized list (Hymes 1983). Dumont d'Urville (1834) compared a number of Oceanic languages (which would today be called Austronesian) and proposed a method for calculating a coefficient of their relationship. When he extended his comparison to a sample of Amerindian languages he correctly concluded that they were not related to Oceanic. Lexicostatistics is associated in more modern times with the work of Morris Swadesh, and was a key tool in the armory of historical linguists in the 1960s and 1970s, before some of its methodological problems began to surface.

A sister discipline to lexicostatistics is glottochronology, the notion that if the differentiation between languages can be assigned numerical status then it might be regularly related to the time-depth of the split between languages (Swadesh 1952). Wotton (1730) had early had the idea of calculating how rapidly languages change, by comparing ancient texts of known date with the modern form of those languages, while Latham (1850) first sketched the possibility of assigning a precise date to the divergence of two languages through the application of a mathematical algorithm.

The attractive aspect of both lexicostatistics and glottochronology is quantification: they seem to represent a scientific approach to the dating and genetic classification of languages. However, few historical linguists now accept these approaches,[4] in part because they have signally failed to tie up with archaeology where the result was not known in advance. More important, improved understanding of sociolinguistics and the reporting of a wide variety of case studies of language creolization and mixture have contributed to the realization that language interactions are complex and diverse and lead to a wide variety of end results (e.g., Thomason and Kaufman 1988). Mathematical methods must assume a standard of lexical purity that does not exist in the real world. The generally accepted methods of historical linguistics make possible only relative dating; for absolute dating, linguists inevitably turn to archaeology.

Testable Hypotheses

One of the attractive aspects of linking historical linguistics with archaeology is that it is possible to generate testable hypotheses. Linguists are usually far in advance of archaeologists in their speculations. Finding an informant for a language is easier and far less costly than mounting an archaeological expedition to search, for example, for the origins of food production. An experienced linguist can often elicit a range of basic and cultural vocabulary in a few hours, whereas excavations often take many years and require a team of researchers combining very different skills. Historical linguists are often tempted to throw off hypotheses on the origins of food production far more quickly and perhaps more casually than would be permissible within another academic framework.

However, when a prediction is made then it can at least be tested. So, for example, if a historical linguist claims that certain species of domestic animal can be reconstructed back to the proto-language of a particular phylum, and at the same time makes a proposal for the homeland of the speakers of the proto-language, then excavations should ideally be able to confirm the presence of those species. A striking example of such a correlation is presented by Green and Pawley (1999), where linguistics is used both to pinpoint the homeland of Oceanic languages and to suggest the features of house forms that should be present. Excavation suggests that structures of the predicted type *are* indeed present. Such correlations are rare in practice, especially when only a small number of sites have been identified, but as the density of well-investigated sites increases, hypotheses can be subjected to more rigorous tests.

The Geography of Interdisciplinary Traditions

To engage with other disciplines, especially those with traditions as different as archaeology and linguistics, requires a positive institutional background. This in turn reflects the intellectual climate and the organization of research in particular countries or regions. It turns out that the system of assigning all research in these areas to universities has often created a major block, probably because of the competitive nature of funding within national systems. Countries with national research centers that unite scholars from different intellectual areas, such as France with the CNRS and IRD, the former Soviet Union with its many Institutes, and Australia with RSPAS, have been far more likely to produce interdisciplinary scholarship than England and America, where researchers must also teach in departments of universities. Generally speaking, where careers depend on publications, and only publications in a specific discipline are highly

valued, there is every incentive to concentrate in one intellectual area to the exclusion of others.

The consequence has been that the conjunction of linguistics and archaeology has developed very different outcomes in different regions. Eurasia and the Pacific lead the field; Eurasia because of the Indo-Europeanist tradition and its remarkable survivals in the former Soviet Union, and the Pacific because of the fortunate support for these approaches in a few key institutions. North America represents a particular paradox, because its all-embracing tradition of anthropology usually brings together archaeology, cultural anthropology, and linguistics in single departments. One might expect, therefore, a whole series of rich syntheses; it seems likely that Boas and Kroeber would have seen this as the end result of their labors. However, their virtual absence rather suggests that the reality has been academic isolationism, a tradition that has been replicated in the literature of the New World as a whole. Within Africa, research traditions are highly variable. A lack of dedicated institutions has meant that most archaeological and linguistic research is either by outsiders or funded by them, and inevitably they bring their own agendas. In addition, a shallow time-depth has meant that consolidated approaches of any type have yet to develop.

What Drives Language Dispersals?

Given that the world shelters a finite and quite small number of language phyla, it is reasonable to ask by what process these have spread. The modern era has seen the expansion of Indo-European, notably Spanish, English, and Russian, and the consequent disappearance of many small language groups. We assume that the spread of Arabic, Chinese, and Hindi was responsible for similar past vanishings and that indeed this process has occurred many times prior to recorded history. What we cannot assume is that the reasons for the expansion of particular languages or language families were similar. The expansion of Indo-European through "guns, germs and steel" (Diamond 1998) may be a misleading model for much of the past. Indeed, it is hard to eliminate the suspicion that Diamond's account is a celebration of American technological triumphalism rather than a description of the diverse patterns of cultural change.

Debate about the process of expansion has centered on a key opposition between migration and cultural shift. The modern spread of Indo-European was a physical expansion; in other words, individuals moved to new regions, notably America and Australia, and their offspring came to dominate those regions numerically. Such physical movements undoubtedly occurred in the past as well. The Austronesian migrations out of Taiwan, for example, seem to have been a population movement, pushing the existing Negrito populations of insular southeast Asia into refuge areas. But languages can also spread by processes of assimilation and language shift – one ethnolinguistic group persuading others to switch languages through force or prestige. The expansion of Hausa in West Africa is probably a good example of this. Today, many minority groups on the fringes of Hausaland are switching to Hausa for prestige reasons and Hausa clan names suggest strongly that this process can be read back into the past. It seems likely that the spread of Pama-Nyungan in Australia was similar (see below). In the end, though, we are likely to have to resort to "mixed" models; people move, but sometimes quite small numbers of people can persuade much larger groups to copy their way of doing things.

In recent years, the broader process of model-making has been intertwined with what may be called the "farming dispersals" hypothesis. Originally developed by Renfrew (1987) as a challenge to the conventional "horse warrior" view of Indo-European origins, it has evolved into a much more general characterization of the dispersals of individual language phyla and particular types of archaeological culture. In particular, the notion has arisen that many language groupings were a consequence of agricultural origins, an idea that has been taken up by Peter Bellwood and promoted in a number of places (e.g., Bellwood 1991, 1996, 1997). Versions of Renfrew's classification of language phyla by modes of dispersal have been published in many places, but Table 4.1 provides a convenient useful recent statement.

There is much detailed comment that could be made about this modelling process, but some more general points emerge:

1   The classification adopts a "tidy" view of world language phyla, derived mainly from Ruhlen (1991), who in turn reproduced whole many of Greenberg's controversial macrophyla hypotheses, notably Indo-Pacific and Amerind. It should be noted that *no* specialized scholars of these regions accept these hypotheses and that both Melanesia and the Americas seem destined to remain highly complex.

2   It mixes very different levels of genetic classification; for example, "Niger-Kordofanian (specifically the Bantu languages)." Bantu is a small subgroup of Niger–Congo despite its geographic dispersal and this formulation makes it unclear whether the other 800 languages in Niger–Congo can be said to take part in this process.

3   Most importantly, it does not engage with the actual linguistic evidence. Published evidence that any type of farming technology can be reconstructed for Sino-Tibetan, Austroasiatic, "Early Altaic," or Elamo-Dravidian (itself a controversial grouping) is non-existent.

This last is probably the most important point; language phyla are intellectual constructs of a very different order of empirical reality from potsherds. If we are to interpret their distribution, then the phyla themselves

Table 4.1 Language phylum dispersals and their stratification

---

CLASS A: MOSAIC ZONE (PLEISTOCENE)

1 *Initial colonization prior to 12,000* BP
"Khoisan," "Nilo-Saharan" (plus later "aquatic" expansion), Northern Caucasian, South Caucasian, "Indo-Pacific" (plus later farming changes), North Australian, "Amerind" (with subsequent spread zone processes), localized ancestral groups of II and III (below)

CLASS B: SPREAD ZONE (POST-PLEISTOCENE)

2 *Farming dispersal after 10,000* BP
Niger-Kordofanian (specifically the Bantu languages), Afroasiatic, Indo-European, Elamo-Dravidian, Early Altaic, Sino-Tibetan, Austronesian, Austroasiatic

3 *Northern, climate-sensitive adjustments after 10,000* BP
Uralic-Yukaghir, Chukchi-Kamchatkan, Na-Dene, Eskimo-Aleut

4 *Elite dominance*
Indo-Iranian, Later Altaic, Southern Sino-Tibetan (Han)

5 *Long-distance maritime colonization since 1400* AD (elite dominance plus farming dispersal)
Mainly Indo-European (English, Spanish, Portuguese, French)

Source: Renfrew (in press)

must contain internal linguistic evidence for the engine of their proposed dispersion. In other words, if you are to assert that the Niger–Congo phylum spread following the adoption of agriculture, then vocabulary in the actual languages must support this assertion, otherwise the identity amounts to little more than a statement that early farming coincides with the present-day distribution of languages. In the case of Niger–Congo, even the archaeological evidence hardly supports this, since recent archaeological data from West Africa all indicate a relatively late adoption of farming (Neumann et al. 1996).

Another problem is picking and choosing the subset of a language family that supports a specific hypothesis. All large, diverse language phyla may have at least one subgroup that depends on livestock-keeping, agriculture, hunting-gathering, or fishing. Nilo-Saharan, Iroquoian, and Altaic represent typical examples of this diversity of subsistence. By selecting the appropriate subgroup, the archaeological evidence can be made to

match the linguistic model. There is nothing wrong with this procedure as long as the scales of the two disciplines remain in parallel; errors arise when the interpretation is expanded to apply to a whole phylum. Mithun (1984: 271) specifically discusses the question of whether agriculture can be reconstructed for the whole of Iroquoian and concludes that it cannot, despite the presence of agricultural terminology in proto-north Iroquoian. Importantly, then, the initial driver of Iroquoian expansion cannot be agriculture, whatever its role in a later era.

Is all this, then, just building castles from the spirits of the upper air? Not entirely, but there has been a speculative leap from cases where such dispersals are well-supported by interdisciplinary evidence, to those where the evidence is at best insubstantial. The guilty party is definitely Austronesian, the only phylum where there are a large number of quite uncontroversial reconstructions of agricultural and livestock-related terms (e.g., Wolff 1994). The great majority of archaeologists working in the region of island southeast Asia accept a general dispersal from Taiwan and most would probably accept a link with a seafaring culture with agricultural skills. At the level of Oceanic, a major subgroup of Austronesian, the correlations are tighter still (Pawley and Ross 1995).

But Austronesian is the exception, not the rule. Not only is there an unparalleled body of descriptive language data and field archaeology, but also Austronesian is sufficiently "young" for its unity to be uncontroversial. Some relatively shallow New World phyla such as Maya (Kaufman 1976) or Mixe-Zoque (Wichmann 1995) are perhaps similar and also support the notion of agricultural expansion. Language phyla of greater antiquity and those in continental zones that have undergone much more extensive interaction with unrelated groups produce much more ambiguous results (cf. Dixon 1997 for an ahistoric view). Afroasiatic is a good example of this. Archaeologists and linguists convinced its origins are to be found in the Near East have taken the generally accepted evidence for reconstructions of agricultural terminology in Semitic (e.g., Fronzaroli 1969) as evidence that agriculture was the engine of Afroasiatic expansion as a whole (e.g., Militarev in press). This type of argument uses scattered look-alikes as a buttress, despite a complete absence of regularly reconstructed items reflecting agriculture in Omotic and Chadic, the most diverse branches of Afroasiatic.

By a strange irony, one language phylum omitted from the above discussion provides some of the most convincing evidence for agricultural expansion. Daic, the phylum to which modern Thai belongs, is today scattered across southern China and adjacent regions of southeast Asia. Its geographical dominance in Thailand is historically recent, for the diversity of the group is situated in China. Ostapirat (2000; in press) has recently shown that a wide range of crops and fruits can be reconstructed for proto-Daic, which is probably slightly "younger" than

Austronesian. Frustratingly, although the archaeology of cereal production in China is beginning to be quite well known, there is as yet no archaeological complex that can be linked with Daic expansion (though see some arguments in Higham and Thosarat 1998).

Attributing Dates to Phylic Dispersals

Even if we are skeptical about the claims of glottochronology, it seems reasonable to want to put dates to the dispersal of individual language phyla for an effective liaison with the archaeological evidence (e.g., Renfrew et al. 2000). Table 4.1 offers this, but without any specific justifications for the assignation of individual phyla. Except perhaps for Austronesian, it is probably too early to make any uncontroversial assertions in this area, but we can look at the evidence to hand and set out the tools and research directions that will bring more convincing results. For the establishment of a convincing timescale for the diversification and spread of language groups and the interpretation of this spread in terms of subsistence systems, there are three essential elements:

1 The development of an internal classification for the phylum with a relative chronology.
2 The reconstruction of lexical items indicative of particular subsistence strategies.
3 An archaeological data set that can be linked to the reconstructed subsistence strategies.

There is nothing very new or surprising about this, but its application in particular cases is a non-trivial task. The first problem is that many language phyla do not have an agreed internal structure. For example, two sub-classifications and reconstructions of Nilo-Saharan have been published (Bender 1996; Ehret 2001) which reach very different results concerning the internal classification of the phylum. In the case of Afroasiatic, questioning its Near Eastern origin is almost a taboo subject among scholars with a Semitic or Egyptological background (e.g., Diakonoff 1988; Orel and Stolbova 1995). Nonetheless, researchers working in the more diverse African branches concluded long ago that its most likely homeland was in Sub-Saharan Africa, most specifically in southwest Ethiopia (Bender 1975; Ehret 1995). Sino-Tibetan, a phylum whose broad internal structure was long accepted in outline, has recently been deconstructed by Van Driem (2001) and now resembles more "fallen leaves" than a tree. While disagreements persist, archaeologists should be extremely wary of attempting to interpret phylic level dispersals and stick with agreed subgroups. In other words, it may be more effective for archaeologists to explore Nilotic or Songhay than Nilo-Saharan as a whole.

The second requirement is that it should be possible to reconstruct lexical items indicative of particular subsistence strategies. For example, the Miao-Yao language phylum, spoken in scattered communities across China and northeast Thailand, has several roots for rice and its preparation that appear to be reconstructible to proto-Miao-Yao (Table 4.2).

These reconstructions suggests that speakers of proto-Miao-Yao were familiar with wetfield rice cultivation rather than simply wild rice. Given the increasingly early dates for cultivated rice in China, it may be that Miao-Yao were the original domesticators of rice and the Han took over as they moved in from further north

Table 4.2 Rice-related reconstructions in proto-Miao-Yao

Lexical item	Reconstruction
Rice plant	#llaŋ
Unhulled rice/sticky rice	#mple
Hulled rice	#coŋ
Cooked rice	#naŋ

Source: Haudricourt (1988)

(cf. Blench, in press, for more detailed discussion).

Another case where there is a convincing body of reconstruction to support a very specific hypothesis concerning the subsistence patterns of speakers of a proto-language is Berber, spoken in north Africa and formerly throughout most of the Sahara. Blench (2001a) shows that all major species of domestic ruminant except the camel can be reconstructed for proto-Berber, suggesting extremely strongly that its earliest speakers were not only livestock producers but also pastoralists. In the absence of other candidates, the diffusion of domestic animals across the desert and into Sub-Saharan Africa, which can be dated through archaeology, should therefore be identified with the Berber expansion. On a scale of greater detail, Schoenbrun (1997, 1998) has reconstructed a raft of cultural vocabulary for the Bantu of the Great Lakes region and linked it with the known archaeology of the region.

Of course, not all the data for the world's language phyla work out so neatly or are indeed available. Still, the detailed reconstructions for Austronesian and Daic mentioned above and the evidence for the inclusion of Hopi in the Northern Uto-Aztecan maize complex (Hill 2001) all suggest these are profitable avenues to explore and can be linked very directly to archaeological evidence. Ross et al. (1998), which contains the first part of a continuing series of explorations of the lexicon of proto-Oceanic, provides a model that could well be emulated in other regions of the world.

Negative evidence is also important here, where the data are adequate. For example, both "bow" and "arrow" have clear reconstructions in Niger–Congo and not in Nilo-Saharan (nor indeed in Afroasiatic or Khoisan). In neither phylum is there incontrovertible evidence for any reconstructions of terms connected with agriculture.[5] This suggests strongly that both Niger–Congo and Nilo-Saharan began to disperse prior to agriculture and that Nilo-Saharan also dispersed before the bow and arrow reached

Sub-Saharan Africa. Negative evidence must be used with care, however. In the case of ceramics, few language phyla anywhere in the world have reconstructed terms for pottery. This does *not* show whether the speakers of the proto-language used pottery, but rather that the great variety of pottery makes the semantic field in which they occur rapidly become very diffuse.

The third requirement is that an archaeological data set be available that can be linked with the reconstructed subsistence strategies. The existence of this is highly contingent and often reflects politics and geography as much as scholarship. Indo-European tends to out-compete other regions, since archaeological coverage is extremely dense across most of its purported range. Uralic, Austronesian, Na-Dene, and Australian are other language groupings where archaeological and linguistic coverage can be matched with some confidence. However, southeast Asian phyla such as Tibeto-Burman, Miao-Yao, Daic, and Austroasiatic all have part of their extension in areas where warfare and political problems restricted archaeology and indeed field linguistics during the twentieth century. This situation is gradually being rectified, but the sort of correlations possible in the eras mentioned previously should not be expected for some time. The situation is similar in much of Africa and South–Central America, not necessarily for political reasons, but rather that few resources have been available for the excavation of non-monumental sites and coverage therefore remains inadequate.

Placing potentially verifiable dates on the dispersal of language phyla must involve building on known historical facts. If we can place *ante quem* dates on particular families or subgroups then at least proposals for dates of phylic expansion can derive from overall estimates of internal diversity. One African phylum, Afroasiatic, is particularly suitable for such an approach, since three of its branches, Egyptian, Semitic, and Berber, have early and datable written texts. Table 4.3 shows the approximate earliest dates for

Table 4.3   Written attestations of Afroasiatic

Branch	Date	Diversity of group
Egyptian	3100 BC	Single language
Semitic	2700 BC	30 closely related languages
Berber	300 BC	Single language changing clinally across its range

written sources and the number of languages in the branch.

These "northern" branches are extremely undiverse compared with the branches without written attestations (Table 4.4).

Not only do the southern branches of Afroasiatic have numerous languages, but they are also extremely internally diverse, normally an indicator of considerable antiquity. Interpretations of Afroasiatic as a tree structure usually assign the Sub-Saharan families as primary branchings (e.g., Ehret 1995). Given the already considerable age of Egyptian, it would be perverse not to see the original dispersal of Afroasiatic as at least 9,000–10,000 years old and probably one or two millennia older still. Disagreements over the homeland of Afroasiatic have arisen because the archaeological data for the Near East and North Africa are so much richer than for southwest Ethiopia that some writers have chosen to privilege this region (e.g., Militarev, in press).

An argument from archaeology along similar lines can derive dates for the dispersal

Table 4.4   Diversity of other branches of Afroasiatic

Branch	Number of languages	Source
Chadic	135	Jungraithmayr and Ibriszimow (1995)
Cushitic	60	Bender and Fleming (1976)
Omotic	35	Bender (2000)

of Niger–Congo (Blench 1999a). The Bantu languages, known for their close internal relationships, are spread from southeast Nigeria to South Africa. They represent the final branching of Niger–Congo, "a subgroup of a subgroup of a subgroup" roughly comparable to Polynesian within Austronesian. Archaeology suggests that Bantu is at least 4,000 years old, if it is to be identified with the Neolithic populations spreading southwards into Northern Gabon ca. 4000 BP, as most scholars suppose (e.g., Oslisly 1992; Clist 1995). Niger–Congo is a rich and complex phylum and it is inconceivable that such complexity could have evolved unless it was at least twice as old.

The settlement of the New World has been the source of a controversy that illustrates the internal problems of historical linguistics and consequent difficulties that arise in linking them to archaeological data. The Americas represent a region of exceptional linguistic diversity and the earliest classifications suggested there were at least 58 distinct phyla (cf. Campbell 1997 for an overview of scholarship and dates), which would make it one of the most diverse regions of the world. Archaeologists, however, have generally considered the occupation of the Americas as relatively recent, with most dates focusing on the so-called "Clovis" horizon, ca. 12500 BP (e.g., Lynch 1990). This creates a major problem, since few linguists would accept such differentiation could evolve in so short a time, especially in the light of what we know about language diversification in Australia and Melanesia. Throughout most of the twentieth century, linguists have been unwilling to reduce significantly the numbers of distinct phyla of Amerindian languages, despite a major expansion in available data, and so have been rather skeptical of the archaeological position. However, in the 1980s, Joseph Greenberg (1987), hitherto known principally for his work in Africa, put forward a radical reclassification of the linguistic situation in the Americas which proposed to reduce the languages to just three distinct phyla. The largest of these, Amerind, would roll up most of the languages of North and South America. Amerind has been widely adopted by both archaeologists and geneticists, since it neatly solves the problem of the contradiction between language and settlement dates. Unfortunately, there seems to be little evidence that it is even partly true. Despite the predictions of many Africanists (e.g., Newman 1995), the years since the publication of *Language in the Americas* have not seen a single major scholar adopt Greenberg's ideas and recent large reference books now uniformly reject it (e.g., Campbell 1997; Mithun 1999; Dixon and Aikhenvald 1999). Amerind now lives on as a fossil conception outside the professional discipline of native American linguistics; an orphan rejected in its natural home, archaeologists have kindly adopted it.

Some mainstream literature on historical linguistics has suggested that there are temporal limits that standard methods cannot breach. A figure sometimes put forward is 10,000 years, although this seems to have little to commend it except a satisfying row of zeroes. Indeed, Nichols (1992) put forward her proposals for innovative methods precisely to try to capture much greater time-depths. However, recent work on Australian languages is challenging previous notions of reconstructibility. It is estimated there were more than 400 languages in Australia prior to European contact, and that of these records remain for at least 280 (Dixon pers. comm.). Australian languages show enormous differentiation, often with lexicostatistical counts as low as values given by random comparison between any two languages. Even on the most optimistic "lumpist" assessment there are still 8–10 language families [here = phyla] (Koch 1997) and skeptics still consider the proto-Australian project methodologically impossible. Evans (in press) shows that the extreme diversity in Australia is gradually yielding up some common features and that a reconstructed proto-Australian is conceivable. Present evidence suggests that modern humans reached modern Papua New Guinea and Australia

60–40 Ky ago (Connell and Allen 1998) and linguistic reconstructions may therefore reach back to this period. If so, there may be no temporal barrier that blocks us at some defined point in the past; we must work with the historical and archaeological materials to hand.

Language Shift

It can seem from standard texts that all language families diversify neatly into branching trees and it would certainly be convenient for proponents of demic expansion if this were indeed so. Moreover, if people would stick to their own language and not engage in multilingual behavior, the life of the archaeolinguist would be easier. But language shift is one of the key processes of cultural change and indeed bound up with prestige institutions and material culture. Any convincing model of the relation between language and prehistory must take such processes into account (Ehret 1988).

A plus about language shift is that it can be seen and documented in the present, which makes it easier to seek its traces in the past. All over the world, ethnic minorities are under extreme pressure to yield their own speech to a national language and in many cases this is occurring (Blench 2001b). The consequences for material culture, though, can be highly variable. In many developed economies, for minority languages such as Breton, Scots Gaelic, or the Amerindian languages of North America, the shift in material culture has already occurred. Language loss trails behind it, perhaps artificially retarded by literacy programs or well-meaning linguists. However, in the developing world, speaking a minority language is often linked to poverty and social exclusion, for example in Indonesia or Mexico. The spread of a dominant language by agencies of the state in such countries reflects as much the impulse towards political control as the inexorable tide of globalization, and consequently there may be no material

change in the state of populations who lose their language, as in many Latin American countries.

To relate this to archaeological interpretation, one of the long-standing puzzles of Australian prehistory is the distribution of Pama-Nyungan languages. Although the language groupings of Australia are highly diverse, indicating long periods of separation, the diversity is all confined to a small region of northern Australia (McConvell and Evans 1998). The rest of the continent is dominated by a single family, Pama-Nyungan, the languages of which are sufficiently close as to be almost inter-intelligible. Given the early settlement dates for Australia, we must imagine that Pama-Nyungan speakers persuaded the resident groups in a large region of the continent to switch languages. Since there is no evidence that this was achieved by violence, we have to assume that either technological superiority or prestige social institutions were the keys to this process. McConvell and Evans (1998) argue that we can see evidence for both. Pama-Nyungan speakers show an innovative type of social organization, linguistic exogamy, linked to possession of song repertoires, that may well be the prestige social institution that impressed the resident groups. At the same time, some 4,000–5,000 years BP, a new type of microlithic technology begins to appear throughout the region. Specifically, backed blades correspond almost precisely with the distribution of Pama-Nyungan languages. The combination of tools and songs[6] seems to have been irresistible and the languages gradually spread through most of the continent, assimilating those already present.

Loanwords as an Underexploited Tool

Historical linguists are rather prone to look for convincing reconstructions that can be assigned to proto-languages. Marcus van Boxhorn (1647) was perhaps the first scholar to draw attention to the study of loanwords:

Niet oock uyt vreemde woorden neffen vreemde saecken ontleent van vreemden, ende dien volgende onder verscheiden vreemde volckeren te vinden, gelijck een *Kemel*, over al by de Romeinen, Griecken, Duitschen, ende andere, genoemt vverdt een *Kemel*, maer uyt in ende aengeboren vvoorden, bediedende saecken ofte dingen, die over al dagelijcx gebruyct, geboren, ende gevonden vvorden.

[Genetic relationship is established] not on the basis of loanwords for foreign objects borrowed from foreigners, which can therefore be found amongst foreign nations, just as a camel is known as a camel to the Romans, Greeks, German and others, but rather on the basis of native, inherited words which denote matters or things which are used, borne or encountered on a daily basis. (Boxhorn 1647: 65; translation by Van Driem 2001: 1045)

Boxhorn (1654: 100) also understood that relationships must have a systematic character and that linguists must be careful to eliminate chance resemblances or look-alikes. He notes that simply because Latin has *sus* for "pig" and Hebrew has *sus* for "horse" we should not construct a historical explanation to relate these two.

The study of lexical items that reflect introductions is definitely perceived as a less prestigious activity, a task for graduate students. However, in terms of the reconstruction of prehistory, the tracking of loanwords can provide much information that is unavailable through other means. A good example is the spread of New World crops in Africa. We know that maize, cassava, groundnuts, and chilis transformed African agriculture long before European presence in the African interior reached significant levels. The main agents for the introduction of American food plants were the Portuguese, who left few records. Using the pattern of loanwords, the spread of individual crops can be tracked from the coast into the hinterland and shows how they were borrowed from one group to another, and often by what agency, whether through trade or farmer-to-farmer spread (cf. Blench et al. 1997 for maize; Blench 1998 for cassava; Phillipson and Bahuchet 1998 for American crops in central Africa). Wichmann (1998) explores many of those same crops in the Mixe-Zoque-speaking regions of Mexico and observes that even where archaeology can establish the antiquity of particular domesticates, linguistics demonstrates that they are regularly borrowed between subsets of a particular language grouping. Brown (1999) has used similar analyses both to track the spread of post-Columbian introductions such as the horse among the indigenous peoples of North America and explore more generally the conditions for borrowing and the different circumstances under which it occurs.

There is another way in which loanwords can be of interest. Their frequency in languages that interact can also indicate the intensity and often the nature of contacts. For example, Papua New Guinea and its offshore islands were inhabited entirely by Papuan speakers prior to the seaborne incursions by Austronesians. The two language groupings are entirely different in structure and lexicon and as a consequence it is relatively easy to detect loan phenomena. And indeed we find a wide variety of linguistic outcomes of this interaction, most strikingly "mixed" languages, such as Maisin or Magori, which derive an almost equal proportion of their grammar and syntax from the two different phyla (Dutton 1976; Ross 1984). This points to situations of intense bilingualism over a long period. In other cases, whole areas of vocabulary illustrate the consequences of contact. On Mailu island, for example, the resident Magi (Papuan) speakers have borrowed all their vocabulary to do with boats and sailing as well as a large proportion of lexemes relating to trade and barter from Austronesian (Dutton 1999). More curiously still, the Magi represent the dominant group and Austronesian languages now only have a fragmentary presence. Even without archaeology, we can conclude that the residents of

Mailu were initially culturally dominated by the technology brought by the incoming seafaring groups, lived in a situation of intense bilingualism, and probably regarded Austronesian as highly prestigious. However, at some point, they must have regained their cultural self-confidence, expanded to overwhelm the Austronesian settlements, and reinvented themselves as traders and seagoing people. Fortunately, however, we also have a good account of the archaeology of Mailu (Irwin 1985) and indeed much of this scenario seems to be paralleled by the archaeological record. For example, the regaining of territory by the Papuan speakers, when the Mailu people took over the Austronesian trading system and disruption ensued, is probably reflected in a radical shift in settlement pattern on the mainland from about 300 BP onwards (Irwin 1985: 204; Dutton 1999). Loanwords remain thus far an underexploited tool; their potential to illuminate the spread of technologies of interest to archaeologists, such as ironworking and ceramics, has been little utilized.

Archaeology, Linguistics, and Genetics: New Synthesis or Wayward Detour?

A discipline which has been the subject of great hopes and even greater claims is genetics, specifically the analysis of mitochondrial DNA. DNA can potentially be recovered from archaeological material, but seems also to offer a way of relating present human populations, both to one another and to past skeletal or other materials. Indeed, to judge by the claims of some of its exponents, the links between language, demographic movement, and genetics in prehistory are well-established. These were enthusiastically promoted at the end of the 1980s and into the early 1990s as the "New Synthesis" and Archaeogenetics (see, for example, Cavalli-Sforza et al. 1988; Renfrew 1992; Cavalli-Sforza 1997; Renfrew and Boyle 2000). The culmination of this trend

was the appearance of *The History and Geography of Human Genes* (Cavalli-Sforza et al. 1994), which essays a major revision of the methodology for exploring human history. Linguistic classifications of human populations purport to offer a tool for outflanking simple racial models; more abstract, they appear to provide an ideal analogue to the classificatory trees drawn from DNA analyses. If DNA trees and language trees were indeed to correspond, then this would provide striking mutual confirmation for models of human prehistory (e.g., Gibbons 2001). This plays well in the pages of *Nature* and hardly at all with most archaeologists and linguists (e.g., Pluciennik 1996; McEachern 2000). Partly this is due to innate conservatism and the fact that no academic career points are to be made in being interdisciplinary, where established disciplines have developed internal structures. But it is also because DNA studies have not delivered credible results; linguists are faced with endless trees that show links quite contrary to established results and contradict one another from one paper to the next (cf. Chen et al. 1995; Blench 1999b, for some particularly egregious cases; McEachern 2000). Claims for a genetic "clock" are endlessly revised and "theoretical" dates seem not to match any actual dates available.[7]

What is going wrong here? Human populations move, interact, spread their genes; there should be a link with the map of language, as Darwin suggested. The sand in the machine is language shift; human populations shift languages for reasons which have no biological analogy. Their marriage patterns may reflect notions of cultural prestige that do not mirror biological advantage. As a consequence, language affiliation and genetic composition rapidly go out of synchronization. Only where a population is expanding into previously uninhabited terrain or is otherwise unable to interact with other, genetically distinct, populations is such a correspondence possible. Genetics seems presently to be confident about its ability to provide useful hypotheses for other disciplines to test, but outside its special arena a healthy skepticism still prevails.

Polynesia represents as simple a case history as exists; linguists all agree that it is an offshoot of Central Pacific, which includes Rotuman and Fiji, and Samoa is the first island in the chain which eventually leads to New Zealand. For most accepted language groupings, notably Austronesian, of which Polynesian is but a small subset, many physical types are represented and much of the genetic interactions in prehistory are still poorly understood. Despite their racial, archaeological, and genetic accretions, terms such as *Polynesian* and *Austronesian* remain purely linguistic classifications and attempts to implant other types of meanings encounter a purely logical gap. To assume that linguistic entities can be mapped one-to-one with constructs from other disciplines is also to implicitly accept that contradictions can occur. In other words, a proposition of the form "genetics shows that Polynesians did not originate in Samoa as commonly supposed, but rather . . . " has an assignable meaning. Bing Su et al. (2000) use genetics to try to decide between a Melanesian or a Taiwanese origin for the Polynesians. This represents a serious confusion; genetics *cannot* show linguistic hypotheses to be "wrong" in this way.

What then can such statements mean? Presumably those who say this have something in mind. The underlying statement seems to be that "certain genetic markers characteristic of the people presently identified as Polynesian are found in important concentrations in *x*," where *x* is different from the agreed homeland of the Polynesians. It seems very doubtful whether enough of the diverse Polynesian-speaking peoples have really been adequately sampled to make this statement unequivocal. However, for the sake of argument, let us suppose that Polynesian-speaking peoples have been so characterized. The geneticists' claim then amounts to the observation that the genetic profile typical of a linguistic group is found among peoples who do not speak those lan-

guages today. Clearly, this can have a number of possible explanations:

- Chance mutation.
- Migration of a population from the present-day Polynesian-speaking region to region *x* and its assimilation.
- Migration of a population from region *x* to the present-day Polynesian-speaking region and its assimilation.
- Both populations deriving from a common source in a third region thus far unidentified.

However, none of these options suggest that linguists are wrong or even confused in their characterization of Polynesian. There are technical problems with the results from DNA analyses, but even more important are logical gaps that are far from being addressed. Moreover, DNA is a large church, with a great variety of haplotypes and significantly different distributions of nuclear and mitochondrial DNA. So a distinctive characterization of Polynesians on this basis is probably as much a chimera as the classification of human races by head types, nasal indices, or many another now-forgotten indicator.

Conclusion

What emerges from all this? If nothing else, that the interaction between archaeology and linguistics is currently extremely lively. The engines are undoubtedly the growth of available data, both putting names and classifications to the languages of the world and ensuring that at least a small scattering of datapoints populate previously blank areas of the archaeological map. Nationalist concerns and the increasing articulacy of indigenous peoples have also played an important role in moving the archaeological agenda along.

For a more fruitful interchange, historical linguists need to consider more carefully what sorts of reconstructions they research, focusing in particular on areas where material remains can be recovered by archaeologists. This in turn may require rethinking certain types of data collection, particularly as regards technological vocabulary. They will also need to find ways to present their results in terms accessible to those outside the discipline. Archaeologists seeking a more rounded prehistory should in turn try to work with linguists to discover what models of language distribution are current for their region of interest and what hypotheses could be tested by further research. It seems unlikely that any archaeologist has ever conducted an excavation solely to explore a linguistic model; the scale of the archaeological endeavor and thereby its inherent inertia militates against this. But it can at least be imagined; this is a topic that won't go away.

Appendix 1: Language Phyla of the World

Table 4.5 presents a synoptic overview of the language phyla of the world to assist in locating the examples given in this chapter.

Table 4.5 Language phyla of the world and their status

Phylum	Usual acronym	Where spoken	Status/comment
Niger–Congo	NC	Western, central, and southern Africa	Accepted
Afroasiatic	AA[a]	Northeast Africa and the Middle East	Accepted
Indo-European	IE	Eurasia	Accepted
Uralic	U	Eurasia	Accepted
Kartvelian	K	Caucasus	Accepted
North Caucasian	NC	Caucasus	Accepted
Chukchi-Kamchatkan	CK	Siberia	Accepted
Karasuk	KS	Siberia/northern Pakistan	Recently proposed
Eskimo-Aleut	EA[b]	Bering Strait	Accepted
Dravidian	DR	India	Accepted
Sino-Tibetan	ST	Central Asia	Accepted
Miao-Yao	MY	China	Accepted
Daic (= Tai-Kadai)	D	Southeast Asia	Accepted
Austroasiatic	AS[a]	Southeast Asia	Accepted
Austronesian	AN	Pacific	Accepted
Trans-New-Guinea	TNG[b]	Papua New Guinea	Accepted, though formulations of membership differ
Pama-Nyungan	PNY	Australia	Accepted
Na-Dene	ND[b]	North America	Accepted, though affiliation of Haida is debated

Table 4.5 (Continued)

Phylum	Usual acronym	Where spoken	Status/comment
Khoisan	KH	Eastern and southern Africa	Usually accepted, but some languages not included
Nilo-Saharan	NS	Eastern and central Africa	Usually accepted, although external scholars have questioned the evidence
Altaic	AT	Eurasia	Usually accepted, although the affiliation of Korean is debated
"Papuan"	PP[b]	Papua New Guinea	Large number of accepted groups, but their unity is not accepted
"Australian"	AU[b]	Australia	Large number of accepted groups, but their unity is not considered proven
"Amerind"	AM[b]	Americas	Large number of accepted groups, but their unity is not accepted
Andamanese	AD[b]	Andaman islands	Inadequate data make effective historical linguistics impractical

This table excludes a number of well-known isolates such as Basque, Ghilyak, Ainu, and Japanese, as well as African and New World isolates and problematic languages of Asia such as Nahali and Kusunda.
[a] AA is unfortunately used for both Afroasiatic and Austroasiatic. AS is adopted here for Austroasiatic to eliminate confusion. PN is applied to Polynesian, hence the use of PP for Papuan here.
[b] Proposed acronym

There are some language phyla whose existence is generally accepted, such as Indo-European or Austronesian, as a result of the weight of scholarly opinion. In a few cases, such as Nilo-Saharan, despite its introduction in the 1950s and a series of conferences since then, a body of scholarly comment exists questioning either its unity as a phylum or the families that compose it. In addition, there are regions of the world where a large number of languages exist which show common features but which have not been shown to be related to the satisfaction of most researchers. These "geo-graphical" names are often shown as phyla in works of synthesis. The most important of these are Papuan, Australian, and Amerind; zones of languages with common features and coherent subgroups where overall genetic relations have proved resistant to the methods of historical linguistics. Similarities of phonology or other features do suggest a common origin, but it is possible that they have so far diversified from a common proto-language that proof will remain a chimera. Finally, in one case, Andamanese, inadequate data make any final judgment impossible at present.

Notes

1 This subject has recently been reviewed in Blench and Spriggs (1999) and I have attempted here not to repeat that discussion but to cover new themes or else to add significant updating. Matthew Spriggs drew my attention to some of the quotations from the archaeological literature.

2 Leonard Bloomfield (1935: 6) noted that no direct source in Voltaire's writings has been discovered and there is more than a suspicion that this is a piece of convenient linguistic folklore.

3 I would like to thank George van Driem for drawing my attention to what is effectively a major revision of the narrative of historical linguistics. This passage draws heavily on his published account (Van Driem 2001).

4 Although regular attempts are made to revise the system of calculation to counter the rather basic objections coming from both archaeology and sociolinguistics. For one modern version, see Greenberg (1987).

5 This is controversial, since Ehret (1993) seems convinced that such terms are found in proto-Nilo-Saharan, but Bender (1996) was unable to confirm his reconstructions.

6 This may seem less improbable once it is compared with the rapid spread of studio-produced popular music from America, which has led to the rapid erasure of many local musical traditions in the last decades.

7 It would be unfair to say that there are no archaeologists who have taken an interest in "Archaeogenetics," the publications of the McDonald Institute constituting a major focus of these ideas (e.g., Renfrew et al. 2000). But publications in this area seem to have taken on a momentum of their own; rather than influencing mainstream practitioners, researchers of the same school spend their time going to conferences with one another.

References

Bellwood, P. 1991. "The Austronesian dispersal and the origin of languages." *Scientific American*, 265 (1): 88–93.

Bellwood, P. 1996. "The origins and spread of agriculture in the Indo-Pacific region: gradualism and diffusion or revolution and colonization?" In D. R. Harris (ed.), *The Origins and Spread of Agriculture and Pastoralism in Eurasia*, pp. 465–98. London: UCL Press.

Bellwood, P. 1997. "Prehistoric cultural explanations for the existence of widespread language families." In P. McConvell and N. Evans (eds.), *Archaeology and Linguistics: Aboriginal Australia in Global Perspective*, pp. 123–34. Melbourne: Oxford University Press.

Bender, M. L. 1975. *Omotic: A New Afroasiatic Language Family*. Carbondale: University Museum, Southern Illinois University.

Bender, M. L. 1996. *The Nilo-Saharan Languages: A Comparative Essay*. Munich: Lincom Europa.

Bender, M. L. 2000. *Comparative Morphology of the Omotic Languages*. Munich: Lincom Europa.

Bender, M. L. and H. C. Fleming (eds.) 1976. *The Non-Semitic Languages of Ethiopia*. Ann Arbor: Michigan University Press.

Bing Su, Li Jin, and P. Underhill et al. 2000. "Polynesian origins: insights from the Y chromosome." *Proceedings of the National Academy of Sciences USA*, 97 (15): 8225–8.

Blench, R. M. 1998. "The diffusion of New World cultigens in Nigeria." In M. Chastenet (ed.), *Plantes et paysages d'Afrique*, pp. 165–210. Paris: Karthala.

Blench, R. M. 1999a. "The languages of Africa: macrophyla proposals and implications for archaeological interpretation." In R. M. Blench and M. Spriggs (eds.), *Archaeology and Language, IV*, pp. 29–47. London: Routledge.

Blench, R. M. 1999b. "Are the African pygmies an ethnographic fiction?" In K. Biesbrouyck, G. Rossel, and S. Elders (eds.), *Challenging Elusiveness: Central African Hunter-Gatherers in a Multi-Disciplinary Perspective*, pp. 41–60. Leiden: Center for Non-Western Studies.

Blench, R. M. 2001a. "Types of language spread and their archaeological correlates: the example of Berber." *Origini*, 23: 169–90.

Blench, R. M. 2001b. *Globalisation and Policies Towards Cultural Diversity*. Natural Resource Paper, 70. London: Overseas Development Institute. Also at http://www.oneworld. org/odi/nrp/70.html.

Blench, R. M. in press. "From the mountains to the valleys: understanding ethnolinguistic geography in southeast Asia." In L. Sagart, R. M. Blench, and A. Sanchez-Mazas (eds.), *Perspectives on the Phylogeny of East Asian Languages*. London: Curzon Press.

Blench, R. M. and M. Spriggs 1999. "General introduction." In R. M. Blench and M. Spriggs (eds.), *Archaeology and Language, IV*, pp. 1–20. London: Routledge.

Blench, R. M., K. Williamson, and B. Connell 1997. "The diffusion of maize in Nigeria: a historical and linguistic investigation." *Sprache und Geschichte in Afrika*, 14: 19–46.

Bloomfield, L. 1935. *Language*. London: Allen and Unwin.

Bonfante, G. 1953. "Ideas on the kinship of the European languages from 1200 to 1800." *Cahiers d'Histoire Mondiale*, 1: 679–99.

Boxhorn, M. van 1647. *Antwoord van Marcus Zuerius van Boxhorn op de Vraaghen, hem voorgestelt over de Bediedinge van de tot noch toe onbekende Afgodinne Nehalennia, onlancx uytgegeven. In welcke de ghemeine herkomste van der Griecken, Romeinen, ende Duytschen Tale uyt den Scythen duydelijck bewesen, ende verscheiden Oudheden van dese Volckeren grondelijck ontdeckt ende verklaert*. Leiden: Willem Christiaens van der Boxe.

Boxhorn, M. van 1654. *Originum Gallicarum Liber. In quo veteris & nobilissimæ Gallorum gentis origines, antiquitates, mores, lingua & alia eruuntur & illustrantur*. Amsterdam: Joannes Jansonius.

Brown, C. H. 1999. *Lexical Acculturation in Native American Languages*. New York: Oxford University Press.

Campbell, L. 1997. *American Indian Languages: The Historical Linguistics of Native America*. New York: Oxford University Press.

Cavalli-Sforza, L. 1997. "Genes, peoples, and languages." *Proceedings of the National Academy of Sciences, USA*, 94: 7719–24.

Cavalli-Sforza, L. L., P. Menozzi, and A. Piazza 1994. *The History and Geography of Human Genes*. Princeton, NJ: Princeton University Press.

Cavalli-Sforza, L. L., A. Piazza, and P. Menozzi et al. 1988. "Reconstruction of human evolution: bringing together genetic, archaeological and linguistic data." *Proceedings of the National Academy of Sciences*, 85: 6002–6.

Chen, J., R. R. Sokal, and M. Ruhlen 1995. "Worldwide analysis of genetic and linguistic relations of human populations." *Human Biology*, 67 (4): 595–612.

Clist, B. 1995. *Gabon: 100 000 ans d'histoire*. Libreville: Sepia.

Connell, B. 1998. "Linguistic evidence for the development of yam and palm culture among the Delta Cross River peoples of southeastern Nigeria." In R. M. Blench and M. Spriggs (eds.), *Archaeology and Language, II*, pp. 324–65. London: Routledge.

Connell, J. F. and J. Allen 1998. "When did humans first arrive in Australia and why is it important to know?" *Evolutionary Anthropology*, 6 (4): 132–46.

Daniel, G. 1962 (reissued 1971). *The Idea of Prehistory*. Harmondsworth: Penguin Books.

Darwin, C. 1859. *On the Origin of Species*. London: John Murray.

Diakonoff, I. M. 1988. *Afrasian Languages*. Moscow: Nauka Press.

Diamond, J. 1998. *Guns, Germs and Steel: A Short History of Everybody for the Last 13,000 Years*. London: Jonathan Cape.

Dixon, R. M. W. 1997. *The Rise and Fall of Languages*. Cambridge: Cambridge University Press.

Dixon, R. M. W. and A. Y. Aikhenvald (eds.) 1999. *The Amazonian Languages*. Cambridge: Cambridge University Press.

Donaldson, J. W. 1839. *The New Cratylus*. Cambridge: Deighton.

Dumont d'Urville, J. S. C. 1834. *Philologie, par M. D'Urville. Seconde Partie. Les autres vocabulaires de langues ou Dialectes océaniens recueillies durant la voyage, et le Vocabulaire comparatif des langues françaises, madekass, malaio, mawi, tonga, taiti et hawaii, suivis de quelques considérations générales sur ces langues*. Paris: Ministère de la Marine.

Dutton, T. 1976. "Magori and similar languages of southeast Papua." In S. Wurm (ed.), *New Guinea Area Languages and Language Study, Vol. 2: Austronesian Languages*, pp. 581–636. Pacific Linguistics C-39. Canberra: Australian National University.

Dutton, T. 1999. "From pots to people: fine tuning the prehistory of Mailu Island and neighbouring coast, southeast Papua New Guinea." In R. M. Blench and M. Spriggs (eds.), *Archaeology and Language, III: Artefacts, Languages and Texts*, pp. 90–108. London: Routledge.

Ehret, C. 1988. "Language change and the material correlates of languages and ethnic shift." *Antiquity*, 62: 564–74.

Ehret, C. 1993. "Nilo-Saharans and the Saharo-Sudanese Neolithic." In T. Shaw, P. Sinclair, B. Andah, and A. Okpoko (eds.), *The Archaeology of Africa: Food, Metals and Towns*, pp. 104–25. London: Routledge.

Ehret, C. 1995. *Reconstructing Proto-Afroasiatic: Consonants, Vowels, Tone and Vocabulary*. Berkeley: University of California Press.

Ehret, C. 2001. *A Historical–Comparative Reconstruction of Nilo-Saharan*. Köln: Rudiger Köppe.

Elichmann, Johann 1640. *Tabula Cebetis Græce, Arabice, Latine. Item Aurea Carmina Pythagoræ cum Paraphrasi Arabica*. Leiden: Ioannis Maire.

Evans, N. in press. "Faint tracks in an ancient wordscape." In J. Moore and W. A. Durham (eds.), *Entering New Landscapes: Comparing the First Human Occupations of Australia, the Americas and Remote Oceania*.

Fronzaroli, P. 1969. "Studi sul lessico comune semitico, VI. La natura domestica." *Rendiconti dell'Accademia Nazionale dei Lincei, Classe di Scienze morali, storiche e filologiche*, 8 (24): 285–320.

Gibbons, A. 2001. "The peopling of the Pacific: archaeologists, linguists, and geneticists struggle to understand the origins of the bold seafarers who settled the remote Pacific Islands." *Science*, 291 (5509): 1735–7.

Gilij, F. S. 1780–4. *Saggio di storia americana, o sia, storia naturale, civile e sacra de'regni e delle provinzie spagnuole di Terra-Firma nell'america meridionale*, 4 vols. Rome: Perigio.

Green, R. and A. Pawley 1999. "Early Oceanic architectural forms and settlement patterns: linguistic, archaeological and ethnological perspectives." In R. M. Blench and M. Spriggs (eds.), *Archaeology and Language, III: Artefacts, Languages and Texts*, pp. 31–89. London: Routledge.

Greenberg, J. 1987. *Language in the Americas*. Stanford, CA: Stanford University Press.

Haudricourt, A. G. 1988. "Les Dialectes chinois." In N. Revel (ed.), *Le Riz en Asie du sud-est*, Vol. 1, pp. 35–42. Paris: EHESS.

Higham, C. and R. Thosarat 1998. *Prehistoric Thailand: From Early Settlement to Sukothai*. Bangkok: River Books.

Hill, J. H. 2001. "Dating the break-up of southern Uto-Aztecan." In J. L. M. Zamarrón and J. H. Hill (eds.), *Avances y balances de lenguas yutoaztecas*, pp. 345–57. Mexico: INAH.

Hymes, D. H. 1983. "Lexicostatistics and glottochronology in the nineteenth century (with notes towards a general history)." In D. H. Hymes (ed.), *Essays in the History of Linguistic Anthropology*, pp. 59–113. Amsterdam: John Benjamins.

Irwin, G. 1985. *The Emergence of Mailu: As a Central Place in Coastal Papuan Prehistory*. Canberra: Department of Prehistory, Research School of Pacific Studies, Australian National University [Terra Australis 10].

Jungraithmayr, H. and D. Ibriszimow 1995. *Chadic Lexical Roots*, 2 vols. Berlin: Reimer.

Kaufman, T. 1976. "Archaeological and linguistic correlations in Mayaland and associated areas of Meso-America." *World Archaeology*, 8: 101–18.

Koch, H. 1997. "Comparative linguistics and Australian prehistory." In P. McConvell and N. Evans (eds.), *Archaeology and Linguistics: Aboriginal Australia in Global Perspective*, pp. 27–43. Melbourne: Oxford University Press.

Latham, R. G. 1850. *The Natural History of the Varieties of Man*. London: John van Voorst.

Lynch, T. F. 1990. "Glacial-age man in South America?" *American Anthropologist*, 55: 12–36.

McConvell, P. and N. Evans (eds.) 1997. *Archaeology and Linguistics: Aboriginal Australia in Global Perspective*. Melbourne: Oxford University Press.

McConvell, P. and N. Evans 1998. "The enigma of Pama-Nyungan expansion in Australia." In R. M. Blench and M. Spriggs (eds.), *Archaeology and Language II*, pp. 174–91. London: Routledge.

McEachern, S. 2000. "Genes, tribes and African history." *Current Anthropology*, 41 (3): 384.

Militarev, A. in press. "Prehistory of dispersal: Proto-Afrasian (Afroasiatic) farming lexicon." In P. Bellwood and C. Renfrew (eds.), *Proceedings of the Meeting on Early Farming Dispersals*. McDonald Institute Monographs. Cambridge: McDonald Institute for Archaeological Research.

Mithun, M. 1984. "The proto-Iroquoians: cultural reconstruction from lexical materials." In M. K. Foster, J. Campisi, and M. Mithun (eds.), *Extending the Rafters: Interdisciplinary Approaches to Iroquoian Studies*, pp. 259–81. Albany: State University of New York Press.

Mithun, M. 1999. *The Languages of Native North America*. Cambridge: Cambridge University Press.

Müller, F. M. 1871. *Lectures on the Science of Language*, 2 vols. London: Longmans, Green.

Muller, J.-C. 1986. "Early stages of language comparison from Sassetti to Sir William Jones (1786)." *Kratylos*, 31 (1): 1–31.

Neumann, K., A. Ballouche, and M. Klee 1996. "The emergence of plant food production in the West African Sahel: new evidence from northeast Nigeria and northern Burkina Faso." In G. Pwiti and R. Soper (eds.), *Aspects of African Archaeology*, pp. 441–8. Harare: University of Zimbabwe Publications.

Newman, P. 1995. *On Being Right: Greenberg's African Linguistic Classification and the Methodological Principles Which Underlie It.* African Studies Program. Bloomington: Indiana University Press.

Nichols, J. 1992. *Linguistic Diversity in Space and Time.* Chicago: University of Chicago Press.

Orel, V. and O. Stolbova 1995. *Hamito-Semitic Etymological Dictionary.* Leiden: Brill.

Oslisly, R. 1992. *Préhistoire de la moyenne Vallée de L'Ogooué (Gabon),* 2 vols. Paris: ORSTOM.

Ostapirat, W. 2000. "Proto-Kra." *Linguistics of the Tibeto-Burman Area,* 23 (1).

Ostapirat, W. in press. "Kra-Dai and Austronesian." In R. M. Blench, L. Sagart, and A. Sanchez-Mazas (eds.), *Perspectives on the Phylogeny of East Asian Languages.* London: Curzon Press.

Pawley, A. and M. Ross 1995. "The prehistory of Oceanic languages: a current view." In P. Bellwood, J. Fox, and D. Tryon (eds.), *The Austronesians: Historical and Comparative Perspectives,* pp. 39–74. Canberra: Department of Anthropology, Research School of Pacific and Asian Studies, Australian National University.

Payne, D. 1993. "Una visión panorámica de la familia lingüística Arawak." In M. L. R. De Montes (ed.), *Estado actual de la classificacion de las lenguas indígenas de Colombia,* pp. 127–64. Santafé de Bogotá: Instituto Caro y Cuervo.

Phillipson, G. and S. Bahuchet 1998. "Les Plantes d'origine américaine en Afrique bantoue: une approache linguistique." In M. Chastenet (ed.), *Plantes et paysages d'Afrique,* pp. 87–116. Paris: Karthala.

Pictet, A. 1859–63. *Les Origines indo-européennes, ou les Aryas primitifs: essai de paléontologie linguistique.* Paris: Cherbuliez.

Pluciennik, M. 1996. "Genetics, archaeology and the wider world." *Antiquity,* 70: 13–14.

Relandus, Hadrianus [Adriaan van Reeland] 1708. *Dissertationum Miscellanearum, Pars Tertia et Ultima,* pp. 55–139. Trajecti ad Rhenum: Guilielmus Broedelet.

Renfrew, C. 1987. *Archaeology and Language: The Puzzle of Indo-European Origins.* London: Jonathan Cape.

Renfrew, C. 1992. "Archaeology, Genetic and Linguistic Diversity." *Man,* 27 (3): 445–78.

Renfrew, C. in press. " 'The emerging synthesis': the archaeogenetics of language/farming dispersals and other spread zones." In P. Bellwood and C. Renfrew (eds.), *Proceedings of the Meeting on Early Farming Dispersals.* McDonald Institute Monographs. Cambridge: McDonald Institute for Archaeological Research.

Renfrew, C. and K. Boyle (eds.) 2000. *Archaeogenetics: DNA and the Population Prehistory of Europe.* McDonald Institute Monographs. Cambridge: McDonald Institute for Archaeological Research.

Renfrew, C., A. McMahon, and L. Trask (eds.) 2000. *Time Depth in Historical Linguistics.* McDonald Institute Monographs. Cambridge: McDonald Institute for Archaeological Research.

Ross, M. 1984. "Maisin: a preliminary sketch." *Papers in New Guinea Linguistics No. 23,* pp. 1–82. Pacific Linguistics A-69. Canberra: Australian National University.

Ross, M., A. Pawley, and M. Osmond 1998. *The Lexicon of Proto Oceanic, Vol. 1: Material Culture.* Canberra: Pacific Linguistics.

Ruhlen, M. 1991. *A Guide to the World's Languages, Vol. 1.* Stanford, CA: Stanford University Press.

Schoenbrun, D. L. 1997. *The Historical Reconstruction of Great Lakes Bantu Cultural Vocabulary.* Köln: Rudiger Köppe.

Schoenbrun, D. L. 1998. *A Green Place, a Good Place: Agrarian Change, Gender and Social Identity in the Great Lakes Region to the 15th Century*. Portsmouth/Nairobi/Kampala/Oxford: Heinemann/Fountain/EAEP/James Currey.

Swadesh, M. 1952. "Lexicostatistic dating of prehistoric ethnic contacts." *Proceedings of the American Philosophical Society*, 96: 453–62.

Téné, D. 1980. "The earliest comparisons of Hebrew with Aramaic and Arabic." In K. Koerner (ed.), *Progress in Linguistic Historiography*, pp. 355–77. Amsterdam: John Benjamins.

Thomason, S. G. and T. Kaufman 1988. *Language Contact, Creolization and Genetic Linguistics*. Berkeley: University of California Press.

Trigger, B. G. 1989. *A History of Archaeological Thought*. Cambridge: Cambridge University Press.

Van Driem, G. 2001. *Languages of the Himalayas: An Ethnolinguistic Handbook*. Handbuch der Orientalistik. Leiden: Brill.

Wauchope, R. 1962. *Lost Tribes and Sunken Continents*. Chicago: University of Chicago Press.

Wichmann, S. 1995. *The Relationship Among the Mixe-Zoquean Languages of Mexico*. Salt Lake City: University of Utah Press.

Wichmann, S. 1998. *A Conservative Look at Diffusion Involving Mixe-Zoquean Languages*. In R. M. Blench and M. Spriggs (eds.), *Archaeology and Language, II*, pp. 297–323. London: Routledge.

Wolff, J. U. 1994. "The place of plant names in reconstructing proto-Austronesian." In A. K. Pawley and M. D. Ross (eds.), *Austronesian Terminologies: Continuity and Change*, pp. 511–40. Pacific Linguistics C-127. Canberra: Australian National University.

Wotton, W. 1730 [1713]. *A Discourse Concerning the Confusion of Languages at Babel*. London: Austen and Bowyer.

5

The Archaeology of Gender

M. L. S. Sørensen

"Archaeology of Gender": What Does it Mean?

The increase in publications on gender, together with its acknowledgment in archaeological literature in general, suggests that gender archaeology is now an established research area. It has, however, an ambiguous aura, as its political roots continue to make this research simultaneously marginal and fashionable. Gender needs to be embedded in archaeology's way of thinking, yet we feel compromised if the arguments are no longer radical. This tension between presentist objectives and disciplinary aims remains a unique dynamic.

The archaeology of gender refers to the explicit inclusion of gender in the study of past societies. The presence of women and men in (pre)history has always been acknowledged in interpretations of the past and they have been assigned different roles and distinct artefacts. Only in the 1980s was this aspect problematized: the first stage towards developing a theoretically informed gender or feminist archaeology (e.g., Wylie 1991). This stage is closely related to the women's movement generally, and is found in particular in Britain, Scandinavia, and the USA. It focused upon the demand for equality, literally and symbolically. It was argued that women had been systematically

suppressed and made invisible, not only within the profession but also in presentations and reconstructions of the past. Contemporaneously, the social sciences introduced a concept of gender as a social construct contrasted to biologically given sex (essentialism), although the relation between biology and culture remained a topic of debate. Many of these initial statements have since been qualified, but they were important for challenging existing ideas of men and women and their respective roles in (pre)history. These relationships needed investigation rather than relying upon stereotypical assumptions. Importantly, gender as a social and cultural construction could vary through time and space. Conkey and Spector's (1984) article firmly argued for the critical introduction of women into our past and into the profession as a distinct concern. This led to an emphasis upon visibility and replacement. It was argued that women had been involved with the same activities as men, had the same status, and similar roles. Examples of this approach are found in connection with the Man-the-hunter model (Hager 1997). The collective presence and importance of women forms an undercurrent in these early arguments, with gender interpreted to mean women. Most of the social and theoretical implications of the idea of gender, such as negotiation and social construction, remained largely unexplored. This, basically political, manifesto was effective; but due to its political overtones many claims were met with suspicion. Gender archaeology remained marginal both in self-perception and in the discipline's responses.

In contrast, discussions have recently and simultaneously become more broadly based in response to contemporary social developments, in particular as regards sexuality, difference, conformity, and rights, and more specifically through attempts to make the concerns more explicit to the discipline. There has also been a geographically wider impact, including recently, for instance, African archaeology (e.g., Kent 1998; Wadley 1997). This stage is characterized by increased problematization of basic concepts, in particular those of sex and sexuality. On the one hand, debates about discipline and practices are now informed by the critiques of science and of essentialist epistemologies which in different ways have been voiced by feminism, queer theory, and masculinist theory (e.g., Baker 1998; Meskell 1999: 61 ff.). On the other hand, a new focus treats material culture as involved with both the construction and reflection of gender relations, and how gender becomes inserted in material discourses with special attention towards its performance (e.g., Arwill-Nordbladh 1998; Joyce 1996; Sørensen 2000). There is also among some archaeologists a distinct interest in embodiment, body politics, and sexuality (e.g., Meskell 1996, 1999) and in the body as an extension of material culture (e.g., Sofaer-Derevenski 1998). One may characterize this change as a move away from a singular political agenda to a more fluid and explorative stage. The later development of gender archaeology has been less straightforward than its first stage, and it has proven more difficult to agree upon the conceptual and analytical tools. It is, therefore, within the basic frameworks that the greatest diversity of opinions and approaches can now be found. This development is often interpreted as part of a general postmodern or poststructuralist phenomenon, with a similar progression of gender research in other disciplines. In archaeology this association was seen in the intertwining of postprocessual approaches and gender archaeology. There are, however, also well-known tensions between them. Thus a strong current in feminist theory is opposed to a postmodernism which results in a negation of women as a special category and therefore also of their claim to a distinct history, rights, and specific ways of thought and feelings. Furthermore, certain approaches within postmodernism (and postprocessual archaeology) stand accused of androcentrism and of undermining women's position within academia (e.g., Engelstad 1991; Wylie 1997).

This development of approaches explicitly concerned with gender is variously called gender archaeology or feminist archaeology. Sometimes these terms are used interchangeably, while others employ them to refer to explicit differences of approach. There is also regional variation, with the term *gender archaeology* being increasingly used in Europe (and for many lecture courses in Britain; cf. Swedish (*genus arkeologi*), and Spanish (*Arqueologia del género*)). In Australia the word *feminist* does not seem to imply a specifically feminist-informed practice (e.g., Du Cros and Smith 1993; Casey et al. 1998). In the USA, on the other hand, feminist archaeology, in contrast to gender archaeology, often signals an explicitly feminist critique. It should be possible to acknowledge that the distinction between feminist and gender archaeology can be a constructive means of preserving a basic difference in emphasis and objectives (see also Lesick 1997: 31).

The aims of feminist archaeology were initially to demonstrate the unfair, inaccurate presentation of women, and also to improve women's position in the present, through means that one may compare to positive discrimination. In up-grading women's history, women are often presumed to have specific qualities. In challenging the control over the production of knowledge claims, feminist archaeologists also become equally concerned with the practice of archaeology (e.g., Gero 1996; Smith 1995; Wylie 1991), analyzing equity issues, epistemology, and the nature of authority. Later concerns are expressed through new lines of critique of science and specific theoretical approaches aimed at investigating the individual. Gender archaeology is more explicitly concerned with the relationship between men and women as a fundamental social dynamic, and also increasingly with how such relationships are expressed in and negotiated through material objects in different constructions of gender. These (political and epistemological) differences have many roots, but there are also certain concerns that are shared, and these will be my main focus. The following reflections are, however, particularly informed by gender archaeology as practiced within European prehistory.

Why Gender Archaeology?

Gender is an important aspect of any society. It was feminism and general social theory which first focused attention on the varied character of gender relations. Through these influences, and informed by ethnographic case studies, gender became understood as a dynamic social construct, and one which needs to be continuously constituted within society (Moore 1986) and acquired by individuals. Gender is not just women and men – it is a result of the ways we live together and construct a universe around us (Sørensen 1988: 17). At the same time, this does not mean that gender concepts do not remain open to different interpretations. In particular, disputed differences between sex and gender raise the question of their relationship and possible interdependence. The dominant interpretation within archaeology sees gender as a social construction responding to socially perceived differences between people's bodies, differences commonly cat-egorized as variations upon male and female but which may include other categories and subgroups within them. While the concept of gender is commonly used as a duality (i.e., an assumption of there always and only being two genders), this is not in itself implied by the concept. Moreover, the reference to sex is usually interpreted in terms of the "sexual appearance" or "functions" of the body (i.e., external genitalia or reproductive capacities), rather than referring to sexuality. It is important to recognize that this social constructivist model of gender does not necessarily negate the significance of biology or sexuality; rather, it attempts to define an identity within which these may be subsumed through their social meaning.

Gender understood like this has neither a specific nor a static form. This is why the negotiation of gender relations is central to social reproduction and the study of societal change. Yet so far our understanding of how gender operates is limited, and we still have far to go in tracing and understanding its spatial and temporal variability. In addition, we need to investigate the ways that gender arrangements affect groups' responses to various conditions in their social or natural environments (Conkey and Spector 1984: 19). I stress again that gender is constituted by context; it does not exist *per se*, but is produced by practice. People are both gendered individuals and social agents; their activities are influenced by several identities, and such distinctions between gender identity, ideology, and roles are important for understanding the continuous interaction between self and society (Sørensen 2000).

Archaeological Gender Research

During the development of gender archaeology two areas of application became distinct: visibility research and (re)interpretation. Each is informed by both gender politics and gender theory.

Visibility research

The demand for visibility, incorporation, and recognition was an early argument for interest in gender, and it was used to ground a concern with visibility within different domains of archaeology. It remains a core question, and research aimed at ascertaining women's position is being conducted both in countries with a long-standing interest in gender, such as Norway (e.g., Engelstad et al. 1992), and in others where this is a newly discovered issue, such as Africa (e.g., Kent 1998; Wadley 1997). Research focuses on a number of sub-areas, as outlined below.

(In)visibility in the profession

The women's movement of the 1960s brought attention to women's access to ladders of employment. Within archaeology this surfaced in print from the early 1970s (for details, see Sørensen 2000). The earliest articles about women and archaeology are, accordingly, about the job market, and show the familiar picture of women decreasing in numbers at the higher levels of career structures. This type of survey was conducted particularly early in Norway (Mandt and Næss 1999) and the USA (e.g., Stark 1991). They have more recently been extended to many other countries, including several in Europe (e.g., Díaz-Andreu and Sanz Gallego 1994; Morris 1992; see also papers in Díaz-Andreu and Sørensen 1998a), South Africa (Wadley 1997), and Australia (papers in Du Cros and Smith 1993; Casey et al. 1998). The employment pattern is slowly changing, although recent research reveals "invisible" barriers to women, which escape an analysis of presence/absence and positions. Even when women are formally at the top of the hierarchy, their academic products tend to be assigned low status (Engelstad et al. 1992).

A particular version of equity research presents historiographic reanalysis of women's presence in and contribution to archaeology. The aim is to reinsert a muted group into our disciplinary past, creating role models and case studies. Women are almost absent from the classic accounts of how "the past" was discovered and how ideas were created for the analysis of *our* past. The subtext this produces presents archaeology as a professional activity created by men. The research now begun shows that women disappear from the discipline due to two mechanisms. At one level gender politics has been ignored by historiographic analysis. At the other level, individual women, who due to their specific contribution to the field cannot be ignored, have been individualized and consistently referred to as unusual, their importance granted to them *despite* their gender, treating them as a kind of honorary man. Only now are such versions being contested. A volume of critical historiographies about female archaeologists in America (Claassen 1994) and another focused on Europe (Díaz-Andreu and Sørensen 1998a) now exist, while a number of articles concerned with Australia have been published (Du Cros and Smith 1993). It is noticeable that other disciplines have also begun to look critically into their biographies (e.g., Ardener 1992). These volumes clearly show that women's contributions have been systematically erased from disciplinary memories, but also that they were considered important in their own time.

Visibility cannot, however, simply be granted, and the question of inclusion and exclusion in itself becomes a challenge. The attempt at reevaluating roles and importance makes it clear that the reasons for assigning prominence to any work are so profoundly shaped by the authoritative nature of disciplinary culture that it is exceedingly difficult to go beyond accepted notions of knowledge and value (Díaz-Andreu and Sørensen 1998b).

(In)visibility in representation and in data

Another area much affected by a concern with visibility is the representation of the past in museums and in depictions. To this has recently been added how gender may also affect the production of data itself. As a result, we now begin to see museum exhibitions and educational material engaging actively with the question of how gender and its importance are assigned to the past. While relatively new, this perspective will doubtless grow in influence within museum culture, as it meets both the needs of the profession and of the public at large (see the arguments in Devonshire and Wood 1996). Again, however, there is a need for more than just a concern with presence/absence. The need for gender critical analysis of such representations has been recognized, and some studies have been carried out (e.g., Porter 1996; for further discussion see Sørensen 1999). Moser's work, in particular, stands out for its thorough analysis of the roots and values that sit behind both the construction and reading of various visual representations of the past (Moser 1998).

The crucial question of how the archaeological record is formed has also recently been drawn into this debate, at the most basic level of what becomes the record of the past. Should the policies and the practices through which we decide what kind of archaeological record we want be gender-aware? Two areas of practice are involved. The first is selection and preservation, i.e., heritage management. Case studies conducted in some countries have begun to show that the selection of our historical record has been systematically biased towards male-associated images, monuments, and activities (e.g., Dommasnes and Mandt 1999; Holcomb 1998; Smith 1995). This is most clearly shown for recent periods, where industrial activities or battlefields are given prominence in scheduling policies, and where the places of women's activities are badly represented, if at all, in the records. In Australia, for example, although thousands of female prisoners came to the colony, little material culture is preserved to witness their history. In Britain, the English Heritage protection strategy for the remains of the coal industry was originally "designed to represent the industry's chronological depth, technological breadth and regional diversity" (Chitty 1995: 3), but explicitly excluded domestic structures. It had not been recognized that this involved any gender issue, although the policy would exclude women from the records or include them mainly in roles that were unrepresentative of the life of the majority associated with the industry. The second area of practices involves the physical creation of our data, and thus indirectly establishing their interpretational possibilities. Gero (1996) has argued for this as an important aspect of the genderization of the past as a disciplinary construction.

Finally, while gender relations in many ways are embedded in our interpretations, this often remains a muted presence, as their analysis is not actively promoted. They are not usually included in the outlines of objectives or policy documents of the discipline and its professional institutions. We see here an interesting contrast between the common use of gender stereotypes and the reluctance to favor it as a topic of study. This is despite the obvious importance of gender within many well-established research areas, such as the origin of modern humans, cognition, the origin of agriculture, and the rise of social complexity, or its involvement in phenomena such as migration, innovation, and acculturation. As a specific example, in English Heritage's 1991 strategy paper (*Exploring the Past*), the theme of the transition from hunter-gatherers to farmers lacks any reference to gender. This is despite the fact that such changes in subsistence obviously affected resource allocation and labor organization within communities, and thus probably also had significant impact upon gender relations. In fact, there are no explicit references to gender issues in the policy documents of English Heritage and most other institutions.

It is, however, also important to critically assess the limitation of visibility research and our reasons for doing it. Equity and visibility have been looked at typically in terms of the social make-up of the profession – who gets what kinds of job, and who, therefore, decides what the past looks like. These concerns have gradually been extended to other issues, and the questioning of representation and representativity now also affects how the archaeological record is shaped and how knowledge is evaluated. The themes raised are substantial, both as a basis for critical self-reflection within the discipline and as a means of understanding how gendered meaning is practised and reproduced. This particular kind of research has nonetheless become dependent upon potentially limiting research practices. Primarily, it commonly collapses the question of gender into being about the presence of women, and at the same time visibility is judged in terms of quantity. This latter totally misses the point that women are not merely made invisible in terms of not being present, but that their invisibility arises out of their assigned insignificance in terms of the interpretive engagement with their presence or representation – whether in data, the profession, or displays.

Visibility research, as outlined above, makes presentist reasons rather than the desire to understand society and gender the main motivations for our studies. The reasons for these studies can, however, easily and beneficially be argued on a much broader and more critical basis. Despite such limitations, fundamental issues – particularly with regard to the production of knowledge and its authorization – have been highlighted. The interest in equity is therefore far from trivial and can make a profound contribution to our understanding of disciplinary culture.

Theoretical advances and (re)interpretation

Certain concepts and theories provide the foundation for our concept of gender archaeology. They originated in the social sciences, in particular social anthropology, with later influences coming from a wider field. While such influences are essential for the continuous development of theoretical concepts, it is nonetheless essential that archaeology respond analytically to differences in our dis-

ciplinary practices and possibilities. In addition, as feminism and gender studies have developed and proliferated, the need to reinvestigate the meaning and implications of central concepts, when used within distinct contexts such as archaeology, has become ever more obvious. Arguably, the most challenging task for gender archaeology at this point is how to develop a theoretical gender framework of relevance to archaeology, past communities, and contemporary society. It is within such debates that much of the most challenging developments in gender archaeology have taken place in recent years (e.g., Meskell 1996; Joyce 1996; Hastorff 1998; Sofaer-Derevenski 1997, 1998).

Possibly the most basic proposition, and one that has caused archaeology some agony, is that sex and gender are not the same. Recent problematization regarding the potential cultural dimension of sex and sexuality has complicated this issue even further. Recall that a central premise for the development of gender archaeology was the proposition that, while sex more or less can be understood as a biological characteristic, gender is a cultural construct. This distinction had several implications for archaeology. First and foremost, gender politics, roles, and ideologies are dependent on the particular cultural contexts in which they are being shaped. Thus, gender is inseparable from other social relations; and the latter cannot be fully analyzed without also acknowledging gender. Secondly, gender becomes an identity composed through practices, attitudes, meaning, and values – structures that affect but do not have a physical form or matter themselves. So archaeologists were blessed with the proposition that gender is culture and at the same time apparently denied the ability to observe and analyze it. In response to this dilemma, archaeologists have commonly returned to the biologically sexed body and assumed it represents the gendered individual, or interpreted objects (singly or as assemblages) as gender-coded, or ignored the difference between sex and gender. One of the main problems arising from all this is that gender tends to be reduced to something which is observed through the biological body. Alternatively, it is equated with the objects associated with such bodies, rather than recognized as acted out (and in that sense embodied) through practices and learned throughout individual life cycles. This also means that research has remained focused on the question of differences between women and men, or on the idea of a limited number of genders, rather than recognizing gender relations as an important dynamic aspect of the interrelations between people, and society's conception and interpretation of them.

Recently, however, discussions within some disciplines, such as literary criticism, psychology, history, and sociology, have argued that both sex and gender are far more complex constructions than our earlier discussions revealed (e.g., Butler 1993; Laqueur 1990). In particular, the status of sex is being debated, and some scholars challenge the separation between sex and gender, insofar as they stress both as cultural constructions. Some even argue that sex and gender are not or cannot be separated (Moore 1994). Another point, which has also been made within archaeology (e.g., Sofaer-Derevenski 1997), is that so-called biological males and females may in their individual life cycles go through stages differently associated with sexual characteristics and notions of sexuality. Women, for example, are not reproductive throughout their lives. There is also wider biological variation than the grouping into male and female implies, and gray areas may either be constructed or recognized culturally. Sexual identity, moreover, may within different cultures be based on a variety of criteria and often has temporal variations. The cultural recognition of sex, therefore, does not necessarily correspond to a biological "reality" and some dispute such realities (e.g., Laqueur 1990); nor is it inevitably a stable characteristic of an individual. In response to such issues much of the social science debate

on gender has turned its attention towards the individual, subjectivity, and embodiment, although others continue to lay stress on conventions and the social arena of performance. Archaeology has only recently begun to react to these debates, which largely happen outside its obvious expertise, and we see different interpretive responses to this challenge (e.g., Lesick 1997; Meskell 1996; Nordbladh and Yates 1990). Nonetheless, the debate will affect gender archaeology and the assumption and central premises upon which it has been based. The prevalent understanding of gender, which emphasizes it as a cultural construction, will have to be reconsidered in view of these arguments about sex and sexuality. In doing so, it seems important that we do not return to views that represent the interwoven, and possibly inseparable, relationship between sex and gender in terms of a static or essentialist quality. Arguments that present gender as a far more flexible dimension of identity than we have been assuming so far offer interesting potential. They allow gender (as a dimension of identity, practice, and experience) to be assigned a certain elasticity, which affects how it is expressed and recognized in different contexts, including the individual's life cycle. Understood in this way, gender is a continuous dialogue taking place within society, between internalized, embodied selves and externalized, learned, and confirmed identities. It also stresses gender as an outcome of ongoing negotiation. Thus, gender is understood not as an essential identity but as an outcome of how individuals come to understand their differences and similarities from others and how this involves material culture.

The recognition of the many dimensions of gender makes it important for archaeology to accept that the aspect we can investigate with the greatest expertise is the way in which gender construction and the living of gender involves and affects material things. In response to the current deconstruction of concepts of gender and sex, archaeology may therefore usefully clarify that our concern is with gender as a dialogue about membership and conventions, and about normative behaviors that comment upon and construct people in terms of difference, as well as the subversive reactions this may provoke. Although much of what constitutes (and gives meaning to) gender is lived through and made sense of by the individual, gender is also always deeply involved in social life, and it is as a social expression that it becomes most obviously apparent in archaeological data.

To utilize the many existing potentials within the archaeological record, and to respond to the urgent questions about the construction and significance of gender in past societies, further research into the complex relationship between sex and gender and about the practice and performance of gender, is still needed. Rather than taking these concepts for granted or ignoring them, we must learn to let them "work" for us. For instance, Sofaer-Derevenski (1997, 2000) has applied a theorization of the body itself as material culture – seeing it as a manifestation of gendered lives and affected by the transformative process of growing up – to the Tiszapolgar-Basatanya cemetery, an Early Copper Age site in Hungary. In her analysis, metal objects, rather than being a reflection of wealth or status, are interpreted as mediating age–gender dimensions at a period of social transformation. The dynamic discursive character of social categories emerges from this study as a significant key to understanding the rupturing of and attempts at social order that characterize central Europe during the third millennium BC. Other propositions or concepts, such as gender negotiation, gender symbolism, the materiality of gender, and the relationship between gender and other structuring principles such as age and ethnicity, clearly also need further consideration to enable a fuller exploration of the past. The basic point, that gender relations participated in shaping and forming the societies that we study, that they influenced decision-making, informed practices, and were

susceptible to change, must remain central and be incorporated in the ways we approach, analyze, and represent the past.

The interpretive impact of gender archaeology has been felt at two distinct levels. At one level, former stereotypic and familiar views of gender relations in different periods and cultures have been severely criticized and are being abandoned, causing interpretation (and analysis) of social organization on a grand scale to be recast. For instance, for the Palaeolithic period, basic assumptions, reflected in notions such as pair-bonding and division of labor on the basis of sex, have been questioned; thus the argued dynamic and evolutionary drives within these societies have come to be challenged (see, for example, papers in Hager 1997). For early historic studies, the effect has been much greater attention towards women's actual (rather than presumed) lives, showing their significant involvement in productive activities and the means they had of independent action (Gilchrist 1999).

At another level, changes to mega-narratives about the past have been fed by detailed analysis of specific sites and types of assemblages or structures that have begun to embellish our insights into society, as they show gender in its integration with other social concerns and relations. Parker Pearson (1996), for example, has argued that the principle behind the layout of Iron Age round houses in England corresponds with a simple gender division, suggesting that domestic architecture was based on a simple metaphor of social relations. As another example, I have used evidence from Bronze Age graves about clothing and accessories to show that distinct dress codes existed, and to argue that a categorical distinction was being made within women, and that this did not relate to differences in wealth (Sørensen 1997). This is interpreted as indicating that the female gender had subgroups within it or that there were at least two distinct categories of women. Such differences may have been the effect of culturally acknowledged life-stage changes, which may be based on a variety of criteria, including physiological or moral criteria. Some specific interpretations gained significance not only from this proposal but also by breaking with established assumptions. Arnold's (1996) discussion of the rich Iron Age grave of Vix in France is a good example of this. In this case the "female" objects among the gravegoods and the identification of the skeleton as female had consistently affected the interpretations of the grave, which avoided presenting one of the richest graves in prehistoric Europe as being that of a woman. Another subtle challenge to established gender interpretations is provided by Nevett's (1994) critical analysis of the conventional interpretation of the seclusion of women in the Ancient Greek house. Reassessing architectural layout in terms of function and access, Nevett proposes that it was designed to limit physical access to and visibility of certain parts of the domestic unit. The seclusion in question was therefore not about women from men as such, but about the separation of women from strangers. The theme of segregation has also been extensively discussed by Gilchrist (1999: 113ff.), whose concern has increasingly become the wider role this plays in social politics. On this basis, she has linked what she calls the "body politic" with various spatial configurations – especially the castle and the nunnery – in medieval times (Gilchrist 1997, 1999).

Such specific, detailed studies that rectify earlier interpretations or introduce new perspectives abound in the literature. Our understanding of the past, both at a general level and in its specific expressions, is beginning to incorporate a far more critical and reflexive understanding of gender. In particular, such studies are increasingly informed by a desire to understand rather than just assume these relationships.

In addition to considering gender interpretations in terms of the level at which their impact is felt, they can also roughly be characterized in terms of their basic approach. What we may call a *gender identifying approach* focuses on women aiming

to reassert their roles and importance, such as demonstrating that females could be blacksmiths in the medieval period, or arguing that women played central roles in food procurement in hunter-gatherer societies (see, for example, papers in Devonshire and Wood 1996; Moore and Scott 1997; Wright 1996). Alternatively, a *gender inclusive approach* discusses how the practices and activities reflected by an archaeological assemblage make it possible to reinsert women into these contexts, due to the mutual dependency, interaction, and interference between activities carried out by different members of the community. The aim is to show gender relations entangled with practical everyday existence.

Gender Identifying Approach

The gender identifying approach has typically been used for activities which are thought to be involved with the communication of gender categories and their evaluation. Many gender studies have been carried out on archaeological data that may be associated with such practices, and within these, burials probably remain the best and most extensively investigated. Among well-known studies from varied parts of European prehistory one may mention, for example, analysis of Neolithic passage graves (Hodder 1984), different methodological investigations of Beaker assemblages and grave structure (Gibbs 1990; Sofaer-Derevenski 1998), and assemblages from Early Bronze Age graves (Shennan 1975). For later periods, there have been several large-scale investigations of Iron Age, Anglo-Saxon, and Viking Age cemeteries from, for example, England (Brush 1988; Lucy 1997), Norway (Dommasnes 1982; Hjørungdal 1991), and Russia (Stalsberg 1991). In the USA, Australia, and Africa the examples can be vastly expanded, ranging over a number of cultures and contexts. Contemporary political concerns regarding the study of human remains, together with characteristics of the archaeological record, may, however, have caused burial analysis to be less prominent in gender research within these areas than they are in Europe (nonetheless, see various papers in Gero and Conkey 1991; Casey et al. 1998; Wadley 1997).

The results of such studies, in terms of reinterpreting women in the past, vary from asserting women's position within particular contexts, to qualifying the determining influence of gender in other contexts. For instance, based on analysis of grave assemblages, it has been shown that women's position in Viking trading centers in Russia needs to be reassessed, suggesting that Viking settlers included women from the beginning and that women gained various positions of importance within the emerging local communities (Stalsberg 1991). Another significant study that challenges accepted interpretations is Rega's (1997) preliminary analysis of Early Bronze Age communities, where various chemical and pathological analyses of human bones from the Morkin cemetery in former Yugoslavia suggest gender/sex was a less important factor in determining differential access to food than was kinship.

In addition to mortuary activities, objects used in the construction of people's appearance have also been recognized as central to notions of identities, including gender (Sørensen 1997; Treherne 1995). Figurines, iconography, and some types of art are also now routinely explored in such terms (see, for example, Conkey 1997; and papers in Gero and Conkey 1991; Whitehouse 1999; Wright 1996). To this we are also slowly adding other situations and resources, such as colonization and innovation, as well as food (Claassen 1992; Sørensen 2000). Some of the areas that we must assume to have been continuously involved with different types and degrees of gender negotiation, and in which gender was commonly performed, have, however, proven difficult to open up for gender analysis. For example, it remains unclear how to investigate the way domestic units and tasks are involved with gender ne-

gotiation, beyond possible symbolic or metaphorical effects upon the "architectural blueprint." In consequence, studies of such activities are often simplistic and tend to rely upon universal assumptions about gender or be based on rather basic binary oppositions. Meanwhile, social anthropological case studies show domestic domains as actively participating in gender negotiation, as food preparation, allocation of resources and labor, rubbish categories, and spatial order may all be involved in reaching agreement about gender rights and responsibilities, and thus reproducing and negotiating the content of gender (e.g., Moore 1994). The particular ways that gender appears to be constructed within these communities are, however, contextually explicit and cannot in themselves provide interpretation of past communities. They help us to understand gender in terms of its temporal existence and constituent parts, but that does not provide insight into how such concerns were negotiated within other societies. The ways in which gender informs, and is maintained through, daily contexts of action, in contrast to possibly quite reified expressions in contexts such as burials and art, must therefore be explored further. This is an aspect of gender archaeology that is ripe for further attention.

Gender Inclusive Approach

In contrast to the above, the gender inclusive approach focuses on recognizing within assemblages the existence of a range of concurrent concerns and activities, which would have been subject to continuous negotiation and interpretation, including gender and its meaning. This coexistence of many activities that are each subject to gender negotiation, and the use of various means in their ongoing interpretation, is often overlooked in gender studies due to our search for importance and status. This approach is exemplified in Conkey's (1991) classic study of a Magdalenian rockshelter in Spain, in which she argues for using evidence "not as a record of some given predetermined social form but to elucidate strategies of social action" (p. 58). This perspective enables her to reach a detailed, genderized discussion of social life, action, and interaction on the site, on the basis of an assemblage within which seemingly both men and women were absent.

A similar exploration of ideas about contexts of meaning and action has been used by Arwill-Nordbladh (1998) in her analysis of the famous Viking ship grave from Oseberg, Norway, in which a woman was buried accompanied by a very rich funerary assemblage. One of Arwill-Nordbladh's aims was to engage with the complexity of gender dynamics, and to explore how different artefacts may have been involved with different aspects of the construction of gender – a view reached when objects are seen to be constituent of gender in distinct ways. On this basis, an interpretation is mounted which presents the Oseberg ship burial as a type of scenographic space or discursive event. The artefacts are analyzed as object-meanings that are brought into the space and reassembled there in a manner aiming to communicate (and constitute) the gender of the body in death, through references to a range of actions which place it within the gender dynamics of a prestige-based, high-ranking society.

A further example of the idea of the context of social action is my own discussion of how we approach the question of metalworking in the Bronze Age (Sørensen 1996). I argue that rather than attempting to insert women as the metalworkers, we can constructively rephrase the research agenda to be about how such practices are only possible as socially agreed and collectively facilitated projects, and that they will therefore always impact on society beyond role allocations. Such an approach would move attention away from the importance of special roles and actions to an appreciation of the involvement of gender with, and its dependency upon, social action.

Using both of the approaches outlined here, as and when appropriate, will help us enlarge our understanding of gender as new venues for research are being recognized. But in order to develop our ability to investigate gender relations as performed and negotiated within various aspects of life, archaeology also needs to renew its attention towards how material culture becomes a partner in the structuring and negotiation of social relations. To understand gender organization as a part of history and historical processes, it is essential to look at social institutions and relations and trace how they are reproduced over time. Material culture plays a special role in such reproduction for several reasons. One particular point is that objects are one of the central means through which generations and events are linked; they are therefore fundamental for mediating tradition. Another central dimension of objects is their materiality, which means that they are also the physical resources within which rights and obligations are invested. I regard the question of the materiality of gender as one of the most promising and important areas in which to pursue further the potential of gender archaeology. This will be the focus of the rest of this chapter.

Gender and Materiality

Archaeology's relevance and contribution to gender studies come from its unique time dimension and its use of material culture. The latter is neglected by other disciplines, where the material and symbolic correlates and impact of gender are assumed, but where little attention is given to either the significance of this association or how it is made. Thus, despite the obvious influences from the social sciences upon the development of gender archaeology, there are also significant analytical potentials that may be generated from within the discipline itself.

Objects and practical action solidify and give physical realities and consequences to thoughts and norms, including gender. This means that we should recognize material culture as constituting contexts or situations through which gender is affected, but also that this involvement can take different forms due to the flexible manner in which objects can be explored. Furthermore, it means that material culture provides both a medium for the practice of gender and resources through which its negotiation can take place. In other words, in its operation gender uses objects and actions, and it is through its articulation in the material domain that gender differences gain a new reality. And it is here that we begin to engage with the link between gender and materiality. It is therefore relevant to further contemplate the materiality of gender, as this may provide the basis for a distinct approach to the investigation of the construction and negotiation of gender.

Gender, as a basic structure and interest of prehistoric societies, would have permeated objects as a means of becoming tangible and significant for the people involved. Objects, however, due to their durability and evocative nature, did not simply reflect gender difference, but were also discursively involved in its creation and (re)interpretation. In addition, due to their capacity to transgress, interconnect, and symbolize, objects would have been one of the mechanisms through which gender differences could irradiate throughout society as a whole and be maintained and recreated through time and between events.

Material things and practices, as the foci for such gender arrangements and negotiations, are significant means of gender construction for several reasons. Prime among these are their fundamental role in the learning, negotiation and enactment of gender, which means that they are critically and substantially involved with how gender comes to be understood, practiced, and recognized within any society. It is the case that objects influence the ways we see ourselves and the roles and rights we presume access to (Sørensen 1999). It is therefore useful to confirm that material culture is also a set of resources (i.e., things that are needed, desired, and distributed), as this emphasizes that

objects are continuously subject to various kinds of production and distribution. The main point to emphasize is that, in their production and distribution, these resources become involved with the construction of gender; they make it tangible and material, giving it physical reality and with real effects upon people's lives and possibilities. In other words, it is through objects and their associated activities that gender becomes enacted. Objects thus both represent and affect gender, and their role in both instances is to embody a code of difference and to provide a means of its recognition and repetition (Sørensen 2000).

The significance – symbolically as well as materially – of such associations between gender and material objects is further augmented by how alternative notions of gender and/or sexuality are commonly expressed through so-called subversive use of material culture, which aims to challenge the restricted association between objects and certain categories of people. Equally, the substantial investment in the suppression of such alternatives, and the effort involved in maintaining the material form of particular gender systems, testify to the importance these objects gain as the expression and enactment of a code. As objects are made into feminine and masculine items they also become associated with notions of their appropriate use, and breaking these codes, however mundane the items seem to be, commonly produces unease or even censorship. Thus, the material expression of gender is not merely its reflection. It is an active element of the experience of self and it is part of the differences that affect people's lives. It is involved with the allocation of rights and responsibilities within communities, and the approbation and prescription of appropriate actions. Gender, one may even argue, is of limited significance unless and until the differences that it contains are associated with evaluations that affect the allocation of resources, and thus become influential elements of social and political discourse (Sørensen 2000).

It is therefore through and with objects that gender becomes performed. The combination of materiality and practices lends itself to the repetitive performance of gender as a difference, as well as providing locales for its negotiation. It is, therefore, through repetitive acts following rules or schemas, and association between these and certain kind of resources (for example, food, clothing, or gravegoods) that people are confirmed as being different. In return they participate in the continuous performance of difference – whether through conformity or subversion. Children, for instance, learn to recognize themselves as belonging to particular groups of people, and witness their negotiation of rights and responsibilities. As each performance may be interpreted as a range of citations to earlier performances, it also provides a means of recognition and learning that goes beyond the isolated event and the specific context. Looking at the archaeological record, we see how structures and objects such as graves, houses, field systems, pots, flint tools, or weapons were produced, maintained, changed, and adapted to the practices and negotiations taking place in connection with them, and how these were about people and their rights and responsibilities. It is within these practices that people express and experience gender.

Conclusion

Gender archaeology, as it has evolved over the last two decades, has been substantially affected by its early roots in the women's movement and its various contemporary political aims. It has therefore largely focused upon identifying places for woman and making her visible within various dimensions of the past, as well as in the discipline. While acknowledging the importance of these roots, it is argued that gender archaeology has other potentials, and that their further exploration is of importance for archaeology as a discipline and for its contribution to the understanding of gender generally.

In order to locate and develop these potentials we need to understand the intersection between individuals, social concerns, and material culture. We need to explicitly explore the "thingness" of objects, and how this quality affects how we experience the world. Basically, one impact of the physicality of material culture is that it brings a distinct dimension to gender: as gender is affected by and affects material conditions, it gains physical consequences and impact. Understanding this, we also see that gender acted out through material discourse affects people's lives in critical ways.

Due to the impact of gender studies we now, in general, accept that gender relations constitute a fundamental social structure in which both men and women (and other variations) participate as partners in the historical process. They react and function in relationship to their mutual similarities and differences, creating, manipulating, and maintaining social institutions such as "marriage," kinship, lines of obligations, and alliances. They co-habit and collaborate. Thus, gender *cannot* be ignored in historical studies, as it constitutes an essential mechanism of society and is embedded in its changes. That is why archaeology needs to incorporate gender in its study of the past, and why it needs to continue laboring with its theoretical basis and methodological implications. The concepts we have learned to use to engage with these critical issues are, however, once again subject to debate within the arts and social sciences. The stable, comfortable notions of sex and gender that we had begun to think with are increasingly challenged, moving debates into realms outside the easy reach of archaeology. The separation of sex and gender, of biology and culture, which to archaeology originally provided the *raison d'être* for gender as a legitimate and necessary research topic, is being challenged, and if not disappearing, new meanings to these differentiations are being evoked. Variability is being emphasized, and negotiation, manipulation, and the strategic use of sex have come to the fore, undermining assumed knowledge, as our entities become slippery and escape easy classification.

These debates affect archaeology, but their practical and intellectual impact is still open for us to clarify and decide. Rather than abandoning the project of engendering the past because "it is getting too difficult," the volatile climate of debate and the shifting and vague form of former solid entities must be recognized, as part of a challenging intellectual climate within which we try to find our own voices and set distinct aims. Gender, we begin to learn, does not just need to be found, identified, and rescued; we need also to think with gender, to investigate it as construction or experience, and analyze its constituent parts and the ways it is maintained and reacted upon. Out of this, a unique contribution from (and challenge to) gender archaeology could be its ability to engage with the question of where and how to locate the insertion of gender in various social practices, and how an object becomes a gendered thing. The recognition of how, in practice, the evaluation and recognition of gender is informed by and affects material conditions is an essential addition to the theoretical discussion of the existence of gender as social understanding.

Acknowledgments

Thanks to John Bintliff for his constructive comments on this chapter. It is with great satisfaction that I note the increase in more broadly based publications on gender archaeology since writing this contribution.

References

Ardener, S. (ed.) 1992. *Persons and Powers of Women in Diverse Cultures: Essays in Commemoration of Audrey I. Richards, Phyllius Kaberry and Barbara E. Ward*. Oxford: Berg.

Arnold, B. 1996. " 'Honorary males' or women of substance? Gender, status and power in Iron Age Europe." *Journal of European Archaeology*, 3 (2): 153–68.

Arwill-Nordbladh, E. 1998. *Genuskonstruktioner i Nordisk Vikingatid. Förr och nu*. Gothenburg: Gothenburg University.

Baker, M. 1998. "Italian gender theory and archaeology: a political engagement." In R. D. Whitehouse (ed.), *Gender and Italian Archaeology: Challenging the Stereotypes*, pp. 23–33. London: Accordia Research Institute, University of London and Institute of Archaeology, University College London.

Brush, K. 1988. "Gender and mortuary analysis in pagan Anglo-Saxon archaeology." *Archaeological Review from Cambridge*, 7 (1): 76–89.

Butler, J. 1993. *Bodies that Matter: On the Discursive Limits of Sex*. London: Routledge.

Casey, M., D. Donlon, J. Hope, and S. Wellfare (eds.), 1998. *Redefining Archaeology: Feminist Perspectives*. Canberra: ANH Publications.

Chitty, G. 1995. *Monuments Protection Programme: The Coal Industry. Recommendations for Protection* (step 4 report). Final Draft. London: English Heritage.

Claassen, C. (ed.) 1992. *Exploring Gender Through Archaeology: Selected Papers from the Boon Conference*. Monographs in World Archaeology 11. Madison, WI: Prehistory Press.

Claassen, C. (ed.) 1994. *Women in Archaeology*. Philadelphia: University of Pennsylvania Press.

Conkey, M. W. 1991. "Contexts of action, contexts for power: Material culture and gender in the Magdalenian." In J. M. Gero and M. W. Conkey (eds.), *Engendering Archaeology: Women and Prehistory*, pp. 57–92. Oxford: Blackwell.

Conkey, M. W. 1997. "Mobilizing ideologies: Paleolithic 'art,' gender trouble, and thinking about alternatives." In L. D. Hager (ed.), *Women in Human Evolution*, pp. 172–207. London: Routledge.

Conkey, M. W. and J. Spector 1984. "Archaeology and the study of gender." *Advances in Archaeological Method and Theory*, 7: 1–38.

Devonshire, A. and B. Wood (eds.) 1996. *Women in Industry and Technology: From Prehistory to the Present. Current Research and the Museum Experience*. London: Museum of London.

Díaz-Andreu, M. and M. L. S. Sørensen (eds.) 1998a. *Excavating Women: A History of Women in European Archaeology*. London: Routledge.

Díaz-Andreu, M. and M. L. S. Sørensen 1998b. "Excavating women: towards an engendered history of archaeology". In M. Díaz-Andreu and M. L. S. Sørensen (eds.), *Excavating Women: A History of Women in European Archaeology*, pp. 1–28. London: Routledge.

Díaz-Andreu, M. and N. Sanz Gallego 1994. "Women issues in Spanish archaeology." In M. C. Nelson, S. M. Nelson, and A. Wylie (eds.), *Equity Issues for Women in Archaeology*, pp. 121–30. Archaeological Papers of the American Anthropological Association 5. Arlington, VA: American Anthropological Association.

Dommasnes, L. G. and G. Mandt 1999. "Feminist perspectives in archaeological research and cultural heritage management: Definitions, survey and remedial action." *K.A.N.* [Kvinner i Arkeologi i Norge], pp. 119–31. (First published in *K.A.N.* 6, 1988, pp. 99–113.)

Dommasnes, L. H. 1982. "Late Iron Age in Western Norway: female roles and ranks as deduced from an analysis of burial customs." *Norwegian Archaeological Review*, 15 (1–2): 70–84.

Du Cros, H. and L. Smith (eds.) 1993. *Women in Archaeology: A Feminist Critique*. Occasional Papers in Prehistory 23. Canberra: Dept. of Prehistory, Research School of Pacific Studies. Canberra: Australian National University.

Engelstad, E. 1991. "Images of power and contradiction: feminist theory and post processual archaeology." *Antiquity*, 65/248: 502–14.

Engelstad, E., G. Mandt, and J.-R. Næss 1992. "Equity issues in Norwegian archaeology", *K.A.N.* [Kvinner i Arkeologi i Norge], 13–14: 67–77.

English Heritage 1991. *Exploring our Past: Strategies for the Archaeology of England*. London: English Heritage.

Gero, J. M. 1996. "Archaeological practice and gendered encounters." In R. P. Wright (ed.), *Gender and Archaeology*, pp. 251–80. Philadelphia: University of Pennsylvania Press.

Gero, J. M. and M. W. Conkey 1991. *Engendering Archaeology: Women and Prehistory*. Oxford: Blackwell.

Gibbs, L. 1990. *Sex, Gender and Material Culture Patterning in Later Neolithic and Earlier Bronze Age England*. Unpublished PhD thesis, Dept. of Archaeology, Cambridge University.

Gilchrist, R. 1997. "Gender and medieval women." In J. Moore and E. Scott (eds.), *Invisible People and Processes: Writing Gender and Childhood into European Archaeology*, pp. 42–58. Leicester: Leicester University Press.

Gilchrist, R. 1999. *Gender and Archaeology: Contesting the Past*. London: Routledge.

Hager, L. D. (ed.) 1997. *Women in Human Evolution*. London: Routledge.

Hastorf, C. A. 1998. "The cultural life of early domestic plant use." *Antiquity*, 72 (278): 773–82.

Hill, E. forthcoming. "The liminal body: mediating the social through sacrifice." *Cambridge Journal of Archaeology*.

Hjørungdal, T. 1991. *Det skjulte kjønn. Patriarkal tradisjon og feministisk visjon i arkeologien belyst med fokus på en jernalderkontekst.* Acta Archaeologica Lundensia. Series in 8°, Nr 19. Lund: Almqvist and Wiksell International.

Hodder, I. 1984. "Burials, houses, women and men in the European Neolithic." In D. Miller, D. Tilley, and C. Tilley (eds.), *Ideology, Power and Prehistory*, pp. 51–68. Cambridge: Cambridge University Press.

Holcomb, B. 1998. "Gender and heritage interpretation." In D. Uzzell and R. Ballantyne (eds.), *Contemporary Issues in Heritage and Environmental Interpretation: Problems and Prospects*, pp. 37–55. London: HMSO.

Joyce, R. 1996. "Performance and inscription: negotiating sex and gender in classic Maya society." Unpublished paper given at Dumbarton Oaks.

Kent, S. (ed.) 1998. *Gender in African Prehistory.* Walnut Creek: AltaMira Press.

Laqueur, T. 1990. *Making Sex: Body and Gender from the Greeks to Freud.* Cambridge, MA: Harvard University Press.

Lesick, K. S. 1997. "Re-engendering gender: some theoretical and methodological concerns on a burgeoning archaeological pursuit." In J. Moore and E. Scott (eds.), *Invisible People and Processes: Writing Gender and Childhood into European Archaeology*, pp. 31–41. Leicester: Leicester University Press.

Lucy, S. 1997. "Housewives, warriors and slaves? Sex and gender in Anglo-Saxon burials." In J. Moore and E. Scott (eds.), *Invisible People and Processes: Writing Gender and Childhood into European Archaeology*, pp. 150–68. Leicester: Leicester University Press.

Mandt, G. and J.-R. Næss 1999. "Who created and recreates our distant past? Structures and content of Norwegian archaeology in the perspective: 'How male is science?' " *K.A.N.* [Kvinner i Arkeologi i Norge], pp. 22–3, 101–17. (First published in *K.A.N.* 3, 1986.)

Meskell, L. 1996. "The somatization of archaeology: institutions, discourses, corporeality." *Norwegian Archaeological Review*, 29 (1): 1–16.

Meskell, L. 1999. *Archaeologies of Social Life.* Oxford: Blackwell.

Moore, H. L. 1986. *Space, Text and Gender.* Cambridge: Cambridge University Press.

Moore, H. L. 1994. *A Passion for Difference.* Cambridge: Polity Press.

Moore, J. and E. Scott (eds.) 1997. *Invisible People and Processes: Writing Gender and Childhood into European Archaeology.* Leicester: Leicester University Press.

Morris, E. 1992. *Women in British Archaeology.* Institute of Field Archaeologists Occasional Paper no. 4. Birmingham: Institute of Field Archaeologists.

Moser, S. 1998. *Ancestral Images: The Iconography of Human Origins.* Stroud: Sutton.

Nevett, L. 1994. "Separation or seclusion? Towards an archaeological approach to investigating women in the Greek household in the fifth to third centuries BC." In M. Parker Pearson and C. Richards (eds.), *Architecture and Order: Approaches to Social Space*, pp. 98–112. London: Routledge.

Nordbladh, J. and T. Yates 1990. "This perfect body, this virgin text: between sex and gender in archaeology." In I. Bapty and T. Yates (eds.), *Archaeology after Structuralism: Poststructuralism and the Practice of Archaeology*, pp. 222–37. London: Routledge.

Parker Pearson, M. 1996. "Food, fertility and front doors in the first millennium BC." In T. C. Champion and J. Collis (eds.), *The Iron Age in Britain and Ireland: Recent Trends*, pp. 117–32. Sheffield: Sheffield Academic Press.

Porter, G. 1996. "Seeing through solidity: a feminist perspective on museums." In S. Macdonald and G. Fyfe (eds.), *Theorizing Museums*, pp. 105–26. Oxford: Blackwell.

Rega, E. 1997. "Age, gender and biological reality in the Early Bronze Age cemetery at Mokrin." In J. Moore and E. Scott (eds.), *Invisible People and Processes: Writing Gender and Childhood into European Archaeology*, pp. 229–47. Leicester: Leicester University Press.

Shennan, S. 1975. "The social organization at Branc." *Antiquity*, 49: 279–88.

Smith, L. 1995. "Cultural heritage management and feminist expression in Australian archaeology." *Norwegian Archaeological Review*, 28 (1): 55–64.

Sofaer-Derevenski, J. 1997. "Engendering children, engendering archaeology." In J. Moore and E. Scott (eds.), *Invisible People and Processes: Writing Gender and Childhood into European Archaeology*, pp. 192–202. Leicester: Leicester University Press.

Sofaer-Derevenski, J. 1998. "Gender Archaeology as Contextual Archaeology: A Critical Examination of the Tensions Between Method and Theory in the Archaeology of Gender." Unpublished PhD thesis, University of Cambridge.

Sofaer-Derevenski, J. 2000. "Rings of life: the role of early metalwork in mediating the gendered life course." *World Archaeology* 31 (3): 389–406.

Sørensen, M. L. S. 1988. "Is there a feminist contribution to archaeology?" *Archaeological Review from Cambridge*, 7 (1): 9–20.

Sørensen, M. L. S. 1996. "Women as/and metalworkers." In A. Devonshire and B. Wood (eds.), *Women in Industry and Technology: From Prehistory to the Present. Current Research and the Museum Experience*, pp. 45–52. London: Museum of London.

Sørensen, M. L. S. 1997. "Reading dress: the construction of social categories and identities in Bronze Age Europe." *Journal of European Archaeology*, 5 (1): 93–114.

Sørensen, M. L. S. 1999. "Archaeology, gender and the museum." In N. Merriman (ed.), *Making Early Histories in Museums*, pp. 136–50. Leicester: Leicester University Press.

Sørensen, M. L. S. 2000. *Gender Archaeology*. Cambridge: Polity Press.

Stalsberg, A. 1991. "Women as actors in north European Viking trade." In R. Samson (ed.), *Social Approaches to Viking Studies*, pp. 75–83. Glasgow: Cruithne Press.

Stark, M. 1991. "A perspective on women's status in American archaeology." In D. Walde and N. D. Willows (eds.), *The Archaeology of Gender: Proceedings of the Twenty-Second Annual Conference of the Archaeological Association of the University of Calgary*, pp. 187–94. Calgary: University of Calgary Archaeological Association.

Treherne, P. 1995. "The warrior's beauty: the masculine body and self-identity in Bronze Age Europe." *Journal of European Archaeology*, 3 (1): 105–44.

Wadley, L. (ed.) 1997. *Our Gendered Past: Archaeological Studies of Gender in Southern Africa*. Johannesburg: Witwatersrand University Press.

Whitehouse R. D (ed.) 1999. *Gender and Italian Archaeology: Challenging the Stereotypes*. London: Accordia Research Institute, University of London and Institute of Archaeology, University College London.

Wright, R. P. (ed.) 1996. *Gender and Archaeology*. Philadelphia: University of Pennsylvania Press.

Wylie, A. 1991. "Gender theory and the archaeological record: why is there no archaeology of gender?" In J. M. Gero and M. W. Conkey (eds.), *Engendering Archaeology: Women and Prehistory*, pp. 31–54. Oxford: Blackwell.

Wylie, A. 1997. "Good science, bad science, or science as usual? Feminist critiques of science." In L. D. Hager (ed.), *Women in Human Evolution*, pp. 29–55. London: Routledge.

6

Archaeology and Social Theory

Matthew Johnson

What is archaeological theory, and how can we describe its terrain? What are the main fault lines in theory today? What are the key issues of difference between competing (or complementary) theoretical schools? When we read different interpretations of the same or similar pieces of archaeological evidence, how are these differences driven by underlying differences in theoretical training, assumptions, and intellectual background? And further, how do these fault lines of theory condition different approaches to the archaeological record – how do they produce concretely different understandings of the material?

Many of those currently writing on theoretical topics would answer these questions with reference to epistemology; that is, they would point to the different nature of the knowledge claims made by different schools (positivist, idealist). Others would refer to differences in positions taken towards other areas of the human sciences (is archaeology "fundamentally" history, or is it "fundamentally" a science? Or, indeed, should we alternatively welcome interdisciplinary assimilation into the human sciences, or preserve our separate identity as a discipline?). Others still might contrast different assumptions made about the nature of the archaeological record, whether it is a fossil record on the one hand or

to be "read" like a text on the other (e.g., Patrik 1985).

In this chapter, I want to concentrate on differences in one key area of archaeological theory, namely that of *social theory*: how we go about understanding how human beings relate to one another, how we explain social stability and change, how archaeologists think about past societies. What form of social theory we choose to use, I suggest, determines which wider archaeological models of social life we find convincing, what sorts of social explanations of the archaeological record we find coherent and compelling. In short, I suggest that our social theory is an important if not central field over which we play out the key intellectual differences that characterize contemporary archaeological debate.

I do not suggest that other debates over epistemology or over method are unimportant, or that social theory is necessarily the one central area of debate in archaeological interpretation. But I do suggest that the way we conceive of past human communities, our use of different social models, is an excellent means of introduction to many areas of contemporary archaeological thought, particularly for those new to the field. There is a very simple reason for this: we all have practical knowledge of contemporary society, of social rules, of how to go about living with and behaving towards other people. As a result, theoretical appeal to different models of how the social world works (the use of phrases like "everyday routine" or "passive resistance," for example) tends to have resonance in our daily lives. It is difficult, as we go about the daily business of living, engaging in daily social transactions, or worrying about social and economic tensions in the world around us, to see how our life experiences relate to different forms of epistemology, but it is much easier to see how they relate to top-down versus bottom-up models of social change, conflict-driven versus consensus models of culture.

It follows therefore that an acquaintance with the central themes of social theory is an essential component of the archaeologists' toolkit, as essential as a trowel or measuring tape. We are, after all, supposed to be studying *Homo sapiens sapiens*; we all remember Mortimer Wheeler insisting "archaeology is a science that must be lived, must be seasoned with humanity" (Wheeler 1956: 13). The North American insistence that "archaeology is anthropology or it is nothing" makes a parallel point (I shall return to this below). Archaeology without human beings is mere antiquarianism, whatever other theoretical views one subscribes to.

It is disturbing therefore to find a widespread ignorance of social theory in many quarters – even pride in ignorance. "Oh, I just dig and use my common sense – I'm too busy doing real archaeology to have time for systems modeling or structuration theory." We would be genuinely shocked if a colleague announced proudly that their grasp of stratigraphy or of seriation was a bit hazy, but when a theorist hears a colleague loudly declaiming his ignorance of agency theory, we have learnt through distasteful experience that it is best not to rise to the bait, to grit one's teeth and make no comment. Tim Champion (1991) has charted admirably some of the more myopic views of "theory" within the discipline as a whole in the British Isles. The everyday practice of archaeology in much of the

Anglo-Saxon world at least remains depressingly anti-intellectual, for reasons I have discussed elsewhere (Johnson 1999: 1–11).

What follows, therefore, is something of a polemic. I will suggest that social theory has been central to our concerns, at least since the advent of the New Archaeology (though Mortimer Wheeler's words remind us that theories of the social world lay implicitly but deeply embedded in much work before that time). I shall go on to look at some recent theoretical developments that interest me, and try to bring out how they have helped us do more fruitful archaeology over the last decade or so. I shall then give a case study – the archaeology of castles – to suggest how, in practice, social theory can influence archaeological interpretation for the better, make our interpretations stronger, more truthful and accurate. I shall conclude by looking at some of the more negative reactions to the literature on social theory and the misconceptions and insecurities that underlie those reactions.

What is Social Theory?

Within the human sciences as a whole, there is no clear, unitary definition of the nature, aims, and purpose(s) of social theory. Bryan Turner writes:

> There is little agreement as to what "theory" is or what would constitute theoretical progress. As a result, theory may be regarded as a broad framework for organizing and ordering research, or as a collection of general concepts which are useful in directing research attention, or as a specific orientation . . . Recent developments in feminism and postmodernism have only confounded much of the existing confusion and uncertainty. (Turner 1996: 11)

This indeterminacy in the nature of social theory is one source, I think, of skepticism and opposition to it. It is often difficult to specify, concretely, how this specific theory leads to that specific better interpretation of the past. A radiocarbon determination appears to have a more solid contribution that no philosophical deconstruction can quite dissolve. As Turner hints, this indeterminacy increases, the more sympathetic one's own intellectual position is to approaches that can loosely be termed "postpositivist."

Positivists, however defined, see theory and data as connected, often in a recursive process, but nevertheless tend towards a quite definite division between theory and data, in which each stands independently of the other. One tests one's theories against the data; data collection itself is a process that positivists often claim can be analytically separated from or stands outside the purview of theory (hence the stress on methodology, and specifically the need for "middle-range theory," without which there is no secure link between theory and data: Binford 1993). Therefore, positivism tends towards a narrow definition of what theory is or might be: it can either be a set of general propositions or rules about how to treat data ("our statements about the past must always be testable"), or generalizing statements about social process ("state formation and factional competition are systemically linked"). Within postpositivist approaches, however, definitions of "the social" and of "theory" itself begin to dissolve into other categories; emphasis is placed, for example, on how the mundane activities of the excavation process are themselves theoretical. Ian Hodder, for example, talks of "interpretation at the trowel's edge" (Hodder 1999: 92).

Let me clarify this last point. For many of those continuing to work within processual or positivist traditions, theory is a set of concrete propositions applicable at the least to more than one ancient society: "state formation is conflict-driven," "risk minimization is a key factor in hunter-gatherer subsistence strategies," "chiefdom societies share the following characteristics . . . " Insofar as such propositions can be explicitly defined, theory is quite easily classified and has definite boundaries. It stands in clear opposition to a body of "raw data." If, however, one is skeptical of our ability to generate such concrete generalities, if one views their apparent certainty and straightforward nature as illusory, then "theory" remains just as important but its edges become fuzzy. If theory thus becomes indeterminate, then so are data. Data are no longer taken raw, in Joan Gero's memorable phrase; they are theory-laden. My concern here is not to argue for one view of theory over another, but rather to demonstrate how different views of archaeology are directly dependent on views of what is or is not theory.

So if theory is difficult to define, let's turn the proposition on its head. Can we do archaeology without social theory? Clearly not; the most basic interpretation of archaeological data – "this was a storage pit; that was an ancillary structure" – involves ideas about how human beings interact with each other and the natural world, and ideas furthermore about what are or are not plausible, understandable ways for human beings to act. Much of Lewis Binford's most exciting work in the 1970s and 1980s was concerned with showing how much archaeological interpretation of the Palaeolithic rested on the foundation of assumptions about what was "normal" or taken for granted for human groups – "home-base" behavior for example (Binford 1993). He drew the moral that these foundations were insecure, as we were not dealing with *Homo sapiens sapiens* in these contexts; I would add that the assumptions Binford was questioning were also statements that were implicitly theoretical, as they relied on notions of how people behaved socially in the past. So however indeterminate our social theory is, it is nevertheless unavoidable. The statement "we are all practicing social theorists whenever we open our mouths to talk about data" is at least as self-evident, important, and undeniable a statement as "theory never specifies concrete explanations."

Anthony Giddens argues that theory is not only indeterminate, but that it is also recursive – that is, social theory draws on contemporary social experience and in commenting on that experience transforms it (Giddens 1984, 1993). The implication is that it is difficult for the historian of archaeological ideas and systems of thought to trace concrete cause-and-effect relations between *this* theory and *that* interpretation, since the formulation of this theory will already affect that interpretation; there is no primacy to one or the other. I will expand and exemplify this point later in relation to the archaeological study of castles.

Culture as a System

For me, the most positive and lasting contribution of New Archaeology was in this realm of social theory. New Archaeology rightly stressed that as students of human culture we must be *anthropological* (Willey and Phillips 1958; Binford 1962). Different things were meant by the use of this phrase by different writers, but part of its meaning lay in the recognition that other cultural systems, both past and present, had to be studied explicitly, analytically, and in their own right. Other cultures were not simply collections of norms or meaningless stylistic traits or, indeed, to be judged on ethnocentric criteria.

Anybody who has worked with a certain type of traditional historian or in areas of archaeological study relatively unaffected by the New Archaeology will appreciate the central importance of this insight, and will understand that it is not simply a statement of the blindingly obvious or indeed something that the archaeological profession has completely accepted. Binford was quite accurate in his comment that many archaeologists did see culture aquatically, with "influences" cross-cutting each other like ripples on a pond – much as many art and architectural historians, and medieval archaeologists, do today (Binford 1962; for the survival of such models of explanation in contemporary archaeology see, for example, Lindley 1997;

Egan and Forsyth 1997). Many traditional archaeologists *were* ethnocentric, peppering their interpretations with commonsensical assumptions about "convenience" that would not last twenty minutes' ethnographic experience of other cultures – just as many archaeologists still do today. Many traditional archaeologists *did* refer to an implicit, untheorized notion of developmental evolution in which technology simply got better and better for no specific reason and barbarian values gave way to "civilized" ones without any clear definition of what made the latter more "advanced."

In this sense, when the noted anti-intellectual Andrew Selkirk termed Clarke's *Analytical Archaeology* (1972) the most dangerous book in British archaeological thought (cited in Champion 1991: 145) he was entirely accurate. Clarke's book remains the most comprehensive, point-by-point challenge to the sleepy complacency, the attitude that a lot of hard digging is somehow a substitute for thinking clearly and self-critically, that continues to pervade much of traditional archaeology. The post-processual critique of New Archaeology did, perhaps, make the error that R. G. Collingwood rightly condemned in his exposition of the "question-and-answer" approach to philosophy. That is, it failed to ask "What were the problems – the intellectual and practical issues – that these early notions of system and process were designed to attack?"

When we go back to early Binford or Clarke or early Renfrew, what shines through their work is an insistence that we can understand social systems, that their properties are knowable, that we can explain patterns of social change, that prehistoric societies had their own trajectories rather than simply submitting to "waves of influence" from "higher cultures." This confidence in the ability of archaeology to take up Mortimer Wheeler's challenge, when he wrote in the 1950s that "I envy the new generation its great opportunity, as never before, to dig up people rather than mere things' (Wheeler 1956: 246), was given to them by social theory – by the potential of systems thinking to infer many variables from the relative few found in the archaeological record, via contemporary thinking on mathematical models and simulation.

Why, then, have such models, at least in their early forms, been so comprehensively abandoned? And can we find avenues to rebuild Binford, Clarke, and Renfrew's confidence in the ability of archaeology to achieve its most basic ambition – to explain and understand past societies – through alternative forms of social theory?

What I want to do here is highlight the recent historical influence of three elements of contemporary social thought. In some ways, to go through their insights is to tell stories already familiar from other elements of the radical critique; these stories reach the same end-point, but by slightly different if parallel routes. My purpose in retelling these stories here is to draw attention to their social elements. I want to stress how different understandings of the way society works were mobilized in order to raise profound questions concerning the credibility of an exclusively systemic view and to introduce other ways of thinking about culture.

Feminism

The achievements of feminist theory in creating an "archaeology of gender" have been reviewed by others, most recently Conkey and Gero (1997). Here, I want to concentrate on what Conkey and Gero identify as the most radical and "dangerous" element of an archaeology of gender: the potential of feminist critiques of the social and human sciences to open up and to question at a very basic level many of the assumptions by which archaeology proceeds.

The first radical element is an opening up of the question of gender identities. No longer are men and women's roles seen as fixed, unchanging, in all times and in all places. In short, a fluid view of gender, in which identities are shifting, has been substituted for a fixed view. As a result, a stable view of social categories and power, in which larger structures of class and ideology rise on top of the "building blocks" of household relations and everyday practice, becomes radically decentered. Now, the moment one uses a general term such as "stratified society" or "the managerial elite" (or for that matter "the working classes"; cf. Wurst and Fitts 1999) one encounters conceptual problems. Thirty years ago, such terms would appear transparent; now they invite critique. In place of such macro-terms, or arguably in complement to them, we get a stress on the micropolitics of power. For social theorists writing after fifteen years of feminist critique in archaeology, power is now a subject for everyday negotiation. It is not just about the building of great monuments and the emergence of managerial elites, but also about everyday practices in and around the household. As a result, power is not only seen all the way up and down the social scale, but it also tugs in different, cross-cutting directions, and is continually renegotiated throughout everyday life.

Much of this reassessment of our understanding of larger structures of power can be grouped under a feminist questioning of essentialism (McNay 1992). Essentialist and reductionist arguments are attempts to reduce the understanding of very complex social situations to a few simple variables. Such a strategy has its attractions, most notably those of simplicity and, arguably, testability. But feminism suggests that such arguments tend to rest on assumptions about what is "essentially true" in all times and in all places about the human species; for example, on reliance on the "mothering instinct" or the neural structuring of the brains of different sexes. If such social categories are "opened up" through the feminist critique of science, so is the biological basis on which gender identities are apparently based.

As a result of the feminist attack on essentialism we get the questioning of either/or thinking of all kinds. For example, power is now neither "secure" nor "insecure." In this view, it can be very coercive, but also and always open to sudden inversion or destabilization. It can't be easily measured, categorized, treated as another variable. As a result, a large number of accepted archaeological categories and ways of thinking are now rendered quite problematic; feminist rewritings of archaeology often look, concretely, very different to earlier accounts of the same material (Spector 1993: esp. 31–2).

I suggest that Lisa Jardine's views on the feminist rewriting of history are true also for archaeology when she writes of this tension between assimilation to old structures and the new difficulty of writing:

> We must unweave the comforting accretions of an incremental historical narrative which have given us marginal categories of women, and assimilated women's voices. Fortified with the great wealth of "incremental women's history," which has recovered and enriched our understanding of women in past time, we must now begin again to reweave the unwoven tapestry, reweave our ruptured historical narrative again and again in pursuit of that new history in which women's and men's interventions in past time will weight equally – permanently and for all time (or at least until the next structural change in the narrative). It is not yet clear where that new historical narrative will lead, but it will surely take us away from the continuing ghettoization, the marginalization of women's history within the traditional discipline of which all of us are too aware. (Jardine 1996: 147)

It is worth glossing this passage. Jardine here is commenting on an attack on Natalie Zemon Davis' historical work, *The Return of Martin Guerre*. As a history book that breaks the rules of traditional, male-centered historical method, *Martin Guerre* comes under fire from Robert Finlay, a traditional historian, who attacks Davis' book on apparently "factual" grounds. After demonstrating with alarming ease that Finlay's attack is in fact underpinned by a theoretical inability on his part to take women's history seriously

and on its own terms, Jardine explores the ruptures and gaps that taking such a history seriously might entail. Using the analogy of Penelope weaving and unweaving her tapestry in front of her bemused male suitors, Jardine insists that we must unweave the historical narrative within which, for example, standard historical terms and categories like "scold" and "witch" are readily understandable. Women like scolds were *created* by the textual record, she insists, and were not a preexisting "problem" to be defined, tabulated, and discussed in the usual historical way.

Now, what goes for history also goes for archaeology (the parallels between Finlay's attack on Davis and, for example, Coppack's critique of Gilchrist's study of nunneries in *Gender and Material Culture* are very striking; see Gilchrist (1996), where Gilchrist points out, as Jardine, that Coppack's "empirical" objections are actually based on a theoretical unwillingness to take a gendered viewpoint seriously). Thinking in this way is often counter-intuitive (particularly, feminist standpoint theorists would point out, if one is gendered male) but must be the first rule of any discipline which relies on empathy, historical or archaeological. The necessity of thinking in counter-intuitive ways leads us on into our second area of social theory, the decentering of society.

The Decentering of Society

If feminists show that many of the building-blocks of classical social theory – the family, gender roles – are not in fact stable categories but are open to endless contestation and renegotiation, what happens to our understanding of the nature of society as a whole?

One of the founding principles of traditional social thought is that society has a definite existence of its own, with social rules, trends, and processes that can be observed. Such social phenomena cannot be reduced to individual behavior and must be studied in their own right. This is an observation that was quite basic to the founding of sociology as a discipline. Emile Durkheim, often resonantly termed "the founding father of sociology," formulated his famous study of suicide in part as a plea for the disciplinary status and social usefulness of sociology. He attempted to demonstrate that the suicide rate was a "social fact," irreducible to particular, individual cases of suicide. He further suggested that such social facts could only be explained with reference to other social facts, not to "the human condition" or to non-social factors (Durkheim 1951). Sociology therefore emerged through Durkheim's argument as a discipline that dealt with observables.

Durkheim's formulation has gone through many vicissitudes, not least from the intellectual challenge of methodological individualism and from the political challenge of Margaret Thatcher's famous assertion that "there is no such thing as society"; it nevertheless formed the underpinning of much positivist and functionalist social anthropology. As such, it has had a profound impact on the human sciences.

It is this formulation that structuration theory sets out in part to challenge. Structuration theory, as set out by Anthony Giddens (1984) and employed in archaeology in various forms (cf. Graves 1989; Dobres and Robb 2000), goes as follows: individual social agents and social structures do not exist independently of one another, but are related:

There is no such thing as a football player, for example, without the game of football with its rules and structured relationships between players. But it is also true that it is individuals who literally create the reality of a football game every time they set out to play it. When individuals play the game, they draw upon shared understandings of the rules associated with the game and use these in order to construct the game as a concrete reality. In this sense, there is what Giddens calls a duality of structure, which is to say, the structure of a system provides

individual actors with what they need in order to produce that very structure as a result. (Johnson 1995: 4)

In this view, the whole idea of "society" becomes decentered. It is always dispersed, referred somewhere else. This does not mean that "society does not exist" as methodological individualists might claim, but it does have radical implications for its study. The result of structuration and related theories, then, is to move us away from the "hard facts" of the social and the collective, towards the "soft" areas of the individual and of agency. Nevertheless, many still refer to certain essential, "underlying" properties of certain social systems, whether in materialistic or idealistic ways – "the economic subsystem" or "the spirit of capitalism."

Consider, for example, the historical explanation of "marriage." In the 1960s and 1970s, as part of the general move away from narrowly conceived political history, social historians became interested in thinking about the institution of marriage below the level of the elite. To this end, they tabulated and scrutinized statistical information on changing ages of marriages and patterns between 1500 and 1800. Many of these changes could be described and modeled statistically, using documentary records. Such scholars attempted to map variables against each other (wealth, age at marriage, number of children, mortality rates). Research showed, however, that such description and modeling was not an end in itself. If we were to *explain* different trends we had to refer to changes in sentiment – the "rise of the modern notion of romantic love," for example. So historical explanation moved away from a Durkheimian correlation of the rates of different social processes, towards an exploration of changes in mentality.

But the critique of structuration theory runs deeper still. The moment we began to look at sentiment and mentality, the individual agent came more clearly into focus. Each individual act of marriage was a renegotiation of what marriage really meant; each time someone said "I love you" or "I do" it had the effect not simply of reflecting a "social reality," but of redefining the reality itself. Even though we continue to use the term as if it were a stable one, "marriage" in 1500 was a very different thing from "marriage" in 1800. Each individual marriage was a renegotiation of the general rule – this marriage was more or less companionate or egalitarian, that marriage was more or less liable to break down. Individual social agents brought their expectations of marriage to the ceremony and the subsequent experience of living together; those expectations were derived from their own cultural background, and may have been different from those of their prospective partner. What each marriage turned out to be "really like" was the result, then, of the clash of these different expectations; and the expectations that their children brought to their own marriages a generation later varied accordingly. So just as Jardine draws attention to the lack of fixity in the concept of "witch" or "scold," so here we can draw attention to the lack of fixity in the concept of "marriage." Both are created and recreated through actions, and both are subject to Giddens' concept of the duality of structure (Joyce 1997).

Many would locate this lack of fixity in specifically textual models of the relationship between structure and practice; to oversimplify, they would see social institutions and practices as a form of text or language. As a result, such developments have been termed the "linguistic turn" in history. Such historians argue that each set of actions can be "read" in different ways, and that actors bring their own "readings" to a given social situation. The notion of society-as-text is a powerful analogy. It is an excellent one for heuristic or learning purposes, in that we all use and manipulate language; and therefore the counter-intuitive understandings of structuration theory can be brought home.

As many have pointed out, however, the analogy between language and social action is flawed as soon as one begins to think about social change at a more sophisticated level. In particular, it is difficult to see how material things can be treated as texts, for a whole series of reasons. If such analogies are limited, what can we put in their place? This need for a theory of social action not dependent on textual analogy directs our attention to a third area of social theory that is of use to us as archaeologists: the study of how material culture is created and used within society; how material objects come to carry meaning; how we apprehend the material world around us.

Society and Material Culture

If, then, social theory leads us towards a questioning of fixed and stable categories of society, can we extend this insight to the stuff of archaeology – the bits and pieces of architecture, material culture, and landscape that make up the "archaeological record"? Are their meanings and definitions just as problematic and opaque as that of society or indeed of social theory?

Inevitably, the answer is "yes." Postprocessual archaeology launched itself around the premise that "material culture is actively constituted." Two intellectual trends came out of this: first, an interdisciplinary interest in material culture studies, seen for example in the work of Danny Miller (1985, 1987, 1999) and the foundation of the *Journal of Material Culture*. Second, a recognition of the historicity of cultural meanings. In other words, things didn't just mean different things in different cultures; the way they came to have meaning was shown to be as historically variable as the meanings themselves. In retrospect, one of the things I was trying to do in *An Archaeology of Capitalism* (Johnson 1996) was not simply to trace changes in material forms as they related to social and cultural changes, but to look at how the configuration between artefact and meaning changed with the transition between feudalism and capitalism, however defined.

In conclusion, then, our three areas of social theory share a number of features in common. They see a lack of fixity or stability, whether in gender roles, social institutions, or in the relationship of meaning and artefact. They all prefer "bottom-up" to "top-down" models of social theory, engaging in the everyday, the apparently trivial and mundane. They all engage in the questioning of boundaries between (ethnocentrically) defined categories. And they all lead towards an insistence that the *a priori* separation between the material and the social is itself an ideological construct, part of an Enlightenment project that is inseparable from the project of modernity. The ultimate irony, therefore, may be that the internal logic of social theory leads us to a dissolution of the concept of "the social" itself (Joyce 1997).

Archaeology of Castles

I want to turn now to a case study in which we can see theory at work: how we might rethink the archaeology of late medieval castles in England (ca. 1350–1500 AD). I have pursued these arguments in more depth elsewhere (Johnson 2002).

There is a story told by traditional scholars of castles, a story with variations between each retelling. Nevertheless its main elements go as follows: the castle is defined by the Royal Archaeological Institute as "a fortified residence which might combine administrative and judicial functions, but in which military considerations were paramount" (Saunders 1977: 2). It was introduced into England by the invading Normans after 1066. The following two centuries saw a steady refinement of techniques of both defense and attack. For example, the great central tower or *donjon* was abandoned in stages; more emphasis was placed on protecting the curtain wall by studding it with flanking towers; square towers, susceptible to sapping, were replaced with round forms; gates ceased to be simple openings and were flanked by pairs of towers, evolving into specialized "gatehouses."

After this pivotal date of ca. 1300, castle design changed. It was not so "serious," late medieval warfare being largely "in the field" rather than siege-based and the growing influence of cannon making many stone defenses obsolete in any case. These post-1300, late medieval castles are often of a courtyard plan, and/or feature a great tower or *donjon* like their earlier counterparts. In this story, these late medieval castles represent an uneasy compromise between "domestic comfort" on the one hand and the continuing need to protect against the "casual violence" of mobs and small armies (as opposed to organized large-scale warfare) on the other.

The courtyard plan also, in this story, marked an interim stage between the classic thirteenth-century castle and the Renaissance country house, built to a compact plan, symmetrical, and with high standards of domestic comfort. "Influence" from Renaissance Italy on English buildings was apparent in architectural design from ca. 1500 onwards, but took more than a century of successive waves to overcome traditional late medieval forms (Figures 6.1, 6.2, 6.3).

The perceptive reader will note that I have not been able to resist putting much of this narrative in quotation marks in order to distance myself from it. What are the problems with this story? Most obviously, it suffers from an almost complete lack of contact with any explicit theory, whether that theory is processual, postprocessual, or any other form. Of course, this does not mean that it is not based on certain theoretical assumptions: four come immediately to mind.

First, what Binford (1964) termed "the aquatic view of culture" is clearly being represented, with its language of successive waves of influence. Here, we see the implicit proposition that a certain set of ideas, termed the Renaissance, started off in Italy and began lapping on English shores in the sixteenth century. As usual, such talk of influence means that the real action takes place

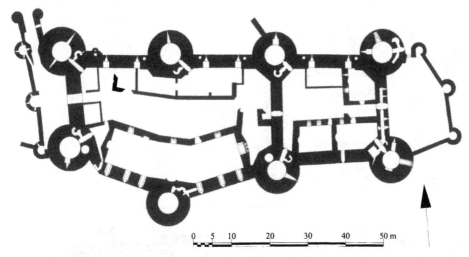

Figure 6.1   Conway Castle, ca. 1300: a royal castle of Edward I. The defenses (curtain wall and towers) are apparently the dominant feature; suites of accommodation are present, but are (it is argued) secondary to the defenses – most obviously in the way the hall is "wrapped round" the curtain wall.

elsewhere, in this case in Italy, thus removing from English scholars the responsibility to account for change in dynamic/processual terms. Second, an implicit narrative of technological or military "progress" is also assumed here, with the defensive qualities of castles getting better and better in response to better and better siege techniques, and the final demise of the castle being in part due to improvements in military technology. Third, reference is made to ideas of evolution – different architectural forms evolve from one another; some are uneasy transition points between one species and another. Fourth, there is reference to a normative view of culture, in which types – "the courtyard house" are expressions of norms, or indeed can be uneasy compromises between different norms.

The very fact that all four of these theoretical views are clearly here suggests, first, that any claim by castle writers to be innocent of theory is disingenuous. But we can go further; anyone with a brief acquaintance with the development of archaeological theory will quickly note that the different ideas listed above are mutually incompatible. Ideas of norms and influence, evolution and

progress, even if they have intellectual credibility on their own, sit uneasily with one another at best and completely contradict each other at worst (Flannery 1967). *The reluctance to explicitly theorize castle studies has, quite demonstrably, led to sloppy thinking on all sides.* If the skeptical reader demands an example of the importance and relevance of theory, here it is.

Another result of its untheorized nature is that the story is almost impervious to testing. It rests in part on a circular and mentalist argument: how do we know that the primary purpose in the minds of the builders was defensive? Because if it was not defensive, it cannot have been a castle. The story rests on an insecure sample base, and uses the technique of narrative rather than analytical description to hold itself together, with individual castles appearing as illustrative anecdotes, "the best examples" of a given type or trend, rather than as sites for potential confrontations of theory and data.

Let me clarify this point. Such accounts of castles appear to be at least 90 percent "empirical," in that they rest on detailed accounts of individual structures. However, certain examples are not discussed, left out

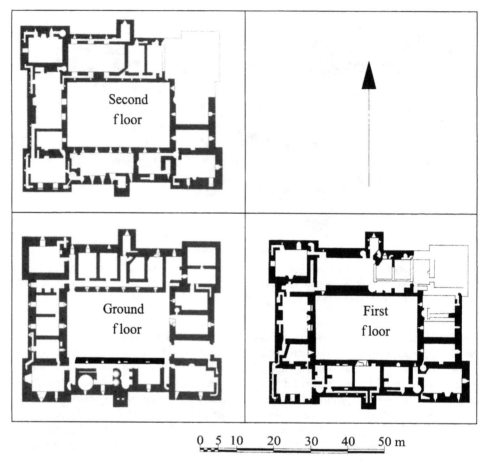

Figure 6.2 Bolton Castle, late fourteenth century: the curtain and towers are still here, but as integrated elements of a courtyard plan, with much more extensive and carefully planned accommodation.

entirely, and others are selected from a range of possible candidates because they are the "best" examples of their "type." But on whose authority is this selection made? On what theoretical justification is this castle discussed, but that one left out? In this way, a purely "descriptive" text, moving from one castle to another, is deeply theoretical – though it masks its theory, and becomes thereby insulated from critique.

But there is an even more basic reaction to the story. In the terms of the New Archaeology it is not *anthropological*. In the first place, castle and Renaissance houses seem to sprout flanking towers, regular courtyard plans, and symmetrical layouts of their own accord, with little reference to contemporary social characteristics and developments – the human beings that built and used the towers and courtyards. More fundamentally, we never get a sense of the social system that produced these archaeological traces, and how changes in castle and house design might relate to changes in that system.

What Theory Might Contribute

How might we understand such a system? There is a series of intellectual moves that are obvious to social theorists but have, in the main, yet to be applied to castle studies. In

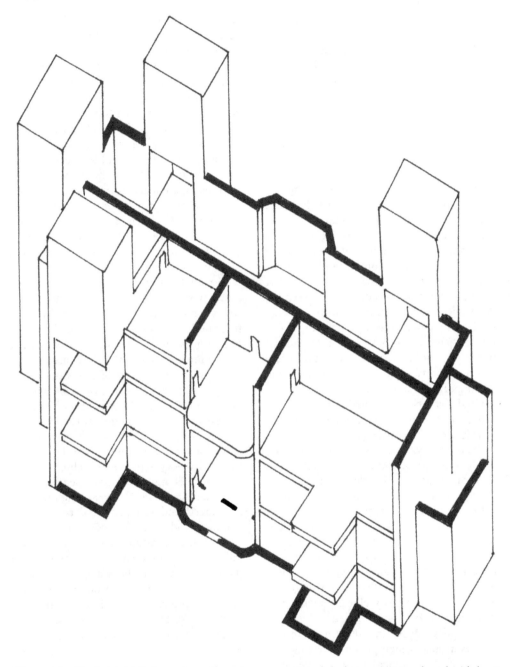

Figure 6.3 Hardwick Hall, later sixteenth century: symmetrical, lacking a courtyard, and with huge windows.

the first place, we might begin to understand castles by stating the obvious: castles are large domestic structures, belonging to the elite. As such, they might stand cross-cultural comparison with elite structures in other times and places. Castles might be considered as one element of a formal settlement hierarchy corresponding to a feudal social hierarchy. Changes in this hierarchy might then be modeled in terms of the structural transition between feudalism and capitalism.

One of the most fruitful avenues of evolutionary analysis in recent years has been a stress on heterarchy and factional conflict (cf. Crumley 1987; Brumfiel 1992). In castles, we might feel that we have a perfect case study of such processes. Feudal England was ruled by the monarch, but the great barons of the land had great power of their own, their own military retainers for example. Competition between barons spilled over into open conflict, and this translated into national dynastic conflicts. For example, the political conflicts between the Percy and Neville families of northeast England, and their respective sets of supporters, formed part of the background to the national Wars of the Roses in the fifteenth century so famously if inaccurately rendered in Shakespeare's history plays.

Castles can be interpreted in terms of this system of factional competition in which the recruitment of followers, exchange of gifts and hospitality, and ideas of dynasty and honor were so important, as they were in other state societies. Castle building and rebuilding might be seen as a process of competitive emulation, creating buildings that served to structure these factional conflicts. Many of these structures have extensive ranges of guest rooms to accommodate followers, and large halls in which to show hospitality to these followers. Such castles also served as centers of elite estate management; they are often surrounded by extensive parks and gardens, and serve as manorial centers around which peasant farming was organized. A theoretical interest in their economic role here might go hand-in-hand with recent "practical" stress on the castles' landscape context.

So such a view of castles derived from current thinking in cultural evolutionary theory, particularly recent stress on factional

conflict and heterarchy, would, I think, redirect our attention in new and exciting ways. It would direct us, for example, away from the details of arrow-slits and to the context of castles – how they related to ancillary settlements, to the often extensive parks and gardens and wider landscape systems that went with them. And it would enable castle scholars to set their work within a cross-cultural frame that would lend it great significance. It would take the story of castles from being a particular one, one that was a just-so story of little wider relevance beyond the shores of a remote rather barbarous island on the fringes of Europe, to one that could be compared with similar processes in other times and places.

Moving to "softer" forms of social theory, much work has already been done on the spatial and social "grammars" underlying these buildings. Such work is linked to functional views of social system and structure, for example Fairclough's (1992) use of Hillier and Hanson's pattern of access analysis to analyze Bolton, following on from that of Faulkner (1958, 1963). Such studies attempt to answer the question: If these castles reflect elite identities, what does social theory direct us to look for with those identities? Structuration theory tells us that elites are not some normal or natural consequence of inevitable developments, but that elite identities are staged and restaged. And the internal planning and landscape context of castles can be understood in these terms. All these buildings are centered around the hall – a piece of space that I have analyzed in other contexts as being framed around contemporary conceptions of social order (Johnson 1989, 1993). They also have extensive suites of guest accommodation in an age when hospitality played a central role in social reproduction.

Theory thus directs our attention towards a more sophisticated understanding of their social context. Vague, normative references to "the values of bastard feudalism" or to "casual violence" simply will not do. The first question we must ask is: What do these terms mean anthropologically? How did such a social system perpetuate itself, and how, structurally, was it transformed? It is notable that for all its recent vicissitudes, the most coherent theory of such a transformation is still the Marxist account of the feudal/capitalist transition. But we could also look at the reformation of manners (Elias 1978), changing notions of self, at power as performative (Butler 1997) – castles acting as stage settings.

It is striking that as we move towards these micro-strategies we also move more towards the detailed analysis of archaeological data. Artefact studies have much to say on the reformation of manners; clothing on the changing notion of the self and body; faunal and botanical assemblages on the practices of elite hospitality. The divisions of space within castles are a relatively well-known subject, and fit in with the notion of power as performative.

Theory also leads us here away from the essentialism of different interpretations. The classic reaction to the "military" interpretation has been to counterpoint the "social." But theory directs us further: to question the category of social, and to question the essentialism of the debate. Castles were not "really military" or "really symbolic"; different castles were different things – there is no unchanging, ahistorical essence to castles any more than there is to marriage, as discussed above. Indeed, one of the most striking things about castles is that they are all *different* – late medieval structures come in a wide variety of different shapes and sizes that are not obviously related to regional traditions, specific builders, or to variables such as social status.

Many of these interpretations are equifinal; that is, they are capable of being explained equally well in different directions. One person's causeway exposing attackers to fire from the battlements is another person's staged processional route leading the visitor to view the castle in a certain way from a certain viewpoint. One of the most exciting things that I have learned from recent

social theory is to question the either/or nature of these arguments. Late medieval warfare, for example, was bound up with contemporary notions of knighthood and more generally masculinity: so to oppose "military" and "symbolic" explanations is to miss the point. The castle reflects gendered identities in a subtle and complex way indicated by theories of material culture. This discussion is necessarily open-ended, but I hope I have said enough to show how theory can open up new questions.

The Role of Theory

As we noted at the beginning of this chapter, theory is recursive. Data do not stand, pristine, prior to theory; we cannot therefore index or measure the effect of theory on our interpretations of "the data" in a readily quantifiable way. Much of this thinking is already penetrating castle studies, though it has not been articulated in these terms. Charles Coulson (1996), David Austin (1984), Graham Fairclough (1992), and David Stocker (1992), among others, are thinking in social terms. And many of these people are not immediately or extensively enthusiastic about Anthony Giddens or theories of the construction of the aesthetic or of medieval masculinities. But their work is part of a shift of mood within which wider currents of theory can be clearly seen to have played their part; if I were to write the intellectual biographies of writers on castles who have questioned the military perspective, we would find much of the intellectual and cultural background that produced specific social theories engaging with their lives and ways of thinking also. Theory, then, does not lead to new insights in a cause-and-effect way, but it does act as a description of what is going on as much as a prescription for its transformation.

In part, theory's role is communicative. This observation will come as a surprise to the practicing archaeologist, whose main reaction to theory is that it is full of impenetrable jargon. But theory here enables us to communicate, to make links between historical observations, architectural data, and anthropological theory, within the purview of the discipline of archaeology. It enables us to take the insights of one discipline and translate them into another. It enables us to show how Coulson's insights from the background of architectural history are situated within a certain disciplinary perspective and background, and therefore how we might translate or modify them to reflect our own concerns. Ultimately, it enables us to write a better version of the past, one more coherent and more sympathetic to the subtleties of the evidence, and more understanding of the differences between the ways various disciplines approach that evidence.

In Place of a Conclusion

For some, the loss of determinacy in social theory is proof of the irrelevance of recent trends. Carneiro sums up the feelings of many in the social sciences when he writes that postmodern ethnographers have failed to contribute to the "broad theories" and "generalizations" of ethnology:

> We debate . . . the invention of agriculture . . . the rise of chiefdoms, and the development of states. What have postmodernists contributed to the solution of these great problems? Nothing. Has anyone even heard of a postmodernist theory of the origin of the state? (Carneiro 1995: 14–15)

It may be worth spelling out precisely why such a demand is misleading. Of course there is no postmodern theory of state origins; postmodernists rather allege that "the postmodern condition" is one in which the intellectual underpinnings of any cross-cultural delineation of a process like "state origins" (or of "chiefdoms" or "agriculture") have been argued to be fatally flawed. Carneiro is asking postmodern thinkers to jump through a series of hoops of his own devising, while the whole point of any critique

informed by postmodernism is that jumping through a set of hoops framed within what is seen by this school as a flawed intellectual tradition is a misguided exercise. To oversimplify a little, to ask for a postmodern theory of state origins is like asking for, say, a Darwinist theory of flying saucers, and then claiming that the failure of Darwinists to account for these phenomena is conclusive proof of the Darwinists' intellectual irrelevance.

Of course, what the Darwinist would do, quite rightly, is to offer a theory of why contemporary "observations" of flying saucers have increased or decreased in frequency; and in this sense postmodern thought can offer some very convincing explanations of why much of Western anthropological thought is so obsessed with the constructed problem of "state origins" and defines some questions as "great" and others as "trivial."

Carneiro's real problem here is his assumption that theory is somehow necessarily a set of concrete propositions; his irritation echoes Schiffer's complaint that postprocessual "thinking is reptilian. You try to get a handle on it and it's like a snake – it slithers away or changes in color" (cited in Thomas 1998: 86). The whole sweep of this chapter has argued that theory is not the formalized, rather dull beast Carneiro and Schiffer would like it to be; but this does not mean that theory has somehow become myopically particular. Social theory informed by postmodernism has a proven track record of contributing to major intellectual questions of wide relevance: one thinks of the work of Rorty (1989) in addressing the questions of moral systems after the certainties of modernism have fallen away, or the work of Giddens (1993) on modernity. If we want to cite examples pertaining to the past, work on cave art, on the domestication of Europe, or on the feudal/capitalist transition can hardly be called narrow in scope or described as failing in its wider responsibilities of saying wide-ranging things of interest to all archaeologists.

I have argued in this chapter that theory is *important*. We all use theory; our work is, whether we like it or not, situated within theoretical discourse; theory structures and defines our project as archaeologists even as we deny its influence. The more reptilian theory becomes, the more slippery it is to get hold of; but the more essential it is as an underpinning to everything we say and do as archaeologists.

References

Austin, D. 1984. "The castle and the landscape." *Landscape History*, 6: 69–81.

Binford, L. R. 1964. "Archaeology as anthropology." *American Antiquity*, 11: 198–200.

Binford, L. R. 1993. *Bones: Ancient Men and Modern Myths*. New York: Plenum.

Brumfiel, E. M. 1992. "Distinguished lecture in archaeology: breaking and entering the ecosystem – gender, class and faction steal the show." *American Anthropologist*, 94: 551–67.

Brumfiel, E. M. 1996. "The quality of tribute cloth: the place of evidence in archaeological argument." *American Antiquity*, 61 (3): 453–62.

Butler, J. 1997. *Excitable Speech: A Politics of the Performative*. London: Routledge.

Carneiro, R. 1995. "Godzilla meets new age anthropology: facing the postmodernist challenge to a science of culture." *Europaea*, 1 (1): 3–22.

Champion, T. 1991. "Theoretical archaeology in Britain." In I. Hodder (ed.), *Archaeological Theory in Europe: The Last Three Decades*, pp. 129–60. London: Routledge.

Clarke, D. 1972. *Analytical Archaeology*, 2nd edn. London: Methuen.

Conkey, M. and J. Gero 1997. "From programme to practice: gender and feminism in archaeology." *Annual Review of Anthropology*, 26: 411–37.

Coulson, C. 1996. "Cultural realities and reappraisals in English castle-study." *Journal of Medieval History*, 22: 171–208.

Crumley, C. 1987. "A dialectical critique of heterarchy." In T. C. Patterson and C. W. Galley (eds.), *Power Relations and State Formation*, pp. 155–9. Washington, DC: American Anthropological Association.

Dixon, P. 1990. "The donjon of Knaresborough: the castle as theatre." *Chateau Gaillard: etudes de castellologie médiévale*, 14: 121–39.

Dobres, M.-A. and J. Robb (eds.) 1999. *Agency and Archaeology*. London: Routledge.

Durkheim, E. 1951. *Suicide*. New York: Free Press.

Egan, G. and H. Forsyth 1997. "Wound wire and silver gilt: changing fashions in dress accessories c.1400–c.1600." In D. Gaimster and P. Stamper (eds.), *The Age of Transition: The Archaeology of English Culture 1400–1600*, pp. 215–38. Oxford: Oxbow.

Elias, N. 1978. *The Civilising Process, Vol. 1: The History of Manners*. Oxford: Blackwell.

Fairclough, G. 1992. "Meaningful constructions: spatial and functional analysis of medieval buildings." *Antiquity*, 66: 348–66.

Faulkner, P. A. 1958. "Domestic planning from the 12th to the 14th centuries." *Archaeological Journal*, 115: 150–83.

Faulkner, P. A. 1963. "Castle planning in the 14th century." *Archaeological Journal*, 120: 215–35.

Flannery, K. 1967. "Culture history versus culture process: a debate in American archaeology." *Scientific American*, 217: 119–20. Reprinted in M. P. Leone (ed.) 1972, *Contemporary Archaeology*, pp. 102–7. New York: Academic Press.

Gaimster, D. and P. Stamper (eds.) 1997. *The Age of Transition: The Archaeology of English Culture 1400–1600*. Oxford: Oxbow.

Giddens, A. 1984. *The Constitution of Society: Outline of the Theory of Structuration.* Cambridge: Polity Press.

Giddens, A. 1993. *The Giddens Reader.* Stanford, CA: Stanford University Press.

Gilchrist, R. 1996. "Review feature: gender and material culture: the archaeology of religious women." *Cambridge Archaeological Journal,* 6 (1): 119–36.

Graves, C. P. 1989. "Social space and the English parish church." *Economy and Society,* 18 (3). 297–322.

Gwilt, A. and C. C. Haselgrove (eds.) 1997. *Reconstructing Iron Age Societies.* Oxbow Monograph 17. Oxford: Oxbow.

Hodder, I. 1985. *Reading the Past.* Cambridge: Cambridge University Press.

Hodder, I. (ed.) 1991. *Archaeological Theory in Europe: The Last Three Decades.* London: Routledge.

Hodder, I. 1999. *The Archaeological Process: An Introduction.* Oxford: Blackwell.

Jardine, L. 1996. *Reading Shakespeare Historically.* London: Routledge.

Johnson, A. G. 1995. *The Blackwell Dictionary of Sociology.* Oxford: Blackwell.

Johnson, M. H. 1989. "Conceptions of agency in archaeological interpretation." *Journal of Anthropological Archaeology,* 8: 189–211.

Johnson, M. H. 1992. "The Englishman's home and its study." In R. Samson (ed.), *The Social Archaeology of Houses,* pp. 245–57. Edinburgh: Edinburgh University Press.

Johnson, M. H. 1993. *Housing Culture: Traditional Architecture in an English Landscape.* Washington, DC: Smithsonian Institution.

Johnson, M. H. 1996. *An Archaeology of Capitalism.* Oxford: Blackwell.

Johnson, M. H. 1997. "Vernacular architecture: the loss of innocence." *Vernacular Architecture,* 28: 13–19.

Johnson, M. H. 1998. *Archaeological Theory: An Introduction.* Oxford: Blackwell.

Johnson, M. H. 2002. *Behind the Castle Gate: From Medieval to Renaissance.* London: Routledge.

Joyce, P. 1997. "The end of social history?" In K. Jenkins (ed.), *The Postmodern History Reader,* pp. 341–65. London: Routledge.

Leone, M. P. (ed.) 1972. *Contemporary Archaeology.* New York: Academic Press.

Lindley, P. 1997. "Innovation, tradition and disruption in tomb sculpture." In D. Gaimster and P. Stamper (eds.), *The Age of Transition: The Archaeology of English Culture 1400–1600,* pp. 77–92. Oxford: Oxbow.

McNay, L. 1992. *Foucault and Feminism: Power, Gender and the Self.* Cambridge: Polity Press.

Meskell, L. 1999. *Race, Gender, Class Etcetera in Ancient Egypt.* Oxford: Blackwell.

Miller, D. 1985. *Artefacts as Categories: A Study of Ceramic Variability in Central India.* Cambridge: Cambridge University Press.

Miller, D. 1987. *Material Culture and Mass Consumption.* Oxford: Blackwell.

Miller, D. 1999. *A Theory of Shopping.* Cambridge: Polity Press.

Patrik, L. E. 1985. "Is there an archaeological record?" In M. B. Schiffer (ed.), *Advances in Archaeological Method and Theory 8,* pp. 27–62. New York: Academic Press.

Patterson, T. C. and C. W. Galley (eds.) 1987. *Power Relations and State Formation.* Washington, DC: American Anthropological Association.

Rorty, R. 1989. *Contingency, Irony and Solidarity.* Princeton, NJ: Princeton University Press.

Saunders, A. D. 1977. "Five castle excavations: reports of the Institute's project into the origins of the castles in England." *Archaeological Journal,* 134: 1–156.

Shanks, M. and C. Tilley 1987. *Social Theory and Archaeology.* Cambridge: Polity Press.

Spector, J. 1993. *What This Awl Means: Feminist Archaeology at a Wahpeton Dakota Village.* St. Paul: Minnesota Historical Society Press.

Stocker, D. 1992. "The shadow of the general's armchair." *Archaeological Journal*, 149: 415–20.

Thomas, D. H. 1998. *Archaeology*. London: Harcourt Brace.

Turner, B. S. 1996. *The Blackwell Companion to Social Theory*. Oxford: Blackwell.

Wheeler, M. 1956. *Archaeology from the Earth*. Harmondsworth: Penguin Books.

Willey, G. R. and P. Phillips 1958. *Method and Theory in American Archaeology*. Chicago: University of Chicago Press.

Wurst, L. and R. K. Fitts 1999. "Introduction: why confront class?" *Historical Archaeology*, 33 (1): 1–6.

7

Materiality, Space, Time, and Outcome

Roland Fletcher

There is no single, agreed upon way of conceptualizing or discussing the organization of space, or of classifying it. Such agreement is badly needed. We need a shared taxonomy, vocabulary, and set of concepts. Without these, progress in the field remains seriously inhibited. The many isolated studies, descriptions and findings (and there are many) cannot be compared or synthesized. In effect they are "lost."

Rapoport (1994: 496)

Introduction

The relationship between the material and "social" is not what we imagined it to be thirty years ago. We have learned that the associations between the material component of social life and the verbal meanings and actions of the members of a community are far from straightforward and are certainly not one-to-one correlations. Nor, on a larger scale, are there simple correlations between an economic phenomenon like agriculture and a social phenomenon like sedentism, or between irrigation and urbanism. When we add to this the still prevailing problem that the label *urban* refers to "no set of precise well-understood additional characteristics for societies so described" (Adams 1981: 81), we might suspect that the current archaeological theories, agendas, and disputes, tied to the conventions of social theory and history, are in some need of redefinition.

The pseudo-differentiation of processual and postprocessual archaeology (Fletcher 1989; Tschauner 1996), which is still prevalent, yet decried by practitioners from varied "sides" (e.g., Cowgill 1993; Feinman 1994; Parker Pearson 1998: 680–1; Preucel and Hodder 1996: xi), has not led to any such reappraisal. While we have moved away from seeing material space as a reflection of social organization, current perspectives with varied flavors still affirm the obvious association. Space is seen as "a primary means of structuring social encounters and so producing and reproducing social relationships" (Laurence 1997: 219); or "the choice of individuals or groups to differentiate themselves stylistically through domestic building shape depends upon their perspective within a local, national and international hierarchy" (Lyons 1995: 351). The house has been perceived as a discursive object (Keane 1995: 102), and the primacy of verbal meanings has been maintained as the basis of interpretation (Prussin 1995). The premise that the material has its function in relation to familiar verbalized expressions of sociality and is to be understood by reference to standard social categories has remained constant through the theoretical tirades and cumulative exhaustion of the past thirty or more years of explanatory dispute.

But what if these familiar general assumptions are an inadequate basis for understanding materiality and sociality? Can we systematize a view that, instead of just reinforcing, maintaining, and complementing active social life, the material possesses pattern in its own right, has the effect of constraining options and creating friction, and is also potentially able to undermine viable social life? The material is then an "actor without intent" with which people try to engage. This would create a dynamic in which the inertial and abrasive impact of the material framework on community life is a key agency in the long-term outcomes we see in the archaeological record. Instead of just associating the material and sociality in some fashion, we would also need to ask how their interaction generated the outcomes, whether good, bad, or indifferent, which become apparent over differing spans of time. Currently, primary significance is allocated to whatever standard verbal meanings are ascribed to the material by the conventions of social analysis. Instead, we might ask what the material does and how the collision of the material with verbal meaning and social action creates what actually happens. In the latter view, the conventional sense of the social, primarily as a suite of verbalized meanings associated with actions and things, should now be extended to include the material as another kind of social phenomenon, with internal patterning and operational characteristics independent of its associated verbal meaning structures and patterns of social action.

We need to treat the material as a class of behavior with its own generative system, its own distinctive heritage constraints, and its own operational impact. What it does and the consequences of this non-correspondence are the theme of this chapter. A gestalt shift is required away from a commonsense viewpoint in which the verbal meanings of a community are treated as statements about the generative basis from which the material is created by actions. After all, Keane, while analyzing Sumbanese descriptions of the "traditional" house, also remarks that "much of what we know about our world remains tacit – it can go unsaid and is often difficult to put into words" (Keane 1995: 102). Perhaps verbal declarations about the material should, instead, be understood as a layer of meaning overlaid on the material at a different replicative rate and only partially and uneasily linked to it. Furthermore, while actions do indeed generate material entities, it cannot then be safely assumed that the words a community uses to refer to the actions are a sufficient description of what is happening, or why. Nor can we assume that the social actions that are concurrent with a material assemblage are necessarily compatible with it. The suites of actions can also be seen as an effort to cope with the inertia and friction generated by the material milieu of community life.

Dissonance between the material and social action–verbal meaning would also lead to the logical possibility that, at a large enough scale, the material could adversely affect viable social life. For instance, the overall material conditions of a settlement, such as its extent and degree of residential compactness, might restrict the maximum span of time over which a community can persist. In addition, if dissonance is inherent to community life, there can be no deterministic connection between what a community is doing and the economic or environmental milieu in which it is attempting to operate, because there could be no single directive agency on which the external circumstances might impact directly. Not only are the intentions of the human beings in a community varied, but also it is well understood that they can be to some degree at odds. We should therefore expect that external circumstances will adversely affect behavior which does not work in that context, but not that circumstances will determine what a community tries to do.

Somehow the inherent patterning and operations of the material component of behavior, i.e., its nature as material behavior (Fletcher 1995: 20–33), should relate to the kind of mismatches we have identified between the phenomena referred to by categories such as urbanism and irrigation, or sedentism and agriculture. From all those mismatches we have identified between our established taxa, we should therefore envisage a quite different relationship between the sociality of words and actions and the material component of behavior, and also between that materiality and the economic/environmental context in which human communities are trying to function.

There is no quick fix which we can borrow from another respectable field to speed the process of creating such a new, systematic approach. Instead, we have to work through the exercise as a discipline, defining issues and refining our analytic skills and our data collection. No short time span perspective will serve as a guide. The emphasis on social action in social anthropology and history will not suffice because analysis must be aimed at understanding the "material as behavior" and its cumulative abrasive impact over years, decades, or centuries. Seeking to comprehend the material as a fundamental and autonomous player in community life – "an actor without intent" – would be a proper construct of archaeological theory. A high-level theoretical structure would be created, one not yet developed by the other social sciences. Their lack of a unified theory (Trigger 1989: 22) may be indicative of the problem which arises when social theory gives primacy to explanations from only a limited portion of the temporal and expressive range of human behavior. Perhaps a high-level theory of human behavior appropriate to archaeology may have more significance than we have supposed.

The Verbal-Action, Material Conundrum

What is contained within the splendid and creative incoherence of conventional social theory in archaeology is a fundamental conundrum about whether the material has a pattern of its own or is merely a derivative of pattern elsewhere in the cultural system, whether environmental, economic, or social. Archaeological practice takes for granted that the material component of human behavior does have pattern in its own right, e.g., the similar settlement plans of interrelated communities (Figure 7.1), and that the pattern can be recognized regardless of our knowledge of the associated actions and verbal meanings of the builders. Since, as is very clear from analyses based on the postmodern perspective, there is no deterministic relationship between material and social action, it follows relentlessly that no external factor or factors can be acting to make those material patterns. If all the varied standard social and environmental factors do not exactly correlate with the material and therefore cannot pattern it, the material must be seen as a fully operational factor in its own right with its own generative patterns. If many factors are involved, then the material can be one in its own right, not merely a foil for sophisticated analyses of verbal meaning and the retrodiction of standard concepts of social action.

The core issue is the relationship between social action and space and time, since all action must be located in space and occur at some point in time. Furthermore, all action occurs in a context of scale or magnitude. Since human action is inextricably attached to meaning, it must also follow that meaning engages with space and time, as is most apparent in rituals but also inheres in daily life. The catch, however, with the conventional view, is the usual perception of meaning as properly residing at some particular scale of human familiarity – the level of verbality. But of course it does not, since, like

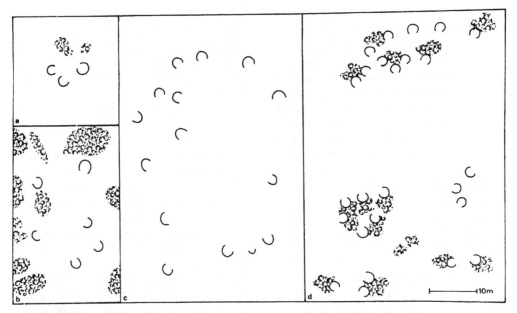

Figure 7.1 (a) San camps, southern Africa, 1960s AD (after Whitelaw 1991).

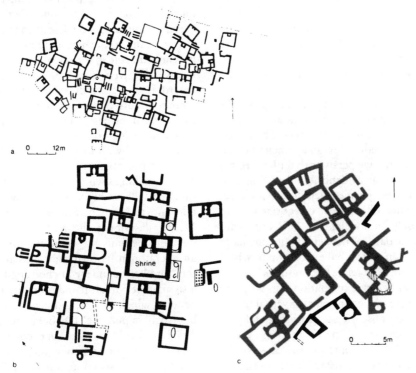

Figure 7.1 (b) Djeitun assemblage settlement plans, central Asia, fifth millennium BC (after Mellaart 1975).

action, it too exists in varied contexts of scale and magnitude. Action has meaning, but the space is extended and a greater passage of time is required to deliver meaning, compared to the potentially very brief utterances of the spoken word. Position also delivers meaning, as we all can discover by trying to sit next to the only other person on the bus at 11 o'clock at night! That condition is not just a function of a unique association. Instead, it involves the cultural, non-verbal patterning of interpersonal space (Argyle 1990).

Meaning, therefore, cannot have a delimited verbal character. The non-verbal component of ordinary and familiar daily life removes that possibility. We have masked that actuality by referring to the non-verbal in verbal terms such as privacy and intimacy, but have, in the process, removed from our awareness that what is being ordered is space and time. The ordering of space and time is a mathematical proposition, not a verbal one. Not surprisingly, the verbal traditions of scholarship have not engaged with this reality. How could they? Without a means of reference what could be discussed? The effect, however, has been to divert our attention from the material, by converting it into verbalized categories of meaning. The prevalent assumption is that such meanings are the index for whatever generates the actions that, in turn, produce material spaces. The material is thereby reduced to an epiphenomenon. Consequently, we persistently fail to see the majority of our evidence, conflated as it is into families, power, dichotomies, sacred, and profane. Either those categories seem to be the only ones which we could use to approach the data, or the actual phenomena of social action and verbal expression to which they purportedly relate are presumed to provide a sufficient explanation for why the spaces were made. But what if verbal meaning taxa are obscuring a surprising and profoundly interesting past? Perhaps verbal meaning does not represent the cause of the spatial patterns, but instead juxtaposes, or is laid over, the available pattern of material space generated by tacit, non-verbal behav-

ior? The verbal may be a means we use to make sense of what we are doing anyway. That this alternative has not formed the basis for a paradigm of human behavior is a monument to the power of the verbal in the scholarly world of the humanities.

If the material is generated separately from the verbal, but the two are juxtaposed in day-to-day life, then collapsing the material via the social into the verbal has removed an entire generative factor from our perception of culture. If correspondence is not inevitable, and material pattern exists and existed independent of verbal meaning, then the obvious point, that the operation of sociality cannot be encompassed by words, can be seen in a new way. An independent generative process creating the material phenomena of culture would have to be envisaged. The content of familiar verbal meaning would not suffice to encompass our understanding of materiality, and social action would not subsume it as an epiphenomenon. Furthermore, we would have to conclude that non-verbal meaning, strictly described in terms of size, amount, frequency, and intensity, plays a significant role in the understanding of our behavior. Given that the archaeological record is a record of such data, perhaps there is a more direct and more fruitful way to approach the past, and thence the present, than converting non-verbality into a partial and potentially notional set of verbal meanings. The prevalent assumption has been that only by making such a conversion could anything socially or humanely worthwhile and relevant to human beings be produced. Merely describing the material would be dull. But perhaps by seeing the material as an operator in its own right we can escape the "familiar quandary of choosing between a significant pursuit based on faulty method or one which is methodologically sound but trivial in purpose" (De Boer and Lathrap 1979: 103). In essence our conventional social assumptions about verbal meaning structures and social action are a liability. They conceal both the content and the fascination of the long-term past as "another country" (Lowenthal 1985). Things were really done differently there. If they were not, why bother to look? For instance, "ancestor worship" as an explanation is liable to become a conservative retrodiction, denying both the historicity of the past and the logical conditions of a rigorous evolutionary perspective. The problem lies in an assumption that material–"social" correlates just are, rather than that they came gradually, perhaps even erratically, into being.

People create their social lives out of actions and verbal declarations. They envisage social relations as well as practice them and they state their ideals of meaning as well as seeking to implement those ideals. They also build space. However, we should beware of the convenient assumption and easy expectation that social actions and verbal meanings have a direct causal connection to the material form of a structure or settlement. Lack of correspondence between the ideals and actuality of social life is well known in social anthropology. There should be no expectation that correspondence will exist for the verbal and the material. The actual actions of people will, of course, have a relationship to the actual content of the archaeological record. But even when post-occupation taphonomic effects are limited, the patterns of movable material items need not have a one-to-one correspondence with the way in which space is subdivided within a house. Allison (1997) shows that in Pompeii, room contents do not correspond to the ideal functions that modern scholars would ascribe to rooms on the basis of Renaissance interpretations of Roman idealized room types, and that movable objects of many different types occur both in any one space and throughout the house. The taxonomy of space cannot be reduced to a taxonomy of functions defined by object types.

Nor can spaces determine the functions they may contain. Rooms may be differentiated by their shape, size, and location, but different functions do not simply map onto them. In Catal Huyuk the distributions of different kinds of micro-debris did not co-

vary in consistent functional zones within a room (Matthew et al. 1996). This is precisely as should be expected in spaces used over many decades where successive, varied, specific social functions will have created complex palimpsests of many different room space functions. No doubt there can be *some* correspondence between space and active social life. All I am specifying here is merely that no direct, continual correspondence exists. That the contents of a space can be rearranged more readily than the frame is a neglected commonplace. In modern houses a bedroom can then become a study. Similarly, as David (1971) showed for the Fulani, the functions of spaces also alter over time in the houses of small-scale agrarian communities. If the shape/size and function linkages are not necessary or determinative, then the assumption that some initial intentions about function, or some intended verbalizable meaning, are the *sufficient* determinative explanation of spatial order and function is untenable.

Patterned space must be something other than just a reflection of verbal categories and do something other than just be a mechanical derivative of functions. An inherent non-correspondence and potential friction exists between the material form of settlement space and its associated actions and verbal meanings. Understanding the consequent operational dissonance will have considerable implications for studying the internal dynamics of community life and the triggers for cultural change.

Implications of Non-Correspondence

That the material does something and is a factor in its own right is recognized (e.g., Braudel 1981; Appadurai 1986) but the next step, to truly constitute mundane materiality as an agent in its own right, has not been taken. Clearly the shift would be of profound significance to archaeology, because the material record is the information about that agency and its role for over

2 million years – a comprehensive record available for all human existence. Like it or not, there are also big cross-cultural issues in the analysis of the past. The information about them resides in the archaeological record, whatever our analytic failures. There are profound matters concerning the formation of very large, enduring aggregates of people in extensive complexes of durable buildings. Even more fundamental are the issues involved in how human communities begin and cease to reside habitually in one settlement site for decades on end. These are far from trivial topics. Nor are they figments of political or philosophical fashion. Instead, they are brutally consequential for the present and the future, if what we call sedentism has some connection to the capacity for intense population growth, and what we label initial urbanism provided the foundations of the built-world of cities that now dominates human social life. Understanding what has happened, and why, is an essential part of comprehending our current dilemma. To do this requires that we comprehend and bring together our understanding of material behavior, both as a patterned structure with its own heritage constraints, and as an operational phenomenon impacting on human social action. Archaeology is the only discipline whose domain of competence covers the relevant data and spans of time.

Spatial Material Behavior: Predictability and Dissonance

Primate behavior: the foundations of spatial predictability

The core social role of spatial patterning is the creation of a predictable milieu for community life (Fletcher 1995: 33–6). The patterning of space by primates other than modern humans exists independent of verbal meaning (Groves and Sabater-Pi 1985; Fruth and Hohmann 1996). The "camps" of Virunga mountain gorilla groups (Schaller 1963; esp. pp. 174–85; Casimir 1979) dis-

play consistency both in the nest spacings within the "camps" and in the degree of variability in the spatial behavior of the groups. Most nests are about 3–4 meters apart with a tail towards larger distances of 15–20 meters (Figure 7.2). There is no marked difference in the mode of the spacings in the successive "camps" of different social groups, suggesting a consistent "cultural" pattern. Such "cultural" patterns are not, of course, unique to primates (for other animal species, see Bonner 1980; Heyes and Galef 1996). What is relevant for this discussion is that "camping" behavior and spatial patterning are a normal component of the behavior of the African great apes and their hominid relatives. An "origin" of spatial patterning in hominids does not, therefore, need a special explanation, any more than tool use and production which are shared by chimpanzees and hominids (McGrew 1992). The behaviors are just part of the evolutionary repertoire of this kind of animal. Furthermore, while tool use is only known among a more limited range of other animal species (Beck 1980), spatial patterning is an inherent part of animal behavior in general (e.g., Manning and Dawkins 1998).

What follows is that spatial patterning, whether of individuals or of the material component of behavior, is an ancestral trait that must predate the evolution of the hominids. In a specifically primate, and then hominid form, it must also predate the evolution of the social organization of modern humans and the use of language in its modern form. Far from our kind of social action generating spatial patterning it is, at best, complementary. It more likely follows from, and is laid on, the elementary spatial format of hominid behavior. To collapse the two together, or to allocate explanatory priority or hegemony to verbal meaning, is neither analytically logical nor behaviorally valid.

The key point is that hominid debris scatters, even 2–2.5 million years old (Kroll and Price 1991), however much redeposited and overlaid, are still visible today and were presumably an enduring marker on the

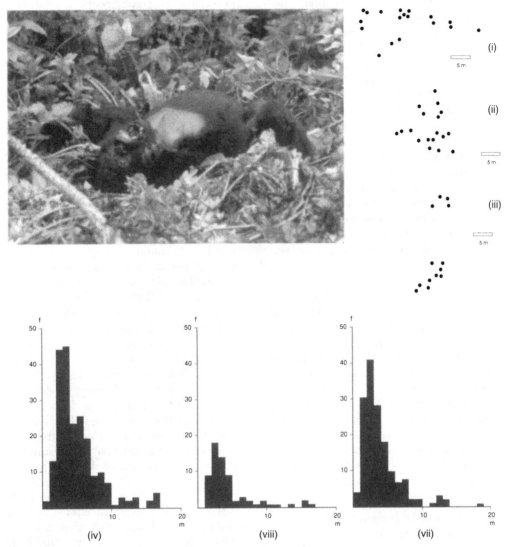

Figure 7.2 (a) upper left, gorilla lying on nest. Dian Fossey Gorilla Fund/Bob Campbell. (b) upper right, plans of camps of mountain gorillas (after Schaller 1963). (c) below, spatial patterning in camps of mountain gorillas (*Gorilla gorilla*) in the Virunga Mountains, Uganda and Rwanda (data acquired from plans in Schaller 1963 by Karen Calley). Aggregate of distances between the nests within the successive "camp" sites of Group IV (left), Group VIII (center), Group VII (right). The distances measured were the nearest neighbor values. Up to three values were measured, depending on the relative position of the nests in the camp.

landscape for the acute hominid eye. The "hard" scatters marked the repeatedly changing loci of hominid activity, providing a map of behavior for the observer (Fletcher 1993).[1] They also constituted a class of

material milieu with some inertia, within which human social action and verbal meaning evolved. In that initial dialectical engagement between material spatial behavior and repeatedly generated variants of social action, both would have changed very slowly, but we should not assume that this occurred in a simple synchrony. However slight, the presence of inertia in the material spatial patterns and the inevitable capacity of active behavior to create variants more rapidly (Fletcher 1992: 47–8; 1996: 64–5) would have generated some non-correspondence between them. Combinations of social action and material spacing that could operate together, would only have become prevalent by selective competition acting on numerous alternative associations over long spans of time. Therefore, we cannot assume that the initial associations of materiality and social action were the long-term workable ones we might now observe. Unless an unusual determinism was defining what the hominids did in a given type of space, the outcome must derive from the impact of selection, whether arbitrary or not, on a range of variants. The social actions and the specific forms of modern hunter-gatherer camps, or the spaces used by the present-day non-human primates, cannot therefore mirror the specific unsuccessful combinations of the material and social action which would have played such a critical role in creating the record of our past. The research questions are legion, and the appropriate methodology to pursue the problem will itself be a major research issue.

The spatial behavior of modern humans: spatial predictability

Modern human beings tacitly pattern space by locating individuals relative to each other (see Hall 1966 for the first description of proxemics), by placing people in relation to their spatial milieu, and by generating consistent arrangements of built space (Fletcher 1977, 1995: 25–42). The ordering of space in human communities has the same overall pattern as the spacing of nests in the gorilla camps, though more elaborate. Instead of one distance (i.e., between nests), human settlements can carry many spatial signals, especially in communities that build substantial structures. A simple example is provided by the distances between the supports of the "latte" in Guam (Craib 1986) (Figure 7.3). When the distance between pillars along a row and the distances between pillars across the width of the building are measured, two simple distributions are apparent. There is a marked spatial consistency, as in gorilla camps. The distributions of distances along and across the "latte" are also very similar, with modes within the same class interval and similar ranges, suggesting that function and mechanical demand do not in themselves generate the spatial consistency. The load-bearing functions across the width and along the length of the building are different, since the crossbeams carry the load of activity on the floor of the building and the lateral beams hold up the load of the walls. Obviously these functions were sustained within the dimensions of the buildings, but could not, in themselves, exactly determine those distances. All the builders had to do was overbuild enough to ensure that the building stayed up. With that freedom, what they actually did was to build according to some consistent set of dimensions. Nor are the dimensions a function of raw material. Palm trees supplied long,

Figure 7.3(a)   Plan (lower left) and reconstruction view (above) of a latte, the elevated houses indigenous to Guam (after Morgan 1988). (b) (right) Spatial patterning in the dimensions of latte in village sites in Guam (data collected by Miffy Bryant). Histogram derived from measurements on "houses" recorded on the plans of several villages prepared by John Craib. Where one of a pair of pillars was obviously missing no measurement was taken. These graphs therefore represent the distances between surviving pairs of pillars. Some of these pillars are as much as 3 meters high. Wooden beams laid between the pillars along the length of a building held up the outer walls. Beams laid across the width of a row of pillars held up the floor. Note: where the absence of a pillar was uncertain, due to some irregularity in the layout, then the distance was included and these account for some of the larger distances.

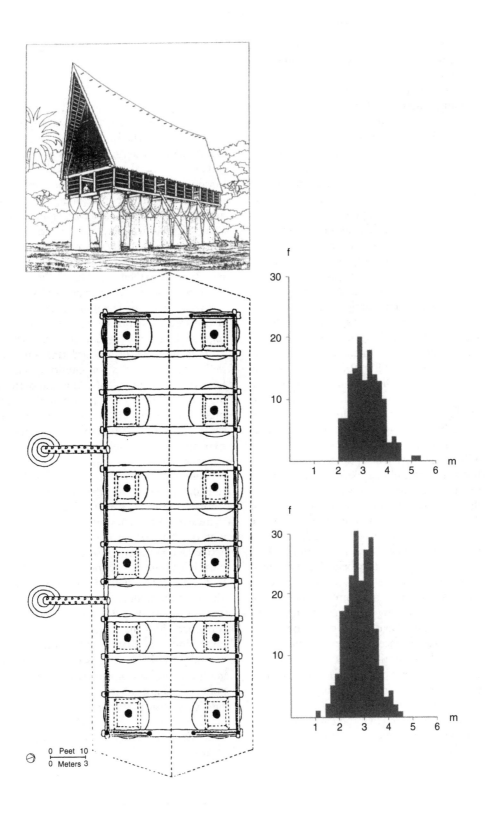

straight timber spars from which the builders cut the much shorter beams that they used.

Spatial pattern consistencies can be seen globally, whether in seventeenth-century AD Franciscan monasteries and Hopi pueblos, New Kingdom workers' settlements in Egypt, or modern Ghanaian villages (Figure 7.4) (Fletcher 1977). Within the spatial pattern unique to each settlement, similar dimensions occur with different functional purposes. In Awatovi pueblos, room lengths were the same as widths (approx 2 meters) or else are about 4 meters long. In the New Kingdom site on the top of the ridge above Deir el Medina on the west bank of Thebes, room widths were either around 1 or 2 meters, and room lengths also had a mode around 2 meters, corresponding with the sizes of the small open yards and small "storerooms" of the main settlement in the valley (Fletcher 1981: 100–3). Clearly, raw materials for roofing are not determinative because builders can opt for differing spans of timber. While the Hopi predominantly chose branches for roofing, the contemporaneous Franciscans, in exactly the same milieu, used tree trunks (Fletcher 1977: 49). If the style of building specifies the use of the raw material, not the other way round, then the consistency of settlement form cannot derive from a determinative function of the supply of raw materials. Instead, it has to derive from some internal operational characteristic of community behavior. This must generate a pattern, on which the impact of external selective pressures operates, to leave us with the enduring arrangements of space that have sufficed to cope with their circumstances. Deterministic statements which ascribe the cause of shapes directly to external forces are easier to state but do not become valid for that reason, just as in biology, declarations that the "animals adjusted to their environment" are a convenient shorthand but utterly infringe neo-Darwinian logic.

The spatial behavior of modern humans: the material, verbal meaning, social action, and dissonance

In essence, the question is whether a community's social organization and values, as expressed in its verbally articulated traditions, create spatial order. *A priori* this would seem unlikely, as social action and verbal declaration are famously non-correspondent. The built space is, of course, a consequence of the actions of people and has a correspondence to what they did to make that material form. However, it is an unwarranted but easy elision to assume that the verbal descriptors people apply to their social life, fully describe those actions, i.e., are the clue to why people did what they did. The non-correspondence of declared and actual behavior leaves one no logical choice but to conclude that declaration is only one form of ordering – not the definitive essence of a community's comprehensive ordering of reality. Material patterning of space is far too complex and multiscaled to be reduced to a verbal descriptor (Figure 7.4). We have to deal with at least two operational levels, each with its own structure and implications. The reductive premise that one can be subsumed by, or fully described by, the other is untenable.

Once the reductive premise is removed, there can be no deterministic link between material features on the one hand and the active components of social life – verbal meaning and social action – on the other. If that is so, then correlations between materiality and the familiar components of social meaning must be partial and episodic. On some occasions the correspondence may be quite close, but that would be only one of several possible kinds of association, including behavioral dissonance. That true correspondence is not inherent to community life can be seen in the mismatches apparent in notable cases of sociospatial "cosmology." In a classic instance, the Bororo village (Lévi-Strauss 1955), which is repeatedly used to

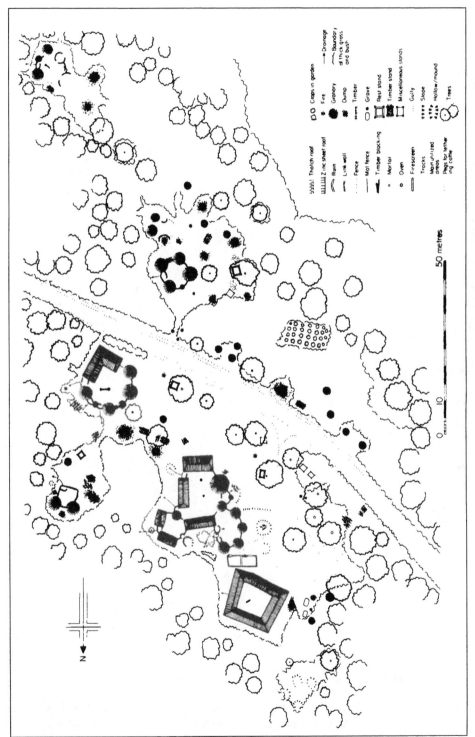

Figure 7.4 (a)   Plan of Munyimba (Ghana), a village of the Konkomba, in the early 1970s (after Fletcher 1977).

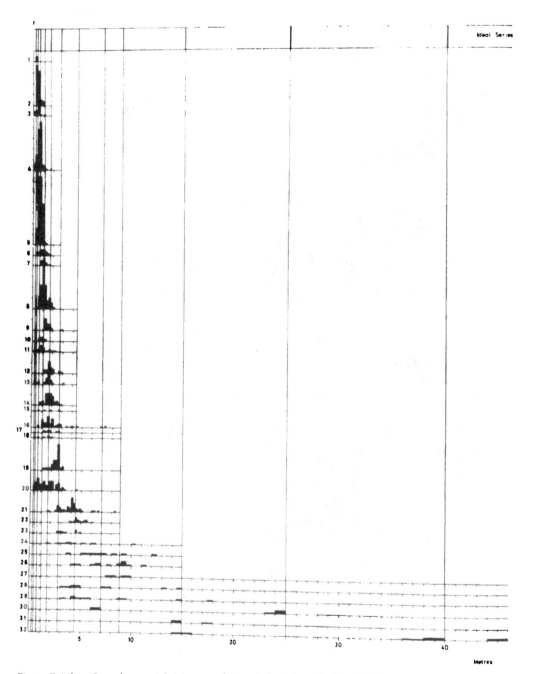

Figure 7.4 (b) Complex spatial signature of Munyimba (after Fletcher 1977).

illustrate the mapping of the social onto the material, the correspondence is only partial (Figure 7.5). The dualities and social groupings identified in words cannot be derived from the plan on its own. This is *precisely* what we should expect if social action and domestic life can change more rapidly than the rate at which the built space is being replaced or replicated. In the case of the Dogon (Griaule 1966), the cosmology is very elaborate, but the actual houses vary in form, a condition that is not in itself contained by, expressed in, or subsumed as meaning in the cosmology. The cosmology does not, and logically cannot, specify to what degree the houses will vary, because words alone cannot encompass quantified statements of variability. If, of course, the "tolerance" of differing degrees of variability is a characteristic that differentiates communities, then verbality fails to describe a fundamental part of cultural mechanisms of adaptation.

It is also worth bearing in mind that any versatile cosmology could, of course, be used to construct *ad hoc* verbalized meanings as a social lubricant for non-correspondence. That is a key virtue of words. But the corollary is that the relationship of words to materiality is liable to be so plastic that such explanations would be almost unfailing and therefore could not be determinative! This kind of non-correspondence can be seen on a large scale in the relationship between ideal cosmologies and urban settlement plans.

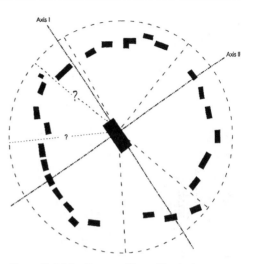

Figure 7.5 (b) Bororo village. Physical structure of axes normal to the central building and house groups defined by gaps in the perimeter row of buildings. Note neither corresponds to the moiety/ clan divisions in Figure 7.5 (a).

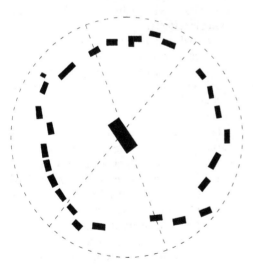

Figure 7.5 (a) The Bororo village, Amazonia, 1950s AD: schematized ideal of the variety of clan divisions and the material/social non-correspondence (after Lévi-Strauss 1955).

Steinhardt's (1990) study of Chinese imperial cities actually shows that despite the overtly declared Chinese cosmology of the idealized Wang Cheng city plan (Figure 7.6 (a)), there are no cases of precise correspondence with the ideal in Chinese urban history. Ironically, the closest correspondence was created by foreign nomadic invaders, the Mongols, who used Chinese planners to create Da-du (Figure 7.6 (b)) and legitimate their control of China (Steinhardt 1990: 160). Given that the Wang Cheng ideal refers to the profound association between the authority of the emperor and the structure of the universe, it is somewhat surprising to find that the wealthiest and most powerful pre-industrial rulers did not effect the ideal.

The current preeminence, indeed the dominance, of verbal meaning as a determinative explanation may appear simple. It even looks, at first, like the Occam's Razor preference, but it does not adequately cope with the repeated observational statements which are available about settlement space. The fallacy of the verbal derives from accepting the primacy of the "ethnographic" and

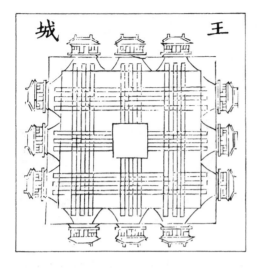

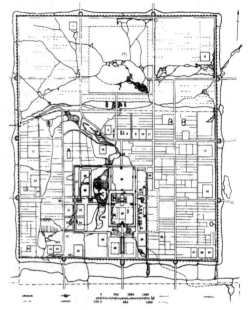

Figure 7.6 (b) Da-du, the Mongol Yuan Dynasty capital in north China where modern Beijing now stands (thirteenth to fourteenth centuries AD) (derived from Steinhardt 1990).

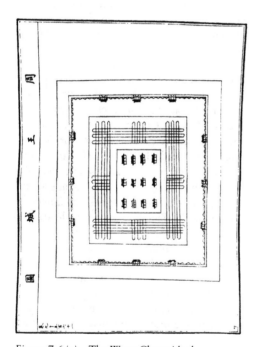

Figure 7.6 (a) The Wang Cheng ideal.

treating the timescales of contemporary experience as definitive. Words are considered to be the window into the mind. Primacy is given to the declaratory, reducing the past to the present and collapsing the timescales over which we might "see" the material having its effects.

If verbal declarations do not specify why settlements have their form, then we might incline to argue that some aggregate of the actual actions of the community must be ascribed the role. Perhaps many variables are involved, such as resource supply and social circumstances. But if these create spatial patterns by their myriad simultaneous interactions, then a curious problem arises. First, if many variables are involved, then tacit, ordered spatial behavior derived from our primate ancestry can be one of them. But this, in itself, supplies a largely sufficient explanation, since that is what settlement space actually is. The syntax of that spatial order would be the equivalent of genetics for life forms (Fletcher 1996).

Secondly, if many independent variables are involved, as we must presume since they range from natural environments to belief systems, then either there is profound restrictive consistency within the region where a settlement is located, or those variables are not, in aggregate, the generative agency. In addition, external variables could act to destroy or ruin the efforts of a community, so we cannot even assume that the sum of the effects is aggregative. The mistake inherent in the "many variables" view is the failure to recognize that the impact of different variables, and the limitations on how they operate, come about over different time spans. What people can say changes far faster than their non-verbal body language (Fletcher 1996: 64–5), and social opinion can impact more rapidly than economic decline on specific features of a community.

The logical solution is provided by the well-founded, irretrievable criticism of Lamarckism as an explanation of the relationship between systems which generate form and the external reality in which those forms operate (Bateson 1972: 324–5). If externals defined form then consistency of heritage and hence traditions would vanish, since every specific external circumstance would be continually introducing arbitrary new variants into the replicative process. This alone suggests that the concept of "culture" as Lamarckian is mistaken. Just as in biological systems, we must envisage that the spatial pattern of culture is replicated by some operation that is capable of generating internal consistency regardless of external factors. Change would arise internally by replicative "error" in the generating system, and from the longer-term selective impact of external circumstances. Some features would thereby become more common than others in the next round of replication. In the case of the material component of social life, the heritage selectivity would be a function, in part at least, of

what remains visible to be observed as a guide to successive generations of observers/builders.

Implications

The key implication of consistency and the heritage effect is that human space is patterned by internally coherent suites of tacit, spatial messages unique to a community. To consistently describe and analyze residential space, we must therefore develop a way of representing material spatial messages composed of the visual distances carried by structures and the location of entities. A theory of non-verbal behavior will also be needed to explain the relationship between settlement form and those spatial messages. The issue is to explain how a suite of visual distances comes to constitute a settlement, in the same sense as we ask the question: how do genes make the form of the living entity that carries them? The further questions, as for example with the design of a Chinese capital city, relate to the factors of social action, other than cosmology, which were involved in the choices of the decision-makers. What cannot be excluded is that what they sought to create was itself influenced by the actuality of their tacit ordering of space, as well as by overt and mystified matters, such as state policy and military planning. The nature and role of settlement space is a far more interesting issue than simple, functional, and/or cosmological deterministic models could lead one to expect. While settlement space is initially created by tacit coherence in spatial positioning, the actual use of settlement space involves a complex relationship between the message systems of the material, the verbal, and social action. What results is a dynamic of engagement and non-correspondence which one might expect to strongly influence the long-term workings of the resident community.

The Dynamics of Settlement Growth and Decline: Operational Dissonance and Outcome

Community life and material/social action dissonance

On an even larger scale the same critique can be applied to the dynamic relationship between the operation of a residential community and the context in which it is functioning. If non-correspondence occurs, then we should find that community life has its own internal, operational limits independent of external conditions. If this were not the case, community functioning would be determined by external variables rather than selectively affected by them. The Lamarckian ban applies again. If the sum of community life derives from the aggregate impact of unique suites of externals in each region of the world, then cross-cultural pattern would disappear and settlement histories could display no global consistencies. The only externality which could create worldwide consistency would be a single type of powerful determinant, but none has ever been demonstrated to exist. By marked contrast, internal operational limits common to all communities, simply because they are residential aggregates of human beings, would generate cross-cultural consistency, and not infringe the Lamarckian ban. An assessment of the duration of pre-industrial cities indicates that there is such consistency (Figure 7.7). Overall, the *maximum* operable duration of the largest compact cities declines as settlement area increases.[2] While settlements of any areal extent can have brief existences of varying duration, cut short by natural, economic, and political disaster, or the mere whim of rulers, only the relatively small cities with areas of less than 20–30 sq km could endure for periods of more than 700 years between their take-off and their nadir or demise. Larger cities, like Abbasid Baghdad (Figure 7.8), with areas of over 60 sq km, had more limited futures. Contextuality cannot, therefore, offer an adequate explanation for the consistent pattern of the upper limit on their duration, since the specific histories of these cities are unerringly unique and cannot therefore specify a cross-cultural consistency. No one supposes that imperial Rome resembled Ming–Ch'ing Beijing in its social particulars or its unique sequence of historical events. But, likewise, conventional processualism is confounded by numerous cases of any one settlement size with extremely different durations, involving unique and idiosyncratic histories. Area and duration do not correlate. Processualism is inadequate because the consistency only occurs for a boundary condition, not for a correlation between the condition of all communities and their settlement sizes. The "universal" condition does not allow a prediction of each case, which is what the generalizing logic of determinative processualism would specify. Neither the logic of contextualized cultural uniqueness, nor that of purported processual cross-cultural consistencies which explain all specific cases, are tenable.

What the diagram of urban histories indicates is that as the areal extent of a compact settlement increases, the potential capacity of the community to endure decreases. How they will decline or fail is not specified, only that they appear to have some extremely strong tendency to do so. The prevalent factor then stares us in the face: obvious, blatant, and all but invisible to conventional social theory. Sheer areal extent and the degree to which people are packed together are material factors which can potentially overwhelm the socially integrative actions of any community. According to this view, the materiality and the social actions of a community are increasingly at odds, as area and density increase. Areal extent overstretches the community's capacity to communicate coherently, while large numbers of people packed close together at high densities overload the capacity to tolerate interaction (Fletcher 1995: 69–98). The decreasing capacity to persist as the aggregate stresses increase, follows from a simple

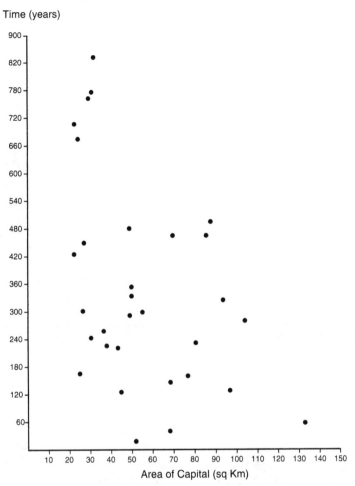

Figure 7.7 The operational ceiling on the duration of compact urban settlements from circa 400 BC to the mid-nineteenth century AD (see note 2).

model of the limits on viable interaction and communication in human communities.

The unique social activities and histories of each community are relentlessly, but not deterministically, connected to the general outcome because interaction and communication stresses pick out each society's unique, internal social contradictions and operational weaknesses. In one community it might be the nexus between a fatalistic cyclical view of time and internal social conflicts about the legitimation of power (perhaps Teotihuacan); in another, the conflict between different sects of the same religion

interlocking with an ambiguous relationship between spiritual and temporal power (perhaps Abbasid Baghdad). In order to understand the specifics, the unique social conditions of each society have to be understood. Then they have to be placed in the context of the cross-culturally consistent behavioral constraints on viable community life. That interaction has then to be located in the vast milieu of altering environments, whether this is collapsing trade networks, soil erosion, or the arrival of militaristic nomads. For instance, in AD 1258 the Mongols were the specific nemesis of

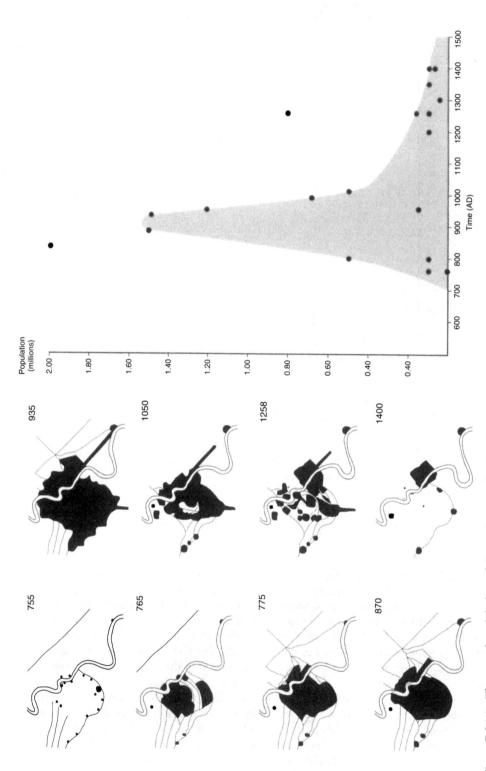

Figure 7.8 (a)   The growth and decline of the areal extent of Abbasid Baghdad, Mesopotamia (after Le Strange 1924; Lassner 1970).   (b) The growth and decline of the population of Abbasid Baghdad. Note that what is recorded are various estimates of the population of the city. The envelope marks the maximum internally consistent estimates for the total population.

Baghdad (Morgan 1988: 144). The contingent and the arbitrary do not preclude pattern and consistency. Vulnerability changes with size and time. Baghdad had suffered several sieges and conquests at the peak of its size in the ninth and tenth centuries AD, after which it endured for several centuries (Lassner 1970). Abbasid Samarra (Northedge 1987), with an areal extent that exceeded 100 sq km, lasted just over fifty years and was destroyed by civil war in AD 892.

An issue to be investigated further is the effect of the deteriorating material infrastructure of a settlement. The inertial cost of such decay may play a critical role in the demise of massive urban systems. The degeneration of space, the deterioration of infrastructure, and problems of maintaining changed social relationships in an old material frame, should play a considerable role in the way a community functions or fails to function in the long term (Fletcher 1995: 51–5). Such dissonance would be especially serious if the material infrastructure of a community is substantial, extremely durable, or hard to alter. That deterioration occurs is well known, both historically and in the modern world (Royce 1984), where concrete cancer in infrastructure, such as bridges, has required serious attention. On occasion, such problems were overtly recognized in the past. In the early 580s AD the new Sui emperor of China decided to reestablish his capital at Ch'ang-an, where the rulers of the prestigious Han dynasty (206 BC to AD 220) had lived. But the councillors declared that the aged town was cramped and run down, its water supply foul (Wright 1967: 143). The place was socially depressing, the scene of lost power, looting, and death, populated by ghosts. It was replaced by a new capital on the open space immediately to the south.

In other cases, however, the inertia is likely to have crept up on the social world, creating problems when there was a lack of political, economic, and technical means to renovate a failing system. This, perhaps, offers a new direction of inquiry into the demise of Angkor in Cambodia, the Khmer capital between the ninth century AD and the mid-second millennium AD (Dayton 2001). The purported sack by the Thai in AD 1431 is now suspect as a neat political fiction (Jacques and Freeman 1997: 229, 195), so uncertainty surrounds the decline and demise of Angkor as an urban complex. Particularly significant is that, like industrial cities with their massive buildings, route systems, and utilities, Angkor consisted of an immense, enduring fabric of fields, canals, reservoirs, tanks, causeways, and interconnected great monuments (Figure 7.9), enmeshing a vast, dispersed, low-density urban complex (Pottier 1999; Fletcher 2001). What is readily apparent is that the functioning of this complex was linked to distributing water, whether for ritual and/or economic purposes or to manage the flow rates of the rivers. Alterations in the flow of water down the streams from the Kulen hills would therefore have had a profound effect on the entire urban complex. Continued expansion of fields and the removal of forest cover was likely to have precisely that effect (Fletcher 2001).[3] Because the level of the entry points for water to flow into the network of channels was utterly immovable, the network was very vulnerable to changes in flow and sedimentation. If the flow rate increased and flooded the system, or the gradient of the streams changed and cut below the level of the channels, then the network, as a whole, would cease to function, even if some parts of it could still be maintained. For example, in central Angkor the Siem Reap river now flows some 5–6 meters lower than its former channel, suggesting that the river regime had become unstable and altered markedly during or just after the demise of Angkor. If this indicates a cumulative problem, then the relationship between the rigid frame of the water network, urban expansion, and the pragmatics of daily life deserves attention. There are two interrelated issues. First, what overall, internal, behavioral conditions affect the ongoing operation of a low-density

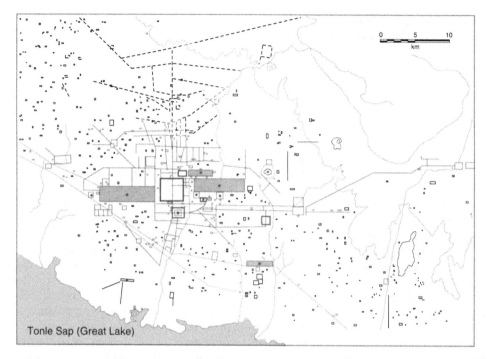

Figure 7.9 The extent of Angkor (Cambodia), late twelfth century to circa sixteenth century AD. Prior to the 1995 Endeavor Space Shuttle flight, which obtained the radar image showing the whole of Angkor in one image for the first time, the urban complex was seen as ending just north of the Preah Khan (see ZEMP plan 1995). Bantei Srei, 25 km off to the northeast, was seen as a distant outlier. By contrast, once the northern route network is plotted, Bantei Srei becomes an integral part of the northeast edge of the urban complex. (The image is copyright of the Greater Angkor Project. The data derive from research by Christophe Pottier of EFEO and Damian Evans of the Spatial Science Innovation Unit (Archaeological Computing Laboratory), University of Sydney. It is published with the kind permission of EFEO.)

urban system (Fletcher 1995: 117–24), and secondly, the relationship between what a community is doing and how long it can keep going if external factors militate against its persistence.

Implications

The collision between slow change in spatial patterning, material factors such as inertia and structural decay, and rapidly transforming social action, would create a powerful nexus of dissonant effects with profound consequences for the prospects of a community. Not only are there several levels of meaning (e.g., verbal and non-verbal), but also there are several operational levels, such as social action and the inertia of the material framework of social life. The implication is that each level of operation has its own coherence, its own suite of effects, and its own particular range of time spans over which impact is felt on the outcome of an activity. If this is so, then a "scientistic" processual, reductive determinism is inappropriate to encompass or describe the operation of human sociality over a range of timescales. But, conversely, contextualism with its emphasis on verbal meaning and its tendency to collapse interpretations of sociality onto the familiar normalcy of the short term, is also insufficient (Murray 1997). Contextualism treats the content, expressions, and concerns of social anthropology and familiar history as an unquestioned and (paradoxically) "natural" way to approach the analysis of community life. Instead of this dichotomy, we might usefully consider whether a hierarchical, non-deterministic view of cultural operations, spanning and interconnecting a range of spatial and temporal scales, would serve us better. The old debate about internal and external causes is really obsolete. A systematic model is required in which change occurs at several different rates of transformation, both in meaning content and in the operations of a community. Not only would these be in some conflict with each other in a society which uses a substantial material frame, but also they could not be altering at the demand of external circumstances. The continually shifting relationships between materiality and the "social," which were generating the internal changes, could not be "directed" in any sense that would logically be deterministic. On a still larger scale, resource supply and environmental change would, in their turn, eventually have a selective effect on the long-term outcome of whatever a community attempted to do.

Communities, Settlement Histories, and Context: Non-Correspondence and Outcome

Given that urban settlements seem to have a broadly consistent, maximum operable duration that decreases as settlement area increases, the possibility has to be considered that the maxima are determined by the duration and/or extent of some other larger factor, e.g., the empires which contained these cities. But even a brief inspection negates this viewpoint. Samarra only persisted for 56 years, in the midst of the first half of the history of the Abbasid empire, while Baghdad began before Samarra and continued for several centuries more. Other great capitals have histories which cannot be reduced to the duration of their empire. Hangchow, in China, the last capital of

the Southern Sung, survived the Mongol conquest in the early 1270s. Marco Polo's travelogue describes it as one of the great, thriving cities of the world in the following decade (Moule 1957). Only when the Mongol's Yuan dynasty collapsed did Hangchow's area and population decline (Fletcher 1995: 206).

Even urban area and population do not simply relate to empire size or extent. Ming–Ch'ing Beijing reached a population of about a million on an overall area of about 70 sq km. But during the Ch'ing dynasty from the seventeenth into the nineteenth century the total population of China increased from 100 million to approximately 400 million without having any appreciable effect, whether increase or decrease, on the population of the capital. The limits on the size of the capital were apparently specified by factors other than the potential supply of people. Nor, for the same reason, can there be a simple claim for a direct link from resource supply and extent of empire to the size, growth, and decline of the capital.

Most obviously, the lack of an invariable correlation between the histories of imperial capitals and the history of their empires is illustrated by the growth and decline of Rome and Constantinople, and the expansion and collapse of the imperial territory from 400 BC to AD 1438.[4] When the various population estimates (up to 1 million[5] for each city) are plotted against the areal extent of the imperial territory, the non-correspondence is very obvious (Figure 7.10). Not surprisingly, Rome grew after the imperial expansion had begun. That expansion fueled the city's growth, neatly illustrating inertia and lag in the transmission of wealth across an empire. More significant and interesting, however, is that while Rome began to decline as the empire contracted, it had already ceased to be the seat of imperial power more than a century earlier. The Diocletian reforms between AD 284 and 305 restructured the management of the empire (Grant 1990: 61) but did little to alter the decline of the increasingly redundant capital. Crucially,

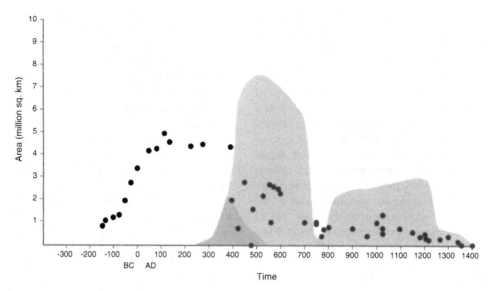

Figure 7.10 The growth and decline of Rome and Constantinople and the Roman and Byzantine empires. The population growth and decline envelopes for Rome and Constantinople enclose the maximum population estimates. The points for the areal extent of the Roman and Byzantine empires record varied reported estimates and areas calculated from maps.

however, once the empire was in its declining trend, Constantine became the new capital that expanded in area and population as the diminution of the empire leveled off. There was finally another recovery in the size of Constantinople's population (to perhaps as much as 400,000 in AD 1204 (Magdalino 1995: 35)) after the seventh-century decline, but the maximum area of the empire scarcely changed and then markedly declined.

Implications

Even on the macroeconomic scale of imperial resource supply, the dynamics of the capitals cannot be reduced to a simple predictable association with the extent of their respective empires. As the duration/size graph (Figure 7.7) indicates, the great cities had their own inertia, related apparently to their internal interaction and communication problems. The external factors of imperial scale and the associated resource supply, display lag and non-correspondence,

however much the end of Constantinople can be ascribed pragmatically to the loss of imperial territory in the thirteenth and fourteenth centuries AD. It is not the point of this example to claim that there is no correspondence between different scales of operation. Rather, the key theme is that they do not inevitably correspond and therefore cannot be linked deterministically. As a corollary, however, it follows that each level of operation has its own characteristic boundary conditions or constraints, which will be general to all societies.

Just as compact cities with large areas and large populations have a limited future, so likewise empires should have limits on their magnitude and economic viability, set by the adequacy of the transmission rate of their communication systems and the degree to which they can balance their acquisition and consumption of resources. Again, this does not mean that empires cannot exceed those limits, only that they should not be able to do so for very long. How long, is the crucial empirical issue. Elvin's proposition about the "high-level equilibrium trap" (Elvin 1973: 298) offers an interesting insight. The Kennedy (1989) argument about military over-commitment and Tainter's (1988) case for the diminishing returns of increased complexity need to be restated in terms of magnitudes and durations. For instance, the stable core of the Chinese empires from 220 BC to the mid/late nineteenth century, China proper, was about 6–8 weeks across by horse courier (Blunden and Elvin 1983: 94). The Mongol empire of the thirteenth and the fourteenth centuries AD, stretching across Asia from the China Sea to the borders of Europe, depended upon high-speed horse couriers, but could not persist as a single working entity, even for a century, before splitting into the effectively autonomous states of the Golden Horde, the Ilkhanids, Chagatai, and Yuan China (Morgan 1988: 103–7, 195–204).

Outcome Analysis

Archaeological data are then the record of the outcomes of a myriad human initiatives and intentions. But as we all know, implemented intentions frequently do not lead to the anticipated outcomes. Many variables intervene. The materiality of social life now has to be taken seriously – not the material as a referent for social action and verbal meaning, but the material itself. The emphasis now should be on asking what the material actually does. Perhaps we can productively analyze large-scale patterns of outcome rather than be trapped by disputes about initiating causes explained in terms of verbal meaning.

The primary point is that contrary to general expectation, the material and the active component of social life do not necessarily correspond with each other at a variety of scales of magnitude, and they have the capacity to become dissonant. Nor are larger-scale social operations determined by their economic or environmental constraints. All this seems rather obvious once stated. There

can be no deterministic effect defining that a given social system will always produce the same material milieu, just as no environment determines what people may try to build. In the real world, cross-cultural ethnographic studies do not show that a particular social system always has a particular material correlate. Even supposedly pragmatic, mundane mechanical associations like pottery and sedentism are insecure (see Rafferty 1985, despite her preference for a correlation). Therefore, the more rarified associations like house form and social organization are unlikely to be universal. Local, specific associations will always be explicable, but they are contingent and circumstantial, not universal (Fletcher 1995: xx–xxii, 21–3). There is no demonstrable determinism at any level or scale of social behavior, nor any reduction of social behavior to any one aspect of its expression, whether material, verbal, or active. There are, however, limits to what will work adequately, whether it is community life within the massive shell of a great city, or an economic system in its environmental context.

Rather than presuming that the material, such as a settlement plan, corresponds with an active social condition, such as family organization, we should instead begin to envisage that the material and the active components of human behavior interact to varying degrees of adequacy. This allows that, in some communities, the material may be incompatible with the active component of daily life and therefore damage the prospects of continued viable social existence. If so, the material–active relationship is not a one-to-one correlation but is part of a triad with the outcome of the relationship (Figure 7.11). The outcome would be describable in terms of a community's duration, magnitude, and degree of sustainability. Just as an economy and an environment can interact either to produce success or failure over some span of time, depending on whether or not the economy will work in the environment, so likewise we should find a similar relationship for social action and

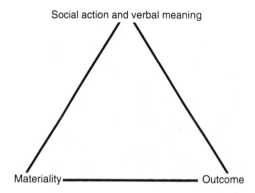

Social action and verbal meaning

Materiality ———————————— Outcome

Figure 7.11 The outcome triad.

the material milieu. If a suite of social action is at odds with its material milieu and cannot readily alter it, then we should find that the conjuncture produces complications and friction. Obviously, the relationship and the analyses will be complex. But the archaeological record contains the necessary clues, such as successive, attempted material alterations and the degree to which the community does or does not persist and in what condition.

Instead of the material reflecting the active, or being in a recursive relationship to it, we should envisage instead that the route to the socially active and therefore invisible component of the archaeological record is via the association of the material with the nature of the outcome of that relationship. This precludes the possibility that substantive examples, whether specific or generalized, can be logically extrapolated into the past (a point which Gould made clear for palaeontology in 1965). The use of associational ethnographic analogies, linking material and social phenomena in the present, to equivalent purported associations in the past is logically untenable. So long as these are only associations, lacking an explanation of why the association *must* occur, they cannot specify the nature of the past. They infringe the elementary condition inherent in any application of neo-Darwinian logic, that the past would have

been different in its particulars and also would have contained some modes of social life which were less effective than others. From the possibility of variation in past social organization it follows that the internal operations of some communities can be, or will have been, defective due to material–social dissonance. If that defectiveness led to selective disadvantage, then the story of the past would gain its specificity and unique quality from the consequent failures. To read those failures, instead, as typical of associations between material and social phenomena that are now prevalent, would be a serious analytic error. The current pattern may be prevalent precisely because it works adequately or even effectively, and has thereby become more common over time. Instead of generalizing a false substantive uniformitarianism into the past and infringing the contextualist ban on cross-cultural generalization, an ethnography of Britain in the sixth to fourth millennium BC might concentrate on asking whether the elaborate constructions of this period, such as long mounds, henges, and causewayed camps, were part of a process of new social relations coming into being from a diverse range of other options, rather than representing a bland extrapolation (as in the form recommended by Tilley 1996) of the currently familiar "ancestor worship" onto the very unusual. The past should be far more interesting. Indeed, because ancestor worship is/was ethnographically quite common, yet rarely occurs with massive stone or timber structures in small-scale societies, several interesting possibilities can be envisaged. Perhaps the structures in Britain were not part of "ancestor worship," but were instead some quite different mode of engaging with the dead. Or they may have been a milieu in which societies played out their relationship to their dead, eventually creating ancestor worship. Perhaps, even, the structures *were* used for ancestor worship, but that specific association did not work![6] Or is the category "ancestor worship" so generalized as to be an unfailing explanatory proposition? By leaving out the possibility of non-correspondence, social theory in archaeology has denied the potential richness of the past, and limited inquiry to a small spectrum of the familiar and the apparently possible.

Conclusions

That nineteenth-century archaeology could not begin its encounter with the past by assuming non-correspondence is understandable. But we now possess enough assurance of our skill and enough sense of the past to give away the flawed assumption about correspondence that has served us well over nearly two hundred years. It has now become an explanatory straitjacket. What is needed is to combine a theory of non-correspondence, the analysis of outcome, and the phenomenon of the material as behavior, to begin developing a true archaeological contribution to social theory which incorporates the relationship between materiality, space and time, and social life in all its versatile expressions of action and verbal meaning. We might then head towards an "Archaeology of Friction," applicable to an immense range of community life, and with a strong resonance in our experience of living in the early stages of industrialization. As a corollary to the significance of residential stress in appalling urban slums and ineptly planned burgeoning cities, or the grinding life and death of our social institutions on the fearsome mechanized battlefields of the industrializing world, the slow friction of space in the highly mobile hunter-gatherer communities

of modern humans may be of more than passing significance. In communities whose movements repeatedly disengage their social actions from flimsy shelters which are readily replicated at each new campsite, there would be relatively little friction between social action and its material milieu. Without much friction, the intense selective impact would be lacking that could strongly alter the likely persistence of slight variants in social action or verbal meaning. The effect would be to minimize transformational change, or to promote change by slight and gradual oscillations, with no strong tendency for marked directional shifts to occur. On the model of internal inconsistencies outlined in this chapter, it would follow that low dissonance between the material and social action will lead to slow rates of cultural transformation, while the bulkier the material frame, the greater the possibility of dissonance and the greater the potential rate of change. My point, at present, is not whether this is correct or incorrect, since that is an empirical issue. Rather, my aim is to show that an entire field of inquiry could be systematized to pursue such issues. The true domain of archaeology is the dynamic relationship between the material and sociality, not, as we have tended to presume, the use of social theory and historical premises to regenerate some semblance of a familiar past from the material. If we ever wish to move on from the prevalent style of social reconstruction, and enhance our aptitude at a form of social analysis which rigorously incorporates the material as an independent actor, there should be no shortage of topics, problems, or insights.

Acknowledgments

My especial thanks to John Bintliff for inviting me to write this chapter and then for some very patient cajoling and insistence to get it from me. The demand and the pressure was much appreciated. Thanks also to the reviewers who did their job at very short notice. As one noted, Heidegger's concept of technology as another "life form" resembles my own arguments, but ends at a quite different explanatory and expository position. Worth pursuing, along with the Marxism suite of propositions, to see why the material behavior concept differs.

For considerable assistance with data collection and technical advice on processing data in Washington DC, my sincere gratitude to the staff of the Natural History Museum and the Freer and Sackler Gallery of the Smithsonian Institution. My year in your company was a deeply satisfying professional experience.

In Cambodia I am particularly indebted to Christophe Pottier for advice and for our collaboration on fieldwork. A delight to work with. Thanks also to Terry Lustig for his vigorous perspective on what I was doing and on the mechanics of the hydraulic system of Angkor.

At home in the University of Sydney, the staff of VISLAB and of the Archaeological Computing Laboratory (ACL) have given much appreciated assistance, especially Ben Simons, Damien Buie, and Andrew Wilson. To Ian Johnson, as always, a great thank you for friendship and the facilities of the ACL. Thanks also to John Craib for directing me to the details of the latte in his thesis. To those who collected data over the years, in particular Miffy Bryant and Karen Calley, my thanks for your enterprise and interest.

Notes

1   The key point is that hominids made and discarded stone tools as they moved about, thereby leaving a durable and enduring set of signals as a record of their location in the landscape. The tool debris was therefore available to function as a spatial marker for hominid positioning in space, and had the potential to transmit a "message" about where hominids had been, and on closer reading of the tools, whether their behavior was like or unlike that of another observer, whether in the past or now. By contrast, though some chimpanzees go to anvil sites to crack nuts (see McGrew 1992), and also engage in distinctively localized cultural behavior, the collections of stones at such sites do not create an extensive and highly consequential "map" of behavior all over the landscape. A locus of lithic scatter produced by chimpanzees is a place to which the chimpanzees are attracted for other reasons and about which they are generally cognizant. This is not a continually transforming extensive landscape in which lithic debris signals to hominids where other hominids once were, with all the profound implications of generating a novel and informative cultural landscape.

2   The diagram is derived from the data on the 30 largest pre-industrial compact cities with areas larger than 15–20 sq km and with 400,000 or more people. Commencement dates are the official foundation dates for all cases other than Rome, for which a date in the fourth century BC is used to mark its take-off into fast growth. The duration of Rome might therefore be longer, but because cities with small areas have very long durations, the effect would not alter the overall pattern of the graph. One city is problematic, and that is Beijing during the Ming and Ch'ing dynasties. The Manchu, who took over Beijing in AD 1644 from the Ming, continued to use it as the capital of their dynasty through to the collapse of their Ch'ing dynasty in the early twentieth century. The city therefore had, in principle, an existence of about half a millennium from its establishment by the Ming in the fifteenth century. However, there is an alternative. Given the massive relocation of people within the city after the Manchu established the Ch'ing dynasty (Wakeman 1985), the city could be considered to have two durations of about 250 to 270 years. In this diagram the maximum duration is plotted for alternative maximum areas of 70 or 86 sq km.

3   Dr. Terry Lustig pointed out to me, while on fieldwork in Angkor, that the natural drainage is from northeast to southwest, but the Khmer of the ninth to sixteenth centuries AD were realigning the water flow into channels running north to south or either direction between

east and west. By taking the water flow and altering its direction of flow, the Khmer engineers and farmers forced the water into a longer and therefore slower route across the landscape, and specifically imposed reduced water flow rates wherever the water had to flow around a right-angle bend. Both the turns and the altered direction of flow would have reduced flow rates and therefore have led to more sedimentation in the system.

4   The convention of a Roman empire followed by a Byzantine one is not how the people or rulers of the two capitals saw their world (Norwich 1988).

5   There are estimates for Rome which exceed 1 million, most notably an estimate of 4 million ascribed to Lipsius by Hermansen (1978: 129). A figure of about a million is now generally considered to be a high and possible, though debated, estimate of the population of imperial Rome. The growth and decline curves represent the pattern of the higher estimates for each city. The actual growth could lie within that range, but the overall non-correspondence of the timing and magnitude of the urban growth and decline, relative to the trends for extent of empire, would not be altered, as their overall pattern through time is well known.

6   Another alternative, that neither the material nor the social affect each other much, so anything goes and any combination will work, has enough implications to make any analyst of the past quite anxious!

References

Adams, R. M. C. 1981. *Heartland of Cities*. Chicago: University of Chicago Press.

Allison, P. M. 1997. "Artefact distribution and spatial function in Pompeian houses." In B. Rawson and P. Weaver (eds.), *The Roman Family in Italy: Status, Sentiment and Space*, pp. 321–54. Humanities Research Centre: Canberra. Oxford: Clarendon Press.

Appadurai, A. (ed.) 1986. *The Social Life of Things: Commodities in Cultural Perspective*. Cambridge: Cambridge University Press.

Argyle, M. 1990. *Bodily Communication*. London: Routledge.

Bateson, P. P. G. 1972. *Steps to an Ecology of Mind: Collected Essays in Anthropology*. St. Albans: Paladin.

Beck, B. B. 1980. *Animal Tool Behavior: The Use and Manufacture of Tools by Animals*. New York: Garland STPM.

Blunden, C. and M. Elvin 1983. *Cultural Atlas of China*. Oxford: Phaidon; New York: Equinox Books.

Bonner, T. 1980. *The Evolution of Culture in Animals*. Princeton, NJ: Princeton University Press.

Braudel, F. 1981. *On History*. London: Weidenfeld and Nicolson.

Casimir, M. J. 1979. "An analysis of gorilla nesting sites of the Mt. Kahuzi region (Zaire)." *Folia Primatologica*, 32: 290–308.

Cowgill, G. 1993. "Beyond criticizing the New Archaeology." *American Anthropologist*, 95: 551–73.

Craib, J. L. 1986. "Casas de los antiguos: social differentiation in protohistoric Chamorro society, Mariana Islands." Unpublished PhD dissertation: University of Sydney.

David, N. 1971. "The Fulani compound and the archaeologist." *World Archaeology*, 3: 111–31.

Dayton, L. 2001. "The lost city." *New Scientist*, 169 (2273): 30–3.

De Boer, W. R. and D. W. Lathrap 1979. "The making and breaking of Shipibo-Conibo ceramics." In C. Kramer (ed.), *Ethnoarchaeology: Implications of Ethnography for Archaeology*, pp. 102–38. New York: Columbia University Press.

Elvin, M. 1973. *The Pattern of the Chinese Past.* London: Eyre Methuen.

Feinman, G. M. 1994. "Towards an archaeology without polarization." In J. Marcus and J. F. Zeitlin (eds.), *Caciques and their People: A Volume in Honor of Ronald Spores. Anthropological Papers. Museum of Anthropology, University of Michigan* 89: 13–43.

Fletcher, R. J. 1977. "Settlement studies (micro and semi-micro)." In D. L. Clarke (ed.), *Spatial Archaeology*, pp. 47–162. London: Academic Press.

Fletcher, R. J. 1981. "Space and community behavior." In B. Lloyd and J. Gay (eds.), *Universals of Human Thought: The African Evidence*, pp. 71–110. Cambridge: Cambridge University Press.

Fletcher, R. J. 1989. "Social theory and archaeology: diversity, paradox and potential." In J. R. Rhoads (ed.), *Australian Reviews of Anthropology. Mankind* 19 (1): 65–75.

Fletcher, R. J. 1992. "Time perspectivism, *Annales*, and the potential of archaeology." In A. B. Knapp (ed.), *Archaeology, Annales and Ethnohistory*, pp. 35–49. Cambridge: Cambridge University Press.

Fletcher, R. J. 1993. "The evolution of human behavior." In G. Burenhult (gen. ed.), *The First Humans, Vol. 1: The Illustrated History of Humankind*, pp. 17–29. St. Lucia: University of Queensland Press.

Fletcher, R. J. 1995. *The Limits of Settlement Growth: A Theoretical Outline.* Cambridge: Cambridge University Press.

Fletcher, R. J. 1996. "Organized dissonance in cultural message systems." In H. D. G. Maschner (ed.), *Darwinian Archaeologies*, pp. 61–86. New York: Plenum Press.

Fletcher, R. J. 2001. "Seeing Angkor: new views of an old city." *Journal of the Oriental Society of Australia*, 32–3: 1–27.

Fossey, D. 1983. *Gorillas in the Mist.* Boston, MA: Houghton Mifflin.

Fruth, B, and G. Hohmann 1996. "Nest building behavior in the great apes: the great leap forward?" In W. C. McGrew, L. F. Marchant, and T. Nishida (eds.), *Great Ape Societies*, pp. 225–40. Cambridge: Cambridge University Press.

Gould, S. J. 1965. "Is uniformitarianism necessary?" *American Journal of Science*, 263: 223–8.

Grant, M. 1990. *The Fall of the Roman Empire.* London: Macmillan.

Griaule, M. 1966. *Dieu d'eau : entretiens avec Ogotemmêli.* Paris: Fayard.

Groves, C. P. and J. Sabater-Pi 1985. "From ape's nest to human fix-point." *Man*, 20 (1): 22–47.

Hall, E. T. 1966. *The Hidden Dimension.* Garden City, NY: Doubleday.

Hermansen, G. 1978. "The population of imperial Rome." *Historia*, 27: 129–68.

Heyes, C. M. and B. G. Galef, Jr. (eds.) 1996. *Social Learning in Animals: The Roots of Culture.* San Diego: Academic Press.

Jacques, C. and M. Freeman 1997. *Angkor: Cities and Temples.* London: Thames and Hudson.

Keane, W. 1995. "The spoken house: text, act, and object in eastern Indonesia." *American Ethnologist*, 22 (1): 102–24.

Kennedy, P. 1989. *The Rise and Fall of the Great Powers: Economic Change and Military Conflict from 1500 to 2000.* London: Fontana Press.

Kroll, E. M. and T. D. Price (eds.) 1991. *The Interpretation of Archaeological Spatial Patterning.* New York: Plenum Press.

Lassner, J. 1970. *Topography of Baghdad in the Early Middle Ages: Texts and Studies.* Detroit, MI: Wayne State University Press.

Laurence, R. 1997. "Space and text." In R. Laurence and A. Wallace-Hadrill (eds.), *Domestic Space in the Roman World: Pompeii and Beyond*, pp. 7–14. *Journal of Roman Archaeology Supplement* 22, Portsmouth.

Le Strange, G. 1924. *Baghdad During the Abbasid Caliphate from Contemporary Arabic and Persian Sources* (reissue of 1900 edition). Oxford: Oxford University Press.

Lévi-Strauss, C. 1955. *Triste tropiques*. Paris: Librairie Plon.

Lowenthal, D. 1985. *The Past is a Foreign Country*. Cambridge: Cambridge University Press.

Lyons, D. 1995. "The politics of house shape: round vs rectilinear domestic structures in Dela compounds, northern Cameroon." *Antiquity*, 70: 351–67.

McGrew, W. C. 1992. *Chimpanzee Material Culture: Implications for Human Evolution*. Cambridge: Cambridge University Press.

Magdalino, P. 1995. "The grain supply of Constantinople." In C. Mango and S. Dagron (eds.), *Constantinople and its Hinterland*, pp. 35–47. Burlington VT: Variorum.

Manning, A. and M. S. Dawkins 1998. *An Introduction to Animal Behavior*. Cambridge: Cambridge University Press.

Matthew, W., C. French, T. Lawrence, and D. Culter 1996. "Multiple surfaces: the micromorphology." In I. Hodder (ed.), *On the Surface: Catalhoyuk 1993–95*: 301–42.

Mellaart, J. 1975. *The Neolithic of the Near East*. New York: Charles Scribner's Sons.

Morgan, D. 1988. *The Mongols*. Oxford: Blackwell.

Moule, A. C. 1957. *Quinsai with other notes on Marco Polo*. Cambridge: Cambridge University Press.

Murray, T. 1997. "Dynamic modelling and new social theory of the mid-to long term." In S. E. van der Leeuw and J. McGlade (eds.), *Time, Process and Structured Transformation in Archaeology*, pp. 449–63. One World Archaeology 26. London: Routledge.

Northedge, A. 1987. "Samarra." *Archiv. Fuer Orient-forschung* 34: 115–24.

Norwich, J. J. 1988. *Byzantium: The Early Centuries*. London: Viking.

Parker Pearson, M. 1998. "The beginning of wisdom." *Antiquity*, 72: 680–6.

Pottier, C. 1999. "Carte archéologique de la region d'Angkor. Zone sud." PhD thesis, 3 vols. Université Paris III – Sorbonne Nouvelle (UFR Orient et Monde Arabe).

Preucel, R. and I. Hodder 1996. "Preface." In R. Preucel and I. Hodder (eds.), *Contemporary Archaeology in Theory*, pp. xi–xii. Oxford: Blackwell.

Prussin, L. 1995. *African Nomadic Architecture: Space, Place, and Gender*. Washington, DC: Smithsonian Institution Press: National Museum of African Art.

Rafferty, J. 1985. "The archaeological record of sedentism: recognition, development and implications." In M. Schiffer (ed.), *Advances in Archaeological Method and Theory 8*: 113–56.

Rapoport, A. 1994. "Spatial organization and the built environment." In T. Ingold (ed.), *Companion Encyclopaedia of Anthropology*, pp. 460–502. London: Routledge.

Royce, H. (ed.) 1984. *Perspectives on Urban Infrastructure*. Washington, DC: National Academy Press.

Schaller, G. 1963. *The Mountain Gorillas: Ecology and Behavior*. Chicago: University of Chicago Press.

Steinhardt, N. S. 1990. *Chinese Imperial City Planning*. Honolulu: University of Hawaii Press.

Tainter, J. A. 1988. *The Collapse of Complex Societies*. Cambridge: Cambridge University Press.

Tilley, C. 1996. *An Ethnography of the Neolithic: Early Prehistoric Societies in Southern Scandinavia*. Cambridge: Cambridge University Press.

Trigger, B. G. 1989. *A History of Archaeological Thought*. Cambridge: Cambridge University Press.

Tschauner, H. 1996. "Middle-range theory, behavioral archaeology and postempiricist philosophy of science in archaeology." *Journal of Archaeological Method and Theory*, 3: 1–20.

Wakeman, F. E. 1985. *The Great Enterprise: The Manchu Reconstruction of Imperial Order in Seventeenth-Century China*. Berkeley: University of California Press.

Whitelaw, T. 1991. "Some dimensions of variability in the social organization of community space among foragers." In C. S. Gamble and W. A. Boismier (eds.), *Ethnoarchaeological Approaches to Mobile Campsites: Hunter-Gatherer and Pastoralist Case Studies*, pp. 139–88. Ann Arbor, MI: International Monographs in Prehistory.

Wright, A. F. 1967. "Changan." In A. Toynbee (ed.), *Cities of Destiny*, pp. 138–49. London: Thames and Hudson.

8

Archaeological Perspectives on Local Communities

Fokke Gerritsen

Introduction

The study of small social formations, while by no means a new area of archaeological interest, has been embraced with renewed enthusiasm in the last decade. In particular, household archaeology is acknowledged as a "certified" field of research, both in processual and postprocessual archaeology (see Hendon 1996 for a review of household archaeology debates up to the mid-1990s; Allison 1999). The archaeology of communities has not had the same recognition and the field is presently amorphous and little theorized. A recent edited volume is a rare attempt to date to address the topic through theoretically informed case studies (Canuto and Yaeger 2000).

In this chapter I want to take a closer look at the archaeology of communities (not to be confused with *community archaeology*, which normally refers to the area of public archaeology that aims to engage contemporary communities with their archaeological heritage). Are we dealing with one of the numerous themes that have been presented in recent years as new and important, have made a brief appearance on the catwalk, only to fall out of fashion even before their empirical potential was thoroughly explored? Or does it have the ingredients for a

longer shelf-life in archaeological practice? I have little doubt that it will keep a place in analysis and interpretation, and believe that this is a positive thing. But I equally feel that in order for the field to retain its current vigor it is necessary to look critically at the directions that have been taken recently and identify areas that are neglected or remain under-theorized.

This chapter is intended as a partial contribution to such an evaluation. It is partial because it is based mostly on literature concerning prehistoric agricultural societies in Western Europe. To a lesser extent the chapter takes an outsider's look at developments in North American archaeology. Moreover, I do not claim to be in any way exhaustive in my treatment of the theory and empirical potential of communities. By and large, I will not deal with matters of methodology. While the chapter touches on developments before the 1990s, it is not meant as a historical overview of the archaeology of settlements or communities.

A general trend in the social sciences of perhaps the last thirty years or so is to critically rethink and often deconstruct conceptualizations of social groups, be they nation, ethnic group, society, kin group, community, or even household. Generalizing greatly, one could say that this involves viewing social groups no longer as bounded units characterized by shared cultural norms. Instead, notions of overlapping, cross-cutting, and non-discrete networks of social relations are considered more pertinent (e.g., Anderson 1991; Kuper 1992; Hannerz 1992; Hutchinson and Smith 1996). Identity, both of individuals and collectives, has become a key concept. Groups mark themselves through the construction of symbolic boundaries, but these are highly permeable and temporal. That is to say that boundaries are felt to exist as they are constructed or maintained, but can be ignored in other situations (Cohen 1985). Boundaries can serve to hide internal contradictions and conflict, emphasizing differences between insiders and outsiders rather than between group members. Also common is the notion that social relationships within groups, down to those within the household, are political in nature.

Archaeology has picked up on this re-thinking of social groups, but to different extents regarding different social collectives. Many archaeologists have abandoned the normative understanding of archaeological cultures as bounded, cohesive entities based on shared material culture, customs, and beliefs. Recent approaches to ethnicity in archaeology emphasize its situational meaning and the importance of origin myths. The concept of ethnogenesis is used to study ethnicity as a historical process (Jones 1997; Derks and Roymans, in press). When it comes to smaller social formations (i.e., households and local communities), there is a remarkable divergence in the way in which archaeologists have incorporated ideas from the social sciences. Household archaeology has developed new ways of thinking about the constitution and social relationships of the domestic group. Archaeologists studying local communities and the settlement spaces they inhabit are just now beginning to engage in debates regarding the theoretical underpinnings of their field.

Recent Trends in Household Archaeology as a Comparison

Why do archaeologists feel that it is necessary to theorize small social formations? This may appear a superfluous question: is there any topic that would not benefit from being thought and written about at a theoretical level? But the question is relevant in another sense. The motivations to investigate, not only empirically, but also theoretically, small social formations provide insights into why some themes are currently addressed, as well as why others are not being addressed. For the reasons mentioned, it is easier to characterize ongoing developments in household archaeology than in the archaeology of the community. It is instructive to look briefly at the motivations that have led archaeologists in recent years to study households, as there are parallels and contrasts with debates on communities.

Household archaeology as it arose within processual traditions in the 1970s and 1980s was prompted largely by interest in socio-economic and ecological issues, leading to the development of themes such as household composition and organization, subsistence and ecological relationships, and household-level specialization (e.g., Flannery 1976; Wilk and Rathje 1982; Wilk and Ashmore 1988; cf. Allison 1999: 1–2, 8–9). One of the attractions of the household for issues such as these is that it can relatively easily be modeled as a building block of larger social and economic systems. As Wilk and Rathje (1982: 617–18) state, households are social groups that articulate directly with economic and ecological processes and therefore provide a level of analysis between individual artefacts and grand narratives. Their behavior can be archaeologically delineated and monitored as a result of the domestic, architectural setting of many of the household's activities of production and consumption. Many studies of settlements and village communities start (albeit often implicitly) from the same principles. At a larger scale, the settlement is also thought about as a socioeconomic unit within a regional or supraregional system of interaction. The local community is also envisaged as a unit that can be equated with an archaeologically definable spatial correlate, in this case usually the site or settlement territory (e.g., Kolb and Snead 1997).

More recently, alternative approaches to the study of small social formations have been developed. The household is felt to be a salient context of analysis because it offers possibilities to provide a theoretically informed counterweight against an archaeology focusing on processes, systems, and social evolution. "Big stories" about social and cultural change almost by definition refer to temporal and spatial scales that would have been meaningless to the people involved in those changes. An archaeology of everyday life allows the archaeologist to narrate smaller stories. The household provides an obvious context of research from this point of view, since the majority of a (prehistoric agricultural) society's population would have spent most of their time being part of a household. Such narratives are thus presumably closer to the experiences of life of people in the past than an archaeologist's reconstruction of long-term change can ever be. Expressed differently, the professed aim of much current household archaeology is to be able to write about a peopled past (Hodder and Preucel 1996: 426), or to do away with Ruth Tringham's (1991) by-now famous "faceless blobs."

For researchers of complex societies, an additional motivation to look at "regular" people and everyday life is to provide a counterweight to the heavy emphasis traditionally put on elite contexts, great monuments, chiefly or royal ceremonial centers, art, or prestige goods exchange (e.g., Pollock 1999).

Closely related are concerns emanating from current theoretical interests in gender issues (e.g., Tringham 1991; Nevett 1994; Lawrence 1999). The household is a logical place to begin increasing the visibility of women on the one hand and to expose and redress androcentric views of the past on the other. It contains the minimum unit of social reproduction, and as such the presence of women is guaranteed (Tringham 1991: 101). Ethnographic cases almost invariably bring out the significance of women in many of the domestic activities of production, consumption, and socialization. Moreover, contrary to views that emphasize the social and economic unity of the household, gender studies have stressed the political nature of domestic relationships (Yanagisako 1979; Hendon 1996: 46–7).

Finally, one can distinguish reasons to turn to households based on the theoretical argument that archaeology needs to develop ways to deal with human agency. Practice or structuration theory now informs many forms of archaeology and, for better or worse, it has been claimed to be the main source of theoretical inspiration since the general demise of systemic models (Dobres and Robb 2000). At least at a theoretical level, agency is generally ascribed by archaeologists to all socialized human beings in a society. This promotes a "bottom-up" perspective, maintaining that relationships between agency and structure need to be studied at very basic social levels, before larger processes of social and cultural change can be understood. Given that most people's agency primarily and most directly relates to the conditions of their daily life, the domestic group and its dwelling spaces are again obvious contexts of archaeological study.

All combined, these motivations to do household archaeology have stimulated a diversity of questions and themes of research. More so than before, households are viewed as socially rather than biologically or economically constituted. They are viewed as dynamic nodes of social relations and practices. Intra-household social relationships are now often the object of study, rather than taken for granted. Next to household production, consumption within the domestic context is being studied (e.g., Allison 1999: 8–9; Meadows 1999), shifting the focus away from the household as a building block of larger entities. The household's social and economic behavior is still an object of study (for example, craft specialization: Wright 1991), but so are issues of gender and identity, symbolic representation, ritual, temporality, and materiality (e.g., Hendon 1996; Brück 1999; Gerritsen 1999).

Partly, a desire can be recognized in these recent approaches to broaden the range of research themes. But a stronger element is the wish to steer archaeology away from the systems thinking and behavioral undertones of earlier approaches. The unfortunate side-effect of this, however, is that some lines of research that in themselves are worthwhile are no longer in vogue.

One area of research can be identified that despite the current popularity of household archaeology is receiving less, rather than more, attention than fifteen years ago. This is the question of the position of households and small communities in social and cultural change. The focus on practices of daily life stimulates detailed, small-scale, and synchronic studies, but at the same time appears to stand in the way of a perspective combining the small social scale with broader diachronic developments. While fully acknowledging the validity of archaeological interpretations that attempt to provide an alternative to dehumanized processes and structures, I would argue that the archaeological contexts of households are important and potentially rich sources for understanding long-term change. I will return to this topic at the end of this chapter, as it is equally an issue for the archaeology of communities.

Concepts of Community in Archaeology

Debates about the community have been a feature of anthropology and sociology for a century or more (Bell and Newby 1971; cf. Cohen 1985: 21–38, for a brief overview). One would have expected archaeologists,

therefore, to have been more explicit in their use of the concept of community. But with few exceptions, this is not the case. The main uses of the concept can be found in New World archaeology, which has focused on the community now and again (Hill 1970; Flannery 1976; Wilk and Ashmore 1988; Kolb and Snead 1997), and it is therefore perhaps not surprising that a recent collection of essays on the archaeology of the community was also given the subtitle *A New World Perspective* (Canuto and Yaeger 2000). In Western European archaeology, community discourses have only haphazardly entered settlement studies.

Settlement archaeology has long worked with a notion of the group of inhabitants of a settlement as a co-residential community. Major topics have traditionally been environmental adaptation, subsistence production, the use of space, and territoriality (cf. Brück and Goodman 1999 for a critique). The local group tends to be envisaged as an entity whose members share not only a common settlement or territory but also values, understanding of the world, interests, and goals. This conceptualization of the local group has been described as the "natural" community notion (Isbell 2000).

The natural community idea can be observed in many themes of settlement archaeology, but those relating to territoriality may be briefly mentioned as an example, because of the relationship between community and landscape that I will return to below. Territorial marker models have been applied to numerous prehistoric agricultural societies, often in conjunction with the use of analytical concepts such as site catchment analysis (Vita-Finzi and Higgs 1970) and Saxe's (1970) postulation regarding the establishment of formal cemeteries in situations whereby land or other critical resources become scarce. For example, Renfrew (1973, 1976) and Chapman (1981; but see also Chapman 1995) studied the appearance of megalithic monuments in the context of the spread of agriculture throughout Europe. According to their models, communities faced with a shortage of prime agricultural land erected megalithic (burial) monuments to demonstrate to outsiders the community's legitimate claim to a territory. The notion that land tenure is about relationships between social groups as much as between people and land was thus recognized by the authors. But the nature of the social group itself was not called into question. The fact that there was a social group was taken as a pre-given, and territoriality was studied as the means by which that group staked out and maintained control over land at the expense of other groups. This represents a form of the "natural" community concept.

There are several problems with the way that the notion of community has been applied in archaeology. One is the fact that a "natural" community concept is difficult to combine with an emphasis on human agency as a factor in shaping social relationships and identities. I am not overly concerned about this, and can accept the fact that the resolution of most archaeological data means that, irrespective of hopes raised by theoretical trends, it will be easier to distinguish collective rather than factional or individual representations of social reality. To me a bigger problem is the matter that social collectives and collective identities are constituted in historically and culturally specific ways. "Natural" community concepts often fail to take this into account. There is a justifiable need for etic definitions of local communities based on archaeological criteria, especially for comparative studies. But the question of the specific constitution of local communities needs to be addressed. This is crucial to be able to build any understanding of such issues as social change as it takes place in local settings, interactions between local groups, and between local groups and larger social networks. This means that we need to come to grips with problems of recognizing indigenous notions of social relationships and the ways in which those contributed to senses of community.

New Perspectives for the Archaeology of Communities

A group of authors that clearly also believe in the value of theorized community concepts are the contributors to the volume *The Archaeology of Communities: A New World Perspective* (Canuto and Yaeger 2000). Being a rare substantial treatment of the archaeology of communities, it deserves to be looked at in some detail in this chapter. In their introduction the editors argue for a study of communities that avoids reifying and essentializing the community, but instead investigates how communities are constructed through social interaction and agency (Canuto and Yaeger 2000: 5–9). One of the strong points of such a perspective is that it can recognize historically and culturally specific forms of communities; groups that form, perpetuate, or dissolve as indigenous definitions of collective and individual identity change. Moreover, it acknowledges that common residence or at least frequent interaction can be an important element of community construction, but holds that the forms of social interaction that foster community identities also take place in other spheres of social life.

Many of the contributors to the volume share these ideas. Their thinking about communities betrays the same concerns that were identified in recent approaches to household archaeology above. Practices of everyday life, agency, gender, and micropolitics figure prominently. Key questions that the authors try to resolve consider the ways in which communities and community identity are constituted. Most of the authors use categories of data that have traditionally been investigated within the realm of settlement archaeology; that is, architecture and the built environment (Preucel 2000; Mehrer 2000), spatial patterning of houses, public buildings and areas, and access routes within and between settlements (Yaeger 2000; Joyce and Hendon 2000; Pauketat 2000). The main differences with the studies of local communities that the authors criticize are therefore not so much in the use of empirical materials or even the forms of analysis, but with the questions asked and the concepts used. This raises the question whether the contributions demonstrate that earlier theories actually lead to empirically inferior images of the past or whether they (do no more than) offer additional perspectives. Not being familiar with the archaeological data that the contributors use, it is not up to me to answer this question.

In a review of the articles at the end of the volume, William Isbell (2000) characterizes the approaches of the contributors by setting up a dichotomy between natural and "imagined" community notions. The latter term he borrows from the anthropologist Benedict Anderson (1991), who used it to denote the ideologically constructed nature of nations, in which people that are often not even aware of each other's existence still share a feeling of solidarity and collective identity. This emotion is open to political manipulation by self-interested factions and individuals. Isbell maintains that similar social and political principles operate in much smaller social collectives. Local communities are equally fluid, cross-cut by other allegiances and competing identities. Its members should be seen as agents involved in promoting their own agendas and opposing those of others (Isbell 2000: 249–52).

Although Isbell divides the contributors into those that embrace the imagined community notion and those that have retained the natural community idea, not all imagined community authors envisage the individualistic, strategically operating agents that Isbell assumes to have populated past communities. Yaeger, for example, distinguishes three categories of practices in the construction of community identity at the Maya site of San Lorenzo (Yaeger 2000: 129–36). Local and supra-local practices of affiliation, including feasting, and the construction of a large house as well as a ritual complex, form two categories of practices that constitute and maintain collective identities in a discur-

sive manner. At the same time, the members of the community share bonds of solidarity and understanding that are based on largely non-discursive practices that form a local *habitus*. Yaeger identifies house orientation and spatial proximity, similarities in food production and processing equipment, and the shared use of a nearby quarry site as the main elements fostering a local sense of community. His perspective appears more balanced than Isbell's imagined community concept, as it offers a departure from assuming a reified, natural community without embracing a postmodern conceptualization of identity as fleeting strategy. To my mind, the dichotomy set up by Isbell is clarifying but ultimately not helpful for understanding premodern communities.

Several useful new directions of research are developed in the volume, but many of the case studies suffer from the fact that the interpretation is based on a single site, a single category of material, or a single phase in the histories of the respective communities studied. This is perhaps not a fair criticism, as one cannot expect authors to present a substantial treatment of a theme in the pages allotted in an edited volume of this kind. However, I bring it up because it seems to me to be symptomatic of much of the current literature dealing with small social formations, inter-human relations, or agency.

Are the questions of the social constitution of the community and the construction of identity the main or even the only issues to be investigated when it comes to communities? What about more "traditional" fields of interest, such as the ecological and economic basis of domestic practices or settlement patterns, the relationships of the community to larger social units and institutions, or the influence of outside historical forces on the development of communities? The danger in steering a field of research towards new perspectives is always that existing perspectives are problematized to a point where even asking the questions associated with an "old" perspective is condemned. But this is not necessary; in fact, it can be quite detrimental. I would argue that even though the conceptualization of communities may have lacked sophistication in the past, the questions that were asked have lost none of their value.

A case can be made that the most promising direction for an archaeology of communities incorporates a perspective of the group as a symbolic construct of identity – and hence puts questions regarding the constitution of the community – into questions considered more traditional. In order to be able to develop such a direction, it is useful to link the field of communities with current themes in landscape and settlement archaeology (e.g., Barrett 1994, 1999; Brück and Goodman 1999; Brück 2000; Gerritsen 1999, 2003; Kealhofer 1999).

Landscape, Locality, and the Study of Communities

Suggestions about relationships between a group's identity and the landscape it inhabits commonly evoke a certain amount of suspicion, and in some cases it should. But I am not concerned here with stereotypes of the kind: "people from around the Mediterranean are temperamental because they live in a warm climate," or "northerners are guarded and unforthcoming because where they live it rains most of the year," or worse. At a much more local scale, the inhabited landscape can be one of the elements constituting one's identity. Ethnographic studies indicate that feelings of belonging to a place, of having roots somewhere, and a sense that such localities are part of one's identity, are not unique to modern Western culture (Lovell 1998; Hirsch and O'Hanlon 1995). Senses of belonging can be highly individual, but they are equally powerful at a collective level. This is also recognized in some of the articles mentioned above (e.g., Bartlett and McAnany 2000; Joyce and Hendon 2000), but the implications of this for the constitution of communities are not further pursued. There is considerable potential

here for a fruitful perspective on local communities. I use the term *local* purposively here, to refer not only to the small scale of the group, but also to the fact that these are communities whose constitution is in some way affected by localities. It is important to keep in mind that local communities will always be cross-cut by identities not directly related to localities or localized social practices.

A basic tenet for such a perspective is that there is a reciprocal and dynamic relationship between humans and the landscape. By dwelling (*sensu*, Ingold 1993, 2000; Gerritsen 2003), humans order a landscape, both physically and mentally. In return, by being inhabited and inscribed with memory and cosmology, a landscape also creates and acts as an instrument in creating identities and social collectives. A crucial difference with a natural community concept is that these identities do not come about automatically through co-residence, but that they are constructed through social practices taking place in shared localities. The nature of these practices can vary greatly, and needs to be investigated.

The concept of dwelling is important because it privileges emic understandings of the world by the groups that are the object of study, without disregarding the insights that can be gained from studies of that world from the outside, for example through ecological research. Moreover, dwelling is an all-inclusive process, incorporating both the habitual, routinized actions of daily life and the discursive practices of ritual, ceremony, monument building, and the like. This forces the archaeologist to apply a broad perspective in the study of the construction of local communities. It is necessary to investigate all activities that ordered the landscape (in an archaeologically traceable way) and that may have contributed to a sense of community – or equally, how it may have been used to contest the community. This incorporates subsistence practices, the establishment of field boundaries, cattle drove-ways, resource procurement, house building and domestic activities, but also burial practices, rituals, or the construction and use of monumental structures. In the sense that all involve social interaction, they can all construct, maintain, or contest collective identities.

Perhaps the value of this perspective for an archaeology of communities can best be demonstrated with a brief case study drawn from my own research concerning the Iron Age (800–1 BC) in the southern Netherlands (Gerritsen 1999, 2003, with references to the relevant literature). Admittedly, this case is methodologically more straightforward than many others. There is some evidence for the presence of elites, some of whom were involved in long-distance exchange networks bringing them objects such as (rare) bronze drinking vessels manufactured in the Alpine regions (Roymans 1991). But until perhaps the very end of the Late Iron Age, there is nothing to suggest that these were land-holding elites or that their authority enabled them to influence the ways in which local communities organized their landscape. Archaeologically, this means that patterns of landscape organization give us a relatively direct insight into the ways in which those landscapes were perceived at a local level, and this in turn can suggest how identities were created through the interaction with the lived-in landscape.

During the Early Iron Age and the beginning of the Middle Iron Age (ca. 800–400 BC), burial practices involved cremation and the interment of the remains under an individual barrow, regularly in a ceramic urn. These mounds are usually round, of varying diameters but rarely exceeding 12–15 meters. Long barrows occur as well, in a few cases well over 100 meters long. In terms of gravegoods, the burial rituals seem to have been rather uniform, as gravegoods are rare and not very distinctive. More remarkable is the concentrated distribution of these barrows in dense urnfield cemeteries. About 260 urnfields have been located to date in the southern Netherlands. For 165 of these there are indications for use during the Early Iron Age or beginning of the

Middle Iron Age, but this figure should be taken as an absolute minimum. Even though the group that used a cemetery typically numbered around 20–40 people (which can be established in a number of cases of cemeteries that were (almost) completely excavated), many cemeteries must have contained well over a hundred or some hundreds of graves. Most urnfields were the collective cemeteries of a local group for the duration of several centuries (often beginning in the Late Bronze Age), suggesting that they formed foci of community identity in which the group's ancestors played a major role. Moreover, the long-standing bond between the community and its territory may have been represented symbolically through the urnfield.

This interpretation of the role of urnfield cemeteries can be reinforced by taking contemporary settlement practices into account. Farmsteads consisting of a farmhouse, in which both humans and animals dwelt, and several small outbuildings lay dispersed over the settlement territory. There is some evidence to suggest that farmsteads lay within extensive field systems, so-called Celtic fields. Typically, Early Iron Age farmsteads contain only a single farmhouse. This may show signs of repair and alteration, but once the timber-built farmhouse was evacuated, the whole farmstead was given up for habitation. This dispersion and lack of permanence in the settlement patterns at the level of individual farmsteads suggest that individual households did not establish long-standing bonds with localities within the settlement territory. I would suggest, therefore, that in this period local community identity was largely constructed through the shared use of a burial place, perhaps expressed in an idiom of shared ancestors. Collective rather than household-level tenurial practices may also have been an element in the constitution of identity.

Shortly after the end of the Early Iron Age (ca. 500 BC), urnfields ceased to be used for burying the dead. Cremation remained the normal form of body treatment, and the cremated remains were buried in a small pit, mostly without an urn. The erection of barrows over graves was much less common than before. Graves of this period tend to be dispersed, occurring singly or in small clusters of (at the very most) some tens of graves. While dating evidence from these clusters is often scarce, their small size makes it unlikely that they were in use for significant periods of time. This suggests that the group of people sharing a location for burying the dead became smaller, and that more frequently than in the Early Iron Age, burial locations were given up in favor of a new place.

If my interpretation of the urnfields as central localities in the construction of local communities and shared identities holds any water for the Early Iron Age, then it follows that a significant change took place in the ways in which communities defined themselves when the urnfields were given up. This could have involved the dissolution of local communities as an element of the social order altogether, but the archaeological evidence suggests that this was not the case. Instead, communities of the Middle and Late Iron Age appear to have used other social practices and symbols in the constitution of communities.

Small ditched enclosures that are generally interpreted as local cult places comprise one type of locality that may have functioned as such. They date to the Middle and Late Iron Age and continue into the Early Roman period, but do not occur in large enough numbers to allow us to ascertain their significance in the constitution of local communities throughout the southern Netherlands. Another change in the organization of the landscape occurring after about 300 BC takes place in the settlement patterns. Farmsteads gradually become more fixed elements in the landscape, the farmhouse being rebuilt at the same location several times. When a farmstead "moves," the distance over which this takes place is smaller than before. This change in settlement patterns may well have been accompanied by the development of more stable agricultural practices, but it would also have made farmsteads more permanent features of the landscape in which local groups dwelt.

Given the absence of collective cemeteries (I do not consider the earlier urnfields that were still part of the landscape but no longer in use, to have continued to function in the same way in the constitution of communities, as that is something that occurs through social interaction), I would interpret the evidence as showing two processes. The first is a change in the way in which local communities defined themselves. Even though size, structure, or place of these communities in larger social networks may not have changed all that much, this alteration in community constitution does raise questions about how and why social practices were transformed during this period. The second is a greater emphasis on the household or family group within local social networks. The long-standing farmstead would have been a highly appropriate symbol to express the identity or permanence of a family group, as well as its long-established relationship with the land surrounding the farmstead. If the urnfields were the territorial markers of local communities during the Early Iron Age, then during the Middle and Late Iron Age the farmstead may have become a symbol expressing the tenurial claims of individual families.

The transition taking place shortly after the middle of the first millennium BC in the southern Netherlands can be understood as a transformation of locally significant identities. Given that social life in this period and region took place to a large extent within local contexts, it must have been a fundamental transformation. It is very much a social and cultural change, the combined result of the intended and unintended outcomes of actions by human agents. But is this the full picture? Does this interpretation give us sufficient insight into why this transformation may have come about? Or should we look further and attempt to identify outside factors that acted as incentives towards change? In this particular case study, such a "search" suggests that this transformation took place during the same period as a region-wide concentration of settlement territories into the more fertile parts of the landscape and an abandonment of many parts of the landscape that were previously inhabited. This suggests that the observed social and cultural changes need to be linked in some way to (long-term) processes of soil degradation and demographic change (Roymans and Gerritsen 2002). These are precisely the kinds of factors that are frequently ignored in many current, agency-theory inspired studies.

Issues of Social and Cultural Change

Taking a comparative (i.e., different types of data) but more importantly a diachronic perspective can strengthen interpretive studies such as the one described above. But there are also other reasons why I think the archaeology of communities and other small social formations should concern itself with issues of social and cultural change.

Human agency, operating within structures and with the inherent potential to change those structures, has come to be seen as a crucial dynamic of social and cultural change. It is a principle that is straightforward enough as a theoretical position, but extremely difficult to put into practice archaeologically outside situations in which the actions of historical figures are known (e.g., Johnson 2000). Prehistoric archaeology is reliant on an application of practice theory, whereby the role of human agency in archaeologically observed changes is assumed rather than demonstrated. It means leaving room in our accounts for self-awareness, for internal contradiction and conflict, and especially for historical contingency, without being able to pinpoint the role and effects of human agency. The longer the time-frame over which changes are studied, the more generalized the incorporation of agency becomes. I would argue that this

need not be so troubling, and certainly that it is no reason to return to models of social change in which humans are passively reacting to outside forces.

But the difficulties in relating the effects of the actions by human agents to archaeologically inferred social and cultural change appear to steer many archaeologists studying small social formations away from considerations of structural change. For example, of the ten case studies in *The Archaeology of Communities*, only three explicitly try to come to grips with the role of human agency in social change (Pauketat 2000; Mehrer 2000; Preucel 2000). It is quite ironic that a theoretical perspective of which the value is supposed to derive from its potential to give better accounts of social and cultural change, leads in current archaeological practice to a paucity of substantial studies of change. It should be noted, however, that agency is being brought into models of social and cultural change in some other fields of archaeology related to the study of increasing social complexity (e.g., Joyce 2000; Clark 2000).

I have no ready suggestions to solve this paradox, other than say that archaeologies of households and communities should not shy away from questions currently considered out of fashion. This includes questions about factors behind social change that are not internal to the community or the outcome of "bottom-up," agency-driven human actions. It is possible to accept that social and cultural change involves human agency, while simultaneously accepting that agency is partly used to react to new situations that humans are confronted with but which have come about outside of their control. Here one has to include quite "traditional" factors: demographic growth, climate change, or changes in the availability of natural resources. Furthermore, one can think of outside political authority, conquest, or long-distance trade. These occur in history, and can forcefully demand human reaction. Accounts of history that only identify root causes and assume that human reactions to them are predictable are clearly falling short of what archaeology should attempt to do. Equally, accounts of history that assign centrality to human agency but fail to identify where and how that agency was used to deal with forces from outside the agents' community, class, or society are not going to bring us any further.

This is true for archaeology in general, but it certainly pertains to the archaeology of households and communities. The point referred to above by Wilk and Rathje (1982: 617–18) that households (and local communities) articulate directly with economic and ecological processes and therefore provide a level of analysis between individual artefacts and grand narratives, may have been expressed in an idiom of processual archaeology, but it is valid nonetheless. Small

social formations may be small. They may be relatively autonomous in their self-definition, the organization of domestic space, or the internal division of labor. But they cannot be studied in a vacuum.

More generally, a question that archaeology needs to deal with in this respect is how views of domestic life as lived by knowledgeable agents can be integrated with models of (long-term) structural change. Or, if integration proves impossible epistemologically, how we can write narratives or reconstructions of the past that accept plurality in explanatory models. These are surely questions without easy answers, but the endeavor should be worth the effort. I believe that a theoretically informed archaeology of communities can offer fruitful ways to make a beginning.

References

Allison, P. M. (ed.) 1999. *The Archaeology of Household Activities*. London: Routledge.

Anderson, B. 1991. *Imagined Communities: Reflections on the Origins and Spread of Nationalism*, 2nd edn. London: Verso.

Barrett, J. C. 1994. *Fragments from Antiquity: An Archaeology of Social Life in Britain, 2900–1200 BC*. Oxford: Blackwell.

Barrett, J. C. 1999. "The mythical landscapes of the British Iron Age." In W. Ashmore and A. B. Knapp (eds.), *Archaeologies of Landscape: Contemporary Perspectives*, pp. 253–65. Oxford: Blackwell.

Bartlett, M. L. and P. A. McAnany 2000. " 'Crafting' communities: the materialization of formative Maya identities." In M. A. Canuto and J. Yaeger (eds.), *The Archaeology of Communities: A New World Perspective*, pp. 102–22. London: Routledge.

Bell, C. and H. Newby 1971. *Community Studies: An Introduction to the Sociology of the Local Community*. New York: Praeger.

Brück, J. 1999. "Houses, lifecycles and deposition on Middle Bronze Age settlements in southern England." *Proceedings of the Prehistoric Society*, 65: 1–22.

Brück, J. 2000. "Settlement, landscape and social identity: the Early–Middle Bronze Age transition in Wessex, Sussex and the Thames Valley. *Oxford Journal of Archaeology*, 19: 273–300.

Brück, J. and M. Goodman 1999. "Introduction: themes for a critical archaeology of prehistoric settlement." In J. Brück and M. Goodman (eds.), *Making Places in the Prehistoric World: Themes in Settlement Archaeology*, pp. 1–19. London: University College London Press.

Canuto, M. A. and J. Yaeger (eds.) 2000: *The Archaeology of Communities: A New World Perspective*. London: Routledge.

Chapman, R. 1981. "The emergence of formal disposal areas and the 'problem' of Megalithic tombs in prehistoric Europe." In R. Chapman, I. Kinnes, and K. Randsborg (eds.), *The*

Archaeology of Death, pp. 71–81. Cambridge: Cambridge University Press.

Chapman, R. 1995. "Ten years after – megaliths, mortuary practices, and the territorial model." In L. A. Beck (ed.), *Regional Approaches to Mortuary Analysis*, pp. 29–51. New York: Plenum.

Clark, J. E. 2000. "Towards a better explanation of hereditary inequality: a critical assessment of natural and historic human agents." In M. A. Dobres and J. Robb (eds.), *Agency in Archaeology*, pp. 92–112. London: Routledge.

Cohen, A. P. 1985. *The Symbolic Construction of Community*. Chichester: Ellis Horwood.

Derks, T. and N. Roymans (eds.) in press. *Ethnic Constructs in Antiquity: The Role of Power and Tradition*. Amsterdam: Amsterdam University Press.

Dobres, M. A. and J. Robb 2000. "Agency in archaeology: paradigm or platitude?" In M. A. Dobres and J. Robb (eds.), *Agency in Archaeology*, pp. 3–17. London: Routledge.

Dobres, M. A. and J. Robb (eds.) 2000. *Agency in Archaeology*. London: Routledge.

Flannery, K. (ed.) 1976. *The Early Mesoamerican Village*. New York: Plenum.

Gerritsen, F. A. 1999. "To build and to abandon: the cultural biography of late prehistoric houses and farmsteads in the southern Netherlands." *Archaeological Dialogues*, 6: 78–114.

Gerritsen, F. A. 2003. *Local Identities: Landscape and Community in the Late Prehistoric Meuse-Demer-Scheldt Region*. Amsterdam: Amsterdam University Press.

Hannerz, U. 1992. "The global ecumene as a network of networks." In A. Kuper (ed.), *Conceptualizing Society*, pp. 34–56. London: Routledge.

Hendon, J. A. 1996. "Archaeological approaches to the organization of domestic labour: household practice and domestic relations." *Annual Review of Anthropology*, 25: 45–61.

Hill, J. N. 1970. *Broken K Pueblo: Prehistoric Social Organization in the American Southwest*. Tucson: University of Arizona Press.

Hirsch, E. and M. O'Hanlon (eds.) 1995. *The Anthropology of Landscape: Perspectives on Space and Place*. Oxford: Oxford University Press.

Hodder, I. 1992. *Theory and Practice in Archaeology*. London: Routledge.

Hodder, I. and R. Preucel (eds.) 1996. *Contemporary Archaeology in Theory*. Oxford: Blackwell.

Hutchinson, J. and A. D. Smith (eds.) 1996. *Ethnicity*. Oxford: Oxford University Press.

Ingold, T. 1993. "The temporality of the landscape." *World Archaeology*, 25 (2): 152–74.

Ingold, T. 2000. *The Perception of the Environment: Essays on Livelihood, Dwelling and Skill*. London: Routledge.

Isbell, W. 2000. "What we should be studying: the 'imagined community' and the 'natural community'." In M. A. Canuto and J. Yaeger (eds.), *The Archaeology of Communities: A New World Perspective*, pp. 243–66. London: Routledge.

Johnson, M. 2000. "Self-made men and the staging of agency." In M. A. Dobres and J. Robb (eds.), *Agency in Archaeology*, pp. 213–31. London: Routledge.

Jones, S. 1997. *The Archaeology of Ethnicity: Constructing Identities in the Past and Present*. London: Routledge.

Joyce, A. A. 2000. "The founding of Monte Alban: sacred propositions and social practices." In M. A. Dobres and J. Robb (eds.), *Agency in Archaeology*, pp. 71–91. London: Routledge.

Joyce, R. A. and J. A. Hendon 2000. "Heterarchy, history and material reality: 'communities' in Late Classic Honduras." In M. A. Canuto and J. Yaeger (eds.), *The Archaeology of Communities: A New World Perspective*, pp. 143–60. London: Routledge.

Kealhofer, L. 1999. "Creating social identity in the landscape: Tidewater, Virginia, 1600–1750." In W. Ashmore and A. B. Knapp (eds.), *Archaeologies of Landscape: Contemporary Perspectives*, pp. 58–82. Oxford: Blackwell.

Kolb, M. J. and J. E. Snead 1997. "It's a small world after all: comparative analyses of community organization in archaeology." *American Antiquity*, 62: 609–28.

Kuper, A. 1992. *Conceptualizing Society*. London: Routledge.

Lawrence, S. 1999. "Towards a feminist archaeology of households: gender and household structure on the Australian goldfields." In P. M. Allison (ed.), *The Archaeology of Household Activities*, pp. 121–41. London: Routledge.

Lovell, N. (ed.) 1998. *Locality and Belonging*. London: Routledge.

Meadows, K. 1999. "The appetites of households in Early Roman Britain." In P. M. Allison (ed.), *The Archaeology of Household Activities*, pp. 101–20. London: Routledge.

Mehrer, M. W. 2000. "Heterarchy and hierarchy: the community plan as institution in Cahokia's polity." In M. A. Canuto and J. Yaeger (eds.), *The Archaeology of Communities: A New World Perspective*, pp. 44–57. London: Routledge.

Nevett, L. 1994. "Separation or seclusion? Towards an archaeological approach to investigating women in the Greek Household in the fifth to third centuries BC." In M. Parker Pearson and C. Richards (eds.), *Architecture and Order: Approaches to Social Space*, pp. 98–112. London: Routledge.

Pauketat, T. R. 2000. "Politicization and community in the pre-Columbian Mississippi valley." In M. A. Canuto and J. Yaeger (eds.), *The Archaeology of Communities: A New World Perspective*, pp. 16–43. London: Routledge.

Pollock, S. 1999: *Ancient Mesopotamia*. Cambridge: Cambridge University Press.

Preucel, R. W. 2000. "Making pueblo communities: architectural discourse at Koyiti, New Mexico." In M. A. Canuto and J. Yaeger (eds.), *The Archaeology of Communities: A New World Perspective*, pp. 58–77. London: Routledge.

Renfrew, C. 1973. "Monuments, mobilization and social organization in Neolithic Wessex." In C. Renfrew (ed.), *The Explanation of Culture Change: Models in Prehistory*, pp. 539–58. London: Duckworth.

Renfrew, C. 1976. "Megaliths, territories and populations." In S. J. de Laet (ed.), *Acculturation and Continuity in Atlantic Europe, Mainly During the Neolithic Period and the Bronze Age. Papers Presented at the 4th Atlantic Colloquium, Ghent 1975*, pp. 198–220. Brugge: De Tempel.

Roymans, N. 1991. "Late urnfield societies in the northwest European plain and the expanding networks of central European Hallstatt groups." In N. Roymans and F. Theuws (eds.), *Images of the Past: Studies on Ancient Societies in Northwestern Europe*, pp. 8–89. Amsterdam: Instituut voor Pre-en Protohistorische Archeologie.

Roymans, N. and F. A. Gerritsen 2002. "Landscape, ecology and *mentalités*: A long-term perspective on developments in the Meuse-Demer-Scheldt region." *Proceedings of the Prehistoric Society*, 68: 257–87.

Saxe, A. 1970. "Social dimensions of mortuary practices." Unpublished PhD thesis, University of Michigan.

Tringham, R. 1991. "Households with faces: the challenge of gender in prehistoric architectural remains." In J. Gero and M. Conkey (eds.), *Engendering Archaeology: Women and Prehistory*, pp. 93–131. Oxford: Blackwell.

Vita-Finzi, C. and E. S. Higgs 1970. "Prehistoric economy in the Mount Carmel area of Palestine: site catchment analysis." *Proceedings of the Prehistoric Society*, 36: 1–37.

Wilk, R. and W. Ashmore 1988. *Household and Community in the Mesoamerican Past*. Albuquerque: University of New Mexico Press.

Wilk, R. and W. Rathje. 1982. "Household archaeology: building a prehistory of domestic life." In R. Wilk and W. Rathje (eds.), *Archaeology of the Household, American Behavioral Scientist* 25: 617–39.

Wright, R. P. 1991. "Women's labour and pottery production in prehistory." In J. Gero and M. Conkey (eds.), *Engendering Archaeology: Women and Prehistory*, pp. 194–223. Oxford: Blackwell.

Yaeger, J. 2000. "The social construction of communities in the Classic Maya Countryside: strategies of affiliation in western Belize." In M. A. Canuto and J. Yaeger (eds.), *The Archaeology of Communities: A New World Perspective*, pp. 123–42. London: Routledge.

Yaeger, J. and M. A. Canuto 2000. "Introducing an archaeology of communities." In M. A. Canuto and J. Yaeger (eds.), *The Archaeology of Communities: A New World Perspective*, pp. 1–15. London: Routledge.

Yanagisako, S. 1979. "Family and household: the analysis of domestic groups." *Annual Review of Anthropology*, 8: 161–205.

9

Archaeology and Technology

Kevin Greene

Why Take an Interest in Technology?

It is a commonplace that one of the principal attractions of archaeology is its focus upon material evidence for the past. Artefacts, structures, and even landscapes made by people have physical dimensions that invite technical description and analysis. I offer one recent example to show why I find the combination of archaeology and technology especially interesting. Excavation (under difficult rescue conditions) of two deep timber-lined pits in London in 2001 revealed remains of Roman mechanical water-lifting equipment (Blair 2002). Greek and Roman mechanical technology is a well-established field of study that until recently was based almost entirely upon documentary sources. Integrated study of written evidence and archaeological finds has transformed not only our understanding of what existed and how it worked, but also the extent to which inventions and innovations were applied in practice (Oleson 1984; Wilson 2002). This London discovery did not just offer an opportunity to investigate the finds from an engineering point of view; it also demonstrated that knowledge of such machinery was not restricted to the sophisticated Greek scholars of Alexandria, and that it was actually put to use in Rome's most northerly province. I had published

articles in 1990 and 1992 that stressed the "appropriateness" of much Graeco-Roman technology and the opportunities that the Roman Empire offered for technology transfer. I was understandably excited to hear that archaeological excavation had contributed more information relevant to this issue.

Unfortunately, publicity about the London bucket-chains also revealed underlying attitudes to the interpretation of technology that I find exasperating. National pride was invoked on the grounds that Britain could now match anything known in Rome or Alexandria, and the *Daily Telegraph* identified the start of the Industrial Revolution in second-century AD London. This demonstrated the strength of a tradition of triumphalism, with an underlying paradigm of progress, that has characterized so much general writing about the history of technology (Greene 1993). Trevor Williams' book *The Triumph of Invention: A History of Man's Technological Genius* (1987) exemplifies this phenomenon. Titles of this kind distract attention from alternative approaches to the history of technology, such as "social construction," and ignore modifications to nineteenth-century linear concepts of biological and social evolution. I acknowledge that there have been major developments in technology (for example, the adoption of metallurgy) and innovative feats of engineering (suspension bridges, steam-powered ships), but I like their study to be placed in a social setting.

Archaeology's unique ability to recover ordinary, everyday data can encourage an alternative approach that pays attention to appropriate technology rather than triumphalism. The Intermediate Technology Development Group (a charity inspired by Schumacher's *Small is Beautiful* (1973)) tackles "Third World" economic problems by encouraging "low" technology solutions that require modest capital investment, use local materials and labor, and improve the incomes of ordinary people. Established businesses are more likely to import "high" technology, which is expensive to purchase and maintain, and may reduce local employment. Economic globalization and climate change (exacerbated by the waste products of industrialized countries) have reinforced Schumacher's message. His book's subtitle – *A Study of Economics as if People Mattered* – underlines the importance of thinking about social circumstances which technical change may enhance, transform, or destroy.

Long-term history, whether written by the "Annales school" in the mid-twentieth century or by Horden and Purcell at the beginning of the twenty-first, creates space within which material evidence gains significance as the effects of short-term political events diminish. In addition, anthropology and cultural studies have placed more emphasis upon physical artefacts and structures in recent years, while historians of modern technology have been looking closely at social contexts and factors – such as gender – that have not been given sufficient prominence in the past. The time is ripe for even greater integration between archaeology, anthropology, and the history of technology. The World Archaeological Congress held at Southampton in 1986 included a theme session about "The social and economic contexts of technological change," subsequently published under the rather more dynamic

title *What's New? A Closer Look at the Process of Innovation* (Leeuw and Torrence 1989). The editors described the session as "the only main theme . . . that was conceived of as being in the non-fashionable, functional and technological sphere" (p. xix). The many contributions to *What's New?* raised the subject of the *context* of technology and innovation to a sophisticated level, drawing upon case studies from all over the world. Michael B. Schiffer has carried the battle forward over the last decade with increasing confidence:

> We need to develop a unified behavioral science in which the technological, social, and ideological aspects of activities are studied together, along with their artefacts, over time. The artificial divisions of scientific inquiry that have arisen in our own society have to be transcended. Technological science, social science, and ideological science are but fragmentary inquiries that must merge if we are to arrive at the laws of behavioral change. (Schiffer 1992: 130–41)

> That, today, there is a coincidence of high interest in technology among both archaeologists and sociocultural anthropologists presents us with a rare opportunity to foster collaboration and synergies . . . More than that, archaeologists and sociocultural anthropologists together can explore technology studies as one possible mechanism for reintegrating a fragmenting field. (Schiffer 2001: 1–2)

I do not share Schiffer's belief in the possibility of determining behavioral laws, but would commend his study of *The Portable Radio in American Life* (Schiffer 1991) to anyone skeptical about the collecting and technical study of modern industrially produced consumer artefacts. This book is actually a radical rewriting of received wisdom about twentieth-century industrial economics, firmly based upon material culture:

> Perhaps only an archaeologist, equally at home in discussions of technical detail and of social change, would be foolhardy

enough to tackle a product history holistically. But we really have no choice if there is to be an alternative to personal histories, narrow technological and social histories, and cryptohistories dished out by corporations. (Schiffer 1991: 4)

History of Technology

Grand narratives

"History of technology" is a dynamic field ranging from technical studies of devices and systems to subtle anthropological observations of the context of their invention and application, but in my experience, few archaeologists know much about it. The discipline is characterized both by superb fine-grained studies of techniques, innovations, and their contexts, and by rather clumsy overviews that ride slip-shod over prehistory, early history, and archaeological evidence. Archaeology and the history of technology share a tradition of drawing upon Grand Narratives such as "progress" or the special character of Western civilization, and both have made use of social and biological concepts of evolution for explanatory purposes (Basalla 1988). Since suspicion about the validity of narratives has been such an enduring feature of American historiography as well as European postmodernism since at least the 1960s, it is surprising to find essentialist progressive studies of technology flourishing in the 1990s. A recent North American overview that took an overtly anthropological perspective came under attack from a British anthropologist, Tim Ingold:

The comparative perspective is entirely absent, so that Adams can discuss the industrial revolution in Britain and the preeminence of American manufacture as though the rest of the world did not exist. Behind this, however, lies the assumption that the history of technology has been one of inevitable and accelerating progress toward modernity. To write in this evolutionary mode, one has only to deal with whatever culture or nation is judged to be at the cutting edge of innovation...From then on, the most adventurous and competent will supposedly pull the remainder of humanity along in their wake. To treat history thus, as a one-way advance from Pleistocene hunting and gathering to modern America, is to write off any alternative trajectories as blind alleys. (Ingold 1999a: 131–2; reviewing Adams' *Paths of Fire* (1996))

Underlying Ingold's criticism is the rarely stated but unavoidable issue of the construction of narratives. This means more than using historiographical analysis to reveal ideologies underlying approaches to archaeology or history (Kehoe 1998); behind everything are Hayden White's persistent and deeply disconcerting questions:

What is involved, then, in that finding of the "true story," that discovery of the "real story" within or behind the events that come to us in the chaotic form of "historical records"? What wish is enacted, what desire is gratified, by the fantasies that real events are properly represented when they can be shown to display the formal coherency of a story? (White 1987: 4)

Technology and culture

Ingold's review was published in this significantly named journal of the (American) Society for the History of Technology, which, according to its website, is "an interdisciplinary organization...concerned not only with the history of technological devices and processes, but also with the relations of technology to science, politics, social change, the arts and humanities, and economics" (http://shot.press.jhu.edu/). *Technology and Culture* began publication in 1958 and is "an interdisciplinary journal, publishing the work of historians, engineers, scientists, museum curators, archivists, sociologists, anthropologists, and others, on topics ranging from architecture to agriculture to aeronautics." Archaeologists are conspicuously absent from this list, but are possibly subsumed within anthropologists. A British equivalent of *T&C* began publication in 1976: "The technical problems confronting different societies and periods, and the measures taken to solve them, form the concern of this annual collection of essays...In addition, *History of Technology* explores the relation of technology to other aspects of life – social, cultural and economic – and shows how technological development has shaped, and been shaped by, the society in which it occurred" (back cover of volume 22 for 2000).

Thus, to judge from the stated aims of two leading periodicals, the history of technology should overlap to a considerable extent with archaeology, for both express a strong concern with social and cultural aspects of technology. After all, historians of technology make use of evidence that may be considered "archaeological" whenever they study material culture, especially sites, structures, or artefacts. In practice archaeologists rarely contribute to *Technology and Culture* or *History of Technology*, and the great majority of papers about early periods that *have* appeared in either journal concern Graeco-Roman engineering (possibly because it has a respectable cousin, Greek science).

The history of technology as an academic discipline has undergone theoretical shifts in recent decades very similar to those that have affected archaeology (Fox 1996). In terms of relevance to archaeology, I would single out social construction of technology (Bijker 1995); its acronym SCOT describes the approach of a number of American and European scholars, primarily concerned with modern technology, who emerged in the 1980s. The *locus classicus* is *The Social Construction of Technological Systems* (Bijker et al. 1987). The zeal of SCOT has not been universally welcomed; like "New Archaeology" in the 1960s, SCOT's claims carried the irritating implication that everyone else engaged in the field had been missing the point.

Phenomenology and actor-network theory

As in archaeological theory, praxis philosophy and phenomenology were particularly influential in the 1980s and 1990s – especially because Heidegger wrote extensively about technology (Lovitt and Lovitt 1995). In common with postprocessual archaeology, the impact of postmodernism (or at least reflexive modernism) is most clearly visible in highly specific cultural/anthropological analyses of individual technologies and their contexts, rather than broader processes. For exponents of actor-network theory, "intuition about the identity of 'technology' is called into question. The distinctions between human and machine, knowledge and action, engineering and the study of engineering practices are all 'blown up.' We find that sociologists of technology are actually contributing to the development of technology!" (Bijker et al. 1987: 6). There is a parallel between this sentiment and the use of structuration theory in archaeology, according to which people create material culture that reproduces social life but are simultaneously structured and constrained by it (Barrett 2001).

Bruno Latour's fascinating study of *Aramis* (a failed French plan for an automated train system) connected technology with another major twentieth-century cultural preoccupation, "the text":

I have sought to offer humanists a detailed analysis of a technology sufficiently magnificent and spiritual to convince them that the machines by which they are surrounded are cultural objects worthy of their attention and respect. They'll find that if they add interpretation of machines to interpretation of texts, their culture will not fall to pieces; instead, it will take on added density. I have sought to show technicians that they cannot even conceive of a technological object without taking into account the mass of human beings with all their passions and politics and pitiful calculations, and that by becoming good sociologists and good humanists they can become better engineers and better informed decision-makers. (Latour 1996: vii–viii)

Gendered and ethnic perspectives

Another parallel with archaeological theory in recent decades can be found in the work of many writers who have examined groups – especially women (Wajcman 1995) – whose importance has been underplayed in traditional accounts of the history of technology. Gendered perspectives take the SCOT position in a new direction, for innovations are not just "socially shaped": "feminists have further demonstrated that this 'social' in which the shaping occurs, often interpreted as class relations, is also a matter of gender relations" (Cockburn and Ormrod 1993: 7). Terry and Calvert's criticism of the narrow material view of technology held by archaeologists and physical anthropologists may do an injustice to those who study the cognitive implications of prehistoric stone tools, but it underlines the danger of a paradigm of progress: "tools signify culture and civilization, distinguishing Man [*sic*] from other species of life and providing evidence of his superior relation to the natural world... Critics of this positivist and laudatory definition of technology begin by asking whose lives are being enhanced through technological development" (Terry and Calvert 1997: 2; the "*sic*" is theirs).

The problem for archaeologists is, as ever, a deficiency in evidence, and this necessitates interpretation based on analogy rather than observation. It is all very well for prehistorians to conduct ethnoarchaeological research among hunter-gatherers, but only modern-world historical archaeologists will ever have the luxury of examining an artefact through all stages – from invention to production to consumption, with testimony from living witnesses – in the manner achieved by Cockburn and Ormrod:

Some of the concepts developed in the social constructivist and actor network studies have furnished us with a language to use in our study of the microwave oven. First, science and technology are culture. Ideas and artefacts are social constructs, the outcome of negotiation between social actors, both individuals and groups. To explain a technological development we need to identify the people involved, observe what they do, what they say and how they relate. (Cockburn and Ormrod 1993: 9)

A question of confidence

"Why is it that our best scholarship gets so little recognition outside our circle?... Among ourselves we stipulate the historical significance of technology and accept without evidence the proposition that technology has enormous explanatory power. Others need to be convinced" (Roland 1997: 713).

The powerful range of approaches to studying technology – social constructivism, actor-network theory, gender – appears to have increased this lack of confidence, even in a recent president of the Society for the History of Technology, who expressed a yearning for simplicity by recommending that "seemingly obsolete approaches to technological history might have more significance and value to certain groups who might have use for our scholarship than our latest, most avant-garde work" (Reynolds 2001: 524). My own perception is exactly the opposite: archaeologists and historians would derive considerable benefit from studying the way in which the history of technology has developed over recent decades. The current editor of *Technology and Culture*, John Staudenmaier, published a book in 1985 that traced trends in articles in that journal up to the 1980s. It acknowledged the issue of narrativization in its metaphorical title, *Technology's Storytellers: Reweaving the Human Fabric*, and concluded with an explicitly reflexive statement that is, surely, the mark of a confident subject:

By its nature contextual history is a vulnerable process in which the historian is deeply affected by the humanity of the subject matter. To reject as ahistorical the ideology of autonomous progress is to recognize that technological designs are intimately woven into the human tapestry and that all of the actors in the drama, including the story-teller, are affected by tensions between design and ambience. By telling the stories of technological developments while re-specting the full humanity of the tale, the contextual scholar rescues technology from the abstractions of progress talk and, in the process, takes part in the very ancient and very contemporary calling of the historian, reweaving the human fabric. (Staudenmaier 1985: 201)

Defining Technology

Defining technology is a complex matter (Sigaut 1994: 422–3). To an archaeologist, the study of "lithic technology" implies much more than simply identifying and classifying stone tools; it will probably involve materials science, use-wear analysis, study of raw ma-terials and waste products, and the experi-mental production and testing of replicas. There may be an attempt to arrange the actions and processes involved into a se-quence (chaîne opératoire) – probably with help from ethnoarchaeology (Sigaut 1994: 426–30; Dobres and Hoffman 1999: 124–46). The terms technology or industry are also a shorthand way of grouping artefacts together in order to highlight changes, for example the use of carefully prepared flakes and blades as opposed to core tools in the Palaeolithic period. Techniques suggesting an increase in manual dexterity are seen as indicators of cognitive development, which is then extrapolated to behavior and commu-nication. Technological change is more easily understood in later periods, for example when ironworking appeared at the end of the Bronze Age. Iron ore occurs very widely, unlike the ores of copper, tin, lead, and other metals that were alloyed into bronze. Iron was smelted, then forged into artefacts in solid form, while molten bronze was poured into molds. The organization and economics of Iron Age metallurgy would thus be likely to differ markedly from those of the preced-ing Bronze Age.

Ingold has emphasized the dangers of extending the definition too far: "Is there anything, the skeptic might ask, about human culture and social life that is not tech-nological? If not, what need is there for the concept of technology at all?" (Ingold 1999b: vii). My reply is that a pragmatically limited concept of technology enhances the import-ance of analyzing material culture with the help of analogy or interpretation derived from any other domain. David Edgerton has highlighted a different problem of defin-ition: "much, probably most, history of technology... was concerned not with the history of technology, but rather with the history of invention, innovation, and so on. That is not to say that histories of invention will not be of interest to historians, only that they will be of interest for different reasons" (Edgerton 2000: 186). Archaeologists working in prehistoric periods focus upon invention and innovation because the lack of contextual information from documen-tary sources restricts the depth in which ap-plication and utilization may be studied.

"Technology" in historical periods has dif-ferent usages and connotations. Classicists have traditionally drawn a clear line between science and technology, retaining something of the value judgments of the ancient world. The attitude expressed in Greek and Roman texts was that work of the mind is noble but that its application is demeaning. Similarly, in cultural regard today, "Greek science" stands in the same relationship to "Roman technology" as the Parthenon does to the Baths of Caracalla: elegance is preferred to utility. The application of water power to agriculture and industry has attracted little attention from classicists in comparison with architecture or science, whereas some medi-eval historians have presented water-powered machinery as a major intellectual step towards modernity, inseparable from religion and philosophy (e.g., Bloch 1935).

Thus, subjective distinctions between high and low technology, and what is considered appropriate in particular economic settings, are imposed upon the past in complicated ways that very much reflect the present.

Some forms of material equipment have long trajectories of development and modification – often invisible in the lifetimes of their makers and users – that most people would be happy to define as technological, and to relate to major economic and social change. Prehistoric axes were a favorite focus for nineteenth-century typological study. Their raw material changed from chipped or ground stone to bronze and finally iron, while their design maximized sharp durable cutting edges and ways of keeping the ax head firmly attached to a handle. Neolithic stone axes facilitated the creation of clearings and building timber structures, but nineteenth-century double-bitted steel axes expanded the industrial exploitation of North American forests and opened up enormous swathes of territory for settlement (Jager 1999). Boats have a long trajectory from dug-out logs to expanded log-boats, and from shell-like hulls constructed from edge-to-edge planks to "skeleton-first" frame-built ships. While the simplest boats might permit humans to reach Australia, frame-built ships with elaborate systems of masts, rigging, and sails were able to create, sustain, and exploit overseas colonies for European states.

Other material items are more difficult to define as technological; how should we regard coins, which came into existence fully-fledged in Asia Minor in the sixth century BC and developed hardly at all? Metallic coinage had profound socioeconomic effects, but having been rapidly popularized in Greece and formalized into a system of denominations in the Roman Empire, it underwent little further change in Europe before the modern period, when fully token currency (especially in the form of paper notes) became accepted. Military technology has similar problems of definition; the design and manufacture of weapons is clearly technological, but may not be as significant as institutional and ideological factors that determine the context and success of their use. In both shipbuilding and arms manufacture, working practices changed dramatically in modern times because of the use of mathematical calculations, drawn designs, and a demand for interchangeable parts, all of which interacted with the introduction of machine tools. Psychological and cognitive factors are as difficult to extricate from "practical" technology in this context as they are in the study of early hominid tool use.

Evolution

It is common for ideas about ages, typology, and social stages to be conflated with evolution, despite the care with which they have been separated in histories of archaeology. Glyn Daniel's (1943) pioneering account of the Three Age System stressed the secondary role of evolutionary thought, and Graslund (1987) pointed out that Christian Thomsen's work in early nineteenth-century Denmark relied on associations between artefacts in closed find contexts, not the application of an abstract evolutionary model. Herbert Spencer and Karl Marx both drew analogies between machinery and organisms, while Pitt Rivers' use of Darwinian evolutionary principles in artefact typology is well known among archaeologists (Channell 1991: 83–4). Schick and Toth used the term "techno-organic evolution" to describe how early stone tools and other synthetic artefacts allowed hominids "to move into new niches in competition with other animals"; thus, a stone flake is an analogue for flesh-cutting carnivore teeth, and a digging stick is an analogue for the snout and tusks of a pig (Schick and Toth 1993: 184–5).

Morgan's *Ancient Society* (1871) and Tylor's *Primitive Culture* (1871) discussed material culture in short introductory chapters before turning to detailed analysis of social structures; Engels made rather more of Morgan's material and economic dimensions for political reasons, of course. It is surprising to me that these great names of nineteenth-century archaeological and anthropological writing used social anthropology and studies of the technical succession of stone, bronze, and iron to provide support *for* biological evolution, rather than using biology as scientific evidence for social and material evolution:

> Among naturalists it is an open question whether a theory of development from species to species is a record of transitions which actually took place, or a mere ideal scheme serviceable in the classification of species whose origin was really independent. But among ethnographers there is no such question as to the possibility of species of implements or habits or beliefs being developed one out of another, for development in culture is recognized by our most familiar knowledge. Mechanical invention supplies apt examples of the kind of development which affects civilization at large. (Tylor 1871: 13)

V. Gordon Childe's influential writings related twentieth-century thinking about Marx and Engels' social stages to material evidence. They combined a Marxist understanding of the relationship between production and the social superstructure with a comprehensive knowledge of European and Near Eastern archaeology. In the 1940s to 1960s in North America, Taylor, Steward, and White also worked on the problems of bridging the gap between material culture and social evolution, and laid the foundations of processual archaeology (Trigger 1989: 289–328). Processualism offered a "scientific" method for relating artefacts, sites, landscapes, and ecosystems to societies, but ran the risk of encouraging determinism (an issue never far from the minds of students of technology: Smith and Marx 1994). However, its breadth of approach and insistence upon causes and effects operating within

an extensive system made processualism a perfect background for the emergence of behavioral approaches (such as Schiffer's) to the archaeology and anthropology of technology.

An idea of inevitability and/or autonomy survives within many evolutionary concepts; Jared Diamond's writing reveals that the specter of the Grand Narrative still looms over studies of technological development:

> Because technology begets more technology, the importance of an invention's diffusion potentially exceeds the importance of the original invention. Technology's history exemplifies what is termed an autocatalytic process: that is, one that speeds up at a rate that increases with time, because the process catalyzes itself. The explosion of technology since the Industrial Revolution impresses us today, but the medieval explosion was equally impressive compared with that of the Bronze Age, which in turn dwarfed that of the Upper Palaeolithic. (Diamond 1997: 258–9)

In contrast, Leonard has turned the tables upon evolution by stressing the value of a specifically archaeological contribution:

> The record of human evolution can be written only by archaeologists or by those working closely with them. Biological anthropologists may of course write evolutionary narratives of morphological changes in the human skeletal structure, but it is only archaeologists who can address the interaction between that biological structure and the technologies that, through time, constituted an ever larger component of the human phenotype. (Leonard 2001: 70)

Archaeology and Technology

Early prehistory

Clive Gamble has encapsulated change in the human past in five "big questions" about origins (of hominids; modern humans; agriculture and domestic animals; urbanism and civilization; modernity) and a sixth about global colonization by the human species (Gamble 2001: 157). Since the first four and much of the sixth took place in prehistoric times, the absence of written sources promotes the importance of material culture in any serious study of their technological dimensions. Tool making began at some point after the origins of hominids and became extraordinarily diverse among anatomically modern humans. The origins have been blurred by increased knowledge of the use of tools by living primates. Nobody watching chimpanzees using anvils and hammer-stones for cracking nuts, or flakes for cutting, could draw a clear dividing line between primate and hominid behavior on the criterion of tools (Schick and Toth 1993; Wynn 1994). The phrase "Man the Tool-Maker" popularized by Kenneth Oakley in the 1950s is a retroprojection of human qualities considered desirable in an industrial age, but it does draw attention to the significance of more systematic selection, modification, curation, and exploitation of chipped pebbles and flakes – alongside, presumably, perishable items such as digging sticks. Portable artefacts such as hand axes suggest more sophisticated concepts of time, distance, and natural resources than the temporary use of nearby stones by primates. This technological development has potentially profound implications for cognitive evolution and (indirectly) for the development of social behavior and language (Gibson and Ingold 1993).

Technology does seem an appropriate term to apply to the accelerating diversity of stone-working methods from the Lower to the Upper Palaeolithic. Mode 1 "Oldowan" pebble tools were supplemented by more carefully flaked Mode 2 "Acheulean" bifaces (Schick and Toth 2001: 54–74). Considerable forethought is revealed by Levallois technology, for cores were prepared so that standard flakes could be removed which could then be worked into a variety of tool types. However, any hope that a succession of modes of tool making might correlate neatly with stages in the physical evolution of human species seems ill-founded. In Europe and western Asia, for example, technical developments do not coincide well with the transition from Neanderthals to "anatomically modern" humans, although the latter went on to produce even more diverse Upper Palaeolithic blade industries (Klein 2001: 129). Although there were additional "modern" cultural practices such as bone carving, cave painting, personal ornamentation, and more careful burial of the dead, the sharp contrast drawn since the late nineteenth century between "Cro-Magnon" people and the Neanderthals they displaced may have been exaggerated. Fine technology, art, flatter foreheads, and prominent chins may promote a sense of continuity between us and our "modern" Upper Palaeolithic counterparts, but some negative assessments of Neanderthal capabilities can sound harsh (e.g., Klein 2001: 122–3). Did Neanderthals use fewer and simpler tools because they were physically stronger than modern humans?

Tools made from stone were only one part of late Stone Age technology (Bettinger 2001: 149–54). The atlatl (a spear-thrower made from bone or wood) multiplied human energy by extending the effective length of a thrower's arm and adding leverage. Much later, the bow propelled projectiles with even greater force by combining the tension of the bow and its string with the strength of both arms of an archer. Hunter-gatherers also extended their efficacy by means of traps and nets, made from organic materials and used on land and in water (Fischer 1995). Thus, the study of Mesolithic stone technology has lower status than that of earlier periods; the understanding of microliths is a matter of ethnoarchaeology rather than imagination. Neolithic polished stone axes are very attractive, and allow interpretation in terms of symbolism and economic anthropology as well as function, but changes in settlement and food production were more significant.

Neolithic revolution to urban revolution

Questions of definition are particularly prominent in the two revolutions identified by Childe in the 1930s, and concern both the nature of these "events" and their technological components (Childe 1936, 1942; Greene 1999). While the New Stone Age was originally defined by the appearance of a new stone toolkit, artefacts now seem of marginal significance beside the fundamental economic change from hunting and gathering to farming (a process long proposed independently by social evolutionists). The Neolithic is visible archaeologically through buildings and tools as well as domestication and settlement patterns, and coincides in many parts of the world with one of the great transforming technologies, the firing of clay to produce pottery. A broad definition of technology that envisages the adoption of settled farming as a "package" of ideas and practices in addition to material objects and structures would acknowledge that the "Agricultural Revolution" was indeed a major technological development. However, the size of the step may have been exaggerated by differences in theoretical approaches; Mesolithic studies are dominated by ecology and Neolithic studies by social anthropology. Postprocessual archaeology has favored ideological rather than technical explanations – for example, the development of concepts of the wild and the tame explored in Ian Hodder's account of neolithicization, *The Domestication of Europe* (1992).

Andrew Sherratt (1997) coined an attractive name – the "secondary products revolution" – for the later ramifications of the Neolithic revolution in which intensification of farming was accompanied by animal traction and long-distance exchange. This makes the "step up" to the urban revolution less clearcut, although Childe always believed that the growth of population made possible by the Neolithic revolution, along with the adoption of metallurgy, were essential preliminary factors in the development of urban settlements and their social hierarchies. Urbanism was frequently accompanied by one of the diagnostic features of civilization: writing. The invention of a means of storing information in the form of symbols impressed into clay tablets or carved on stone surfaces underlines the difficulty of differentiating between the role of the physical technology itself and the implications of the behavior involved. Unlike the printing press with movable type, the technological component of cuneiform is unsophisticated in comparison with the concept; nevertheless the invention of writing always appears with a flourish in general histories of technology: "The advent of writing is generally regarded as marking the transition from barbarism to civilization" (Williams 1999: 31).

Bronze Age and Iron Age

The introduction of metallurgy in the Old World has long been linked to narratives of social development. Bronze supposedly favored the emergence of elites controlling resources and skilled manufacture, while iron was a "democratic metal" that placed a cheap and widely available raw material into the hands of ordinary people, who could use it to improve everyday life through more efficient craft tools and farming implements (not to mention lethal weapons). However, the potential for developing and expressing social complexity has also been detected in stone tools, for example in Iberia during the transition from the Neolithic to the Copper Age (Forenbaher 1999). Steven Rosen's general study has contested the notion of a "simple 'rise' of metallurgy accompanied by a correspondingly simple 'fall' of flint" in the Levant (Rosen 1996: 131). He identified a phase of around 1,000 years before there was any decline in lithics; after this, flint axes were replaced by copper ones as a result of exchange systems and ease of manufacture rather than superior functional properties; the final decline occurred only with the ready availability of iron.

> Thus the primarily cultic functions of Chalcolithic metallurgy did not displace flint technology. Copper axe replacement of flint is a later occurrence, in essence a by-product of a technology initially developed for other purposes...Complex, long-term, undirected technological change, in many ways like biological evolution, can appear to be progressive and linear. This illusion can mask far more important cultural developments. (Rosen 1996: 151, 153)

Vandkilde's (1996) highly specific study of the stone to bronze transition in Denmark placed the whole process into a context of social power, ritual action, and increasing external contacts within which metalwork and metallurgy acted as a catalyst rather than a single causal agent. Furthermore, the conclusions of this analysis accord with the SCOT approach, and not only contradict Diamond's generalizations cited above, but also make a modest claim for broader application:

> Technology does not develop by itself (how could it possibly?); it has evolved due to human choices...One might therefore say that technology gains meaning only from its social context, and although we distinguish analytically between technology and social practice, this separation is hardly real. Hence, technology is probably devoid of any autonomy as a driving force in social transformation, whilst it is the fusion between technology and its social context that may be potentially important. Being aware of these relationships, it should still be legitimate to study the history of technology, in this case the earliest metallurgy. It may even prove useful to examine – in so far as data are available – the production of metalwork and the technological achievements of the early metal age, since the ever-present social link would imply that

information of wider significance may present itself. (Vandkilde 1996: 262)

Taylor (1999) has reminded us that modern preconceptions are informed both by ethnographic knowledge about contact between Europeans and non-metal using peoples and by modern industrial perceptions of the significance of metals. We should examine "materials-related behaviors" among the first metal-using communities and their archaeological correlates (p. 30). In the same way that students of cognitive evolution make much of the appearance of Oldowan stone tools, Taylor stresses the impact of copper:

> ...the first truly laterally cyclable artefactual product, which could be unmade and remade at will virtually *ad infinitum* without any necessary loss of basic material value. I believe that it is to be expected that there will be dramatic shifts in the depositional pattern of such a revolutionary material through time, and especially during the period of its inception. Such shifts would be underscored by the fact that the new material was also "good for thinking." (Taylor 1999: 29)

Taylor's appeal for awareness of "otherness" is reinforced by the purposes to which metallurgical technology was put in different societies, for instance China or pre-Columbian Mexico. The production of elaborate cast bronze ritual vessels in China is unparalleled in the West, while in Mexico functional requirements demanded artefacts that produced sound, rather than tools or weapons. Furthermore, the link between metallurgy, social complexity, and the emergence of urban civilizations detected by Childe in the Near East does not fit the American sequence at all.

Metallurgy based on copper developed in Mexico around AD 800 (Hosler 1988, 1995), 4,000 years after plant domestication and hundreds of years after complex sociopolitical organization and urban centers.

Furthermore, the artefacts produced could not be more different from the axes and spears of Europe: 60 percent of those studied by Hosler were bells, 20 percent open loops or rings. The remaining 20 percent comprised tweezers, sheet metal ornaments, axes, sewing needles, awls, and miscellaneous ornaments:

> Thus the two types of metal artefacts that appear most frequently in ancient West Mexico and that comprise almost 80 percent of the objects fabricated are symbols of elite status. Elite status was conveyed through sounds and through the golden color accomplished with the copper–tin bronze alloy and, less frequently, through the silvery color imparted by the copper–arsenic alloy. In both artefact types the alloy, although mechanically necessary to the design, was used in concentrations far higher than necessary to confer mechanical advantage. (Hosler 1988: 334)

This metallurgy was different from that found in the Andes, lower Central America, or Colombia; the technology constituted "an original regional experiment in metallurgy," which, while stimulated by developments in other areas, expressed "the particular cultural realities and requirements of West Mexican societies of the time" (p. 331). More recently, Heather Lechtman (1999) has explored ways in which Andean materials and procedures carried and conveyed meaning according to whether metal was worked as a solid or plastic material, or in the form of alloys. Color and layering seem to have been an important link to similar technical processes used in managing woven cotton and animal fibers (pp. 227–8). I feel that there is much potential for interaction between interpretations of "ethnocategories" made by anthropologists and contextual approaches to modern-world technology such as Cockburn and Ormrod's (1993) study of microwave ovens cited above, building upon Michael Schiffer's work.

Greece and Rome

The minor role played by technology in classical archaeology may be explained by the long and close association between Classics and high culture. The recreation of classical art forms and structures, from bronze equestrian statues to the new St. Peter's in Rome, relied upon extensive empirical observation of Greek and Roman works of art and buildings, but this took place before the practice of archaeology was defined as an independent academic pursuit. It was left to historians of science and medicine, following the model of philosophy and literature, to wonder at Greek achievements and to lament Roman imitations. This narrative construction is alive and well: "Very consciously the heir of the Greek idea of civilization...her [Rome's] success derived not from any great technological originality but rather from the systematic and effective exploitation of existing technologies" (Williams 1999: 24). This is not praise: "The very success of the Roman administration was a disincentive to change and the abundance of cheap labor, including slaves, gave no encouragement to the development of power-driven machinery." The story is normally rounded-off in the tradition of Gibbon, with a sideswipe at Late Roman Christianity.

Only recently have studies of Greek science made much overt reference to its practical application (Rihll 1999; Cuomo 2000). A considerable amount of officially supported research appears to have lain behind a range of devices invented or improved in Greek and Roman contexts, notably surveying instruments, water-lifting machinery, and mechanical mills (Lewis 2001; Wikander 2000). It is surprising that their significance in supporting the apparatus of royal or imperial government and economic exploitation had not received more emphasis. Mathematical skills may be applied to taxes and accounting, surveying instruments to building roads and measuring land, and pumps and processing equipment to maximizing returns in mining and agriculture. Moses Finley dominated the field of Greek and Roman economics for fifty years because his narrative (like Childe's) was powerful and attractive; unfortunately, he placed a prominent stamp of stagnation and failure upon technology early in his career, and barely mentioned it again (Finley 1973; Greene 2000).

Medieval Europe

Medieval technology has received considerable attention despite the comparatively recent emergence of medieval archaeology as a distinct field. Some of the most influential writings on Greek and Roman society and economy ignored, minimized, or actually denigrated ancient technology (Rostovtzeff 1926; Finley 1965). In contrast, post-Roman historians have claimed medieval origins for inventions and innovations characteristic of the modern world, or have at least given technical factors a greater causal role in historical or economic change (Usher 1929; Bloch 1935; White 1962; Gimpel 1976). These writers not only drew attention to medieval inventions, but also used them to show that a change in mentality had taken place since classical times, as a result of which labor came to be valued, time measured, and the human spirit freed from animism – all under the influence of Christianity. I view this as a late efflorescence of Romanticism, building upon the nineteenth-century rediscovery of Norman and Gothic architecture as a major source of inspiration with roots in northern Europe rather than the Mediterranean. According to this narrative, pioneers of modern industrialization and science broke free from the restraints of classicism and Catholicism (represented by ancient and modern Rome) by mechanizing milling and mining in Britain, Germany, and France, rather than in the sybaritic slave societies of the classical world. Similarly, idealistic nineteenth-century reactions to industrialization expressed by John

Ruskin or William Morris were attracted to the *medieval* past, where they detected free and honest craftsmanship, rather than to the non-industrial and leisured classical world.

Some of the interest in medieval technology sprang from a wish to investigate social evolution, notably the transition from slavery to feudalism. Mechanization was seen as a correlate of this movement, an interpretation reinforced by the notion that classical slavery had inhibited invention and progress. Marc Bloch took the "triumph and conquest" of the water mill as the epitome of this process. Lynn White Jr. focused upon other internal and external inventions, such as the stirrup and the wheeled plow, in a long series of books and articles with arresting titles, erudite footnotes, and a seductive narrative. He built upon the opinions put forward by Lefebvre des Noëttes (1931), who had attributed the stagnation of the ancient world both to slavery and to specific technical limitations, notably defective horse harnessing. Unlike the views of Finley, Rostovtzeff, or Childe, these propositions (and criticisms of them) were rarely based upon material evidence; until recently, medieval archaeology was concerned predominantly with art, architecture, and only the finest end of metalwork and ceramics. Hilton and Sawyer's (1963) critical review of White's *Medieval Technology and Social Change* objected to determinism and wayward use of written sources, rather than the nature of the evidence itself. The Roman background of much "medieval" technology has only become evident as a result of detailed archaeological study (Greene 1994), with considerable help from experimental reconstructions in the case of animal harnessing and traction (Raepsaet 2002).

Industrial archaeology

In contrast to classical or medieval archaeology, industrial archaeology is perhaps *too* closely identified with the study of technology. Its claim to intellectual value has been diminished by a focus upon the survival and preservation of material evidence rather than its significance. The case for industrial archaeology has not always been helped by antagonism towards theory among some of its pioneers, notably Angus Buchanan (1991), who seems to blame excessive interest in the social context of technology for winning only "some marginal recognition, mainly for illustrative purposes" (Buchanan 2000: 33). Is it a genuine discipline in its own right, or simply a part of modern-world historical archaeology? Gordon and Malone (1997: 13–14) claim that the material record is independent and lacks inherent bias, and they value the appreciation of skill and strength to be gained from experiencing tools and machinery, as well as the sense of place and scale to be gained from industrial landscapes: "The tactile experiences of making and shaping materials are being replaced by manipulation of images on video screens and by work in the so-called service or leisure industries...While industrial archaeology informs us about the past, it can also contribute to better use of human resources in industry today" (pp. 14–15). Gordon and Malone have a somewhat nostalgic view of the purpose of studying modern-world material culture that contrasts with Schiffer's fervent desire to correct misleading political interpretations of economic change.

If industrial archaeology remains a mere "provider of solid physical evidence, well presented and analyzed, about the forces of industrialization which have transformed modern conditions of life" (Buchanan 2000: 33), it will not increase its appeal in a society in which technical products (such as mobile phones) are more deeply embedded in everyday social practices than ever, but whose production has become increasingly distant and invisible to their users. Palmer and Neaverson's (1998) discussion of the scope of industrial archaeology acknowledges the dichotomy between the social approaches of archaeologists and the functional approaches of industrial archaeologists, but may have made matters worse rather than better by stating that at present they "concentrate on the interpretation of sites, structures and landscapes rather than artefactual material. This does not, of course, mean that they are excused from working within a theoretical framework but that the data used is rather different from that of the prehistoric archaeologist" (p. 4). Although they may *look* different, I believe that both industrial and prehistoric data have exactly the same potential for theoretical and practical investigation.

A problem for industrial archaeologists is that because of an abundance of information of all kinds, explanations of the Industrial Revolution (in particular its origins in the "first industrial nation," England) have become even more numerous and varied than those of the Neolithic revolution. Where some identify revolution, others describe transition; where some detect technological causes, others prioritize social factors. Were the agricultural revolution of the eighteenth century and the scientific revolution of the seventeenth century actually where the critical changes took place that allowed a workforce to be fed and engineers to acquire essential knowledge? If so, what precisely is the purpose of investigating the industrial monuments of the last 250 years, apart from a somewhat suspect sense of nostalgia and the growth of the heritage industry? If the answer lies not in the technology itself, but the circumstances in which it was practiced, this removes the distinct identity of industrial archaeology and returns the subject to the fold of a socially constructed history of technology, or (more simply) modern-world archaeology.

Might some aspects of industrial archaeology be made to coincide with the postprocessual interest in "otherness"? Industrial museums could stress differences rather than continuities, and more attention could be devoted to byways, dead-ends, and failures rather than the successful antecedents of modern technology. Physical artefacts and monuments that happen to have survived should not be given precedence over those that have not; reading about the spectacular but long-decayed monuments of America's Wooden Age (Hindle 1975) has changed my perception of Roman wooden machinery and timber architecture, for example.

Conclusions

The contribution of technological studies in archaeology will continue to vary according to the relative salience of material culture in different periods. Archaeologists of all periods could gain much by exploring the social construction of technology, because it is compatible with many strands of postprocessual archaeology, from phenomenology to agency. A few studies of prehistoric artefacts, for example Perea's (1999) investigation of goldwork, have made good use of SCOT theory. Perea noted that previous research had been either based upon typology, which answered questions related to time, or upon art-historical comparison, which answered questions related to space:

Typology and style, time and space, were integrated into a positive theoretical framework which became weakened in the 1970s and was discarded in the 1980s... If they are multidirectional, selective and flexible, the techniques or technological processes do not respond to random or evolutionary phenomena but to man's capacity for making choices and decisions; and this implies intentionality and meaning. In short, technology can be interpreted and manipulated; it thus becomes a potential political weapon. (Perea 1999: 68–9)

SCOT's contextual basis was a reaction against a mechanistic worldview that was also present in processual archaeology; in both cases the reaction encouraged approaches centered upon people and experience rather than systems theory, with its dangers of ecological determinism. Historians of technology have concentrated on the recent past because of the wealth of documentary information that accompanies scientific and technical developments, and have failed to apply equally sophisticated thinking to earlier periods.

Archaeology's combination of theoretical depth and practical methodology (helped by materials science) enriches long-term studies of technology and could improve the presentation of the history of technology to a wider academic and public audience. Industrial archaeology could form a better bridge between both fields; the history of technology demands careful observation and analysis of material structures and artefacts, just as much as it requires an understanding of industrial processes drawn from the history of science. Archaeology and the history of technology must continue to exploit cultural studies, anthropology, social theory, and the philosophy of science in order to broaden explanations and to evaluate interpretations. Both subjects will also benefit from pursuing "otherness" by taking fuller account of ideology, gender, and ethnicity, and by exploring the role of technology in different contexts, whether real (Mesoamerica, China) or artificial (Samuel Butler's *Erewhon*, William Morris' *Nowhere*, science fiction). Contemporary non-Western and "alternative" technologies also deserve more attention because lessons may be drawn from their failure to conform to Western expectations of growth. Technology is such an integral component of human existence that all possible sources of information, methods of investigation, and approaches to explanation should be exploited to improve our understanding of it.

References

Barrett, J. C. 2001. "Agency, the duality of structure, and the problem of the archaeological record." In I. Hodder (ed.), *Archaeological Theory Today*, pp. 141–64. Cambridge: Polity Press.

Basalla, G. 1988. *The Evolution of Technology*. Cambridge: Cambridge University Press.

Bettinger, R. L. 2001. "Holocene hunter-gatherers." In G. M. Feinman and T. D. Price (eds.), *Archaeology at the Millennium: A Sourcebook*, pp. 137–95. Dordrecht: Kluwer Academic.

Bijker, W. E. 1995. "Sociohistorical technology studies." In S. Jasanoff et al. (eds.), *Handbook of Science and Technology Studies*, pp. 229–56. Thousand Oaks, CA: Sage Publications.

Bijker, W. E., T. P. Hughes, and T. Pinch (eds.) 1987. *The Social Construction of Technological Systems: New Directions in the Sociology and History of Technology*. Cambridge, MA: MIT Press.

Blair, I. 2002. "Roman London's waterworks: the Gresham Street discoveries." *Current Archaeology*, 180: 509–16.

Bloch, M. 1935. "Avènement et conquêtes du moulin à eau." *Annales: Économies, Sociétés, Civilisations*, 7: 538–63. Translated as "The advent and triumph of the water mill." In J. E. Anderson (ed.) 1967. *Land and Work in Medieval Europe: Selected Papers by Marc Bloch*, pp. 136–68. London: Routledge and Kegan Paul.

Buchanan, R. A. 1991. "Theory and narrative in the history of technology." *Technology and Culture*, 32: 365–76.

Buchanan, R. A. 2000. "The origins of industrial archaeology." In N. Cossons (ed.), *Perspectives on Industrial Archaeology*, pp. 18–38. London: Science Museum.

Channell, D. F. 1991. *The Vital Machine: A Study of Technology and Organic Life*. New York: Oxford University Press.

Childe, V. G. 1936. *Man Makes Himself*. London: Watts Library of Science and Culture.

Childe, V. G. 1942. *What Happened in History*. Harmondsworth: Penguin Books.

Cockburn, C. and S. Ormrod 1993. *Gender and Technology in the Making*. London: Sage Publications.

Cuomo, S. 2000. *Pappus of Alexandria and the Mathematics of Late Antiquity*. Cambridge: Cambridge University Press.

Daniel, G. 1943. *The Three Ages: An Essay on Archaeological Method*. Cambridge: Cambridge University Press.

Diamond, J. 1997. *Guns, Germs and Steel*. London: Chatto and Windus.

Dobres, M.-A. and C. R. Hoffman (eds.) 1999. *The Social Dynamics of Technology: Practice, Politics, and World Views*. Washington, DC: Smithsonian Institution Press.

Edgerton, D. 2000. "Reflections on the history of technology in Britain." *History of Technology*, 22: 181–7.

Finley, M. I. 1965. "Technical innovation and economic progress in the ancient world." *Economic History Review*, 18: 29–45.

Finley, M. I. 1973. *The Ancient Economy*. London: Chatto and Windus.

Fischer, A. (ed.) 1995. *Man and Sea in the Mesolithic: Coastal Settlement Above and Below Present Sea Level*. Oxford: Oxbow Monograph 53.

Forenbaher, S. 1999. *Production and Exchange of Bifacial Flaked Stone Artifacts during the Portuguese Chalcolithic*. Oxford: British Archaeological Reports S756.

Fox, R. 1996. "Introduction: methods and themes in the history of technology." In R. Fox, *Technological Change: Methods and Themes in the History of Technology*, pp. 1–15. Amsterdam: Harwood Academic.

Gamble, C. 2001. *Archaeology: The Basics*. London: Routledge.

Gibson, K. R. and T. Ingold (eds.) 1993. *Tools, Language and Cognition in Human Evolution*. Cambridge: Cambridge University Press.

Gimpel, J. 1976. *The Medieval Machine: The Industrial Revolution of the Middle Ages*. New York: Pimlico.

Gordon, R. B. and P. M. Malone 1997. *The Texture of Industry: An Archaeological View of the Industrialization of North America*. Oxford: Oxford University Press.

Graslund, B. 1987. *The Birth of Prehistoric Chronology: Dating Methods and Dating Systems in Nineteenth-Century Scandinavian Archaeology*. Cambridge: Cambridge University Press.

Greene, K. 1990. "Perspectives on Roman technology." *Oxford Journal of Archaeology*, 7: 22–33.

Greene, K. 1992. "How was technology transferred in the Roman empire?" In M. Wood and F. Queiroga (eds.), *Current Research on the Romanization of the Western Provinces*, pp. 101–5. Oxford: British Archaeological Reports S575.

Greene, K. 1993. "The study of Roman technology: some theoretical constraints." In E. Scott (ed.), *Theoretical Roman Archaeology: First Conference Proceedings*, pp. 39–47. Aldershot: Avebury.

Greene, K. 1994. "Technology and innovation in context: the Roman background to mediaeval and later developments." *Journal of Roman Archaeology*, 73: 97–109.

Greene, K. 1999. "V. Gordon Childe and the vocabulary of revolutionary change." *Antiquity*, 73: 97–109.

Greene, K. 2000. "Technological innovation and economic progress in the ancient world: M. I. Finley reconsidered." *Economic History Review*, 53: 29–59.

Hilton, R. H. and P. H. Sawyer 1963. "Technical determinism: the stirrup and the plough." *Past and Present*, 24: 90–100.

Hindle, B. (ed.) 1975. *America's Wooden Age: Aspects of its Early Technology*. New York: Sleepy Hollow Restorations.

Hodder, I. 1992. *The Domestication of Europe: Structure and Contingency in Neolithic Societies*. Oxford: Blackwell.

Horden, P. and N. Purcell 2000. *The Corrupting Sea: A Study of Mediterranean History*. Oxford: Blackwell.

Hosler, D. 1988. "The metallurgy of ancient West Mexico." In R. Maddin (ed.), *The Beginnings of the Use of Metals and Alloys*, pp. 328–43. Cambridge, MA: MIT Press.

Hosler, D. 1995. "Sound, color and meaning in the metallurgy of ancient West Mexico." *World Archaeology*, 27 (1): 100–15.

Ingold, T. 1999a. Review of R. M. Adams (1996) *Paths of Fire: An Anthropologist's Enquiry into Western Technology*. Princeton University Press. *Technology and Culture*, 40: 130–2.

Ingold, T. 1999b. "Foreword." In M.-A. Dobres and C. R. Hoffman, *The Social Dynamics of Technology*, pp. vii–xi Washington, DC: Smithsonian Institution.

Jager, R. 1999. "Tool and symbol: the success of the double-bitted axe in North America." *Technology and Culture*, 40: 833–60.

Kehoe, A. B. 1998. *The Land of Prehistory: A Critical History of American Archaeology*. London: Routledge.

Klein, R. G. 2001. "Fully modern humans." In G. M. Feinman and T. D. Price (eds.), *Archaeology at the Millennium: A Sourcebook*, pp. 109–35. Dordrecht: Kluwer Academic.

Latour, B. 1996. *Aramis, or, the Love of Technology*. Cambridge, MA: Harvard University Press

Lechtman, H. 1999. "Afterword." In M.-A. Dobres and C. R. Hoffman, *The Social Dynamics of Technology*, pp. 223–32. Washington, DC: Smithsonian Institution.

Leeuw, S. E. van der and R. Torrence (eds.) 1989. *What's New? A Closer Look at the Process of Innovation*. London: Unwin Hyman: One World Archaeology 14.

Lefebvre des Noëttes 1931. *L'attelage, le cheval de selle à travers les âges*, 2 vols. Paris: A. Picard.

Leonard, R. D. 2001. "Evolutionary archaeology." In I. Hodder (ed.), *Archaeological Theory Today*, pp. 65–97. Cambridge: Polity Press.

Lewis, M. J. T. 2001. *Surveying Instruments of Greece and Rome*. Cambridge: Cambridge University Press.

Lovitt, W. and H. B. Lovitt 1995. *Modern Technology in the Heideggerian Perspective 1*. Lewiston, NY: Edwin Mellen Press.

Morgan, L. H. 1871. *Ancient Society, or Researches in the Lines of Human Progress from Savagery through Barbarism to Civilization*. New York: Henry Holt.

Oakley, K. P. 1949. *Man the Tool-Maker*. London: British Museum.

Oleson, J. P. 1984. *Greek and Roman Mechanical Water-Lifting Devices: The History of a Technology*. Buffalo: Reidel.

Palmer, M. and P. Neaverson 1998. *Industrial Archaeology: Principles and Practice*. London: Routledge.

Perea, A. 1999. "Project Au for the study of goldwork technology and the concept of techno-logical domain systems." In S. M. Young et al. (eds.), *Metals in Antiquity*, pp. 68–71. Oxford: British Archaeological Reports S792.

Raepsaet, G. 2002. *Attelages et techniques de transport dans le monde gréco-romaine*. Brussels: Le Livre Timperman.

Reynolds, T. S. 2001. "Presidential address: on not burning bridges: valuing the past." *Technology and Culture*, 42: 523–30.

Rihll, T. E. 1999. *Greek Science*. Oxford: Oxford University Press/Classical Association.

Roland, L. 1997. "Presidential address: what hath Kranzberg wrought? Or, does the history of technology matter?" *Technology and Culture*, 38: 697–713.

Rosen, S. A. 1996. "The decline and fall of flint." In G. H. Odell (ed.), *Stone Tools: Theoretical Insights into Human Prehistory*, pp. 129–58. New York: Plenum.

Rostovtzeff, M. 1926. *Social and Economic History of the Roman Empire*. Oxford: Oxford University Press.

Rothschild, J. 1983. *Machina ex dea: Feminist Perspectives on Technology*. New York: Pergamon Press.

Schick, K. D. and N. Toth 1993. *Making the Silent Stones Speak: Human Evolution and the Dawn of Technology*. New York: Simon and Schuster.

Schick, K. D. and N. Toth 2001. "Paleoanthropology at the millennium." In G. M. Feinman and T. D. Price (eds.), *Archaeology at the Millennium: A Sourcebook*, pp. 39–108. Dordrecht: Kluwer Academic.

Schiffer, M. B. 1991. *The Portable Radio in American Life*. Tucson: University of Arizona Press.

Schiffer, M. B. 1992. *Technological Perspectives on Behavioral Change*. Tucson: University of Arizona Press.

Schiffer, M. B. (ed.) 2001. *Anthropological Perspectives on Technology*. Dragoon, AZ: Amerind Foundation, New World Studies 5.

Schumacher, E. F. 1973. *Small is Beautiful: A Study of Economics as if People Mattered*. London: Blond and Briggs.

Sherratt, A. 1997. "Plough and pastoralism: aspects of the secondary products revolution." In A. Sherratt, *Economy and Society in Prehistoric Europe: Changing Perspectives*, pp. 158–98. Edinburgh: Edinburgh University Press.

Sigaut, F. 1994. "Technology." In T. Ingold (ed.), *Companion Encyclopedia of Anthropology*, pp. 420–59. London: Routledge.

Smith, M. Roe and L. Marx (eds.) 1994. *Does Technology Drive History? The Dilemma of Technological Determinism*. Cambridge, MA: MIT Press.

Staudenmaier, J. M. 1985. *Technology's Storytellers: Reweaving the Human Fabric*. Cambridge, MA: Society for the History of Technology/MIT Press.

Taylor, T. 1999. "Envaluing metal: theorizing the Eneolithic 'hiatus'." In S. M. Young et al. (eds.), *Metals in Antiquity*, pp. 22–32. Oxford: British Archaeological Reports S792.

Terry, J. and M. Calvert (eds.) 1997. *Processed Lives: Gender and Technology in Everyday Life*. London: Routledge.

Trigger, B. G. 1989. *A History of Archaeological Thought*. Cambridge: Cambridge University Press.

Tylor, E. B. 1871. *Primitive Culture*. London: John Murray.

Usher, A. P. 1929. *A History of Mechanical Inventions*. Cambridge, MA: Harvard University Press.

Vandkilde, H. 1996. *From Stone to Bronze: The Metalwork of the Late Neolithic and Earliest Bronze Age in Denmark*. Jutland Archaeological Society.

Wajcman, J. 1995. "Feminist theories of technology." In S. Jasanoff et al. (eds.), *Handbook of Science and Technology Studies*, pp. 189–204. Thousand Oaks, CA: Sage Publications.

White, H. B. 1987. *The Content of the Form: Narrative Discourse and Historical Representation*. Baltimore, MD: Johns Hopkins University Press.

White, L. T. 1962. *Medieval Technology and Social Change*. Oxford: Clarendon Press.

Wikander, O. (ed.) 2000. *Handbook of Ancient Water Technology*. Leiden: E. J. Brill.

Williams, T. I. 1987. *The Triumph of Invention: A History of Man's Technological Genius*. London: Macdonald.

Williams, T. I. (ed. W. E. Schaaf, Jr.) 1999. *The History of Invention: From Stone Axes to Silicon Chips*. London: Little, Brown.

Wilson, A. 2002. "Machines, power and the ancient economy." *Journal of Roman Studies*, 92: 1–32.

Wynn, T. 1994. "Tools and tool behavior." In T. Ingold (ed.), *Companion Encyclopedia of Anthropology*, pp. 133–61. London: Routledge.

10

Time, Structure, and Agency: The Annales, Emergent Complexity, and Archaeology

John Bintliff

Introduction: Giddens' False Trail

A central dispute that separates the two major movements in late twentieth-century archaeological theory – the new or processual ("modernist") and the postprocessual ("post-modern") approaches to the past – lies in the importance of the "individual" in the creation of the archaeological record. Like many such internal disputes, the polarization is a manifestation of an older argument in the human sciences, in this case the "structure and agency" debate within sociology.

From within sociology, and thence by direct importation into archaeology, has come recently a theory offering to resolve this dichotomy: structuration theory, proposed by Anthony Giddens. We quote from an early formulation:

> In sum, the primary tasks of sociological enquiry . . . [include] explication of the production and reproduction of society as the accomplished outcome of human agency. (Giddens 1976: 162)

It follows that in the (new) rules of sociology,

> The production and reproduction of society thus has to be treated as a skilled perform-

ance on the part of its members, not as merely a mechanical series of processes. To emphasize this, however, is definitely not to say that actors are wholly aware of what these skills are . . . or that the forms of social life are adequately understood as the intended outcomes of action. (Giddens 1976: 160)

Despite the bold step of locating the source of significant social action in "skilled members," one feels unease at the final sentence's ambiguity. If human agents are to an uncertain degree unconscious of what they are doing, and if actions have consequences separate from intentions, is it appropriate to envisage the forms of society as the "accomplished outcome" and "skilled performance" of human agency?

Further doubts arise from informed commentary within sociology on the merits of Giddens' theory. Archaeological theorists enamored of structuration assume that the theory rests on observational evidence from modern society. Not so, for we find that structuration

proved not to be closely related to research programs of empirical data collection . . . What is the use of theory which never dirties its hands with data? (Clegg 1992: 583)

So where did the theory originate? In another theory, in another discipline, it seems:

His attempt to account for the relationship between structure and agency is modeled after Saussure's . . . discussion of the relationship between *langue* (grammar) and *parole* (utterance) . . . Giddens' reliance on . . . *parole* contributing to the continual reproduction of *langue* leads to the formulation of agents who reproduce existing structures which are part of the ongoing practices of agency. (Baber 1991: 227)

Colleagues within sociology also question the success of Giddens' bridging between individual human agency and persistent social structures:

Despite the stated claim, Giddens' account of action is clearly derived from the voluntarist perspective . . . [What we get is] not a reconceptualization of structure and agency but rather the obliteration of structure and exaggeration of the power and capacity of agents . . . [Since according to Giddens] social systems only exist insofar as they are continually created and recreated in every encounter, as the active accomplishment of human subjects . . . [many critics have agreed that in the last analysis] the "structure" and "systems" concerned are inchoate and evanescent, appearing and disappearing at the behest of specific individuals in specific encounters. (Baber 1991: 224, 226)

Despite these criticisms of structuration's claims to go beyond its clear focus on free-willed human agents in accounting for social structures, a number of archaeological theorists have been seduced by it, notably John Barrett, in arguing against "the dichotomy which has been erected in life as lived in the immediate and the short term, and the history of the long-term social institutions." Barrett proposes instead:

Biographies are not determined by the external conditions which they inhabit but are created by the possible ways the actor can move into that world and operate effectively through an ability to read the world for meaning . . . Agency . . . transforms and reproduces its material conditions . . . We have been concerned to develop an archaeology of agency. (Barrett 1994: 3, 169–70)

Conscious human individuals here dominate social structures, with little respect for "external conditions which they inhabit." This existential view of the world leads him into implausible claims. Take the case of Ötzi the "Ice Man," whose violent death on an Austrian Alp in prehistory led to refrigerated preservation, allowing modern-day voyeuristic tabloid speculation and intensive scientific study. Barrett claims this shows

how events, such as that ill-fated journey into the Alps, reworked the structural conditions which gave them their significance . . . we must consider the conditions which enabled certain events to reach out in this way to extend deeply through time and space. (Barrett 1994: 3)

Well, frankly, mischance for Ötzi, fortunate chance for archaeologists, but irrelevant for the philosophy of history. We sympathize with Barrett's idealism, but like Giddens, structure has disappeared, and all is ultimately individual agency. An alternative path might envisage social structures as more than the sum of their parts, providing scope for mutual interactions, and asking more realistically how each human agent and human act forms partial rather than total explanation for the way people lived in the past.

Enter the Annales . . .

Barrett refers in passing to a theory of history offering a contrasting methodology, which *does* place individual agents and actions as part of a much larger nexus: the Annales School of French historians. Table 10.1

represents a central aspect of Annaliste thought: structural history, as elaborated by Fernand Braudel (1972; Bintliff 1991a, 1991b).

The past is created by interacting forces or "conjunctures," processes which operate in parallel but on different wavelengths of time: the short term of individuals and events, the medium term of a century to several centuries (the time of socioeconomic and demographic cycles and lasting world-views), and finally the long term (several hundred to thousands of years) where we can observe the effect of environmental constraints, the spread and impact of new technologies, and very long-lasting ways of seeing the world.

To illustrate the relevance of Annaliste thinking for archaeological interpretation, a summary regional case study may serve. One major pattern emerging from a long timescale analysis of a province of Greece (Boeotia) is the cyclical rise and fall of urban and rural populations (Bintliff 1997b; 1999a, 1999b). Much of this structure can be interpreted through a neo-Malthusian (demographic–ecological) model, noting the connections between population waves, land use, erosion, and declining soil productivity, alongside an underlying trend to denser populations following improvements in agricultural productivity. Such an approach has the advantage of synthesis and the identification of central recurrent processes.

Thus it is significant that one Malthusian population wave in Boeotia, and other regions of Archaic–Classical southern Greece with complex city-based political systems, peaks earlier (seventh to fourth centuries BC) than one developing in the tribal regions of Aetolia, Epiros, and Macedonia, in the north of Greece, where an aggressive externally directed population climax occurs during the Hellenistic era, from the late fourth to the second centuries BC. In the context of a larger, Mediterranean scale, a peak of Italian peninsular rural prosperity, as in most of the western Roman provinces, is reached later again, in the first century AD – and now southern Greece is generally in severe demographic decline. The weakening of the Western European Roman economy by the third century AD is matched by the florescence, first of North Africa, then in the fifth to sixth centuries AD of the eastern provinces – including Greece once again.

This simple neo-Malthusian model is attractive and plausible for the data available, but looks at just one kind of temporal trend, ignoring the details, indeed ignoring the historical complexity behind such useful descriptions of observable processes. This is why the Annales School argues that historical sequences are created by the interaction of processes occurring at different wavelengths of time. Firstly for Boeotia (Bintliff 1991b), there is the *longue durée*, the long term, where we document the progressive rise in human population and the accompanying development of more productive economies from the hunter-gatherer bands

Table 10.1 Braudel's model of historical time

History of events	Short term – *événements* Narrative, political history; events; individuals
Structural history	Medium term – *conjonctures* Social, economic history; economic, agrarian, demographic cycles; history of eras, regions, societies; worldviews, ideologies (*mentalités*)
Structural history	Long term – structures of the *longue durée* Geohistory: "enabling and constraining"; history of civilizations, peoples; stable technologies, worldviews (*mentalités*)

of the Palaeolithic to the complex economies of the classical city-states. Secondly, at a more detailed level we observe as archaeologists those characteristic cyclical fluctuations of demography and prosperity whose wavelength of growth and decay is the *moyenne durée*, the medium term, of the order of half a millennium. Here we see most clearly the ecological cycles of Malthusian type and the erection and dismantling of sophisticated urban, political, and cultural structures that grow and decay with them.

Yet both long-term and medium-term wavelengths are normally beyond the cognizance of contemporaries, the human actors whose decisions we have yet to create space for. Here lies the necessity for the wavelength of the short term, the world of *événements*, events and personalities, and unpredictable chance.

Thus in Boeotia, between the Geometric and the Roman imperial eras (ca. 800 BC to AD 300), short-term processes are crucial to the way each city reacts to general trends in the medium term. At the beginning of this long time-swathe, the role of chance and individual personalities will have influenced the way that some pioneer villages or small towns rose to power over their neighbors, even if others, like the city of Thebes, had inbuilt geographic and historic advantages. Later, the cities of Tanagra and Thespiae had good luck in recurrently backing the winning side in the conflicts of the late Roman republic, and escaped the fate of most other towns in the region – pillage or heavy indemnities; this explains in large part their unique relative prosperity through the early Roman imperial era. In contrast, the city of Haliartos suffered total destruction by the Roman army in the early second century BC, an event from which it never recovered in antiquity. On the other hand, the decisions of human actors may in the end mold themselves to the logic of the geopolitics of the medium to long term. Alexander the Great's willful destruction of Thebes, like that of other conquerors at Corinth and Carthage, proved to be a short interruption in the city's

long history: it was refounded a generation later by Cassander.

Challenging the Annales: Response from Montaillou

Barrett nonetheless was quick to find fault with this promising inclusive Annales model of the past, through its apparent failure to specify the way in which the processes operating at the three time-levels interact: "We would appear still to be left with the problem of refining our understanding of the way in which processes, operating in each timescale, are routinely structured in relation to each other" (Barrett 1994: 7)

Barrett thus rejects structural history in favor of a much simpler explanation of how the time of the individual and the event can be linked to longer-term historical processes – through the role of memory. The handing on of memories of people, places, and things – either verbally, through texts, or through monumentalization – provides Barrett with a means to perpetuate Giddens' daily acts of reproduction of society by individual human agents into a potentially infinite future time.

I have serious difficulties with the hypothesis that individual or collective memory – oral, textual, or monumental – systematically conveys the time of *événements* into the medium and long term without being transformed in the process, through memory loss, selective survival, and reinterpretation. Take this example: for some ten years I taught at the University of Durham in northern England. The small city square is dominated by two monumental statues, one of which, a giant equestrian bronze, is reproduced in Figure 10.1.

Ask a typical passer-by, or 99 percent of the very numerous Durham students, what "memories" these statues perpetuate, or even whom they literally portray, and you will get a blank response. They have become, despite the earnest intent of the Victorian magnate and city council who

Figure 10.1 Monumental equestrian statue in Durham marketplace, northeast England.

respectively are the cause of their erection, merely part of the historic wallpaper of the city center, but the specific meanings originally attached to the art – and they are many – are lost to all but the erudite modern-day antiquarians.

I am not saying that some memories cannot survive well beyond their historic agents (some monuments *do* retain their first meanings), but it seems to me – and I could cite many other instances from history, anthropology, and archaeology (such as the Parthenon or Stonehenge) to justify my view – that more often it is the case that stories and objects from the past have undergone drastic transformation over time. One can recall Jacquetta Hawkes' fine and witty comment: "Every age gets the Stonehenge it desires – or deserves."

It is time to return to the Annales and take up John Barrett's challenge to explain how one can analyze the parallel effects of processes operating on different wave-

lengths of time. I shall do this by taking apart and amplifying with archaeological detail a *tour de force* of Annales scholarship: the classic study by Le Roy Ladurie (1978) of a rural community in southwest France, Montaillou, in the years around AD 1300. It is based on a highly detailed picture of village life over a single generation, as revealed by the records of the Catholic Inquisition, which exhaustively interviewed its predominantly "heretic" Cathar inhabitants. Figure 10.2 shows the location of the village, an agropastoral community in the Pyrenean foothills near the Spanish border.

Through careful reading of Ladurie's monograph and more recent archaeological and historical literature it is possible to simplify the analysis for our purposes and tabulate the ways in which the different *durées* or wavelengths of processes molded the life of the village before, during, and after the short period in which the people and events

Figure 10.2 Location of Montaillou, Ariège, southwestern France (after Ladurie 1978).

recorded by the Inquisition occupied the regional stage.

Elements in the Montaillou scenario, ca. AD 1300:

1 The *longue durée*

- Agropastoral adaptation.
- Marginal district.
- Low social differentiation.
- Emphasis on household social and economic autarchy.
- Power struggle between families or *domus*.
- Progressive nucleation from Roman era.
- Mentality of "timelessness," "no other age," fatalism.

From the perspective of the long term, the people of Montaillou ca. AD 1300 were in part the creation of far older processes at work in their region and on a wider scale in Western Europe. Their everyday way of life or *mode de vie* (a deeply embedded form of economy tied to a specific environment and level of technology), is well adapted to the marginal agricultural potential of their region and its natural potential for special-

ized pastoralism, utilizing both the high summer pastures of the Pyrenees and alternative lowland grazing on both the French and Catalan sides of those mountains. Related to the marginal regional character and its *mode de vie* is the low level of class differentiation within local communities, both between families and also between the peasantry, community officials, and the local feudal gentry. In contrast to the rich farmlands of northern France, which nourished in the Middle Ages cohesive corporate peasant communes (and a well-differentiated, wealthy lordship), the poorer and more diversified potential of the Pyrenean margins favors an emphasis on the social and economic independence (autarchy) of each household (*domus*).

Our documents have enabled us to burrow beneath the rich but superficial crust of feudal . . . relationships which for so long . . . nourished the histories that were written of early peasant communities . . . We have got down to the basic unit . . . of the people . . . the *domus* . . . the unifying principle that linked man and his possessions . . . The *domus* . . . constituted a formidable reservoir of power which could hold out with some degree of success against the external powers surrounding it . . . But the *domus* had marked tendencies towards anarchy and subsistence economy . . . and thus militated against the growth of a civic sense of community. (Ladurie 1978: 353–4)

The centrality of the household creates identification with the physical structure of the extended family residence: "the family of flesh and blood and the house of wood, stone or daub were one and the same thing" (Ladurie 1978: 25).

A natural result of this fragmented society is competition within the rural community for what limited wealth and status its leading families below the level of lordship can accrue. In Montaillou this position is held by the Clergue family, maintaining power through manipulating minor administrative positions, marriage links, and extramarital sexual politics:

> All the women of Montaillou "deloused" and admired the Clergues. These bonds of blood, marriage or concubinage provided the Clergue family with indispensable support or complicity both in the time of their splendor and the time of their decline. (Ladurie 1978: 57)

Nonetheless, Montaillou was a nucleated community presided over by the feudal keep of its lord, and in this respect we can see it as the product of a long drawn out process of settlement concentration. Archaeological evidence goes beyond Ladurie's historical evidence (see Figure 10.3) to show that in many parts of the later Roman Empire a landscape of mixed nucleated and dispersed settlement was becoming reduced to population concentrations. This focus on villages remains through the succeeding Early Middle Ages, despite vigorous population growth from around AD 1000; we merely see the

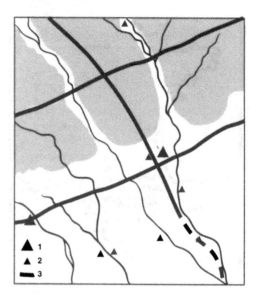

(b) Late Roman and Early Medieval Settlement pattern.
  Key:
  1=nucleated   2=dispersed   3=roads

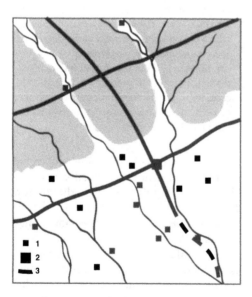

(a) Early Roman Settlement pattern.
  Key:
  1=dispersed   2=nucleated   3=roads

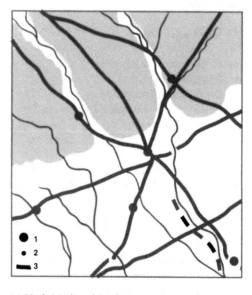

(c) High Medieval Settlement pattern.
  Key:
  1=nucleated   2=dispersed   3=roads

Figure 10.3 a–c Settlement evolution in the territory of Lunel Viel, Languedoc (after Favory and Fiches: 1994, figs. 39–42).

multiplication of villages across the landscape in the final centuries up to the time of the Montaillou archive. In the later stages at least of this process of an expanding network of nucleated settlements (as we shall see in the *moyenne durée*, below), a role has been identified for intervention by rising feudal elites, since concentrations of population favor domination and exploitation by a land-based aristocracy; indeed, often the final stages of this phenomenon witness pairing of village and feudal fortification, sometimes with a wall enclosing both (such as the excavated village of Rougiers in central Provence: cf. Goudineau and Guilaine 1991: 308–9; for a pioneer study of this process of *incastellamento* in Italy, see Toubert 1973).

So deeply embedded in this carefully adapted *mode de vie* are the inhabitants of Montaillou, that they have almost no sense of deep historical memory:

> The memories of the farmers scarcely went back further than the previous Comte de Foix, who had been kind to his subjects but an enemy to tithes and the Church . . . Apart from a few very rare passages about, for example, the great age of some genus or lineage . . . the witnesses . . . took no interest in decades earlier than 1290 or 1300 . . . So the people of Montaillou lived in a kind of "island in time," even more cut off from the past than from the future. "There is no other age than ours," said one. This absence of a historical dimension went with a general use in speech of the present indicative tense without logical connections with past and future. (Ladurie 1978: 282)

For the character who most catches the empathy of Ladurie – Pierre Maury – this limitation becomes a form of fatalism. Thus Belibaste, the heretic Cathar priest, says to the migrant shepherd Maury:

> Your regular returns to the Comté de Foix for the summer pasturing may make you fall into the hands of the Inquisition, to which Maury replies: "I cannot live otherwise than the way I was brought up . . . I must follow

my fate . . . my destined path." (Ladurie 1978: 132)

This attitude to time and memory appears widespread among traditional rural societies, as we see by comparison with a recent discussion of memory among the non-elite on Malta by an anthropologist:

> The memory of the populace appears to have little depth, no collective focus, not much dynamism . . . Their own unofficial private memories are memories of family rather than family memories. In this they resemble peasants, whose memories are based "less on historically relevant events than on the recurrent processes of the life cycle or the family" [Fentress and Wickham 1992: 98]. (Sant Cassia 1999: 252)

I am also reminded of Lynn Foxhall's (1995) description of family life in ancient Athens, where family cemetery plots and other evidence suggest an absence of household continuity beyond two to three generations.

2 *Moyenne durée*

- Spread of lordship and feudalism from northern Italy and northern France.
- *Incastellamento* enhances older nucleation of villages ca. tenth to thirteenth centuries.
- Divergent feudal outcomes, northern versus southern France; initial ecological and sociocultural contrasts are central.
- Contrast between fragmented village and family focus versus corporate community and managed land.
- Power struggle between rising nation-states, city-states, and minor feudal lords.
- Agro-demographic population cycles with a wavelength in several centuries.
- And for the modern era: rise of global capital, consumerism, and the EEC – Pyrenean pastoral lifestyle in rapid decline.

During the centuries leading up to the era of the Montaillou archive, from around the year AD 1000, a stronger network of feudal lordship was diffusing through Western Europe out of centers in northern Italy and northern France, enhancing the nucleation of communities under the watchful eye of feudal keeps, particularly when a second fortification enclosed the subordinate village. As can be seen in Montaillou today, the ruined keep looks down from a nearby height onto the modern and medieval locations of the village.

However, important distinctions between the initial local conditions into which high feudalism spread, led to broadly divergent developments between lordship in the rich cereal plains of northern France and the diversified terrain of the south (the Midi). Lordship was less powerful in class and wealth distinctions in the Midi compared to the status and income of the subordinate rural classes. In Montaillou this encouraged far more social interaction between the keep and the village, even of the most intimate kind, and minor rather than great distinctions in lifestyle. At the same time, however, the more variable and marginal a landscape, the more fragmented and factional are its communities. In this era, in regions such as the Pyrenean foothills, such factors prevented the formation of powerful rural corporate communities, such as arose elsewhere in both England and France as a counterpoise to a centralizing state.

In the latter part of this same period (ca. 1000–1300) there occurred a growing tendency towards the formation of competitive nation-states and territorial city-states in Western Europe. A result of these political developments was a policy by both a centralizing kingship and the urban patriciates in the major city-states to reduce the authority of provincial feudal lords. In France, the relentless expansion of the royal Capetian dynasty from its slender possessions during the tenth century in the Île de France to its ubiquitous possessions by the early fourteenth century portend the ultimate total control of the country that was to follow (Figure 10.4), and yet an alternative and at times more

likely outcome was a division of France between the Capetians and an aggressive English kingship (Figure 10.5).

These competing dynasts at the head of emergent nation-states, who utilized any excuse to remove power from the semi-autonomous lords of the French provinces, were intent on bringing the lax and poorly differentiated Midi lords into their more absolute grip, as well as tightening the efficiency of surplus extraction. The earlier Albigensian Crusade in the Midi has been seen by modern historians as cynical cover for large-scale intervention by the French crown into areas where it had minimal formal control, claiming that local lords were insufficiently ruthless in suppressing the heresy, or even party to it themselves. The subsequent Cathar heresy found ready rural support in the same region, as a conscious resistance to this perceived threat to a local form of political coexistence which both rulers and ruled found congenial, or which at least offered many freedoms and opportunities for advancement. In a recent study of the High Medieval Midi ("Occitania," a term from its Early Medieval past), Paterson has written: "Occitania was not Utopia . . . But it was the first spectacular casualty of the 'formation of a persecuting society,' the victim of a desire on the part of outsiders to dominate and control" (Paterson 1993: 344).

The medium-term timescale typifies population cycles in Europe, a powerful and (until the modern era) seemingly irresistible combination of Malthusian economics, warfare, and disease. This is clearly documented for the whole of France in earlier publications by Ladurie (1966, 1971; Ladurie and Goy 1982). By way of illustration, Figure 10.6 shows population waves in Provence. In accordance with well-known cycles of European demographic change, we see the end of the boom that began around AD 1000 (1315), the nadir from the after-effects of the Black Death and the Hundred Years War (1471), then a new rise in the latter eighteenth century (1765). Not shown here is an intervening high in the sixteenth cen-

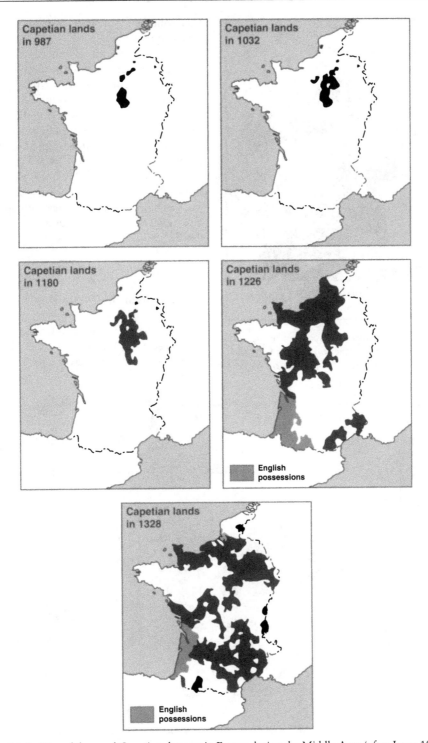

Figure 10.4   Rise of the royal Capetian dynasty in France during the Middle Ages (after Jones 1994).

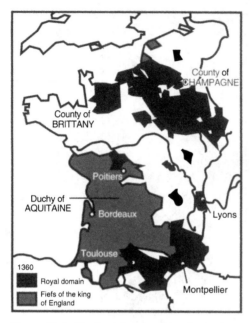

Figure 10.5 Territorial competition in the later Middle Ages between the kingdoms of England and France within the boundaries of modern France.

tury, followed by a phase of stagnation in the seventeenth century.

The most recent development is a phase of demographic and economic decline in the agropastoral communities of the Pyrenean foothills, linked to novel forms of disruption through global capitalism and EEC planning. In the 1970s, Ladurie saw this decay as perhaps terminal rather than a trend to be reversed in the future: "Now its people are abandoning the fields up in the mountains, and so threatening the stability of an ancient habitat which neither repression nor contagion were able to destroy" (Ladurie 1978: 356).

3   Short term – événements

- Albigensian heresy, catalyst for French expansion.
- Southern resistance and Cathar heresy.
- Gregorian reform of the Catholic Church, a new player against secular power.

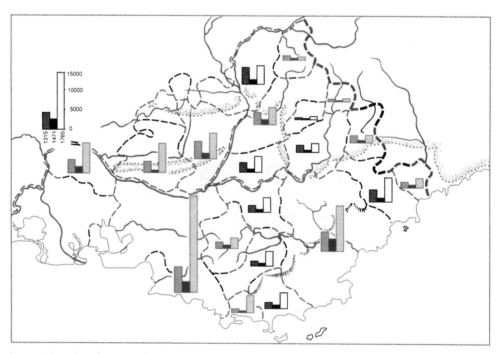

Figure 10.6 Population cycles in Provence, fourteenth to eighteenth centuries AD (after Duby and Wallon 1975: 556).

- Black Death, enhanced warfare in the fourteenth century.
- Family choices, imperfect knowledge.

Within the time of living memory and conscious evaluation, even if not informed evaluation of the full circumstances (i.e., the time of events and personalities; of the short term) specific processes of a distinctive period-bound nature are identifiable. Firstly, two waves of popular "heresy" which found great favor in southern France: the Albigensians and later the Cathars. At one level, they represent popular provincial resistance, both to the encroachment of centralizing states and a newly aggressive Catholic establishment keen to stamp out unorthodoxy and vie for authority and income with secular powers. At another level (and this emerges strongly from the first-person narratives of the Montaillou archive), these "heresies" represented grassroots personalized mysticism spread by renegade priests or laypersons, such as frequently punctuate the history of stratified institutional religions.

Although it is argued that population and food production were severely out of balance in Europe by the fourteenth century, favoring negative Malthusian forces and an inevitable (medium-term) downturn, the appalling impact of the Black Death in mid-century was nonetheless an autonomous event capable in itself of causing massive loss of life and societal disruption. In combination, of course, the effects of this short-term and other medium-term negative processes manifested in the Midi after the time of the Montaillou archive, delayed recovery and may have hastened the transformation out of feudalism in Western Europe. The prolonged episodes of warfare in the fourteenth to sixteenth centuries are also on the one hand distinctive historic processes related to the struggles between emergent nation-states and larger territorial city-states, and on the other hand reactions to medium-term forces to do with the Black Death, climatic fluctuations, and related factors.

Finally, also very clear from the Montaillou archive, we can see the way that individuals and families make choices, or follow the limited alternatives – or no choices – available to them, more often unaware of the wider context of their actions, but nonetheless striving to come to terms with fate – either as active or passive participants in its foreseen and unforeseen twists and turns.

Retrospect: Learning from Montaillou and the Annales

What insights follow from our elaboration of Annales methodology and in particular the case study of Montaillou in its wider Mediterranean and European context, as regards our initial search for the ways in which individuals and societies, places and regions, events and trends in the medium and long term, come together to make specific pasts?

A primary result has to be that indeterminacy dominates – not predictable outcomes, developments, or changeless ways of life. The factors exposed are too complex and variable over time and space to meet John Barrett's expectation to see processes in time that are "routinely structured in relation to each other." Nor is it likely that perpetuations of memory carry forward individual consciousness and action to forge the longer-term structures of society. What we have seen is certainly evidence of people striving to comprehend their lives and the world about them, but their knowledge is imperfect, their choices narrowly circumscribed, the processes at work resistant to a daily potential for disruption through existentialist human actors, as Giddens would have us believe.

This scenario of past time closely matches a thought-provoking analysis by the anthropologist Paul Sant Cassia of how and why contemporary Mediterranean populations conform consciously and subconsciously to their stereotypes:

These examples . . . seem to bring out the ultimate irony and final paradox in the depiction of social life as "theatre" in the Mediterranean. In all the above examples . . . men and women are not just actors in search of characters in order to define and project their own true selves. They are also writing and acting out a play about their predicament as characters within a wider social drama over which they sometimes have little control, except in the way they act their parts. (Sant Cassia 1991: 14)

A second realization is this: if social structures are more than the sums of their parts, that is to say, if the human actor is more often than not constrained in choice and direction rather than being socially creative, then structure cannot be merged into a variant of agency.

These considerations lead us to question the importance of sourcing the origin of a lasting social or economic institution, way of thought, or *mode de vie* to an event or person and place. More informative is to comprehend how significant numbers of individuals opt in, or choose from limited pathways, or are merely conditioned to accept a trend or persistent shape to social behavior. At the same time, the undeniable appearance at irregular time intervals of waves of change leading to new forms of life, and the quite unforeseen effects of the conjunctive clashing of processes operating at all three Braudelian timescales, show the necessity of formulating a character for the direction or course of history which is fundamentally unpredictable. Yet unpredictability operates *despite* the equally undeniable evidence for the regular creation of persistent forms and shapes to human social life.

Paradoxically, then, the story of the past is not, as some postmodern historians seem to portray it, "one damn thing after another" (Kuzminski, quoted in Steinberg 1981), but neither can it conform to any predictive model. All of which brings us to reformulate the problem of structure and agency into this question: "How do we reconcile scenarios which are beyond prediction and yet full of trends, alternately persistently shaped and shapelessly disordered?"

Punctuated Equilibrium, Chaos, and Complexity

Remarkably, at this critical point the burden can be shifted from the powerful shoulders of the Annales historians onto – surprisingly – those of theorists in the natural sciences. Two bodies of contemporary theory will take us towards a solution of our reformulated research issue of structure and agency. The first is the theory of punctuated equilibrium first outlined by Eldredge and Gould in 1972, and most influentially in Stephen Jay Gould's modern classic, *Wonderful Life* (1989). Gould explores the wider implications of this theory of zoological evolution, extending it into a general theory of the nature of history on earth itself: the past is the result of the uncertain interplay between chance occurrences and the adaptive pressures which lead to lasting and ever more complex ecological and biotic structures. We can "postdict" but never "predict" the outcomes. In a much-quoted aphorism, Gould states that if we were to rewind the tape of life again, things would probably turn out quite differently.

If Gould emphasizes the devastating shifts of historical trajectory that follow sudden disruptions to biotic communities, a fellow evolutionary theorist utilizing the same data, Conway-Morris (1998), places a contrary emphasis on the enormous adaptive pressures to create shapes that persist, trends that chain rather than disconnect. Yet both accept the unpredictability of detailed evolutionary outcomes. The wider implications of these ideas have recently been explored by Gould himself, fellow evolutionary biologists, physical and social anthropologists, and an archaeologist (Bintliff 1999e; see also Chippindale 1990).

Complementary to, and enriching, the theory of punctuated equilibrium, is the interdisciplinary theory termed *chaos-complexity* (Gleick 1987; Lewin 1993; Reed and Harvey 1992; Kaufmann 1995; Van der Leeuw and McGlade 1997). A networking of empirical and theoretical observations and ideas running from the world of pure mathematics and computer simulations to the everyday problems of predicting the weather, the stock market, traffic jams, and the best location for shopping malls, its interest for us lies in its central postulates, which present a radical reformulation of the structure–agency debate. In very general terms, complexity – elaborate and persistent interacting constellations made up of many diverse but discrete "players" – arises, exists, and disappears over time, as a result of the non-linear, non-determined, and unpredictable conjunction of arbitrary, agent-based variability *and* adaptive pressures to give duration to inclusive structures. For history and prehistory, read: individuals, events, places, in a dialectic with societies, cross-cultural convergent processes, and trends of the *moyenne* and *longue durée*. The resultant structures are termed *attractors*.

Archaeologists have already explored the possibilities of comparing social change to mathematical trends, where small changes can produce dramatic system shifts – notably Colin Renfrew's discussion of catastrophe theory (Renfrew and Cooke 1979). The particular advance presented by research into complexity is the recognition that small differences are a constant component of structure: they cause increasing divergence of forms over time even when structures look remarkably similar and the major variables are constant between networks being compared, and they threaten the dissolution of structures at arbitrary moments of time. Minor contrasts in initial conditions tend to enlarge into radically divergent pathways of development. The more complex a system becomes, the further it tends to be from equilibrium and nearer to the "edge of chaos." At the same time, positive feedback to adaptive structures forms a counterbalancing force favoring the crystallization of

persistent inclusive structures or networks – the attractors. In societal terms, we can sidestep the possible too-limited reading of "adaptation" as an extra-human process akin to Darwinian species-survival by enlarging the means of "adaptation" of a structure to include elements such as a regional *mode de vie* or a set of social institutions. This allows us to go beyond the mere physical prosperity of the human group under study, into forms of behavior which satisfy the collective conscious and subconscious needs and aspirations of the individual human agents concerned.

Archaeologists, notably in the United States, have been involved at an early stage in the potential applications of chaos-complexity approaches to the archaeological record (cf. Lewin 1993), and there have been two edited volumes exploring this theme for the human sciences, including archaeology (Van der Leeuw and McGlade 1997 Bentley and Maschner 2003). I have explored the potential of both punctuated equilibrium and chaos-complexity in a number of studies, on the one hand to suggest that they nullify the supposed incompatibility of processual and postprocessual approaches to the human past, and on the other hand in more applied terms to deploy them to analyze regional development pathways from archaeological survey (Bintliff 1997b), the rise and fall of cities (Bintliff 1997a), the emergence of villages, territories, and city-states (Bintliff 1999a, 1999c), and the "attractors" associated with city-states, Roman villas, and English parish churches (Bintliff 1999d). Some insights from these studies follow.

The village-state

Over a period of a few centuries in Iron Age Greece there arose a dense carpet of tiny city-states or *poleis*. The "normal" polis had an average population of 2,000–4,000, not by chance large enough to be virtually endogamous and hence control all its lands (Bintliff 1999a, 1999c). Ernst Kirsten (1956) demonstrated that the astonishing abundance of these tiny states is explained by revealing their true status as large villages. The network of mature villages from which the cities emerge (the *Dorfstaat*, as Kirsten termed it) betrays cross-cultural regularity in its modal territory of some half-hour radius of land. Over time more powerful villages expanded their authority over neighbors, and many once-independent villages and small cities became subordinate to a minority of dominant poleis. With pressure to make land more productive, a minority of citizens moved out to live in farms and villas outside of the city. Thus by ca. 500 BC there was established through southern Greece a "structure" of village-towns within natural territories, often focused on larger cities and at the same time having their own satellite rural sites. This general pattern will persist without serious modification for some 1,100 years until the late sixth century AD. To be sure, the towns will grow and shrink, the farms and villas multiply and decrease, but the structure of life remains little altered.

However, the structural timelessness goes deeper than mere settlement pattern, into the sociopolitical sphere. The anthropologist Robin Dunbar (1992, 1996) argues that unstratified human communities tend to adapt to our biological limits of not being able to process social relationships with more than some 200 individuals. If a village does not undergo fission at this point but grows far larger, it is because it has overcome this face-to-face organizational constraint through horizontal or vertical subdivision of the community. In the case of our typical Greek polis, we find that the normal form of government limited power to the nobles and wealthier farming class: some 200–400 or so adult males. Since only a certain proportion of these men would have regularly participated in the political process, it can be claimed that a vertical power hierarchy was well adapted to biological constraints. And once again we find that the power structure of the Greek landscape for some 1,100 years remained one where characteristically an elite minority controlled the cities.

If we find here a structure with an underlying persistence reminiscent of Ladurie's (1974) "timeless history," we may expect to find it in very different places and times (Bintliff 1999c, 1999d). Indeed, a similar structure recurs as a focus of interest to historians of Medieval Western Europe researching into the origin of the village community. During the late first millennium and early second millennium AD there emerged a widespread trend towards nucleated villages organized as "corporate communities" by village councils with wide-ranging powers. For example, study of over 13,000 English villages recorded in the Domesday Book of 1086 shows that they were typically still at the face-to-face level of 150 people or less, but population growth in the following three centuries could be accommodated through the crystallization of communal power around a minority of adult male yeoman farmers. The territorial scale of these expanding villages is commonly some half-hour radius. But although these corporate communities may have been responsible across wide swathes of Western Europe for the restructuring of land use into the two-and three-field system, they did not, at the village scale, transform themselves into city-states of the *Dorfstaat* type or develop an artistic and intellectual life in any way comparable to the normal Greek polis. For here, historical contingency cuts through structural tendencies.

Archaic Greece with its proliferating village-states was a power vacuum, lacking significant dominant states and still beyond the reach of external colossi such as the Persian Empire. This chance circumstance opened an almost unique dimension to the otherwise familiar process of population growth following a cultural collapse (in this case the fall of Bronze Age palace civilization). The development of a landscape of corporate village communities might have been predicted, but the contingent absence of any superstructure of power freed villages to assume total authority over their small worlds, to invent the state in the compass of a large English parish, with all the cultural impetus that such autonomy brought.

In complete contrast, the corporate villages of Medieval Western Europe were almost entirely created under the watchful eyes of powerful states and their feudal lordship; real and important though the village councils were for land management and everyday law, there were always clear limits to freedom of action and investment of surplus wealth and labor. Only in Italy, where feudal powers were weaker and divided, can we see a mushrooming of city-states (200–300 by the twelfth century AD).

Chaotic structures in complex equilibrium?

The application of chaos-complexity ideas in the social sciences, including archaeology, is at a pioneer stage, but one can identify areas of considerable potential for future research. For example, if very complex entities such as extensive civilizations are closer to the "edge of chaos" than less hierarchical, geographically more confined forms of sociopolitical structure, the contrasts between those civilizations with strong temporal persistence and those that are short-lived, raise fundamental questions about the processes sustaining these forms of life. In the case of relatively ephemeral civilizations, such as that of Mycenaean Greece or Chalcolithic southeastern Spain, the potential effectiveness of even minor perturbations (which could well include the actions of individual historical actors) can become magnified into large-scale political breakdown, as predicted by chaos theory. What, though, are the implications of chaos-complexity for the prolonged survivors: Minoan Bronze Age civilization on Crete, Pharaonic Egyptian civilization, and even more strikingly, the Roman Empire?

The search for such contrasts as a source of historical insight forms a further intellectual link with the Annales School, since also in that tradition it has been stated that an effective way to probe the interactions of multiple temporal processes is to focus on a specific historical problem (*problème histoire*; cf. Bintliff 1991b: 13–15).

A useful point of departure for the specific question asked here – persistence or temporal fragility of complex societies – is the use of thermodynamics in the study of complex systems. The study of energy sources indicates that the "arrow of time" allows only one ultimate path for energy – its dispersal (entropy). There is underlying pressure to disaggregate foci of energy and spread it evenly through space. Chaos-complexity theorists focus on the counter-intuitive observation that almost all developmental trajectories exhibit this predicted property and at the same time the emergence of energy foci. Most notable is the currently perceived history of the universe itself (Coveney and Highfield 1990), where the unparalleled ball of energy of the Big Bang has been followed by endless entropic dispersal with the expanding physical universe, and yet the creation of generations of high-energy suns. For the leading thinkers of chaos-complexity, numerous small-scale physical experiments confirm that, provided the relevant systems are open, intermediate "traps" of energy can arise, in so-called "dissipative structures" in between energy focus and thermodynamic dissolution (Prigogine 1996; Stengers and Prigogine 1997). *Autocatalytic processes, emergent complexity*, and *self-organization* are all terms for this formation of structures.

Thus one critical factor which might allow a vast and complex structure such as a civilization to achieve unusual persistence, would be its ability to capture additional energy flows for its own sustenance from those sustaining its initial growth. The civilization should then be adaptable, "open," so as to circumvent the expected disruption from enhancement of minor perturbations in its internal structure and external context.

Although I can speculate at this high level of generalization about possible ways to approach ancient civilizations, you might now reasonably accuse me of the mirror-failing to structuration theory: sacrificing all agency to structure. However, as discussed earlier, it is self-evident that elaborate human social forms cannot be vulnerable to dissolution on a day-to-day, individual agent basis. Those social networks which do exhibit the limitations of extreme brevity, or persistent instability, probably remain so as a result of such small-scale interventions and challenges, but by definition, any social structure with significant temporal persistence should have achieved a significant degree of resistance to recurrent variabilities within itself. One mechanism we have already investigated is continual reinforcement of the structure by its constituent human agents, although we have expressed doubts as to whether conscious choice is the dominant motive (Bourdieu's 1977 concept of *habitus* is a happier, more neutral term, preferable to Giddens' implication of an important degree of conscious planning). The second form of process would be adaptability: we would expect evidence of trends of renewal and transformation in persistent complex social structures. Thirdly, *dissipative far from equilibrium systems* – to use the jargon of chaos-complexity – should be open rather than closed systems and continually trap new energy supplies to stave off their entropic fragmentation.

I shall conclude this discussion with preliminary comments on the relevance of these ideas to the *problème histoire* of the Roman Empire and its remarkable temporal and spatial scale (cf. Bintliff 1997a: 87–88). First, something on the role of individual human agents.

In keeping with my comments on continual disruptive threats by human agency, it would be expected that the principle "the whole is greater than the sum of its parts" ought to hold true for a vast society with a trajectory of some 1,200 years. In one of the classic in-depth studies of the mature Empire, it is significant that Fergus Millar (1977) concludes that the internal mechan-

isms regulating the Roman imperial system were sufficient to guarantee a high probability of its survival regardless of the brilliance or madness of the current emperor. At the same time, there is a reasonable case to be made that the predicted requirement of structural transformation was met on critical occasions by an individual agent. Octavian-Augustus, for example, rescued the failing republic from unstable dictatorship by formulating a different form of centralized government – the principate – which generally managed to avoid the structural weaknesses of those other alternatives (Zanker 1988). Constantine the Great, in the fourth century AD, consciously put his personal weight behind the growing fragmentation of the empire into regions of varying strength and weakness by relocating the imperial capital to Constantinople (effectively loosening dependency on the declining western provinces and tying the Empire's fate to the increasingly flourishing eastern provinces). If this was a calculated reading of earlier tendencies marked by the decline of Italy and the marginalization of the city of Rome in favor of multiple imperial capitals (Milan, Trier, Thessaloniki), another decision of Constantine was more historically contingent or even "arbitrary": his promotion of the Christian religion, then still an obscure minority sect opposed to the established religion of the Empire (Elsner 1998).

Indeed, although the Western Roman Empire collapsed definitively in the fifth century AD, and the Eastern Empire all but did so in the seventh century, it is unquestionable that Constantine's individual intervention made possible a "bifurcation" of societal development – the West being molded into regional kingdoms and ultimately emergent nation-states based around barbarian tribal states, the East witnessing a radical further transformation of the rump sixth–seventh century Roman Empire into the Byzantine Empire. The latter political unit – which thus correctly would always term itself "Roman" – was to survive (but with further significant adaptive reformings) for a further

800 years, till its dissolution with the Ottoman conquest of 1453.

Nonetheless, focusing on "emergent complexity," the challenge is to account for the effective survival of the wider Roman Empire to the fourth to sixth centuries AD, despite its theoretical position on the "edge of chaos." An element already predicted would be the punctuated injection of new adaptive transformations into its structure. Indeed, the political organization of imperial rule underwent occasional critical transformations. Early republican aristocratic rule changed to that of late republican warlords; this was followed in early imperial times (in large part due to Augustus) by a careful balance between the decisions and initiatives of a single autocrat – the emperor – and the more effective and lasting day-to-day practical control by the imperial army and bureaucracy and provincial town elites. In the late Empire the failings of this system led to a total reorganization of provinces, the army, and the roles of bureaucracy and town elites (notably inaugurated by Diocletian), and finally, when the Eastern Empire entered into its own period of threatening extinction in the seventh century, once again a political restructuring (the "theme" organization) of the provinces created survival capsules which ensured a further 800 years for the Empire.

A second element which we have seen to be relevant to "emergent complexity" is the prevention of systemic – in this case sociopolitical – fragmentation due to internal diversification and resource depletion, through tapping external flows of energy. It has often been observed that there is a potential causative link between the stabilization of frontiers, cessation of expansion, and internal decay, both for the Roman and other imperial systems (e.g., the Ottoman). As I have noted elsewhere (Bintliff 1997a), we can bring this observation into relation with that school of thought which sees ancient imperialism as a process of predator–prey expansion cycles, growth of the core being conditioned by expansion of the resource catchment supporting the system. In complexity terms, the Roman Empire avoided "chaos" in at least two ways. Firstly, by irregularly undergoing major alterations in the rules of its structure, as we have seen; and secondly and perhaps more importantly, through trapping new energy sources (through conquest or incorporation, and also through stimulating increased surplus production of human and natural resources in newly acquired territories). Nonetheless, by the third century AD territorial stabilization had occurred and began indeed to give way to defensive strategies, as the Empire came under increasing predatory attack from external tribal and alternative civilizational systems.

We witness an unpredictable bifurcation of political pathways in the late Empire. The East retained a strongly modified autocratic imperial system and over time underwent internal homogenization centered on Greek culture and language, hastened by the progressive loss of provinces dominated by other cultures and languages. In the West, the opposite pattern – the deliberate settlement of distinct clusters of barbarian peoples (Goths, Vandals, Franks, Anglo-Saxons), or their unstoppable colonization within the imperial provinces, and the increasing dominance of these elements in the Roman army – laid the basis for the dismemberment of the Western Empire into a series of barbarian states, from which would emerge the outlines of the early modern nation-states. But contingency is always a potent "wild card" – the Balkan core of the Eastern Empire was overrun by Slav tribes in the sixth to seventh centuries AD, and only with difficulty (not least as a result of imperial reorganization noted above) was most of it reincorporated into the Eastern Empire.

Conclusions

In this chapter I have argued that the human past cannot be predicted because it is not determined by the physical environment or by conscious human actors, either individually, or through the activities of social structures. It can, however, be postdicted through the careful taking apart of the evidence in accordance with these methodologies:

- Annaliste structural history with its overlapping temporalities of actions and mentalities.
- Punctuated equilibrium with its nonlinear interplay between contingency and persistent tendencies for the creation of formal structures.
- Chaos-complexity theory, with its subtle openness to the full potential of both human and other individual agent interventions in the world, and simultaneously its empirical support for the "constraining and enabling" effects of the more dominant "attractors" – the structures (social, cultural, ecological, technological) – on developmental trajectories over time.

How can archaeologists deploy this new understanding?

Firstly, it is now apparent that an investigation of the past which commences with grand models is inappropriate. We must assemble the varied data from our region, site, or landscape without interpretive preconceptions as to its "predictableness." Notwithstanding the fact that we must consider carefully how much we are limited by our technologies and forms of data collection and analysis (something learnt from postprocessualism). At the same time, we require a breadth of anthropological, historical scenarios: these are valuable for purposes of comparison with any patterns or trends which become visible as we order the archaeological evidence. A major focus remains the identification of time-persistent "shapes" – the "attractors" – which may emerge out of the purely unique, non-recurrent events met with in the data.

Secondly, after this stage of study we hope to have clarified a sequence of stabilities and transformations in society and landscape for the area and period which are our research focus, graded against varied timescales, with the aim of separating out the different wavelengths of Braudelian time-process. If we are fortunate in the resolution of our evidence, it may be possible to compare structures and their lack, both at the level of whole societies or communities and at the level of the household, or even the individual (Bintliff 1989).

When we come to try and account for the temporal sequence (i.e., "what happened") we would have to accept a vital role both for contingency and for emergent and constraining attractors. The result would become a mapping of interactions between temporal processes and societal and ecological structures, with discrete events and individual people, without predictable and *a priori* interrelations. We expect that balanced against the tendency for scenarios to be drawn gravitationally into adaptively successful modes of life (Conway-Morris 1998), we would find sequences of changes which defy simplification into trends or structures and whose forms can merely be documented through "thick description" of the evidence (Gould 1989) – akin to "chaos." In the most extreme circumstances, the lack of lasting trends and structures which pull human behaviors into dominant shape would provide a historical record which cannot be modeled and where archaeological analysis would contain little less than a full description of the dynamics of the material culture evidence over time and space. In reality, the archaeological record can be argued to be remarkably similar to that of the geological fossil record (cf. examples in Bintliff 1999e), in that it offers strong indications of punctuated equilibrium processes. Episodes of unstructured events are irregular and unpredictable in timing, but much shorter-lived than the intervening phases of structural coherence, represented either by stability or evolving and transforming complexity.

References

Baber, Z. 1991. "Beyond the structure/agency dualism: an evaluation of Giddens' theory of structuration." *Sociological Enquiry*, 61: 219–30.

Barrett, J. 1994. *Fragments from Antiquity: An Archaeology of Social Life in Britain, 2900–1200 BC*. Oxford: Blackwell.

Bentley, R. A. and H. D. G. Maschner (eds.) 2003. *Complex Systems and Archaeology*, Salt Lake City: The University of Utah Press.

Bintliff, J. L. 1989: "Cemetery populations, carrying capacities and the individual in history." In C. A. Roberts, F. Lee, and J. L. Bintliff (eds.), *Burial Archaeology*, pp. 85–104. Oxford: British Archaeological Reports, Brit. Ser. 211.

Bintliff, J. L. (ed.) 1991a. *The Annales School and Archaeology*. Leicester: Leicester University Press.

Bintliff, J. L. 1991b. "The contribution of an Annaliste/structural history approach to archaeology." In J. L. Bintliff (ed.), *The Annales School and Archaeology*, pp. 1-33. Leicester: Leicester University Press.

Bintliff, J. L. 1997a. "Catastrophe, chaos and complexity: the death, decay and rebirth of towns from antiquity to today." *Journal of European Archaeology*, 5: 67–90.

Bintliff, J. L. 1997b. "Regional survey, demography, and the rise of complex societies in the ancient Aegean: core–periphery, neo-Malthusian, and other interpretive models." *Journal of Field Archaeology*, 24: 1–38.

Bintliff, J. L. 1999a. "The origins and nature of the Greek city-state and its significance for world settlement history." In P. Ruby (ed.), *Les Princes de la protohistoire et l'émergence de l'etat*, pp. 43–56. Rome: Ecole Française de Rome.

Bintliff, J. L. 1999b. "Pattern and process in the city landscapes of Boeotia, from Geometric to Late Roman times." In M. Brunet (ed.), *Territoire des cités Grecques*, pp. 15–33. Athens: Ecole Française d'Athénes, BCH Supplement.

Bintliff, J. L. 1999c. "Settlement and territory." In G. Barker (ed.), *The Companion Encyclopedia of Archaeology*, pp. 505–45. London: Routledge.

Bintliff, J. L. 1999d. "Structure, contingency, narrative and timelessness." In J. L. Bintliff (ed.), *Structure and Contingency in the Evolution of Life: Human Evolution and Human History*, pp. 132–48. London: Cassell.

Bintliff, J. L. (ed.) 1999e. *Structure and Contingency in the Evolution of Life: Human Evolution and Human History*. London: Cassell.

Bourdieu, P. 1977. *Outline of a Theory of Practice*. Cambridge: Cambridge University Press.

Braudel, F. 1972. *The Mediterranean and the Mediterranean World in the Age of Philip II*, 2 vols. London: Fontana/Collins.

Chippindale, C. 1990. "Editorial." *Antiquity*, 64, September: 448–50.

Clegg, S. 1992. "How to become an internationally famous British social theorist." *Sociological Review*, 576–98

Conway-Morris, S. 1998. *The Crucible of Creation*. Oxford: Oxford University Press.

Coveney, P. and R. Highfield 1990. *The Arrow of Time*. London: W. H. Allen.

Duby, G. and A. Wallon (eds.) 1975. *Histoire de la France rurale, t.1*. Paris: Seuil.

Dunbar, R. 1992. "Why gossip is good for you." *New Scientist*, November 21: 28–31.

Dunbar, R. 1996. *Grooming, Gossip and the Evolution of Language*. London: Faber and Faber.

Eldredge, N. and S. J. Gould 1972. "Speciation and punctuated equilibrium: an alternative to phyletic gradualism." In T. J. Schopf (ed.), *Models in Paleobiology*, pp. 82–115. San Francisco: Freeman, Cooper.

Elsner, J. 1998. *Imperial Rome and Christian Triumph*. Oxford: Oxford University Press.

Favory, F. and J. L. Fiches (eds.) 1994. *Les Campagnes de la France Méditerrannéene dans l'antiquité et le haut moyen age*. Paris: Editions de la Maison des Sciences de l'Homme.

Fentress, J. and C. Wickham 1992. *Social Memory*. Oxford: Blackwell.

Foxhall, L. 1995. "Monumental ambitions: the significance of posterity in Greece." In N. Spencer (ed.), *Time, Tradition and Society in Greek Archaeology: Bridging the "Great Divide"*, pp. 132–49. London: Routledge.

Giddens, A. 1976. *New Rules of Sociological Method*. London: Hutchinson.

Gleick, J. 1987. *Chaos: Making a New Science*. London: Hutchinson.

Goudineau. C. and J. Guilaine (eds.) 1991. *De Lascaux au grand Louvre. Archéologie et histoire en France*. Paris: Editions Errance.

Gould, S. J. 1989. *Wonderful Life*. London: Hutchinson.

Jones, C. 1994. *The Cambridge Illustrated History of France*. Cambridge: Cambridge University Press.

Kaufmann, S. 1995. *At Home in the Universe: The Search for the Laws of Complexity*. Harmondsworth: Penguin Books.

Kirsten, E. 1956. *Die Griechische Polis Als Historisch-Geographisches Problem Des Mittelmeerraumes*. Bonn: Colloquium Geographicum 5.

Ladurie, E. Le Roy 1966. *Les Paysans de Languedoc*. Paris: École Pratique des Hautes Études SEVPEN.

Ladurie, E. Le Roy, 1971. *Times of Feast and Famine: A History of the Climate Since the Year 1000*. New York: Doubleday.

Ladurie, E. Le Roy 1974. "L'histoire immobile." *Annales*, 29: 673–92.

Ladurie, E. Le Roy 1978. *Montaillou: Cathars and Catholics in a French Village 1294–1324*. London: Scolar Press.

Ladurie, E. Le Roy and J. Goy 1982. *Tithe and Agrarian History from the Fourteenth to the Nineteenth Century*. Cambridge and Paris: Cambridge University Press/Editions de la Maison des Sciences de l'Homme.

Lewin, R. 1993. *Complexity: Life at the Edge of Chaos*. London: J. M. Dent.

Millar, F. 1977. *The Emperor in the Roman World*. London: Duckworth.

Paterson, L. 1993. *The World of the Troubadours*. Cambridge: Cambridge University Press.

Prigogine, I. 1996. "Life's expectancy." *Times Literary Supplement*, April 5: 17.

Reed, M. and D. L. Harvey 1992. "The new science and the old: complexity, and realism in the social sciences." *Journal for the Theory of Social Behaviour*, 2 (4): 353–80.

Renfrew, C. and K. L. Cooke (eds.) 1979. *Transformations: Mathematical Approaches to Culture Change*. London: Academic Press.

Sant Cassia, P. 1991. "Authors in search of a character: personhood, agency and identity in the Mediterranean." *Journal of Mediterranean Studies*, 1: 1–17.

Sant Cassia, P. 1999. "Tradition, tourism and memory in Malta." *Journal of the Royal Anthropological Institute*, 5: 247–63.

Steinberg, J. 1981. " 'Real Authentick History' or what philosophers of history can tell us." *Historical Journal*, 24 (2): 453–74.

Stengers, I. and I. Prigogine 1997. *The End of Certainty: Time, Chaos, and the New Laws of Nature*. New York: Free Press.

Toubert, P. 1973. *Les Structures du latium mediéval*. Paris: Bibliothèque des Écoles françaises d'Athènes et de Rome.

Van der Leeuw, S. E. and J. McGlade (eds.) 1997. *Time, Process and Structured Transformation in Archaeology*. London: Routledge.

Zanker, P. 1988. *The Power of Images in the Age of Augustus*. Ann Arbor: University of Michigan Press.

Part III
Major Traditions in Archaeology in Contemporary Perspective

11

Archaeological Dating

J. A. J. Gowlett

Introduction: Measuring Time Change in Archaeology

"How old are things?" is one of the fundamental questions of archaeology, as was discovered by Willard F. Libby, the creator of radiocarbon dating, when he first sought to test his new method against samples of known age: he soon found that there were precious few objects truly so well dated that they could meet his needs (Libby 1955: 107).

Chronology, in a dictionary definition, is the science of computing time or periods of time and of assigning events to their true dates. In archaeology, most of which is prehistory, this can present many challenges. This chapter is about the issues of archaeological timescales, and about the way they affect archaeological interpretation. Today, archaeology is dominated by social ideas, and the building blocks of the subject are admitted somewhat grudgingly. It could be said that people prefer to be on the bridge rather than in the engine room.

If "ideas archaeologists" can take a somewhat lofty view that they do not need the detail, it is only because of the enormous contribution made by dating scientists within the last fifty years: these have shaped the framework within which ideas have the scope to flourish. Moreover, theoreticians should not be proud of the extent to which archaeology has polished its own theory yet failed to address many aspects of chronological methodology in the areas where archaeology has an interface with other sciences (often the task has fallen to radiocarbon specialists, e.g. Waterbolk 1971; Bronk Ramsey 1998).

Indeed, it could be said that most archaeologists are perhaps uninterested in chronology for its own sake. A dating problem such as "When did Thera erupt?" is fascinating when we do not know the answer. But when we do, the interest passes, just like the result of last year's horse race or lottery. If so, the enduring interest of chronology is that in archaeology we do not know all the results; and that each new achievement makes another one necessary.

There are two main ways of looking at chronology, which affect the fundamental organization of this chapter. The first is that we look back from the present. We can establish continuity so far – and then the breaks begin. We use all the means at our disposal to peer back and assemble a coherent record. Second, however, the arrow of time runs forward. To follow events as they affect one another, we start at the beginning and run forwards in a logical succession. Who, in general, would read a novel from back to front? But archaeology is not just a story or narrative, and so our actual interest as chronologists lies in the whole time spectrum as mapped out for us. There are of course many ways of looking at time apart from those of Western science, which has conditioned those who use clocks and calendars. Hallowell (1937) describes the cyclical nature of time as perceived by the Ojibwa; Ingold (1986) the concepts of time as they affect anthropology more generally. Bailey (1983) discusses notions of archaeological time, and Bintliff (1991) the Annaliste school of thought and its relevance to archaeological approaches. As a matter of practical convenience, this chapter uses some recent examples to establish principles, and then in the following chapter I shall give content to the timescale from early to late.

Let us start with a simple outline of chronology. This will make plain a few of the problems. Figure 11.1 provides an overview of the main techniques and data. In essence we are interested in a human past. We shall see in chapter 12 that hominid ancestors probably diverged from apes 5–8 million years ago. Technology – a first mark of human activity – becomes visible less than 3 million years ago. There follow about 2.5 million years of Stone Age, during which early humans spread around the world, and at some stage within the last 500,000 years more modern humans appeared. There is a marked change of pace in the last 100,000 years, with evidence of symbolism and new technologies. Then domestication and agriculture begin around 10,000 years ago; cities and civilizations appear in some areas from about 5,000 years ago; human activity flourished on an immensely greater scale – but much of the world has remained in prehistory until the last few hundred years (Semaw et al. 1997; Harris 1983; Gamble 1993; Klein 1999; Rightmire 1990, 1996; papers in Aitken et al. 1993; Harris 1996; Oates 1993).

Almost the entire modern framework for looking at these events has been provided

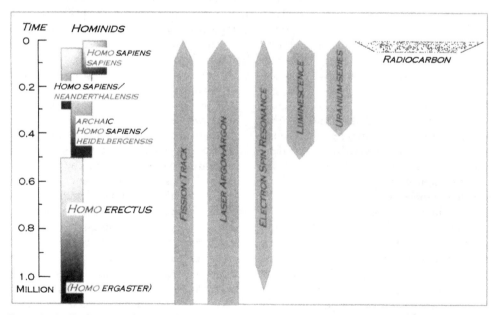

Figure 11.1 Radiometric dating techniques available through the Pleistocene, showing the approximate time ranges of their application.

for us by radiometric dating methods. These have given accurate scale to an earlier framework which was built up painstakingly on the basis of stratigraphy, from the early days of archaeology in the early 1800s, to about 1950. A spate of new techniques came in the 1950s: radiocarbon dating, potassium-argon, and uranium-series (Libby 1955; Evernden and Curtis 1965; Curtis 1981; Stearns and Thurber 1965; Broecker and Bender 1972; Aitken 1990). Later came Thermoluminescence, fission track, and other experimental techniques (Fleming 1979; Aitken 1990; Gleadow 1980).

In the last twenty years, rather than entirely new techniques, there have come in numerous refinements, often based on a "micro" approach (Aitken 1998; Tuniz 1998). The development of radiocarbon dating by accelerator mass spectrometry (AMS) has reduced sample size a thousand-fold, while lasers have brought added precision to potassium-argon, U-series, and luminescence (OSL) dating (Hedges et al. 1997; Walter et al. 1991; Schwarcz 1993; Aitken and Valladas 1993; Aitken 1998; Tuniz 1998).

From such techniques we know the outline sketched in above quite definitely, but subject to certain limitations of resolution, accuracy, and precision. In archaeological dating there are three main components: one, to ask "how old is it?", the next, in respect of sites and sequences, to ask "how long does it go on?", and the third to ask "how fast does it change?" Often we can achieve the first, have little clue of the second, and struggle to gain sight of the third. Yet this last, the business of rates of change, is at the very heart of cultural interpretation in archaeology. In practical terms the main factor is the available precision of dating techniques. In percentages, the techniques which we possess achieve similar success all the way through 2 million years. If we compare the age (mean or average) and the uncertainty value attached to it, the answer is usually in the range 5–10 percent. For radiocarbon in the last few millennia, the error usually

works out as 100–200 years (which can seem a lot). But for the early Pleistocene, the same error ratio reflects uncertainties of +/− 20,000 years. Just occasionally we can do better, but sometimes the result is what Mike Baillie (1994, 1995) the dendrochronologist has called "needless precision" – precision that an archaeologist cannot actually use.

Just how much precision does archaeology need? This depends on many things, particularly whether we need to (or can hope to) operate on the scale of the individual life, or whether a more general view of events is actually more desirable (cf. Bintliff 1991). In general, beginnings are always hazy, largely as a matter of sampling: there are few sites, and small chance of finding them. These factors, and vagaries of preservation, may be more important in determining archaeological resolution than the precision available in the techniques of dating. Even so, the dating techniques available for different periods give different precisions. These may or may not mesh well with the available archaeological resolution. In each case archaeology has a duty to adjust its own questions and methodology to what is realistically available. For example, human occupations may have expanded and contracted through time – perhaps many times over – but direct evidence of this may be lacking (Bar-Yosef 1996; Gamble 1993).

Thus we have to be aware of the changes of scale in archaeology. There are far more events to record in the last 250,000 years than the previous 2.5 million; far more again in the last 100,000; and probably a hundred times as many again in the last 10,000 (the Recent or Holocene). In later times the increase becomes exponential. Although archaeologists are sometimes happy to hand over to historians the burden of events in the last three or four thousand years, archaeological evidence of any period can on occasion be precise enough to confront us with individuals and moments in their lives.

Establishing a Framework

The Mary Rose

The *Mary Rose*, flagship of Henry VIII, heeled over and sank in AD 1546 in the Solent, soon after the beginning of a war with France. It gives in microcosm a picture of the processes and inferences of dating (McKee 1982; Rule 1983).

How do we know when the *Mary Rose* sank? From records that give the day. They are reliable because they are linked to the present on a calendar in which every day is accounted for. Continuity is therefore the guarantee of accuracy.

In the 1980s the hull of the *Mary Rose* was salvaged. It is a kind of time capsule, but many of the items have a history going back beyond 1546, and their origins may not be known with historical certainty. It seems likely from records that the ship was built in 1510. Dendrochronology (tree ring dating) is consistent with this, but also shows evidence of later refits, perhaps more work than is recorded historically (Bridge and Dobbs 1996). So without the historical evidence, some precise history of the ship could still be compiled; but even with it, archaeological chronology adds to the picture. Any inconsistency, of course, would be shattering. Coins would be expected to show a spectrum of dates up to 1546. What if some had been dated 1548? Then everything would be put into doubt, and every link of evidence would have to be scrutinized in a search for the weakest one. We can say that such a conundrum would be impossible for the *Mary Rose*, but there are many other cases where lines of evidence do conflict, and often it is very hard to resolve the problem.

Even in the case of the *Mary Rose*, some ideas were destroyed. It had been thought that naval guns had solid wheels in their carriages, but those of the *Mary Rose* were spoked. If some such conflict of ideas carried enough weight, one could say this could not be a sixteenth-century wreck, because the evidence was inconsistent (i.e., it did not fit the accepted framework). In this case, it would be absurd to contest the archaeological evidence, which is overwhelming.

Then, without the historical frame, the *Mary Rose* would be just another sunken warship – perhaps related to a particular war, perhaps not. The dates for the *Mary Rose* matter, in that they have a historical significance. In contrast, those for Pompeii do not. Pompeii and Herculaneum were destroyed by an eruption of Vesuvius starting on August 24 AD 79. Again, we know the precise date – once more because an eyewitness account, by Pliny, fits into a calendar (Pliny, *Ep.* vi, 16 and 20 – two letters to the historian Tacitus) – but the catastrophe has virtually no bearing on Roman history: the picture is clear, but not related to a hypothesis (although the preservation of complete townscapes allows many archaeological hypotheses to be formed and tested).

In these examples the date of the main event – the sinking of the ship, the eruption of the volcano – is astonishingly clear. In many archaeological instances, however, there is no equivalent historical frame; it is necessary to establish even the simple idea that some appropriate event is being dated, and the weighting of evidence can be much more troublesome. For help in assessing such factors, we can adapt a system devised by the Dutch archaeologist H. T. Waterbolk for looking at radiocarbon associations: these measure certainty of association between a dated sample and the event of interest (Waterbolk 1971). Waterbolk gives us a scale from A to D:

A   The sample and the event are the same (e.g., a hominid is dated by a technique using a sample from its bone).

B   There is a very good direct or functional association (e.g., the date is on volcanic ash from an eruption which clearly terminated the archaeological occupation of interest).

C   There is a reasonable association (e.g., charcoal is dated from a layer containing bones).

D   There is a weak or limited association (e.g., there is a K/Ar [Potassium-Argon] date, but from a layer underlying the level of archaeological interest).

Such associations help us to work out the validity of individual dates in their site context, without reference to a broader framework. Often, however, a perceived broader hypothesis affects the acceptability of dates. The main factors can be given as follows, in a scale which works from the most specific to the most general:

1   Date: single determination (the product of a dating technique, its validity largely a question of dating assumptions).
2   The date in its context (onus on the archaeologist to verify relations between date and event to be dated – as in Waterbolk's scheme, above).
3   The pattern of dates on a site (overall interpretation of dates which may be obtained by varied methods).
4   The regional pattern of dates (governs regional archaeological hypotheses about the meaning of archaeological events).
5   The global constraints (hypotheses allowable by dint of consideration of the general framework of knowledge).

Where there are conflicts in dating evidence they can usually be examined in this framework. Waterbolk's scheme helps to establish (2) as a vital link between the individual dates (1) and an overall site interpretation (3). Equally important is the broader pattern of perceived events, given by levels 4 and 5.

When a date or dates have been obtained, there is often a measure of doubt. Perhaps the dates seem not to fit, there is a large declared error margin, or the conclusions, if accepted, involve a major reassessment. Quite often, material from a newly dated site (3) appears to conflict with regional (level 4) or global models (level 5)

Which should then be believed? Such problems are a challenge to archaeological methodology. In the end, levels 4 and 5 are also based strictly on dating evidence, although this may not be so evident. Levels 4 and 5 are usually strongly grounded in people's minds, usually as a result of cumulative research over a long period, though sometimes as a result of some single hypothesis, which may or may not have been rigorously tested.

Archaeology has not done much to come to terms with such problems, perhaps because of the frequent difficulty of deciding how to partition errors between archaeology and scientific method. How do you decide whether a date is more likely to be wrong because of a freak context, or because of an error of measurement? Few people will be expert in both areas, and there will be little background for comparison. But it is possible to build up case studies of problems, and to use these for reference.

These points about context and levels embrace the old scheme of *relative* and *absolute* dating (refined by the late K. P. Oakley; see, for example, Oakley 1966). An absolute date provides a value in calendar years; a relative date gives an age relative to something else. This important conceptual distinction is now blurred in practice, because we can almost always place absolute limits on relative dates, and many absolute dates – as in radiocarbon – are not quite absolute (see, for example, Bard et al. 1990; Hughen et al. 1998, and discussion below). Gradually, on a grand scale, two major records are being intercalibrated with ever-greater precision: the astronomical record of predictable variations in the earth's orbit; and the marine records of oxygen isotopes and palaeomagnetism, dated via radioisotopes. This is the process of "orbital tuning" (Renne et al. 1993, 1994; Shackleton 1996) which helps to pinpoint the places where gaps do exist in the records. It can be said that we now possess an absolute framework, but that our dates are estimates which nearly always fall short of the absolute.

In the next chapter I shall try to illustrate and test the interplay of these principles.

Ceaselessly, we must ask: "What events do we want to recognize?", "What nature of change is important?", "What resolution do we need?"

On this last point, it is the case that archaeology has usually been able to seek greater resolution almost as an end in itself: always we need more. Yet life is too short to relive all the past, so sampling has to be imposed. Generally, it has been dictated simply by the work archaeologists have done. An ideal might be to know something about every year in the last 5,000 (although the Annaliste approach mentioned above has introduced to history the idea that notions of detail can be excessive). But 2 million years ago we can scarcely be aware of even a thousand year interval. Nobody has yet suggested that we should distinguish carefully between the prehistory of 365,000 and 364,000 years ago.

Dating the Past, Looking to the Future

Almost every problem in archaeology has a chronological aspect. Although there is a natural tendency to consider areas where there are the biggest chronological problems – the biggest margins of doubt, the greatest differences of hypothesis, partly because these present the most gripping issues of interest, and partly because they offer insights into dating problems which operate on a small scale – there is no doubt that smaller problems can be equally crucial – fifty years can also matter.

The dating model of five levels, as outlined at the beginning of this chapter, can help in evaluating such problems, although its principal function is to assess the larger areas of uncertainty. As we have seen, dating techniques themselves have progressed greatly over just such a period, the *last* fifty years. The micro-tendency has greatly improved precision in several techniques, especially radiocarbon, U-series, and potassium-argon (or argon-argon as it now is). Luminescence

techniques are likely to make similar strides forward in accuracy and precision.

The early development of radiometric dating techniques coincided with a time when archaeologists were interested in quantification. Through the 1950s and 1960s the refinement of dating techniques and the development of the New Archaeology or processual archaeology went hand in hand. Superficially, the more recent emphasis on postprocessual (or humanistic) archaeology may seem to have detracted from the development of chronological theory. The approach to higher precision demands an emphasis on process, by both dating scientist and archaeologist. Greater precision in dating – even down to a few years – implies archaeological narrative and objective description, rather than a concentration on ideas. Yet things are rarely quite as they seem. For one thing, behind the frontrunners of archaeological theory there is a great continuity of development in chronology, tied to the unending cycle of excavation and date production. Then, also, different points of view always have something to contribute, and in the long run are assimilated into the mainstream. One might imagine the dating of an individual, such as King Shamsi-Adad, to be the ultimate aim of precision, and look in despair at the uninformative stone tools of early periods, or of recent Australia. This, though, is where the best processual and postprocessual archaeology combine to give a warning. Individuals were as important in Australia, or in the distant past, as in a record where they are named (cf. Gamble 1998). To prefer the archaeology of individuals is to make a choice, among many possible choices (compare again the deliberate dialectic between coarse, medium, and fine-grain chronologies favored by the Annaliste approach, with that of a conventional history). In prehistory we can choose the site where the refitting of stone tools shows actions of an individual through the short chronology of a few minutes; or we may prefer to learn from a palimpsest site, which shows the general pattern of events through thousands of years. Archaeologists choose according to interests. The same is true for any period.

Now that an absolute framework has been roughed out through 50 years of work, superimposed on the previous 150 years of formative study, it can be said that we need new questions of chronology. If so, what are they? In the modern world of collective research, funding initiatives are encouraging archaeologists to address such matters through general strategies. These are helpful for concentrating resources on particular problems (such as dating the origins of the Upper Palaeolithic), but in a broader sense it

is more likely that the new questions will be found by a kind of natural selection. Dates cost money, and for field archaeologists the dating budget is one among various competing requirements. As archaeologists will not pay for dates that are too imprecise, so there is a continuing thrust towards greater precision – which is also what dating scientists seek to provide, simply as good scientists. Sometimes – quite rarely – this process delivers "needless precision," but in the long run there may be no such thing: it is possible to conclude on the optimistic note that new chronological data will always furnish archaeologists with new ideas.

References

Chronology presents the most enormous of bibliographies, since it ranges through every area and period of archaeology. There are hundreds of thousands of radiocarbon dates, alone. The references below give pointers only. A good starting point for detailed searching is the website of the journal *Radiocarbon*. Since AMS and laser work are tending to link different fields of dating at the technical level, their bibliographies are becoming more interrelated.

Aitken, M. J. 1990. *Science-based Dating in Archaeology*. London: Longman.

Aitken, M. J. 1998. *Introduction to Optical Dating*. Oxford: Clarendon Press.

Aitken, M. J. and H. Valladas 1993. "Luminescence dating relevant to human origins." In M. J. Aitken, C. B. Stringer, and P. A. Mellars (eds.), *The Origin of Modern Humans and the Impact of Chronometric Dating*, pp. 27–39. Princeton, NJ: Princeton University Press.

Aitken, M. J., C. B. Stringer, and P. A. Mellars (eds.) 1993. *The Origin of Modern Humans and the Impact of Chronometric Dating*. Princeton, NJ: Princeton University Press.

Bailey, G. 1983. "Concepts of time in quaternary prehistory." *Annual Review of Anthropology*, 12: 165–92.

Baillie, M. G. L. 1994. "Dendrochronology raises questions about the nature of the AD536 dust-veil event." *The Holocene*, 4 (2): 212–17.

Baillie, M. G. L. 1995. *A Slice Through Time*. London: Routledge.

Bard, E., B. Hamelin, R. G. Fairbanks, and A. Zindler 1990. "Calibration of the 14C timescale over the past 30,000 years using mass spectrometric U-Th ages from Barbados corals." *Nature*, 345: 405–10.

Bar-Yosef, O. 1996. "The role of climate in the interpretation of human movements and cultural transformations in Western Asia." In E. S. Vrba, G. H. Denton, T. C. Partridge, and L. H. Burckle (eds.), *Palaeoclimate and Evolution, With Emphasis on Human Origins*, pp. 507–23. New Haven, CT: Yale University Press,

Bintliff, J. 1991. "The contribution of an *Annaliste*/structural history approach to archaeology." In J. Bintliff (ed.), *The Annales School and Archaeology*, pp. 1–33. Leicester: Leicester University Press.

Bridge, M. C. and C. T. C. Dobbs 1996. "Tree ring studies on the Tudor warship *Mary Rose*." In J. S. Dean, D. M. Meko, and T. W. Swetnam (eds.), *Tree Rings, Environment and Humanity: Proceedings of the International Conference Tucson, Arizona, 17–21 May 1994*, pp. 491–6. Arizona: *Radiocarbon*.

Broeker, W. S. and M. L. Bender 1972. "Age determinations on marine strandlines." In W. W. Bishop and J. A. Miller (eds.), *Calibration of Hominoid Evolution*, pp. 19–38. Edinburgh: Edinburgh University Press.

Bronk Ramsey, C. 1998. "Probability and dating." *Radiocarbon*, 40 (1): 461–74.

Curtis, G. H. 1981. "Establishing a relevant timescale in anthropological and archaeological research." In J. Z. Young, E. M. Jope, and K. P. Oakley (eds.), *The Emergence of Man*. London: Royal Society and the British Academy (*Phil Trans. R. Soc. Lond.* B 292, 7–20).

Evernden, J. F. and G. H. Curtis 1965. "Potassium-argon dating of late Cenozoic rocks in East Africa and Italy." *Current Anthropology*, 6: 343–85.

Fleming, S. J. 1979. *Thermoluminescence Techniques in Archaeology*. Oxford: Oxford University Press.

Gamble, C. 1993. *Timewalkers*. London: Alan Sutton.

Gamble, C. 1998. "Handaxes and Palaeolithic individuals." In N. Ashton, F. Healy, and P. Pettitt (eds.), *Stone Age Archaeology: Essays in Honour of John Wymer*, pp. 105–9. Oxbow Monograph 102, Lithic Studies Society Occasional Paper 6. Oxford: Oxbow Books.

Gleadow, A. J. W. 1980. "Fission track age of the KBS Tuff and associated hominid remains in northern Kenya." *Nature*, 284: 225–30.

Hallowell, I. 1937. "Temporal orientation in western civilization and in a preliterate society." *American Anthropologist*, 39: 647–70.

Harris, D. R. (ed.) 1996. *The Origins and Spread of Agriculture and Pastoralism in Eurasia*. London: University College London Press.

Harris, J. W. K. 1983. "Cultural beginnings: Plio-Pleistocene archaeological occurrences from the Afar, Ethiopia." *African Archaeological Review*, 1: 3–31.

Hedges, R. E. M., P. B. Pettitt, and M. S. Tite 1997. "Luminescence and radiocarbon dating at Oxford." *Techne*, 5: 54–60.

Hughen, K. A., J. T. Overpeck, S. J. Lehman, M. Kashgarian, J. R. Southon, and L. C. Peterson 1998. "A new 14C calibration data set for the last deglaciation based on marine varves." *Radiocarbon*, 40 (1): 483–94.

Ingold, T. 1986. *Evolution and Social Life*. Cambridge: Cambridge University Press.

Klein, R. G. 1999. *The Human Career: Human Biological and Cultural Origins*, 2nd edn. Chicago: University of Chicago Press.

Libby, W. F. 1955. *Radiocarbon Dating*. Chicago: University of Chicago Press.

McKee, A. 1982. *How We Found the Mary Rose*. London: Souvenir Press.

Oakley, K. P. 1966. *Frameworks for Dating Fossil Man*. London: Weidenfeld and Nicolson.

Oates, J. (ed.) 1993. "Ancient trade: new perspectives." *World Archaeology*, 24 (3).

Renne, P. R., A. L. Deino, R. C. Walter, B. D. Turrin, C. C. Swisher, T. A. Becker, G. H. Curtis, W. D. Sharp, and A.-R. Jaouni 1994. "Intercalibration of astronomical and radioisotopic time." *Geology*, 22: 783–6.

Renne, P. R., R. C. Walter, K. L. Verosub, M. Sweitzer, and J. L. Aronson 1993. "New data from Hadar (Ethiopia) support orbitally tuned time scale to 3.3 million years ago." *Geophysical Research Letters*, 20: 1067–70.

Rightmire, G. P. 1990. *The Evolution of Homo Erectus*. Cambridge: Cambridge University Press.

Rightmire, G. P. 1996. "The human cranium from Bodo, Ethiopia: evidence for speciation in the Middle Pleistocene?" *Journal of Human Evolution*, 31: 21–39.

Rule, M. H. 1983. *The Mary Rose: The Excavation and Raising of Henry VIII's Flagship*, 2nd edn. London: Conway Maritime Press.

Schwarcz, H. P. 1993. "Uranium-series dating and the origin of modern man." In M. J. Aitken, C. B. Stringer, and P. A. Mellars (eds.), *The Origin of Modern Humans and the Impact of Chronometric Dating*, pp. 12–26. Princeton, NJ: Princeton University Press.

Semaw, S., P. R. Renne, J. W. K. Harris, C. S. Feibel, R. L. Bernor, N. Fesseka, and K. Mowbray 1997. "2.5 million-year-old stone tools from Gona, Ethiopia." *Nature*, 385: 333–6.

Shackleton, N. J. 1996. "New data on the evolution of Pliocene climatic variability." In E. S. Vrba, G. H. Denton, T. C. Partridge, and L. H. Burckle (eds.), *Palaeoclimate and Evolution, with Emphasis on Human Origins*, pp. 242–8. New Haven, CT: Yale University Press.

Stearns, C. E. and D. L. Thurber 1965. "Th230/U234 dates of late Pleistocene marine fossils from the Mediterranean and Moroccan littorals." *Quaternaria*, 7: 29–42.

Tuniz, C. (ed.) 1998. *Accelerator Mass Spectrometry: Ultrasensitive Analysis for Global Science*. New York: Harcourt.

Walter, R. C., P. C. Manega, R. L. Hay, R. E. Drake, and G. H. Curtis 1991. "Laser-fusion 40Ar/39Ar dating of Bed I, Olduvai Gorge, Tanzania." *Nature*, 354: 145–9.

Waterbolk, H. T. 1971. "Working with radiocarbon dates." *Proceedings of the Prehistory Society*, 37 (2): 15–33.

12

Chronology and the Human Narrative

J. A. J. Gowlett

Hominid Origins

When did the first hominid ancestors diverge from an ape stem? When did the first members of our own genus *Homo* appear? These are fundamental and intriguing questions which can be answered only in general terms, and through the interplay of several techniques. Broadly, we are talking about the period 12–6 million years ago, the later part of the Miocene period and the Pliocene, and there is no great problem in dating the periods as such (papers in Vrba et al. 1996 give a recent view). Through this time, there are sediments on land, and ocean cores. Accurate dating of volcanic events is offered by potassium-argon both in Europe and Africa, and deep sea cores provide a vital additional record that can be cross-linked through palaeomagnetism (Shackleton and Opdyke 1973, 1977; Shackleton 1996). The record of past changes in the earth's magnetism also aids cross-linking or correlation between regions, between sea and land. The ocean cores preserve a palaeotemperature record, and information about wind intensities on land (de Menocal and Bloemendahl 1996). In Africa and Eurasia, the evolution of faunas can be traced, for example the first arrival of the three-toed Hipparion horses in Africa, and then of true horses within the last 10 million years (Bernor and Lipscomb

1996; Hill 1996; Opdyke 1996); or the evolution of primates, which can be seen on and off through the last 40 million years (Simons 1995; Delson 1994).

In this frame, the earliest hominids were long represented just by a gap. The picture has been transformed by the spectacular finds of *Orrorin tugenensis* in Kenya (Senut et al. 2001) and *Sahelanthropus tchadensis* in Chad (Brunet et al. 2002), which at a stroke drive the record back to 7 million years. Otherwise, they are largely absent – as are fossil apes within the last 8 million years, although earlier apes are much more visible. This is partly chance, partly a result of biases in the record, caused by the favored preservation of some habitats over others, and of rocks from some periods rather than others. In general the great Rift Valley system of eastern Africa gives exceptional preservation of sediments through the last 20 million years, but some periods such as 5–10 million years ago are preserved in limited areas (Opdyke 1996; Hill 1996; Hill and Ward 1988).

The new fossil finds can be compared with results of a "molecular clock." Comparisons of DNA and proteins of living species allow good estimates to be made of their relative divergence dates, provided that one or two divergence dates are well established in the fossil record. The divergence date of apes and monkeys at least 30 million years ago allowed calculation of the divergence of apes and hominids, in the range 5–8 million years ago (Sarich and Wilson 1968; Goodman et al. 1989; Jeffreys 1989) (more recent calibrations have not refined these estimates).

The new fossil evidence supports dates at the older end of this range. At present, other well-documented hominid fossils go back to around 4.2–4.6 million years. These are the finds of *Ardipithecus ramidus* from the Awash valley in northern Ethiopia, and of *Australopithecus anamensis* from the south end of Lake Turkana in Kenya (White et al. 1994, 1996; Leakey et al. 1995). Fragmentary remains of a hominid jaw from Lothagam in Kenya (Patterson et al. 1967) suggested the possibility of somewhat earlier hominids, as indicated by the newest finds.

Most early hominids have been found in the Rift Valley of East Africa, but the discovery of finds in Chad confirms that this could be an effect of sampling. With the previous isolated find of *Australopithecus afarensis* from Lake Chad, more than 1,000 kilometers from the Rift, this suggests that the actual hominid distribution may have been much broader, and that sampling factors limit their visibility (Brunet et al. 1995). Even so, the Rift Valley is unparalleled both for preservation and the application of dating methods. The extent of rain forest (the ideal ape habitat) and of savanna and denser bush all varied immensely in the past, so that modern biotopes provide little reliable information about past distributions.

From about 3.5 million years, hominids are well represented down the length of Africa from Ethiopia to South Africa, but there are still intriguing gaps and variations in the quality of dating. There is a lacuna from 2.5–2 million years, with very few fossil finds of any substance. In South Africa the cave sites are very hard to date, although ESR (electron spin resonance) and palaeomagnetism are beginning to help: recent finds of early *Australopithecus* from Sterk-fontein have been dated from 2–3.5 million years (Schwarcz et al. 1994; Partridge et al. 1999).

Within the radiation of Australopithecine species, the origin of *Homo* – our own genus – should be a matter of special interest. But this is perhaps as much a problem of classification as of chronology. It may be that scholarship tends to focus on the origins of *Homo* and then of *sapiens* as a direct result of the Linnaean system of classification. This is owed to the eighteenth-century scholar Linnaeus, used universally, and emphasizes the levels of genus and species. Yet palaeontologists are always looking for distinctive features which will help them in arriving at a classification. In this way classification tends to fit itself to the major evolutionary events that are recognizable.

Until recently there were thought to be three species of early *Homo*, present in East Africa at around 1.9 million years ago. These were *Homo habilis*, *Homo rudolfensis*, and *Homo ergaster* (or *erectus*) (Wood 1991, 1992; Rightmire 1990). The implication of such diversity is that a considerable span of time would be needed if these species were to be traced back to some ancestral form of *Homo*, perhaps at 2.5 Ma (millions of years ago) or earlier.

Recent reclassifications – in some ways a return to older views – suggest that the three early species of "*Homo*" are not linked by characters attesting a common origin within *Homo* (Wood and Collard 1999). This implies that two of them should be regarded as varieties of *Australopithecus*, and that *Homo* does not "need" such long chronological roots. On the basis of the evidence now available, it seems that true *Homo* first appears at about 1.9 Ma, around East Turkana in northern Kenya.

In this area the dating of such finds was formerly controversial in itself. Dates for the crucial volcanic ash at East Turkana ranged from 1.8–2.6 million years (Fitch and Miller 1970; Fitch et al. 1976). By 1980 the position was resolved, and a date of around 1.88 million years was established both by potassium-argon and fission track dating (Drake et al. 1980; McDougall et al. 1980; Gleadow 1980). Now the use of the laser-fusion argon technique, the production of large numbers of dates, and chemical "fingerprinting" of volcanic ashes have combined to make the chronologies of East Africa among the most solid. Indeed, the volcanic ashes can also be traced in Arabian Sea cores, providing additional dating evidence and a measure of climatic change. Thus Frank Brown (1996) was able to chart out 25,000 years of deposition with an accuracy and precision which is rarely available except in the last few thousand years.

For most purposes, this record of millennia is more resolution than can be used. There are relatively few early archaeological sites, and we do not understand the variations in their technology. At first, scholars were inclined to suggest that earlier sites would be simpler than later ones. Research in Ethiopia and western Kenya in the 1990s, however, has shown that the early Oldowan tradition has a duration from as much as 2.7 million years down to 1.7 million, and that within this span the very earliest industries show all the skills that were present through almost the next million years (Semaw et al. 1997; Plummer et al. 1999; Harris 1983).

Advances in technological design come only later, with a Developed Oldowan that is dated to ca. 1.6 million years, and the beginnings of the Acheulean hand-ax tradition soon afterwards (Asfaw *et al.* 1992; Isaac and Curtis 1974; Leakey 1971). These developments are reasonably well dated along the Rift Valley, although the greatest site sequences – at Olduvai Gorge and East Turkana – have a discontinuous record of the events. Olduvai Gorge remains in general the best yardstick for early archaeology (Leakey 1971; Leakey and Roe 1995; Walter et al. 1991), but many other sites have to be linked in to provide a fuller picture.

For the next million years, the main problem for chronology is one of dating sites and distributions rather than "new" phenomena of culture – of these there are very few.

The Spread Around the World

The next great problem is "when did humans spread around the world?" In reality this is a thousand problems (and more). The most accepted outline is that humans originated in Africa, that within the last 2 million years they appear in many parts of the globe, and that in the present day they have a broader distribution than any other mammal (Bar-Yosef 1996a; Clark 1992; Gamble 1993).

Our world has a peculiar geography, which dictates that Africa can be left only through a fairly narrow corridor, unless water transport is used. This position has held for about 5 million years, since the straits opened at the south end of the Red Sea. In glacial phases, however, sea level drops, so that the corridor "out of Africa" would be wider than its present 70 kilometers. Once beyond Africa, there are various routes to the east and north – and ultimately to Europe in the west. Landbridges may have given occasional access to Europe across the Mediterranean, but there is little solid evidence of these. Hominids moving to the north would be pushing into the temperate regions, needing new adaptations to cope with autumn and winter. At times of climatic deterioration, pushing up against glaciers and fearsomely low temperatures, they would certainly be forced south again. The east would seemingly offer easier adaptations – climate, flora, and fauna have more in common with Africa (Cox and Moore 1993). Even so, there is a huge ecological variety to cope with (Clark 1993). As modern hunter-gatherers are supremely well adapted to their environments, it is hard to see how earlier hominids, with far lower cultural capabilities, could have flitted easily from environment to environment. They would need time – but how much time? Here theory is not enough to provide the answers, and a dated archaeological record is the only thing that can do so.

To weigh up the problem, the main dating tools are palaeomagnetism and K/Ar (Potassium Argon), as for earlier periods. Unfortunately, this limits most dating to areas of Pleistocene volcanic activity. Fortunately, surprisingly many of the areas in question do have some vulcanism, though this is rare in China. Here, however, great sequences of loess sediment are available, which can be dated with high resolution by palaeomagnetism – specifically, magnetostratigraphy (Sun Donghuai et al. 1998). Loess, a fine-grained sediment made up of wind-blown materials transported from the front of ice sheets, can accumulate in thicknesses of thousands of meters, and preserves many archaeological sites (e.g., in Tadzikistan: Schäfer et al. 1996). The main evidence from this period is of stone artefact sites, with very occasional hominid remains.

Assuming that they went first into Asia, when did hominids spread into the Middle East? This question highlights the sampling problem. In the Levant, there are possible stone tools in the Yiron gravels of northwest Israel, dated to about 2.4 million years (Ronen 1991). Thereafter, only the sites of 'Ubeidiya in Israel and Latamne in Syria may break the barrier of 1 million years (Bar-Yosef and Goren-Inbar 1992; Bar-Yosef 1996a). Neither of them is pinned closely by absolute dates, but further north another remarkable site has emerged: Dmanisi in Georgia (Gabunia et al. 2000). Here remains of early *Homo*, early Pleistocene fauna, artefacts and argon-argon dates of 1.8 Ma combine to force a reassessment.

Further afield, however, there are apparently older dates, in an arc, spreading from Spain, across to the Caucasus, China, and through to Java (Swisher et al. 1994). They are spread very wide but very thin, and none is beyond doubt. On the other hand, we can state with some confidence that dates of 1 million years or more are reliable across this huge area. One fairly firm baseline is the Brunhes/Matuyama palaeomagnetic boundary, at 780,000 years (Cande and Kent 1995). There is a far denser pattern of dates which extend again from Spain to China. Here we have no need to doubt Atapuerca in the west, 'Ubeidiya in the center, or Lan-tien in the east (Bermudez de Castro et al. 1997; Bar-Yosef and Goren-Inbar 1992; An and Ho 1989; Shaw et al. 1991).

Thus a sort of foundation is emerging: that dates of a million years (or so) can be accepted across a huge zone of the Old World. Considering that the occupation probably did not happen overnight, does this license us to accept any of the older dates? One complication is that occupations may have come and gone with climate change. Truly, resolution of every kind is limited, but here is a tentative evaluation.

First, our global model (level 5) has very few constraints. There are no known archaeological sites older than 2.5 Ma in Africa, but whether or not these exist, there is nothing to rule out equally early sites in parts of Asia and Europe. An implicit model emerged that because the earliest hominids arose in Africa, so should the earliest stone technology – but this is untested assumption.

Then, regional patterns (level 4) in several areas point to dates of greater than 1 million years. Those furthest from Africa – Western Europe and Java – surely increase the likelihood that yet earlier dates should be found in the regions closer to Africa – Dmanisi seems to add support to this idea.

Much more is to appear, but in terms of ideas, it is good to stand back and see what has happened. In the 1950s, people thought that early technology everywhere belonged in the last half-million years. Then compelling scientific dating evidence from Olduvai pushed the African record back to 2 million years – so that the rest of the world had to be occupied later. Now its dates may be catching up (or perhaps we should say "catching back").

Yet these changes of date do not necessarily provide us with a record of progress, such as seen in later periods. Between about 1.5 million and 250,000 years ago, there are very few "new" events to be recorded. Mostly life seems to go on in such a repetitive fashion that – dare we say it – dating is hardly needed. Variations in preservation account for some of the differences which we do see.

The "first" wooden artefacts are clearly not the oldest ever made (400,000 year-old spears are reported by Thieme 1996 from Schöningen in Germany). It is not certain whether humans were building huts, but structures were exceedingly rare until about 400,000 years ago (Nadel and Werker 1999).

Fire offers another controversy: but although the chronology of fire is of great interest, the limits are provided by sampling, and even more by the difficulties of distinguishing between wild fire and domestic fire (Bellomo 1993). There are clusters of sites with fire traces around 1.5–1.0 million years ago in Africa, and at around 0.5 million within Europe and Asia, but between them there is a great gap in the evidence. Nor is there any real prospect, for now, of dating the origins of language, since there is little agreement about what evidence to look for. Anatomists see evidence for and against language in the early Pleistocene, and so have archaeologists (Davidson 1991; Davidson and Noble 1993; Deacon 1997; Dunbar 1996; Graves 1994; Tobias 1991).

Origins of Modern Humans

At some time within the last 200,000 years human beings have emerged who are like us – anatomically modern *Homo sapiens sapiens*. The origins of modern humans present one of the greatest problems of chronology, also introducing new factors of evolutionary process. Broadly speaking, we can state with certainty that the humans of 200,000 years ago around the world were not fully modern; by 100,000 years ago some populations were modern in most details (AMHs=anatomically modern humans), while others, such as the Neanderthals, were considerably more "archaic" looking, and perhaps on their own evolutionary trajectory; and by 30,000 years ago, modern humans prevailed almost everywhere (Mellars and Stringer 1989; papers in Aitken et al. 1993; D'Errico et al. 1998).

The main factors are much as before: sampling problems, and those of obtaining accurate and precise dating. There is, however, a new component: in the case of a process such as colonization, the task is primarily one of finding the events and dating them. Here we have something more – an evolutionary change, that has to be characterized and assessed both during and through the dating process. To add spice to the problem, there is also the presence of genetic studies – of mitochondrial and nuclear DNA (Richards et al. 1993; Krings et al. 1997). These give information about present-day and some past population relationships, but cannot quite be treated as an additional dating method. Linked directly with dated evidence – especially fossil hominids – they become a far more powerful tool.

Add to this a window of difficulty in applying techniques and the dating picture becomes complex. Potassium-argon is applicable in only a few areas, and there are no major palaeomagnetic boundaries in this period. The main techniques which can be used are those related to uranium-decay: thermoluminescence (TL), ESR, and U-series itself (Aitken 1990; Grün 1989; Grün and Stringer 1991; Schwarcz 1993).

In temperate regions it is also possible to recognize on land the cold and warm stages which appear very clearly in deep sea cores. These oxygen isotope stages are numbered in series backwards from the present interglacial (the Holocene, stage 1), so that warm stages have odd numbers and cold stages even ones. Thus sediments from a warm period can be ascribed first to one of a series of interglacials (say Isotope Stage 9, 11, or 13), and then other dating factors can be brought into play to help decide which stage is involved in particular cases (cf. Shackleton 1996).

From all this a summary of "facts" can be made. Humans of 250,000–200,000 years ago are clearly not modern, anywhere. They have the large brow ridges, flattened cranial vaults, and massive limbs of Middle Pleistocene hominids. By 100,000 years ago, some humans are roughly modern-looking: a little robust in places, but evidently "like us."

They are found scattered across Africa, and in the Middle East, but both sampling and dating is poor elsewhere (Rightmire 1996). In Europe it is good enough to show the continued presence of Neanderthals (Stringer and Gamble 1993; Stringer 1995).

Over the same period, archaeology reveals the adoption of the sophisticated Levallois technique for making stone tools, and the beginnings of regional diversification in tool traditions (Wendorf and Schild 1974; Tuffreau 1992). By 100,000 some stone points look like projectile tips. Burials also appear (Harrold 1980; Bar-Yosef et al. 1991). There is not much else that clearly changes during this period. Thus, both crucial sets of evidence that we are trying to date *change* – perhaps with waves of humans moving around the world – without our being able to characterize very clearly what we are dating (and without having very precise techniques for doing the dating). It is easy to fall back to modern genetic distributions and to use them as a sort of blueprint, adding authority to statements about the past. Thus we have to ask what is the key evidence that certainly belongs in the past, rather than to build a pleasing and plausible story by combining all kinds of evidence at will.

By region the basic evidence can be summarized as follows.

Europe

Neanderthals are widespread and well dated, starting with ancestral forms 300,000 years ago, and continuing as the only hominids until about 40,000 years ago. Modern humans then begin to appear. In our finds there is virtually no overlap between the two populations. There is a possible hybrid find from Portugal, where Neanderthals may have hung on until about 25,000 BP (before present) (Duarte et al. 1999).

Africa

Scattered finds are reasonably well dated on some sites. Finds around 200,000, such as Kabwe or Ndutu, are of *Homo sapiens*, but still robust; those around 100,000 such as Omo, Ngaloba, or Jebel Irhoud are more modern-looking but not entirely so (Hublin 1993).

Middle East

Finds are almost absent until the period about 100,000 years ago, when a tight group of finds occurs in the caves of Israel, all representing early modern humans (*Homo sapiens sapiens*). The only two finds which could give a picture of a trajectory through time – Tabun and Zuttiyeh – are fragmentary or poorly stratified. At about 60,000 Neanderthals appear in the Middle East; soon afterwards, they appear to be replaced by early modern humans (Vermeersch et al. 1998; Marks 1990; Jelinek 1990).

Asia

There are remarkably few fossil finds except in Java, China, and then (later) in the region of Australia. In Java, the Solo or Ngandong finds may represent a late *Homo erectus*, but others would see them as an early *sapiens*. In China, early *sapiens* finds date back to 300,000 (Chen and Zhang 1991; Chen et al. 1994), and there is a case for seeing an *in situ* modernization (Stringer 1993). The Australian finds are all of moderns, of varying degrees of robustness, but almost all fall within the last 30,000 years, with the probable exception of one burial from Lake Mungo (Thorne et al. 1999; Stringer 1999).

Two views dominate discussions: (1) that there was a diaspora starting from Africa, the so-called "Out of Africa 2" (or Garden of Eden theory), in which modern humans spread out and replaced all more archaic populations; (2) of multiregionalism, in which the populations of all areas "modernize" in parallel, with a certain amount of gene flow occurring between areas.

It is not plain now that the majority of specialists hold to such simply expressed views. The main planks of replacement are as follows:

1 That genetics points this way: there is less diversity in modern populations than might be expected, but more in Africa than in other regions, suggesting that Africa has the longest history of modern population.
2 African specimens became modern early on, and can be dated reasonably well.
3 Middle Eastern specimens appear modern at an early date (around 100,000).
4 There was replacement in Europe: almost indisputably, Neanderthals in Europe are followed by modern humans at a late date – after 40,000 years ago.

The central difficulty for the replacement scenario is one of chronology: it has had to happen around the whole Old World – and all diversification of modern populations has had to happen since. Australia, for example, has had an occupation by modern humans for at least 40,000 years, perhaps much longer; and yet early modern humans apparently came out of Africa only within the last 100,000 years, and are not clearly seen in the Middle East between 90,000 and 50,000. This pattern creates many global constraints at level 5, some of them glossed over in the replacement debate: was there really enough time for replacement to happen, given the huge distances, and the variety of adaptations that would be needed in the face of varied climates and resources? On the other hand, multiregionalism does not work in Europe – it has a time problem, and now also a genetic problem. First, Neanderthals cannot evolve into modern humans in Europe 40,000 years ago, because modern humans had already evolved somewhere else (Africa or the Middle East): it is exceedingly unlikely that the same species should evolve twice, from different ancestors. The idea of a real and substantial difference between the human varieties is now given extra force by the genetic evidence of mitochon-

drial DNA. At the very least this shows clearly that the mtDNA of one Neanderthal (the specimen from Neandertal itself) does not resemble that of modern humans (Krings et al. 1997). Some gene flow between populations of course remains a possibility, but the sudden late appearance of a hybrid population would not affect the basic argument that modern humans appeared first outside Europe (cf. Tattersall and Schwartz 1999).

Would the dates allow alternative interpretations to the most favored scenarios? It is difficult to free ourselves of preconceptions, but there is no doubt that everything hangs not just on a framework of ideas, but also on the dates themselves which have shaped the ideas. Hardly anywhere are Neanderthals and moderns stratified in single sequences, so our trust in the reliability of the dates is crucial. They are amply good enough to make some points about *rates of change*. We can be sure that in Europe Neanderthals evolved gradually over a long period, but that (relatively) the change from Neanderthal to modern came quite fast.

Everything would look simpler if there were a straightforward seriation, especially in the Middle East. In fact we pass from "no evidence" before 200,000; to "equivocal evidence" around 150,000 (Tabun and Zuttiyeh); to early moderns at 100,000; to Neanderthals at 60,000; then apparently around 50,000 to moderns who, apart from their archaeology, are almost invisible for the first few thousand years. This is a great challenge, and a warning not to expect simple solutions elsewhere in the world. In the Middle East, early moderns occur earlier than most if not all Neanderthals – all current explanation has to work around this. They are also older than many European Neanderthals. The Skhul hominids of Israel had been dead for 50,000 years when the Neanderthals of La Ferrassie in France were alive.

African modernization may occur earlier than that of the Middle East. Fragmentary hominid remains are well dated at Klasies River Mouth in South Africa, but few of the other African sites with human remains are very well dated (Smith 1993). What Africa offers is the appearance of continuity, through most of the last half-million years, culminating in modern humans – a gradient that is dated overall, although its detail lacks precision. The greatest difficulty lies in interpreting events in Asia and beyond – in having time for the diaspora which most scholars now accept. First, there is an almost complete lack of dated hominid finds from the Middle East to China. Then there is the puzzle of the late Neanderthals in the Middle East, around 60,000 years ago. It is almost inconceivable that the eastwards spread of moderns could have come later than this. The alternative is to invoke an earlier spread (or even multiregional origin) of modern humans across Asia, one that is almost invisible in the record, and therefore difficult to date.

The Upper Palaeolithic

Dating of the Upper Palaeolithic can be seen as a sub-problem in the dating of modern humans. Modern humans spread across the world, but the Upper Palaeolithic is a regional phenomenon of Eurasia. It also brings us into the realm of radiocarbon – the chief dating technique of the last 40,000 years – and brings into focus this key question of rates of change. In earlier periods cultural change was so fundamentally slow that a lack of dating precision hardly matters, but as events speed up the need for higher resolution becomes more and more pressing.

The Upper Palaeolithic is a technical and perhaps social phenomenon of a particular part of the world. Historically, it has attracted great attention because it is found in Europe and because of its rich material culture, which embraces symbolism in the record of art. With a lack of knowledge and of chronologies in other parts of the world, the Upper Palaeolithic long stood proxy for the arrival of modern humans in the world. It was the front door to modernity. This picture is now circumscribed and eroded – by newer finds, but just as much so by new dates.

To date it, we must first determine what the Upper Palaeolithic is. In practice archaeologists have tended to treat it as a package of characteristics which occur in the record more or less together. Just as the Neolithic became a package of agriculture and elements of material culture such as pottery, so have ideas of the Upper Palaeolithic moved beyond blade technology. In Europe there are several features in this classic package, including blade industries, prismatic cores, elaborate bone and antler work, arts, and evidence of personal decoration. In contrast, in the Middle East, the chief evidence is of blade industries, with less bonework and art, but again with evidence for social complexity.

It is hard to be utterly consistent in dealing with such a package – even the blade component itself is not always major. But if the term is to be used – and dated – the stone industries have to be taken as having primacy, because they survive the most, and on the most sites. Unfortunately, the beginnings are just too old to be covered reliably by radiocarbon. The oldest known sites are in the Levant, and the likelihood is that they reach back to 50,000 years. This can be said on the basis of radiocarbon dates older than 45,000 from a few sites, and from rare comparisons with uranium-series dates, as at Nahal Zin in Israel (Schwarcz et al. 1979; Schwarcz 1993). Although the number of sites is very small, and there are difficulties in relating the techniques, there is little doubt that the actual technical change from Levallois point to blade industries began at around 50,000 years ago. Once established, the Upper Palaeolithic seems to have spread north and west into Europe, and to have provided the cultural matrix for the introduction of modern humans (Kozlowski 1992, 1999; Rigaud 1989; Mellars 1992).

What chronological problems does all this pose? From the 1980s there came a new demand to think of modern human origins and the origins of the Upper Palaeolithic as separate events. Especially important were dates which broke established patterns, such as those of about 90,000 BP for early bone harpoons at Katanda in the western Rift Valley of Africa (Brooks et al. 1995; Yellen et al. 1995). The implication is that not only were modern humans here, but also with them the technical advances which add up to "modern behavior" – in this case signaled by the advanced bone toolkit. If this is correct, we have a set of site evidence (level 3) changing the global view (level 5), but not unassisted by other finds. The early presence of art and bone tools elsewhere suggests that these may have earlier dates than expected, and that in fact they are nothing to do with the "Upper Palaeolithic package," as was always assumed.

There is of course a resistance to reinterpretation. Most prehistorians recognize the need to see the problems of "modern humans" and "Upper Palaeolithic" separately, but the issues tend to recombine. If the central idea is that modern humans emerge from Africa, then it leads to a pressure either to (a) ignore the question of dated archaeological evidence as a tiresome thorn in the side; or (b) find changes of culture which can be linked with the supposed population movement.

Thus, one might link the 90,000-year-old harpoons with 50,000-year-old stone toolkits in the Levant, as the pathway of new "modern" behavior. But there is virtually no material justification for this, given that the African stone toolkits are so different and no harpoons have been found in the Middle East. Much of the problem is a preoccupation with "modern behavior." As it cannot be defined, it cannot be dated. It seems much better to concentrate on evidence trait by trait, and to wait for patterns to emerge (Reynolds 1990, 1991; Rigaud 1989). Thus the development in stone tools that leads to blade industries can be documented and dated where it happens and need not be confused with the origins of bone tools, art, or

even of modern humans, all of which may have distinct origins, perhaps in different places.

Even accepting this, the dating of the Upper Palaeolithic presents many puzzles. There is a strong tendency, conscious or unconscious, to accept "wave propagation" models when looking at Europe. These are emphasized by the triad of first colonization of the continent (~1 million years?), the appearance of the Upper Palaeolithic and modern humans (~40,000 years), and then of farming (~10,000 years). Europe's shape as a peninsula begs this interpretation, as does the fact that all these phenomena start outside Europe at earlier dates.

Perhaps, of course, the Upper Palaeolithic had a broad origin outside Europe, but dates across Asia are not good enough to pin this down. What we see (or imagine we see) is the thrust across Europe. But here there is another double puzzle. First, the initial Upper Palaeolithic is localized and varied (Kozlowski 1992, 1999). Then there appear to be dates that buck the general trend. If we take one view, dates appear around 45,000 in the southeast, and Spain is not reached until 25,000 years ago. So this Upper Palaeolithic movement takes nearly half of the last 50,000 years. The other view is that hardly a date over 40,000 is firmly established – but that dates of this age appear as early in the extreme west, in northern Spain, as in southeast Europe. This picture is of an Upper Palaeolithic which appears explosively fast across Europe, but then leaves local areas of delayed occupation to be explained (as in the Dordogne in France, or parts of the Peloponnese in Greece).

These differences are huge and have profound implications, not least concerning the demise of the Neanderthals. The difficulties, however, could largely be an artefact of limitations in our dating techniques. Archaeologists need resolution of about 1,000 years, and radiocarbon superficially provides this. Yet the technique is close to its limits. Roughly speaking, these are the activity levels of samples through this period:

32,000: 2 percent modern
37,000: 1 percent modern
42,000: 0.5 percent modern

This means that to achieve accurate measures, laboratories have to reduce contamination levels well below these figures (Olsson 1991; Olsson and Possnert 1992). Although the best laboratories can do this most of the time, it is plain from many dated sequences both that (a) there is variation in dates at a single level, and (b) dates stop getting plainly older towards the bottom of a sequence. The Abri Pataud in southwest France exemplifies both points (Movius 1975; Mellars et al. 1987), which are prima facie evidence that contamination is present.

On this basis one can suggest a model that the Upper Palaeolithic occupation of Europe began by 45,000, and was largely complete by 40,000; in the far reaches of the continent it may have come later, but most variation departing from these figures is probably produced by unduly late dates.

Into New Worlds

As the Upper Palaeolithic was unfolding in Europe, similarly momentous events were taking shape in other corners of the globe – modern humans were making their way far and wide. That these events were contemporaneous is known to us mainly through radiocarbon, but as in Europe, this technique cannot reach back quite far enough to solve some of the major questions.

Australia

Recent studies show that *Homo erectus* had reached far out onto the island chains of Indonesia (Morwood et al. 1999), but it was left to *sapiens* to cover the last 100 kilometers of open water to Australia – or rather the landmass of Sahul (Australia and New Guinea combined).

Australia gives us pure prehistory, undisturbed until 1788. The prehistory of Austra-

lia again illustrates the problems of sampling resolution. Here the handicap is provided by the scarcity of alternatives to radiocarbon, which clearly does not reach back far enough to chart the earliest occupation. The first archaeological investigators thought that humans had reached Australia within the last few thousand years. Then in the 1960s deep excavations began to show occupations of 20–30,000 years ago (Mulvaney 1969). Eventually, archaeology began to push beyond this framework, but as only radiocarbon was available for dating, there was no means of extending the timescale.

Thus, archaeologists were able to develop a regional chronology (level 4), extending to about 30,000 years. The global constraint at level 5 was that modern humans had been "available" for only 30–40,000 years. In the 1980s this constraint was lifted by earlier dates for modern humans (see above). Older dates in Australia then became a reasonable hypothesis. (Alongside this is the marginal possibility that some premodern population might be found in Australia. Possible hints of this have come through the robust nature of some hominid finds not only in Indonesia but also in Australia itself, but no convincing pattern of evidence has emerged.)

Although deeper roots to the human occupation of Australia have seemed likely, the opportunities for use of appropriate dating techniques are quite restricted. Circumstances allowing the use of K/Ar and palaeomagnetism are minimal. U-series is possible in coastal contexts, but most attempts have been made with thermoluminescence (TL). Unfortunately, this cannot be regarded as a routine dating technique when based on sediments. Fierce arguments have resulted from attempts to date sites such as Jinmium rock-shelter in the north (Fullagar et al. 1996; Spooner 1998). The dates in dispute have ranged from 140,000 to 40,000 years. The early occupation of Australia has become as controversial as that of the Americas.

Assessment is not easy at present because the framework is not very tight. Is there reason for doubting that the oldest radiocarbon dates give a true picture? It seems unlikely that they should do so, given that very old dates on the limits of the technique occur on opposite sides of the landmass – from Upper Swann close to Perth, from Ngarrabullgan cave on the Cape York peninsula, and from the Huon peninsula in New Guinea, none of them likely to be first ports of call for early colonists (Pearce and Barbetti 1981; David et al. 1997; Groube et al. 1986).

This is not to say that far older dates are correct. The best chances of occupation of Australia are likely to have come in a cool (glacial) period when sea levels were depressed. The oceans were high, overall, from about 130,000 through to 80,000 years ago. Therefore the period 80–40,000 appears to give the best window of opportunity. Neither the regional pattern of dates, nor the global constraints, argues strongly for an earlier date. This puts the onus on excavators and dating scientists to come up with dated site evidence. At the moment this seems to extend up to 50–60 ka (thousands of years ago). Malakunanja rockshelter in the north has dates in this range (Roberts et al. 1990). These are now supported by dates of approximately 60,000 obtained by a combination of techniques for a human skeleton at Lake Mungo, much further south (Thorne *et al.* 1999; Stringer 1999). Techniques such as ESR, luminescence, and U-series rarely offer high security when used singly, but in combination they are gradually changing perceptions of the regional model; it seems likely that modern humans were present in Australia long before they reached Europe.

The long aboriginal occupation of Australia provides other challenges to interpretation (Lourandos 1997). What actually happened in this vast field of prehistory? Study requires painstaking application of many hundreds of radiocarbon dates over the whole continent. There are few highlights, but certain important ones in establishing a worldwide picture. These include the dating of rock art (Chippindale et al.

2000; Hedges et al. 1998; Rosenfeld and Smith 1997); also, the extinction of megafauna, which appears in some of the early art. The replacement of technologies can sometimes be charted, but among the myriad cultural events there appear to have been only few that led to distinctive changes in the archaeological record (see below).

The Americas

The chronology of the first settlement of the Americas has long appeared particularly controversial. Many scholars have believed that the occupation goes back only some 12,000 years, whereas others have argued for a far earlier date (see Bonnichsen and Steele 1994; Bonnichsen 1999). The 12,000 BP benchmark was defined by the dates of ice barriers in the north, the lack of early occupations in the plains of North America, and the "cranky" nature of some claims for earlier sites. For long, the problem of late versus old has appeared to be one for American archaeology specifically, or even for American archaeologists. Now however, it must be admitted that the margins of doubt for the early occupation of Europe, or for the first colonization of Australia, have become at least as great in percentage terms. The unusual feature in the Americas is the "fork" of choice set out by atrocious conditions of the last glacial maximum from about 20,000–15,000 BP. The Bering landbridge was exposed at this time, but initial colonization would be extremely unlikely during the most extreme climate, so perforce it should come earlier or later. Later colonization is problematic, given the huge diversity of subsequent cultures across the Americas, and the short timescale available for achieving it. Earlier colonization also remains problematic, although some sites such as Pedra Furada in Brazil would probably be accepted without question if they were found elsewhere in the world (Guidon and Arnaud 1991). There is one major difference from the Australian controversy. There the early site evidence has been characterized to general satisfaction, but the dates are in dispute. In the Americas, the dates are often acceptable, as at Pedra Furada, but the evidence for human occupation is disputed. Normally, stone age "traditions" can be characterized satisfactorily once a few sites have been found, but it must be admitted that no such recognizable persona has emerged for early American sites. This comes only with the distinctive stone points of the Clovis tradition, beginning about 11–12,000 years ago in the Great Plains, or for material of similar age in South America (Lynch 1980). Human remains are usually recognizable beyond controversy, but in the Americas they have provided little help. Initial amino acid dates proved misleading (Bada and Helfman 1975). None of the radiocarbon dates made possible by accelerator mass spectrometry is so far older than 11,000 BP (Bada et al. 1984; Taylor et al. 1985), although Stafford (1994) has pointed out that poorly preserved older samples would not necessarily yield valid old radiocarbon dates. Perhaps the strongest pointers towards an early occupation via a coastal route (Gruhn 1994) are dates in the south of <10,000 years, which presuppose an earlier entry (e.g., Athens and Ward 1999; Roosevelt et al. 1996). Older dates in North America such as for Tlapacoya or Meadowcroft rockshelter provide further but controversial support for this interpretation (Mirambell 1978; Carlisle and Adovasio 1982).

Again, the global perspective (level 5) can no longer be held as a reason for denying the possibility of early occupation: modern humans were "available" at least 30,000 years ago. As with Australia, the debate is significant partly because of later developments. The Americas – the New World – make up almost 25 percent of total global land area. Although the great majority of recognizable archaeological events fall in the Holocene, the last 10,000 years, the depth of the roots is a critical matter, considering that this region of the world saw its own sequence of megafaunal extinctions, domestication of plants and animals, and the

rise of civilizations. Recent years have seen a strengthening of the case for early occupation: perhaps the time has come to accept it as a working hypothesis which still presents curious puzzles.

Problems of Domestication

Amid a host of events that become ever more complex, archaeologists, geologists, and botanists like to have some timelines that are utterly reliable, and that set a frame for further inquiry. The change from Pleistocene to Holocene about 11,000 years ago has long provided one such event on a worldwide scale. The world warmed up, sea levels rose, vegetation changed, and – as it were – humans began to get ready to change everything. Domestication and the origins of agriculture are a large part of this, and have transformed human existence. This makes the chronology of their development an important issue: it reflects other problems. There is space here only for some very general points, the aim being to stand back and consider the frame, rather than looking at the detail. Until the 1950s the view did not depend on radiocarbon – lake varves and pollen plotted out the Holocene. Radiocarbon then showed the Holocene to be about 10,000 years long, and calibration of radiocarbon dates through dendrochronology has added precision to the figures – about 11,600 years BP, "real time" (see Kromer and Spurk 1998; Kromer et al. 1998). The need for such radiocarbon calibration has now been appreciated for thirty years. The basic equations of the technique employ the assumption that past levels of radiocarbon production in the upper atmosphere were equivalent to those of recent times. Dating of tree rings of known age showed that this was not quite the case, and chronologies based on the annual rings of European oaks or American bristlecone pines now allow corrections to be made right through the Holocene. Approximate calibrations of earlier periods can be made from comparisons of U-series dates on coral and radiocarbon dates of the same specimens.

The domesticated plants and animals can be studied in the present in all their diversity, which can now be mapped genetically. To an extent this allows reading of the past, as with human genetics, but crucial archaeological evidence is surprisingly scarce or poorly sampled, or hard to date (Hillman et al. 1993; papers in Gowlett and Hedges 1986). Most plant and animal remains do not survive, and in some of the most critical instances, interpretations may depend upon just one or two charred grains or a few scraps of bone. Direct dating of these by AMS (accelerator) radiocarbon has improved reliability and precision. Wet sieving has also transformed the rates of recovery of plant remains and bone fragments in more recent excavations, such as that at Abu Hureyra in Syria, so that the potential for accurate dating and interpretation has been much improved.

A further problem is that morphological change in early domesticates may be extremely rapid – after many generations, perhaps, of selection and genetic change there may come a virtually instantaneous change in the phenotype, or external appearance (see Hillman 1996). Early maize seems to belie this, as growth in the size of the cobs can be traced through a long period (Beadle 1978), but locally the introduction of maize could be very rapid. Fortunately, it can be pinpointed through studies of stable isotopes of carbon in the bones of people or animals from the relevant sites (Van der Merwe and Vogel 1978; Blake et al. 1992).

Around the world, domestication and agriculture appeared during the early Holocene, so it seemed natural to see this great readjustment as an adaptation to the change: stimulus and response. The near-synchronization of events in the Old and New Worlds appeared to need no more explanation, because this was the start of a new era.

This no longer seems the appropriate frame. A picture is beginning to emerge of continuous developments in the Middle East since the glacial maximum of 20,000 years ago (Harris 1996; Hillman 1996; Sherratt 1997). Radiocarbon dating shows the sophistication of early sites, such as Ohalo II in Israel, dated to 19,000 BP (Nadel and Werker 1999), and Wadi Kubbaniya in Egypt of similar age (Wendorf et al. 1988). At Ohalo there can be seen a range of crafts and signs of intensive food collection, especially of seeds. The following Natufian phase in Israel is also now well dated to the period before the beginning of the Holocene. The question arises: if the Holocene itself was not the trigger of all these developments, why the synchronism at all? Why do comparable developments towards agriculture happen around the world in so many areas, with such synchronism? After precursor phases from about 20,000 to 12,000, all this occurs, broadly, between 12,000 and 8,000 years ago (e.g., Harris 1996). Why not at 30,000, when modern humans were already widely distributed and sophisticated in behavior? These are questions of chronology which go beyond chronology, but their resolution must depend upon high-resolution dating.

There is a growing appreciation that the glacial maximum itself may have been the principal trigger for change. Worldwide, the downturn into atrocious conditions 20,000 years ago, the lowering of sea levels, and then their rapid rise as climate ameliorated, perhaps forced a roughly synchronous set of changes. It may have come naturally to modern humans to react similarly, though independently, in parallel. This may be speculation, but dating evidence – especially unexpectedly early dating evidence for precocious developments, as with yam horticulture in New Guinea – plays a key part in forcing reassessments.

The Home Straight

The last 5,000 years are in many ways the most crucial period of all for chronological study, since they embrace the great bulk of archaeological effort, as well as of developed economies and literate civilization. Clearly, these times need resolved, precise dating, but equally it is a fact that much of the world was in prehistory until the last thousand years, and even within civilizations some circumstances are far fuller with chronological sensitivity than others. A Roman military structure will relate to particular campaigns, and the finds of coins may precisely reflect their span. In contrast, a contemporary native farmstead in the fort's hinterland may remain effectively in Iron Age prehistory, and preserve no equivalent evidence. Glimpses of clarity may be surrounded by utter ignorance. Q. Laberius Durus, a young officer, was killed in a skirmish during Caesar's second expedition to Britain in 54 BC, the first named casualty of any event in Britain, the known rather than the unknown soldier, among all those who must have fallen in this campaign (Caesar, *Gallic Wars* V, 16).

How does archaeology proceed? First, we must understand that approximately three quarters of the world lie outside the historical chronologies; but on the other hand, the period is close enough that (as an ideal) we can look for real calendrical precision (tree rings and ice cores date the entire period at ~1 year precision). Thus, in general:

1   Historical chronologies of ancient civilizations must provide a backbone.
2   Wherever possible, precise natural science chronologies must be brought into play, such as those provided by dendrochronology or volcanic eruptions.
3   In most other circumstances radiocarbon will provide the mainstay of absolute dating, with reasonable precision (usually 100–300 years).
4   There should be numerous opportunities to cross-link dating methods, although on particular sites or in particular areas these may be hard to apply.

The examples given below attempt to follow these points across selected areas of the globe. The chronologies of early civilizations can provide a backbone for the dating of adjacent cultural provinces, but the Egyptologist Ken Kitchen also notes the difficulties (Kitchen 1989, 1991). For the earliest Egyptian dynasties, the errors are potentially of the order of ~300 years – a similar range to that of an average radiocarbon date (+/– 80 years gives a 95 percent confidence range of about 300 years). Thus, if a group of radiocarbon determinations could be associated well enough, the set of dates could give at least equal precision to that of earliest "history."

Cursory study shows that the ancient chronologies are not built up merely from juggling the surviving lists of kings. There is an interplay with archaeological evidence, which can assist in various forms. Some of the best documentary evidence can come when archaeological finds are made in sealed contexts, perhaps related to other datable material. Apart from the manuscripts of the classical world, which have survived in libraries, most other archives have actually been found by archaeological work. This may provide a feedback loop, in which the interpretation of discovered documents allows further fruitful excavation.

Kitchen (1991) stresses the value of synchronisms, or timelines. Those of correspondence, or artefacts, can provide information as effectively as a layer of volcanic ash. Diplomatic exchanges between two monarchs can prove their contemporaneity, even if neither is precisely dated. Similarly, Bronze Age wrecks in the Mediterranean, such as that at Uluburun off Turkey, have provided trade goods from several sources, linked in "systemic context" (cf. Schiffer 1976 for the idea of systemic contexts).

Astronomers were active in early civilizations through the last four to five thousand years, but their observations are not always accurate enough, or precisely described, to allow correlations with known events. Some are easy to pin down, such as the eclipses of the sun, but so many of these happened that confusion can arise. Further back, there are disputes – perhaps this report is a supernova, that one an unknown comet. To summarize, at 2000 BC in Egypt and the Near East, historical chronology is constrained to around ten years. A figure such as King Shamsi-Adad (ca. 1813–1781 BC) can be traced through cuneiform letters found in archaeological excavations, and there is even documentation for his interactions with the kingdom of Dilmun further south in the Gulf (the modern Bahrein), which has not itself yielded documents from this period (Eidem and Hojlund 1993).

If we turn west in the Mediterranean, the record is less precise, notwithstanding the presence of early civilizations such as Mycenae. The resolution is just good enough that Sherratt and Sherratt (1993) can treat the period from 2000 BC onwards roughly by century, the dating based on a mixture of radiocarbon and transferred historical evidence (dated artefacts, including metalwork and pottery, etc.).

European chronologies are stiffened further by dendrochronology, based after all chiefly on the European oak sequences (Baillie 1995). For 2000 BC this could give great precision to the dating of, say, wooden finds preserved in the Swiss lakes. It has the broader importance of providing a precise framework which extends beyond individual finds: dendrochronology is exact. To an extent this record can be cross-linked with the record from Arctic ice cores. Both can give an indication of major volcanic eruptions. Acidity or tephra are recorded in the ice, while the growth of trees is impaired by reduced sunlight and harsh frosts. Mike Baillie has isolated a series of timelines which seem to point to events of climatic catastrophe. One such, at around 1640 BC, may coincide with, or represent, the eruption of Thera (Santorini), although this is generally no longer considered to have been "catastrophic" for the contemporary Minoan civilization of which Thera was an outpost (see Baillie and Munro 1988; Baillie 1998). Yet such coincidences of events can be deceptive, and disasters can be multiple – Pompeii was rocked by a great earthquake less than

twenty years before the eruption of Vesuvius (Potter 1987; Laurence 1994; Fulford and Wallace-Hadrill 1998). Thera erupted in the second millennium BC, but so also did the volcanoes of Iceland, which might be even more likely to affect the Arctic ice cores (see Zielinski and Germani 1998; Buckland et al. 1997). Ultimate precision may be lacking here, but the general picture can be striking in its impact. Lead aerosol records from the ice cores provide a quite remarkable impression of the rises and falls of smelting through the last five thousand years (Figure 12.1).

Such a record treats prehistory and history alike. Elsewhere, there is only prehistory to grapple with. Of hundreds of parts of the globe, we can take for comparison central Africa, and parts of Sahul – the landmass which separated into Australia and New Guinea as seas rose during the early Holocene.

Domesticated plants and animals crept down Africa from about 9,000 years ago, as well evidenced by dated sites from the Sahara down to southern Africa (Robertshaw 1992). At some time came the great expansion that has led to the many Bantu languages of today. Archaeology cannot relate the two. It can aim to date material evidence, such as the earliest pottery in an area, or first traces of domestic animals (Robertshaw 1992). In northern Congo, brave efforts along the tributaries of the Congo River have located "Iron Age" sites, and given a series of dates on pottery, ranging from about 4,000 to 2,000 BP (Eggert 1992). These are probably evidence of an agricultural economy, but they do not date particular peoples. They do not tell us, for example, about the origins of the pygmies. Direct evidence of the latter is provided only by Egyptian tomb paintings – another example of a link between early history and prehistory (Clark 1971).

In Australia and New Guinea the circumstances are somewhat similar, but there can be even less "handle" in terms of material culture, except where rock art is abundant,

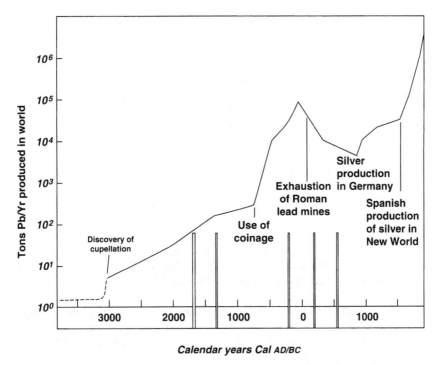

Figure 12.1   The lead aerosol record of Arctic ice cores gives a dated index to production of lead and silver through the last 5,000 years (after Settle and Patterson 1980). Marker dates noted by Baillie can be studied against this record. It seems that the effects of volcanic eruptions and dust veils were too localized and short term to have a measurable impact on industrial production (cf. Baillie 1995; Baillie and Munro 1988).

or where environmental evidence provides a framework. Even within the region, there can be great differences between records. On the north coast of New Guinea, the rising Holocene sea flooded a gulf at the mouths of the Sepik and Ramu rivers, producing a shoreline of 6,000 BP which is now some 125 km inland (Swadling 1997). Gradually the shallow embayment silted up, creating a geomorphological history which includes a record of human activity. Midden sites near the shoreline date from 5800 BP onwards. They preserve fish and plant remains in some variety. Pottery, too, is known, from the Lapita tradition, and perhaps an earlier tradition (Swadling 1997; Gosden 1992). A distinctive kind of pottery such as Lapita serves to generate its own controversies of origin and dating, much as have the Beakers of Europe (Ambrose 1997; Sand 1997).

This picture, rich in detail, contrasts with southern Australia, where stone tools are virtually the entire record, and do not exhibit much obvious sequential development. There is a dichotomy between early large stone and later small stone or microlithic tool traditions, the latter found in the last three or four thousand years (Bird and Frankel 1991). This means that patterns have to be evaluated without "events." In some areas of Australia traditions of rock art help to furnish such events (Chippindale et al. 2000), although their radiocarbon dating has proved difficult (Hedges et al. 1998; Gillespie 1997). Again, the relationship between humans and environmental change can sometimes help to shape a picture. Dortch (1997a) has studied the distribution of stone fish weirs in the southwest. These would be hard to date by radiocarbon, as they were probably rebuilt many times, but generally they would be set in tidal embayments. Multiple radiocarbon dates show that Lake Clifton, for example, was tidal up to about 4000 BP, when it became a lagoon, thus providing by indirect means a probable minimum age for the weirs. At much the same time in Western Australia, the rising waters of Lake Jasper covered other sites, probably the result of higher water tables as postglacial sea levels rose (Dortch 1997b)

In each area prehistorians have the duty of building up a local record. This brief sampling of examples shows that although their basic task is similar worldwide, the nature of the record varies enormously, even, or perhaps especially, in the last five thousand years – in cultural repertoire, rates of change, in resolution of the events that can be dated, as well as in the means of dating them.

References

Aitken, M. J. 1990. *Science-based Dating in Archaeology*. London: Longman.

Aitken, M. J., C. B. Stringer, and P. A. Mellars (eds.) 1993. *The Origin of Modern Humans and the Impact of Chronometric Dating*. Princeton, NJ: Princeton University Press.

Ambrose, W. R. 1997. "Contradictions in Lapita pottery, a composite clone." *Antiquity*, 71: 525–38.

An Zhizheng and Ho Chuan Kun 1989. "New magnetostratigraphic dates of Lantian Homo erectus." *Quaternary Research*, 32: 213–21.

Andel, T. H. van 1990. "Living in the last high glacial – an interdisciplinary challenge." In O. Soffer and C. Gamble (eds.), *The World at 18000 BP, Vol. 1: High Latitudes*, pp. 24–38. London: Unwin Hyman.

Andel, T. H. van 1998. "Middle and Upper Palaeolithic environments and the calibration of 14C dates beyond 10,000 BP." *Antiquity*, 72: 26–33.

Andrews, P. and P. Banham (eds.) 1999. *Late Cenozoic Environments and Hominid Evolution: A Tribute to Bill Bishop*. London: Geological Society.

Asfaw, B., Y. Beyene, G. Suwa, et al. 1992. "The earliest Acheulean at Konso-Gardula." *Nature*, 360: 732–5.

Asfaw B., T. D. White, C. O. Lovejoy, et al. 1999. "*Australopithecus garhi*: a new species of early hominid from Ethiopia." *Science*, 284: 629–35.

Athens, J. S. and J. V. Ward 1999. "The Late Quaternary of the Western Amazon: climate, vegetation and humans." *Antiquity*, 73: 287–302.

Bada, J. L. and P. M. Helfman 1975. "Amino acid racemization dating of fossil bones." *World Archaeology*, 7: 160–83.

Bada, J. L., R. Gillespie, J. A. J. Gowlett, and R. E. M. Hedges (1984). "Accelerator mass spectrometry radiocarbon ages of amino acid extracts from Californian Palaeoindian skeletons." *Nature*, 312: 442–4.

Bailey, G. (ed.) 1997. *Klithi: Palaeolithic Settlement and Quaternary Landscapes in Northwest Greece, Vol. 1: Excavation and Intra-site Analysis at Klithi*. Cambridge: McDonald Institute for Archaeological Research.

Baillie, M. G. L. 1995. *A Slice Through Time*. London: Routledge.

Baillie, M. G. L. 1998. "Bronze Age myths expose archaeological shortcomings? A reply to Buckland et al. 1997." *Antiquity*, 72: 425–7.

Baillie, M. G. L. and M. A. R. Munro 1988. "Irish tree rings, Santorini and volcanic dust veils." *Nature*, 332: 344–6.

Bard, E., M. Arnold, R. G. Fairbanks, and B. Hamelin 1993. "230Th–234U and 14C ages obtained by mass spectrometry on corals." *Radiocarbon*, 35: 191–9.

Barton, C. M., G. A. Clark, and A. E. Cohen 1994. "Art as information: explaining Upper Palaeolithic art in Western Europe." *World Archaeology*, 26 (2): 185–207.

Bar-Yosef, O. 1992. "The role of western Asia in modern human origins." In M. J. Aitken, C. B. Stringer, and P. A. Mellars (eds.), *The Origin of Modern Humans and the Impact of Chronometric Dating*, pp. 132–47. Princeton, NJ: Princeton University Press.

Bar-Yosef, O. 1996a. "The role of climate in the interpretation of human movements and cultural transformations in Western Asia." In E. S. Vrba, G. H. Denton, T. C. Partridge, and L. H. Burckle (eds.), *Palaeoclimate and Evolution, With Emphasis on Human Origins*, pp. 507–23. New Haven, CT: Yale University Press.

Bar-Yosef, O. 1996b. "The impact of Late Pleistocene–Early Holocene climatic changes on humans in Southwest Asia." In L. G. Straus, B. V. Eriksen, J. M. Erlandson, and D. R. Yesner (eds.), *Humans at the End of the Ice Age: The Archaeology of the Pleistocene–Holocene Transition*, pp. 61–78. New York: Plenum Press.

Bar-Yosef, O. and N. Goren-Inbar 1992. *The Lithic Assemblages of the Site of Ubeidiya, Jordan Valley*. Jerusalem: Qedem 34.

Bar-Yosef, O., B. Vandermeersch, B. Arensburg, et al. 1992. "The excavations in Kebara Cave, Mt Carmel." *Current Anthropology*, 33 (5): 497–550.

Beadle, G. W. 1978. "The origin of Zea mays." In D. L. Browman (ed.), *Cultural Continuity in Mesoamerica*, pp. 24–42. The Hague: Mouton.

Belfer-Cohen, A. and O. Bar-Yosef 1999. "The Levantine Aurignacian: 60 years of research." In W. Davies and R. Charles (eds.), *Dorothy Garrod and the Progress of the Palaeolithic*, pp. 118–34. Oxford: Oxbow Books.

Bellomo, R. V. 1993. "A methodological approach for identifying archaeological evidence of fire resulting from human activities." *Journal of Archaeological Science*, 20, 525–55.

Bermudez de Castro, J. M., J. Arsuaga, E. Carbonell, et al. (1997). "A hominid from the lower Pleistocene of Atapuerca, Spain: possible ancestor to Neandertals and modern humans." *Science*, 276: 1392–5.

Bernor, R. L. and D. Lipscomb 1996. "A consideration of Old World hipparionine horse phylogeny and global abiotic processes." In E. S. Vrba, G. H. Denton, T. C. Partridge, and L. H. Burckle (eds.), *Palaeoclimate and Evolution, With Emphasis on Human Origins*, pp. 164–77. New Haven, CT: Yale University Press.

Bird, C. F. M. and D. Frankel 1991. "Problems in constructing a regional sequence: Holocene southeast Australia." *World Archaeology*, 23 (2): 179–92.

Bischoff, J. L., J. F. Garcia, and L. G. Straus 1992. "Uranium-series isochron dating at El Castillo cave (Cantabria, Sapin): the 'Acheulean'/'Mousterian' question." *Journal of Archaeological Science*, 19: 49–62.

Bischoff, J. L., R. Merriam, W. M. Childers, and R. Protsch 1976. "Antiquity of man in America indicated by radiometric dates on the Yuha burial site." *Nature*, 261: 128–9.

Bischoff, J. L., and R. J. Rosenbauer 1981. "Uranium series dating of human skeletal remains from the Del Mar and Sunnyvale sites, California." *Science*, 213: 1003–5.

Bishop, W. W. and J. D. Clark (eds.) 1967. *Background to Evolution in Africa*. Chicago: University of Chicago Press.

Blake, B., B. S. Chisholm, J. E. Clark, B. Voorhies, and M. W. Love 1992. "Prehistoric subsistence in the Soconusco region." *Current Anthropology*, 33: 83–94.

Blockley, S. P. E., R. E. Donahue, and A. M. Pollard 2000. "Radiocarbon, calibration and Late Glacial occupation in northwest Europe." *Antiquity*, 74: 112–19.

Bonnichsen, R. (ed.) 1999. *Who Were the First Americans?* Peopling of the Americas Publications. Corvallis: Oregon State University.

Bonnichsen, R. and D. G. Steele (eds.) 1994. *Method and Theory for Investigating the Peopling of the Americas*. Peopling of the Americas Publications. Corvallis: Oregon State University.

Brooks, A. S., D. M. Helgren, J. S. Cramer, et al. 1995. "Dating and context of three Middle Stone Age sites with bone points in the Upper Semliki Valley, Zaire." *Science*, 268: 548–53.

Brown, F. H. 1996. "The potential of the Turkana basin for palaeoclimatic reconstruction in East Africa." In E. S. Vrba, G. H. Denton, T. C. Partridge, and L. H. Burckle (eds.), *Palaeoclimate and Evolution, With Emphasis on Human Origins*, pp. 319–30. New Haven, CT: Yale University Press.

Brown, T. A., R. G. Allaby, K. A. Brown, and M. K. Jones 1993. "Biomolecular archaeology of wheat: past, present and future." *World Archaeology*, 25 (1): 64–73.

Brunet M., A. Beauvilain, Y. Coppens, et al. 1995. "The first australopithecine 2,500 kilometres west of the rift valley (Chad)." *Nature*, 378: 273–5.

Brunet M., F. Guy, D. Pilbeam, et al. 2002. "A new hominid from the upper Miocene of Chad, central Africa." *Nature*, 418: 145–51.

Buckland, P. C., A. J. Dugmore, and K. J. Edwards 1997. "Bronze Age myths? Volcanic activity and human response in the Mediterranean and North Atlantic regions." *Antiquity*, 71: 581–93.

Cande, S. C. and D. V. Kent 1995. "Revised calibration of the geomagnetic polarity timescale for the late Cretaceous and Cenozoic." *Journal of Geophysical Research*, 100: 6093–5.

Carlisle, R. C. and J. M. Adovasio 1982. *Collected Papers on the Archaeology of Meadowcroft Rockshelter and the Cross Creek Drainage*, 7th Annual Meeting of the Society for American Archaeology, Minneapolis.

Chen Tiemei, Y. Quan, and W. En 1994. "Antiquity of *Homo sapiens* in China." *Nature*, 368: 55–6.

Chen Tiemei and Zhang Yinyun 1991. "Palaeolithic chronology and the possible coexistence of *Homo erectus* and *Homo sapiens* in China." *World Archaeology*, 23 (2): 147–54.

Chippindale, C., J. de Jongh, J. Flood, and S. Rufolo 2000. "Stratigraphy, Harris matrices and relative dating of Australian rock-art." *Antiquity*, 74: 285–6.

Clark, J. D. 1969. *Kalambo Falls Prehistoric Site, Vol. 1: The Geology, Palaeoecology and Detailed Stratigraphy of the Excavations*. Cambridge: Cambridge University Press.

Clark, J. D. 1971. "A re-examination of the evidence for agricultural origins in the Nile valley." *Proceedings of the Prehistoric Society*, 37 (Part 2): 34–79.

Clark, J. D. 1992. "African and Asian perspectives on the origins of modern humans." In M. J. Aitken, C. B. Stringer, and P. A. Mellars (eds.), *The Origin of Modern Humans and the Impact of Chronometric Dating*, pp. 148–78. Princeton, NJ: Princeton University Press.

Clarke, D. L. 1968. *Analytical Archaeology*. London: Methuen.

Clarke R. J. and P. V. Tobias 1995. "Sterkfontein member 2 foot bones of the oldest South African hominid." *Science*, 269: 521–4.

Cox, C. B. and P. D. Moore 1993. *Biogeography: An Ecological and Evolutionary Approach*, 5th edn. Oxford: Blackwell.

Crawford, G. W. and C. Shen 1998. "The origins of rice agriculture: recent progress in East Asia." *Antiquity*, 72: 858–66.

Dark, P. 2000. "Revised 'absolute' dating of the early Mesolithic site of Star Carr, North Yorkshire, in the light of changes in the early Holocene tree-ring chronology." *Antiquity*, 74: 304–7.

David, B., R. Roberts, C. Tuniz, R. Jones, and J. Head 1997. "New optical and radiocarbon dates from Ngarrabullgan Cave, a Pleistocene archaeological site in Australia: implications for the comparability of time clocks and for the human colonization of Australia." *Antiquity,* 71: 183–8.

Davidson, I. 1991. "The archaeology of language origins: a review." *Antiquity,* 65: 39–48.

Davidson, I. and W. Noble 1993. "Tools and language in human evolution." In K. R. Gibson and T. Ingold (eds.), *Tools, Language and Cognition in Human Evolution,* pp. 363–88. Cambridge: Cambridge University Press.

Deacon, T. 1997. *The Symbolic Species: The Co-Evolution of Language and the Human Brain.* London: Allen Lane.

Delson, E. 1994. "Evolutionary history of the colobine monkeys in palaeoenvironmental perspective." In A. G. Davies and J. F. Oates (eds.), *Colobine Monkeys: Their Ecology, Behaviour and Evolution,* pp. 11–43. Cambridge: Cambridge University Press.

DeMenocal, P. B. and J. Bloemendahl 1996. "Plio-Pleistocene climatic variability in subtropical Africa and the paleoenvironment of hominid evolution: a combined data-model approach." In E. S. Vrba, G. H. Denton, T. C. Partridge, and L. H. Burckle (eds.), *Palaeoclimate and Evolution, With Emphasis on Human Origins,* pp. 262–88. New Haven, CT: Yale University Press.

D'Errico, F., J. Zilhao, M. Julien, D. Bafier, and J. Pelegrin 1998. "Neanderthal acculturation in Western Europe? A critical review of the evidence and its interpretation." *Current Anthropology,* 39: 1–44

Dortch, C. E. 1997a. "New perceptions of the chronology and development of Aboriginal fishing in southwestern Australia." *World Archaeology,* 29 (1): 15–35.

Dortch, C. E. 1997b. "Prehistory down under: investigations of submerged Aboriginal sites at Lake Jasper, Western Australia." *Antiquity,* 71: 116–23.

Drake, R. E., G. H. Curtis, T. E. Cerling, B. W. Cerling, and J. Hampel 1980. "KBS tuff dating and geochronology of tuffaceous sediments in the Koobi Fora and Shungura formations, East Africa." *Nature,* 283: 368–72.

Duarte C., J. Mauricio, P. B. Pettitt et al. 1999. "The early upper Paleolithic human skeleton from the Abrigo do Lagar Velho (Portugal) and modern human emergence in Iberia." *Proceedings of the National Academy of Sciences USA,* 96: 7604–9.

Dunbar, R. 1996. *Grooming, Gossip and the Evolution of Language.* London: Faber and Faber.

Edwards, R. L., J. W. Beck, G. S. Burr et al. 1993. "A large drop in atmospheric 14C/12C and reduced melting in the Younger Dryas, documented with 230^{Th} ages of corals." *Science,* 260: 962–7.

Eggert, M. K. H. 1992. "The Central African rain forest: historical speculation and archaeological facts." *World Archaeology,* 24 (1): 1–24.

Eidem, J. and F. Hojlund 1993. "Trade or diplomacy? Assyria and Dilmun in the eighteenth century BC." *World Archaeology,* 24 (3): 441–8.

El Mansouri, M., El Fouikar, A., and B. Saint-Martin 1996. "Correlation between 14C ages and aspartic acid racemization at the Upper Palaeolithic site of the Abri Pataud (Dordogne, France)." *Journal of Archaeological Science,* 23: 803–9.

Ericson, J. E., L. Pandolfi, and C. Patterson 1982. "Pyrotechnology of copper extraction: methods of detection and implications." In T. A. Wertime and S. F. Wertime (eds.), *Early Pyrotechnology: The Evolution of the First Fire-Using Industries,* pp.193–203. Washington, DC: Smithsonian Institution Press.

Fitch, F. J., P. J. Hooker, and J. A. Miller 1976. "Argon-40/Argon-39 dating of KBS Tuff in Koobi for a formation, East Rudolf, Kenya." *Nature,* 263: 740–4.

Fitch, F. J. and J. A. Miller 1970. "Radioisotopic age determinations of Lake Rudolf artefact site." *Nature,* 226: 226–8.

Fulford, M. and A. Wallace-Hadrill 1998. "Unpeeling Pompeii." *Antiquity,* 72: 128–45.

Fullagar, R. L. K., D. M. Price, and L. M. Head 1996. "Early human occupation of northern Australia: archaeology and thermoluminescence dating of Jinmium rock-shelter, Northern Territory." *Antiquity*, 70: 751–73.

Gabunia, L., A. Vekua, D. Lordkipanidze, et al. 2000. "Earliest Pleistocene hominid cranial remains from Dmanisi, Republic of Georgia: taxonomy, geological setting, and age." *Science*, 288: 1019–25.

Gamble, C. 1993. *Timewalkers*. London: Alan Sutton.

Geel, B. van, J. van der Plicht, M. R. Kilian, et al. 1998. "The sharp rise of Δ14C ca. 800 cal BC: possible causes, related climatic teleconnections and the impact on human environments." *Radiocarbon*, 40 (1): 535–50.

Geyh, M. A. and C. Schlüchter 1998. "Calibration of the 14C time scale beyond 22,000 BP." *Radiocarbon*, 40 (1): 475–82.

Gibert, J., L. Gibert, A. Iglesias, and E. Maestro 1998. "Two 'Oldowan' assemblages in the Plio-Pleistocene deposits of the Orce region, southeast Spain." *Antiquity*, 72: 17–25.

Gillespie, R. 1997. "On human blood, rock art and calcium oxalate: further studies on organic carbon content and radiocarbon, age of materials relating to Australian rock art." *Antiquity*, 71: 430–7.

Gleadow, A. J. W. 1980. "Fission track age of the KBS Tuff and associated hominid remains in northern Kenya." *Nature*, 284: 225–30.

Goodman M., B. F. Koop, J. Czelusniak, et al. 1989. "Molecular phylogeny of the family of apes and humans." *Genome*, 31: 316–35.

Görsdorf, J., G. Dreyer, and U. Hartung 1998. "New 14C dating of the archaic royal necropolis Umm el-Qaab at Abydos (Egypt)." *Radiocarbon*, 40 (1): 641.

Gosden, C. 1992. "Production systems and the colonization of the western Pacific." *World Archaeology*, 24 (1): 55–69.

Gowlett, J. A. J. and R. E. M. Hedges (eds.) 1986. *Archaeological Results from Accelerator Dating*. Oxford: Oxford University Committee for Archaeology Monograph Series, No. 11.

Gowlett, J. A. J., J. W. K. Harris, D. Walton, and B. A. Wood 1981. "Early archaeological sites, hominid remains and traces of fire from Chesowanja, Kenya." *Nature*, 294: 125–9.

Gowlett, J. A. J., R. E. M. Hedges, and R. A. Housley 1997. "Klithi: the AMS radiocarbon dating programme for the site and its environs." In G. Bailey (ed.), *Klithi: Palaeolithic Settlement and Quaternary Landscapes in Northwest Greece, Vol. 1: Excavation and Intra-site Analysis at Klithi*, pp. 27–39. Cambridge: McDonald Institute for Archaeological Research.

Graves, P. 1994. "Flakes and ladders: what the archaeological record cannot tell us about the origins of language." *World Archaeology*, 26 (2): 158–71.

Groube, L., J. Chappell, J. Muke, and D. Price 1986. "40,000-year-old human occupation site at Huon Peninsula, Papua New Guinea." *Nature*, 324: 453–5.

Gruhn, R. 1994. "The Pacific coast route of initial entry: an overview." In R. Bonnichsen and D. G. Steele (eds.), *Method and Theory for Investigating the Peopling of the Americas*, pp. 249–56. Peopling of the Americas Publications. Corvallis: Oregon State University.

Grün, R. 1989. "Present status of ESR-dating." *Applied Radiation and Isotopes*, 10–12, 1045–55.

Grün, R. and C. B. Stringer 1991. "Electron spin resonance dating and the origin of modern humans." *Archaeometry*, 33: 153–99.

Guidon, N. and B. Arnaud 1991. "The chronology of the New World: two faces of one reality." *World Archaeology*, 23 (2): 167–78.

Harris, D. R. (ed.) 1996. *The Origins and Spread of Agriculture and Pastoralism in Eurasia*. London: University College London Press.

Harris, J. W. K. 1983. "Cultural beginnings: Plio-Pleistocene archaeological occurrences from the Afar, Ethiopia." *African Archaeological Review*, 1: 3–31

Harrold, F. B. 1980. "A comparative analysis of Eurasian Palaeolithic burials." *World Archaeology*, 12 (2): 195–211.

Hay, R. L. 1976. *Geology of the Olduvai Gorge*. Berkeley: University of California Press.

Hedges, R. E. M. and J. A. J. Gowlett 1986. "Radiocarbon dating by accelerator mass spectrometry." *Scientific American*, 254: 100–7.

Hedges, R. E. M., C. Bronk Ramsey, G. J. van Klinken, et al. 1998. "Methodological issues in the 14C dating of rock painting." *Radiocarbon*, 40 (1): 35–44.

Hedges, R. E. M., M. J. Humm, J. Foreman, G. J. van Klinken, and C. R. Bronk 1992. "Developments in sample combustion to carbon dioxide, and in the Oxford AMS carbon dioxide ion source system." *Radiocarbon*, 34 (3): 306–11.

Hedges, R. E. M. and G. J. van Klinken 1992. "A review of current approaches in the pretreatment of bone for radiocarbon dating by AMS." *Radiocarbon*, 34 (3): 279–91.

Heinzelin J. de, J. D. Clark, T. White, et al. 1999. "Environment and behavior of 2.5 million-year-old Bouri hominids." *Science*, 284: 625–9.

Hill, A. 1996. "Faunal and environmental change in the Neogene of East Africa: evidence from the Tugen Hills sequence, Baringo District, Kenya." In E. S. Vrba, G. H. Denton, T. C. Partridge, and L. H. Burckle (eds.), *Palaeoclimate and Evolution, With Emphasis on Human Origins*, pp. 178–93. New Haven, CT: Yale University Press.

Hill, A. and S. Ward 1988. "Origin of the Hominidae: the record of African large hominoid evolution between 14My and 4My." *Yearbook of Physical Anthropology*, 31: 49–83.

Hillman, G. 1996. "Late Pleistocene changes in wild plant-foods available to hunter-gatherers of the northern Fertile Crescent: possible preludes to cereal cultivation." In D. R. Harris (ed.), *The Origins and Spread of Agriculture and Pastoralism in Eurasia*, pp. 159–203. London: University College London Press.

Hillman, G., S. Wales, F. McLaren, J. Evans, and A. Butler 1993. "Identifying problematic remains of ancient plant foods: a comparison of the role of chemical, histological and morphological criteria." *World Archaeology*, 25 (1): 94–121.

Housley, R. A., C. S. Gamble, and P. Pettitt 2000. "Reply to Blockley, Donahue and Pollard." *Antiquity*, 74: 119–21.

Housley, R. A., C. S. Gamble, M. Street, and P. Pettitt 1997. "Radiocarbon evidence for the late glacial human recolonization of northern Europe." *Proceedings of the Prehistoric Society*, 63: 25–54.

Huang, W., R. Ciochon, Y. Gu, R. Larick, Q. Fang, H. P. Schwarcz, et al. 1995. "Early *Homo* and associated artefacts from Asia." *Nature*, 378: 275–40.

Hublin, J.-J. 1993. "Recent human evolution in northwestern Africa." In M. J. Aitken, C. B. Stringer, and P. A. Mellars (eds.), *The Origin of Modern Humans and the Impact of Chronometric Dating*, pp. 118–31. Princeton, NJ: Princeton University Press.

Hublin, J., F. Spoor, M. Braun, F. Zonneveld, and S. Condemi 1996. "A late Neanderthal associated with Upper Palaeolithic artefacts." *Nature*, 381: 224–6.

Huxtable, J. and R. M. Jacobi 1982. "Thermoluminescence dating of burned flints from a British Mesolithic site: Longmoor Inclosure, East Hampshire." *Archaeometry*, 24 (2): 164–9.

Isaac, G. L. and G. H. Curtis 1974. "Age of Early Acheulian industries from the Peninj Group, Tanzania." *Nature*, 249: 624–7.

Jeffreys, A. J. 1989. "Molecular biology and human evolution." In J. R. Durant (ed.), *Human Origins*, pp. 217–52. Oxford: Clarendon Press.

Jelinek, A. J. 1990. "The Amudian in the context of the Mugharan tradition at the Tabun Cave (Mount Carmel), Israel." In P. A. Mellars (ed.), *The Emergence of Modern Humans*, pp. 81–90. Edinburgh: Edinburgh University Press.

Johanson, D. C., F. T. Masao, G. G. Eck, et al. 1987. "New partial skeleton of *Homo habilis* from Olduvai gorge, Tanzania." *Nature*, 327: 205–9.

Khan, F. and J. A. J. Gowlett 1997. "Age-depth relationships in the radiocarbon dates from Sanghao Cave, Pakistan." *Archaeological Science, Conference Proceedings, Liverpool 1995*: 182–7.

Kimbel, W. H., D. C. Johanson, and Y. Rak 1994. "The first skull and other new discoveries of *Australopithecus afarensis* at Hadar, Ethiopia." *Nature*, 368: 449–51.

Kimbel, W. H., R. C. Walter, D. C. Johanson, et al. 1996. "Late Pliocene *Homo* and Oldowan tools from the Hadar formation (kada hadar member), Ethiopia." *Journal of Human Evolution*, 31: 549–61.

Kitagawa, H. and J. van der Plicht 1998. "Extension of the 14C calibration curve to ca. 40,000 cal BC by a 40,000-year varve chronology from Lake Suigetsu, Japan." *Radiocarbon*, 40 (1): 505–15.

Kitchen, K. A. 1989. "The basics of Egyptian chronology in relation to the Bronze Age." In P. Aström (ed.), *High, Middle or Low? Acts of an International Colloquium on Absolute Chronology held at the University of Gothenburg, 1987*, pp. 37–55. Gottenburg: Paul Aströms Förlag.

Kitchen, K. A. 1991. "The chronology of ancient Egypt." *World Archaeology*, 23 (2): 201–8.

Kozlowski, J. K. 1992. "The Balkans in the Middle and Upper Palaeolithic: the gate to Europe or a cul-de-sac?" *Proceedings of the Prehistoric Society*, 38: 1–20.

Kozlowski, J. K. 1999. "The evolution of the Balkan Aurignacian." In W. Davies and R. Charles (eds.), *Dorothy Garrod and the Progress of the Palaeolithic*, pp. 97–117. Oxford: Oxbow Books.

Krings, M., A. Stone, R. W. Schmitz, et al. 1997. "Neandertal DNA sequences and the origin of modern humans." *Cell*, 90: 19–30.

Kromer, B. and M. Spurk 1998. "Revision and tentative extension of the tree-ring based 14C calibration, 9200–11955 Cal. BP." *Radiocarbon*, 40: 1117–25.

Kromer, B., M. Spurk, S. Remmele, M. Barbetti, and V. Toniello 1998. "Segments of atmospheric 14C change as derived from Late Glacial and Early Holocene floating tree-ring series." *Radiocarbon*, 40 (1): 351–8.

Kuhn, S. L., M. C. Stiner, and E. Güleç 1999. "Initial Upper Palaeolithic in south-central Turkey and its regional context: a preliminary report." *Antiquity*, 73: 505–17.

Kuzmin, Y. V. and L. A. Orlova 2000. "The Neolithization of Siberia and the Russian Far East." *Antiquity*, 74: 356–64.

Lange, M. 1998. "Wadi Shaw 82/52: 14C dates from a predynastic site in northwest Sudan, supporting the Egyptian historical chronology." *Radiocarbon*, 40 (1): 687.

Laurence, R. 1994. *Roman Pompeii: Space and Society*. London: Routledge.

Leakey, M. D. 1971. *Olduvai Gorge, Vol. 3: Excavations in Beds I and II, 1960–1963*. Cambridge: Cambridge University Press.

Leakey, M. D. and D. A. Roe 1995. *Olduvai Gorge, Vol. 5*. Cambridge: Cambridge University Press.

Leakey, M. G., C. S. Feibel, I. McDougall, and A. C. Walker 1995. "New four-million-year-old hominid species from Kanapoi and Allia bay, Kenya." *Nature*, 376: 565–71.

Lourandos, H. 1997. *Continent of Hunter-Gatherers*. Cambridge: Cambridge University Press.

Lynch, T. F. (ed.) (1980). *Guitarrero Cave: Early Man in the Andes*. New York: Academic Press.

McBurney, C. B. M. 1967. *The Haua Fteah*. Cambridge: Cambridge University Press.

McDougall, I., R. Maier, P. Sutherland-Hawkes, and A. J. W. Gleadow 1980. "K-Ar age estimate for the KBS Tuff, East Turkana, Kenya." *Nature*, 284: 230–4.

McHenry, H. M. and L. R. Berger 1998. "Body proportions in *Australopithecus afarensis* and *A. africanus* and the origin of the genus *Homo*." *Journal of Human Evolution*, 35: 1–22.

Malone, C. (ed.) 1998. "Rice domestication: special section." *Antiquity*, 72: 857–907.

Manning, S. W. and B. Weninger 1992. "A light in the dark: archaeological wiggle matching and the absolute chronology of the close of the Aegean Late Bronze Age." *Antiquity*, 66: 636–63.

Marks, A. E. 1990. "The Middle and Upper Palaeolithic of the Near East and the Nile Valley: the problem of cultural transformation." In P. A. Mellars (ed.), *The Emergence of Modern Humans*, pp. 56–80. Edinburgh: Edinburgh University Press.

Mellars, P. A. 1992. "Archaeology and the population dispersal hypothesis of modern human origins in Europe." In M. J. Aitken, C. B. Stringer, and P. A. Mellars (eds.), *The Origin of Modern Humans and the Impact of Chronometric Dating*, pp. 196–216. Princeton, NJ: Princeton University Press.

Mellars, P. A. 1996. *The Neanderthal Legacy*. Princeton, NJ: Princeton University Press.

Mellars, P. A., H. M. Bricker, J. A. J. Gowlett, and R. E. M. Hedges 1987. "Radiocarbon accelerator dating of French Upper Palaeolithic sites." *Current Anthropology*, 29 (1): 128–32.

Mellars, P. and C. Stringer (eds.) 1989. *The Human Revolution: Behavioral and Biological Perspectives on the Origins of Modern Humans*. Edinburgh: Edinburgh University Press.

Mercier, N., H. Valladas, G. Valladas, et al. 1995. "TL dates of burnt flints from Jelinek's excavations at Tabun and their implications." *Journal of Archaeological Science*, 22: 495–509.

Mirambell, L. (1978). "Tlapacoya: A late Pleistocene site in central Mexico." In A. L. Bryan (ed.), *Early Man in America from a Circum-Pacific Perspective*, pp. 221–30. Occasional Papers No. 1, Department of Anthropology, University of Alberta, Edmonton.

Morwood, M. J., F. Aziz, F. Nasruddin, et al. 1999. "Archaeological and palaeontological research in central Flores, east Indonesia: results of fieldwork 1997–98." *Antiquity*, 73: 273–86.

Movius, H. 1949. "The Lower Palaeolithic cultures of southern and eastern Asia." *Transactions of the American Philosophical Society*, n.s. 38 (4): 329–420.

Movius, H. L., Jr. 1975. "A summary of the stratigraphic sequence." In H. L. Movius, Jr. (ed.), *Excavation of the Abri Pataud, Les Eyzies (Dordogne)*. American School of Prehistoric Research, Bulletin No. 30: 7–18.

Mulvaney, J. 1969. *The Prehistory of Australia*, 1st edn. London: Thames and Hudson.

Nadel, D. and E. Werker 1999. "The oldest ever brush hut plant remains from Ohalo II, Jordan Valley, Israel (19,000 BP)." *Antiquity*, 73: 755–64.

Neftel, A., H. Oeschger, J. Scwander, B. Stauffer, and R. Zumbrunn 1982. "Ice core sample measurements give atmospheric CO_2 content during the past 40,000 yr." *Nature*, 295: 220–3.

O'Connor, T. P. 1997. "Working at relationships: another look at animal domestication." *Antiquity*, 71: 149–56.

Olsson, I. U. 1991. "On the calculation of old ages and the reliability of given ages." In B. G. Andersen, and L.-K. Königsson (eds.), *Late Quaternary Stratigraphy in the Nordic Countries 150,000–15,000 BP. Striae* (Uppsala) 34: 53–8.

Olsson, I. U. and G. Possnert 1992. "The interpretation of 14C measurements on pre-Holocene samples." *Sveriges Geologiska Undersökning*, Ser. Ca. 81: 201–8.

Opdyke, N. 1996. "Mammalian migration and climate over the last seven million years." In E. S. Vrba, G. H. Denton, T. C. Partridge, and L. H. Burckle (eds.), *Palaeoclimate and Evolution, With Emphasis on Human Origins*, pp. 109–14. New Haven, CT: Yale University Press.

Palmqvist, P. 1997. "A critical re-evaluation of the evidence for the presence of hominids in lower Pleistocene times at Venta Micena, southern Spain." *Journal of Human Evolution*, 33: 83–9.

Partridge, T. C., J. Shaw, D. Heslop, and R. J. Clarke 1999. "The new hominid skeleton from Sterkfontein, South Africa: age and preliminary assessment." *Journal of Quaternary Science*, 14: 293–8.

Patterson, B. and W. W. Howells 1967. "Hominid humeral fragment from early Pleistocene of northwestern Kenya." *Science*, 156: 64–6.

Patterson, B., A. K. Behrensmeyer, and W. D. Sill 1970. "Geology and fauna of a new Pliocene locality in northwestern Kenya." *Nature*, 226: 918–21.

Pearce, R. H. and M. Barbetti 1981. "A 38,000-year-old archaeological site at Upper Swan, Western Australia." *Archaeology in Oceania*, 14, 18–24.

Pearson, G. W., J. R. Pilcher, and M. G. L. Baillie 1983. "High precision 14C measurement of Irish oaks to show the natural 14C variations from 200 BC to 4000 BC." *Radiocarbon*, 25: 179–86.

Pettitt, P. R. 1997. "High resolution Neanderthals? Interpreting Middle Palaeolithic intrasite spatial data." *World Archaeology*, 29 (2): 208–24.

Plicht, J. van der 1999. "Radiocarbon calibration for the Middle/Upper Palaeolithic: a comment." *Antiquity*, 73: 119–23.

Plummer, T., L. C. Bishop, P. Ditchfield, and J. Hicks 1999. "Research on Late Pliocene Oldowan sites at Kanjera South, Kenya." *Journal of Human Evolution*, 36: 151–70.

Potter, T. W. 1987. *Roman Italy*. London: British Museum Publications.

Raynal, J.-P., L. Magoga, F.-Z. Sbihi-Alaoui, and D. Geraads 1995. "The earliest occupation of Atlantic Morocco: the Casablanca evidence." In W. Roebroeks and T. van Kolfschoten (eds.), *The Earliest Occupation of Europe: Proceedings of the European Science, Foundation Workshop at Tautavel (France), 1993. Analecta Praehistorica Leidensia*, 27: 255–62. Leiden: University of Leiden.

Renfrew, A. C. 1968. "Wessex without Mycenae." *Annual of the British School at Athens*, 63: 277–85.

Reynolds, T. 1990. "The Middle-Upper Palaeolithic transition in southwestern France: interpreting the lithic evidence." In P. A. Mellars (ed.), *The Emergence of Modern Humans*, pp. 262–75. Edinburgh: Edinburgh University Press.

Reynolds, T. E. G. 1991. "Revolution or resolution? The archaeology of modern human origins." *World Archaeology*, 23 (2): 155–66.

Richards, M., K. Smalley, B. Sykes, and R. Hedges 1993. "Archaeology and genetics: analysing DNA from skeletal remains." *World Archaeology*, 25 (1): 18–28.

Rigaud, J.-P. 1989. "From the Middle to the Upper Palaeolithic: transition or convergence?" In E. Trinkaus (ed.), *The Emergence of Modern Humans*, pp. 142–53. Cambridge: Cambridge University Press.

Rightmire, G. P. 1990. *The Evolution of Homo Erectus*. Cambridge: Cambridge University Press.

Rightmire, G. P. 1996. "The human cranium from Bodo, Ethiopia: evidence for speciation in the Middle Pleistocene?" *Journal of Human Evolution*, 31: 21–39.

Roberts, R. G., R. Jones, and M. Smith 1990. "Thermoluminescence dating of a 50,000-year-old human occupation site in northern Australia." *Nature*, 345: 153–6.

Robertshaw, P. 1992. "Radiocarbon dating and the prehistory of sub-saharan Africa." In R. E. Taylor, A. Long, and R. S. Kra (eds.), *Radiocarbon, After Four Decades: An Interdisciplinary Perspective*, pp. 335–51. New York: Springer-Verlag.

Roebroeks, W. 1996. "The English Palaeolithic record: absence of evidence, evidence of absence and the first occupation of Europe." In C. S. Gamble and A. J. Lawson (eds.), *The English Palaeolithic Reviewed*, pp. 57–62. Salisbury: Wessex Archaeology.

Roebroeks, W., N. J. Conard, and T. van Kolfschoten 1992. "Dense forests, cold steppes, and the Palaeolithic settlement of northern Europe." *Current Anthropology*, 33: 551–86.

Roebroeks, W. and T. van Kolfschoten (eds.) 1995. *The Earliest Occupation of Europe: Proceedings of the European Science Foundation Workshop at Tautavel (France), 1993. Analecta Praehistorica Leidensia*, 27. Leiden: University of Leiden.

Ronen, A. 1991. "The Yiron-Gravel lithic assemblage: artifacts older than 2.4 My in Israel." *Archäologisches Korrespondenzblatt*, 21: 159–64.

Roosevelt, A. C., M. Lima da Costa, C. L. Machado, et al. 1996. "Paleoindian cave dwellers in the Amazon: the peopling of the Americas." *Science*, 272: 373–84.

Rosenfeld, A. and C. Smith 1997. "Recent developments in radiocarbon and stylistic methods of dating rock-art." *Antiquity*, 71: 405–11.

Sand, C. 1997. "The chronology of Lapita ware in New Caledonia." *Antiquity*, 71: 539–47.

Sarich, V. M. and A. C. Wilson 1968. "Immunological time scale for hominid evolution." *Science*, 158: 1200–2.

Schäfer, J., P. M. Sosin, and V. A. Ranov 1996. "Neue Untersuchungen zum Lösspaläolithikum am Obi-Mazar, Tadzikistan." *Archäologisches Korrespondenzblatt*, 26: 97–109.

Schick, K. and D. Zhuan 1993. "Early Paleolithic of China and eastern Asia." In J. D. Fleagle (ed.), *Evolutionary Anthropology*, 2 (1): 22–35. New York: Wiley-Liss.

Schiffer, M. B. 1976. *Behavioral Archaeology*. New York: Academic Press.

Schild, R., F. Wendorf, and A. Close (1992) "Northern and eastern Africa climate changes between 140,000 and 12,000 years ago." In F. Klees and R. Kuper (eds.), *New Light on the Northeast African Past*, pp. 81–96. Köln: Heinrich-Barth-Institut.

Schwarcz, H. P. 1993. "Uranium-series dating and the origin of modern man." In M. J. Aitken, C. B. Stringer, and P. A. Mellars (eds.), *The Origin of Modern Humans and the Impact of Chronometric Dating*, pp. 12–26. Princeton, NJ: Princeton University Press.

Schwarcz, H. P., B. Blackwell, P. Goldberg, and A. E. Marks 1979. "Uranium series dating of travertine from archaeological sites, Nahal Zin, Israel." *Nature*, 277: 558–60.

Schwarcz, H. P., R. Grün, and P. V. Tobias 1994. "ESR dating studies of the australopithecine site of Sterkfontein, South Africa." *Journal of Human Evolution*, 26: 175–81.

Sealy, J. C. and N. J. van der Merwe 1985. "Isotope assessment of Holocene human diets in the southwestern Cape, South Africa." *Nature*, 315: 138–40.

Semaw, S., P. R. Renne, J. W. K. Harris, et al. 1997. "2.5 million-year-old stone tools from Gona, Ethiopia." *Nature*, 385: 333–6.

Senut, B., M. Pickford, D. Gommery, et al. 2001. "First hominid from the Miocene (Lukeino Formation, Kenya)." *Comptes rendus des séances de l'académie des sciences*, 332: 137–44.

Settle, D. M. and C. C. Patterson 1980. "Lead in Albacore: guide to lead pollution in Americans." *Science*, 207: 1171.

Shackleton, N. J. 1996. "New data on the evolution of Pliocene climatic variability." In E. S. Vrba, G. H. Denton, T. C. Partridge, and L. H. Burckle (eds.), *Palaeoclimate and Evolution, With Emphasis on Human Origins*, pp. 242–8. New Haven, CT: Yale University Press.

Shackleton, N. J. and N. D. Opdyke 1973. "Oxygen isotope and palaeomagnetic stratigraphy of Equatorial Pacific core V28–238." *Quaternary Research*, 3: 39–55.

Shackleton, N. J. and N. D. Opdyke 1977. "Oxygen isotope and palaeomagnetic evidence for early Northern Hemisphere glaciation." *Nature*, 270: 216–19.

Shaw, J., Z. Hongbo, and A. Zisheng 1991. "Magnetic dating of early man in China." *Archaeometry*, 90: 589–95

Sherratt, A. 1997. "Climatic cycles and behavioral revolutions: the emergence of modern humans and the beginning of farming." *Antiquity*, 71: 271–87.

Sherratt, S. and A. Sherratt 1993. "The growth of the Mediterranean economy in the early first millennium BC." *World Archaeology*, 24 (3): 361–78.

Simons, E. 1995. "Egyptian Oligocene primates: a review." *Yearbook of Physical Anthropology*, 38: 199–238.

Smith, F. H. 1993. "Models and realities in modern human origins: the African fossil evidence." In M. J. Aitken, C. B. Stringer, and P. A. Mellars (eds.), *The Origin of Modern Humans and the Impact of Chronometric Dating*, pp. 234–48. Princeton, NJ: Princeton University Press.

Soffer, O. and C. Gamble (eds.) 1990. *The World at 18000 BP*, 2 vols. London: Unwin Hyman.

Spooner, N. 1998. "Human occupation at Jinmium, northern Australia: 116,000 years ago or much less?" *Antiquity*, 72: 173–8.

Stafford, T. W. 1994. "Accelerator C-14 dating of human fossil skeletons: assessing accuracy and results on New World specimens." In R. Bonnichsen and D. G. Steele (eds.), *Method and Theory for Investigating the Peopling of the Americas*, pp. 45–55. Peopling of the Americas Publications. Corvallis: Oregon State University.

Stern, N. 1994. "The implications of time-averaging for reconstructing the land-use patterns of early tool-using hominids." In J. S. Oliver, N. E. Sikes, and K. M. Stewart (eds.), *Early Hominid Behavioral Ecology. Journal of Human Evolution*, 27: 89–105.

Stocker, T. F. and D. G. Wright 1998. "The effect of a succession of ocean ventilation changes on 14C." *Radiocarbon*, 40 (1): 359–66.

Straus, L. G., B. V. Eriksen, J. M. Erlandson, and D. R. Yesner (eds.) 1996. *Humans at the End of the Ice Age: The Archaeology of the Pleistocene-Holocene Transition*. New York: Plenum Press.

Stringer, C. B. 1993. "Reconstructing recent human evolution." In M. J. Aitken, C. B. Stringer, and P. A. Mellars (eds.), *The Origin of Modern Humans and the Impact of Chronometric Dating*, pp. 179–95. Princeton, NJ: Princeton University Press.

Stringer, C. B. 1995. "Replacement, continuity and the origin of *Homo sapiens*." In G. Bräuer and F. H. Smith (eds.), *Continuity or Replacement*, pp. 9–24. Rotterdam: Balkema.

Stringer, C. B. 1999. "Has Australia backdated the Human Revolution?" *Antiquity*, 73: 876–9.

Stringer C. B. and C. Gamble 1993. *In Search of the Neanderthals*. London: Thames and Hudson.

Sun Donghuai, A. Zhisheng, J. Shaw, J. Bloemendal, and S. Youbin 1998. "Magnetostratigraphy and palaeoclimatic significance of Late Tertiary aeolian sequences in the Chinese Loess Plateau." *Geophysics Journal International*, 134: 207–12.

Suwa, G., B. Asfaw, Y. Beyene, et al. 1997. "The first skull of Australopithecus boisei." *Nature*, 389: 489–92.

Svoboda, J. 1994. *Paleolit Moravy a Slezska (The Paleolithic of Moravia and Silesia)*, vol. 1. Brno: Dolni Vestonice Studies

Swadling, P. 1997. "Changing shorelines and cultural orientations in the Sepik-Ramu, Papua New Guinea: implications for pacific prehistory." *World Archaeology*, 29 (1): 1–14.

Swisher, G. C., G. H. Curtis, T. Jacob, et al. 1994. "Age of the earliest known hominids in Java, Indonesia." *Science*, 263: 1118–21.

Tattersall, I. and J. H. Schwartz 999. "Hominids and hybrids: the place of Neanderthals in human evolution." *Proceedings of the National Academy of Sciences*, 96: 7117–19.

Taylor, R. E., L. A. Payen, C. A. Prior, et al. 1985. "Major revisions in the Pleistocene age assignments for North American human skeletons: None older than 11,000 14C years BP." *American Antiquity*, 50 (1): 136–40.

Terrell, J. E. and R. L. Welsch 1997. "Lapita and the temporal geography of prehistory." *Antiquity*, 71: 548–72.

Thieme, H. 1996. "Altpaläolithische Wurfspeere aus Schöningen, Niedersachsen – ein Vorbericht." *Archäologisches Korrespondenzblatt*, 26 (4): 377–93.

Thorne, A., R. Grün, G. Mortimer, et al. 1999. "Australia's oldest human remains: age of the Lake Mungo 3 skeleton." *Journal of Human Evolution*, 36: 591–612.

Tobias, P. V. 1991. "The emergence of spoken language in hominid evolution." In J. D. Clark (ed.), *Approaches to Understanding Early Hominid Life-ways in the African Savanna*, pp. 67–78. Römisch-Germanisches Zentralmuseum Forschungsinstitut für Vor-und Frühgeschichte in Verbindung mit der UISSP, 11 Kongress, Mainz, 31 August – 5 September 1987, Monographien Band 19. Bonn: Dr Rudolf Habelt GMBH.

Tuffreau, A. 1992. "L'Acheuléen en Europe occidentale d'après les données du bassin de la Somme." In C. Peretto (ed.), *Il più antico popolamento della valle Padana nel quadro delle conoscenze Europee: Monte Poggiolo*, pp. 41–5. Milan: Jaca Book.

Tuffreau, A., A. Lamotte, and A.-L. Marcy 1997. "Land-use and site function in Acheulean complexes of the Somme valley." *World Archaeology*, 29 (2): 225–41.

Tushingham, A. M. and W. R. Peltier 1993. "Implications of the radiocarbon timescale for ice-sheet chronology and sea-level change." *Quaternary Research*, 39: 125–9.

Valladas, H. 1981. "Datation par thermoluminescence de grès brûlés de foyers de quatre gisements du Magdalénien final du Bassin Parisien." *Comptes rendus de l'académé de sciences, Paris*, series 11, 292: 355–8.

Van der Merwe, N. J. and J. C. Vogel 1978. "13C content of human collagen as a measure of prehistoric diet in woodland North America." *Nature*, 276: 813–16.

Vermeersch, P. M., E. Paulissen, S. Stokes, et al. 1998. "A Middle Palaeolithic burial of a modern human at Taramsa Hill, Egypt." *Antiquity*, 72: 475–84.

Voelker, A. H. L., M. Sarnthein, P. M. Grootes, et al. 1998. "Correlation of marine 14C ages from the Nordic Seas with the GISP2 isotope record: Implications for 14C calibration beyond 25 ka BP." *Radiocarbon*, 40 (1): 517–34.

Vrba, E. S., G. H. Denton, T. C. Partridge, and L. H. Burckle (eds.) 1996. *Palaeoclimate and Evolution, With Emphasis on Human Origins*. New Haven, CT: Yale University Press.

Walter, R. C., P. C. Manega, R. L. Hay, et al. 1991. "Laser-fusion 40Ar/39Ar dating of Bed I, Olduvai Gorge, Tanzania." *Nature*, 354: 145–9.

Wanpo, H., R. Ciochon, G. Yumin, et al. 1995. "Early Homo and associated artefacts from Asia." *Nature*, 378: 275–8.

Wendorf, F. and R. Schild 1974. *A Middle Stone Age Sequence from the Central Rift Valley, Ethiopia*. Warsaw: Institute for History and Material Culture, Polish National Academy.

Wendorf, F., R. Schild, A. E. Close, et al. 1988. "New radiocarbon dates and Late Palaeolithic diet at Wadi Kubbaniya, Egypt." *Antiquity*, 62: 279–83.

White, T. D., B. Asfaw, and G. Suwa 1996. "Ardipithecus ramidus: a root species for Australopithecus." In F. Facchini (ed.), *The First Humans and Their Cultural Manifestations. The Colloquia of the XIII International Congress of Prehistoric and Protohistoric Sciences, Forli, Italy*, pp. 15–23. Forli: ABACO.

White, T. D., G. Suwa, and B. Asfaw 1994. "*Australopithecus ramidus*, a new species of early hominid from Aramis, Ethiopia." *Nature*, 371: 306–12.

WoldeGabriel, G., T. D. White, G. Suwa, et al. 1994. "Ecological and temporal context of early Pliocene hominids at Aramis, Ethiopia." *Nature*, 371: 330–3.

Wolpoff, M. H. 1992. "Theories of modern human origins." In G. Bräuer and F. H. Smith (eds.), *Continuity or Replacement: Controversies in Homo Sapiens Evolution*, pp. 25–63. Rotterdam: A. A. Balkema.

Wood, B. A. 1991. *Koobi Fora Research Project, Vol. 4: Hominid Cranial Remains*. Oxford: Clarendon Press.

Wood, B. A. 1992. "Origin and evolution of the genus Homo." *Nature*, 355: 783–90.

Wood, B. A. and M. Collard 1999. "The human genus." *Science*, 284: 65–71.

Yellen, J. E., A. S. Brooks, E. Cornelissen, et al. 1995. "A Middle Stone Age worked bone industry from Katanda, Upper Semliki Valley, Zaire." *Science*, 268: 553–6.

Zaitseva, G. I, S. S. Vasiliev, L. S. Marsadolov, et al. 1998. "A tree-ring and 14C chronology of the key Sayan-Altai monuments." *Radiocarbon*, 40 (1): 571–80.

Zhimin, A. 1991. "Radiocarbon dating and the prehistoric archaeology of China." *World Archaeology*, 23 (2): 193–200.

Zielinski, G. A. and M. S. Germani 1998. "New ice-core evidence challenges the 1620s BC age for the Santorini (Minoan) eruption." *Journal of Archaeological Science*, 25: 279–89.

13

Archaeology and Indigenous Peoples: Attitudes Towards Power in Ancient Oaxaca

Maarten Jansen[1]

More than a generation ago, Vine Deloria wrote a penetrating critique of "anthropologists and other friends":

> The fundamental thesis of the anthropologist is that people are objects for observation, people are then considered objects for experimentation, for manipulation, and for eventual extinction . . . The massive volume of useless knowledge produced by anthropologists attempting to capture real Indians in a network of theories has contributed substantially to the invisibility of Indian people today. (Deloria 1969: ch. 4)

With these words the Lakota author invites anthropologists, as well as archaeologists and other investigators of the world of indigenous peoples, to reflect seriously on their work and to become conscious of the way we are embedded in a conflict-ridden reality of historical trauma and social injustice. Far from having a frustrating effect, such soul-searching should lead to a new and more positive practice. The space of this chapter allows only for a summary and exemplary treatment of some aspects of this complex matter. Making several huge leaps, passing over many discussions about colonialism and the relations between past and present, I mainly want to indicate how interpretive archaeology can benefit and be beneficial by situating itself in the very heart of this problem and from changing its perspective accordingly.

The Setting of International Standards

Comparable to the classic anti-colonial and anti-racist writings of Frantz Fannon and Albert Memmi, Deloria's manifesto marked the beginning of a new era in the struggle for emancipation by indigenous peoples of the Americas. It was followed by the occupation of Wounded Knee and a series of actions at a national and international level, which denounced the continued existence of *internal colonialism*, reinforced through new forms of economic and cultural domination by "Western" states. First ignored and not taken seriously, then despised and ridiculed by the very anthropologists and bureaucrats it attacked, Deloria's radical protest against colonial substrates and Eurocentric perspectives was echoed and continued by other indigenous activists (e.g., Pérez Jiménez 1989; Mamani Condori 1996; Churchill 1998; Smith 1999). As many Native

American movements organized themselves in the 1970s and 1980s, political awareness also mounted among anthropologists, lawyers, priests, and other concerned citizens of "Western" countries. This created a context in which the issue could receive general and serious attention.

Pitching their tepees in front of the Palais des Nations in Geneva, North American Indians forced the international community to open its doors. By 1982 the UN (ECOSOC, the Commission of Human Rights) installed a Working Group on Indigenous Populations in order to review developments and to formulate standards. In a parallel process the International Labor Organization revised its convention 107 and drafted a new convention 169 (1989), shifting from paternalist strategies of integration and "assistentialism" towards indigenous peoples, to a framework of respect, collaboration, and partnership. After a series of annual consultations with representatives of indigenous movements and other experts, the UN working group produced a Draft Declaration of the Rights of Indigenous Peoples (E/CN.4/1995/2 and E/CN.4/Sub.2/1994/56). This remarkable document establishes key principles and guidelines for cultural policies and research:

Article 12. Indigenous peoples have the right to practice and revitalize their cultural traditions and customs. This includes the right to maintain, protect and develop the past, present and future manifestations of their cultures, such as archaeological and historical sites, artefacts, designs, ceremonies, technologies and visual and performing arts and literature, as well as the right to the restitution of cultural, intellectual, religious and spiritual property taken without their free and informed consent or in violation of their laws, traditions and customs.

Article 13. Indigenous peoples have the right to manifest, practice, develop and teach their spiritual and religious traditions, customs and ceremonies; the right to maintain, protect and have access in privacy to their religious and cultural sites; the right to use and control of ceremonial objects; and the right to the repatriation of human remains.

In the 1990s, postmodernism and postcolonialism advanced in the work of literary critics and social scientists (Loomba 1998). It is now widely recognized that anthropology, as a product of the nineteenth century, was formed to serve the interests of (neo)colonial powers. Operating from a positivist and evolutionist perspective, its discourse could be used to legitimize "Western" expansion scientifically as a civilizing effort. The distinction between the dominant Self and the dominated Other was conceived and presented in terms of "civilized, developed" versus "primitive, underdeveloped," or simply – with an essentialist twist – of "normal, active, superior" versus "strange, passive, inferior." This political and intellectual legacy haunts anthropology. It is implicit in terms such as "myth" (a story which is sacred or otherwise of special significance for the Other, but in which the researcher, Self, does not believe) or "informant" (the Other, expert in his/her own culture, reduced to a mere *object* of study by Self as the more rational *subject*). Many anthropologists, however, participating in postcolonial thought, are now aware of the dangers of Eurocentrism and asymmetrical relationships in their research. Critiques like those formulated by Vine Deloria are – at least intellectually – accepted as part of a necessary reflexivity and multivocality. Theoretical norms now seem well defined; putting them into practice, however, is quite a different matter:

Since the publication of *Custer* there has been no concerted effort by the academic community, or by anthros themselves, to open the ranks of the discipline to American Indians. (Deloria, in Biolsi and Zimmerman 1998: 211)

Archaeology in the Anglo- and Latin American nations is part of anthropology. The logic behind this connection is that both disciplines from the perspective of the dominant groups in those societies deal with the Other, i.e., the colonized native peoples. A more idealistic motivation would be the direct continuity of ancient cultural traditions in the present. This circumstance creates special opportunities for archaeology, as indigenous knowledge, experience, and views offer a wealth of valuable data and crucial insights for understanding the archaeological record. One may actually experience the past in a living environment. Ethnoarchaeology, especially the "continuous model" or the "direct historical approach," calls for collaboration between the interested outsiders and the indigenous experts. Structures and mentalities inherited from colonialism, however, still form concrete obstacles, the more so where archaeologists are accustomed to see themselves as the sole "owners" or "caretakers" of the past. The encounter with other voices and claims often provokes a shock.

The developments sketched briefly above have obliged archaeology to reconsider its position, especially in the US. The most commented upon event is without doubt the passing of the Native American Grave Protection and Repatriation Act (NAGPRA) by the US Congress in 1990. Simultaneously, the World Archaeological Congress formulated some principles and rules, focusing on the acknowledgment and protection of the indigenous cultural heritage, as well as on the need to seek the informed consent and active involvement of indigenous peoples in research. Soon after, the Society of American Archaeology elaborated its ethical standards, focusing on concepts like stewardship, accountability, and the recognition of intellectual property.[2] The question remains how much of this really transforms research practice and its outcome.

Obviously it is quite a challenge to translate indigenous demands and international protocols into concrete archaeological projects. Political and ethical concerns are important ingredients of our actual situation, but often difficult to accommodate in a trad-

itional research design. In fact, the claims of "neutrality" and "objectivity" of scientific discourse tend to shut them out systematically. Going against this mainstream may even be detrimental to one's career. Many authors in this field, therefore, avoid connecting the study of the culture and history of indigenous peoples to an active engagement with their problems in present-day reality. The consequence is often a scholarly monologue, which excludes the peoples concerned, silences their voices, and impedes their possible contributions. Paradoxically, many intellectuals are focusing so much on their specific interests that they only move further away from the culture and people they study.

Cultural Continuity in Mexico

In Middle and South American countries the social sciences have a tradition of sociopolitical criticism (Benavides 2001), but here too we see little repercussion of the international standards outlined above, and even less true partnership. This is more noticeable as the indigenous population in this part of the world is quite significant, both in quantity (in some regions an absolute majority) and in cultural influence. Mexico is a particularly interesting case. Archaeologically and anthropologically speaking, most of its territory belongs to the large culture area known as Mesoamerica, of which the Nahuas (Mexica or "Aztecs") and the Mayas are the most emblematic peoples. Scores of Mesoamerican languages continue to be spoken throughout the country. On the one hand, the prehispanic civilizations are valued as the root and pride of the nation; on the other hand, their present-day descendants in practice are victims of all kinds of racist and other negative prejudices, so that they are treated as second rank citizens or strangers in their own land (cf. Bartolomé 1997; Bonfil Batalla 1989). Their living conditions are often characterized by economic exploitation, marginalization, alcoholism, violence, and ethnicide, as well as by the lack of work, medical care, good schools, and other elementary facilities. Many people simply have to migrate and leave their region. The typical future of indigenous girls is to become a servant somewhere in the city, often in circumstances that resemble slavery.

The double attitude of admiring the monuments and artefacts of the indigenous past, while discriminating against indigenous people in the present, has a correlate in the reluctance to consider cultural continuity as a relevant framework for studying Mesoamerica. On the popular level there is even a widespread belief that the prehispanic civilizations cannot have been created by the ancestors of "those Indians," but must have been the work of other peoples, coming from Egypt, Atlantis, or Outer Space! A more scholarly version of the same view is the opinion that the ancient culture was *decapitated*: it had been developed by an elite of wise priests, advanced astronomers, and refined princes, who were all killed during or shortly after the Spanish conquest (1521). Contemporaneous indigenous peoples would "merely" be the descendants of the peasants and slaves, not deemed capable of carrying on the achievements of their leaders. The Native American heritage is thus seen and treated as a dead culture, a view particularly promoted by archaeologists. This disjunction may be observed in many major exhibitions, which usually focus on the sensational presentation of ancient treasures, while limiting attention to "cultural survivals" to some isolated and secondary elements, such as motifs in folk art, or leaving them out altogether.[3]

Another, more sophisticated form of disjunction is produced by emphasizing and exaggerating the cultural diversity of ancient Mesoamerica, and so calling into question the very idea of a coherent cultural tradition. Indeed, there were many local differences and, likewise, there were dramatic changes during the colonial era, but in spite of all that, we find a profound constant or "core"

both in the archaeological cultures and in the cultural heritage of present-day indigenous peoples of Mexico. This "core" may be understood from a Braudelian perspective as a long duration process (*histoire structurale*). It is not limited to ecological conditions and other cyclical processes, but is especially manifest in daily life experience, cognition, and mentality.[4] Archaeologists can only ignore it at their own cost.

Characteristic of internal colonial structures is the complete nationalization of archaeological remains. Most research, preservation, and management are concentrated in the Instituto Nacional de Antropología e Historia (INAH). Although some of its investigators have indigenous roots, and many have good relations with indigenous communities, the institution as such is not pursuing indigenous aims nor practicing an indigenous cultural policy.[5] Instead, we see ancient shrines and holy places become tourist attractions, where nearly everything is permitted except the continuation of the native spiritual tradition. Similarly, cult images, archaeological objects venerated until this very day, still may end up in a museum, alienated from their devotees.

Changes are imminent, however. Despite all the odds, more and more young Native American men and women follow professional education and start to take a keen interest in these questions. Furthermore the Zapatista uprising at the beginning of 1994 has pushed the plight of indigenous peoples to the foreground, raising consciousness of Mexico's internal contradictions in all segments of society.

This is the context for research in Oaxaca, a mountainous state in southern Mexico, bordering on the Pacific Ocean, and a specific culture area, centrally located within the wider context of Mesoamerica. It is a state with a large indigenous population, the Ñuu Savi (Mixtec) and Beni Zaa (Zapotec) being the most numerous peoples. A crucial role in its archaeology is played by the site of Monte Albán, an impressive acropolis near Oaxaca City, located in the heart of the so-called

Central Valleys.[6] Founded in the late Formative or Preclassic period around 500 BC, it became a major capital and flourished throughout the Classic period (ca. AD 200 – ca. 800), at the end of which it was largely abandoned. During the Postclassic (ca. AD 900–1521) it held only a ceremonial function, mainly as a site for elite burials and related cults. Throughout the state of Oaxaca there are many archaeological sites, the majority of which have not yet been explored. After significant excavation projects in the past decades, both on Monte Albán and other locations (such as Huamelulpan and Yucu Ita in the Ñuu Savi region), at present the research coordinated by the Regional Center of INAH in Oaxaca City focuses on non-destructive archaeology: identification and delimitation of zones, surveys, documentation, maintenance, conservation, and protection. The Center functions as a broker or gatekeeper for projects of foreign institutions or individuals, which also tend to engage in surveys or, at the most, small-scale excavations. Generally, the collaboration of local communities and their authorities is sought explicitly, as without their permission any work would be impossible.[7] An interesting project is the foundation of community museums.

All of this results in a complex interaction of different interests and perspectives, not without tensions. In some cases local communities, following a legitimate tradition of distrust, may be opposed to the idea of outsiders walking through their lands or excavating special places, acts which arouse the suspicion of perpetrating some robbery or damaging the cultural heritage. The natural impression is that at the end of the day the archaeologists, and foreign intellectuals in general, are much better off than the poor villagers. Other communities precisely welcome such interventions, however, and want their monuments to be excavated and exposed in full splendor, as a boost to pride in local identity, to the level of education, and/or to the promotion of tourism. In all cases archaeology is clearly expected to be inter-

active and to tell a story with a meaning for the descendants and stewards of this patrimony.

Which Story?

Narrative plays a prominent role in all interpretive archaeology, both in conceptualization and in method. Drawing attention to the subjective and mythic nature of scientific discourses and to the circumstances under which knowledge is constructed, the postmodern perspective qualifies many disciplines as forms of storytelling. Far from dismissing archaeological work as cheap fiction, such a definition points towards the profound social responsibilities, tasks, and problems of research. Storytelling is a very serious activity. It has been said, "If the stories disappear, our people ceases to exist."[8] Subjective experience and creativity are not brought in as a justification for flights of fantasy, but as a call for personal engagement. The Past and the Other are not objects of free speculation, but have an independent existence, which demands recognition and *respect*. The archaeology of living cultures especially has to open up to intercultural communication and active intersubjectivity, the more so where the process of colonial domination profoundly determines the relationships between the peoples concerned. This sets the stage for a story about sovereignty, in the telling of which we all participate. Linda Tuhiwai Smith clarifies:

> The research agenda is conceptualized here as constituting a program and set of approaches that are situated within the decolonization politics of the indigenous peoples' movement. The agenda is focused strategically on the goal of self-determination of indigenous peoples. Self-determination in a research agenda becomes something more than a political goal. It becomes a goal of social justice which is expressed through and across a wide range of psychological, social, cultural and economic terrains. It

necessarily involves the processes of transformation, of decolonization, of healing and of mobilization as peoples. (Smith 1999: 115–16)

Self-determination, as a goal and a point for orientation in the studies of indigenous cultures, calls for a change in the attitudes, theories, and methods of archaeologists. If we reflect on the story that archaeology has been telling in Oaxaca, and for that matter in Mesoamerica as a whole and in many other regions, we notice that it has been to a large extent a "biography of the state," giving a great deal of attention to the evolution of social complexity. Comparing the discourse of traditional archaeology with that of human rights, one cannot help but feel struck by the contrast in the evaluation of the state: in the former, it is hailed as the great hallmark of civilization and progress, creating law, social order, and efficiency; in the latter, it is denounced as one of the great dangers to fundamental human freedoms and as the main culprit in the violations of our common rights.

When Sanders and Price (1968) introduced the evolutionary scheme of Elman Service and others (Band-Tribe-Chiefdom-State) to the archaeology of Mesoamerica, the idea of being able to trace such a development using the hard data of material remains appealed to many and gave a new sense and direction to research and debates. Such a mission statement fitted the evolutionary perspective and conservative interests of archaeology as a product of the nineteenth century. Moreover, the discipline had developed in intimate connection with the state and its nationalist ideology. Concrete projects were often organized and/or financed by a direct executive branch of the state, generally through the mediation of a national institution which monitored all activity, granted permits, etc., and thereby was able to put forward a nearly exclusive claim on the past and its remains. In other words most archaeologists were and are directly or indirectly paid by the state.

The material bias of archaeology further programs a tendency towards (neo)positivism with a high appreciation for descriptive and quantitative analysis. The formulation and testing of hypotheses derived from general principles of social evolution and behavior (the nomothetic approach) was a hallmark of the New Archaeology, which has had its influence on projects in Oaxaca from the 1970s onwards. In such theories, economy and politics are intimately related. An admirable level of synthesis within this tradition, both of concrete fieldwork data and of theoretical reflection, was reached in *The Cloud People* (Flannery and Marcus 1983), which still influences archaeological thinking and practice today. Catchment areas, market systems, and long-distance trade routes to extract elite goods and commodities, became central concerns, as well as military endeavors to protect these interests and to establish law and order. The special attention to war-related aspects may in part be explained by the circumstance that archaeological practice from its origins had been rather militarily structured and conceived; traditionally, it was (and to a large extent still is) a world dominated by men, working in planned expeditions, with research strategies, maps, trenches, camps, and a clear hierarchy of site supervisors.

With a focus on the state, one tends to interpret the intellectual and aesthetic achievements of the indigenous cultures as manifestations of ideology. Precious objects were thus studied as markers of status and indicators of elite exchange systems. Iconography and writing were deemed to reflect propaganda, in order to legitimate the position of the ruling class, while religion itself was also seen as manipulated to serve the interests of power (Marcus 1992: 12–16). In connection with this framework, a regional perspective may be constructed using world systems theory (cf. Blanton et al. 1999). Its emphasis on asymmetrical core-periphery relationships and exploitation as one of the main dynamics in society was originally intended by Wallerstein as a critical view on the modern economy. Curiously, its introduction in archaeology tends to have the opposite effect. The projection of exploitative imperialist structures and their legitimating ideologies onto the past, may lead to a feeling that this condition is somehow normal, and so may justify and reaffirm those structures in the present.

This body of theories certainly has made valuable contributions, making us aware of important processes in human society. On the other hand, it echoes the interests in the thinking and practices of present-day "Western" national elites and is quite far removed from the experiences and concerns of indigenous peoples, inheritors of the past onto which these theories are projected. In fact, one often gets the impression that the construction of abstract models and hypotheses gets in the way of communication and empathy with the people in question.

Present-day indigenous society may view the "biography of the state" as a rather hollow topic, of limited interest. In creating a communicative, multicultural discourse, new roads need to be explored. Established theories and methods do not automatically have to be discarded, but they must at least be complemented. Other perspectives have to be accommodated. The focus of research accordingly may shift from chronology and the use of resources to (for example) the cultural landscape experienced as a source of identity and power, a locale where the community connects with nature, where the ancestors live, and where one's umbilical cord has been buried; from the evolution of status hierarchy to social drama and the experience of *communitas* (cf. Turner 1990); from the politics of exploitation and legitimation to the realm of the sacred and the moral. Where stratigraphic excavation is essential for the evolutionary perspective, it is conversation and interaction, the talking to and working with people (not as "informants" but in collaboration and *convivencia*), which is the main method for this approach.

Start with Learning the Language

Archaeology is not dealing with some "survival groups" of possible interest as a source of information, but with active and creative *peoples*, protagonists with a project for the future. A first step, therefore, is to recognize their proper names, instead of the names given to them by others: Ñuu Dzavui (nowadays pronounced as Ñuu Savi) instead of Mixtecs, *Beni Zaa* instead of Zapotecs, *Ngigua* instead of Chocho-Popoloca, etc. Most of the terms now widely used come from Nahuatl, the language of the Mexica empire, which was used as a broker language by the Spaniards during the early phases of colonization. Thus *Mixtec* means "inhabitant of the land of the clouds," but Ñuu Dzavui has a more profound sense as "People and Land of the Rain God," referring to the unity of land and people (*ñuu*) and to the concept of a community formed by the devotion for and protection of a common patron deity. The same applies to the toponyms in the region, which in later times were combined with the names of Christian saints and historical heroes of the Mexican republic. An example of such a stratigraphy is the place-name Chalcatongo de Hidalgo. The latter part honors the initiator of Mexican independence. It took the place of the patron's name Santa María de la Natividad that had been added in the viceroyal era. Chalcatongo itself is probably a corruption of the Nahuatl toponym Chalco Atenco, "Precious Place on the Lake Shore," referring to the existence of a lake in the valley where the town is located. Its name in Dzaha Dzavui (the Mixtec language) is Ñuu Ndeya, often translated today as "Town of Abundance." In the sixteenth century it still was Ñuu Ndaya, "Place of the Underworld," probably named after the sacred cave where the precolonial rulers of the Ñuu Dzavui city-states were centrally buried.

In order to be able to participate in the circuit of cultural communication and to develop an incipient understanding of another meaningful universe, investigators have to study the native tongue. Names, concepts, convictions, sentiments – they are all formulated in a particular language. The same is true for material culture, the traditional focus of archaeology: forms, functions, production technologies – all are described and classified in that language. Surveys and excavations, as well as the study of the ancient chronicles, have to be combined with listening carefully to the oral tradition related to the landscape and with serious and committed participation in present-day indigenous society in order to promote awareness of its cultural dynamics, values, and challenges. Present-day traditions and concepts inform intents of a postprocessual, contextual, cognitive, and hermeneutic archaeology, which may surpass artefact fetishism by focusing on the immaterial aspects of the cultural heritage, particularly on the messages registered in iconography and writing. Metaphors and art are central to this line of research. Carved stones, figurative ceramic vessels, frescoes, incised bones, and particularly pictographic manuscripts (codices) may be read as statements and narratives. Here again the use of terms, phrases, and literary conventions in the native language may be extremely relevant and revealing. The character of the protagonists of the historical pictorial manuscripts, for example, was for a long time a matter of debate among scholars: were they deities, supernatural beings, or humans? Colonial glosses demonstrate that their titles were *iya*, "Lord," and *iyadzehe*, "Lady." Today, these terms are used for Christian saints and spirits of nature, in some villages also for priests and authorities. A contextual analysis clarifies that the protagonists of ancient dynastic history were considered human personages but with a special, divine status. Reading the codices in these terms (re)creates for present-day Ñuu Dzavui people the experience of a "Sacred History," similar to the holy scriptures of Christianity.[9] And the political domain of those rulers – should we call it a chiefdom or a state? In Dzaha Dzavui

terms it was a *yuvui tayu*, "mat and throne," a seat of rulership for the royal couple. Several events have a very special significance in the indigenous cosmovision. When we see a young warrior and a princess travel to a Death Temple, the scene is easily identified as a visit to the *Vehe Kihin*, a cave where daring people go to ask the fear-inspiring spirits of the Underworld for special favors, success, wealth, or power. But in exchange they have to hand over their soul. Such an act functions as a turning point in a dramatic narrative, announcing its tragic outcome, and thereby uncovers the literary composition of the historical source (cf. Jansen and Pérez Jiménez 2000).

The focus on archaeological sites has to be extended to all features of the constructed and natural landscape that are significant in people's worldview and experience.[10] The village Santiago Apoala is a good example. Its original name in Dzaha Dzavui is Yuta Tnoho (now Yutsa Tohon), taken from the river that flows through the small plain in which the village is located. Tonal and nasalization differences account for different translations of the toponym as "River that Plucks or Pulls Out," "River of the Lords," or "River of the Stories." All meanings refer to the root story of this place: it was on the bank of this river that the Sacred Mother Tree (a ceiba) stood, from which the first lords and ladies were "pulled out," the founders of the dynasties that ruled the city-states of Ñuu Dzavui. The village itself is clearly an archaeological area, but what the historical sources focus on is a series of points in the landscape: the cave with a subterranean lake and spring "at the head" of the valley, the waterfall where the river plunges over a cliff "at the foot" of the valley, a high mountaintop to the east, called the Mountain of Heaven, where the First Mother and Father are reported to have lived, "in the year and on the day of darkness and obscurity, before there were days or years." A precolonial painting (Figure 13.1) represents this landscape as the body of a feathered serpent, a divine being, the emblem of the main culture

Figure 13.1   Codex Tonindeye (Nuttall), p. 36: the landscape of Yuta Tnoho (Apoala).

hero and a symbol of visionary experience in Mesoamerica (Anders et al. 1992). An archaeological study simply cannot hope to do justice to the ideological importance of this village if it does not take into account its awe-inspiring natural surroundings, central to a cosmovision and riddled with stories about the time of origins.

The same is true for a widely debated problem in Oaxacan archaeology: that of the rise of Monte Albán as the capital of a Classic Beni Zaa state. The location of this site, on a mountain in the center of the three-lobed valley of Oaxaca, clearly defies the suggestion that it was chosen for economic reasons: the acropolis is not particularly suited for farming or for establishing a market. Considering political motivations and taking into account some later carved stones that refer to conquests and captives, several scholars have proposed that Monte Albán was constructed as the "disembedded capital" of a (military) alliance of valley towns. Militarism at Monte Albán indeed must have been an important ingredient in creating a state organization. In fact one of the most remarkable buildings in the central plaza has the form of an arrow and may represent an arrow temple, dedicated to the Divine Force of Arms.[11] Trying to understand the motivations for its foundation, however, we should be aware of the dominant role of religion in Mesoamerican culture, in particular the devotion towards mountaintops documented by historical sources and observable today. The mountain is alive, full of power. It holds the underground water streams that feed the lands and the community, as it contains the caves of origin and the caves where the Rain God lives. It is here that the first sunrays of morning hit and create a daily hierophany in the change from darkness to light – a central motif in Mesoamerican thinking. The rocky outcrops on slopes and mountaintops are often considered the spiritual Owners (*Ñuhu* or *Ndodzo* in Dzaha Dzavui) of the lands around. They are invoked at harvesting rituals. Religious specialists seek their help in healing patients who suffer from "fright" or traumatic shock. Such a place rapidly becomes a focal point of pilgrimages from the surrounding valleys and adjacent areas. Taking into account this worldview, we understand immediately the religious importance of Monte Albán as a prime motivation for the construction of a ceremonial center there. The ubiquitous presence of the Beni Zaa rainstorm deity, Cocijo, molded on ceramic vessels ("urns") of the Classic period, suggests that the site was considered to be his house, the source of all abundance.[12] The sacred place was honored and formalized through the building of different temples and altars. The large processions so popular in Mesoamerican cult determined the layout of courtyards and a huge central plaza.

Experiencing the Other World

From an outsider perspective, with a critical view to modern power-holders, one might focus on the manipulative pretensions of the elites, who may have used their success in war in combination with ideological claims, ritual prominence, and the accumulation of esoteric knowledge, to establish lasting control over the non-elites (Joyce and Winter 1996). An empathetic look at community life, or an insider's perspective, problematizes the idea of a sharp elite–non-elite dichotomy, at least in the smaller city-states with their strong internal interdependence. The kings, queens, heads of leading lineages, priests, merchants, warlords, and artists formed quite a heterogeneous group, with varying degrees of education and intellectual capacity. Certainly they distinguished themselves from the tributaries, those who worked the fields, but at the same time all shared one frame of reference, one sphere of communication, one "cognitive map," one social and moral code. It would have been very difficult for an elite to locate itself outside this shared worldview for the purpose of cynical manipulation.

To understand ancient mentality, we should assimilate present-day Mesoamerican cosmovision. One of its most relevant aspects is *nahualism*, the dream sensation of transforming into a *nahual*, i.e., an alter ego (companion animal) in nature. This set of experiences explains the frequent representations of humans with animal traits in precolonial iconography. Shamans use this state of mind to speak with the ancestors and other spirits. The symbol of their ecstatic vision is the serpent. As visual expressions of liminality, sculptured serpents enclose the temples as homes of the gods. Already in the iconographic corpus of the earliest civilization of Mesoamerica, that of the Olmecs, these references are present: rulers represented in their nahual aspect with the traits of jaguars and other fierce animals, a priest encircled by a vision serpent. Especially powerful nahual animals are the plumed serpent, a metaphoric designation of the whirlwind, and the so-called fire serpent, which is a ball of lightning. The latter, with its characteristic upward curved snout, came to be used as the emblematic nahual, accompanying Mexica gods such as Huitzilopochtli, encircling the famous Sun Stone. The Dominican monks translated the ancient Dzaha Dzavui title *yaha yahui*, "Eagle, Fire Serpent," as "necromancer," i.e., shaman. Probably the heavily beaked or snouted flying animals in Classic Oaxaca art represent this same concept.

On Stela 1 of the South Platform of Monte Albán (Figure 13.2) we see a ruler in front of a large inscription and a series of carved slabs with the representation of captives (Marcus 1992: 325–8; Urcid 2001: 317). He is seated on a cushion of jaguar skin on top of a mountain with a mat design, i.e., on the "mat and throne" of the community. Outward looking heads of nahual animals, flanking the mountain – supposedly Monte Albán itself – stress its divine power. The

Figure 13.2 Monte Albán, South Platform, Stela 1: the ruler seated on the mat and the throne, with his staff and nahual attributes (Caso and Bernal 1952).

same value is given to the seated individual himself, as the same nahual animal forms part of his headdress. Evidently we are dealing with an important ruler of Monte Albán, portrayed with his regalia and symbols of charismatic power. His dress, a jaguar skin, is again a reference to this ruler's nahual. The staff in his hands is a common attribute of rulers. In Postclassic pictorial manuscripts the founders of dynasties carry similar staffs. Their configuration and context leave no doubt that we are dealing with the precolonial antecedent of the staffs of authority, so important in all communities today.

A related iconography is found on the carved slabs from the Mixteca Baja area, belonging to the so-called Ñuiñe style of the Late Classic Period (Rodríguez Cano et al. 1996/99). Some of them show jaguars seated on mountains. In view of the above these may be interpreted as representations of the names of rulers, connoting their nahual aspect. A confirmation is found in the feather crowns some of these animals are wearing. A particularly interesting example is the representation of a feathered jaguar emitting speech scrolls topped with flints, which have been interpreted as a "feather-crested tiger on place glyph utters twice the name of

1 Flint or declares war in words as cutting as flint knives" (Paddock 1970: 187). Looking at similar conventions in Postclassic codices we prefer a reading as a name: "Lord Jaguar saying 'knife,' i.e., Who Threatens to Kill," "Feathered Jaguar Gnashing his Teeth," or "Lord Growling or Roaring Jaguar." The knife may also represent the quality of "sharp," "brave," or "much" (*dzaa*), a word which in combination with the verb "to speak" means "convincing," "eloquent." This would result in the reading: "Lord Jaguar, who is an eloquent speaker" (Figure 13.3). Other slabs portray a "Feathered Jaguar Holding a Mountain in its Paw," i.e., "Lord Jaguar Ruler of the Mountain" and "Feathered Jaguar Holding a Man in its Paw," i.e., "Lord Jaguar Ruler of the People" or maybe "Lord Man-Eating Jaguar." The event commemorated on these slabs must have been an important one. Victories were eternalized this way, but not the simple declaration of war. Probably the fact that the feline is climbing a mountain or seated on top is the significant action. As the mountain (*yucu*) is usually the nucleus of a toponym, we may read it here as "our place." Actually it may be short for our "mountain and water" (*yucu nduta*), a well-known Mesoamerican expression for our "community." Sometimes a pyramid is added, probably as an explicit reference to the town's ceremonial center. As the seating is a convention for rulership, for taking control of the polity,

probably all these cases show an enthronement statement.

The nahual transformation itself is depicted on a Ñuiñe "urn," found in Tomb 5 of Cerro de las Minas, Ñuu Dzai (Huajuapan), now in the Museo Regional of Oaxaca (Winter 1994: 34). The vessel is modeled in the form of a man. The base on which he is seated contains a stepped fret motif which, as we know from Postclassic codices, is to be read *ñuu*, "town" (Figure 13.4). Being seated on this glyphic sign, the man can be identified as the ruler of the city-state. The gourd or small vessel he holds in his hands before his chest is decorated with a precious stone. The same object also occurs with priests in Postclassic codices, where it represents a gourd (*tecomate*) that contains the hallucinogenic *nicotiana rustica* (*piciete*). The animal snout in the face of the ruler and the wings on his arms, calling our attention

Figure 13.4 Ceramic urn from Tomb 5, Cerro de las Minas, Ñuu Dzai (Huajuapan): the transformation of a ruler into a fire serpent.

Figure 13.3 Yucu Ndaa Yee (Tequixtepec), Carved Stone 19: Lord "Roaring Jaguar" climbs the throne in the year 6 L (Rodríguez Cano et al. 1966/99).

because of their sensational colors, indicate that under the effects of an ecstatic ritual he is becoming a winged fire serpent (*yahui*) and entering the nahual world. The anthropomorphized vessel itself may be considered a "god pot," which became alive during such a specific ritual.[13]

We may use this vessel as the key to interpret a whole series of Classic urns from Monte Albán and the valley of Oaxaca, which show very similar scenes of seated humans transforming into powerful nahuales, even taking the identity of divine ancestors or deities, the most important of whom is the ubiquitous Cocijo. Some of these figures also hold those small gourds in their hands. One actually is the typical old priest. In other cases a vessel from which vapors rise replaces the gourd.[14] In one religious pictorial manuscript, known as the Codex Borgia (Figure 13.5), we see a comparable scene of autosacrifice and the preparation of the hallucinogenic priestly ointment: vapors rising from a vessel in the center of the pyramid take the form of vision serpents, consisting of night and wind, the mysterious essence of the gods, and bring those standing in the corners of the room into ecstasy (cf. Jansen 1998). If we are correct in our interpretation, the Classic "urns" are references to similar royal rituals involving vision quest and direct contact with the other world. Such activities were crucial moments in the lives of the rulers. Possibly these vessels accompanied them into their graves as a commemoration of their vision and as a point of recognition on their very last journey, which would bring them again face to face with the ancestors and the gods.

Conclusion

Modern Mestizo references to nahualism are often fanciful, and stress the element of suspense and strange magic, as in werewolf and vampire stories. Looking at the social function of those who have strong nahuales today, we should not see such representations as expressing cruel dominance. The evaluation of this phenomenon in traditional indigenous communities is quite different: it is the moral force of the nahuales which is important here, their responsibility to safeguard the village and to collaborate with the spirits of nature in order to bring water to the lands and make a good harvest possible. Nahuales usually are protectors of the community, just as shamans do their work for the benefit of the people, generally to heal. Sometimes a traditional healer will send his nahual animal to accompany and protect the nahual animal of another person who is in distress or suffering illness. In this way they are very similar to the *Benandanti* of sixteenth-century northern Italy, analyzed by Carlo Ginzburg (1966).

The nahual representations of rulers, therefore, seem to reiterate the religious and moral nature of rulership, stressing the devotion and ceremonial obligations of the lords and ladies as least as much – if not more – than the aspect of conquest, coercion, and surveillance. Having themselves portrayed as strong animals, the rulers emphasized that they dedicated all their strength and efforts to the well-being of the community. From a present-day standpoint one may interpret those statements as propaganda and ideological manipulation, but in their own iconographical vocabulary the rulers stressed their efforts to protect their people, their moral obligation to perform sacrifice, also self-sacrifice, and express devotion to the True Powers. That same moral discourse still characterizes the traditional passing on of power to newly elected authorities today. In the ceremony of handing over the staff of office, much emphasis is put on the sacred surroundings (invoking God and the patron saint) as well as on morality: the authority should guide the people as a father–mother, along a straight and correct road.

Connecting the past with the present deepens our understanding of both. Studying the ancient manifestations of an ongoing cultural tradition offers unique insights into

Figure 13.5 Codex Borgia, p. 29: the preparation of a hallucinogenic ointment in the Temple of the Death Goddess Cihuacoatl.

mentalities and values, but at the same time implies an encounter with the traumatic impact of colonialism and the persistent structure of social injustice. One of the consequences of colonization in the Amer-icas, just as elsewhere, has been the denial and destruction of local historiography and historic memory, at least to a large extent, converting the native nations into "people without history" (cf. Wolf 1982). Here lies an important social responsibility and challenge for archaeology. Developing a postcolonial perspective and emancipatory practice, archaeologists can and should contribute to the dignifying and so to the empowerment and continuity of the cultures they study and love. On this road their interests and those of the indigenous peoples go hand in hand:

If we were to talk of an Aymara philosophy of history, it would not be a vision of forward progress as a simple succession of stages which develop by the process of moving from one to the next. The past is not inert or dead, and it does not remain in some previous place. It is precisely by means of the past that the hope of a free future can be nourished, in which the past can be regenerated. It is this idea which makes us believe that an Indian archaeology, under our control and systematized according to our concepts of time and space, could perhaps form part of our enterprise of winning back our own history and freeing it from the centuries of colonial subjugation. Archaeology has been up until now a means of domination and colonial dispossession of our identity. If it were to be taken back by the Indians themselves it could provide us with new tools to understand our historical development, and so strengthen our present demands and our projects for the future. (Mamani Condori 1996: 644)

Notes

1 The reflections expressed in this chapter have come up in the context of research carried out together with Gabina Aurora Pérez Jiménez. Our work at the Faculty of Archaeology, Leiden University, has received support from the Netherlands Organization for Scientific Research (NWO). In recent years the collaboration of Laura van Broekhoven and Alex Geurds has been crucial. Thanks are due to the director and staff of the regional centre of INAH in Oaxaca, especially to Alicia Barabas, Miguel Bartolomé, and Raúl Matadamas, for their help, orientation, and positive input. Chatino archaeologist Ninfa Pacheco and Ñuu Savi archaeologist Iván Rivera also contributed significantly to the development of these ideas.

2 Biolsi and Zimmerman (1998) demonstrate the influence of Deloria's work on anthropology and archaeology. For the ethical principles, see Lynott and Wylie (1995). From the indigenous side, efforts were also made to find some middle ground, or as White Deer put it, a mutually inclusive landscape (Swidler et al. 1997).

3 The absence of living people is quite common in museum contexts; but very different concepts are manifest in, for example, the exposition of the National Museum of the American Indian, New York (West et al. 1994) and in the museum of the Mashantucket Pequot reservation. In the first case the presence of many indigenous experts who give explanations on video and in the catalogue, emphasizes the living tradition. In the second the large-scale reconstruction of a sixteenth-century Pequot village, with native voices on the accompanying cassette guide, absorbs the visitor into indigenous life; the subsequent 3D movie of the historical violent destruction of that community creates empathy with its descendants.

4 Needless to say, the very concept of continuity also implies change. We should not think of it as an anachronistic fossilization of society but, on the contrary, as a dynamic diachronic relationship of the present with the past. Let us keep in mind that history, as remembered by the people, has an accumulating and evaluating effect: collective memory stores the experiences of the past, draws conclusions and installs behavioral norms (leading to what Bourdieu calls the *habitus*). In this way a cultural tradition can remain true to its "core,"

its "profound identity," in a subjective way, although over time its subsystems have suffered major transformations.

5   Typically, this issue is not even hinted at in the otherwise so-critical review of the development of Mexican archaeology by Vásquez León (1996).

6   An overview of the archaeology of Oaxaca is beyond the scope of this chapter. Important reference works are Paddock (1970), Flannery and Marcus (1983), Dalton Palomo and Loera y Chávez (1997), Blanton et al. (1999), and Robles García (2001).

7   A traumatic experience in the early 1960s was the excavation of tombs in Zaachila, executed against the will of the town's inhabitants, under military protection, resulting in a lot of anger and a permanently disturbed relationship (see Jansen 1982).

8   See Sambeek et al. (1989). Cf. Tilley (1993: 13–15) and Last in Hodder and Shanks et al. (1995: 141–57).

9   The names of the manuscripts themselves are testimonies of the colonial process of alienation. For example, the book painted in the early viceroyal period on orders of Lord 10 Grass "Spirit of the Earth" (*iya Sicuañe "Yoco Anuhu"*), ruler of Añute, the "Place of Sand" (now known as Magdalena Jaltepec), is now preserved in the Bodleian Library in Oxford under the name "Codex Selden 3135 (A.2)" (cf. Jansen and Pérez Jiménez 2000).

10 The subjective experience of the ancient cultural landscape, as outlined by Shanks (1992) and Tilley (1994), may sound highly speculative in the context of European prehistory, but imposes itself as very real precisely in a situation of cultural continuity such as Mesoamerica.

11 Such a cult is well demonstrated for the Postclassic in several pictorial manuscripts. The directionality provided by the pointing arrow has often been interpreted in archaeoastronomical terms, but without convincing results.

12 Monte Albán seems to have had the quality of the Mesoamerican Cave of Origin and Mountain of Sustenance (known in Nahuatl as *Chicomoztoc* and *Tonacatepec* respectively). See also Anders and Jansen (1994) as well as Jansen and Pérez Jiménez (2000).

13 For the representation of vision quest and "god pots" in Maya art, see Freidel et al. (1993: 247–51 and throughout).

14 Caso and Bernal (1952: figs. 16, 151, 159, 161, 241, 328, 363).

References

Anders, F., M. Jansen, and G. A. Pérez Jiménez 1992. *Crónica Mixteca: El rey 8 Venado, Garra de Jaguar, y la dinastía de Teozacualco-Zaachila. Libro explicativo del llamado Códice Zouche-Nuttall*. Mexico: Fondo de Cultura Económica.

Anders, F. and M. Jansen 1994. *Pintura de la Muerte y de los Destinos. Libro explicativo del llamado Códice Laud*. Mexico: Fondo de Cultura Económica.

Bartolomé, M. A. 1997. *Gente de costumbre y gente de razón. Las identidades étnicas en México*. Mexico: Siglo XXI and INI.

Benavides, O. H. 2001. "Returning to the source: social archaeology as Latin American philosophy." *Latin American Antiquity*, 12 (4): 355–70.

Biolsi, T. and L. J. Zimmerman (eds.) 1998. *Indians and Anthropologists: Vine Deloria Jr. and the Critique of Anthropology*. Tucson: University of Arizona Press.

Blanton, R. E., G. M. Feinman, S. A. Kowalewski, and L. M. Nicholas 1999. *Ancient Oaxaca: The Monte Albán State*. Cambridge: Cambridge University Press.

Bonfil Batalla, G. 1989. *México profundo. Una civilización negada*. Mexico: Grijalbo.

Caso, A. and I. Bernal 1952. *Urnas de Oaxaca*. Mexico: INAH.

Churchill, W. 1998. *Fantasies of the Master Race: Literature, Cinema and the Colonization of American Indians*. San Francisco: City Light Books.

Dalton Palomo, M. and V. Loera y Chávez (eds.) 1997. *Historia del Arte de Oaxaca I. Arte prehispánico*. Oaxaca: Gobierno del Estado.

Deloria, V. 1969. *Custer Died For Your Sins*. New York: Avon Books.

Flannery, K. and J. Marcus (eds.) 1983. *The Cloud People: Divergent Evolution of the Zapotec and Mixtec Civilizations*. New York: Academic Press.

Freidel, D., L. Schele, and J. Parker 1993. *Maya Cosmos: Three Thousand Years on the Shaman's Path*. New York: Morrow.

Ginzburg, C. 1966. *I Benandanti. Stregoneria e culti agrari tra Cinquecento e Seicento*. Turin: Giulio Einaudi editore.

Hodder, I., M. Shanks, et al. 1995. *Interpreting Archaeology: Finding Meaning in the Past*. London: Routledge.

Jansen, M. 1982. "Viaje al Otro Mundo: La Tumba I de Zaachila." In M. Jansen and T. J. J. Leyenaar (eds.), *Los Indígenas de México en la época precolombina y en la actualidad*, pp. 87–118. Leiden: Rijksmuseum voor Volkenkunde.

Jansen, M. 1998. "Ein Blick in den Tempel von Ciuacoatl." In C. Arellano Hofman and P. Schmidt (eds.), *Die Bücher der Maya, Mixteken und Azteken*, pp. 257–306. Frankfurt am Main: Vervuert Verlag.

Jansen, M. and G. A. Pérez Jiménez 2000. *La Dinastía de Añute. Historia, literatura e ideología de un reino mixteco*. Leiden: CNWS.

Joyce, A. and M. Winter 1996. "Ideology, power, and urban society in pre-Hispanic Oaxaca." *Current Anthropology*, 37 (1): 33–47.

Loomba, A. 1998. *Colonialism/Postcolonialism*. London: Routledge.

Lynott, M. J. and A. Wylie (eds.) 1995. *Ethics in American Archaeology: Challenges for the 1990s*. Washington, DC: Society for American Archaeology.

Mamani Condori, C. 1996. "History and prehistory in Bolivia: what about the Indians?" In R. W. Preucel and I. Hodder (eds.), *Contemporary Archaeology in Theory: A Reader*, pp. 632–45. Oxford: Blackwell.

Marcus, J. 1992. *Mesoamerican Writing Systems: Propaganda, Myth and History in Four Ancient Civilizations*. Princeton, NJ: Princeton University Press.

Marcus, J. and K. Flannery 1996. *Zapotec Civilization*. London: Thames and Hudson.

Paddock, J. (ed.) 1970. *Ancient Oaxaca: Discoveries in Mexican Archaeology and History*. Stanford, CA: Stanford University Press.

Pérez Jiménez, G. A. 1989. "Somos víctimas de una ciencia colonialista y de un indigenismo internacional." In Musiro (ed.), *La Visión India: tierra, cultura, lengua y derechos humanos*, pp. 421–6. Leiden: Archeologisch Centrum.

Robles García, N. M. (ed.) 2001. *Procesos de Cambio y conceptualización del tiempo. Memoria de la Primera Mesa Redonda de Monte Albán*. Mexico: CONACULTA-INAH.

Rodríguez Cano, L., A. I. Rivera Guzmán, and J. Martínez Ramírez 1996/99. "Piedras Grabadas de la Mixteca Baja, Oaxaca." *Anales de Antropología*, 33: 165–205. UNAM, Mexico.

Sambeek, P. van, R. de Vries, J. de Vries, and R. Manning (eds.) 1989. *Als de verhalen verdwijnen, verdwijnt ons volk. Indiaanse Literatuur*. Wampum 9. Leiden.

Sanders, W. T and B. J. Price 1968. *Mesoamerica: The Evolution of a Civilization*. New York: Random House.

Shanks, M. 1992. *Experiencing the Past: On the Character of Archaeology*. London: Routledge.

Smith, L. T. 1999. *Decolonizing Methodologies: Research and Indigenous Peoples*. London: Zed Books.

Swidler, N., K. E. Dongoske, R. Anyon, and A. S. Downer (eds.) 1997. *Native Americans and Archaeologists: Stepping Stones to Common Ground*. Walnut Creek: Altamira Press.

Tilley, C. (ed.) 1993. *Interpretative Archaeology*. Oxford: Berg.

Tilley, C. 1994. *A Phenomenology of Landscape: Places, Paths, and Monuments*. Oxford: Berg.

Turner, V. 1990 [1974]. *Dramas, Fields and Metaphors: Symbolic Action in Human Society*. Ithaca, NY: Cornell University Press.

Urcid, J. 2001. *Zapotec Hieroglyphic Writing*. Washington, DC: Dumbarton Oaks.

Vázquez León, L. 1996. *El Leviatán Arqueológico. Antropología de una tradición científica en México*. Leiden: CNWS.

West, W. R. et al. 1994. *All Roads Are Good: Native Voices on Life and Culture*. New York: Smithsonian Institution.

Winter, M. 1994. *Tesoros del Museo Regional de Oaxaca*. Ayuntamiento de Oaxaca.

Wolf, E. R. 1982. *Europe and the Peoples without History*. Berkeley: University of California Press.

14

Classical Archaeology

Ian Morris

The Problem

My goal in this chapter is simple: to explain what classical archaeology is. I first present a simplified account of the classical archaeology of the past two centuries, then discuss changes since the 1970s. I close with thoughts on the directions the field is taking in the new century.

This sounds straightforward, but there is more to it than meets the eye. In opening his 1984 Sather Lectures, Anthony Snodgrass noted:

> Elementary grammar might suggest that "classical archaeology" is a subdiscipline that forms an integral part of one subject – archaeology – and has especially close links with another – classics. But elementary grammar, here as in some other instances, is profoundly misleading. (Snodgrass 1987: 1)

In fact, Snodgrass observed, classical archaeology in the 1980s had more in common with classical philology and an unusual kind of art history than with the ferment then taking place in prehistoric archaeology. Classical archaeologists generally asked different questions than other archaeologists, used different methods in the field, attended different conferences, published in different journals, and wrote in

a different technical language. Classical archaeologists rarely mentioned even the most influential works of the 1960s–1970s archaeological revolution, and prehistorians returned the compliment. My impression as a graduate student in Britain in the 1980s was that most prehistorians thought of classical archaeology as a sad relic, a living museum of archaeology's embarrassing past. Yet in terms of the number of scholars employed, the size of its audience, its lavish financial support, and the sheer scale of academic output, classical archaeology was stronger than ever. Nearly twenty years later, this is still the case – so assessing classical archaeology at the century's turn is no simple matter.

Consider Figure 14.1, a cartoon by Simon James published in Paul Bahn's *Archaeology: A Very Short Introduction* (1996), and reproduced in Matthew Johnson's *Archaeological Theory: An Introduction* (1999). This may make it the most widely seen image of what classical archaeology is all about. In the center, labeled "core," a group of archaeologists fights furiously. Men and women, some bearded, some barefooted, mostly young, denounce each other in the vocabulary of 1990s theoretical archaeology: "processualist reactionary," "poststructuralist pseud," "burn all neo-Marxist heretics," and even "phallocrat scum-bag." But to the left, on

Figure 14.1 Archaeological theory in 1988 (cartoon by Simon James).

the "periphery," a balding, pipe-smoking gentleman in an ill-fitting suit wonders what all the noise is about. He gives his identity away by reading a book called *Classical Archaeology* and sitting on a pile of "*CIL*," the *Corpus Inscriptionum Latinarum*, a series of tomes dedicated (for more than a century) to publishing the text of every Latin inscription. In front of him is an even higher pile of Loebs, bilingual editions of Greek and Latin literary texts. Finally, cowering off to the right, is an "irritating distraction": Joe, Josie, and Josie Jr. Public, looking on in horror as one theoretician (busy strangling another) yells at them: "What the hell do *you* want?"

Bahn spells out his point:

Theoretical archaeology should not be taken too seriously – it's easy to laugh at those who do become obsessed with it: in fact, it's essential. The worst part is that so many of them seem to become grumpy and bitchy and have forgotten what a great, extravagant, glorious treat it is to be in archaeology . . . Other areas, such as classical or historical archaeology, are still far more orientated towards fieldwork, analysis of texts, and the handling of real evidence. For example, some archaeologists in Germany, where little attention has been devoted to theory, tend to consider the theoreticians as eunuchs at an orgy (especially as they are most uncertain to have any successors). (Bahn 1996: 69–70, 62–3)

According to the cartoon, the feuding theoreticians have little to say to the public; but the classical archaeologist musing on his stack of *CIL* speaks to no one at all.

Cultural theorists have taught us that humor is a complicated thing; and obvious as the cartoon seems, Johnson reads it differently. Bahn's ideal archaeologist seems down-to-earth, blokey, and empirical, while Johnson's is apparently one of the eunuchs at the orgy. He historicizes the cartoon, labeling it "Archaeological theory in 1988," and suggesting that it lampoons the

generally low standard of debate [which] means that uninformed position statements, platitudes and "straw people" abound with very little critical analysis on all sides of the debate. There is also an assumption that one's own position has been intellectually victorious to the extent that scholars working in other traditions are mere intellectual dinosaurs or intellectual poseurs rather than serious archaeologists with genuine concerns. (Johnson 1999: 182)

He contrasts this situation with a drawing of his own, captioned "Archaeological theory in 1998" (Figure 14.2). Here, the battling theorists have decomposed into three huddles, happily talking to themselves, some about Foucault, others about Darwin, and others still about cultural resource management. The Publics are wandering off, but the saddest figure is the same pipe-smoking scholar, still sitting on his *CILs*, now reading *More Classical Archaeology*. Johnson labels the drawing "No core/periphery: just fragments," but some of his fragments are more equal than others. The feminists, evolutionists, and technocrats all have their support groups; the Publics appear to have a happy home; but the classicist is alone with his pipe and his books.

What is wrong with this picture? It is a joke, and like most of the best ones, works by mistaking a part-truth for the whole truth. There is something to its representation of classical archaeology, but this is a huge and varied field. James' cartoon gives a false impression, in that classical archaeologists, far from musing contemplatively, can shout just as loud and hit just as hard as the best theoreticians, and any classical archaeologist rash enough to write such a simplifying essay as this one can only expect to generate still more noise to wonder about.

Figure 14.2   Archaeological theory in 1998 (cartoon by Matthew Johnson).

Even a glance at Nancy de Grummond's (1996) *Encyclopedia of the History of Classical Archaeology* shows that the field has had more than its share of colorful characters, but serious analysis of an academic field must go beyond the wondrous variety of its denizens. Max Weber, while recognizing that the basis of all social action is individual, also saw that some of the most important parts of society are collectives. To think about group phenomena, whether labor movements, religious sects, or academic specialties, we have to agree on what our terms mean. So Weber developed the notion of the *ideal type*. Analyzing a subject like classical archaeology, composed of the practices of thousands of individuals who consider themselves or are considered by others to be classical archaeologists, requires explicit definitions. A good ideal type advances understanding, but only does so by leaving out of consideration many of the empirical realities of the groups being studied. Weber explained:

> An ideal type is achieved by the one-sided *accentuation* of one or more points of view and by the synthesis of many diffuse, discrete, more or less present and occasionally absent *individual* phenomena, which are arranged according to those one-sidedly emphasized viewpoints into a unified mental construct. In its conceptual purity, this mental construct can never be found empirically in reality. It is a *utopia*. (Weber 1949: 90)

I set up an ideal type of what I think classical archaeology was in the century after its institutionalization around 1870. Probably few archaeologists fitted this model exactly; only that the model accommodates many of the attitudes we find in classical archaeologists' books, letters, and diaries. I conclude that apart from a brief period in the 1960s and 1970s, the relationship between classical archaeology and the rest of archaeology was different from James' cartoon. Far from wondering absent-mindedly about the pre-

historians' noise, classical archaeologists looked down on these others with scorn and slight regard, addressing a higher message to the more educated families of J. Public. Classical archaeologists gave themselves the mission of revitalizing Western art and saving modernity from itself. Next to this, prehistorians' activities deserved little attention.

My second argument is that the classical archaeologists' role as heroic defenders of culture began to break up a generation ago. The world was changing. Prehistorians started making noise in the 1960s, and a decade later a small but influential group of classical archaeologists started taking it seriously, assimilating their own work to what they heard. They pointed a new way forward, albeit at the cost of abandoning traditional claims to superiority. Most classical archaeologists ignored this splinter group even into the 1990s, but with growing unease.

Third, I suggest that a wholly new kind of archaeology is taking shape out of the old classical archaeology, bearing no resemblance to Figure 14.2. The core of this shift is the collapse of the notion that Greeks and Romans created timeless classics that define Western civilization. The J. Publics and the battling theoreticians seem to agree on this, and as classicists take dialogues with both groups more seriously, they redefine their whole enterprise. Figure 14.2 is a representation of how archaeology would have been in 1998 if a particular strain in postprocessualism had won the arguments; but it did not. Certainly, many archaeological theorists retreated into self-congratulatory encounter groups, but if anything, factional struggle intensified, and classical archaeology became actively involved. As Greek and Roman archaeology moves away from being "classical" in the sense I define below, it joins a broader movement within historical archaeology, which will increasingly dominate the discussion/fistfight in the twenty-first century. Overall, classical archaeologists have not been wondering what all the noise is. They went from despising it, to listening to it, to being part of it.

A Simple Model of Classical Archaeology

I begin with a one-sentence definition of what the traditional practices of classical archaeology comprise, then unpack it. Classical archaeology has been (1) the study of ancient Greek and Roman artefacts with the aim of (2) showing how Graeco-Roman culture was expressed in material terms, (3) focusing on the connections between Greek and Roman works of art (4) and Greek and Latin literary culture.

1 The study of ancient Greek and Roman artefacts with the aim of . . .

"Ancient Greek and Roman": the field is defined in temporal and spatial terms, not theoretical or methodological ones. But immediately things get complicated. "Ancient Greek and Roman" is a moving target, founded on weighty yet largely implicit assumptions.

Probably all classical archaeologists agree that the "Archaic" period of Greek history, beginning around 750 BC, falls within their purview. Most also accept the Greek Early Iron Age, beginning around 1200 BC. But many think that the Late Bronze Age (ca. 1600–1200 BC) is not the territory of classical archaeologists; it belongs to prehistorians. Some see Middle Bronze Age Minoans of early second-millennium Crete as classical, but as we move back into the third millennium, there are few claimants. And by the time we get to the Neolithic, there is virtual unanimity in Western Europe and North America that we have left classical archaeology behind. In Greece itself, though, some scholars see more continuities than differences between the world of Dimini and that of democratic Athens.

Romanists draw similar boundaries. According to the Romans' own stories, Rome was founded in 753 BC. The Regal period lasted until 509 BC, and is classicists'

territory. Many embrace the Iron Age of the ninth and earlier eighth centuries; but the Final Bronze Age is problematic. Few classicists claim the Late Bronze Age as their own, and the Middle Bronze Age is firmly prehistoric.

Time is complicated by space. Eighth-century BC Rome belongs to classical archaeology, but the contemporary Po valley usually does not. Only in the second century BC did the Romans conquer this area. Similarly, eighth-century Athens is a classical subject, but debates (in the current climate, sometimes fierce) rage over whether eighth-century Macedonia has more in common with the Balkans or peninsular Greece.

An archaeologist working on seventh-century Sparta, or the west coast of Turkey (planted with Greek cities in the Early Iron Age), is a classicist, but one working on the contemporary Assyrian provinces of eastern Turkey is not. Yet with Alexander's conquest of the Middle East by 323 BC, everything up to Afghanistan can be added to the classical archaeologist's territory. But this is even more complicated, because while most classicists automatically count the Hellenistic cities of the Middle East as classical, they seem less certain about non-urban areas.

With the Roman armies' bloody march around the Mediterranean from 200 BC onward, swallowing up Greece, the western parts of Alexander's world, and eventually much of Western Europe, the sphere becomes wider still. By the first century AD, everything from the Irish Sea to the Euphrates is the classical archaeologist's back yard, and remains so at least until Constantine I (306–37). We then begin to move into late antiquity. In the last twenty years, classicists have reclaimed this as legitimate turf, but the gradual Germanization of the western empire and the Byzantine transformation of the east mark breaks for most scholars. Few would take classical archaeology beyond Justinian (527–65), and none beyond the Arab conquests of the seventh century. By then we are in a different, early medieval, world.

So, "ancient Greek and Roman" in the first component of my definition depends on "Graeco-Roman culture" in the second. Similarly, "artefacts" depends on "Greek and Roman works of art" in the third component; and all three depend on the fourth, "Greek and Latin literary culture."

2 Showing how Graeco-Roman culture was expressed in material terms . . .

The movable feast of ancient Greece and Rome rests on what we mean by Graeco-Roman culture. Look up "classic(al)" in any dictionary: the definition will probably refer both to cultural productions of timeless relevance and to the culture of ancient Greece and Rome. Hence the label "classical": these times and places constitute an exemplary moment in world history.

This is an old story (I explain my views on it more fully in Morris 2000: 37–106). The Germanic warlords who settled Western Europe from the fourth century AD rarely distinguished themselves sharply from the Romans they sometimes fought against, and when Charlemagne proclaimed himself ruler of these lands in 800 it made sense for him to claim to be restoring the Roman Empire. The Holy Roman Empire kept this idea alive in central Europe throughout the Middle Ages, but there was a serious rupture in the fourteenth century. Some Italian thinkers suggested that continuity from Rome no longer made sense. Rather, a gulf separated modern man from the ancients. The cutting-edge scholars of the Renaissance argued that the present was inferior to antiquity, but proposed that through sustained study of Roman literature and ruins, the moderns might appropriate the excellence of the past, and even improve on it.

Sixteenth- and seventeenth-century scholarship and art gave Western educated European elites a sense of mastery over the best that had been thought or made in the one true Christian empire. Inspired by the emergence of organized natural science, some

dared suggest that modern Europeans were surpassing the ancients. These were times of epochal change: by the mid-eighteenth century, some enlightened minds even claimed that Europeanness counted for more than Christian identity. In such a context, Roman literature and the New Testament did not satisfy everyone as foundation charters, and some radical intellectuals – proto-Romantics – looked elsewhere for the origin of European excellence. Given the debt that Roman authors expressed to Greece, they found this source in fifth-century BC Athens.

This was a broad trend, but its principal author was Winckelmann (1717–68). He wrote chiefly about Greek sculpture (although it is debatable whether he ever saw a genuine example), finding here the origin of a distinctive European spirit. In the nineteenth century, the idea that a dynamic European identity took shape on the slopes of the Acropolis in the fifth century BC and was generalized by the Roman Empire won acceptance in the West. This set of ideas, or "Hellenism" (Morris 2000: 41–8), became the mirror image of what Said (1978) calls "Orientalism," a vision of the Middle East as static and degenerate – everything Europe was not.

Winckelmann made Greek art a tool for defining European vitality, and over following generations Westerners tried to revitalize contemporary art by drinking at the fountain of Europe's childhood. This encouraged extraordinary scenes, from Lord Elgin and Choiseul-Gouffier intriguing to tear statues off the Parthenon, to French, Bavarian, and English agents chasing a shipload of sculptures from Aegina around the Mediterranean. But throughout, material culture was subordinated to philology, the rigorous study of classical texts. Art illuminated the classical spirit already revealed in literature, and inspired contemporary artists to reach the same heights.

In the late nineteenth century an intellectual revolution struck Western Europe and North America. Germany excepted, most leading thinkers about antiquity had been independent men of letters. But about 1870 the idea of research universities, pioneered at Göttingen in the 1730s and promoted all over Germany after 1808, began to take hold. Governments and rich donors endowed Professors and surrounded them with Lecturers, Assistants, and cadres of advanced students learning skills in seminars en route to professional accreditation.

Here was born the academic framework we still live with. Classical archaeologists had to make some big decisions. Where should they stand in the modern university? As a free-standing discipline? Associated with philologists in departments of Classics? Or with the growing numbers of prehistorians, entering departments of Archaeology in Europe and of Anthropology in North America?

In fact, few classical archaeologists thought very hard about these questions. The answer was obvious: stay with the classicists. There were good reasons. Classicists had higher status and funding than anthropologists or prehistorians. Classical philology was arguably the most scientific of the humanities: German *Altertumswissenschaft*, the science of antiquity, was a model to everyone.

But there were other compelling intellectual reasons. Classicists claimed to answer *the* burning issue of the Age of Empire: why Europeans and their white colonists were superior to the rest of the world. Joining a Classics department meant a subsidiary role to philologists, who controlled the texts that held the answers; but it also meant playing in the major leagues. Bruce Trigger (1984) characterizes Americanist prehistory in these years as "colonialist," justifying the right of white settlers to displace natives, and European prehistory as "nationalist," seeking the origins of specific peoples. But classical archaeology was "continentalist," explaining the roots of European civilization as a whole.

Hence the importance of the rolling frontier of classicism described above. The real classics belonged to Aegean Greece between 700 and 300 BC and Italy between 200 BC and AD 200. Around these cores extended temporal and spatial tails, going back in some places to the Bronze Age, and continuing in others into the sixth century AD. By World War I the main attitudes and institutions were in place. They were to survive without serious challenge for two generations.

3   Focusing on the connections between Greek and Roman works of art . . .

It was generally agreed that not all Graeco-Roman objects expressed the classical spirit. Architecture, sculpture, and painting – in short, high art – were what mattered. Painted pottery was debated, but Hamilton's astute marketing of his collection in the 1770s established Greek vases as a major medium for connoisseurs, even if they probably were not in antiquity (Vickers and Gill 1994).

American prehistorians formerly described the goal of archaeology as understanding the Indian behind the pot, and then as the system behind the Indian behind the pot; but in classical archaeology, the pot itself was the focus. The object here and now mattered, and what it might do for contemporary artistic taste. The first large excavations, begun at Herculaneum in 1738, illustrate this. The site was excavated through tunnels: literally mined for statues. Work only shifted to Pompeii when the Herculaneum mines got too dangerous.

Each age gets the field archaeologists it deserves. Winckelmann criticized these digs in 1762, begging for attention to architectural context and proper preservation of wall paintings, and work steadily improved. But recovering fine art remained the reason to dig classical sites, and little changed for a hundred years, when the rigor of classical philology and rising standards in prehistoric excavations inspired archaeologists to consider context and stratigraphy. Morelli transformed research at Pompeii in the 1860s, and within a decade Conze and Curtius did the same in Greece.

In the 1880s classical archaeologists began to see conflicts between scientific excavation and uplifting public taste. The new "big digs" generated vast quantities of objects which artists and the public found uninteresting: tiles, bricks, potsherds, etc. But science demanded that archaeologists treat all facts seriously. An 1880 newspaper dismissed the objects Furtwängler published from Olympia, the greatest scientific dig, as "on the whole merely ancient rubbish, small objects that were worthless then or single fragments of larger objects" (quoted in Marchand 1996: 91).

Conceivably, classical archaeologists could have rejected the focus on high art, asking new questions (or borrowing prehistorians' questions) about the ordinary artefacts they found. But the preference for philology meant this rarely happened. Instead, a successful division of labor emerged. Most practitioners devoted themselves to cataloguing data, producing series of volumes along the same lines as the *CIL*s in Figure 14.1, listing all known Roman lamps, Greek coins, etc., divided into categories. The most extraordinary are Beazley's catalogues of Archaic and classical Athenian black and red figure vase painting (Beazley 1942, 1956). Beazley attributed a high proportion of known paintings to artists, schools, and styles. His astounding achievement dominated the study of vase painting in the English-speaking world for half a century (Kurtz 1985). Debates about alternative methods were muted, and even now, suggesting that Beazley had an implicit theoretical model (as opposed to simply reacting to data) provokes denunciations that make the fight in Figure 14.1 look mild (compare Whitley 1997 with Oakley 1998, 1999).

By 1900 some classical archaeologists were paying about as little attention to the public as the one in Figure 14.1, but most still saw reaching a large audience as their goal. Charles Eliot Norton founded the Archaeological Institute of America in 1879, and tirelessly promoted public appreciation of classical art. He worried about scientific archaeology, cautioning the AIA in 1899 that "a pitfall has opened up before the feet of the archaeologist . . . there is a risk in the temptation, which attends the study of every science, to exalt the discovery of trifling particulars into an end in itself" (Norton 1900: 11). Norton was eager that Americans should excavate at Delphi in order to bring back great statues for the Metropolitan Museum in New York, and as Dyson (1998: 122–57) shows, the wealth and prestige of the great museums played an enormous part in the early history of American classical archaeology.

The result of these developments between the 1870s and 1910s was that classical archaeologists maintained scientific standards in excavation, publication, and typology, without abandoning their role in presenting classical art to the public to redeem the world from the cancer of modernism; and also without challenging the Hellenist worldview. Throughout the twentieth century, high art dominated the archaeological agenda.

4   . . . and Greek and Latin literary culture

"Graeco-Roman civilization" was consistently defined through language and literature. The Greek of Sophocles was the highest form of classicism; to the extent that other writers fell short of it, they diverged from the core. The Romans built their high culture through a particular appropriation of the Greek East; the Latin of Cicero provided a new peak of classicism, once again with earlier strivings toward it, and later fallings away. Hellenistic settlers took Greek to the Near East, and to the degree that it took root, these areas became classical. With the gradual failure of the Hellenistic cities across most of the Middle East in the third and second centuries BC, and the disappearance of Greek speakers, the classical frontier rolled back. But the Romans then carried Latin into Britain, Spain, and Africa, classicizing these regions.

A mechanical model of language, ethnicity, and culture dominated classicists' thought (see Hall 1997: 1–16): material culture expressed a preexisting linguistic formation, classical civilization.

By 1914, classical archaeology was settling into what Thomas Kuhn (1970) called "normal science," a period of agreement about the questions, methods, and major answers. The goal was to communicate to the world the excellence of classical art, which illustrated the spirit of Graeco-Roman civilization. Some archaeologists excavated, ideally doing big digs at famous cities, sanctuaries, or cemeteries, producing museum-worthy art. Architecture, sculpture, inscriptions, and painted pottery should be published lavishly, but classical archaeology's scientific ideals required that a wide range of artefacts also needed thorough publication, even if no one but other professionals publishing similar materials from their own sites would read these tomes. Large scholarly teams pursued these activities, producing knowledge at a density unparalleled in other archaeologies. However, excavators rarely strayed outside the public and elite areas of sites, and entire categories of evidence were ignored. Sieving and flotation were virtually unknown, and practically no seeds and bones were recovered. Classicists who wanted to know what people ate could read Aristophanes or Juvenal; archaeology was not about this kind of information.

To sum up: classical archaeologists worked within a controlling model of Hellenism which determined their subsidiary models of how fieldwork, publication, and interpretation should operate. The notion of "the classical" set archaeologists of the core periods of Greece and Rome above all others. North European prehistorians could tell their publics what had made them Danish, Germans, or French; and as the twentieth century wore on, prehistorians could say more and more about the origins of humanity. But that did not matter. Classical archaeology was about what was *best* in humanity.

Listening to the Noise

At a high level of abstraction there are certain similarities between classical and prehistoric archaeology in the early twentieth century. The controlling model was ethnic, and its working assumption was that archaeological cultures represented "peoples." But there the similarities ended. Classical archaeologists were concerned with classical art in the present, while prehistorians traced movements and influences among the ancient peoples that the artefacts revealed. This required different working practices and publication styles.

The gap was both sociological and intellectual. Hellenism had once been a subversive force. The governments of some German states in the 1820s feared that classical education radicalized students through admiration for Greek freedom and equality; and Greek democracy was a major weapon in liberal ideological critiques in Britain until the 1870s. But by the 1920s Hellenism was a force for cultural and political conservatism.

> Classical archaeology was no longer considered a humanistic science, meeting the late nineteenth-century challenge of modernism with a combination of socially improving aestheticism and inductive scientific rationalism. Rather, it was seen as a conservative discipline providing support for the traditional order, and hence playing an essential role in preserving intellectual and social stability. (Dyson 1998: 159)

Classical archaeology was congenial to the world's most powerful people, who supported it accordingly. Kaiser Wilhelm II intervened to help German archaeologists; Rockefeller donated a million dollars to the Agora excavations; and Mussolini expropriated downtown Rome to expose the imperial fora. The classical legacy was ambiguous in Nazi Germany, given the strength of alternative genealogies from German prehistory (Marchand 1996: 325–54); but the imperial past was unproblematic in Fascist Italy (Manacorda and Tamassia 1985).

But the gap between classical and prehistoric archaeology before and after World War II pales into insignificance compared to their divergence in the 1960s. In North America and Western Europe "new" or "processual" archaeologists attacked the verities of culture history, arguing instead for a systemic, ecologically oriented approach, explicit model building, and quantitative testing.

If classical archaeology ever resembled James' cartoon, it was in the 1960s and earlier 1970s. The classical establishment simply ignored the furious arguments over the "new" archaeology. In 1971 the ancient historian Moses Finley argued that "new" archaeology did little to aid social history, but only in 1982, as the postprocessual critique began in earnest, did Paul Courbin offer a bad-tempered rebuttal. As Dyson observes, "New Archaeology . . . would be middle-aged before most classical archaeologists even noticed it" (Dyson 1998: 247–8).

But prehistorians in Greece and Italy certainly noticed the new archaeology. Colin Renfrew developed a systemic model for Bronze Aegean Age civilization, later embedding this in a larger narrative of European prehistory and contributing to processual theory (Renfrew 1972, 1973, 1984). Similarly, John Bintliff approached the Aegean Bronze Age from a natural-science perspective, working out toward a larger synthesis of early European dynamics (Bintliff 1977, 1984).

Classical archaeologists might consider new archaeology as a fad, but in the 1970s hardly anyone outside Classics departments agreed. From purveyors of timeless truths, classical archaeologists had become old-fashioned. The world was changing; in the age of Biafra, Belfast, and Mylai, the questions new archaeologists asked – about food supply, demography, and exploitation – appeared more relevant than glorifying a unique Western aesthetic and moral superiority that students and many members of the public no longer felt.

Anders Andrén has shown that most regional forms of historical archaeology have developed in similar ways. Following initial interest in ancient art as inspiration for contemporary styles and with using artefacts to illustrate texts, archaeologists move to social and economic issues. This happens first in protohistorical periods, where there are texts, but not enough to write continuous histories (Andrén 1998: 107–26). Classical archaeology conforms precisely. Although historians of the Greek and Roman core periods foregrounded social and economic questions in the 1960s (e.g., Jones 1964; Finley 1973), it was chiefly archaeologists of the Early Iron Ages of Greece (e.g., Snodgrass 1977, 1980) and Italy (e.g., Ampolo et al. 1980, 1984) who took up the new archaeologists' lead. They highlighted state formation, adapting systems theory, neo-evolutionism, model-building, and quantitative testing, often via earlier applications in Bronze Age Aegean studies. Snodgrass provided a manifesto for this new classical archaeology, arguing:

> Once historians extend their interests from political and military events to social and economic processes, it is obvious that archaeological evidence can offer them far more; once Classical archaeologists turn from the outstanding works of art to the totality of material products, then history (thus widely interpreted) will provide them with a more serviceable framework. (Snodgrass 1980: 13)

Protohistorical archaeologists asking these questions discovered that field archaeologists had rarely collected the data they needed, particularly about rural settlement. There had been large-scale surface surveys in Greece and Italy since the early 1950s, but in the 1970s Aegean archaeologists drew on methods pioneered by American new archaeologists, with intensive coverage of transects sampling all the different microenvironments in the survey area, to reconstruct the overall settlement pattern in all periods. Not surprisingly, much of the stimulus came from Bronze Age archaeologists (Renfrew and Wagstaff 1982), but Snodgrass and Bintliff began their Boeotia survey in the mid-1970s (Bintliff and Snodgrass 1985); and Michael Jameson, then best known as an epigrapher, began the first such survey in 1972 (Jameson et al. 1994).

Surveys undermined classical archaeology's boundaries in three important ways. First, the focus moved from the artefact itself. Excavations needed experts on coarseware and tiles, because science required their publication; but they were rarely central to the project. On surveys, by contrast, most data fell into these categories; and further, the explicit goal was to move beyond humble objects to vanished settlement patterns. Second, serious survey was impossible without soil science (e.g., Bintliff 1977). Classical archaeology needed new kinds of specialists, which meant accepting that more than one kind of education could be appropriate. Third, surveys could not preserve the same boundaries around the classical past that choice of site (or deliberate disregard of finds of the wrong periods) allowed to excavators. Surveys led by Bronze Age archaeologists generated data forcing social historians to rethink classical settlement patterns, agriculture, and economics; and archaeologists who had begun working on ancient Greece found themselves immersed in Byzantine and Turkish history (e.g., Bintliff 1996, 1997; Cherry et al. 1991; Davis 1991, 1998). There were experiments in the 1970s in classical archaeology graduate programs in the US, notably at Boston and Indiana universities and the universities of Minnesota and Pennsylvania (Dyson 1998: 251–4), aimed at opening the field to new kinds of classical archaeologists. But these programs lacked the resources or prestige of older centers of classical archaeology like Princeton and Oxford.

The emergence of postprocessual archaeology in the early 1980s made the noise of the theoreticians' fights even more interesting to many classical archaeologists. Ancient historians were already asking questions about ideology and power, and postprocessual ideas gave classical archaeologists an opportunity to join the debates. Cambridge University, where Finley, Snodgrass, and Renfrew all held chairs, where Hodder was initiating the postprocessual critique, and where resources and connections were strong, became the center for exploring the intersections of these traditions. Snodgrass encouraged his students in this, concentrating particularly on the Early Iron Age (e.g., Morris 1987; Morgan 1990; Whitley 1991; Osborne 1996; Hall 1997; Shanks 1999), but also entering the central periods of Greek (Osborne 1985, 1987; Gallant 1991) and Roman history (Alcock 1993; Woolf 1998).

The postprocessual turn also opened up Anglo-American classical archaeology to approaches pioneered in France in the most traditional of all fields, Athenian vase painting. Inspired by Vernant's development of structuralism and psychoanalysis in Greek literary criticism, a "Paris School" of art history emerged (e.g., Bérard 1989; Lissarrague 1990), which impacted classical art history in other countries (e.g., Sourvinou-Inwood 1991; Elsner 1994, 1998; Hoffman 1997; Stewart 1997; Osborne 1998).

Classical archaeology has changed dramatically since the 1960s, but we should keep events in perspective. After the 13th International Congress of Classical Archaeology in Berlin in 1988, John Boardman (Beazley's successor at Oxford) commented: "Many of the papers treated subjects in a traditional way, trying to make sense of new discoveries, and making better sense of some of the long familiar, including some radical revisions . . . There were no signs of anxiety. Should there have been?" After consideration, he answered no (Boardman 1988: 795). The organizers of the 15th Congress, in Amsterdam in 1998, clearly disagreed. In the conference *Program*, Herman Brijder suggested: "On the threshold of the third millennium basic questions arise: where is Classical Archaeology heading, how 'Classical' is it still, what remains of the once strong ties with *Altertumswissenschaft*?" (Brijder 1998: 5). This surely points to a serious change during the 1990s. But Rasmus Brandt, President of the Associazione Internazionale di Archeologia Classica, felt forced to conclude:

> None of these questions were answered at the congress. Many felt this as a disappointment, but for this the organizers cannot be blamed. The theme was intended as a challenge to the classical archaeologists to see their studies in a historical context, but to look at them from new scientific angles. Unfortunately, in many ways the congress became more a presentation of the status quo of the discipline than the presentation of visions for the future, i.e., more reflections than perspectives. (Brandt 1999)

Anxiety was unmistakable in Amsterdam, but most speakers still preferred traditional questions, methods, and answers.

Quo Vadis?

If the field is no longer about the classics of Western culture, providing a beacon in the darkness of modernity, what is left of it? Is it still a distinctive intellectual endeavor? When Snodgrass delivered his 1984 Sather Lectures the issue was that of reorientation toward questions and methods pioneered outside classical archaeology. The tension in Amsterdam in 1998 suggests that this is no longer at issue. The question is now not whether change is a good idea, but what its outcome will be. In this final section I consider what classical archaeology might look like without the concept of "the classical."

Snodgrass suggested that

> the present dignified remoteness of the subject on the academic plane could give way to the kind of acknowledged intellectual vitality that attracts attention across a range of

other disciplines. If this happens, I believe that classical archaeology will still be found to be an exceptional discipline; but exceptional in its capacity to contribute to the fulfillment of new aims rather than in its fidelity to old ones. (Snodgrass 1987: 3)

He was surely right that the opportunities presented by the shake-up of the last twenty years outweigh the losses following the crumbling of the old paradigm, and the outlines of a new classical archaeology are emerging. By 1900 classical archaeologists had earned a safe niche by surrendering to philologists the right to tell the story of the Graeco-Roman world. As this position lost credibility from the 1980s, classical archaeologists began *repeopling* the field, using material culture to reinterpret antiquity more broadly. One manifestation has been the colonization of the core of art history by poststructuralist questions; another the turn toward economic, social, and cultural questions. By bringing people back in, classical archaeology becomes more historical, to the point that the boundaries between history and archaeology become difficult to define (Morris 1994).

This is where I see the greatest contribution of classical archaeology in the new century. The major archaeological debates since the 1960s were among prehistorians, and historical archaeologists have been marginalized, plowing ahead with agendas no one else cares about (like many classical archaeologists), or struggling to contribute modestly to the great battles over the more distant past. Binford (1977) suggested that the best use for historical archaeology was to test models developed in prehistory, where the real action was; and Kathleen Deagan (1988: 19) felt that as American historical archaeologists became more theoretically and methodologically self-conscious in the 1980s, they had moved from being the "handmaiden to history" to being a "handmaiden to prehistoric archaeology."

Postprocessualism criticized new archaeology for dehumanizing the past, and in the

1990s postprocessualists tried to address individual agency (e.g., Hodder 1999). The most original work focused on Neolithic northern Europe and showed the limitations of processualism; but the thinness of the evidence, its lack of variety (most obviously, the lack of written sources) and its chronological imprecision made it impossible for prehistorians to produce the kind of work postprocessualism demanded (Morris 2000: 3–33). But historical (in the sense of text-aided) archaeology *can* work at the required level, whether in Pharaonic Egypt (Meskell 1999), post-1500 America (McGuire and Paynter 1991; Orser 1996), medieval and modern Europe (Gilchrist 1994; Johnson 1996; Tarlow 1999; cf. Insoll 1999) – or Greece and Rome.

Classical archaeologists have created a huge database, and chronologies are often known in detail. Further, the questions classical archaeologists address, ranging from imperialism (e.g., Alcock 1993; Webster and Cooper 1996; Mattingly 1997; Woolf 1998) to the meanings of domestic space (e.g., Wallace Hadrill 1994; Laurence 1994; Nevett 1999), matter for archaeologists of complex societies everywhere. The material and textual records are less detailed than those from the industrial world, but on the other hand, the ancient Mediterranean provides greater time-depth and a range of phenomena unrepresented in modern times. The basic structures of the Greek city-states challenge archaeological theories about social complexity (Morris 1997), and I believe that classical archaeology can play a major role in putting historical archaeology at the forefront of theoretical debates in the next generation (Morris 2000).

Like Snodgrass, I see a strong future if classical archaeologists work toward new aims rather than clinging to old ones. But engaging with both archaeological theory and ancient social history to remake the field as part of a broad movement in postprocessual historical archaeology means speaking to very different audiences from those of the past; and the more we do so, the less "classical" classical archaeology will be.

The major debate to have emerged so far challenges the pairing of Greek and Roman civilization, in opposition to Egypt and the Near East. If we discard the notion of an exemplary Graeco-Roman classical civilization, there is no *a priori* reason for this arrangement. In his influential *Black Athena*, Martin Bernal (1987) argued that the interest since the eighteenth century in tracing Europeanness back to the Greeks was partly a racist conspiracy, concealing the Greeks' own acknowledgment to be descendants of Egyptian and Semitic colonists. His grasp on classical literature and the methods of intellectual history is shaky (Lefkowitz and Rogers 1996; Marchand and Grafton 1997), but mainstream classicist philologists also suggest that Greek culture had more in common with the Near East than with Rome (Burkert 1992; West 1997). Sarah Morris (1992) argues that before the Persian War of 480 BC, Greek material culture was within a Near Eastern *koine*. Afterwards, the Greeks deliberately distanced themselves from their oriental heritage.

These arguments have generated noise and abuse that would shame the theorists in Figure 14.1, drawing more media coverage than prehistorians' debates over the relationship between archaeology and nationalism, and raising more serious issues. Where prehistorians worry about the involvement of their forebears with Ruritanian (or any other nation's) identity, and how globalism affects nationalist agendas (e.g., Kohl and Fawcett 1995; Díaz-Andreu and Champion 1996; Atkinson et al. 1996; Meskell 1998; Hodder 2000), classicists focus on the larger question of the role of their studies in the construction of European identity as a whole. Only rarely (e.g., Graves-Brown et al. 1996) do prehistorians raise their sights to this level.

On the other hand, prehistorians read more broadly in social theory than the classicists, whose arguments are undertheorized (Morris 2000: 102–5). Thinking about classical archaeology without "the classical" calls for a second step, at a very practical level. Arguments over the structure of classical archaeology a century ago combined cultural politics with pedagogical issues, and we should follow their lead. How we teach classical archaeology in universities, how we present it to non-professional audiences, how we conceive our fieldwork, how we write our books: all are interlinked.

Professional classical archaeologists usually sit in Classics departments. But as Snodgrass (1987: 2–6, 132–4) notes, classical archaeologists have not only kept their distance from other archaeologists; they have also had little to say to other classicists or art historians. Traditional philologists or philosophers, working on text editions or commentaries, learned little from archaeologists engaged in attribution studies or excavation reports. Even ancient historians stayed away while their main concern was political narrative. As the historians' turn toward social, economic, and cultural questions accelerated in the 1980s, and as classical archaeologists moved in the same direction, these barriers weakened, and with the belated impact of new historicism on classical literary criticism and philosophy in the 1990s, a surprising situation has developed. By responding to the kinds of questions raised by new archaeologists, postprocessualists, and modern historians, classical archaeologists are finding themselves *more*, not less, integrated into the intellectual currents within classics as a whole. Archaeologists working on panhellenism or provincial responses to Roman imperialism find their work cited by literary critics, and vice versa. Similarly, as art historians of more recent periods turned first to social and economic questions and then to ones informed by poststructuralist literary criticism, the classical archaeologists in their midst grew increasingly isolated, but in the 1990s there is again convergence.

It is no easy thing to define the natural audience or institutional location for a changing classical archaeology. There is much to be said for the 1970s experiments at Indiana and Minnesota, embedding classical archaeology (or at least Aegean prehistory) in a broader program involving natural and social scientists. UCLA has similar aims in its Cotsen Institute, as does the Stanford Archaeology Center, both with strong Graeco-Roman presences. Boston University has a single Archaeology department with several Mediterranean archaeologists. Archaeology departments are of course common in Europe, where it is not unusual for a specialization in Graeco-Roman archaeology to lead to a B.Sc. degree. But every institutional confinement creates as many problems as it solves. The more time students spend on osteology or statistics, the less they have for cultural anthropology and social theory. And the more they spend on any of these approaches, the less time they have for ancient languages or surveys of Greek and Roman material culture.

The diversity of some university systems and students' partial freedom of choice provide some solutions. Some programs emphasize science, others fieldwork, others still historical or artistic approaches. Some require high linguistic standards, others strong quantitative skills. The best programs might allow students to work out their own balance by moving between several different departments while sharing a common core (all students will need a basic grasp of archaeological theory and method, comparative anthropology and history, history of the discipline, statistics, social theory, etc.), and still leaving room for substantial field-specific components. Archaeologists of Greece, India, and Peru should all be able to talk to each other, but should also be able to talk just as effectively with historians, literary critics, philosophers, and art historians of their own region of the world. The precise institutional structures may matter less than freedom of movement across them, but if historical archaeologies are to recognize their potential, we should avoid decoupling archaeologists and historians.

The fear of classical archaeologists that their students will not find jobs unless they have spent years learning Greek and Latin will be justified only so long as classical archaeologists define their primary audience as other classical archaeologists, embedded in a hermetically sealed classics environments. But this is something we can change, by challenging nineteenth-century paradigms at all levels, not just in research and graduate education. Undergraduates come to classical archaeology without preconceptions that the field is distinct from other regions of the Mediterranean or from ancient history. Some seek a degree in ancient history and archaeology, others to major in archaeology with a Mediterranean concentration. If classical archaeologists and ancient historians decide to explode the inherited limits of their fields, only institutional inertia can stop them. The main cost is the effort to prepare new materials for teaching, or to write new kinds of textbooks (e.g., Whitley 2001). The same is true of the public arena. The huge non-professional audience for classical archaeology (the AIA's periodical *Archaeology* has a circulation over 100,000) is highly varied. Some people strongly support traditional models of classical excellence and its role in upholding the social hierarchy; but far more of those who attend lectures in local chapters of the AIA or watch *Ancient Mysteries* on television are just fascinated by the Mediterranean. The barriers to a new role for classical archaeology lie almost entirely within the professional community itself.

There was much unhappiness in classical archaeology at the end of the nineteenth century. In the rapidly changing environment that the expansion of the scientific university created, some scholars squeezed out others in the competition for status, tenure, and rewards (e.g., Marchand 1996: 116–51; Dyson 1998: 61–121). The changes that classical archaeology is currently passing through may be just as traumatic. Ambitions will be thwarted and careers ruined as some people leap too quickly to radical reinter-pretations of the field, and others hang on too long to outdated ideas. But the most important point is that the field *is* changing. The only questions now are by how much, and in what directions.

Conclusions

Returning to Snodgrass' observation, quoted at the beginning of this chapter, we might say that a new classical archaeology is putting elementary grammar straight. The field is moving toward being an integral part of archaeology, with especially close links with classics. But as classics itself changes, substituting a broad social, economic, and cultural approach to the ancient Mediterranean and its larger place in world history for the old idea of elucidating the paradigm for Western civilization, so too must classical archaeology. Stripped of the idea of a foundational "classical" moment in history, Greek and Roman (and Near Eastern and west Mediterranean) archaeology makes most sense as part of a broader historical archaeology of complex societies. In teaching, writing, and fieldwork, the new classical archaeology speaks to central debates in archaeology as a whole.

James' cartoon (Figure 14.1) is a good entry-point for the philosophy of classical archaeology. But like many models, its greatest value may be to throw into sharp relief those dimensions of the field that it *cannot* accommodate. Classical archaeologists have rarely, if ever, sat on their *CIL*s wondering about the theoreticians' noise. For most of the twentieth century they looked down haughtily on the shallow posturing of those who studied savages. In the wake of the 1960s, some began to listen to the ruckus; and at the century's end they are joining in. For better or for worse, classical archaeologists are staking out their own claims to be poststructuralist pseuds and phallocrat scum-bags.

References

Alcock, S. 1993. *Graecia Capta: The Landscapes of Roman Greece*. Cambridge: Cambridge University Press.

Ampolo, C., G. Bartoloni, A. Bedini, G. Bergonzi, A. M. Bietti Sestieri, M. Cataldi Dini, and F. Cordano 1980. *La formazione della città nel Lazio (Dialoghi di Archeologia 2: 1–2)*.

Ampolo, C., G. Bartoloni, and A. Rathje (eds.) 1984. *Aspetti delle aristocrazie fra VIII e VII sec. a.C. (Opus 3.2)*.

Atkinson, J. A., I. Banks, and J. O'Sullivan (eds.) 1996. *Nationalism and Archaeology*. Glasgow: Cruithne Press.

Bahn, P. 1996. *Archaeology: A Very Short Introduction*. Oxford: Oxford University Press.

Beazley, J. 1942. *Attic Red-Figure Vase Painters*, 1st edn. Oxford: Clarendon Press.

Beazley, J. 1956. *Attic Black-Figure Vase Painters*. Oxford: Clarendon Press.

Bérard, C. (ed.) 1989 [1984]. *A City of Images: Iconography and Society in Ancient Greece*. Trans. D. Lyons. Princeton, NJ: Princeton University Press.

Bernal, M. 1987. *Black Athena I: The Fabrication of Ancient Greece 1785–1985*. New Brunswick, NJ: Rutgers University Press.

Binford, L. 1977. "Historical archaeology: is it historical or archaeological?" In L. Ferguson (ed.), *Historical Archaeology and the Importance of Material Things*, pp. 13–22. Tucson: Society for Historic Archaeology.

Bintliff, J. 1977. *Environment and Settlement in Prehistoric Greece*, 2 vols. Oxford: British Archaeological Reports (BAR S28).

Bintliff, J. L. (ed.) 1984. *European Social Evolution*. Bradford: Bradford University Press.

Bintliff, J. L. 1996. "The Frankish countryside in central Greece." In P. Lock and G. Sandars (eds.), *The Archaeology of Medieval Greece*, pp. 1–18. Oxford: Oxbow Press.

Bintliff, J. L. 1997. "The archaeological investigation of deserted medieval villages in Greece." In G. De Boe and F. Verhaege (eds.), *Medieval Europe (Rural Settlement)*, pp. 21–34. Zellik: Instituut voor het Archeologisch Patrimonium.

Bintliff, J. L. and A. Snodgrass 1985. "The Cambridge/Bradford Boeotia Expedition: the first four years." *Journal of Field Archaeology*, 12: 123–61.

Boardman, J. 1988. "Classical archaeology: whence and whither?" *Antiquity*, 62: 795–7.

Brandt, J. R. 1999. "The XVth International Congress of Classical Archaeology: some reflections and perspectives." In R. F. Docter and E. M. Moorman (eds.), *Proceedings of the XVth International Congress of Classical Archaeology, Amsterdam, July 12–17, 1998*, p. xiv. Amsterdam: Allard Pierson Museum.

Brijder, H. A. G. 1998. "Introduction." In R. F. Docter and E. M. Moorman (eds.), *XVth International Congress of Classical Archaeology – Abstracts*. Amsterdam: Allard Pierson Museum.

Burkert, W. 1992 [1984]. *The Orientalizing Revolution: Near Eastern Influence on Greek Culture During the Early Archaic Period*. Trans. W. Burkert and M. Pinder. Cambridge, MA: Harvard University Press.

Cherry, J., J. L. Davis, and E. Mantzourani (eds.) 1991. *Landscape Archaeology as Long-Term History: Northern Keos in the Cycladic Islands*. Los Angeles: University of California Press.

Courbin, P. 1982. *Qu'est-ce que l'archéologie?* Paris. English translation, *What is Archaeology?* Chicago: University of Chicago Press, 1988.

Darnton, R. 1984. *The Great Cat Massacre and Other Episodes in French Cultural History*. New York: Basic Books.

Davis, J. L. 1991. "Contributions to a Mediterranean rural archaeology: historical case studies from the Ottoman Cyclades." *Journal of Mediterranean Archaeology*, 4: 131–216.

Davis, J. L. (ed.) 1998. *Sandy Pylos: An Archaeological History, Nestor to Navarino*. Austin: University of Texas Press.

De Grummond, N. (ed.) 1996. *Encyclopedia of the History of Classical Archaeology*. Westport, CT: Greenwood Press.

Deagan., K. 1988. "Neither history nor prehistory: questions that count in historical archaeology." *Historical Archaeology*, 22: 7–12.

Díaz-Andreu, M. and T. Champion (eds.) 1996. *Nationalism and Archaeology in Europe*. Boulder, CO: Westview Press.

Docter, R. F. and E. M. Moorman (eds.) 1999. *Proceedings of the XVth International Congress of Classical Archaeology, Amsterdam, July 12–17, 1998*. Amsterdam: Allard Pierson Museum.

Dyson, S. 1998. *Ancient Marbles to American Shores*. Philadelphia: University of Pennsylvania Press.

Elsner, J. 1994. *Art and the Roman Viewer*. Cambridge: Cambridge University Press.

Elsner, J. 1998. *Imperial Rome and Christian Triumph*. Oxford: Oxford University Press.

Finley, M. I. 1971. "Archaeology and history." *Daedalus*, 100: 168–86. Reprinted in M. I. Finley, *The Use and Abuse of History*, pp. 87–101. London: Chatto and Windus.

Finley, M. I. 1973. *The Ancient Economy*, 1st edn. Berkeley: University of California Press.

Gallant, T. 1991. *Risk and Survival in Ancient Greece*. Stanford, CA: Stanford University Press.

Gilchrist, R. 1994. *Gender and Material Culture: The Archaeology of Religious Women*. London: Routledge.

Graves-Brown, P., S. Jones, and C. Gamble (eds.) 1996. *Cultural Identity and Archaeology: The Construction of European Communities*. London: Routledge.

Hall, J. 1997. *Ethnic Identity in Greek Antiquity*. Cambridge: Cambridge University Press.

Hodder, I. 1999. *The Archaeological Process: An Introduction*. Oxford: Blackwell.

Hodder, I. 2000. *Archaeology and Globalism*. Bloomington: Indiana University Press.

Hoffman, H. 1997. *Sotades*. Oxford: Clarendon Press.

Insoll, T. 1999. *The Archaeology of Islam*. Oxford: Blackwell.

Jameson, M. H., C. Runnels, and T. van Andel 1994. *A Greek Countryside: The Southern Argolid from Prehistory to the Present Day*. Stanford, CA: Stanford University Press.

Johnson, M. 1996. *An Archaeology of Capitalism*. Oxford: Blackwell.

Johnson, M. 1999. *Archaeological Theory: An Introduction*. Oxford: Blackwell.

Jones, A. H. M. 1964. *The Later Roman Empire*, 2 vols. Oxford: Blackwell.

Kohl, P. and C. Fawcett (eds.) 1995. *Nationalism, Politics, and the Practice of Archaeology*. Cambridge: Cambridge University Press.

Kuhn, T. 1970. *The Structure of Scientific Revolutions*, 2nd edn. Chicago: University of Chicago Press.

Kurtz, D. C. (ed.) 1985. *Beazley and Oxford*. Oxford: Oxford University Committee for Archaeology.

Laurence, R. 1994. *Roman Pompeii*. London: Routledge.

Lefkowitz, M. and G. Rogers (eds.) 1996. *Black Athena Revisited*. Durham, NC: University of North Carolina Press.

Lissarrague, F. 1990. *The Aesthetics of the Greek Banquet*. Princeton, NJ: Princeton University Press.

McGuire, R. and R. Paynter (eds.) 1991. *The Archaeology of Inequality*. Oxford: Blackwell.

Manacorda, D. and R. Tamassia. 1985. *Il piccone del regime*. Rome: Armando Curcio.

Marchand, S. 1996. *Down from Olympus: Archaeology and Philhellenism in Germany, 1750–1970*. Princeton, NJ: Princeton University Press.

Marchand, S. and A. Grafton 1997. "Martin Bernal and his critics." *Arion*, 3rd series, 5: 1–35.

Mattingly, D. (ed.) 1997. *Dialogues in Roman Imperialism. Journal of Roman Archaeology*, supplement 23.

Meskell, L. (ed.) 1998. *Archaeology Under Fire*. London: Routledge.

Meskell, L. 1999. *Archaeologies of Social Life: Age, Sex, Class Et Cetera in Egypt*. Oxford: Blackwell.

Miller, M. 1997. *Athens and Persia in the Fifth Century* BC. Cambridge: Cambridge University Press.

Morgan, C. 1990. *Athletes and Oracles: The Transformation of Olympia and Delphi in the Eighth Century* BC. Cambridge: Cambridge University Press.

Morris, I. 1987. *Burial and Ancient Society*. Cambridge: Cambridge University Press.

Morris, I. (ed.) 1994. *Classical Greece: Ancient Histories and Modern Archaeologies*. Cambridge: Cambridge University Press.

Morris, I. 1997. "An archaeology of equalities? The Greek city-states." In D. Nichols and T. Charlton (eds.), *The Archaeology of City-States: Cross-Cultural Approaches*, pp. 91–105. Washington, DC: Smithsonian Institution Press.

Morris, I. 2000. *Archaeology as Cultural History*. Oxford: Blackwell.

Morris, S. 1992. *Daidalos and the Origins of Greek Art*. Princeton, NJ: Princeton University Press.

Nevett, L. 1999. *House and Society in the Ancient Greek World*. Cambridge: Cambridge University Press.

Norton, C. E. 1900. "The progress of the Archaeological Institute of America: an address." *American Journal of Archaeology*, n.s. 4: 1–16.

Oakley, J. 1998. "Why study a Greek vase-painter?" *Antiquity*, 72: 209–13.

Oakley, J. 1999. " 'Through a Glass Darkly' I: some misconceptions about the study of Greek vase-painting." In R. F. Docter and E. M. Moorman (eds.), *Proceedings of the XVth International Congress of Classical Archaeology, Amsterdam, July 12–17, 1998*, pp. 286–90. Amsterdam: Allard Pierson Museum.

Orser, C. 1996. *A Historical Archaeology of the Modern World*. New York: Plenum Press.

Osborne, R. 1985. *Demos: The Discovery of Classical Attika*. Cambridge: Cambridge University Press.

Osborne, R. 1987. *Classical Landscape with Figures*. London: George Philip.

Osborne, R. 1996. *Greece in the Making, 1200–479* BC. London: Routledge.

Osborne, R. 1998. *Archaic and Classical Greek Art*. Oxford: Oxford University Press.

Renfrew, A. C. 1972. *The Emergence of Civilisation*. London: Methuen.

Renfrew, A. C. 1973. *Before Civilisation*. London: Cape.

Renfrew, A. C. 1984. *Approaches to Social Archaeology*. Edinburgh: Edinburgh University Press.

Renfrew, A. C. and M. Wagstaff (eds.) 1982. *An Island Polity: The Archaeology of Exploitation on Melos*. Cambridge: Cambridge University Press.

Said, E. 1978. *Orientalism*. New York Pantheon Books.

Shanks, M. 1999. *Art and the Early Greek State*. Cambridge: Cambridge University Press.

Snodgrass, A. M. 1977. *Archaeology and the Rise of the Greek State*. Cambridge: Cambridge University Press.

Snodgrass, A. M. 1980. *Archaic Greece*. London: Dent.

Snodgrass, A. M. 1987. *An Archaeology of Greece: The Present State and Future Scope of a Discipline*. Berkeley: University of California Press.

Sourvinou-Inwood, C. 1991. *"Reading" Greek Culture: Texts and Images, Rituals and Myths*. Oxford: Clarendon Press.

Stewart, A. 1997. *Art, Desire and the Body in Ancient Greece*. Cambridge: Cambridge University Press.

Tarlow, S. 1999. *Bereavement and Commemoration: An Archaeology of Mortality*. Oxford: Blackwell.

Trigger, B. 1984. "Alternative archaeologies: nationalist, colonialist, imperialist." *Man*, 19: 355–70.

Vickers, M. and D. Gill 1994. *Artful Crafts: Ancient Greek Silverware and Pottery*. Oxford: Clarendon Press.

Wallace Hadrill, A. 1994. *House and Society at Pompeii and Herculaneum*. Princeton, NJ: Princeton University Press.

Weber, M. 1949. *The Methodology of the Social Sciences*. Trans. E. Shils and H. Finch. Glencoe, IL: Free Press.

Webster, J. and N. Cooper (eds.) 1996. *Roman Imperialism: Post-Colonial Perspectives*. Leicester: School of Archaeological Studies, Leicester University.

West, M. L. 1997. *The East Face of Helicon: West Asiatic Elements in Greek Poetry and Myth*. Oxford: Clarendon Press.

Whitley, J. 1991. *Style and Society in Dark Age Greece*. Cambridge: Cambridge University Press.

Whitley, J. 1997. "Beazley as theorist." *Antiquity*, 78: 40–7.

Whitley, J. 2001. *The Archaeology of Ancient Greece*. Cambridge: Cambridge University Press.

Woolf, G. 1998. *Becoming Roman*. Cambridge: Cambridge University Press.

15

The Archaeologies of Recent History: Historical, Post-Medieval, and Modern-World

Charles E. Orser, Jr.

Introduction

The archaeology of the past 500–650 years is one of the most exciting and potentially rewarding kinds of archaeology now being practiced. Unlike their colleagues who study the far distant past, archaeologists of recent history do not make discoveries of majestic, ancient sites or present bold new interpretations about the cultures of deepest antiquity. They focus, instead, on the archaeology of our immediate ancestors. The archaeology they conduct generally concentrates on the examination of processes, issues, and events that are usually still relevant today. Archaeologists working throughout the world have made significant advances in knowledge about the cultures and histories of the men and women who inhabited the most recent past.

Before explaining some of the contributions of the archaeology of recent history, we must briefly linger on the issue of definition. The archaeology of the recent past is commonly referred to as "historical archaeology," a term with a surprisingly unclear meaning. A universal understanding among archaeologists is elusive, and today's archaeologists use "historical archaeology" in at least three different senses depending upon

their disciplinary backgrounds and perspectives. As a result, archaeologists are constantly shifting and renegotiating the borders of historical archaeology in a process of reconstitution that is vibrant, alive, headstrong, and sometimes even feisty.

An exciting reshifting of historical archaeology's boundaries is currently underway. This reworking goes to the heart of the discipline, even involving the way in which we define and conceptualize the field's goals and mission. It is likely that the resultant stretching of the limits of historical archaeology will have far-reaching, lasting consequences for the future of archaeological research.

The Senses of Historical Archaeology

Today's archaeologists impart three prominent meanings to "historical archaeology." Some practitioners define the term simply as any archaeological practice in which an archaeologist bases his or her interpretations on the combination of excavated data and textual information. Others relate the term to the archaeology of a distinct historical period, a segment of time delineated by literacy. For still others, the focus of historical archaeology commences with modernization, a process often but not necessarily associated with the global spread of Europeans beginning in the fifteenth century.

Many of the conceptual distinctions between the three senses of historical archaeology occur because of the presence of the word "historical" in the field's name. Archaeologists interested in recent history engaged in a protracted debate around this issue in the 1960s, with Lewis Binford (1977: 13) offering a succinct expression to the problem: "Why should I be uncomfortable and indecisive as to an appropriate subject or way of treating a problem . . . That word 'historical' again!" Even Binford, who early in his career excavated at an eighteenth-century French and British colonial fortification in the United States, was perplexed by the close combination of "history" and "archaeology."

Binford's confusion is understandable because the question "What is History?" has occasioned unceasing debate among historians since the days of Herodotus. The precise details of the argument must be left to professional historians, but the definitions presented by Italian philosopher Benedetto Croce (1921) are instructive. Croce defined *history* simply as what happened in the past, and *chronicle* as the retelling or writing of history. In Croce's terminology, historians create chronicles from history. Archaeologists know Croce's distinction mainly through Walter Taylor's (1948) classic *A Study of Archaeology*. Relying largely on the work of revisionist historian Charles Beard (1934), Taylor (1948: 30–1) termed history "past actuality," and chronicle, "historiography." Croce stressed, and historian Carl Becker (1955) made popular, the idea that historians produce chronicles through the conscious selection of events from the broad sweep of past actuality. When historians choose events from the past to write histories, the collected events become "historical facts" by virtue of their selection.

Philosophers may debate the profound implications of fact selection, but the practical need for the choice of historical facts is read-

ily apparent because a complete retelling of the past "would take as long as the happenings" themselves (Kroeber 1935: 547). Faced with this reality, "no chronicler nor historian can attempt to record all events; from the superfluity of happenings he must select what he regards as memorable" (Childe 1947: 22).

The link between chronicle and archaeology is obvious. Famed historian Frederic Maitland observed in the late 1890s: "an archaeology that is not history is somewhat less than nothing" (Hazeltine et al. 1936: 242). Despite Willey and Phillips' (1958: 2) famous paraphrase of Maitland – stressing the indispensability of anthropology to archaeology – most archaeologists today would probably agree with him. In Anglo-American archaeology, the intellectual genealogy of Maitland's understanding begins with the pioneering cultural historians of the nineteenth century. In British archaeology, the relationship between history and archaeology largely begins with such names as Layard, Flinders Petrie, and Evans, and extends through Childe and Collingwood. More recently, Ian Hodder (1986: 77) reaffirmed the link between archaeology and chronicle by stating "archaeology should recapture its traditional links with history." In fact, Hodder (1986: 101) envisioned the union of history and archaeology as being effected by "transposing many of the methods and assumptions of historical archaeology into prehistory."

Hodder's statement was undoubtedly appreciated by historical archaeologists throughout the world, but it is problematic because we do not know precisely what he means by "historical archaeology." We can assume from the context that he means something distinct from prehistoric archaeology, but how and why?

Hodder may not have required greater explicitness because archaeologists for the most part can easily imagine the distinction between "history" and "prehistory." Knowing that this difference exists, however, does not necessarily translate into an understanding that the archaeology of history is operationally distinguishable from the archaeology of prehistory. On the contrary, many archaeologists have tenaciously held onto the notion that the archaeology of history is a mirror image of the archaeology of prehistory, such that historical archaeology is "not a different kind of archaeology from any other" (South 1977: 2). Prehistorians usually make this claim when they discover the interpretive power of an approach that combines excavated information with textual sources (e.g., see Kepecs 1997; Lightfoot 1995). The prehistorians' enlightened realizations are nothing new, and many historical archaeologists often find their wide-eyed revelations to be charmingly naive.

In truth, some archaeologists have recognized for years that the distinction between history and prehistory has never been "clean cut through time" (Hogarth 1899: vi). But to create a division between the two, archaeologists have usually identified "history" as a time of literacy, and "prehistory" as a pre- or non-literate time. When so conceptualized, history and prehistory exist as elements of time conceived typologically, because the defining measure is rooted "in terms of socioculturally meaningful events" (Fabian 1983: 23) – the advent of literacy.

The inherent truth that the distinction between history and prehistory is based on literacy is usually perceived as so irrefutable in archaeology that it has become something of a truism. Textbook authors regularly propose the prehistory/history dichotomy as the natural state of affairs. The authors of one popular text state, for example, that historical archaeology "refers to archaeological investigations carried out in conjunction with analyses of written records" (Sharer and Ashmore 2003: 29). They include all forms of written expression in their catalogue: "clay tablets marked in cuneiform writing, Egyptian hieroglyphic texts on papyrus, and inscriptions carved on Maya stone monuments are just as much documents as are the books published in seventeenth-century Europe" (Sharer and Ashmore 2003: 27).

Based on this formulation, we may imagine that archaeologists of the Maya became historical archaeologists – or we might say that the Mayas entered history – when scholars learned to decipher the Maya's intricate glyphs. The importance of literacy to historical archaeology was made most explicit by James Deetz (1977: 7): "The literacy of the people it studies is what sets historical archaeology apart from prehistory."

Based on such comments, it would appear that archaeologists understand "history" not as Croce's "what happened in the past," or even as Taylor's "past actuality," but as that segment of time for which literacy exists, as expressed by textual documentation. We can say accordingly that Western history began with the Sumerians and extends to the present, whereas prehistory is literally all the time before "history."

The distinction between history and prehistory based on writing is not confined to the West. Chinese archaeologists regularly make the distinction between these two periods (Cultural Artifacts Administration 1985; Xia Nai 1985), with prehistory beginning sometime around 600,000 BC and extended to history, which began around 1600 BC, with the production of incised oracle bones during the Shang dynasty (Fitz-Gerald 1978: 40; Gernet 1982: 47). As a result, most Chinese archaeology is "historical" in orientation, with most archaeologists working in departments of history (Feinman 1997: 368). The same theoretical orientation obtains in India (see Dhavalikar 1999).

The understanding that historical archaeology rests on a methodology that combines textual documentation with archaeological sources at sites associated with literacy is indeed widespread (see Andrén 1998). Not all archaeologists who combine textual information with archaeological remains, however, refer to themselves as historical archaeologists. In fact, rather than describe themselves by their methodology, most archaeologists prefer identifiers that have either temporal or cultural meaning. Classical archaeologists investigate Greek and

Roman history, European medieval archaeologists study the years between AD 400 and 1400, post-medieval archaeologists focus on the 1450–1750 period, and industrial archaeologists mostly concentrate on sites and properties inhabited before, during, and after the Industrial Revolution. Mesoamericanists almost never refer to themselves as historical archaeologists unless they are engaged in some facet of post-Columbian Spanish contact and conquest.

Other archaeologists who make extensive use of documents in their research, however, do describe themselves as historical archaeologists. These archaeologists examine those parts of the globe that witnessed the clash between colonizing Europeans and indigenous peoples in the Columbian and post-Columbian eras. The sites of interest for these historical archaeologists are situated largely in global locales that experienced colonialist activities within the past few hundred years. Thus, instead of examining the entirety of literate human history, self-identified historical archaeologists study sites with far less time-depth, usually between 500–650 years.

Anthropologically trained archaeologists tend to understand historical archaeology as focusing on post-Columbian history. Literacy is an undeniable part of this history, but not its defining characteristic. The vast majority of Europe's agents of colonialism and imperialism – fur trappers, traders, merchants, artisans, craftspersons, indentured servants, and slaves – were illiterate. The literacy of a group's home country is much less important than what happened when the agents of colonialism encountered indigenous peoples in what were for them new worlds. In this perspective, historical archaeologists use a broadly multi- and transdisciplinary research program to examine fur trade posts, abandoned colonial settlements and military outposts, industrial plants, urban tenements, Native American villages, and other kinds of human settlements.

The understanding that historical archaeology should be defined in this manner has roots that extend to the earliest structured thinking about the creation of a formalized historical archaeology in the United States. The 13 men who founded the Society for Historical Archaeology in January 1967, decided to limit the scope of the organization "to the following periods: Exploration and Settlement; Contact Aboriginal; Colonial; National Development; and Modern" (Pilling 1967: 6). The main focus of the new society would thus be "the era since the beginning of the exploration of the non-European world by Europeans. The areas of prime concern are in the Western Hemisphere, but consideration of Oceanic, African, and Asian archaeology during the relatively late periods" would also fall within the purview of the new organization (Anonymous 1967: 509).

We must not place too strong an emphasis on the ability of a few men to define an entire field, but before 1967 the archaeological examination of post-Columbian history was negligible at best, only being relegated to a few carefully selected sites prominent within the dominant national ideology of the United States or to small numbers of essentially prehistoric sites that contained post-Columbian components. The understanding of historical archaeology by the founding members of the Society for Historical Archaeology was that the field should focus on the post-Columbian expansion of Europeans into the non-European world.

Three Strengths of Historical Archaeology

As a distinct field of serious study, historical archaeology did not develop in a standardized manner until the late 1960s (Orser and Fagan 1995: 23–37). Since this time, historical archaeologists have made impressive advances in interpreting the post-Columbian world. Three contributions are especially significant: (1) the solidification of a transdisciplinary approach that emphasizes the careful combination of archaeological and textual sources of information; (2) the presentation of rich details about post-Columbian material culture; and (3) the documentation of the lives and living conditions of recent history's poor, disadvantaged, and forgotten men and women.

The historical archaeologists' reliance on a transdisciplinary approach to the past has been one of their greatest triumphs. Trans- and multidisciplinary approaches have become commonplace in much archaeology, and it is not unusual for today's archaeologists to collaborate with cultural and social anthropologists, historians, geophysicists, geohydrologists, botanists, and many other specialists whose fields of expertise have relevance to archaeology. Prehistorians may frequently conduct multidisciplinary research, but it is not necessarily required. They can conduct perfectly elegant site-specific, artefact-focused, and even regional investigations without the assistance of any "non-archaeological" sources of information.

Most historical archaeologists find archaeological chauvinism to be unwise and so they typically revel in the presence of textual sources relevant to their research. So important is the union of history and archaeology in historical archaeology that the field is sometimes termed *documentary archaeology* (Beaudry 1988) or even *text-aided archaeology* (Little 1992). Historians have taught historical archaeologists that they must approach documentary collections cautiously. Producers of documents often lied, were misinformed, unknowledgeable, and incomplete in their recitation of past events. As a result, most historical archaeologists resist "the tyranny of the historical record" (Champion 1990), recognizing that they can use chronicles and documents but that they need not be constrained by them.

Historical archaeologists need not rely exclusively on written records. Many excavators have presented insightful studies by combining their excavated findings with oral interviewing, photographic and cartographic materials, governmental treatises, religious tracts, and many other supposedly "non-archaeological" sources of information. The unabashed appropriation of information from any useful source is an especially fulfilling aspect of historical archaeology. The most successful historical archaeologists do not make judgments about what is properly "archaeological," and smugly ignore what is not.

A second strength of historical archaeology is its focus on the material culture of recent history. An interest in the physical things of the immediate past is deeply buried in historical archaeology's heritage, with its roots extending to the field's earliest practitioners, individuals originally trained as culture historians. Fledgling historical archaeologists, educated for the most part as prehistoric archaeologists of Native America, knew little if anything about the artefacts they encountered at post-Columbian sites. Many archaeologists were uncomfortable knowing they could classify artefacts made thousands of years in the past, but that they could not do the same for those produced only a hundred years earlier: "with few exceptions colonial artefacts have not been analyzed or classified by a method suitable for the archaeologist to handle. Therefore, it is up to us to do so" (South 1964). J. C. Harrington (1994: 7), the excavator of Jamestown, Virginia, in the 1930s, summarized the situation well when he admitted: "My greatest deficiency was in my dismal ignorance of non-architectural artefacts."

Presented with the stark reality that they knew little if anything about the physical objects they excavated from post-Columbian sites, many archaeologists began intensive, long-term study of the material objects made and used during the past 500 years. In the United States, the first organization to devote itself to the study of post-Columbian artefacts was the Conference on Historic Site Archaeology (South 1967: 135). In England, the study of post-medieval artefacts began with ceramics, a focus that has retained a central place in post-medieval archaeology for the past 25 years (Crossley 1990: 243). The "Post-Medieval Ceramic Research

Group," launched in Bristol in 1963, established its temporal focus on the 1450–1750 period (Barton 1968: 102). Only three years later, the Group was recreated as the Society for Post-Medieval Archaeology. The founders of the new society downplayed their former preoccupation with ceramics, but kept the same temporal interests, arguing that the 1450–1750 period was historically significant because it was characterized by "the unification of states within the British Isles, the establishment of Britain upon the path of maritime colonial expansion and the initial stage of industrial growth" (Anonymous 1968: 1). The examination of ceramics continues to be a primary focus of post-medieval archaeology (Gaimster 1994: 285).

In addition to providing specific information about manufactured objects from the past 500 years, many historical archaeologists have used the changes in artefact design or the differential rates of artefact usage to make important statements about such cultural processes as acculturation, resistance, inequality, and cultural maintenance. Several historical archaeologists have also interpreted the symbolic meanings of portable artefacts, as well as those of settlements and landscapes. One of the earliest and best-known symbolic studies is Mark Leone's (1984) classic interpretation of the underlying meaning of William Paca's garden in Annapolis, Maryland. Leone's interpretation has not been without its critics (Hall 1992; Hodder 1986; Beaudry et al. 1991; see further comments in Orser 1996: 164–82), but studies such as his have appreciably added to our understanding of recent history and have demonstrated the broad-based interpretive power of historical archaeology.

A third significant strength of historical archaeology concerns its ability to provide unique information about men and women who have been largely overlooked in history. Since the 1960s, several archaeologists have concentrated on documenting the daily lives and living conditions of peoples largely silenced by the sweep of post-Columbian, recorded history.

The first historical archaeologists in the United States worked almost exclusively to illuminate the lives of the rich and the famous in American history, with their earliest research focusing on such notable places as Williamsburg, Jamestown, George Washington's Fort Necessity, and other prominent historic properties. After about thirty years of this research strategy, several insightful American historical archaeologists, trained in the anthropological tradition of studying non-Western peoples, quickly realized that whole groups of men and women were simply ignored in most written documents. Thus erased from the official telling of history, these people had also been overlooked by historical archaeologists.

Urged forward by the Civil Rights Movement in the United States and elsewhere, and cognizant of their own anthropological education, some archaeologists began to imagine that they could turn their considerable talents toward the elucidation of the lives of the overlooked and the forgotten. In the United States this investigation began with the study of slave life, as some archaeologists began to wonder how, in the face of unspeakable degradation and oppressive racism, New World slaves of African descent had survived in the slave-holding world (e.g., Fairbanks 1984; Ferguson 1992). Before this realization, however, historical archaeologists who excavated at southern plantations were drawn almost exclusively to the planter's mansions, spending much of their time providing architectural details for physical reconstruction programs.

Since the late 1960s, the archaeology of African American slaves has become one of the most developed kinds of historical archaeology practiced in the New World. Scholars around the globe are today diligently engaged in the archaeology of the African diaspora, providing important new information about diet and nutrition, religion, settlement patterns, material culture, and many other facets of slave life (for full citations see Orser 1990, 1994, 1998a). The archaeology of the forgotten, the dispossessed, and the poor is the "noblest of causes in archaeological research" (Orser 1996: 161).

Archaeology and the Poor

Robert Ascher (1974), in an early though usually unrecognized plea for what would later be termed "interpretive archaeology" (Hodder 1986), encompassed the poor by his term "the inarticulate." By "inarticulate," Ascher (1974: 11) meant men and women "who did not write or who were not written about" in the chronicles of the past. An interest in the so-called inarticulate soon became prominent in historical archaeology (Deagan 1982: 171; Feder 1994: 16), and by the early 1980s, historical archaeologists had shed much light on several groups who can be considered to have been neglected and poor. Even so, poverty itself has never been a major topic of long-term interest within the discipline.

The need to study men and women who can be situationally defined as "poor" is slowly gaining acceptance in the field (see Mayne and Murray 2001), but most historical archaeologists have seldom mentioned this group directly. The poor often exist in historical archaeology, as they do in society, as an acknowledged (albeit largely invisible) group. For example, Deetz (1991: 6) mentioned the poor only indirectly when he noted that historical archaeology focuses on more than just "a small minority of deviant, wealthy, white males." We can infer from this comment that poor men and women can constitute a focus of much historical archaeological research.

While intellectually recognizing their ability to study men and women typically ignored in documentary history, most historical archaeologists have sidestepped any overt study of poverty. They have accomplished this avoidance in two ways: either by examining impoverished peoples first and foremost as members of cultures (the culturalogical position), or by hiding poverty

as a "socioeconomic status" (the sociological position). The way in which archaeologists have used these two approaches can be easily demonstrated by reference to the archaeology of African Americans, one of the peoples often considered "inarticulate."

When Charles Fairbanks (1983) first decided to conduct archaeological research at African American slave sites in coastal Georgia and Florida, his interest largely mirrored that of general American anthropology. His main concern was to augment knowledge about the cultural lives of slaves by employing the archaeological findings as a contribution "to defining the total picture of black lifeways in America" (Fairbanks 1983: 22). Fairbanks' vision was prescient because future archaeologists would provide a wealth of new information about the entire range of African American slave life (also see Fairbanks 1984). His ideas, coming as they did in the politically turbulent late 1960s, were voiced at an opportune time, and the archaeology of African Americans quickly expanded.

Surprisingly, however, few studies of slave life have explicitly mentioned poverty. Archaeologists usually portray slaves first and foremost as members of cultures and ethnic groups. Historical archaeologists thus began by seeking to identify the material markers of the slaves' ethnicity, searching for African survivals in the archaeological deposits where slaves had lived. The researchers' logic was simple. African slaves crossing to the New World brought their cultural knowledge with them, and when they made physical things in their new environments they generally made them using the techniques and designs that were consistent with their homeland's cultural rules. Using this logic as a base, it was reasonable for archaeologists to imagine that they could identify the markers of ethnic peoplehood in excavated material culture.

Archaeologists soon learned, however, that the discovery of Africanisms was a difficult task because the cultures created in the New World had not existed in isolation.

Instead, they were creolized blends of elements from Africa, the Native New World, and Europe (see Dawdy 2000). Before this realization, many archaeologists established stereotypic links between artefacts and ethnic groups: Irish men and women smoked pipes decorated with harps, while Chinese immigrants used opium pipes. Such facile interpretations have not been entirely expunged from archaeology, even though several historical archaeologists have adopted much more sophisticated perspectives. Archaeologists using more complex cultural models understand that men and women can use material culture to manipulate the social order, while also promoting a sense of peoplehood among themselves (e.g., Praetzellis 1991; Staski 1993; Mullins 1999).

In most studies of enslaved African American ethnicity, we obtain an intuitive notion that the people under investigation were poor, but their economic condition is seldom in the foreground. We learn instead that the people were culturally rich; that they were able to survive and to build vibrant, living cultures from the wreckage of human bondage. We understand poverty as an inherent condition of their enslavement, and we are asked to focus on their achievements in spite of it. This understanding comes through clearly in Deetz's (1977: 154) brief examination of the Parting Ways settlement in New England, in which he portrays the African Americans who lived there as "bearers of a lifestyle, distinctively their own" rather than as "simple folk living in abject poverty." Deetz's culturalogical treatment elevates these individuals in our minds from the realm of poor, disadvantaged members of a hierarchical, racially based social system to people who struggled to carry on their cultural traditions in the face of poverty, cruelty, and enslavement. Poverty is epiphenomenal to culture; it gets in the way, but does not inhibit it.

In terms of African American archaeology, the sociological position has come closest to confronting poverty. The position is best exemplified in the oft-cited but much

misunderstood research of John Solomon Otto (1977, 1980, 1984). Otto devised three social "statuses" to relate the material culture of plantation sites with past social conditions. A "racial/legal status" separated plantation inhabitants on the basis of skin color. Planters and overseers were in a free white class, while African American slaves were in an unfree black class. A "social status" separated people on the basis of occupation. Planters as managers, overseers as supervisors, and slaves as workers were each in different classes. Finally, an "elite/subordinate status" separated people on the basis of their power within the plantation regime. Planters, as members of the elite, were at the top of the hierarchy, while overseers and slaves, as subordinates, were at the bottom (Otto 1980: 8).

The theoretical foundation for much of Otto's analysis was rooted in the idea that on any large plantation one could reasonably expect to find wealthy planters, working managers, and the laboring enslaved all living side by side. For Otto, it was only logical to conclude that archaeologists could discern the distinctions between the material culture of these three social groups. Poverty did not figure in his study in any significant way, however. The central issue for him was simple social inequality: white vs. black, managers vs. supervisors, managers vs. workers, and elites vs. subordinates. His interest was in "socioeconomic status" as something that could account for the material inequalities found at the homes of plantation owners, overseers, and slaves.

The apparent logic of Otto's analysis undoubtedly accounts for its wide acceptance (but see Orser 1988). But by abandoning the spatial confines of the antebellum, southern plantation, we can discern its conceptual problem.

In 1943, Adelaide and Ripley Bullen (1945) excavated a homesite in Andover, Massachusetts, that had been inhabited by a freed slave named Lucy Foster, who died in 1845 at the age of 88. Several years after the Bullens' pioneering excavation, Vernon

Baker (1978, 1980) analyzed the ceramics from the Foster site. In addition to describing the pieces owned and used by a freed African American slave, Baker (1980: 29) hoped to illuminate "patterns of material culture distinctive of Afro-American behavior." In other words, he wanted to identify those elements of the ceramic collection that were indicative of African American ethnicity. To make this culturalogical determination, Baker compared the ceramics from Foster's home with those excavated from Otto's slave cabin and from Deetz's Parting Ways site. When his analysis was completed, however, Baker (1980: 35) faced an unforeseen problem: he could not determine whether the artefacts reflected poverty or ethnicity. Thus stymied, Baker stated that an answer could be devised only after the excavation of a number of sites inhabited by poor whites. Baker began his analysis hoping to discover the material aspects of African American life as they were reflected in ceramics, but ended wondering whether poverty was more important than cultural expression. Bullen (1970: 128) had expressed the same attitude in an earlier paper when he noted that Foster, "although she was a person of low status, possessed a large collection of ceramic materials, much larger than might be expected." Assuming that a poor person could not command many ceramics, he reasoned that she had probably obtained cast-off pieces from her employers as handouts. He concluded: "the assessment of a person's social or economic status by the items found in their cellar hole or well must be done discretely" (Bullen 1970: 128).

The connection between economics and ethnicity was addressed most directly by several archaeologists in the late 1980s and early 1990s. Subsuming their research under the rubric of consumer choice studies, these scholars attempted to discern the subtlest of differences within artefact collections as a clue to understanding the socioeconomic positions of their owners (Klein and LeeDecker 1991; Spencer-Wood 1987). The idea behind this research seemed reason-able because it only made sense that men and women would purchase objects that both appealed to them and were affordable. The same economic decisions are repeatedly played out every day in every capitalist society around the world, and it is a process that archaeologists personally understand quite well. The efforts of the consumer-choice archaeologists began with great promise, but they have been less than successful in their overall research program, and most of them have not been able to progress beyond Baker and Bullen. The complexities inherent in correlating material culture with poverty were explicitly expressed by two archaeologists who were asked to comment on consumer-choice research: "the poor are often not poor in their own eyes, and may also be despised in the eyes of the rich. They are often also an ethnic group, that is, they are not only different, they are sometimes thought of as profoundly other. And the otherness can be an escape as well as a source of integrity amidst exploitation" (Leone and Crosby 1987: 405).

The issue of whether material culture reflects class, ethnic affiliation, or some complex combination has been an expanding topic in historical archaeology since the 1980s and it will surely continue to grow in importance over the next several years. Any kind of concrete understanding, however, is only further complicated by the introduction of race, one of the most complex, albeit most important, issues now facing historical archaeology (see Orser 2001).

Until now, most historical archaeologists have been willing to accept the widely held though incorrect conception that race equals ethnicity. This facile conception of race has made it possible for politically conservative historical archaeologists to downplay or even to ignore race and racism as a means of creating and upholding the social inequalities in capitalist societies. In the United States, for example, politically conservative scholars have sought to prove that the nation is race-blind. Regrettably, in keeping with this trend, race perception, though a major contributor to inequality, has been largely excluded from historical archaeological research (Orser and Fagan 1995: 213–19). But race and poverty are inexorably linked in the kinds of sociohistorical contexts typically studied by historical archaeologists, and this linkage can no longer be ignored.

Linking Poverty and Race: A Major Challenge for Historical Archaeology

Poverty is a complex issue, but scholars typically agree that economic deprivation figures prominently among its major characteristics (Citro and Michael 1995: 19; Sen 1982: 22). The idea that poverty is linked to the consumption of tangible goods and services has obvious relevance to historical archaeological research because, with growing frequency the nearer one comes to our own time, most of the artefacts excavated at post-Columbian sites around the world were once commodities produced as part of a capitalist exchange system. Examples of large-scale commodity manufacture can be found among ancient empire-states, but only after the rise of the Ming dynasty in China in 1368 did large numbers of men and women have the opportunity to purchase objects manufactured in faraway places (but see Frank and Gills 1993). Within this global network of commerce, commodities that were once out of reach soon became "objects of desire" for the masses (Forty 1986: 6–10).

Stating that poverty refers to economic deprivation makes it abundantly clear why many archaeologists may hesitate to examine the poor: after all, archaeology is at least on some level about things. Given the high cost of excavation, archaeologists generally avoid investigating places where they suspect they will find little or nothing in the way of material culture. Using this practical logic, the argument against the archaeology of poverty seems straightforward: since the poor in all capitalist societies suffer economic deprivation, we can assume that they could

not have been able to purchase large numbers of tangible commodities. As a result, the argument goes, the archaeology of their homesites should contain little in the way of material culture. The excavation of sites known to have been inhabited by economically disadvantaged men and women thus seems intellectually risky.

The logic of this argument seems unassailable. Still, archaeology has progressed far beyond the simple search for artefacts, no matter how important objects from the past continue to be in all archaeological interpretation. And surprisingly, archaeology conducted at sites where the inhabitants were known to have been economically deprived has produced artefacts, often in large numbers. For example, the Bullens recovered fragments from 113 individual ceramic vessels from Lucy Foster's homesite (Baker 1978: 109), and Otto (1977: 115) found the remains of 80 tableware vessels in a slave cabin at Cannon's Point Plantation. It is thus clear that the correlation between the presence of artefacts and poverty defies easy, universal interpretation.

Any understanding of poverty becomes increasingly complicated when we introduce race. The complex, mutable relationship between race and consumerism presents a major challenge to today's historical archaeology. One of the most concise statements about the linkage between race and economics was voiced by heavyweight boxing champion Larry Holmes: "I was black once – when I was poor" (Oates 1987: 62). Holmes' comment suggests the complexities of race in living populations, and obliquely implies that the interpretive problems expand exponentially when we think about race in archaeological terms. It seems only reasonable, then, that any kind of archaeological search for "racial markers" would be as intellectually unsatisfying as the search for "ethnic markers." Historical archaeologists must acknowledge the importance of the intersections of race and class, and be prepared to interpret the material manifestations of these interactions at the sites they study. This kind of interpretation represents a major challenge to all archaeologists who investigate post-Columbian history (see also Orser 1998b).

Another Challenge for Today's Historical Archaeologists: Creating a Global Historical Archaeology

When historical archaeologists examine important elements of post-Columbian social history – such as dispossession, racism, gender relations, and class designation – they must constantly remind themselves that they are investigating elements of the modern world, or in other words, their world. Operationalizing this realization has the potential to lead to the development of a new kind of historical archaeological practice, an archaeology that may be termed "global historical archaeology" (Orser 1996) or "modern-world archaeology" (Orser 1999). Globalization is not only extremely interesting from a purely intellectual standpoint, but also many scholars consider it to be centrally important to understanding the realities of today's world. Archaeology has an important role to play in the developing discourse about globalization by illustrating the material dimensions and historical antecedents of some of today's most pressing problems.

Modern-world archaeology has two overarching perspectives and four central characteristics. Each one of these elements, when taken together, sets this kind of archaeology apart from all other historical archaeologies, no matter how they are defined. The two overarching perspectives of modern-world archaeology are: (1) that it focuses on a particular subject, the process of modernization or globalization, and (2) that it presents a particular way of thinking about its temporal and spatial focus. The four central characteristics of this archaeology are that it is (1) mutualistic, (2) globally focused, (3) multi-scalar, and (4) reflexive.

Modern-world archaeology unabashedly studies the process of becoming modern, or to put it another way, the spread of globalization. For many observers, the rising tide of globalization represents humanity's greatest challenge to date (McMurtry 1998; Mander and Goldsmith 1996). As raw materials disappear, as once-pristine environments give way to industrial plants and sprawling ranches, and as the world's population continues to grow, humanity will be faced with many serious choices. Modern-world archaeology recognizes the importance of globalization and seeks to examine its historical and material roots. One way to examine these roots is through the linked processes of colonialism, Eurocentrism, capitalism, and modernity (Orser 1996: 57–88). Each one of these historical features has a direct bearing, to different degrees and in different ways depending upon sociohistorical context, on the men and women who lived during the past 650 years. Within this perspective, the "modern world" is the time when colonialism, Eurocentrism, capitalism, and modernity all came together. The precise beginning of the modern world need never be concretely associated with a date, but the final culmination of the process is the "full world," that time when the globe has reached its maximum limit of environmental exploitation, population growth, and market expansion (Korten 1996: 23). Part of the goal of modern-world archaeology is to provide localized (micro) historical and cultural information about the process of globalization (macro), illustrating and interpreting its material dimensions.

The second overarching perspective of modern-world archaeology involves time and space. Many historical archaeologists have attempted to establish the relevance of their research projects by consciously linking past and present. They hope to demonstrate through this course of action that archaeology has importance to living men and women. Modern-world archaeologists must think differently. Instead of looking from past to present, modern-world archaeologists must explicitly engage in multiple temporalizations and spatializations. Examining an archaeological site that dates, for example, from 1600 to 1650, the modern-world archaeologist must confront a bidirectional history that looks backward in time from 1600 and forward in time from 1650. At the same time, the modern-world archaeologist must be prepared to perceive the space beyond the artificial boundaries of the site itself. He or she must be willing to engage the idea that the site's inhabitants operationalized a diverse, intersecting network of connections, each one with a potentially wider spatiality. This referential modification is more than a semantic convention, because it serves to empower modern-world archaeology as a fore-grounded subject, rather than simply as an archaeological study appended to prehistory.

When history is viewed bidirectionally the initial limit of modern-world archaeology appears indistinct. On the near side, it always exists within our own time, a time loosely referred to as "today." On the other side, the end-point of the subject matter of modern-world archaeology is unknown. It is unsatisfying to argue that modern-world archaeology should employ the Eurocentric beginning date of 1492 or even 1415, the date the Portuguese reoccupied Ceuta on the African mainland. World history has far too many unique, local manifestations to permit such a fixed artificiality. The aim of modern-world archaeology is thus not to take a subject like urbanization and to show how it bridges history, but rather to examine the key, site-specific conditions of urbanization and to show its historical antecedents and descendants. The goal is not to establish the central features of urbanization through time as a theoretical construct, but to demonstrate how concrete urban centers, with their unique problems and solutions, developed as they did. The modern-world archaeologist, engaged in such an analysis, must investigate, at a minimum, the local and global environments within which the site's inhabitants are enmeshed.

Mutualism provides a conceptual base for modern-world archaeology. Mutualism holds that the social relationships men and women create and maintain throughout their lifetimes are "the basic stuff of human life" (Carrithers 1992: 11). As an idea, mutualism is deeply rooted within the history of anthropological thought (e.g., see Lesser 1961; Radcliffe-Brown 1940: 3; Wolf 1982, 1984). Modern-world archaeology is thus based on a social-structural understanding of human networks of interaction and association, and constitutes a kind of social archaeology.

Proposing that modern-world archaeology is globally focused means that its practitioners must be constantly aware of the links a site's inhabitants had with the outside world, however that world is defined. This perspective is particularly challenging to archaeologists because rarely can an archaeologist excavate more than one site at a time. Modern-world archaeology rejects the view that historical archaeologists must restrict themselves to the study of single sites only. The interconnectedness of the world is one of the hallmarks of globalization, and to ignore it in the exclusive name of site-specific study ignores the realities of modern history. In many cases, the transnational connections that are being pressed around the world today have antecedents in the earliest days of multicultural, global expansion, and they are worthy of serious archaeological consideration in their own right (Frank 1998).

Mutualism does not mean, however, that all links are transnational or global in scope. On the contrary, mutualism holds that human connections are multiscalar, existing on successive levels. By adopting a multiscalar approach, archaeologists can strive to interpret the complexity of the connections in local, regional, national, and even international terms. To effect this kind of investigation, archaeologists must remember that men and women create social relations across various slices of space and through diverse segments of time. The basis of this understanding is rooted in the idea that men and women "comprehend patterns, recognize homogeneity, plan for the future, and operate in the present at specific scales" (Marquardt 1992: 107). The job of the modern-world archaeologist is to find the effective scales (after Crumley 1979: 166) at which they can observe interpretable patterned regularity, acknowledging all the while that they may contradict the findings at one level with those from another level. Multiscalar research also allows archaeologists to redefine their notion of the geographic region and recognize that in global history, any particular region may effectively cross natural boundaries and encompass many diverse peoples (see Orser 1996: 139–140).

Reflexivity, one of the key elements of modern-world archaeology, includes the idea that archaeologists can provide useful and important information to living men and women (Shanks and Tilley 1987: 66). This proposition is particularly meaningful to modern-world archaeology because archaeologists of globalization have a responsibility to make their research relevant beyond the narrow confines of their own discipline. In these days of shrinking funds and increased destruction of archaeological sites, it becomes even more imperative for archaeologists to demonstrate the societal significance of their research. Professional bureaucrats responsible for distributing funds are unlikely to be swayed by the timeworn knowledge-for-knowledge's-sake argument. This assertion is not meant to suggest by any means that pure, scholarly research is unimportant or that archaeologists should abandon it. On the contrary, we only suggest that modern-world archaeology is difficult to ignore because it holds societal relevance as a primary tenet, even though its goals are consistent with committed scholarship.

The ability to stress the importance of archaeological research begins with the archaeologist's own self-reflection. Self-reflection empowers archaeologists to think about their research in contemporary terms and to understand that their interpretations can impact large numbers of non-archaeologists (Biolsi and Zimmerman 1997; Leone et al. 1995; Mackenzie and Shanks 1994; Potter 1991, 1994; Swidler et al. 1997). One goal of reflexivity is to make it impossible for non-archaeologists to push archaeology aside as trivial. Without question, "every society is a battlefield between its own past and its future" (Wolf 1959: 106), and modern-world archaeology demands a place in the front lines of this intellectual field of battle.

Conclusion

The archaeology of history is an exciting area of focus within archaeology, and the field will undoubtedly grow over the next several years. Numerous scholars around the globe are already beginning to engage the archaeology of the past 650 years (e.g., DeCorse 2001; Funari et al. 1999; Wesler 1998). No one knows, of course, precisely where the future of archaeology will lead in this rapidly changing world, but the archaeology of recent history holds tremendous promise. Creative scholars will unquestionably continue to make advances in effecting transdisciplinary approaches to the past, just as they will provide new information about the material culture of the modern world. At the same time, historical archaeologists will offer new information about the lives of men and women silenced too long by history's official scribes and documentarians. These silenced people will include both the "poor" and the "middle class" (e.g., see Wurst and Fitts 1999).

Historical archaeologists have much to offer both to archaeology and to the world beyond archaeology. Many archaeologists are only now beginning to appreciate the true potential of their field to investigate recent history. An exciting and intellectually rewarding future lies ahead for historical, post-medieval, and modern-world archaeologists. It may not be hyperbole to state that generations yet unborn may well judge today's archaeology by what its practitioners have had to say about our recently created, historical world and how we sought to establish and to explain our place within it.

References

Andrén, A. 1998. *Between Artifacts and Texts: Historical Archaeology in Global Perspective.* New York: Plenum.

Anonymous 1967. "Institutions." *Current Anthropology,* 8: 509.

Anonymous 1968. "Editorial." *Post-Medieval Archaeology,* 1: 1–2.

Ascher, R. 1974. "Tin can archaeology." *Historical Archaeology,* 8: 7–16.

Baker, V. G. 1978. *Historical Archaeology at Black Lucy's Garden, Andover, Massachusetts: Ceramics from the Site of a Nineteenth Century Afro-American.* Andover, MA: Phillips Academy.

Baker, V. G. 1980. "Archaeological visibility of Afro-American culture: an example from Black Lucy's garden, Andover, Massachusetts." In R. L. Schuyler (ed.), *Archaeological Perspectives on Ethnicity in America: Afro-American and Asian American Culture History,* pp. 29–37. Farmingdale, NY: Baywood.

Barton, K. J. 1968. "Origins of the Society for Post-Medieval Archaeology." *Post-Medieval Archaeology,* 1: 102–3.

Beard, C. A. 1934. "Written history as an act of faith." *American Historical Review,* 39: 219–29.

Beaudry, M. C. (ed.) 1988. *Documentary Archaeology in the New World.* Cambridge: Cambridge University Press.

Beaudry, M. C., L. J. Cook, and S. A. Mrozowski 1991. "Artifacts and active voices: material culture as social discourse." In R. H. McGuire and R. Paynter (eds.), *The Archaeology of Inequality,* pp. 150–91. Oxford: Blackwell.

Becker, C. 1955. "What are historical facts?" *Western Political Quarterly,* 8: 327–40.

Binford, L. R. 1977. "Historical archaeology: is it historical or archaeological?" In L. Ferguson (ed.), *Historical Archaeology and the Importance of Material Things,* pp.13–22. Tucson: Society for Historical Archaeology.

Biolsi, T. and L. Zimmerman (eds.) 1997. *Indians and Anthropologists: Vine Deloria, Jr. and the Critique of Anthropology.* Tucson: University of Arizona Press.

Bullen, A. K. and R. P. Bullen 1945. "Black Lucy's garden." *Bulletin of the Massachusetts Archaeological Society,* 6 (2): 17–28.

Bullen, R. P. 1970. "Comments on Garry W. Stone's paper: 'Ceramics in Suffolk County, Mass., inventories, 1680–1775.' " *The Conference on Historic Site Archaeology Papers,* 3: 127–8.

Carrithers, M. 1992. *Why Humans Have Cultures: Explaining Anthropology and Cultural Diversity.* Oxford: Oxford University Press.

Champion, T. 1990. "Medieval archaeology and the tyranny of the historical record." In D. Austin and L. Alcock (eds.), *From the Baltic to the Black Sea: Studies in Medieval Archaeology,* pp. 79–95. London: Unwin Hyman.

Childe, V. G. 1947. *History.* London: Cobbett.

Citro, C. F. and R. T. Michael (eds.) 1995. *Measuring Poverty: A New Approach.* Washington, DC: National Academy Press.

Croce, B. 1921. *Theory and History of Historiography.* Trans. D. Ainslie. London: George G. Harrap.

Crossley, D. 1990. *Post-Medieval Archaeology in Britain.* Leicester: Leicester University Press.

Crumley, C. L. 1979. "Three locational models." In M. B. Schiffer (ed.), *Archaeological Method and Theory,* vol. 2, pp. 141–73. New York: Academic Press.

Cultural Artifacts Administration (of Guangzhou and the Archaeological Specialty, Zhougshan University) 1985. "A test excavation of the remains of a Qin-Han boat yard in Guangzhou."

In A. E. Dien, J. K. Riegel, and N. T. Price (eds.), *Chinese Archaeological Abstract, 3: Eastern Zhou to Han*, pp. 971–9. Los Angeles: Institute of Archaeology, University of California.

Dawdy, S. L. (ed.) 2000. "Creolization." *Historical Archaeology*, 34 (3): 1–133.

Deagan, K. 1982. "Avenues of inquiry in historical archaeology." In M. B. Schiffer (ed.), *Advances in Archaeological Method and Theory*, vol. 5, pp. 151–77. New York: Academic Press.

DeCorse, C. R. (ed.) 2001. *West Africa During the Atlantic Slave Trade: Archaeological Perspectives*. Leicester: Leicester University Press.

Deetz, J. 1977. *In Small Things Forgotten: The Archaeology of Early American Life*. Garden City, NY: Anchor Press/Doubleday.

Deetz, J. 1991. "Introduction: archaeological evidence and sixteenth-and seventeenth-century encounters." In L. Falk (ed.), *Global Historical Archaeology Perspective*, pp. 1–9. Washington, DC: Smithsonian Institution Press.

Dhavalikar, M. K. 1999. *Historical Archaeology in India*. New Delhi: Books and Books.

Fabian, J. 1983. *Time and the Other: How Anthropology Makes its Object*. New York: Columbia University Press.

Fairbanks, C. H. 1983. "Historical archaeological implications of recent investigations." *Geoscience and Man*, 23: 17–26.

Fairbanks, C. H. 1984. "The plantation archaeology of the southeastern coast." *Historical Archaeology*, 18 (l): 1–14.

Feder, K. L. 1994. *A Village of Outcasts: Historical Archaeology and Documentary Research at the Lighthouse Site*. Mountain View, CA: Mayfield.

Feinman, G. M. 1997. "Thoughts on new approaches to combining the archaeological and historical records." *Journal of Archaeological Method and Theory*, 4: 367–77.

Ferguson, L. 1992. *Uncommon Ground: Archaeology and Early African America, 1650–1800*. Washington, DC: Smithsonian Institution Press.

FitzGerald, P. 1978. *Ancient China*. Oxford: Elsevier-Phaidon.

Forty. A. 1986. *Objects of Desire: Design and Society, 1750–1980*. London: Thames and Hudson.

Frank, A. G. 1998. *ReOrient: Global Economy in the Asian Age*. Berkeley: University of California Press.

Frank, A. G. and B. K. Gills (eds.) 1993. *The World System: Five Hundred Years or Five Thousand?* London: Routledge.

Funari, P. P. A., M. Hall, and S. Jones (eds.) 1999. *Historical Archaeology: Back from the Edge*. London: Routledge.

Gaimster, D. 1994. "The archaeology of post-medieval society, c. 1450–1750: material culture studies in Britain since the war." In B. Vyner (ed.), *Building on the Past: Papers Celebrating 150 Years of the Royal Archaeological Institute*, pp. 283–312. London: Royal Archaeological Institute.

Gernet, J. 1982. *A History of Chinese Civilization*. Trans. J. R. Foster. Cambridge: Cambridge University Press.

Hall, M. 1992. "Small things and the mobile, conflictual fusion of power, fear, and desire." In A. E. Yentsch and M. C. Beaudry (eds.), *The Art and Mystery of Historical Archaeology: Essays in Honor of James Deetz*, pp. 373–99. Boca Raton, FL: CRC Press.

Harrington, J. C. 1994. "From architraves to artifacts: a metamorphosis." In S. South (ed.), *Pioneers in Historical Archaeology*, pp. 1–14. New York: Plenum.

Hazeltine, H. G., G. Lapsley, and P. H. Winfield (eds.) 1936. *Maitland: Selected Essays*. Cambridge: Cambridge University Press.

Hodder, I. 1986. *Reading the Past: Current Approaches to Interpretation in Archaeology.* Cambridge: Cambridge University Press.

Hogarth, D. G. 1899. "Prefatory." In D. G. Hogarth (ed.), *Authority and Archaeology, Sacred and Profane: Essays on the Relation of Monuments to Biblical and Classical Literature,* pp. v–xiv. London: John Murray.

Kepecs, S. 1997. "Introduction to new approaches to combining the archaeological and historical records." *Journal of Archaeological Method and Theory,* 4: 193–8.

Klein, T. H. and C. H. LeeDecker (eds.) 1991. "Models for the study of consumer behavior." *Historical Archaeology,* 25 (2): 1–91.

Korten, D. C. 1996. "The failures of Bretton Woods." In J. Mander and E. Goldsmith (eds.), *The Case Against the Global Economy and for a Turn Toward the Local,* pp. 20–30. San Francisco: Sierra Club Books.

Kroeber, A. L. 1935. "History and science in anthropology." *American Anthropologist,* 37: 539–69.

Leone, M. P. 1984. "Interpreting ideology in historical archaeology: using the rules of perspective in the William Paca garden, Annapolis, Maryland." In D. Miller and C. Tilley (eds.), *Ideology, Power, and Prehistory,* pp. 25–35. Cambridge: Cambridge University Press.

Leone, M. P. and C. A. Crosby 1987. "Epilogue: middle range theory in historical archaeology." In S. M. Spencer-Wood (ed.), *Consumer Choice in Historical Archaeology,* pp. 397–410. New York: Plenum.

Leone, M. P., P. R. Mullins, M. C. Creveling, L. Hurst, B. Jackson-Nash, L. D. Jones, G. Kaiser, C. Logan, and M. S. Warner 1995. "Can an African-American historical archaeology be an alternative voice?" In I. Hodder, M. Shanks, A. Alexandri, V. Buchli, J. Carman, J. Last, and G. Lucas (eds.), *Interpreting Archaeology,* pp. 110–24. London: Routledge.

Lesser, A. 1961. "Social fields and the evolution of society." *Southwestern Journal of Anthropology,* 17: 40–8.

Lightfoot, K. G. 1995. "Culture contact studies: redefining the relationship between prehistoric and historical archaeology." *American Antiquity,* 60: 199–217.

Little, B. J. (ed.) 1992. *Text-Aided Archaeology.* Boca Raton, FL: CRC Press.

Mackenzie, I. M. and M. Shanks 1994. "Archaeology: theories, themes, and experiences, a dialogue between Iain Mackenzie and Michael Shanks." In I. M. Mackenzie (ed.), *Archaeological Theory: Progress or Posture?* pp. 19–40. Aldershot: Avebury.

McMurtry, J. 1998. *Unequal Freedoms: The Global Market as an Ethical System.* Toronto: Garamond Press.

Mander, J. and E. Goldsmith (eds.) 1996. *The Case Against the Global Economy and for a Turn Toward the Local.* San Francisco: Sierra Club Books.

Marquardt, W. H. 1992. "Dialectical archaeology." In M. B. Schiffer (ed.), *Archaeological Method and Theory,* vol. 4, pp. 101–40. Tucson: University of Arizona Press.

Mayne, A. and T. Murray (eds.) 2001. *The Archaeology of Urban Landscapes: Explorations in Slumland.* Cambridge: Cambridge University Press.

Mullins, P. R. 1999. *Race and Affluence: An Archaeology of African America and Consumer Culture.* New York: Kluwer Academic/Plenum.

Oates, J. C. 1987. *On Boxing.* Garden City, NY: Dolphin/Doubleday.

Orser, C. E., Jr. 1988. "The archaeological analysis of plantation society: replacing status and caste with economics and power." *American Antiquity,* 53: 735–51.

Orser, C. E., Jr. 1990. "Archaeological approaches to New World plantation slavery." In M. B. Schiffer (ed.), *Archaeological Method and Theory,* vol. 2, pp. 111–54. Tucson: University of Arizona Press.

Orser, C. E., Jr. 1994. "The archaeology of African-American slave religion in the antebellum South." *Cambridge Archaeological Journal*, 4: 33–45.

Orser, C. E., Jr. 1996. *A Historical Archaeology of the Modern World*. New York: Plenum.

Orser, C. E., Jr. 1998a. "Archaeology of the African diaspora." *Annual Review of Anthropology*, 27: 63–82.

Orser, C. E., Jr. 1998b. "The challenge of race to American historical archaeology." *American Anthropologist*, 100: 661–8.

Orser, C. E., Jr. 1999. "Negotiating our 'familiar' pasts." In S. Tarlow and S. West (eds.), *The Familiar Past? Archaeologies of Later Historical Britain*, pp. 273–85. London: Routledge.

Orser, C. E., Jr. (ed.) 2001. *Race and the Archaeology of Identity*. Salt Lake City: University of Utah Press.

Orser, C. E., Jr. and B. M. Fagan 1995. *Historical Archaeology*. New York: Harper Collins.

Otto, J. S. 1977. "Artifacts and status differences: a comparison of ceramics from planter, overseer, and slaves sites on an antebellum plantation." In S. South (ed.), *Research Strategies in Historical Archaeology*, pp. 91–118. New York: Academic Press.

Otto, J. S. 1980. "Race and class on antebellum plantations." In R. L. Schuyler (ed.), *Archaeological Perspectives on Ethnicity in America: Afro-American and Asian American Culture History*, pp. 3–13. Farmingdale, NY: Baywood.

Otto, J. S. 1984. *Cannon's Point Plantation, 1794–1860: Living Conditions and Status Patterns in the Old South*. Orlando, FL: Academic Press.

Pilling, A. R. 1967. "Beginnings." *Historical Archaeology*, 1: 1–22.

Potter, P. B., Jr. 1991. "Self-reflection in archaeology." In R. W. Preucel (ed.), *Processual and Postprocessual Archaeologies: Multiple Ways of Knowing the Past*, pp. 225–34. Carbondale: Center for Archaeological Investigations, Southern Illinois University.

Potter, P. B., Jr. 1994. *Public Archaeology in Annapolis: A Critical Approach to History in Maryland's Ancient City*. Washington, DC: Smithsonian Institution Press.

Praetzellis, A. C. 1991. "The archaeology of a Victorian city: Sacramento, California." Unpublished doctoral dissertation, University of California, Berkeley.

Radcliffe-Brown, A. R. 1940. "On social structure." *Journal of the Royal Anthropological Society of Great Britain and Ireland*, 70: 1–12.

Sen, A. 1982. *Poverty and Famines: An Essay on Entitlement and Deprivation*. Oxford: Clarendon Press.

Shanks, M. and C. Tilley 1987. *Re-Constructing Archaeology*. Cambridge: Cambridge University Press.

Sharer, R. J. and W. Ashmore 2003. *Archaeology: Discovering Our Past*, 3rd edn. Boston: McGraw-Hill.

South, S. 1964. "Preface." *Florida Anthropologist*, 17 (2): 34.

South, S. (ed.) 1967. *The Conference on Historic Site Archaeology Papers*, vol. 1. Columbia, SC: Conference on Historic Site Archaeology.

South, S. 1977. *Method and Theory in Historical Archaeology*. New York: Academic Press.

Spencer-Wood, S. M. (ed.) 1987. *Consumer Choice in Historical Archaeology*. New York: Plenum.

Staski, E. 1993. "The overseas Chinese in El Paso: changing goals, changing realities." In P. Wegars (ed.), *Hidden Heritage: Historical Archaeology of the Overseas Chinese*, pp. 125–49. Amityville, NY: Baywood.

Swidler, N., K. E. Dongoske, R. Anyon, and A. S. Downer (eds.) 1997. *Native Americans and Archaeologists: Stepping Stones to Common Ground*. Walnut Creek, CA: AltaMira.

Taylor, W. W. 1948. *A Study of Archaeology*. Washington, DC: American Anthropological Association.

Wesler, K. W. 1998. *Historical Archaeology in Nigeria*. Trenton, NJ: Africa World Press.

Willey, G. R. and P. Phillips 1958. *Method and Theory in American Archaeology*. Chicago: University of Chicago Press.

Wolf, E. 1959. *Sons of the Shaking Earth*. Chicago: University of Chicago Press.

Wolf, E. 1982. *Europe and the People Without History*. Berkeley: University of California Press.

Wolf, E. 1984. "Culture: panacea or problem?" *American Antiquity*, 49: 393–400.

Wurst, L. and R. K. Fitts (eds.) 1999. "Confronting class." *Historical Archaeology*, 33 (1): 1–195.

Xia Nai 1985. "Chinese archaeology during the past thirty years." In A. E. Dien, J. K. Riegel, and N. T. Price (eds.), *Chinese Archaeological Abstracts, 2: Prehistoric to Western Zhou*, pp. 1–3. Los Angeles: Institute of Archaeology, University of California.

Further Reading

Australasian Historical Archaeology. Sydney: Australasian Society for Historical Archaeology.

Barber, R. J. 1994. *Doing Historical Archaeology: Exercises Using Documentary, Oral and Material Evidence*. Englewood Cliffs, NJ: Prentice-Hall.

Connah, G. 1993. *The Archaeology of Australia's History*. Cambridge: Cambridge University Press.

De Cunzo, L. A. and B. L. Herman (eds.) 1996. *Historical Archaeology and the Study of American Culture*. Winterthur, DE: Henry Francis du Pont Winterthur Museum.

Falk, L. (ed.) 1991. *Historical Archaeology in Global Perspective*. Washington, DC: Smithsonian Institution Press.

Fitzhugh, W. W. and J. S. Olin (eds.) 1993. *Archaeology of the Frobisher Voyages*. Washington, DC: Smithsonian Institution Press.

Geier, C. R., Jr. and S. E. Winter (eds.) 1994. *Look to the Earth: Historical Archaeology and the American Civil War*. Knoxville: University of Tennessee Press.

Gibb, J. G. 1996. *The Archaeology of Wealth: Consumer Behavior in English America*. New York: Plenum.

Hall, M. and A. Markell (eds.) 1993. "Historical archaeology in the Western Cape." *South African Archaeological Society Goodwin Series*, 7: 3–7, 55.

Historical Archaeology. Tucson: Society for Historical Archaeology.

International Journal of Historical Archaeology. New York: Plenum.

Johnson, M. 1996. *An Archaeology of Capitalism*. Oxford: Blackwell.

Leone, M. P. and P. B. Potter, Jr. (eds.) 1988. *The Recovery of Meaning: Historical Archaeology in the Eastern United States*. Washington, DC: Smithsonian Institution Press.

Leone, M. P. and P. B. Potter, Jr. (eds.) 1999. *Historical Archaeologies of Capitalism*. New York: Kluwer Academic/Plenum.

Leone, M. P. and N. A. Silberman (eds.) 1995. *Invisible America: Unearthing Our Hidden History*. New York: Henry Holt.

McEwan, B. G. 1993. *The Spanish Missions of La Florida*. Gainesville: University Press of Florida.

McGuire, R. H. and R. Paynter (eds.) 1991. *The Archaeology of Inequality*. Oxford: Blackwell.

Noël Hume, I. 1972. *Historical Archaeology*. New York: Alfred A. Knopf.

Noël Hume, I. 1993. *Martin's Hundred: The Discovery of a Lost Colonial Virginia Settlement*. New York: Delta.

Noël Hume, I. 1994. *The Virginia Adventure: Roanoke to James Towne – An Archaeological and Historical Odyssey.* New York: Alfred A. Knopf.

Orr, D. G. and D. G. Crozier (eds.) 1984. *The Scope of Historical Archaeology: Essays in Honor of John L. Cotter.* Philadelphia: Laboratory of Anthropology, Temple University.

Orser, C. E., Jr. (ed.) 1996. "Current perspectives on historical archaeology." *World Archaeological Bulletin,* 7. Southampton: World Archaeological Congress.

Orser, C. E., Jr. (ed.) 1996. *Images of the Recent Past: Readings in Historical Archaeology.* Walnut Creek, CA: AltaMira.

Schavelzon, D. 1991. *Arquelogia Histórica de Buenos Aires, 1: La Cultura, Material Porteña de los Siglos XVIII y XIX.* Buenos Aires: Corregidor.

Schrire, C. 1995. *Digging Through Darkness: Chronicles of an Archaeologist.* Charlottesville: University Press of Virginia.

Schuyler, R. L. (ed.) 1978. *Historical Archaeology: A Guide to Substantive and Theoretical Contributions.* Farmingdale, NY: Baywood Press.

Scott, E. M. 1994. *Those of Little Note: Gender, Race, and Class in Historical Archaeology.* Tucson: University of Arizona Press.

Shackel, P. A. 1993. *Personal Discipline and Material Culture: An Archaeology of Annapolis, Maryland, 1695–1870.* Knoxville: University of Tennessee Press.

Shackel, P. A. 1996. *Culture Change and the New Technology: An Archaeology of the Early American Industrial Era.* New York: Plenum.

Shackel, P. A. and B. J. Little (eds.) 1994. *Historical Archaeology of the Chesapeake.* Washington, DC: Smithsonian Institution Press.

South, S. (ed.) 1977. *Research Strategies in Historical Archaeology.* New York: Academic Press.

South, S. (ed.) 1994. *Pioneers in Historical Archaeology: Breaking New Ground.* New York: Plenum.

Spector, J. D. 1993. *What This Awl Means: Feminist Archaeology at a Wahpeton Dakota Village.* St. Paul: Minnesota Historical Society Press.

Wall, D. diZ. 1994. *The Archaeology of Gender: Separating the Spheres of Urban America.* New York: Plenum.

Yentsch, A. E. and M. C. Beaudry (eds.) 1992. *The Art and Mystery of Historical Archaeology: Essays in Honor of James Deetz.* Boca Raton, FL: CRC Press.

16

Animal Bones and Plant Remains

Peter Rowley-Conwy

Introduction

If you are turning to this chapter without much previous knowledge of archaeology, the chances are that you are doing so out of surprise: what are the remains of animals and plants doing in a book about archaeology? Even if these things do turn up on archaeological sites, aren't they studied by zoologists and botanists rather than archaeologists?

Only a generation ago, most archaeologists would have agreed. Potsherds and stone tools were thought effortlessly to yield up their meanings to archaeologists, while bones and plants had to be studied scientifically by laboratory-based specialists. This dichotomy has largely vanished in the last thirty years or so, as archaeologists have realized that things are not so simple: bones and plants are, like potsherds and stone tools, the products of complex human behavior. The study of stone tools is not geology even though the tools are made of stone. Likewise, studies of bones and plants are not zoology or botany – they are *archaeology* in the truest sense, because they tell us about people. As a result, they are now studied mostly by archaeologists with the necessary skills. The fortunate practitioners can find things out about the past that most other lines of evidence cannot, and they can travel

worldwide to do so. A specialist on (say) the Roman pottery of southeast England is not going to be much use on a Palaeolithic excavation where there is no pottery, nor for that matter on a medieval Japanese site even if it does have pottery. But deer bones look pretty much the same whether they come from the French Palaeolithic or the Japanese medieval period – or from Roman London.

In this chapter I am therefore going to look at a broad selection of results from all periods. The bone and plant specialist contributes a lot more than just a knowledge of what people ate. The arrangements by which different human cultures provided themselves with food are one of the most fundamental factors that determined what those cultures were like – and they are our subject matter. As our methods and ideas improve, so we amend or correct the conclusions of our predecessors, just as surely as our successor will correct ours. A lot of what follows will be a discussion of how conclusions have changed, and how our views of what people did in the past have changed as a result.

The Shape of Things

The study of bones and plants is not rocket science. But it is an organized skill that has its own way of describing and going about things. Figure 16.1 shows the basic layout of a cereal ear and an animal skeleton, with some of the associated nomenclature. A cereal ear consists of a series of spikelets (grains and their enveloping glumes or husks), attached to a segmented stem or rachis. The basic layout of a skeleton is familiar (we each have one, after all), but the distribution of meat is less so: most is on the trunk and upper limbs. This does not mean that the lower limbs are waste, however. Marrow is found inside the tubular leg bones, the metapodials containing some of the best. These are also some of the best bones for making into artefacts, and they carry much useful sinew. *Proximal* describes the upper ends of the leg bones, *distal* the lower ends.

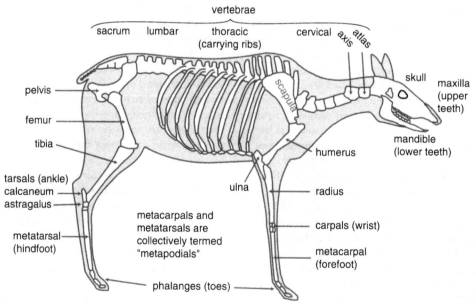

Figure 16.1 Diagrammatic views of a cereal ear and spikelet (top) and an animal skeleton (bottom), showing nomenclature used in the chapter.

Processing plants and animals into food involves their destruction. In wild cereals the rachis breaks into segments naturally when ripe, dispersing the seeds. But domestic cereals do not shatter, and the intact harvested ears must be broken up and the grains separated out before they can be eaten. This is done by threshing, which breaks up the ears; the result is then winnowed, sieved twice to remove larger and smaller waste fragments, and finally searched by hand. Animals are butchered in various ways. A hunter who kills a deer 10 miles from home cannot carry the whole thing back with him, but must decide which bits to take and which to leave; but he can carry a complete rabbit – and a farmer with a domestic sheep can kill it anywhere that suits him. The bones are almost always broken for marrow, so we find the proximal and distal ends separated, and many other fragments; complete animal skeletons are very unusual.

After processing and consumption, bone fragments are dumped. Some will be destroyed by dogs or other causes; a small proportion will become buried as the rubbish accumulates, and (unless soil conditions are too acidic) will survive for the archaeologist to find. Plant remains do not however survive unless they have been burnt and charred (a few dry sites like Tutankhamun's tomb, or wet sites like peat bogs, are the only exceptions). Waste products like glumes or rachis segments may be deliberately thrown on a fire and burnt, but edible grains or pulses are usually only burnt by accident. Every bone thus represents a success – something was eaten; but every grain is a small disaster – something intended to be eaten was destroyed. Two hundred bone fragments from a rubbish midden may well come from 200 different animals, eaten over a period of years; but 200 wheat grains found together were probably all burnt in one accident and represent a single intended meal. The human behaviors behind our samples were thus very different.

Bones and plants have been responsible for some of the major improvements in excav-ation technique. It was realized in the 1960s and 1970s that, contrary to popular myth, the trowel-wielding archaeologist does not spot every object he excavates; many small items are missed. This is bad news for people studying bones because small fragments are missed more often than large ones, so for example sheep bones are missed more often than cow bones. If we are trying to understand the relative importance of cows and sheep, our samples may become skewed during the very act of excavation. Most dig directors put some or all the excavated soil through sieves, which makes smaller items easier to spot – something that archaeologists specializing in small objects like coins or beads have only belatedly come to recognize! Charred cereal grains will hardly even be found by these means, unless a complete grain store has been burnt down and the grains are present in large dense masses. Flotation is now routinely used: the excavated soil is poured into a tank containing water, so the charred grains float to the surface while everything else sinks (Payne 1972; Jarman et al. 1972).

We are now ready to look at some results. Ancient rubbish is our raw material, ancient human behavior our goal.

Early Pioneers

One of the people who first examined animal bones from archaeological sites was the Dane Japetus Steenstrup, one of the more colorful polymaths on the nineteenth-century scene. As a young man he studied peat bogs, and was the first to realize that different forest types had succeeded one another in quite recent times – pine coming before oak, for example. We now recognize these periods as the succession that followed the end of the last ice age, but the existence of continent-wide glaciers was not recognized until after Steenstrup published in 1842. Steenstrup also worked on topics as diverse as flatfish, coral reefs, and giant octopuses, but his peat bogs contained both archaeological finds and animal bones, which he identified by comparing them to modern skeletons in the Zoological Museum in Copenhagen.

He was thus an ideal member of an interdisciplinary team set up in 1848 to examine certain large masses of oyster shells that occur above sea level in various parts of Denmark. These oyster masses were known to contain both animal bones (hence Steenstrup's involvement) and ancient artefacts, so an archaeologist, J. J. A. Worsaae, was also a member. The team's first publication speculated that the shell heaps were natural oyster banks that had grown when sea level was higher, but by 1851 their true nature had become clear: they were the rubbish middens of ancient coastal dwellers who also hunted deer, wild cattle, and wild boar – the only domestic animal present was the dog. Steenstrup recognized that the bones had been butchered by people: there were cut marks inflicted by stone tools, and they had been broken so the marrow could be extracted. He had animal bones from Eskimo rubbish middens in Greenland sent to him, and saw that his Danish examples had been processed in exactly the same way.

The results were presented by Steenstrup (1851), but both Steenstrup and Worsaae claimed priority in realizing the true nature of these "shell middens." Animosity flared between the two men. When Worsaae claimed that the Stone Age comprised two distinct periods (Worsaae 1860), Steenstrup refused to accept it and the two men wrote a series of articles disagreeing with each other. But Worsaae was right: his Later Stone Age we now call the Neolithic, and it was soon established that people had by then domesticated sheep, cattle, and pigs.

At the same time, dry winters in 1853 and 1854 caused the water in the Swiss lakes to fall to unusually low levels. Remains of wooden structures became visible, and among them were artefacts of stone and bronze – and many plant remains. The Swiss botanist Oswald Heer identified a series of wheat and other cereal species, as well as numerous nuts, fruits, and other seeds

(Heer 1865). The artefacts and the presence of bones of domestic livestock made it clear that these settlements were contemporary with and younger than Worsaae's Later Stone Age. In a short time, therefore, it was established that humans lived by hunting and gathering for the early part of the Stone Age (soon termed the Palaeolithic and Mesolithic), and by agriculture in the Neolithic and Bronze and Iron Ages.

Bones and plants continued to be found and studied during the later nineteenth and early twentieth centuries, but the study became ever more specialized and remote from more "conventional" archaeology. The great days when men like Steenstrup and Worsaae crossed swords in the academic arena were over; only more recently have bones and plants come back to center stage.

Lifestyles of the Earliest Humans

Raymond Dart joined the University of Witwatersrand in South Africa as an anatomist in 1922. At this time fossils were being found in quarries, and some were sent to Dart. In 1924 he identified a skull from Taung as that of an ancestral human. This brought him into conflict with the London establishment, which preferred theories based on the Piltdown skull. But Dart was right: Piltdown was later revealed to be a forgery, and the South African finds are now classified as *Australopithecines*, bipedal hominids living around 2–3 million years ago.

What was life like in southern Africa 2 million years ago? No stone tools were found with the hominids, and (contrary to Dart's belief) they did not use fire, so charred remains of plant foods are not found either. But the bones of zebra and a variety of antelope and other species were found at Taung and elsewhere, and they gave Dart some vital clues. The hominids evidently hunted these animals; Dart portrayed this vividly:

Man's predecessors differed from living apes in being confirmed killers: carnivorous creatures that seized living quarries by violence, battered them to death, tore apart their broken bodies, dismembered them limb from limb, slaking their ravenous thirst with the hot blood of victims and greedily devouring livid writhing flesh. (Dart 1953: 209)

They were also violent to each other:

The most shocking specimen was the fractured lower jaw of a 12-year-old . . . The lad had been killed by a violent blow delivered with calculated accuracy on the point of the chin, either by a smashing fist or a club. The blow was so vicious that it had shattered the jaw on both sides of the face and knocked out the front teeth. (Dart 1956: 325–6)

But how had they managed this without stone tools? Dart argued that they used tools made from the skeletons of the animals they killed – dubbed the *Osteodontokeratic* industry, from the Greek words for bone, tooth, and horn (abbreviated to ODK). Most of the animal bones were fractured for use as artefacts: jaws were used as scrapers, broken leg bones as clubs and pounders, bone splinters as daggers, and so on.

This picture of man the primeval killer was powerful, and still finds echoes in some popular literature. But is it correct? Greater understanding was slowly being gained about how carnivores like leopards and hyenas deal with their prey. Bones are often chewed and damaged, and may be collected in hyena dens or end up in natural fossil traps – this is a field of study known as *taphonomy* (from the Greek words for "laws of burial"). Dart's case was demolished by another South African, C. K. Brain, in a book entitled *The Hunters or the Hunted?* (1981). As the title implies, Brain argued that the hominids were not hunters, but were actually the victims of carnivores. Brain's taphonomic studies included the examination of bones at lion kills and in hyena dens, and he demonstrated that the ODK "tools" – and indeed the damage to the hominid bones – were created

by carnivores, not humans. Dart had noted that the animal bones were unevenly represented through the skeleton; for example, distal humerus was much more common than proximal humerus. In a remarkable experiment, Brain demonstrated that this was a carnivore creation. To the bemusement of the inhabitants, he collected all the animal bones lying around in a series of villages of goat herders at Kuiseb River in the Namib desert. The goats were slaughtered on the spot, so all the bones were originally present; the crucial factor was that dogs roamed freely and gnawed discarded bones, destroying many. Brain demonstrated that softer bones (e.g., proximal humerus) are usually destroyed, while harder bones (e.g., distal humerus) survive more often. When arranged in frequency of survival, the goat bone pattern is so similar to that of antelopes from hominid sites like Makapansgat that carnivore gnawing must have been responsible for the prehistoric pattern too (Figure 16.2).

So the *Australopithecines* were not, it appears, the hunters of Dart's envisioning; to judge from their large molar teeth, they may have lived on hard plant foods like seeds, though as mentioned none of these have survived. Hunting evidently came later in the human career.

For a time, the best candidates as the first hunters were other hominids living at East African sites like Olduvai Gorge around 1.5–2 million years ago. These were smaller and slighter individuals than the *Australopithecines*, but with rather larger brains, known as *Homo habilis*. Unlike their southern African cousins, they definitely made and used stone tools – but these were crude choppers and cutting flakes, not spearheads. But where these tools are found, there are also animal bones, and these have definitely been cut and split by stone tools. The hominids must have brought the bones there; here is one scenario:

Far across the plains, a group of four or five men approach . . . A group of creatures have been reclining on the sand in the shade

percent survival

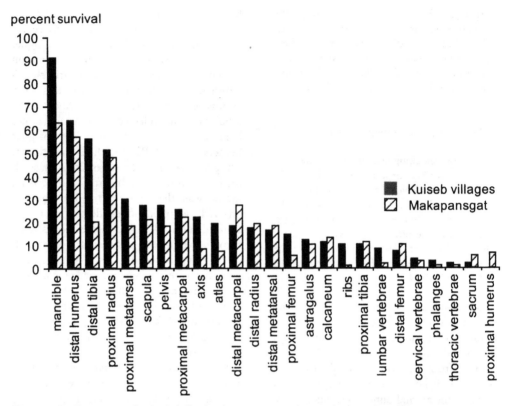

Figure 16.2 Frequency of animal skeletal parts, comparing the goat bones collected by C. K. Brain from modern herders' villages at Kuiseb River with frequencies of antelope and other animal bones from the hominid site of Makapansgat. Data from Brain (1981: tables 5, 8).

of a tree while some youngsters play around them. As the men approach these creatures rise . . . They seem to be female, and they whoop excitedly as some of the young run out to meet the arriving party . . . The object being carried is the carcass of an impala and the group congregates round this in high excitement . . . The stone worker . . . selects two or three pieces. Turning back to the carcass the leading male starts to make incisions . . . each adult male finishes up with a segment of the carcass, and withdraws to a corner of the clearing, with one or two females and juveniles congregating around him. They sit chewing . . . One of the males gets up, stretches his arms, scratches under his armpits and then sits down. He leans against the tree, gives a loud belch and pats his belly. (Isaac 1976: 483–5)

The males hunt; the women wait at home; the men share the carcass among themselves; each then shares his portion with his family. A lot of the "humanness" in this scenario depends on the assumption of hunting being correct.

It was not long before this scenario came under attack. In a book entitled *Bones: Ancient Men and Modern Myths* Lewis Binford (1981) argued that the predominance of animal heads and feet at the Olduvai sites indicated a very different activity. Heads and feet are often left at lion and leopard kills after the rest of the carcass has been consumed; the carnivores lack the crushing teeth needed to get inside these bones, which however contain useful edible material (brains and marrow). Binford argued that the hominids were scavenging the leftovers from big cats' kills and taking them away to eat in safety – hence the concentrations of bones and stone tools. Some have argued that hominids had access to more of the carcasses than Binford's model would allow (Bunn and Kroll 1986), but most now accept the scavenging model, at least in part. Some details of the archaeological record remain unclear, but a study of the superimposition of carnivore gnaw marks and cut marks from stone tools has shown a *threefold* sequence: gnaw marks come first, followed by cut marks, supporting the scavenging hypothesis – after which came another round of tooth marks, indicating renewed attack by scavenging carnivores after the hominids discarded the bones (Selvaggio 1998).

If the Olduvai hominids 1.5 million years ago were not hunting, when *did* humans start to kill large animals? In the wake of the Olduvai discussion, Binford sought to bring scavenging into the much more recent past. In the period from about 100,000 to 50,000 years ago, Neanderthals occupied Europe while anatomically modern humans lived in southern Africa. Binford (1984, 1985) argued that scavenging played a major part in the lives of both. More recently, evidence has emerged that both in fact hunted actively. In Europe, a spectacular find of wooden spears from Schoeningen in Germany indicates hunting 400,000 years ago (Thieme 1997), while the animal bones from some Neanderthal sites show that they had access to the entire skeleton – which suggests hunting rather than scavenging (e.g., Burke 2000). In southern Africa, a long-running debate has surrounded the site of Klasies River Mouth. Klein (1976) identified a head-and-foot pattern among the larger mammals. He argued that this resulted from hunting, and the *schlepp effect* (derived from an American word meaning to drag): the animal was butchered at the kill-site; most meat was cut from the bones, and dumped in the animal's hide, which was used as a carrying container – with the foot bones left attached for use as handles.

Binford (1984) applied his Olduvai argument to the head- and-foot pattern to argue for scavenging. The discussion has subsequently increased in complexity: not all bones were collected during the excavation, so the assemblage may be unrepresentative (Turner 1989); the tips of stone projectile points are embedded in the bones of even the largest animals, showing that these were hunted (Milo 1998); many fragments of the shafts of upper leg bones (the meat-bearing ones) are present, showing the humans had access to these even though the ends are missing and therefore not counted by Klein or Binford (Bartram and Marean 1999); but if the animals were hunted, why is the meat-rich scapula so rare (Outram 2001)?

These debates will continue; but in the meantime they direct our attention to the period 400,000 years and before, when the earliest human hunting of large animals is likely to have occurred.

Landscape Use and Society of Hunter-Gatherers

Modern humans like ourselves have spread from Africa across the entire globe in the past 50,000 years, replacing other hominids such as the Neanderthals. In some places these people created remarkable art and technology just as sophisticated as that of modern hunter-gatherers. For the first time, therefore, we are dealing with the archaeology of *ourselves*.

The most important outcome of this is that the anthropology of modern-day hunter-gatherers can give us some idea of the range of behaviors we might expect in the past, although many prehistoric ways of life will have no modern analogue. There is much variability: some modern hunter-gatherers move their campsites very often and cover huge distances in the course of a year; others move little or not at all, but live in one central base camp supplied by foraging parties using temporary camps. This "nomadic vs. sedentary" variability has ramifications for other aspects of life. The more sedentary a group is, the larger its population is likely to be; such groups often store food, which is individually owned; they also own particular resource-rich territories; and as a result, individual wealth and a stratified society may emerge (e.g., Keeley 1988).

Animal bones and plants can help us examine this sort of thing in prehistory. They do this by allowing us to determine the time of year in which a settlement was occupied, so we can see if it was a temporary camp or a permanent settlement – and if we can apply the modern situation just described to the prehistoric past, this distinction allows us to make some guesses about other areas of society. The key is the time of year different resources are available: if an excavation yields bones and plants that between them must have been collected in different seasons, the site was probably occupied through all those seasons; but if the resources all point to one season, the site may have been temporarily occupied – although we must always remember that not all foodstuffs survive in the archaeological record, so some periods of occupation may remain invisible to us.

Most plant foods were collected in particular seasons. Some animal species migrate, and these too can give valuable information. Other animals remain resident all year, but these can also provide seasonal information. The method is to look at their teeth to determine their age at death. Animals erupt their teeth at particular ages just as humans do. For example, wild boar grow their milk teeth in the first couple of months of life; the first molar appears at 4–7 months, the second at 9–12 months, and so on. This allows the death of juveniles – but not of adults – to be placed in a particular season *if the animals were born in a restricted season* (Rowley-Conwy 1993).

This approach was pioneered by a group of researchers led by Eric Higgs in the late 1960s and 1970s. An early focus of their work was the Upper Palaeolithic: modern human hunter-gatherers living in ice age Europe in the period ca. 35,000–11,000 years ago. In various areas they concluded that people practiced long-range migration. In southwestern France, for example, it was suggested that people spent the winter in the low-lying Dordogne region, and followed the reindeer up into the Pyrenean and Massif Central mountains during the summer (Bahn 1977). Sturdy (1975) used antler growth and shedding to examine central Europe. Male reindeer killed in the season October to December would be carrying their antlers, and this is mostly what he found at the site of Stellmoor near Hamburg. A few growing male antlers and cast female ones indicated early spring killing. This suggested a winter occupation in the north. Sturdy used corresponding evidence from sites further south to argue that the reindeer moved to the Danube in summer, and that the people from Stellmoor followed them.

These long-range seasonal migrations have been questioned as our methods have improved. Hardly any migrations on this scale are known among recent hunter-gatherers (Burch 1972), although that of course is not proof that they did not take place in prehistory. Reindeer-dominated sites in the Dordogne were indeed winter settlements, but sites just a few kilometers away containing horse and red deer bones show *summer* occupation. This suggests that people moved much smaller distances, and that the sites in the Pyrenees were occupied by different groups of people (Burke and Pike-Tay 1997). In central Germany, a similar short-range migration pattern involving various species has been identified (Weniger 1987).

One unresolved question concerns ice age people's use of the sea and its resources. This is not easy to examine because when glaciers covered large areas of the northern hemisphere, they in effect removed a lot of water from the world's oceans. Consequently, the Upper Palaeolithic coastline lies some 100 meters or more below present sea level. It will be a while before we are able to examine these directly! But it is certainly possible that people from southwest France or northern Germany might have visited the (then) coast at certain times of year. This is an important consideration, because some of the most sedentary and socially complex hunter-gatherers known in recent times were coastal, and much of their wealth came from the sea. This becomes easier to examine after the glaciers melted and seas approached their modern levels. Postglacial groups in Europe are termed Mesolithic, and in areas like Portugal and Denmark they made great use of marine foods. In Denmark at least the bones and plants testify to large sedentary settlements, and radial movement from these out to temporary hunting and fishing camps (Rowley-Conwy 1999).

Hunter-gatherers of course did not just live in Europe. At the Wadi Kubbaniya sites on the Nile in southern Egypt, people 16,000 years ago hunted land mammals and caught fish – and also made great use of gathered plants, which would have been much more common here than in glacial Europe. The seasons of availability of the plants cover much of the year, and if the plant foods were stored (something very hard to detect in the archaeological record), all-year occupation is likely (Hillman et al. 1989). At Abu Hureyra 1 on the Euphrates in Syria around 11,500 years ago, people made little use of fish, but hunted gazelle and collected plant foods. Gazelles give birth seasonally; their jaws include newborn and 12-month-old specimens, but none in between. If our estimations were based only on the bones, Abu Hureyra 1 would be identified as a short-lived seasonal camp, occupied only in April and May. The wide range of plant foods reveal otherwise, however, because their seasons of availability cover much of the year (Figure 16.3). It is likely that food was stored, and the site occupied all year; apparently the gazelle were migratory, appearing only in spring, while people lived there permanently (Hillman et al. 1997). This is of particular interest because the wild plants included wild rye and wild wheat; and Abu Hureyra 2, lying above, was one of the world's first agricultural settlements.

The Earliest Agriculture

The origin of agriculture was the single most significant step in human history. Agriculture emerged in several areas of the world. In the Near East, wheats, barley, and rye

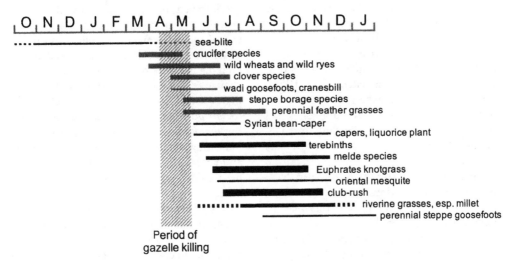

Figure 16.3 Seasonality of hunting and gathering at Abu Hurayra 1, Syria. Line thickness indicates how common the plant seeds were. Modified from Hillman et al. (1997: fig. 1).

formed the basis, along with several pulses, including peas and broad beans. In Mexico, maize was the cereal staple, although other plants were cultivated earlier. Africa, India, and China added various species (including the cereals sorghum and rice), but these may have been taken into cultivation after the arrival of Near Eastern wheat and barley. Peru cultivated quinoa, an annual goosefoot, rather than a cereal. Most added animals, but only in two areas were these large herd species: sheep, goat, cow, and pig in the Near East, llama and alpaca in Peru. Elsewhere, animals were less important, such as the turkey in Mexico.

Recent developments in archaeological dating methods have brought agricultural origins into sharper focus. Early methods of radiocarbon dating required quite large samples before an age could be produced; as a result, individual very early domestic cereal grains or bones could not themselves be dated by radiocarbon, but only by being found in layers which produced ages on other material. More recently, a new method of radiocarbon dating using linear accelerators has made it possible to date individual grains or bones, with interesting results. In some cases, apparently very early examples have turned out to be *younger* than the layers in which they are found. For example, a few barley grains in the 16,000-year-old layers at Wadi Kubbaniya (see above) are actually just a couple of thousand years old (Hillman et al. 1989). "Early" maize in Mexico has produced similarly young dates (Fritz 1994). This highlights one aspect of taphonomy (the "laws of burial" – see above): small objects can occur in the "wrong" archaeological layers. They may be moved by ants or rodent burrowing – or be displaced during excavation. As a result, archaeologists have become more cautious about advancing claims for early farming until the relevant items are directly dated.

Recognizing domestic animals and plants is an interesting problem for archaeologists. Definite recognition depends on some genetic change taking place in the plant or animal, which in turn requires that the domesticated individuals were isolated from their wild cousins and bred only among themselves – because otherwise wild genes would continually come into the domestic population and prevent it changing.

In cereals such as wheat, grain size increases in domestic varieties. Occasional large grains occur in wild populations, but their frequency increases under domestication for reasons that are not well understood. Currently the earliest Near Eastern domestic cereal grains are rye, from Abu Hureyra 1 in Syria (see above), alongside many wild species (Hillman 2000). In the New World, enlarged seeds of domestic squash are nearly as old, occurring at Guilá Naquitz cave 8,000–10,000 years ago (Smith 1997). The dates of both have been confirmed by radiocarbon accelerator. Lentils may also have been cultivated late in the occupation of Abu Hureyra 1: they unexpectedly increase in frequency despite a developing drought. However, no morphological change is visible (Hillman 2000).

Animals in contrast get smaller when domesticated, though whether due to deliberate or unintentional selection by their owners is unclear. The problem is made more complex by other factors: various non-domestic species such as foxes also show a size decrease, for environmental reasons, at the end of the last ice age, just when sheep and goats were being domesticated, and disentangling natural from human-induced size change is problematic; also, in some species males are larger than females, so a change in the *proportion* of the sexes killed can change the *average* bone size without this necessarily indicating a real change in the size of the animals. Currently the earliest domestic herd animal appears to be the goat. This is based not on size but on kill pattern: a change towards the selective killing of young males in western Iran 10,000 years ago implies that the animals were under close human control – otherwise such selective killing would be impossible (Zeder and Hesse 2000).

Farmers, Flocks, and Crops

Farming spread rapidly from the centers of origin described above. Studies of animal bones and plants change their focus when studying farming: the questions now concern the ways in which domestic animals and plants were exploited.

The nature of animal husbandry in Neolithic Europe has been the subject of debate. The wild forms of cattle and pigs were native to Europe. This raises the problem of how the wild and domestic forms should be separated archaeologically. It is of course possible that Neolithic farmers might have domesticated these species locally, rather than import them from the Near East. We also need to know whether animals were closely husbanded and kept separate from their wild cousins, or whether they were loosely herded and interbred with them.

These are questions that have been raised in particular with reference to the pig. Jarman (1976) argued that pigs were herded so extensively that the distinction between wild and domestic became meaningless both behaviorally and genetically. Recent advances have however cast new light on this. Payne and Bull (1988) studied the metrical attributes of a single population of modern wild boar from Turkey. Any particular measurement displays a certain range of variation from smallest to largest, allowing the coefficient of variation to be calculated. When their results are compared to pig bone assemblages from Neolithic Europe an interesting pattern emerges. Figure 16.4 plots the length of the mandibular second molar, and the modern Turkish specimens form a tight group with a coefficient of variation of 4. By comparison, those from Neolithic Gomolava, in Serbia, are spread much wider and have a coefficient of variation of 12. Clearly, there is a wider range of sizes at Gomolava than can be encompassed by a single population – which should look much more like the Turkish one. The implication is that there must be *two* populations at Gomolava, which did *not* interbreed with

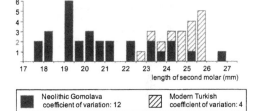

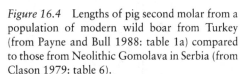

Figure 16.4 Lengths of pig second molar from a population of modern wild boar from Turkey (from Payne and Bull 1988: table 1a) compared to those from Neolithic Gomolava in Serbia (from Clason 1979: table 6).

each other or their sizes would have converged. The only way this appears possible is if one population is under close human control (i.e., is fully domestic) and the other wild hunted animals. Many but not all areas of prehistoric Europe show a similar pattern, suggesting that close domestic control was widespread. This picture goes back to the start of farming in Europe – we do not see a gradual divergence of two populations within Europe. This suggests that the domestic animals were introduced, not locally domesticated.

Domestic animals may be kept for a variety of purposes; sheep, for example, may be kept for meat, milk, or wool. Kill patterns in the three strategies vary, allowing specialization – or compromises between specializations – to be detected (Payne 1973). Cattle similarly may be kept primarily for meat or for milk. An elegant demonstration of a milk specialization comes from the Bronze Age site of Grimes Graves in Britain. From the jaws, Legge (1992) calculates the percentage of animals remaining alive at various ages (Figure 16.5). Many animals were killed while very young, hence the steep drop almost parallel to the vertical axis in the upper part of the figure. This, he argues, would represent mostly the killing of male calves: if these calves were left alive they would need to consume the milk. More female calves would remain alive into adulthood to form the breeding – and

A. Age data from jaws

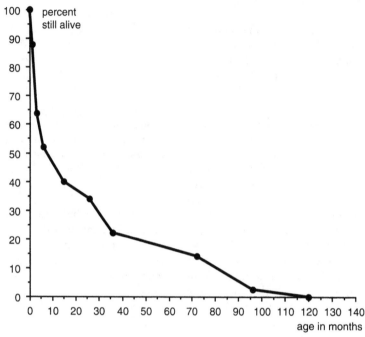

B. Sex data from metacarpals

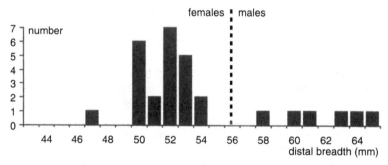

Figure 16.5 Animal husbandry from Bronze Age Grimes Graves, Norfolk. Top: kill pattern derived from mandibular teeth. Bottom: sex ratio derived from distal metacarpal. Information from Legge (1992).

lactating – nucleus of the herd. Jaws, however, cannot be used to determine sex. For this Legge uses the distal metacarpals. The ends of these bones only fuse onto the shafts when the animals are 24–30 months old, and the lower part of Figure 16.5 shows that there is a clear preponderance of females by this age. The conclusion is that most males were killed *under* 24 months in age, confirm-

ing Legge's suggestion that the males were being killed young. This conforms so well with the age/sex pattern expected in a milking herd that dairy products must have been very important (Legge 1992). Other European sites reveal that in some cases meat was the desired product. These methods should in due course show how far back into prehistory the use of dairy products goes – and another method will be discussed below.

It was mentioned above that a sample of bones may accumulate over many years, while a sample of plants may result from a single event occurring on a particular day. Cattle bones are most numerous at Grimes Graves, and we may reasonably conclude that this species was more common there in the Bronze Age. But if barley is the most numerous plant in one particular Bronze Age sample, we cannot draw the corresponding conclusion: other species may have been more important overall. Many samples are needed from a settlement before we can say much about overall crop frequencies. A good example comes from a Bronze Age site at Assiros in Greece, where some storerooms were burnt, charring a series of containers containing a variety of crops. In different samples einkorn wheat, emmer wheat, spelt wheat, bread wheat, barley, millet, and bitter vetch each predominate. Even with so many samples it is difficult to say which crop was originally the most important; certainly, no single sample gives the overall picture (Jones et al. 1986).

Even more fundamental problems may arise. Figure 16.6 shows the plant remains from two Bronze Age settlements in Denmark. That from Lindebjerg comes from a building destroyed by fire, while that from Voldtofte comes from a rubbish midden. The purity of the Lindebjerg sample suggests that it was a cereal store. But does the Voldtofte sample indicate that nearly half the plants (from brome round to campion in the pie chart) were collected from the wild rather than cultivated? Almost certainly not; it was mentioned above that crops must be processed to render them edible, and this includes sieving them to remove small weed seeds. It is likely that the Voldtofte sample represents *waste* from this activity, not an intended *end product* – something supported by its being found in a refuse midden. The Neolithic of Britain has produced relatively few plant samples. These mostly contain some cereal grains, but also many weed

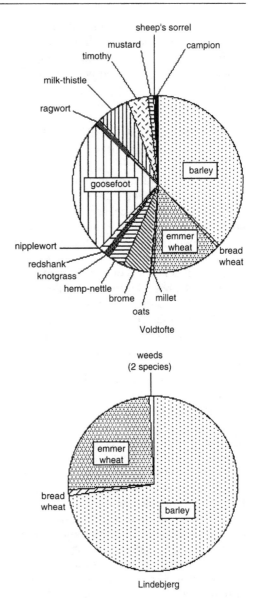

Figure 16.6 Pie charts showing plant frequencies at two Bronze Age settlements in Denmark: Lindebjerg (from Rowley-Conwy 1978) and Voldtofte (from Rowley-Conwy 1982).

seeds and hazelnut shells. Some argue that these can be read at face value, and that the British Neolithic therefore lived mainly on wild plant foods (Thomas 1999). Others, including this writer, suspect that they may be waste from cereal cleaning, so that cereals were of more importance than their actual frequency would suggest (Rowley-Conwy 2000). Improved excavation and sampling should resolve the situation one way or the other.

City Dwellers, Specialists, and Social Elites

With the rise of cities, occupational specialization, and social elites, the focus of bone and plant studies again changes. We are often no longer dealing with primary producer sites, but with the end use of animals and plants by people who were not primary producers of them. The bones and plants can reveal much about the complexities of these societies. Cities are also much more complex archaeological sites: construction work often results in the dumping and redumping of waste materials, so many bone and plant samples are mixtures of residues from many kinds of activities. Some, however, remain undisturbed, providing snapshots of particular activities.

Cities are supported mainly by supplies from their hinterlands (even though some animals like goats or pigs may be kept by the city dwellers themselves). Economic forces are often important. In medieval Britain, for example, the increasing importance of the wool trade meant an increasing number of sheep in the countryside. Sheep towards the end of their working lives were often sold into the cities for consumption, so there is a general trend for sheep to increase in frequency through time. Cattle sold into the cities were mostly also old animals, presumably draught oxen and milking cows coming to the end of their useful lives in the surrounding villages (e.g., Gidney 2000). Plants may also reflect economic trends. In Germany, the arrival of the Romans parallels an increase in the cultivation of spelt wheat at the expense of emmer wheat, possibly reflecting increased cultivation on poorer soils so the crop could be sold (Kreuz 1999). In northern England, spelt wheat increases in

frequency *before* the arrival of the Romans, although whether this reflects economic forces or ethnic differences is unresolved (Van der Veen 1992).

Urban bones may reveal occupational specialization. Several deposits in Roman Lincoln contain thousands of bones of very small fish, mainly sand eels and the herring family; these are probably waste from the manufacture of *garum*, a Roman fish sauce (Dobney et al. 1996). Hides were tanned during leather manufacture; the bone residues from this activity are mainly heads and feet, as these bones were often left attached to the hide. Concentrations of cattle heads and feet in rubbish dumps suggests a tannery in the vicinity (Serjeantson 1989). A high frequency of cat bones in pits belonging to one particular late medieval town house in Leicester indicates the presence of a furrier specializing in cats; pits at an adjacent house contained many sawn fragments of horse bone, indicating a bone craftsman (Gidney 2000). The bones are usually the only way to detect these since such activities are rarely discussed in documentary sources. A different kind of occupational specialization is revealed by fish bones from sites around the North Sea. Early in the medieval period, most fish are coastal, but later on more and more are from large deep-sea species. This reflects the development of the relevant technology by full-time fishermen, who sold their catch (often dried or salted) to towns far inland (Enghoff 2000). Towards the end of the medieval period, the decline in the wool trade meant that sheep also decreased in many English cities. Cattle become more common – and many are now from very young individuals, in contrast to the earlier situation. This probably indicates the growth of dairies inside the towns themselves, providing dairy products for the inhabitants; as at Bronze Age Grimes Graves (see above), young calves were a waste product, hence the high frequency of their bones (Gidney 2000).

Other aspects of society may also be revealed. The Jewish quarter in post-medieval Amsterdam is definable by an absence of pig bones (Ijzereef 1989). The Roman commandant at South Shields Roman fort in northern England ate better cuts of beef that the common soldiery, and also had more hens, ducks, and geese, as well as deer (Stokes 2000). Bones from two Roman temples in southern England show clear signs of the sacrifice of many young lambs (Legge et al. 2000). Refuse pits at the sixteenth and seventeenth-century town house in Leicester of the Earl of Huntingdon contained more deer and wild birds like woodcock than other sites in the city (Gidney 2000). Long-term decline in the social status of the inhabitants of Launceston Castle in Cornwall between the twelfth and nine-teenth centuries is reflected in a decline in deer bones, and wild bird species including woodcock (Albarella and Davis 1996). Peacocks, turkeys, and figs are found in Newcastle upon Tyne in deposits dating from the sixteenth century, testifying to the growing purchasing power of the mercantile elite (Graves and Heslop in press).

Agricultural improvement in the last 300 years has been documented by historians. Animal bones show that the process actually began as early as the sixteenth century, before any evidence appears in documentary sources (Albarella 1999). Bones and plants will in due course reveal other aspects of this process. In northern Switzerland, late medi-eval cultivation is known to have involved three-course rotation (spelt wheat harvested in autumn, followed by spring-sown oats, followed by fallow). Weed seeds contain both summer and winter annuals, clearly re-flecting the growing seasons of the two cereals. Use of this methodology on earlier samples will ultimately reveal when this rotation originated (Karg 1995). By the nine-teenth century, pigs routinely double-farrowed (i.e., produced two litters of piglets each year, one in spring, one in autumn), but it is unknown when this practice started. Defects may form in dental enamel when the animal is subjected to the stresses of winter while the tooth is forming. If all the defects occur at the same point in a tooth,

this may suggest that all pigs were born at the same time of year, whereas if they are vari-able, more than one birth season may be implied. This method indicates that medieval pigs in Belgium gave birth in spring only, so double-farrowing is presumably later than this (Dobney and Ervynck 2000).

This discussion completes our consider-ation of bones and plants. However, one new and very exciting development must be mentioned before the close of this chapter.

Ancient Biomolecules: A New Field

Recent advances in methods mean that it is becoming possible for us to extract and study ancient biomolecules from archaeological bones and plants. DNA, for example, decays quite rapidly, and if it survives at all does so not in its entirety but only in short segments – which means that *Jurassic Park* is not going to be a viable possibility for a long time to come! But the information that can be re-trieved may be very useful nonetheless. If two lineages of a species are kept apart, their DNA will gradually diverge, so measur-ing the DNA difference between individuals gives an approximate "molecular clock" showing how long ago they shared a common ancestor.

Studies of modern cattle reveal two DNA lineages that have been separate for over 100,000 years. This ancient divergence is much older than the origins of cattle domes-tication, and must indicate that cattle were domesticated twice, in eastern and western Eurasia (Bradley et al. 1996). DNA has re-cently been extracted from a few prehistoric wild cattle bones from Britain, and is similar but not identical to the west Eurasian strain. This reinforces the east–west dichotomy of domestication and also suggests that cattle were *not* domesticated in Britain, because if they were, modern cattle DNA should be similar to that from the prehistoric wild spe-cimens (Troy et al. 2001).

Sorghum is an important cereal of African origin; little is known of its history, but it is often thought to have been domesticated over 5,000 years ago. Much well-preserved material was recovered from Qasr Ibrim in southern Egypt (all domestic varieties being under 2,000 years old), and DNA extracted from the three domestic forms identified and compared to that from modern sorghum varieties. All the DNA from both ancient and modern specimens was identical. If the crop had a long domestic history, some divergence would be expected; this could suggest that the crop was domesticated much more recently (Rowley-Conwy et al. 1998).

Other molecular information is also useful. Various isotopes of carbon and nitrogen are present in different forms of food, and consumers of those foods take different proportions into their bones. This may be examined, and the proportions of foods of marine vs. terrestrial origin, and plant vs. animal origin, in the ancient diet may be calculated. This is mostly useful for human diets, but other species may be studied. One early Mesolithic dog from Yorkshire consumed significant amounts of marine foods; sea level at this time had not reached modern levels, so it is unknown whether humans settled on the coasts. The dog is important in suggesting that there was a coastal connection (Schulting and Richards 2002).

Lipids (fatty acids) vary between various forms of food. Analysis of lipids from prehis-toric potsherds in Britain indicates that some contained dairy products, from the Neolithic onwards (Dudd and Evershed 1998). This helps confirm the dairy evidence from the animal bones presented by Legge (1992) at Grimes Graves (see above).

These studies reveal a little of the potential of these methods. Many future developments may be awaited. For example, when European colonists reached the New World, many of their diseases decimated the native populations. Some of these diseases, such as smallpox and measles, were mutations of diseases of animals, presumably acquired by Eurasian people after the animals were domesticated. Did similar epidemics sweep through early farming populations in Asia? Biomolecular work may in future be able to tell us.

Conclusion

I hope it is now clear why I stressed that bone and plant archaeologists have major contributions to make to almost all areas of archaeology. Our chronological scope ranges from 2.5 million years ago to the present; geographically, we cover the entire world. If this canter through a few of the major results and debates has made this point, it has served its purpose.

Acknowledgments

I am very grateful to John Bintliff for asking me to write this chapter, and to Glynis Jones for suggesting references.

References

Albarella, U. 1999. "The mysteries of husbandry: medieval animals and the problem of integrating historical and archaeological evidence." *Antiquity*, 73: 867–75.

Albarella, U. and S. Davis 1996. "Mammals and birds from Launceston Castle, Cornwall: decline in status and the rise of agriculture." *Circaea*, 12: 1–156.

Bahn, P. 1977. "Seasonal migration in southwest France during the late glacial period." *Journal of Archaeological Science*, 4: 245–57.

Bartram, L. E. and C. W. Marean 1999. "Explaining the 'Klasies Pattern': Kua ethnoarchae-ology, the Die Kelders Middle Stone Age archaeofauna, long bone fragmentation and carnivore ravaging." *Journal of Archaeological Science*, 26: 9–20.

Binford, L. R. 1981. *Bones: Ancient Men and Modern Myths*. New York: Academic Press.

Binford, L. R. 1984. *Faunal Remains from Klasies River Mouth*. New York: Academic Press.

Binford, L. R. 1985. "Human ancestors: changing views of their behavior." *Journal of Anthro-pological Archaeology*, 4: 292–327 (reprinted in *Debating Archaeology*, ed. R. L. Binford, pp. 301–28).

Bradley, D. G., D. E. MacHugh, P. Cunningham, and R. T. Loftus 1996. "Mitochondrial diversity and the origins of African and European cattle." *Proceedings of the National Academy of Science*, 93: 5131–5.

Brain, C. K. 1981. *The Hunters or the Hunted?* Chicago: University of Chicago Press.

Bunn, H. and E. Kroll 1986. "Systematic butchery by Plio/Pleistocene hominids at Olduvai Gorge, Tanzania." *Current Anthropology*, 27: 431–52.

Burch, E. S. 1972. "The caribou/wild reindeer as a human resource." *American Antiquity*, 37: 339–68.

Burke, A. 2000. "The view from Starosele: faunal exploitation at a Middle Palaeolithic site in western Crimea." *International Journal of Osteoarchaeology*, 10: 325–35.

Burke, A. and A. Pike-Tay 1997. "Reconstructing 'l'âge du renne'." In L. J. Jackson and P. T. Thacker (eds.), *Caribou and Reindeer Hunters of the Northern Hemisphere*, pp. 69–81. Aldershot: Avebury.

Clason, A. T. 1979. "The farmers of Gomolava in the Vinca and La Tène period." *Palaeohis-toria*, 21: 41–81.

Dart, R. A. 1953. "The predatory transition from ape to man." *International Anthropological and Linguistic Review*, 1: 201–18.

Dart, R. A. 1956. "Cultural status of the South African man-apes." *Smithsonian Report*, 4240: 317–28.

Dobney, K. M. and A. Ervynck 2000. "Interpreting developmental stress in archaeological pigs: the chronology of linear enamel hypoplasia." *Journal of Archaeological Science*, 27: 797–807.

Dobney, K. M., S. D. Jaques, and B. G. Irving 1996. *Of Butchers and Breeds: Report on Vertebrate Remains from Various Sites in the City of Lincoln*. Lincoln Archaeological Studies 5. Lincoln: City of Lincoln Archaeology Unit.

Dudd, S. N. and R. P. Evershed 1998. "Direct demonstration of milk as an element of archaeological economies." *Science*, 282: 1478–81.

Enghoff, I. B. 2000. "Fishing in the southern North Sea region from the 1st to the 16th century AD: evidence from fish bones." *Archaeofauna*, 9: 59–132.

Fritz, G. J. 1994. "Are the first American farmers getting younger?" *Current Anthropology*, 35: 305–9.

Gidney, L. 2000. "Economic trends, craft specialization and social status: bone assemblages from Leicester." In P. Rowley-Conwy (ed.), *Animal Bones, Human Societies*, pp. 170–8. Oxford: Oxbow Books.

Graves, C. P. and D. Heslop, in press. *The Archaeology of Newcastle upon Tyne*. London: English Heritage.

Heer, O. 1865. "Die Pflanzen der Pfahlbauten." *Neujahrsblatt der Naturforschenden Gesellschaft Zürich*, 68: 1–54.

Hillman, G. C. 2000. "Abu Hureyra 1: the Epipalaeolithic." In A. M. T. Moore, G. C. Hillman, and A. J. Legge (eds.), *Village on the Euphrates: From Foraging to Farming at Abu Hureyra*, pp. 327–99. Oxford: Oxford University Press.

Hillman, G. C., A. J. Legge, and P. A. Rowley-Conwy 1997. "Food or fuel? The charred seeds from Epipalaeolithic Abu Hureyra." *Current Anthropology*, 38: 651–9.

Hillman, G. C., E. Madeyska, and J. Hather 1989. "Wild plant foods and diet at late Paleolithic Wadi Kubbaniya: the evidence from charred remains." In F. Wendorf, R. Schild, and A. E. Close (eds.), *The Prehistory of Wadi Kubbaniya, Vol. 2: Stratigraphy, Paleoeconomy and Environment*, pp. 162–242. Dallas: Southern Methodist University Press.

Ijzereef, F. G. 1989. "Social differentiation from animal bone studies." In D. Serjeantson and T. Waldron (eds.), *Diet and Crafts in Towns*, pp. 41–53. Oxford: British Archaeological Reports. British Series 199.

Isaac, G. L. 1976. "The activities of early African hominid." In G. L. Isaac and E. R. McCown (eds.), *Human Origins*, pp. 482–514. Menlo Park, CA: Benjamin.

Jarman, H. N., A. J. Legge, and J. A. Charles 1972. "Retrieval of plant remains from archaeological sites by froth flotation." In E. S. Higgs (ed.), *Papers in Economic Prehistory*, pp. 39–48. Cambridge: Cambridge University Press.

Jarman, M. R. 1976. "Prehistoric economic development in sub-Alpine Italy." In G. de G. Sieveking, I. H. Longworth, and K. E. Wilson (eds.), *Problems in Economic and Social Archaeology*, pp. 375–99. London: Duckworth.

Jones, G., K. Wardle, P. Halstead, and D. Wardle 1986. "Crop storage at Assiros." *Scientific American*, 254 (3): 96–103.

Karg, S. 1995. "Plant diversity in late medieval cornfields of northern Switzerland." *Vegetation History and Archaeobotany*, 4: 41–50.

Keeley, L. H. 1988. "Hunter-gatherer economic complexity and 'population pressure': a cross-cultural analysis." *Journal of Anthropological Archaeology*, 7: 373–411.

Klein, R. 1976. "The mammalian fauna of the Klasies River Mouth sites, Southern Cape Province, South Africa." *South African Archaeological Bulletin*, 31 (123 and 124): 75–98.

Kreuz, A. 1999. "Becoming a Roman farmer: preliminary report on the environmental evidence from the Romanization project." In J. D. Creighton and R. J. A. Wilson (eds.), *Roman Germany, Studies in Cultural Interaction*, pp. 71–98. *Journal of Roman Archaeology*, Supplementary Series 32.

Legge, A. J. 1992. *Excavations at Grimes Graves, Norfolk, 1972–1976, 4: Animals, Environment and the Bronze Age Economy*. London: British Museum Press.

Legge, A. J., J. Williams, and P. Williams 2000. "Lambs to the slaughter: sacrifice at two Roman temples in southern England." In P. Rowley-Conwy (ed.), *Animal Bones, Human Societies*, pp. 152–7. Oxford: Oxbow Books.

Milo, R. G. 1998. "Evidence for hominid predation at Klasies River Mouth, South Africa, and its implications for the behavior of early modern humans." *Journal of Archaeological Science*, 25: 99–133.

Outram, A. K. 2001. "The scapula representation could be the key: a further contribution to the 'Klasies Pattern' debate." *Journal of Archaeological Science*, 28: 1259–63.

Payne, S. 1972. "Partial recovery and sample bias: the results of some sieving experiments." In E. S. Higgs (ed.), *Papers in Economic Prehistory*, pp. 49–64. Cambridge: Cambridge University Press.

Payne, S. 1973. "Kill-off patterns in sheep and goats: the mandibles from Asvan Kale." *Anatolian Studies*, 23: 281–303.

Payne, S. and G. Bull 1988. "Components of variation in measurements of pig bones and teeth, and the use of measurements to distinguish wild from domestic pig remains." *ArchæoZoologia*, 2: 27–65.

Rowley-Conwy, P. 1978. "The carbonized grain from Lindebjerg." *Kuml*, 1978: 159–71.

Rowley-Conwy, P. 1982. "A new sample of carbonized grain from Voldtofte." *Kuml*, 1982–3: 139–52.

Rowley-Conwy, P. 1993. "Season and reason: the case for a regional interpretation of Mesolithic settlement patterns." In G. L. Peterkin, H. Bricker, and P. Mellars (eds.), *Hunting and Animal Exploitation in the Later Palaeolithic and Mesolithic of Eurasia*, pp. 179–88. Archaeological Papers of the American Anthropological Association no. 4.

Rowley-Conwy, P. 1999. "Economic prehistory in southern Scandinavia." In J. Coles, R. M. Bewley, and P. Mellars (eds.), *World Prehistory: Studies in Memory of Grahame Clark*, pp. 125–59. Oxford: Oxford University Press. (Proceedings of the British Academy 99).

Rowley-Conwy, P. 2000. "Through a taphonomic glass, darkly: the importance of cereal cultivation in prehistoric Britain." In S. Stallibrass and J. Huntley (eds.), *Taphonomy and Interpretation*, pp. 43–53. Oxford: Oxbow Books.

Rowley-Conwy, P., W. Deakin, and C. H. Shaw 1998. "Ancient DNA from archaeological sorghum (*Sorghum bicolor*) from Qasr Ibrim, Nubia: implications for domestication and evolution and a review of the archaeological evidence." *Sahara*, 9: 23–34.

Schulting, R. and M. P. Richards 2002. "Dogs, sucks, deer and diet: new stable isotope evidence on early Mesolithic dogs from the Vale of Pickering, northeast England." *Journal of Archaeological Science*, 29: 327–33.

Selvaggio, M. M. 1998. "Evidence for a three-stage sequence of hominid and carnivore involvement with long bones at FLK Zinjanthropus, Olduvai Gorge, Tanzania." *Journal of Archaeological Science*, 25: 191–202.

Serjeantson, D. 1989. "Animal remains and the tanning trade." In D. Serjeantson and T. Waldron (eds.), *Diet and Crafts in Towns*, pp. 129–46. Oxford: British Archaeological Reports. (British Series 199).

Smith, B. 1997. "The initial domestication of *Cucurbita pepo* in the Americas 10,000 years ago." *Science*, 276 (9 May): 932–4.

Steenstrup, J. J. S. 1851. "Beretning om Udbyttet af nogle ved Isefjordens Kyster og i Jylland sidste Sommer anstillede geologisk-antiquariske Undersögelser angaaende Landets ældste Natur-og Cultur-Forhold." *Oversigt over det kongelige danske Videnskabernes Selskabs Forhandlinger*, 1851: 1–31.

Stokes, P. 2000. "A cut above the rest? Officers and men at South Shields Roman fort." In P. Rowley-Conwy (ed.), *Animal Bones, Human Societies*, pp. 145–51. Oxford: Oxbow Books.

Sturdy, D. 1975. "Some reindeer economies in prehistoric Europe." In E. S. Higgs (ed.), *Palaeoeconomy*, pp. 55–95. Cambridge: Cambridge University Press.

Thieme, H. 1997. "Lower Palaeolithic hunting spears from Germany." *Nature*, 385 (27 February): 807–10.

Thomas, J. 1999. *Understanding the Neolithic*. London: Routledge.

Troy, C. S., D. E. MacHugh, J. F. Balley, et al. 2001. "Genetic evidence for Near-Eastern origins of European cattle." *Nature*, 410 (26 April): 1088–91.

Turner, A. 1989. "Sample selection, schlepp effects and scavenging: the implications of partial recovery for interpretations of the terrestrial mammal assemblage from Klasies River Mouth." *Journal of Archaeological Science*, 16: 1–12.

Van der Veen, M. 1992. *Crop Husbandry Regimes*. Sheffield: J. R. Collis Publications, Department of Archaeology and Prehistory (Sheffield Archaeological Monographs 3).

Weniger, G.-C. 1987. "Magdalenian settlement pattern and subsistence in central Europe." In O. Soffer (ed.), *The Pleistocene Old World*, pp. 201–15. New York: Plenum.

Worsaae, J. J. A. 1860. "Om en ny deling af steen-og broncealderen." *Oversigt over det kongelige danske Videnskabernes Selskabs Forhandlinger,* 1860: 93–129.

Zeder, M. A. and B. Hesse 2000. "The initial domestication of goats (Capra hircus) in the Zagros Mountains 10,000 years ago." *Science,* 287 (24 March): 2254–7.

17

Ecology in Archaeology: From Cognition to Action

Fekri A. Hassan

A Historical Synopsis

The relationship between people and their environment has a long history in archaeology.[1] At first, archaeologists sought the help of geologists and geographers (which included palaeontologists and eventually palynologists) to give accounts of the geological environment, fauna and plants. In the late nineteenth century, earth scientists in archaeological research were linked with the establishment of the prediluvial antiquity of humankind and later as a means of dating Pleistocene cultural events. The use of geological and palaeontological data as a means of dating the past became, in the 1950s, a key element of environmental archaeology (cf. Zeuner 1952).

By the 1930s, an interest in the economic aspects of prehistoric societies strengthened the pursuit of environmental archaeology to obtain data on subsistence and palaeoclimatic conditions. In the United Kingdom, economic prehistory and environmental archaeology were popularized by Childe's *Man Makes Himself* (1936), and by Clark's *Prehistoric Europe* (1952), works strengthened and perhaps inspired by Daryll Forde's *Habitat, Economy and Society* (1934). His work was influenced by British geographer H. J. Fleure, who with others developed a regional approach to the geog-

raphy of Britain during the 1920s and 1930s. In 1923, Sir Cyril Fox published his archaeology of the Cambridge region, showing how the pattern of settlement had changed in relation to natural vegetation. In *The Personality of Britain* (1947) he combined environmental-settlement ideas with locational geography and the "personality" idea of French geographers (Daniel 1964). Their interests were focused on races and peoples as a fundamental structuring concept.

According to Clark, Kossinna (1858–1931) pioneered cultural groupings to supplement the preexisting focus on periods. This approach was manifest in Childe's (1925) *Dawn of European Civilization* (see Clark 1968: 34). The identification of specific peoples with languages, physical traits, and cultures was linked to their particular environment. The region as the focal point of geographical research emanated from France and Vidal de la Blache (1845–1918), who argued that a natural landscape cannot be studied separately from its culture; a region was constituted from the intimate relationships between human beings and nature through centuries of development (Holt-Jensen 1999: 45–6). Rejecting environmental determinism in favor of opportunities and ways of life (*genres de vie*) (Broek 1965: 24), his work led to regional monographs widely admired in Britain. British geographers were also influenced by French sociologist Le Play (1806–82) through his Scottish follower Geddes (1854–1932). Le Play and Geddes stressed the importance of studying social phenomena, such as households, in the context of the character of work and the nature of the environment (place). Geddes also emphasized the role of regional surveys and analysis in town planning. A pioneer regional archaeological survey covering 1,000 square kilometers, providing a model of the changing landscape of south Etruria on the basis of the distribution of 2,000 sites, was carried out in the 1950s by the British School in Rome (Potter 1979).

The ideas of Geddes, Le Play, and Vidal de la Blache were adopted by Fleure, involved with Peake in the publication (in 1927) of *Peasants and Potters*, explicating the link between geographical regions and cultural developments. According to Holt-Jensen (1999: 54), Fleure reconceptualized the region by taking into account living experiences, including the shifting relationships between people. Intrigued by the geographical aspects of the region in the "Middle East," Peake and Fleure (1927) considered the possible impact of climatic change (cold conditions ca. 4500 BC) and the distribution of wild cereals on the emergence of cultivation. The early history of agriculture has since been closely linked with geographical/environmental research, and this was one of the first major research projects undertaken by the British Academy, the project being set up in Cambridge under the direction of E. S. Higgs. Cambridge was selected because of the pioneering work in economic prehistory at Star Carr (1949–51), in which 25 students from the department were involved (Clark 1972). Higgs developed one of the most influential schools in environmental and economic prehistory, arguably the most prominent coherent theoretical group in Britain during the 1960s and 1970s. The influence of that school has been clear in the works of many eminent British archaeologists, including Geoff Bailey, Graeme Barker, John Bintliff, Robin Dennell, Clive Gamble,

Charles Higham, Mike Jarman, Tony Legge, and Pete Rowley-Conwy. The ruthless and patently uninformed polemic by Julian Thomas (1993) on the lack of theory in British environmental archaeology and the need to subsume environmental archaeology under (cultural) archaeology is inexplicable. Already in Peake and Fleure, the link between culture and the environment was emphasized. Furthermore, attention to environmental conditions was not due to a brainless, atheoretical fascination with bees and birds, but was instead a result of a theoretical perspective on the causal links between climatic conditions, environmental parameters, and lifestyles as practical modes of culture (manifest already in the concept of region as developed by Vidal de la Blache, Le Play, and Geddes). In addition, the concept of site catchment analysis (Vita Finzi and Higgs 1970) was the first attempt to develop a theory of landscape archaeology on the basis of the spatial range of subsistence activities by a specific group of people, a precursor to more recent attempts to consider landscapes as a function of the perceptions and practices of human groups.

In North America, the anthropologist Franz Boas (1858–1942) reacted against rampant evolutionism and diffusionism, calling instead for particularistic historical studies of culture, especially mindful of the interaction between a people and their physical environment (Harris 1968: 263). Clark Wissler in 1926 and Kroeber in 1939 highlighted the relationship between natural and cultural areas of Native North Amerca (Harris 1968: 339). By the late 1940s and early 1950s, environmental archaeology had become a major strand in American archaeology. Seminal works included those by Wedel, Haurey, Johnson, Heizer, and Cook. At that time, in 1949, Steward placed environmental issues well within an evolutionary paradigm (Willey and Sabloff 1973: 151–6).

The next generation of American archaeologists, in the 1960s, benefited from the emergence of ecology, a sensational field in biology, signaled particularly by the first edition of Odum's *Fundamentals of Ecology* in 1953. Archaeologists and collaborating scientists became involved in modeling subsistence, settlement, and culture change utilizing an ecological perspective. This fitted well with the objectives of the New Archaeology, which sought explanations of what happened in prehistory rather than drafting lists of tool types, and treating artefact assemblages as "cultures" to be arranged in a temporal sequence in order to establish historical connections. What mattered in the New Archaeology was not culture history as a sequence of archaeological units, but the ability to provide credible explanations of various aspects of prehistoric societies, placing archaeology within the domain of anthropological functionalist, structural–functionalist, and neo-evolutionary models. Also, instead of the traditional alliance with history, archaeologists were exhorted to apply scientific methods, guided by a small selection of works on the philosophy of science. Explanations of archaeological phenomena should derive from empirical observations, a clear exposition of the problem and the criteria for testing a hypothesis. Ecology, as a science, thus fitted the perspective of the New Archaeology. Accordingly, concepts such as *ecosystem, niche, ecotone, energy, selection strategy, population, deme, carrying capacity,* and *optimal foraging* were imported as operational notions in archaeology (see Harris and Thomas 1991). In anthropology, the initial formulations by Julian Steward, who coined the term *cultural ecology,* were becoming an influential strand in anthropological theory (Hardesty 1980). Culture and environment were viewed as interactive spheres in dialectical interplay, a Marxization of the concepts of feedback and servodynamic reciprocity developed in the cybernetic approaches to systems (Kaplan and Manners 1972). Interlinkage between culture and environment was particularly emphasized by Andrew Vayda and Roy Rappaport (1967), reacting to the view that cultures were shaped by the environment, and that environmental change *causes*

culture change, as propagated by geographer Ellsworth Huntington in 1945, a stray offshoot of German *Anthropogeographie.* Anthropologists like Clifford Geertz (1963, 1965) rejected a simplistic feedback between environment and culture, and realized the power of the concept *system.* The focus shifted to the complex causal networks of interdependent parts. Geertz considered *ecosystem* as a device integrating biology, environment, and culture. This approach was best illustrated by the work of Roy Rappaport (1968) on the Tsembaga Maring farmers of New Guinea.

The *ecosystem* concept was soon to be broadened from its original ecological context under the influence of general systems theory to become fundamental to ecological archaeology. The most influential figure was Kent Flannery, whose research in Oaxaca in Mexico, and explanations of agricultural origins in Mesoamerica and the Near East (e.g., Flannery 1965, 1968, 1969), were instrumental in shaping ecological discourse in contemporary archaeology. In parallel, David Harris' (1969) masterful overview of agricultural origins introduced the concept of ecosystem and the ecological approach as "a unifying conceptual framework within which to investigate the origins of agriculture and the evolution of all agricultural systems" (p. 3). K. W. Butzer (1982) institutionalized this perspective, supplanting his previous landmark textbook, *Environment and Archaeology* (Butzer 1964; revised in 1971 and subtitled "an ecological approach to prehistory").

With the intrusion of postmodern perspectives into archaeology, the concept of *landscape* has been highlighted in the 1990s as a particular creation of social experience (e.g., Tilley 1994, borrowed mostly from Cosgrove 1984 and Daniels and Cosgrove 1988; Bender 1993b; Thomas 1993). In this approach, landscapes belong more to politics than to palynology and palaeoecology. Although landscape was used in environmental archaeology to denote the topographic configuration, geomorphic elements, and biotic features of a region, "landscape" in postmodern archaeology often refers to the built environment (for example, prehistoric monuments in the Avebury area, megalithic monuments in Sweden, cultivated fields in Melanesia, or the urban setting of Belfast: see papers in Bender 1993a; also Tilley 1994). However, landscape not as a physical actuality, but as a symbolic construct, had already been employed in the study of Australian aborigines and their natural habitat (Morphy 1993). The concept of landscape has also been particularly significant in current examinations of rock art (e.g., Mithen 1991; Bradley 1994; Layton 1999; Ouzman 1998).

To broaden landscape studies in archaeology, Ashmore and Knapp (1999) assembled contributions addressing (1) *constructed* landscapes – intentionally designed or historically constituted; (2) *conceptualized* landscapes – natural landscapes of cultural significance; and (3) *ideational* landscapes – "mental images of something" and "emotional" (cultivating or eliciting some spiritual value or ideal) (Knapp and Ashmore 1999: 9–12).

The current usage in archaeology of *landscape* is concordant with the proliferation of this term in various disciplines. In media arts (as in landscapes of body), Platt and Livingston (1995) remark that the recent global struggle for decentralization or separatism has redefined the notion of locale and increased the importance of place. The current appropriation of the *landscape* (a term first used of landscape paintings, to differentiate them from portraits and other scenes in the 1600s) derives from transformations of its meaning in different disciplines and the convergence of the domains of place, locale, habitat, environment, and region. The regionalization of environment, e.g., in land-use planning, regional ecology, and socioeconomic geography (e.g., Dickinson 1970; Chorley and Haggett 1967; McAllister 1973) coincided with the rise of a sentiment celebrating subjective experiences and "nature." In geography, Frenkel (1994) attributes the emergence of bioregionalism in the

1970s, a movement promoting an ecologically sustainable land ethic, to dissatisfaction with a deteriorating environment and diminishing quality of life. The extension of *landscape* to a whole range of human activities and intangible social concerns in the 1970s appears in Nuttgens' (1972: 14) commentary on architecture and town planning, *The Landscape of Ideas*:

> The landscape in its widest sense, the environment, is literally our surroundings. It is the backcloth against which we can measure the importance of our personalities. It is the physical setting of our lives, the moral and intellectual climate in which we work out our destinies, the emotional wilderness or tamed landscape of feeling with which we develop the particulars of our experiences. Yet it is of our making; and we are part of a process shared with our ancestors and our descendants, which modifies our surroundings at every movement in time.

However, landscape as a social, conceptual construct prefigures the current postmodern interest in Jacquetta Hawkes' (1959) masterful "biography" of the British landscape from its geological formation through prehistoric times to the epoch of "Land and Machines" and beyond. Narrated with romantic subjectivity, it rests on solid scholarship. In her preface, the story of the British landscape becomes a creation of the storyteller's mind, with the counterpoint to the creation of the land being the growth of consciousness, its gradual concentration and intensification within the human skull.

The unsung pioneer of landscape archaeology, and for that matter symbolic archaeology, is D. H. Lawrence, whose *Etruscan Places* (1950) narrates his experiences of walking through what was once the Etruscan landscape. Thrilled by the tomb paintings, Lawrence offers interpretations of their symbolism, chastizing a young German archaeologist who is "a modern, and the obvious alone has true meaning to him" (p. 103). Paradoxically, Richard Aldington, in the book's 1950 Introduction, warns the reader: "it is best to think of this as a poet's holiday among the relics of that far-distant past." Aldington underestimated the contribution of Lawrence, who expresses his disdain for museums crammed with objects, although they are instructive for object-lessons. "But who wants object-lessons about vanished races? What one wants is a contact. The Etruscans are not a theory or a thesis. If they are anything, they are an experience" (Lawrence 1950: 167).

Cognition, Communication, and Action

Cognition, the sphere of generating knowledge, is situated in a bodily matrix, and consists of interactive data processing systems, including at one extreme symbolic logic, and at the other extreme aesthetics and feelings. Cognition is inseparable from bodily actions, through necessary sensory inputs. Human cognition is also governed by human biological endowments which find expression within a social milieu. Communication within society and with other societies, as well as between generations, provides a flow of knowledge and beliefs. Cultures emerge and are recognized from the persistent performance of certain actions and adherence to a set of fundamental beliefs, always dependent on their acceptance, passive or active, willingly or under duress, by a majority of individuals. Individuals struggle with their creative impulse, which may work with or against the prevailing order, and may also face unprecedented life situations. New solutions may be accepted, rejected, or modified by others, causing minor or major changes in the social milieu. Certain changes may lead rapidly to radical consequences, altering relations among people (social organization). However, changes may accumulate until a significant alteration in the structure of social relations is achieved.

Cognition, action, and communication are interrelated, yet operate differently and at different scales. The cultural landscape, inherited and actively modified by its inhabitants, constitutes a map of social memory, as well as psychodynamic features creating nodes of social discourse (e.g., the Nile and the Sphinx in Egypt). The prominence of certain physical or cultural features and their durability form social attractors, but oral memories may endow loci lacking visible remains with meanings. This socially constructed materiality of a landscape concerns us when we explore how "cultural" landscapes legitimate power structures. Landscape nodes also serve to launch social changes (e.g., when the pyramids were used during the millennial celebrations to signal Egypt's transition to an age of rock music, laser shows, commercial tourism, and globalization).

A population's long-term viability depends on its ability to live within its range of environmental possibilities; beliefs or bodies of knowledge undermining the reproduction of a breeding population bring its doom, especially during severe environmental fluctuations. An environment's tolerance range, however, is not fixed, and is subject to change via cultural practices. However, there are ultimate constraints. This coexistence of practices and concepts constitutes what we call a *structure*. Yet the survival of a community may depend on adopting new traits that could eventually lead to the emergence of a novel structure.

Thus "adaptation," as the molding of human populations by *external* environmental parameters, and *natural* selection are unacceptable. There is so much latitude within a habitat that would allow "suboptimal" solutions to the complexity of constraints imposed given any specific mode of habitation and environmental exploitation. Several solutions are possible within a "feasible domain." Evolution is guided more by deletion than selection. This leads to indeterminacy and to evolutionary trajectories governed by the previous state of affairs, the current situation, and decisions adopted by a society from each generation. Choices follow social considerations as well as ideology.

We must reformulate *biological* adaptation to fit the human situation, and re-examine natural selection in explaining evolutionary cultural change. This challenges the application of optimization models (see Smith and Winterhalder 1992) that do not consider the behavior of individuals, acting in small communities, in real time. In this situation, where information gathering is by chance (not systematic), geographically localized (to home range and informal networks), and temporally limited (to personal experiences or oral accounts of history), choices fall within a satisfactory domain (cf. Chisholm 1979: 157–69).

Ingold (1996) has likewise argued that it is imperative to acquire sound ecological understanding of how real people relate to their environment. This has far-reaching implications for our perceptions of the world and the cognitive strategies that ensure human survival. One implication is that our mental abilities develop schemata to relate information from different contexts in order to overcome fixations with localized conditions. Our survival and expansion as a species clearly reside in our ability to move between environments and social contexts.

Picturing Landscapes

Before its use in archaeology, landscape was an art subject. Paintings of landscapes in Europe, before abstract expressionism, are portraits of a stretch of country. They differ in style historically and culturally, and are presentations by skilled artists whose sensibilities shape and are shaped by (along with or contrary to) the modes of thought and aesthetics cherished by their generation. Landscape paintings may appear subjective, but were not independent of predominant worldviews. The painting of landscapes also contributed to the perpetuation and modification of their cultures.

In ancient Egypt, an exquisite "landscape" is the scene of marshes from Userkaf's temple (2465–2322 BC), a theme of religious significance but also often associated with scenes of fowling and hunting (Malek 1986). Such scenes are prominent in the Middle Kingdom (Gombrich 1951) and in the New Kingdom. Scenes in tombs also include cultivation and herding, so that the deceased will not be deprived in the afterworld of the good life once enjoyed on earth (Mekhitarian 1978).

In Rome, landscapes occur on the walls and floors of Roman villas, including a Nilotic landscape adorning the villa of a physician at Pompeii, and the pictorial map of the Nile Valley from Palestrina (Silotti 1998: 18, 22–3). Gombrich (1951: 77–8) regarded landscape painting as the greatest innovation of the Hellenistic period. The landscapes were painted to conjure the pleasures of the countryside for sophisticated town dwellers – shepherds and cattle, distant villas and mountains, forming an idyllic scene. Landscape painting also appears as background in medieval illuminated manuscripts of the Middle Ages.

In China, landscape as a genre of painting was cultivated very early. Influenced by the Buddha and Chinese philosophers, artists painted water and mountains in a spirit of reverence and contemplation (Gombrich 1951: 106). In the Song dynasty (960–1276 AD) the Chinese established standards of idyllic nature painting, and became the pioneers of a long tradition that eventually merged with European art in the nineteenth century.

In the seventeenth century, landscapes figured conspicuously in the works of Bril, Elsheimer, Carracci, Lorrain, Van Goyen, and Dürer. The Dutch painters popularized the words *landskip* and *landscap*, which became *landscape* in English and *landschaft* in German. Lorrain (1600–82) painted the landscapes of the Roman Campagna, with majestic reminders of a great past creating a dreamlike vision of antiquity, dipped in a golden or a silvery air.

Rich Englishmen modeled their parks on Lorrain's conception of landscapes (Gombrich 1951: 295).

The emergence of landscape paintings in modern Europe is linked with the development of a worldly art, associated with the rise of crowded commercial towns and factories, and inspired partly by nostalgia for the "country," and partly through the "discovery" of other landscapes and classical antiquity. Klee and Macke traveled to North Africa in 1914, following in the footsteps of Delacroix, who went to Spain and Morocco in 1832. By contrast, Van Gogh (1853–90) was inspired by the Japanese artist Hiroshige (1797–1858), yet although Hiroshige captures the mood of nature in a sympathetic observation of everyday life, Van Gogh used the landscape as an expression of his own tormented self.

Before Van Gogh, Dutch painters like Van Ruisdael (1628?–82) who specialized in the northern forest landscape of Holland, also began to discover the beauty of their own scenery. In England, initial attempts by Reynolds (1723–92) and Gainsborough (1727–88) were followed by the great landscape paintings by Turner (1775–1851) and Constable (1776–1837). Light and shade were employed with sensational effects by Monet (1840–1926) and the Impressionists, who were fascinated with light's ephemeral effects on natural scenery. By contrast, landscapes prominent in the paintings of Cézanne (1839–1906) were inspired by a desire to create a sense of durability instead of the transient sensations created by the Impressionists.

The substratum of the modern European attraction to landscapes thus may be traced to changing social conditions and worldviews that created a break with medieval sensibilities during the Enlightenment, and the appropriation of a sense of the classical past. Nature was contrasted with towns as a source of wonder and legitimation on its own (not as a religious icon or as a backdrop to human activities). Landscapes of "beauty" were valued among the wealthy, natural settings becoming "picturesque." Landscape paintings were also embedded in regional distinctions and national identification with "places." Landscapes became thus a medium for social and political expression.

The European artistic landscape tradition is quite different from that among Australian aborigines, where paintings express the relationship between clans and the land in spiritual terms. Aboriginal art is neither distant contemplation nor self-expression by individual artists; it is instead an art of spiritual communion and social solidarity (cf. Short 1991: 221–2).

Landscape paintings are thus hardly pictorial *representations* of a stretch of land. Artists paint what *they* see, or even as Picasso said, what they "think." Critics do not ask if an artist succeeds or fails in producing a facsimile of the subject, whether a woman or a landscape; instead, they emphasize more the artist's ability to move the viewers, or inspire them with an idea, or evoke moral or religious sentiments. Philosopher John C. Gilmour in *Picturing the World* (1986) rejects the notion that artists champion subjectivity and individual creative expression, asserting that it is misleading to separate the world into objective and subjective spheres: "Artists' works are as historical as anything can be, and that is just what enables us to comprehend them, since we share cultural meanings with them" (Gilmour 1986: 6). Like Gombrich, Gilmour rejects the idea that artworks merely record artists' feelings. Gombrich sees artists as guided by universal visual structures silently operative in our experience. Gilmour adds that artists' visions are not independent of the existing culture, but reflect imaginative expansions (and, I suggest, follow universal transformational rules) beyond the forms of comprehension already at hand (Gilmour 1986: 63). Similarly, Dolgin, Kemmitzer, and Schneider (1977: 91) criticize Merleau-Ponty's essay on Cézanne because of his failure to see the artist's world as shaped by concrete historical and cultural forces. They add that Merleau-Ponty's phenomenology, by setting aside historical and cultural factors, *assumes* a universal existential dilemma.

Social Landscapes

Landscapes in the lives of people are not simply paintings. The landscape is a habitat, the localized environment in which organisms (in this case people) live, where people obtain food and shelter, seek mates, and satisfy their needs, desires, and pleasures.

In contemporary archaeology (particularly in the UK) landscape vies with the more established environment for the attention of a new generation of archaeologists (Bender 1993a; Gosden and Head 1994; Ingold 1986, 1993; Rowlands 1996; Tilley 1994; Ucko and Layton 1999). Bender (1993b: 1) asserts that " 'landscapes' are created by people through their experience and engagement *with the world around them*" (my italics) and other contributors to the book provide examples of this. The concept of landscape becomes an antidote and a substitute to that of the *environment* (see Layton and Ucko 1999: 3), a term introduced into archaeology from ecology to refer to the conditions affecting a particular organism, including physical surroundings, climate, and other living organisms.

The subjective approach to landscapes may be novel in archaeology, but it has a long history in geography. In German geography, landscape science (*Landschaftenkunde*) began with Wimmer in 1885 and was advanced by Schlüter in 1906 and his students Passarge, Waibal, Bobek, Lautensach, and Banse. Schlüter recognized the importance of intangible racial, social, and political conditions on the visible landscape. Banse claimed that "scientific" regional geographies failed, since their authors suppressed their emotional impressions of the country and the people, an approach dubbed *Gestaltende Geographie* or creative geography (Rose 1981: 113–14). In the lands of classical antiquity, the German Landschafts or Landeskunde was influential via Alfred Phillipson

and his follower Ernst Kirsten (Bintliff, pers. comm.).

Kropotkin (1824–1922), who found refuge in Britain for his anarchistic views, highlighted the need to include human relations and issues of human development in geography, and to show the link between the phenomena of the physical world and the feelings and emotions that develop before the eyes and ears (Kropotkin 1885). The role of emotions has been articulated by Yi-Fu Tuan (1974a, 1974b; see also Lowenthal 1961, 1967; Lynch 1972), identifying "places" with their social significance and emotional character: a place is a product of lived experiences over time, which include those that serve as public symbols (e.g., monuments and sacred places) and those, like homes, taverns, and marketplaces, which are "fields of care." In China, the emotional influences of an environment are employed in Feng Shui, the art of arranging one's environment or locating a grave to maximize beneficial psychological effects and minimize harmful effects (Geddes and Grosset 1999). Knowledge of these traditional arts are now in vogue in the United States and Europe, as people seek harmony and look for healing in "nature" from the ailments of modern living.

At present, applications of "cognized" or "ideational" landscapes focus on the ideological, mythical, ritual, and ceremonial construction of landscapes, as well as the landscape as a medium for social interactions. Although not inspired directly by *Landschaftskunde*, the similarities and differences between the two approaches are noteworthy. I am personally wary of trumpeting ethnic identities and the role of landscapes in creating social identity (see Tilley 1996: 162) in the same manner that Banse and other German ideationalists aimed to do with "national" identity. However, I am encouraged by approaches exploring how a landscape is created through bodily experiences and embodied thinking (cf. Mark Johnson's *The Body in the Mind* 1987; also Gould and White's *Mental Maps* 1974).

Without such explicit principles of how a land is perceived and how land features are identified and linked in an image schema, attempts to develop "phenomenological" models of the "operational" environment of a group remain speculative and inadequate.

On a more mundane level, before one develops models of how landscapes are socially or symbolically cognized, the environmental parameters of an area must be adequately known for the period of occupation. Chapman and Gearey (2000) note that Tilley's (1995) phenomenology of landscape on Bodmin Moor in prehistory was based on an erroneous consideration of palaeoecological conditions, warning that if "scientific" sources of data are a low priority for landscape theoreticians, meaning gained will be incomplete. Field methods must also be sound. Fleming (1999) has already questioned this for the studies by Tilley (1994, 1995, 1996) and Bender (Bender et al. 1997).

Landscapes and the World

By contrast to social landscapes, which may be merely artistic achievements or abstract notions of the character of a terrain, an environment refers to the physical and biological parameters that sustain or constrain human life. The environment may be compared with the body in contrast with the social landscape as the image. No matter how Van Gogh's rain is different from that of Hiroshige's, the physical properties of rain, its role in supporting life, causing soil erosion, and its susceptibility to acidification by pollutants, are the same in Japan, China, and Holland.

The study of the hydrological cycle may not be as moving an experience as Van Gogh's brushwork in depicting rain, but hydrological studies are indispensable, as the world faces a water crisis. For example, Egypt cannot overcome water shortages without precise calculations of the Nile's water. No amount of scholarship aimed at treating the Nile as a landscape could allevi-

ate misery or decide whether to build dams, modify crops, or cope with loss of water from canals.

Intersubjective Landscapes: Landscapes and Action

The concept of a social landscape is, in my opinion, inadequate if it cannot be articulated with landscape, environment, and habitat in the ecological sense, and if it does not aim to utilize our understanding of the landscape to solve environmental problems, develop strategies to alleviate poverty, and find food and water for more than a billion human beings who have no clean water. Not only do we need to relativize "our" experiences of a landscape, but we also need to ascertain the *relevance* of specific conceptions of the environment for the task at hand. Such tasks may include overcoming water scarcity in Egypt, dealing with floods in China, or managing waste disposal in Mexico.

The concept of social landscape is not spurious or inconsequential. On the contrary, it is important for understanding the role of worldviews and conceptions on action. But the concept is inadequate without integration into the world of action. It is instructive to inquire about the processes by which a landscape is created in its particularity.

Bender (1993b: 3–10) cites V. S. Naipaul's experience of the Stonehenge English landscape in his book *The Enigma of Arrival* as a case study of how a landscape changes as engagement with the *land* changes. The land with which Naipaul engages is presumably "outside" Naipaul. Not that we should necessarily claim that it (the land) is the "objective" correlate of Naipaul's landscape. All we require is that the land conceived by Naipaul should refer to a place where the local inhabitants have developed certain notions about the significant elements of the landscape. Their notions would also include the way such elements are related, as well as whatever views and beliefs they have on how the land came to be, its history, and significance.

Communities and people are never isolated islands; nothing can ever be strictly and solely particular. The particularity of a landscape is the result of a reworking of traditional, common ways of conceiving a habitat. A landscape as construed by the local inhabitants of Wiltshire or as Naipaul's dislocated, fragmentary landscape are not a matter of whim or individual subjective flight of fancy, even in a novel. Landscapes and environments do not refer to a reality independent of a subject or a subject independent of others. Notions of "reality" are created *collectively* by cognizant, interactive subjects. Our commonsense "realism" need not be an accurate picture of the world, but we could not have survived as a species if our notions of reality were not compatible with the world. Conceptions of land, environment, and habitat as configurations of tangible, physical (biotic and abiotic) elements belong to a knowledge suitable for empirical examination. These conceptions differ from those of a social landscape, which belong to the ethereal domain of transcendental knowledge. Land, rather than landscape, thus may form a common denominator among different individuals or groups, regardless of their "perspective." It is thus easier for two groups to find a common ground when discussing issues related to tangible features of a stretch of land, than if they are dealing with metaphysical or aesthetic concepts.

Landscape Ecology

The Egyptian landscape remains inseparable from the Nile in the mind of Egyptians. Their beliefs and imagery of the Nile landscape may also differ from those of other countries of the Nile Basin. However, agreement about Egypt's share of water depends on measures of Nile flood discharge accepted by all concerned countries and outside observers. In the archaeological past, as now, social interactions were unsustainable if individuals could not put aside their differences to arrive at a common vision and standard canons of engaging with the world. Ecology, as a science, is developing such canons for dealing with the environment.

What is remarkable is that ecology provides common ground to *integrate* the various landscapes created by the "unique" experiences of the various organisms in a habitat. It is important here to emphasize the new development in ecological theory stressing the concept of "landscape" as the combination of various populations, communities, and ecosystems in a heterogeneous environment at different spatial scales. Landscape ecologists describe, analyze, and model the movement of individuals and materials of different organisms between and among communities and ecosystems in space. They are concerned with how a landscape is structured, how it functions, and how it changes (Forman and Godron 1986; Barrett and Peles 1999; Lidicker 1995). In archaeology, landscape as *paysage* was used by Crumley and Marquardt (1990) to provide a similar approach, but with a focus on the spatial manifestations of the ecological relations between humans and their environment. The concept of landscape in geomorphology and geography (Gentilli 1968) falls within the domain of an ecological landscape. However, we must be cognizant of the problem of scale (from large regions to small microhabitats), time (landscapes as a collective manifestation of a configuration that evolved over time), and materiality (inclusion of intangible constructs). The most controversial is the latter point. However, it would appear that the invisible factors belong to the domain of interpretation, which cannot be attempted without reference to tangible phenomena.

An (ecological) landscape may thus be regarded as a tract of land distinguished by its vegetation, animals, landforms, and human activities. Its characteristics and genesis may be analyzed in terms of long-term concatenated additions, deletions, and modification as a consequence of inter-related geological, biological, and human activities and processes.

Butzer's (1982) paradigmatic shift in *Archaeology as Human Ecology* leads to a recognition of the role of cognition in archaeological ecology, amending the short-comings of ecosystems as sets of formal abstract equations (Hassan, in press). Pion-eer work by William Kirk, a British geographer, is particularly significant (see also Clark 1950). Kirk (1952) asserted that it is necessary to analyze the environment as it was observed and thought to be, because physical features acquire values and potenti-alities which attract or repel action. The importance of environmental perception in geography has also been examined by other geographers, including Wright (1947), Lowenthal (1967), Buttimer (1969), Watson (1969), and Brookfield (1969).

In 1979 Rappaport explicated "cognized environment" as the sum total of the phe-nomena that influence an organism's life, ordered into meaningful categories by a population. He contrasts this with the "oper-ational environment" used by Marston Bates (1960) to refer to the sum total of the phe-nomena that enter a reaction system of the organism or otherwise directly impinge upon it to effect its mode of life at any time throughout its life cycle. The application of the "cognized environment" in archaeology is problematic, since inadequacy of relevant data on cognition often forces us to fall back on general models for expectable behavior in the milieu in question (Sprout and Sprout 1965). Nevertheless, this difficulty is intrin-sic to archaeology, which is circumvented through "middle-range" theories. Unless we assume that people of the past were alien creatures, we should be able, using a system-atic methodology and insights from how we perceive the world and how we think and use metaphors and symbols, to explain and understand the cultural and social phenom-ena of the past. We need not fall back on "creative," subjective proclamations, when

our insights can be grounded in empirical evidence, using explicit methods of analysis that can be cross-examined and replicated by any other researcher, as I attempted in deal-ing with the rock art of Nubia (Hassan 1993c). Indeed, it is also possible, as I hope I demonstrated, to link the symbolic inter-pretation of Nubian rock art with the impact of climatic change on territoriality, inter-group aggression, and gender relations. The remedy to uncritical positivism is not exces-sive idealism that detaches ideas from their worldly context (cf. Ley 1980; Berger and Luckman 1966: 186).

The challenge is not new. Carl O. Sauer (1925) defined landscape as an area made up of a distinct association of physical and cultural forms, but rejected particularism and idiographic geography. He asserted that every landscape has individuality as well as other relations to other landscapes. Although Sauer was clearly thinking within the tradition of *Landschaftskunde*, he regarded Banse's notions of "soul" to lie beyond any organized process of acquiring knowledge, which is how he defined science.

Sauer's approach to the landscape did not examine the social processes by which a cul-tural landscape is generated, but his em-phasis on habitat value, on the union of physical and cultural elements of the land-scape, and most importantly on the processes that relate one landscape to another, are par-ticularly relevant in any attempt to forge a new synthesis.

Landscapes: A Transcultural Perspective

An ecological landscape is historical and transcultural. In archaeology, we would be at a loss if we could not compare the way Romans, Arabs, Persians, and Greeks experi-enced the Nile in order to sharpen our under-standing of the transcultural modalities of a landscape, thus allowing us to discern resili-ent features of the landscape, which may be of persistent symbolic and social significance (regardless of culture-specific forms of symbolism and social organization).

This approach was adopted in my examination of the Nile and civilization from prehistoric times to the present (Hassan 1993a; cf. Hassan 1997a, 1997b). The Egyptian landscape was considered in terms of short- and long-term variations in Nile discharge, the impact of such variability on the geological landscape (geomorphic features) and in turn on food productivity, transportation, settlement location, revenues and taxation, and hence the sustainability of people's life-support systems. In another contribution, the demographic and settlement aspects of the landscape in ancient Egypt were modeled on the basis of ethnographic, historical, and archaeological parameters (Hassan 1993b). The different cultural landscapes of the Nile created by successive generations of Egyptians provided a historical landscape that was continually rehearsed as each generation dealt with the memory or lived through episodes of catastrophic overflooding or droughts. The remaking of the Nile floodplain landscape was also subject to prevailing social circumstances, notably the religio-political system and available technology.

Hassan (1981) showed that episodic changes in Nile flood discharge in the magnitudes of several decades were commonplace. This "natural" aspect of the Nile ecology amounts to an environmental constant. Farmers, regardless of who ruled Egypt, faced this natural condition (cf. also Hameed 1984; Fraedrich et al. 1997; Quinn 1993). However, the religio-political organization and water technology played a key role in dealing with the vagaries of Nile floods.

Conceiving Landscapes: Social Models

The sciences do not try to explain, they hardly even try to interpret, they mainly make models. By a model is meant a mathematical construct, which with the addition of certain verbal interpretations, describes observed phenomena. The justification of such a mathematical construct is solely and precisely that it is expected to work. (John van Neumann, cited in J. Gleick 1987)

For me, landscape archaeology is only viable if it reveals the processes by which landscapes are recreated and by which they become transsubjective "realities" to impede or channel change. This understanding must begin through realizing the different scale of the human dimension relative to other ecological phenomena, then by acknowledging that interactions between human beings and their habitat, unlike that of most other organisms, involves (1) gathering information, (2) collating information in (abstract) mental categories, (3) generating mental constructs of the relationships between such categories (e.g., causal, functional, teleological models), and (4) utilizing mental constructs in acting in and upon the habitat.

"Landscapes" created from experience are working models subject to change to accommodate more or different kinds of information (cf. Layton and Ucko 1999: 14). Certain models (for example, that the Nile is fed by a subterranean river, or its source) are irrelevant to how Egyptians in ancient times irrigated their fields. Today, the sources of Nile water and the causes of water flow variations from such sources, and specific details of the Nile Basin, are of paramount importance to Egypt and to other countries that share the Nile, as well as international agencies financing hydraulic projects or concerned with international conflicts.

The key elements in this paradigm are cognition, action, and the interactive feedback dynamics that link these in dealing with the perceived world. In an insightful examination of actions in human geography, Benno Werlen (1993) concludes that objective and subjective perspectives are not mutually exclusive, but they are too general to use in social theory for geography. Reviewing action theories in sociology, he concluded that only subjective agency, however constrained, could move the structures that constrain it.

I am not personally interested in the objective–subjective debate, because of the vagueness of these terms. Rephrasing Werlen, I emphasize agents attempting to *sustain* their lives in whatever shape they construe the objectives of such lives. Agents *act*, individually or with others, based on *their* knowledge of the possibilities and consequences of such actions. Actions generate information, engendering a new state of the knowledge-base, and an awareness of successful or disastrous courses of action.

Landscapes: Models of Scale

The Egyptians were gathering information on the height of Nile floods perhaps even before the first known records dating to the first and second dynasties. Agricultural productivity was, they surmised, linked to flood height, and since revenues to the government followed agricultural productivity it was important to record Nile floods.

The emergence of kingship and state government represents a change in the size of the political unit, and is also a scale of environmental perception quite different from the peasant community. The village, the "elementary" unit of food production, had a worldview based on a local pool of knowledge, in addition to what was introduced by visitors, officials, or neighbors. The king and his court, on the other hand, had a different cognitive map that encompassed a broader spatial scale (approximately 2,500–4,000 villages) of about 700 people each (Hassan 1993b) and a more diverse spatial universe (e.g., farms, mines, transport arteries, national borders). The rulers and priests also developed concepts of time that included a long-term, historical time (evident in their dynasty lists and chronologies tied to a solar calendar) and a cosmic time, which celebrated a "First time" linking the living king to the moment of Creation.

Differences in conceiving the world emerged in a complex hierarchical society between local communities and cosmopolitan urban rulers. However, the "landscapes" of both groups converged on the Nile and the link between flood discharge and food production. In addition, successive rulers, whether Arab, Roman, or Greek, regardless of their particular culture, shared the view that the Nile was the gift of life; that pragmatically, the Nile was the main feature of the Egyptian landscape; and that the landscape was dynamic, reflecting dramatic interannual and episodic fluctuations in Nile flood discharge. However, these cultures could differ on the source of the Nile, its causes and cosmic significance, because such issues had no pragmatic consequences for them.

A related evolutionary perspective on the scale and meaning of social space has also been attempted by Roberts (1996).

Supralocal Landscapes and Power

Models of the land vary in functional power and practical utility. The scale of information gathering and evaluation by the king's intellectual establishment was supralocal and could integrate information from small-scale habitats and thus provide a more adequate basis for *regional* or *national* action, e.g., large-scale hydraulic operations of the Middle Kingdom and the Ptolemaic period in the Faiyum region (Hassan 1997b).

This kind of supralocal knowledge is often regarded as "true" or "objective," but we are concerned here with how in particular localities the "grand" models (e.g., the current genome project, or global climate research) influence action in specific situations. We also want the most adequate explanatory models of specific, significant ecological phenomena in the past (e.g., the transition from foraging to farming and the resilience of the agricultural mode of subsistence in ancient Egypt). Here we are informed by models that belong to a supralocal and supranational intellectual tradition. Initially linked with the kings, dynasties, and religion, this tradition, though still linked to national institutions, is virtually supranational and probably "universal," i.e. intercultural and trans-historical. Within that tradition, the split, since the fifteenth century in Europe, into an explicitly "scientific" stream and a "humanistic" stream drove a chasm between the two in recent times as a result of industrialization.

Scientists, handmaidens of commerce and industry in a world of transnational spatial mobility and communication, developed models of the world remote from social encounters and human agents and closely tied to "grand," transcultural, "universal" models independent of nation-specific religious cosmogony or particularistic ethnic ideology. In dispensing with theogenic models of the land (religious and magical landscapes) scholars embarked on a project with its own cosmogony – efficacious functional power manifest in pragmatic applications in medicine, food production, transportation, communication, manufacture, and energy generation. In geography, standard transsubjective methods developed for making maps and recording geographical phenomena, which eventually led to a quantitative revolution.

Today, the preoccupation with "landscape" as a subjective, social construct is symptomatic of a sentiment that blames science and positivism for all the ills of industrial society. This guilt by association reveals a surprisingly oversimplistic understanding of history and an equally naive approach to philosophy and politics. The ills of the world are caused by poverty and inequality. These are perpetuated by the power to persuade and coerce, keeping a billion human beings hungry and deprived of safe drinking water. Science was not responsible for the demagoguery of Hitler, the fanaticism of fundamentalists, chauvinistic nationalism, or colonialism. Our woes arose out of religious, nationalistic, and partisan notions based on emotional and sentimental persuasion.

Today, the passion for status and consumer goods is a major cause of unhappiness.

As Rosenau (1992: 169) contends

the cost and benefit of modern science must be weighed. More people are alive today than ever before, and a good many of them live better and longer than in the past . . . To question the philosophic and intellectual tradition that gives rise to and sustains this achievement, as the affirmative postmodernists do, is one thing; but to dismiss it altogether, as so many postmodernists do, is quite another.

The attacks on science are elements of antinomial social movements which develop in times of transition and crisis. They accompany feelings of anxiety and exaggerate the terror of disruption, strife, and famine. Such movements provide a platform for status-hungry intellectuals facing political frustrations (Adler 1972: 21). The dissociation between the observing and acting self induces a sense of alienation and a loss of what is deemed essential or sacred. In the early nineteenth century the Romantic movement in literature, art, and philosophy was a reaction to industrialization and the accompanying change in political and social orders. In this movement, as in the postmodern movements, introspective experiences become juxtaposed with the world outside and the social order. Questions of Being become central to intellectual inquiries (Adler 1972: xi, 36–42). Both Romantic and postmodern movements are antipathetic to the Enlightenment, which emphasized order, regularity, and rules. Hence landscape in modern European paintings was linked with the expression of emotions and individual experiences of the phenomenal world. Landscape, as the fusion of self and nature, as a means to grapple with social and political issues, clearly fits the romantic, antinomial tendencies manifest in postmodernism. More telling also is the obsession with the spiritual meaning of landscapes, contrasted against the emphasis on subsistence, population, and settlement in ecological studies. Ten of twelve case studies in *Archaeologies of Landscape* (Ashmore and Knapp 1999) deal with sacred and mythological landscapes. The postmodern and Romantic movements invoked the sacred to heal cognitive dissonance and alleviate personal anxieties.

Reviewing landscape architecture, Bell (2000) stresses the legacy of Wordsworth and Ruskin in the British perception of landscape, particularly Ruskin's view that access to the country was spiritually necessary for the victims of industrialization, exiled from the land to live in factory towns. The current interest in landscapes in archaeology and other disciplines derives from the transition from an industrial to a post-industrial world and from nationalism to globality. Its critique of the modern condition is not without merit, but it is sentimental, legitimated through antinomial philosophers who wrote during the transition to industry and nationalism. It sits in a dead-end populated by fictive dualities of spirit and matter, mind and world, capitalism and Marxism.

In my opinion, the strength of the Romantic and postmodern movements lies in critiquing social issues and mapping subjects that are "normalized" or marginalized. Highlighting power structures in knowledge systems, postmodernism forces scientists to examine the ethos and consequences of modern science. This should not be confused with the epistemological bases of scientific inquiry, but examines the instrumentality of science.

Reexamining landscapes to unmask the social and political mechanisms that legitimate certain political orders is welcome in order to address injustices. Edward Said's *Orientalism* exposed an imaginative geography of Orient and Occident to further political agendas; it was not intended to dismiss positive knowledge, but to add to it.

Studying landscapes and power utilizes spatial information to discuss social inequality based on age, gender, health, occupation, religion, ethnicity, or other social constructs. So far, emphasis has been placed in European studies on gender (e.g., Rose 1992). Future studies should go beyond social issues that concern Europeans, to those critical in non-Western societies. Pluralism in postmodern thought celebrates one's own particular concerns, rather than those of others.

Finally, we should note the power of media in landscape studies, especially the success of GIS in management and the possibilities of multimedia analysis. Presentation and communication of spatial data provide new potentials (Openshaw 1991; Forte and Silotti 1997) through combining factual and imaginative data to examine conceptual notions of landscapes, and to visually apprehend archaeological models of "reality." This power, together with the power of information processing and communication, is central in the new allocation of political power between countries and scholars in various privileged and underprivileged institutions.

Information, Knowledge, and Wisdom

That science has its limits does not imply that it is "wrong." Science is a transnational knowledge-base, a *resource* for making decisions and explaining the world. The wise person knows when to find pleasure in the sunset or comfort in friends, but also when to call a plumber (instead of a poet) or seek the doctor when a child is ill. "Subjectivism" is laudable for illuminating the gaps in scientific knowledge, since, as astutely noted by T. S. Eliot (1961), wisdom may be lost in knowledge.

Ascertaining the state of phenomena (as in the philosophy of science) differs fundamentally from evaluating the adequacy of specific decisions (the domain of wisdom). Wisdom remains outside the arena of scientific falsifiability, because wisdom is a judgment on issues where utility is subjective, involving feelings and morals.

Human Actions Under Uncertainty: The Importance of Being Social

Endowed with the capacity to make choices, acquire skills, and significantly alter their habitat, human beings have crossed a threshold beyond the evolutionary dynamics of other organisms. Although *ultimately* bound with their biological inheritance (which we are now actively redesigning), nonetheless changed via (non-genetic) cultural acquisitions (artificial limbs, eyeglasses, organ transplants, medicine), human beings are proactive agents in a co-evolutionary trajectory with "nature," rendering simplistic dualities of culture and nature invalid and undermining "natural selection." Human ecosystems differ from primarily biological ecosystems in kind and degree (Butzer 1982: 32). Human actions may involve intentionality and purpose, and can transcend local circumstances to create integrative models of fragmentary sensory inputs, and store and recall information at will (cf. Bennett 1976: 35–6; cited in Butzer 1982: 32).

Our ability to overcome our physical habitats, however, is constrained by (1) our partial and subjective (i.e., "biased") knowledge of "others" and "nature"; (2) our inability to foresee the long-term and *all* the tangential consequences and ramifications of our actions; and (3) our frequent inability to do what is "optimal," "rational," or "wise" in favor of what is expedient, satisfactory, and feasible.

What usually saves us is our creative abilities combined with inborn and learned devices to transform personal, subjective knowledge into shared social experience, as well as the aptitude for curating (collective) knowledge and wisdom across generations. The survival of a group in crisis depends on its knowledge capital and individual creativity to find adequate solutions (e.g., modifying social institutions or even worldviews).

Ecology Is Not Destiny, or Is It?

I wished I could have had standing next to me, a Sumerian farmer from about 2500 BC. I wished I could have seen his expression as he looked upon that blasted ruin and the miles of desert about it. There is nothing like standing on the ruins of this distant past to make one wonder what the future will hold. (Seymour and Girardet 1990: 40)

Climate often features as a cause of culture change. However, environmental changes are not necessarily within the perceptual scope and temporal span of the community and its memory, where actions depend on the perceived social and economic costs and benefits from the vantage point of individual actors. Not until a majority take similar actions can we identify a community act, and it requires practices by successive generations over a large area to leave archaeological traces of a cultural tradition. Similar climatic events may thus not inaugurate the same cultural developments in different regions. This reflects regional particularities (opportunities and constraints) and differences in the social and technological aptitude of local inhabitants. Also, regional opportunities and constraints change in response to internal social developments, innovations from elsewhere, or hosting or being replaced by other groups or individuals. Culture change may thus be totally independent of environmental change. A cultural practice can even be imposed in areas that are normally unsuitable for such a mode (e.g., farming in desert regions utilizing wells, or forests where trees are felled).

People also create, willfully or inadvertently, novel environmental conditions. Witness our own current situation of resource depletion, soil erosion, deforestation, and pollution. In engaging with the world today we can ill-afford to shirk our responsibilities, talking about "politics" and "empowerment" whilst retreating into lax relativism, nihilistic subjectivism, and linguistic solipsism. If we genuinely wish to alleviate poverty and combat greed and violence, we cannot undermine human communication and collective action. We should seriously examine our privileged position as "intellectuals" who have a disdain for manual labor and the marketplace. Reexamining our position in the power structure implies that we cannot continue to be cavalier about issues of serious consequence, and we must think of the social ramifications of our discourse. How can we influence policy-makers? We have to judge our ideas, if we wish to redress social inequalities, in terms of their *ground truth*, a term used to refer to the correspondence between interpretations based on remote sensing data and what is actually on the ground. To explain or understand is a means, not an end. Our intellectual wanderings should be guided, as long as they are funded by society, by some social objectives (cf. Rosenau 1992: 168–9).

Quinlan (1996), discussing sustainable development in South Africa, observes that postmodernism is viewed as a distanced analysis of society, a luxury enjoyed by academics from Cambridge and North America. He notes that anthropologists from the North (and we would include archaeologists) disdain applied research, amounting to a retreat from the reality of the social contexts in which they work.

Science provides a method that encourages skepticism, demands evidence, calls for means by which sources are scrutinized and transculturally acceptable canons of reasoning. There are various specific procedures by which this method is actualized. New developments in cognitive sciences and psychology advance our knowledge of intangible domains once regarded beyond science. We must welcome these developments, as we welcome critiques of current scientific procedures and method. We must also keep our wits when confronted with conflicting models of knowledge, and aim to alleviate cognitive dissonance by a genuine search for

means by which various models can be integrated. In the long run we are neither served by trivializing competing models nor by an *ad hoc* agglutination of extreme positions. Historical insights and philosophical inquiries are creative leaps from habitual ruts. They may alert us to take a different direction or to reconsider our positions. In the end, we are not alone and we are in the world. Our attempts to come to grips with how we relate to our habitats have benefited from insights and ideas generated in various social and cultural contexts and in tandem with various historical transformations. In our own lives the emergence of the environmental movement as a grassroots phenomenon, the rise of ecology and population studies as major disciplines of great significance in international relations, and the current reorganization of the world economy and reformulation of the role of the nation-state, require a pause for reflection. Although I am convinced that we cannot solve many of our current problems without major benign technological and scientific breakthroughs, I am equally convinced that without a change of heart such breakthroughs can only perpetuate current inequalities and human misery (Hassan 1983; 1995: 43). Such a change of heart entails no less than a new global ethic that recognizes that environmental objectives are closely linked to the politics of inequality and the economics of greed (cf. Redclift 1984).

The way forward does not lie in a misplaced repudiation of science, but in directing science from the vantage point of our humanistic understanding toward the good of humankind. By exposing the links between ecology and empire (Griffiths and Robin 1997) and tracing the history of ecology, we can evaluate our predicament as dwellers of degraded habitats with colonial environmental habits. Ecological studies, like the surgeon's knife, can hurt or heal. With the vantage point of history we can dispel colonial ecological doctrines, but we may also realize that sound ecological knowledge is indispensable for rehabilitating our impoverished habitats.

Archaeologists can significantly contribute to our understanding of the long-term aspects of ecological change, as well as to the elucidation of how our social institutions and "subjectivity" create and shape our visions of the environment, and how such visions can lead to disaster or help us in overcoming ecological damage and hazards, whether directly related to our misdeeds, or to flares of the sun or the rotation of the earth.

Conclusion

Archaeologists who wish to understand the relationship between culture and environment cannot ignore the role of the cognitive matrix of environmental perception and decision-making. However, cognition must be considered within the context of human actions and their consequences. In addition, although individuals are the elementary units of thinking and action, a society is not sus-

tainable without a coordination of differences and a modicum of contextualized, situational conventions and consensual norms. From this perspective, the usage of the terms *environment* and *landscape* may be clarified as a difference between complementary models of habitats. However, *landscape* has been used in various contexts (e.g., art, geography, geology, and anthropology). Its use in archaeology today as a "social construct" has a long and chequered history in geography, and is arguably insufficient, by comparison with *ecological landscape*, for explaining the relationships between people and their habitats.

Various models of human habitat differ in the scale of their intersubjective domains and relevance, as well as in their scope and purpose. It would be wise to apply various models to their proper domain of activity. In doing so, it would be foolish to lose sight of the ongoing destruction of our human habitat and not to use our archaeological knowledge of social change and historical ecology to find solutions to our current predicament.

Note

1   This contribution does not aim to provide a comprehensive or even a partial bibliographic overview, but one that expresses my own reflections and experiences. For recent worldwide coverage of the archaeology of landscape with ample bibliographic citations, see the contributions in Ucko and Layton (1999).

References

Adler, N. 1972. *New Lifestyles and the Antinomian Personality: The Underground Stream.* New York: Harper.
Ashmore, W. and A. B. Knapp (eds.) 1999. *Archaeologies of Landscape: Contemporary Perspectives.* Oxford: Blackwell.
Barrett, G. W. and J. D. Peles (eds.) 1999. *Landscape Ecology of Small Mammals.* New York: Elsevier.
Bates, M. 1960. "Ecology and evolution". In S. Tax (ed.), *Evolution after Darwin*, vol. 1, pp. 547–68. Chicago: University of Chicago Press.
Bell, S. 2000. *Landscape: Pattern, Perception, and Process.* London: E. and F. Spon.
Bender, B. (ed.) 1993a. *Landscape: Politics and Perspectives.* Oxford: Berg.

Bender, B. 1993b. "Introduction: landscape – meaning and action." In B. Bender (ed.), *Landscape: Politics and Perspectives*, pp. 1–17. Oxford: Berg.

Bender, B., S. Hamilton, and C. Tilley 1997. "Leskernick: stone worlds; alternative narratives; nested landscapes." *Proceedings of the Prehistoric Society*, 63: 147–78.

Berger, P. and T. Luckmann 1966. *The Social Construction of Reality*. New York: Doubleday.

Bradley, R. 1994. *Rock Art and the Prehistory of Atlantic Europe: Signing the Land*. London: Routledge.

Broek, J. O. M. 1965. *Geography: Its Scope and Spirit*. Columbus, OH: Merrill Books.

Brookfield, H. C. 1969. "The environment as perceived." *Progress in Geography*, 1: 51–80.

Buttimer, A. 1969. "Social space in interdisciplinary perspective." *Geographical Review*, 1969: 417–26.

Butzer, K. W. 1964. *Environment and Archaeology: An Introduction to Pleistocene Geography*. Chicago: Aldine Press.

Butzer, K. W. 1982. *Archaeology as Human Ecology*. Cambridge: Cambridge University Press.

Chapman, H. P. and B. R. Gearey 2000. "Palaeoecology and the perception of prehistoric landscapes: some comments on visual approaches to phenomenology." *Antiquity*, 74: 316–19.

Childe, V. G. 1925. *The Dawn of European Civilization*. New York: Vintage Books.

Childe, V. G. 1936. *Man Makes Himself*. New York: Mentor.

Ching-Wei, W. 1938. *Poems*. London: Shenval Press.

Chisholm, M. 1979. *Human Geography: Evolution or Revolution*. Harmondsworth: Penguin Books.

Chorley, R. J. and P. Haggett (eds.) 1967. *Socio-Economic Models in Geography*. London: Methuen.

Clark, G. 1952. *Prehistoric Europe: The Economic Basis*. London: Methuen.

Clark, G. 1968 [1939]. *Archaeology and Society*. London: Methuen.

Clark, G. 1972. "Foreword." In E. S. Higgs (ed.), *Papers in Economic Prehistory*, pp. vii–x. Cambridge: Cambridge University Press.

Clark, K. G. T. 1950. "Certain underpinnings of our arguments in human geography." *Transactions and Papers, Institute of British Geographers*, 16: 15–20.

Cosgrove, D. 1984. *Social Formation and Symbolic Landscape*. London: Croom Helm.

Crumley, C. and W. H. Marquardt 1990. "Landscape: a unifying concept in regional analysis." In K. M. S. Allen, S. W. Green, and E. B. W. Zubrow (eds.), *Interpreting Space: GIS and Archaeology*, pp. 73–9. London: Taylor and Francis.

Daniel, G. 1964. *The Idea of Prehistory*. Harmondsworth: Penguin Books.

Daniels, S. and D. Cosgrove 1988. "Introduction: iconography and landscape." In S. Daniels and D. Cosgrove (eds.), *The Iconography of Landscape*, pp. 1–10. Cambridge: Cambridge University Press.

Dickinson, R. E. 1970. *Regional Ecology: The Study of Man's Environment*. New York: Wiley.

Dolgin, J. L., D. S. Kemmitzer, and D. M. Schneider 1977. *Symbolic Anthropology: A Reader in the Study of Symbols and Meanings*. New York: Columbia University Press.

Eliot, T. S. 1961. *Selected Poems*. London: Faber and Faber.

Flannery, K. V. 1965. "The ecology of early food production in Mesopotamia." *Science*, 147: 1247–56.

Flannery, K. V. 1968. "Archaeological systems theory and early Mesoamerica." In B. S. Meggers (ed.), *Anthropological Archaeology in the Americas*, pp. 67–87. Washington, DC: Anthropological Society of America.

Flannery, K. V. 1969. "Origins and ecological effects of early domestication in Iran and the Near East." In G. W. Dimbleby and P. J. Ucko (eds.), *The Domestication and Exploitation of*

Plants and Animals, pp. 73–100. Chicago: Aldine Press.

Fleming, A. 1999. "Phenomenology and the megaliths of Wales: a dreaming too far." *Oxford Journal of Archaeology*, 18: 119–25.

Forde, C. D. 1934. *Habitat, Economy and Society*. London: Methuen.

Forman, R. T. T. and M. Godron 1986. *Landscape Ecology*. New York: Wiley and Sons.

Forte, M. and A. Silotti 1997. *Virtual Archaeology: Great Discoveries Brought to Life Through Virtual Reality*. London: Thames and Hudson.

Foucault, M. 1977. *Discipline and Punish*. New York: Vintage Books.

Fox, C. 1923. *The Archaeology of the Cambridge Region*. Cambridge: Cambridge University Press.

Fox, C. 1947. *The Personality of Britain*, 4th Edn. Cardiff: National Museum of Wales.

Fraedrich, K., J. Jiang, F.-W. Gerstengarbe, and P. C. Werner 1997. "Multiscale detection of abrupt climate change: applications to River Nile flood levels." *International Journal of Climatology*, 17: 1301–15.

Frenkel, S. 1994. "Old theories in new places? Environmental determinism and bioregionalism." *Professional Geographer*, 46: 289–95.

Geddes and Grosset [publishers] 1999. *Feng Shui*. Lamark, Scotland: Geddes and Grosset.

Geertz, C. 1963. *Agricultural Involution: The Process of Ecological Change in Indonesia*. Berkeley: University of California Press.

Geertz, C. 1965. "Religion as a cultural system." In M. Banton (ed.), *Anthropological Approaches to the Study of Religion*, pp. 1–84. ASA Monograph 3. London: Tavistock.

Gentilli, J. 1968. "Landscape, geographical." In R. W. Fairbridge (ed.), *The Encyclopedia of Geomorphology*, pp. 629–34. New York: Reinhold.

Gilmour, J. C. 1986. *Picturing the World*. Albany: State University of New York Press.

Gleick, J. 1987. *Chaos: Making a New Science*. New York: Viking.

Gombrich, E. H. 1951. *The Story of Art*. New York: Phaidon.

Gosden, C. and L. Head 1994. "Landscape – a usefully ambiguous concept." *Archaeology in Oceania*, 29: 113–16.

Gould, P. and R. White 1974. *Mental Maps*. Harmondsworth: Penguin Books.

Griffiths, T. and L. Robin (eds.) 1997. *Ecology and Empire: Environmental History of Settler Societies*. Edinburgh: Keele University Press.

Hameed, S. 1984. "Fourier analysis of Nile flood levels." *Geophysical Research Letters*, 1: 843–5.

Hardesty, L. 1980. "The use of general ecological principles in archaeology." *Advances in Archaeological Theory*, 3: 157–87.

Harris, D. R. 1969. "Agricultural systems, ecosystems and the origins of agriculture." In G. W. Dimbleby and P. J. Ucko (eds.), *The Domestication and Exploitation of Plants and Animals*, pp. 3–15. Chicago: Aldine Press.

Harris, D. R. and K. Thomas 1991. "Modelling ecological change in environmental archaeology." In D. R. Harris and K. Thomas (eds.), *Modelling Ecological Change*, pp. 91–102. London: Institute of Archaeology.

Harris, M. 1968. *The Rise of Anthropological Theory*. New York: Crowell.

Hassan, F. A. 1981. "Historical Nile floods and their implications for climatic change." *Science*, 212: 1142–5.

Hassan, F. A. 1983. "Earth resources and population: an archaeological perspective." In D. J. Ortner (ed.), *How Humans Adapt: A Biocultural Odyssey*, pp. 191–226. Washington, DC: Smithsonian Institution Press.

Hassan, F. A. 1993a. "Population ecology and civilization in ancient Egypt." In C. L. Crumley (ed.), *Historical Ecology*, pp. 155–81. Santa Fe, NM: School of American Research Press.

Hassan, F. A. 1993b. "Town and village in ancient Egypt: ecology, society and urbanization." In T. Shaw, P. Sinclair, B. Andah, and A. Okpoko (eds.), *The Archaeology of Africa: Food, Metals and Towns*, pp. 551–69. London: Routledge.

Hassan, F. A. 1993c. "Rock art: cognitive schemata and symbolic interpretation." In G. Calegari (ed.), *L'Arte d l'Ambiente del Sahara Prehistorico: Dati e Interpretazioni*. Memorie della Societa Italiana di Scienze Naturali e del Museo Civico di Storia Naturale di Milano, Milan, 26 (2): 269–82.

Hassan, F. A. 1995. "The ecological consequences of evolutionary cultural transformations: the case of Egypt and reflections on global relevance." In S. Ito and Y. Yasuda (eds.), *Nature and Humankind in the Age of Environmental Crisis*, pp. 29–44. Kyoto: International Research Center for Japanese Studies.

Hassan, F. A. 1997a. "The dynamics of a riverine civilization." *World Archaeology*, 29: 51–74.

Hassan, F. A. 1997b. "Nile floods and political disorder in early Egypt." In H. N. Dalfes, G. Kukla, and H. Weiss (eds.), *Third Millennium* BC *Climatic Change and Old World Collapse*, pp. 1–23. Berlin: Springer-Verlag.

Hassan, F. A., in press. "Environmental perception and human responses in history and prehistory." In J. Tainter, R. McIntosh, and S. McIntosh (eds.), *The Way Wind Blows: Climate, History and Human Action*. New York: Columbia University Press.

Hawkes, J. 1959 [1951]. *A Land*. Harmondsworth: Penguin Books.

Holt-Jensen, A. 1999. *Geography: History and Concepts*, 3rd edn. London: Sage Publications.

Huntingdon, E. 1959 [1945]. *Main Springs of Civilization*. New York: Mentor Books, Wiley.

Ingold, T. 1986. *The Appropriation of Nature: Essays on Human Ecology and Social Relations*. Manchester: Manchester University Press.

Ingold, T. 1993. "The temporality of the landscape." *World Archaeology*, 25: 152–74.

Ingold, T. 1996. "The optimal forager and economic man." In P. Descola and G. Pálsson (eds.), *Nature and Society*, pp. 25–44. London: Routledge.

Johnson, M. 1987. *The Body in the Mind*. Chicago: University of Chicago Press.

Kaplan, D. and R. Manners 1972. *Culture Theory*. Englewood Cliff, NJ: Prentice-Hall.

Kirk, W. 1952. "Historical geography and the concept of the behavioral environment." *Indian Geographical Society*. Silver Jubilee and N. Subrahmangam Memorial Volume: 52–160.

Knapp, A. B. and W. Ashmore 1999. "Archaeological landscapes: constructed, conceptualized, ideational." In W. Ashmore and A. B. Knapp (eds.), *Archaeologies of Landscape: Contemporary Perspectives*, pp. 1–30. Oxford: Blackwell.

Kropotkin, P. 1885. "What geography ought to be." *The Nineteenth Century*, 18: 940–56.

Lawrence, D. H. 1950 [1932]. *Etruscan Places*. Harmondsworth: Penguin Books.

Layton, R. 1999. "The Alawa totemic landscape: ecology, religion and politics." In P. Ucko and R. Layton (eds.), *The Archaeology and Anthropology of Landscape*, pp. 219–39. London: Routledge.

Layton, R. and P. Ucko 1999. "Introduction: gazing on the landscape and encountering environment." In P. Ucko and R. Layton (eds.), *The Archaeology and Anthropology of Landscape*, pp. 1–20. London: Routledge.

Ley, D. 1980. *Geography Without Man: A Humanistic Critique*. School of Geography Research Paper 24. Oxford: Oxford University.

Lidicker, W. Z., Jr. (ed.) 1995. *Landscape Approaches in Mammalian Ecology and Conservation*. Minneapolis: University of Minnesota Press.

Lowenthal, D. 1961. "Geography, experience, and imagination: toward a geographical epistemology." *Annals of the Association of American Geographers*, 51: 241–60.

Lowenthal, D. (ed.) 1967. *Environmental Perception and Behavior*. Research Paper, University of Chicago, Department of Geography, No. 109.

Lynch, K. 1972. "What time is this place?" *Cambridge University Forum*, 9: 27–32.

McAllister, D. M. (ed.) 1973. *Environment: A New Focus for Land-Use Planning*. Washington, DC: National Science Foundation.

Malek, J. 1986. *In the Shadow of the Pyramids: Egypt During the Old Kingdom*. Cairo: American University in Cairo Press.

Mekhitarian, A. 1978. *Egyptian Painting*. New York: Rizzoli.

Mithen, S. 1991. "Ecological interpretations of Palaeolithic art." *Proceedings of the Prehistoric Society*, 57: 103–14.

Morphy, H. 1993. "Colonialism, history and the construction of place: the politics of landscape in northern Australia." In B. Bender (ed.), *Landscape: Politics and Perspectives*, pp. 205–43. Oxford: Berg.

Nuttgens, P. 1972. *The Landscape of Ideas*. London: Faber and Faber.

Odum, E. P. 1959. *Fundamentals of Ecology*, 2nd edn. Philadelphia: Saunders.

Openshaw, S. 1991. "A view on the GIS crisis in geography, or, using GIS to put Humpty Dumpty back together again." *Environment and Planning A*, 23: 621–8.

Ouzman, S. 1998. "Towards a mindscape of landscape: rock-art as expression of world-understanding." In C. Chippindale and P. S. C. Taçon (eds.), *The Archaeology of Rock Art*, pp. 30–41. Cambridge: Cambridge University Press.

Peake, H. and H. J. Fleure 1927. *Peasants and Potters*. Oxford: Clarendon Press.

Platt, L. and J. Livingston 1995. "(Pre) text. In landscape(s)." *Felix: A Journal of Media, Arts and Communication*, 2 (1): 8.

Potter, T. W. 1979. *The Changing Landscape of South Etruria*. London: Paul Elek.

Quinlan, T. 1996. "Circumscribing the environment: sustainable development, ethnography and applied anthropology in Southern Africa." In V. Hubinger (ed.), *Grasping the Changing World: Anthropological Concepts in the Postmodern Era*, pp. 74–99. London: Routledge.

Quinn, W. H. 1993. "The large-scale ENSO event, the El Niño, and other important regional features." *Bulletin de l'Institut Française d'Etudes Andines*, 22 (1): 13–34.

Rappaport, R. A. 1968. *Pigs for the Ancestors: Ritual in the Ecology of a New Guinea People*. New Haven, CT: Yale University Press.

Rappaport, R. A. 1979. *Ecology: Meaning and Religion*. Berkeley, CA: North Atlantic Books.

Redclift, M. 1984. *Development and the Environmental Crisis: Red or Green Alternatives?* London: Methuen.

Roberts, B. K. 1996. *Landscapes of Settlement*. London: Routledge.

Rose, C. 1981. "Wilhelm Dilthey's philosophy of Historical Understanding: a neglected contemporary of heritage of humanistic geography." In R. Stoddart (ed.), *Geography, Ideology and Social Concern*, pp. 99–133. Oxford: Blackwell.

Rose, G. 1992. "Geography as a science of observation: the landscape, the gaze, and masculinity." In F. Driver and G. Rose (eds.), *Nature and Science: Essays in the History of Geographical Knowledge*. Historical Geography Research Series, No. 28, pp. 8–18.

Rosenau, P. M. 1992. *Postmodernism and the Social Sciences: Insights, Inroads, and Intrusions*. Princeton, NJ: Princeton University Press.

Rowlands, M. 1996. "Looking at financial landscapes: a contextual analysis of ROSCAs in Cameroon." In S. Ardener and S. Burman (eds.), *Money Go Rounds*, pp. 111–24. Oxford: Berg.

Said, E. 1978. *Orientalism*. New York: Vintage.

Sauer, C. O. 1925. "The morphology of landscape." *University of California Publications in Geography*, 2: 19–54.

Seymour, J. and H. Girardet 1990. *Far From Paradise: The Story of Human Impact on the Environment*. London: Green.

Short, J. R. 1991. *Imagined Country: Society, Culture and Environment*. London: Routledge.

Silotti, A. 1998. *Egypt, Lost and Found*. London: Thames and Hudson.

Smith, E. A. and B. Winterhalder (eds.) 1992. *Evolutionary Ecology and Human Behavior*. Chicago: Aldine Press.

Sprout, H. and M. Sprout 1965. *The Ecological Perspective on Human Affairs*. Princeton, NJ: Princeton University Press.

Thomas, J. 1993. "The politics of vision and the archaeologies of landscape." In B. Bender (ed.), *Landscape: Politics and Perspectives*, pp. 19–48. Oxford: Berg.

Tilley, C. 1994. *A Phenomenology of Landscape: Places, Paths and Monuments*. Oxford: Berg.

Tilley, C. 1995. "Rocks as resources: landscapes and power." *Cornish Archaeology*, 34: 5–57.

Tilley, C. 1996. "Power of rocks: topography and monument construction on Bodmin Moor." *World Archaeology*, 28: 161–76.

Tuan, Y.-F. 1974a. "Space and place: humanistic perspective." *Progress in Geography*, 6: 233–46.

Tuan, Y.-F. 1974b. *Topophilia: A Study of Environmental Perception, Attitudes, and Values*. Englewood Cliffs, NJ: Prentice-Hall.

Ucko, P. J. and R. Layton (eds.) 1999. *The Archaeology and Anthropology of Landscape*. London: Routledge.

Vayda, A. P. and R. A. Rappaport 1967. "Ecology, cultural and non-cultural." In J. Cliffton (ed.), *Introduction to Cultural Anthropology*, pp. 456–79. Boston: Houghton Mifflin.

Vita-Finzi, C. and E. S. Higgs 1970. "Prehistoric economy in the Mount Carmel area of Palestine: site catchment analysis." *Proceedings of the Prehistoric Society*, 36: 1–37.

Watson, W. 1969. "The role of illusion in North American geography: a note on the geography of North American settlement." *Canadian Geographer*, 13: 10–27.

Werlen, B. 1993. *Society, Action and Space: An Alternative Human Geography*. London: Routledge.

Willey, G. R. and J. A. Sabloff 1973. *A History of American Archaeology*. San Francisco: Freeman.

Wright, J. K. 1947. "Terrae incognitae: the place of imagination in geography." *Annals of the Association of American Geographers*, 37: 1–15.

Zeuner, F. E. 1952. *Dating the Past*. London: Methuen.

18

The Archaeology of Landscape

T. J. Wilkinson

Introduction

Landscape archaeology examines how the land has been shaped and organized for economic, social, religious, symbolic, or cultural processes. It also explores the role of landscape in the construction of myth and history, as well as the shaping of human behaviors (Metheny 1996: 384). This definition stresses cultural factors, but landscape is in reality a combined product of the "natural environment" and cultural factors. In order to get a balanced view of how any archaeological landscape was formed, we should be familiar not only with the ecosystems and geoarchaeology of the area in question, but also with the cultural record. This includes settlement sites as recorded by archaeological survey, traces of economic activity (fields, roads, quarries, etc.), and inferences concerning symbolic or ritual landscapes.

Landscape archaeology has a history that covers much of the twentieth century. In Britain and the Middle East major advances were made with the introduction of aerial photography in the 1920s. Thus O. G. S. Crawford and John Bradford built upon this early opportunity by developing the field around a pragmatic set of techniques and within a historical context. The historical approach has since been followed by studies such as *The Making of the English*

Landscape by W. G. Hoskins (1955) and *Les Caractères originaux de l'histoire rural français* by M. Bloch (1952). Another strand built upon the work of locational geographers such as Haggett and Chorley, which itself resulted in a new wave of response from the postprocessual school, such as Christopher Tilley, Barbara Bender, and others. Today, all three strands continue to be followed, often using different data sets, but to be most effective landscape archaeology should follow a more integrated approach which combines landscape history, aerial survey, and space imagery, as well as more humanistic phenomenological approaches, and environmental archaeology.

The focus here is upon Near Eastern landscapes, but the analysis will range widely, starting with some observations on aspects of archaeological landscapes in the British Isles. The objective here is not to provide a review article on the subject of landscape archaeology, but rather to demonstrate how the record of ancient off-site features and settlement can be critically interpreted to provide a meaningful interpretation of past societies. Although much archaeological data inevitably derive from the excavation of individual sites, it is the landscape that provides the context for much of those data. For example, carbonized plant remains and animal bones before they became "ecofacts" spent most of their existence within the landscape. Not only did surrounding fields, pastures, marshlands, and so on provide the economic context for human survival, but also many natural places beyond the site provided additional ritual and religious foci for the inhabitants.

One attraction of landscape archaeology is that it can encompass the extremes of both positivist processualist archaeologies and that of postprocessualist thought; contrast, for example, chapter 1 of Rossignal (1992) with its quest for a scientifically compatible "landscape approach" to Tilley's (1994) chapter 1 which emphasizes an understanding of how things are experienced by a subject. To some, such a divergence of approaches can be construed as a disadvantage, as old certainties are thrown away and new uncertainties introduced. Nevertheless, a brief perusal of the literature suggests that there are many landscape archaeologies, often with little to connect them but the term *landscape* itself. The field can be divided in many ways, ranging from subspecialties whose practitioners see the subject from the standpoint of local or landscape history (Aston 1985; Taylor 1983), to those who look at more ancient landscapes from a symbolic and more abstracted perspective (Tilley 1994). To others, landscape is a convenient term for settlements, such that non-settlement features are hardly considered. Even when landscape features such as fields are considered, they are sometimes studied as artefacts in their own right and are divorced from the settlements that they relate to (Rippon 1997: 3). Clearly, a more holistic approach is required, and although the often exclusive focus upon settlement pattern is understandable, the terms *settlement* and *landscape* should not be viewed as interchangeable.

Landscapes of various ages have been tackled using a wide range of approaches, ranging from data-oriented techniques of intensive archaeological survey (e.g., Cherry et al. 1991) to more subjective, phenomenological standpoints which place a major emphasis on social action. It can be argued, however, that landscape archaeology has the potential to be truly unifying, bridging the gulf between "scientific" or positivist archaeologies and those that approach it from the perspective of social theory or the humanities (Thomas 1993: 20). Here I make a case for more integrated studies of landscapes in which ecological, economic, cultural, political, and symbolic features of landscapes are all treated to provide a broader and more varied pattern than has been hitherto possible. One should be careful, however, to avoid being too inclusive, otherwise the study would become so vague or indeed vacuous that the only advantage would be that there was room enough for all (Thomas 1993: 20). Beneath such an umbrella, even if certain topics are neglected, the framework that has been erected should still allow other interpretations to be made. My own approach has concentrated on the use of off-site records to infer the spatial layout of economic landscapes. Although this has been undertaken apparently at the expense of symbolic or ritual elements, the overall structure laid down should still allow for additional layers of data and interpretation. The progressive updating of the landscape record is illustrated by the example quoted below from Tell Sweyhat, Syria.

Although the landscape record holds intrinsic interest, it will not necessarily be meaningful because it may represent an uninterpretable mixture of information of various ages. Analysis of the integrity of the available record is therefore a critical first step prior to its interpretation. One productive approach is to examine the integrity of the landscape record for the Near East within a taphonomic framework (outlined below), emphasis being placed first on the material record of landscape features, second on its loss by attrition, third on the inference of various land-use types, and fourth on more abstract components of the landscape such as open areas and symbolic space. At the outset it is necessary to emphasize the potential complexity of the landscape record, which incorporates both human and physical processes, as well as phases of abandonment and settlement shift, all of which leave their characteristic imprints on the land.

- The material record: through the combination of air photo analysis, satellite imagery, and intensive archaeological survey, it is possible to infer the pattern of sedentary settlements, route systems, and irrigation canals, as well as patterns of intensive land use.
- Taphonomy and geoarchaeology are relevant to the recognition of processes that result in the steady loss of earlier landscape features and sites.
- Bearing taphonomic considerations in mind, landscapes can be reconstructed for certain time periods. These landscapes can then be compared with other sources of on-site data (for example, carbonized plant and faunal remains), to provide a more robust interpretation of where, for instance, specific crops were grown or animals pastured. Such approaches to the cultural landscape are well illustrated by the Scandinavian school of ecological landscape analysis (e.g., Berglund 1988; and various essays in Birks et al. 1988).
- Open spaces in the landscape may be inferred as forming merely negative space around the other types of land use, but alternatively these negative spaces can be "read" as potentially having had specific functions. In addition to their contribution to the rural economy, open spaces could have served as points of exchange, gathering places in general, ritual areas, pastoral zones, or of course could have been entirely unused.

By viewing landscapes within a taphonomic framework we may be able to understand why fundamental landscape features have remained in place or been lost from view. However, when doubt exists regarding the description, date, or function of any landscape element, excavation should be undertaken to provide confirmation (Bradford 1980). Such controls have been employed for many years in parts of the Old and New World, but elsewhere, including in the Near East, there is an urgent need to excavate off-site features such as canals, linear hollows, etc. in order to confirm both their function and date. It is also necessary to supplement processualist economic landscape models with models that recognize foci of social power and symbolic places in the landscape. The latter approaches have been neglected by many landscape archaeologists working in the Near East, who instead have wrestled to make sense of the vast array of landscape data and material remains which refer more to economic activities. For landscape archaeology, as in archaeological survey and regional studies in general, it is best to employ a multi-stage methodology over many seasons, in order to reexamine the landscapes described and to remap them if necessary to bring fresh insights to bear upon their interpretation.

Cultural Transformations of the Landscape

Transformations of the landscape fall into two basic components: cultural and environmental process (Schiffer's *c* and *n* transformations: Schiffer 1987: 22). I shall deal first with cultural processes, geoarchaeological transformations being touched upon below.

Early landscape archaeologists were well aware of the problems of transformation of the landscape record. For example, Bradford (1980: 208) describes the progressive loss by attrition of key elements in a system of centuriated fields (also Guy and Passelac 1991: ill, 3). In this chapter the notion of taphonomy is employed in order to understand how the present landscape got to be the way it is today. Strictly speaking, taphonomy is the systematic study of death assemblages of bioarchaeological materials so that we can know what processes and biases operated to produce the fossil record.

The problem confronted by landscape archaeologists is that both modern and ancient landscapes provide a palimpsest of features which have resulted from both progressive additions of features and a selective loss through time, so that any one feature, be it modern or ancient, could be of many different dates. Any given landscape feature may therefore include a number of components that reflect a long history of use. In Britain, for example, although a "modern" field boundary is in use today, part of it may be truly ancient, with a continuous history extending back to the first millennium BC or much earlier, or it might follow an earlier ditch or boundary and be separated from that feature's use by an unknown interval of time. Conversely, certain field boundaries could be as late as the parliamentary enclosures of the later eighteenth and nineteenth centuries. Roberts points out that earlier features, such as sectors of ancient boundaries, can persist in the landscape as antecedent features; these are then added to by accretions of later elements, such as additional boundaries that he terms successor features (Roberts 1987: 28). Fundamental to landscape analysis, therefore, is the principle of retrogressive analysis, which views historical landscapes as consisting of a series of layers that can be peeled off one by one (Williamson 1987; Rippon 1997: 24).

In order to make sense of the very complex record that remains, it is necessary to build up some general principles of landscape taphonomy. Some twenty-five years ago Christopher Taylor elaborated a landscape theory which recognized two basic landscape components: zones of survival and zones of destruction (Taylor 1972: 109–10; 1983: 17–20; Williamson 1998). Taylor's admittedly pessimistic scenario considered that it was not possible to recover settlement patterns in pre-Saxon Britain because an unknown and unknowable portion of the record had been lost within these zones of destruction that constitute the lion's share of the land surface. Although partially true, some of Taylor's misgivings have been addressed by the increase in intensive survey and field walking, topics that are beyond the scope of this chapter.

At the most general level it can be argued that any given landscape feature (such as a field boundary or canal) will survive in the landscape until there is a force of sufficient magnitude (social, political, or physical) to erase or obscure it. In addition, in the context of ecological landscape systems, it is much easier to maintain a given ecosystem than to recreate it once it has been lost (Emanuelsson 1988: 116); examples being the maintenance or recreation of a wooded meadow, or cleaning out canals rather than their initial excavation.

In Britain, Christopher Taylor's model can be modified to include the following zones (Williamson 1998):

1 Uplands above the moorland edge form zones of survival because there has been little subsequent occupation to remove the earlier landscape features. Contained within such landscapes are relict field systems such as the Dartmoor Reaves, that can date back to the Bronze Age (Fleming 1988).

2 The lowland zone, although long settled, may be regarded as the zone of destruction (or as I prefer it, the zone of attrition). The degree of relict or "perpetuated" landscapes (see below) in such areas is still poorly understood, but it is clear that many early landscape features have been erased by later occupations. What remains is a meshwork of features from many periods within the modern field patterns.

3 Finally, there is a coastal zone which provides a complex mosaic of landscapes, some preserved in fine detail with abundant waterlogged remains, while elsewhere the record can be grossly eroded and bereft of all traces of ancient occupation. Burial is a key element in tidal landscapes; features such as ancient salt-evaporation hearths, wooden platforms and trackways, or even human

footprints, fish traps, boats, and related installations (Fulford et al. 1997) can often be recorded in a sedimentary context within such landscapes. Although coastal landscapes frequently lack the spatial extent to rival the dryland record, in some cases wide exposures of intertidal features such as fields that existed prior to submergence can extend the dryland record (Thomas 1978). In general, intertidal landscapes make up for any loss of spatial extent by detail that can amplify and extend the eroded and degraded record of the drylands.

In addition, special types of landscape include:

4   Inland wetland landscapes (e.g., Coles and Coles 1989; Purdy 1988), which include raised bogs, lakeshore landscapes with dwellings, and other wetlands that provide extraordinary levels of preservation of both sites and landscapes.

Other "landscapes of protection" might also include:

5   Buried landscapes, which usually provide information that is of limited spatial extent, but in which features are contained within a sedimentary context that has considerable potential for environmental analysis (Crowther et al. 1985). Although spatial extent may often be sacrificed for a good sedimentary context, in certain circumstances complete landscapes can be buried, such as the Neolithic field systems buried below blanket bog in County Mayo, Ireland (Caulfield 1978: 138–9).

Landscapes of protection also include areas that have become reforested, as in the case of sites in the Mayan lowlands and other parts of the New World. In such locations, although the reestablishment of woodland protects the sites, the terrain is difficult to survey, and because landscape elements are not visible over large areas and are difficult to relate to each other, such landscapes remain difficult to analyze. However, in key areas of patchy forested lowlands, causeways and roads are readily visible (Denevan 1991).

Of the above, zone 2 requires elaboration because it probably has the longest history of continuous human settlement and presents the greatest problem in terms of attrition of archaeological features. Relatively little analytical work has been done on this zone in the Near East, but the methodologies discussed could fruitfully be employed in future and hence are elaborated here.

Relict Field Systems Enshrined Within the Modern Landscape

Earlier this century air photography was a driving force behind the development of landscape archaeology, and the technique resulted in the recognition of complex landscapes of crop marks. When combined with detailed cartographic analysis of modern field boundaries, this approach has pinpointed entire relict landscapes enshrined within the agricultural lowlands of England. In addition to crop marks of settlements and droveways, crop marks of Roman or Iron Age coaxial or brickwork field systems have been recognized, for example in Nottinghamshire (Riley 1980) and in East Anglia.

It is necessary to investigate ancient field systems using as many different sources of information as possible. Williamson (1987) and Rodwell (1978) employed relationships between dated features such as Roman roads to provide a horizontal stratigraphy of East Anglian field systems. Some rectilinear field systems may not be as old as they appear, however, and recent studies in Essex show that certain rectilinear field systems were more likely mid-or late Saxon (Rippon 1991: 55), contrary to the widespread belief that they date to the late Iron Age or Roman period (Rodwell 1978: fig. 11.3). Furthermore, in the area of Grays Thurrock these "relict landscapes" do not constitute a single entity, because there are various morphologically distinct landscapes in the area that include both Roman and Saxon/medieval elements. Nevertheless, individual morphological zones appear to have been deliberately planned out. It is therefore necessary to analyze such systems using a large battery of techniques: early maps, air photography, palynology, documentary records, sites and monuments data, and hedge dating. If such systems have accreted through time by progressive increments of additions, as well as having degraded by some removals, it becomes important to date by excavation as many parts of the landscape as possible, rather than simply seeing them as comprising one overall system.

If field systems grow piecemeal then any visible system will include relicts of earlier fields. Thus in Penwith, Cornwall, patterns of small, irregular, strongly lynchetted, stone-walled fields seem to perpetuate ancient field patterns (Smith 1996). Such fields, which are likely to be no later than the nearby courtyard house settlement of Chysauster, are termed by Smith *perpetuated* because the existing patterns appear to perpetuate earlier ones. Although the investigator considers this extensive system to be rare within the British landscape, the presence of such fields raises the question that many other Old World field systems may similarly be perpetuations of earlier systems (Williamson 1998: 20).

If they have not been subjected to a single phase of land reorganization, agricultural lowlands of the Old World can frequently be seen to contain a complex pattern of earlier field systems. Some elements may be enshrined within modern field boundaries (i.e., Smith's perpetuated fields), others remain as crop marks within and discordant to existing field systems, while an unquantifiable number are lost entirely. Questions for future investigation are: just how old are existing features of the landscape in these areas? Thus, can features such as sunken lanes be traced back thousands or merely hundreds of years? Given that major realignments of field systems can be socially traumatic (e.g., the parliamentary enclosures in Britain in the eighteenth and nineteenth centuries), the recognition of such events may imply major political and social upheavals. Such traumas, if independently dated, may be related either to the on-site record recovered by excavation, or may be more evident in the landscape. Alternatively, the persistence of certain landscapes over many millennia may imply a more stable history than is perceived by the rough and tumble of political histories. This is illustrated for Britain by the evolution of pre-Roman landscapes into their Roman counterparts without any apparent major changes (Fulford 1990: 26).

Physical Transformations of the Landscape Record

Geomorphological processes can result in either the wholesale disturbance of archaeological sites and landscape features or their loss as a result of burial beneath a blanket of later sediments. It is therefore crucial for the landscape archaeologist to be able to estimate how much of the cultural record has been lost in this way. In addition, landscape archaeology provides a range of evidence and theoretical approaches that can contribute to the development of geoarchaeology as a mature and autonomous field.

For example, in the Near East, hollow way routes partly develop along long-used tracks, which then became paths for concentrated overland flow (Tsoar and Yekutieli 1993). The resultant hollows contributed to the development of drainage nets, flood runoff, and sediment yield, and therefore fed into the "environmental" record of sedimentary sequences. Apparently unrelated are large pits that normally developed around Near Eastern sites as a result of the extraction of vast amounts of clay for the construction of mudbrick buildings (Wilkinson and Tucker 1995). These pits then became filled as a result of the rapid deposition of sediments washed from the adjacent sites and along tracks that led towards those sites. Because the tracks directed water to the sites, they contributed to the sedimentary infilling of the adjacent clay pits, which then formed water holes or remained as fetid swamps. The reason that these features are not always visible on the surface is that the erosion products from both the site's catchment and the tell will have infilled them.

Other culturally induced geoarchaeological processes include differential flows of soil minerals and nutrients that result from agricultural activities around archaeological sites (Dodgshon 1994). Just as intensively cultivated fields and manured fields can accumulate phosphates and certain trace metals which then form a halo surrounding the sites (Bintliff et al. 1992), so we may expect to see zones of depletion where replenishment has not kept up with removal of nutrients and certain soil minerals. As hierarchical settlement patterns grew up and staple foods such as cereals were exchanged between communities, we would therefore expect to see asymmetrical flows of minerals, trace elements, and nutrients develop. As a result of such commodity flows, settlement catchments that are in the long term net exporters of grain to neighboring communities will also be net exporters of nutrients and minerals. Although seemingly trivial in the short term, over the long periods involved in Near Eastern archaeology (for example, 3,000 years from the Halaf to the end of the Early Bronze Age occupations), we may expect to see a naturally determined distribution of soil-forming minerals being replaced progressively by a patchy, culturally determined distribution.

Overflow from lowland rivers and ancient canals can discharge large quantities of water into flood basins, with the result that extensive shallow lakes and swamps can develop, together with their associated sedimentary accumulations (Adams 1981). These deposits then remained as a stratigraphic marker, until the locus of canal irrigation shifted, which then resulted in new sedimentary bodies. Such developments provide an explicit link between cultural processes and sedimentary systems, the latter normally being regarded as natural in origin.

Social Memory

Just as the physical remains of features such as relict or perpetuated fields imply that the landscape acts as a memory bank, both storing and losing features through time, so human inhabitants also provide a long-term memory. As long-term actors in the landscape, humans are intimately acquainted with their own landscapes, both through tradition and experience. In *A Phenomenology of Landscape* (1994), Tilley notes that all locales and landscapes are embedded in social and individual memories. Thus human activities become inscribed in the landscape, and every cliff, large tree, stream, and other topographic feature becomes a familiar place, until the landscape effectively becomes a biographic encounter. This is well illustrated in Yemen in southwest Arabia, where seemingly every topographic feature has a name. Together, such features provide a grid of reference points, which unlike our own grid systems also has time-depth. Toponyms also include archaeological features such as dams, monumental terrace walls, and cross-valley walls dated to the Himyarite state that existed some 2,000 years ago. Discussion with the local inhabitants shows that names of specific topographic features are often the same as mentioned in the writings of the Islamic historian al-Hamdani of the tenth century AD, who in turn refers to these features as being of Himyarite date.

Tells may also have played a similar role as a memory bank, and John Chapman (1997: 40) has pointed out that tells in the Hungarian plain have a strong presence of public symbolism. The longevity of the tell, combined with its visibility and its "place-value," contribute to a sanctity of place which flat sites cannot match. This sanctity increases the social power of those in place to deal with ritual and ceremony (visibility, sanctity, and permanence). From a more positivist standpoint, tells show considerable time-depth, and their surrounding landscapes should be expected to show signs of long-term degradation as well as "embedded" features that result from long continued use of selected areas (such as paths or routeways). Therefore, whether one has a post-processual or processual viewpoint, tells are special features that should exhibit social depth, embedded landscape features, and enhanced traces of physical transformation.

Landscape Archaeology in the Near East

The landscape record on the ground

The landscape of the Near East shows considerable potential for the reconstruction of ancient landscapes back to at least the fourth to fifth millennia BC. Such reconstructions are possible because many parts of the Near East were densely populated some 4,000–5,000 years ago, to such a degree that urban sites of up to 50, 100, or even 400 ha (in the case of early third millennium BC Warka) left a fairly heavy imprint on the landscape. By combining air photo and satellite remote sensing with intensive archaeological survey, selective excavation, geoarchaeology, and the use of ancient cuneiform texts, estimates can be made of landscape signatures for certain time periods. Although still at a preliminary stage, these reconstructions take us some way beyond either settlement pattern studies or the inferential approaches of site catchment analysis.

Principles of landscape taphonomy can be applied to Near Eastern landscapes using a variant on Christopher Taylor's model (discussed above). Deserts, if they were ever settled, provide classic examples of landscapes of survival. Where subsequent settlement has been minimal, buildings, field boundaries, marker cairns, water supply

tanks, and other features can be preserved virtually intact. In contrast, in more humid areas such as the Levant or highland Yemen, the landscape may have been occupied more or less continuously, so that later landscapes have either accreted onto or erased earlier landscapes. As a result, palimpsests of features have accumulated. Later features may therefore have either followed, replaced, crossed, or partly erased earlier features (see below: Yemen). More humid areas can show the imprint of relict or perpetuated landscapes such as Roman centuriation (in western Syria), or massive suites of terraces (in highland Yemen). In the latter case the construction of fields results in the recycling of many landscape elements, so that only the most robust remain. As a result of the complexity of cultural patterning, taphonomic zones are patchy, with zones of attrition and survival alternating.

Landscape taphonomic zones can be illustrated for a hypothetical transect across the Fertile Crescent from the moist steppe to the desert. In this model, settlement and landscape preservation increase toward the desert, whereas the potential for long-term settlement and agriculture (as well as for landscape transformation) increases toward the moist climatic zone. Because settlement is often increasingly dispersed in the desert margins, paradoxically, in areas that are precarious for long-term settlement, the total number of archaeological sites can be higher than in the well-watered zones. Thus recent surveys show a "site" density of 8 per sq km for a part of the Negev, 2.5 per sq km for the Jordanian semi-desert fringe, and < 1 site per sq km in the moist agricultural steppe of northern Iraq (Avner 1998: 148; Kennedy 2001: 41; Wilkinson and Tucker 1995). This patterning occurs, in part, because the type of settlement in marginal zones is different: for example, what is often declared to be a site in the desert can be a small activity area, whereas settlement in the well-watered plains of the Fertile Crescent is frequently nucleated into prominent and frequently extensive tells. Although this model oversimplifies a more complex reality, it serves to illustrate that archaeological remains do not necessarily decrease in a linear manner toward the desert. Tentatively, this trend can be seen to be partly the result of changing types of settlement (dispersed, sometimes episodic versus nucleated) within different physical landscapes and partly because of the operation of different degrees of physical attrition that prevail in different landscape regions (Figure 18.1).

The zone of preservation in deserts, and some uplands (zones 1 and 2)

Although deserts are not normally occupied by long-term sedentary settlement, if settlement has occurred there is little chance of it being erased by subsequent settlement. As a result, archaeological remains can be remarkably well preserved. Indeed, some of the first steps in landscape archaeology were conducted in the hyperarid regions of the Gobi and Takla Makan deserts where relict canals, off-site sherd scatters, and fos-

silized orchards, dating from the first millennium AD, were all recorded in fine detail (Stein 1921).

Probably the best examples of zones of preservation occur where economic or political factors have encouraged the extension of settlement into otherwise marginal areas. For example, behind the early Islamic port of Sohar in Oman, until a late twentieth-century re-expansion of agriculture erased their remains, field scatters of pottery, wells, lines of old water channels, and other features remained in remarkable detail. This landscape zone represents a zone of preservation, whereas closer to the coast, within the modern palm gardens, all traces of the former landscape had been obscured either by the activities of the last millennium of cultivation or by sedimentation (Figure 18.2; Costa and Wilkinson 1987).

The deserts of Jordan, Saudi Arabia, Iran, and southern Israel, with rainfall < 200 mm pa, provide numerous examples of landscapes of preservation (Figure 18.3). Despite the high quality of preservation of surface

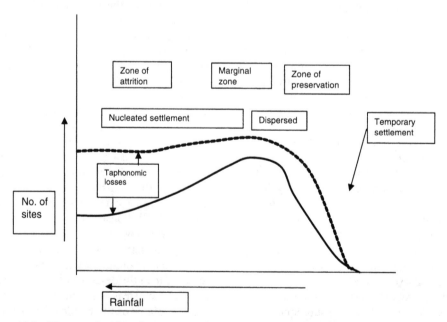

Figure 18.1 Diagram showing the nature and preservation of archaeological sites along a transect through the rainfed, marginal, and desert zones.

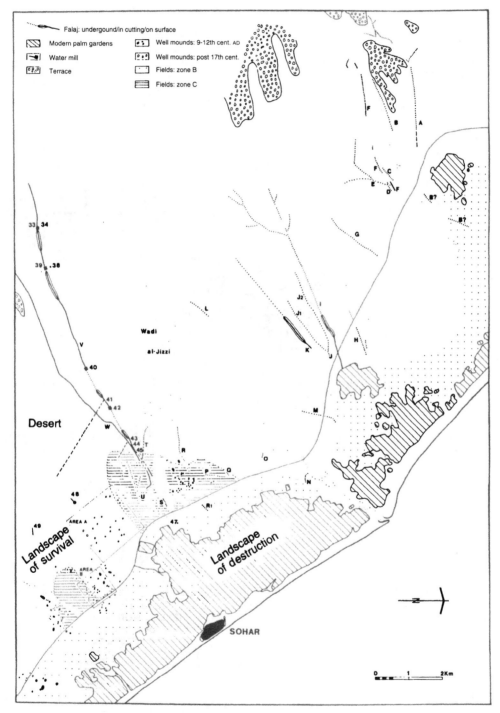

Figure 18.2   The hinterland of Sohar Oman showing landscape features in the desert, zone of survival, and zone of destruction (redrawn from Costa and Wilkinson 1987).

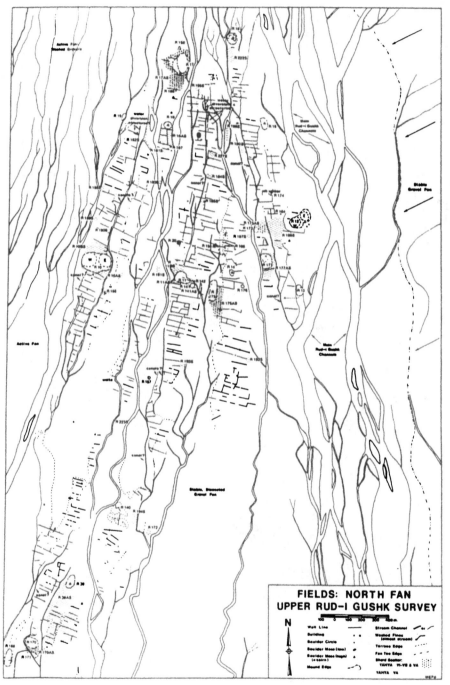

Figure 18.3 Prehistoric field systems near Daulatabad, southeast Iran (from Prickett 1986: fig. 9.5; by kind permission of the Tepe Yahya Project, Peabody Museum, Harvard University).

features, establishing a date for them is frequently difficult. For example, in Jordan numerous field systems associated with Nabataean, Roman, or Byzantine remains are partly of that date, but locally include relics of earlier settlement or land use (Kennedy and Freeman 1995: 39; Barker et al. 1997).

At the other extreme, and representing an island within an otherwise well-watered area in northwest Syria near Aleppo, the limestone uplands of the "Massif Calcaire" present an almost complete landscape of late Roman/Byzantine date. Settlements, oil presses, trackways, and fields are all preserved with remarkable clarity, because there has been little settlement since the ninth century AD to remove the remains. Studies by Tchalenko (1953) and Tate (1992) record both landscapes and architecture in considerable detail, but demonstrate competing interpretive theories: that the area was a commercial olive-growing region exporting goods to the surrounding cities (Tchalenko), or more self-sufficient farms and villages with a more generalized agriculture (Tate). The record from this small area therefore provides a remarkable degree of archaeological preservation that stands in stark contrast to the nearby lowlands, where the remains of the same period usually take the form of anonymous mounds that have been partially erased by later cultural activity.

Where historical landscapes such as parks, race courses, and other features occur, their often large-scale but lightly demarcated features can only be preserved within the zone of survival (Northedge 1990, for ninth-century AD Samarra).

A special case of desert landscapes can be found in the apparently featureless plains of southern Mesopotamia, where the alluvium masks a landscape of considerable complexity. In addition to settlement patterns, the surveys of Robert Adams (1981) recorded relict canals and natural river channels. Archaeological features can remain on the present ground surface (where the remains have often suffered severe deflation), are pedestalled above it, or are buried beneath meters of alluviation deposited by the shifting channels of the Tigris and Euphrates rivers. Where the burial of archaeological sites does prevail, the number of archaeological sites is almost certainly underestimated, and it is one of the challenges of future geoarchaeological research to understand how such complex landscapes were formed.

Recent remote sensing and geomorphological studies by a Belgian team demonstrate the extraordinary complexity of the Mesopotamian landscape (Gasche and Tanret 1999). In the northern alluvium sinuous strings of sites follow along microtopographic rises that form the remains of relict channel levees. These were investigated by coring to demonstrate a history of alluviation and channel development spanning much of the Holocene (Cole and Gasche 1998: map 3; Verhoeven 1998). To supplement this record, recent satellite image analysis by Robert Adams and Jennifer Pournelle has extended the original record (Adams 1981) of early channel patterns, and added an additional layer of data in the form of field boundaries of Parthian, Sasanian, and Early Islamic date. Such macro studies can, in turn, be related to small-scale studies that show windows of landscape visibility. For example, around Old Babylonian Abu Duwari (Mashkan Shapir: Stone and Zimansky 1994) the plain is strewn with varying densities of sherd scatters, a rough grid of small post-Seleucid silt-filled canals, and a large earlier infilled canal (Figure 18.4). According to surface ceramics, such a pattern, which includes archaeological sites and occasional buildings (point 42 on Figure 18.4), mainly relates to occupations of Seleucid and later date. Augering by Lisa Wells within the site of Abu Duwari demonstrated that the original plain level is buried several meters below present plain level. Therefore the extant visible landscape may represent only the last few thousand years; a point supported by the dates of most of the surface ceramics. A strong off-site record is

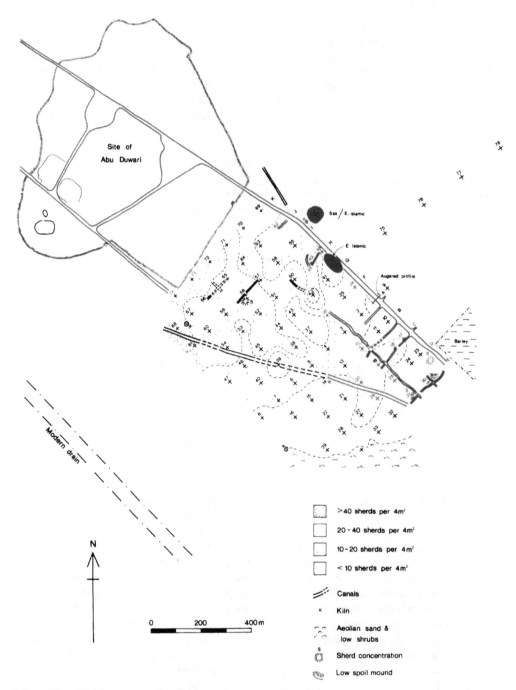

Site of
Abu Duwari

Sas / E. Islamic

E. Islamic

Augered profile

Barley

Modern drain

N

0   200   400 m

>40 sherds per 4m²

20 - 40 sherds per 4m²

10 - 20 sherds per 4m²

< 10 sherds per 4m²

Canals

K   Kiln

Aeolian sand &
low shrubs

S
Sherd concentration

Low spoil mound

Figure 18.4 Field scatters and infilled canals near Mashkan Shapir, Iraq (from Stone and Zimansky, forthcoming).

apparent within the uncultivated desertic parts of the plain, but is virtually obscured

where modern cultivation has encouraged sedimentary aggradation and the disturbance of off-site features. Therefore the Southern Mesopotamian plains represent a complex of alternations of sedimentary aggradation and aeolian degradation, cultivation and desert. Although the pattern of archaeological landscapes is extraordinarily variable and complex, the Mesopotamian plains provide considerable potential for future landscape investigations.

Intermediate zone of marginal rainfed steppe (zone 3)

The north Syrian and Iraqi Jazira is dominated by tells that often attained their maximum size during the middle part of the third millennium BC. For landscape archaeologists this marginal zone of rainfed cultivation in Upper Mesopotamia holds special significance, because it houses an unusual combination of large sites and related landscape features. The area has experienced several phases of settlement decline, which appear to result from a complex and still debated pattern of climatic, social, economic, and political changes (see papers in Dalfes, Kukla, and Weiss 1997). By limiting the amount of later settlement that would obscure or erase the earlier record, any retreat in the margin of settlement may have allowed the early phases of settlement and landscape to be visible. This situation of survival has also been encouraged because the later settlement pattern (roughly post-Late Bronze Age) was dispersed, and consequently has left a lighter print on the landscape than earlier nucleated settlement. Hence the occasional gaps or declines in settlement have resulted in diminished attrition of landscape features.

With a mean annual rainfall ranging from ca. 200–500 mm, zone 3 can exhibit well-preserved off-site features, such as linear hollows (of ancient tracks) and extensive sherd scatters, as well as relict canals. The presence of linear hollows and off-site sherd scatters enables intensively cultivated land, other cultivated land, and open space (potentially devoted to pasture) to be reconstructed

(Wilkinson and Tucker 1995). Other landscape features, such as ancient relict fields, are usually absent, except where "windows" of the landscape of preservation may be visible on localized uplands. In zone 3, satellite imagery, aerial photography, and field survey can all be harnessed to provide a well integrated body of data covering very large areas. Furthermore, in some cases cuneiform texts provide information on the landscapes as they once existed, and it is even possible to match features of the landscape with elements of the textual record (Fales 1990).

Zone 3 harbors a wide range of conditions of landscape survival, and landscape taphonomy is particularly significant along the Syrian Euphrates around Tell es-Sweyhat. Located at the margin of rainfed cultivation, Tell Sweyhat falls within a zone of preservation, a situation which is however complicated by local geomorphology. Three broad landscape zones are evident (Figure 18.5): (1) along the Euphrates valley the braided and occasionally meandering river has eroded and reworked most of the floodplain, to form a geomorphic landscape of destruction in which rare tells (dating back to at least the early third millennium BC) remain on limited uneroded residuals of ancient floodplain; (2) Pleistocene terraces on both left and right banks of the entrenched alluvial plain form a zone of survival, which therefore forms the optimum zone for preservation of landscape and settlement remains; (3) the dry steppe beyond the Pleistocene terraces is the domain of nomadic pastoralists. This is presumably the zone that provided much of the pasture and wild game recorded in the bioarchaeological record from Sweyhat.

In the area of Tell Sweyhat most landscape information comes in the form of off-site features within zone 2, namely linear hollows (probably relict routes), cemeteries, wine presses, quarries, and off-site sherd scatters. Of these, "field scatters," which are interpreted as being the result of applications of settlement-derived refuse as manure to fields to sustain yields, imply that during

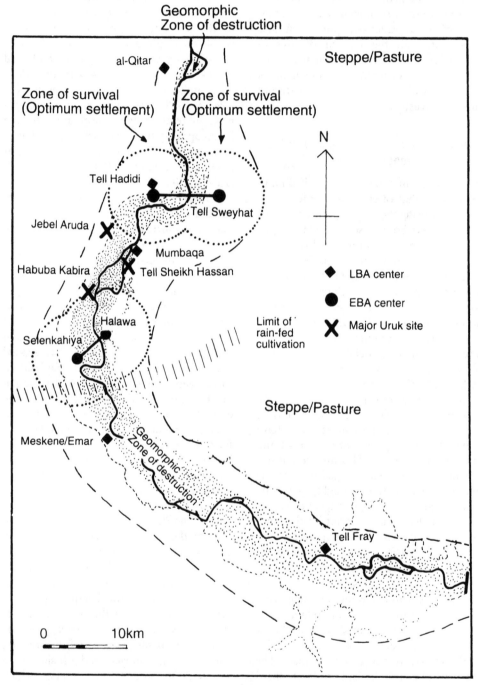

Figure 18.5 Landscape zones in the area of Lake Assad, Tabqa Dam, Syria, showing shifts in the locations of major Uruk (fourth millennium BC), Early Bronze Age (EBA), and Late Bronze Age (LBA) centers.

the late third millennium BC the area was intensively cultivated. Recent bioarchaeological studies suggest that the economy had a major pastoral component, comprising grazing of sheep and goats on steppe pasture, as well as a significant component of hunting of wild animals (Miller 1997; Weber 1997). The original survey (Wilkinson 1994), now elaborated and extended by Michael Danti, recorded small ephemeral sites which suggest that Early Bronze Age pastoral activity occurred on the plateau to the east (Danti and Zettler 1998). In addition, early third millennium BC structures interpreted as grain silos may have stored barley for feeding flocks. These data suggest that the zone of intensive cultivation on Pleistocene terraces could have been devoted to crops for the people of the town, as well as grazing on the cereal stubble, and flocks would then have been sent out to the steppe, where their diet included a high proportion of steppe legumes (Miller 1997: 102–3). The significant amount of wild fauna can be accommodated within the existing model because Sweyhat lies at the limit of rainfed cultivation, in a position where there was access to abundant steppe for hunting.

The combined picture painted by landscape archaeology, surveys, excavation, geophysical survey, and bioarchaeology, suggests therefore that Sweyhat was a truly marginal settlement that could only survive by the optimum harnessing of a broad spectrum of resources, which included both pastoral systems and intensive cultivation (Wilkinson 1994; Miller 1997; Weber 1997; Danti and Zettler 1998).

Zone 4 : zone of attrition

Whereas zone 3 exhibits a partial landscape record with occasional earlier features remaining, in the "zone of attrition" there is a more complex imprint of long-term landscape features which may have continued almost uninterrupted until the present day. This vast zone includes the Levantine coastal plain and much of Israel, Lebanon, and west-ern Syria, as well as parts of Turkey, Jordan, and Yemen. Although it is impossible to do justice to such a complex zone, it is likely that its degree of complexity is comparable to the landscape of Western Europe. For example, areas of the Biqa Valley, Lebanon, that have a virtually continuous pattern of archaeological settlement from the Neolithic, also show complex patterns of fields on 1:20,000 topographic maps. Finding meaningful patterns in such a maze of features seems almost impossible, but in Syria formally laid out patterns of fields have been recognized in the form of Roman and Hellenistic land allotments around Emesa (Homs) and Damascus (Van Liere 1958–9; Dodinet et al. 1990), as well as in other parts of western and southern Syria (Wirth 1971: 375–412). Although not as well developed as relict systems in other parts of the Mediterranean (Bradford 1980; Alcock 1993: 139–40, for Roman; Gaffney, Bintliff, and Slapsak 1991, for Hellenistic), such systems can supply a datum for estimating the ages of yet earlier field systems and landscape features.

In the Levant, Shimon Dar and co-workers have demonstrated that Roman, Hellenistic, and Iron Age landscapes can be recognized within uplands that might be described as part of the landscape of survival. In these often marginal uplands, the pattern of villages, farmsteads, and associated radial tracks, forms part of an extensive network of hundreds of rural roads which connected settlements both with outlying fields and with their neighboring communities (Safrai 1994: 57). Traditional tracks are often built along ancient tracks, which in the rocky uplands were 3–4 meters wide, and edged with stone "fences." Landscape features include farm buildings, field towers, cisterns, wine and olive presses, threshing floors, lime kilns, and (in the Mount Herman area of Jebel al-Sheikh) various cultic installations (Dar 1986, 1993). The process of transformation of rural sites is hinted at in the site descriptions of the Southern Samaria Survey, which frequently note sites as being "dismantled ruin" or "ruins incorporated into terrace walls" (Finkelstein and Lederman 1997: 339, 699, 702, 725).

The highlands of Yemen provide a classic example of a landscape of destruction in which early settlements and landscapes have usually been eroded away or transformed by later occupations. These highlands (altitude >2,000 meters above sea level), with rainfall often in excess of 500 mm per annum, are densely populated today, and the inhabitants farm majestic staircases of terraced fields on hillsides and valley floors. Despite their high potential for settlement, the wetter parts of the highlands often show few conspicuous archaeological sites or ancient landscape features. Instead, many sites consist of little more than scatters of sherds, because the component stones of buildings have been removed and incorpor-

ated into later walls and post-occupational terracing.

In contrast, where rainfall is <200 mm, surveys have demonstrated the existence of numerous small Bronze Age villages, usually on hilltops and rocky slopes (Wilkinson et al. 1997) or on wadi terraces (de Maigret 1990). Such sites were preserved mainly because there appears to have been little subsequent settlement in these drier regions. Taphonomic factors therefore appear to have contributed to the archaeological invisibility of the Yemeni Bronze Age: in moist areas, settlements were less conspicuous because many had been transformed by later activities which denuded them of building stones. In marginal semi-arid areas a rich palimpsest of features is enshrined within the existing system of fields, much of which incorporates later elements (Figure 18.6). From their deep

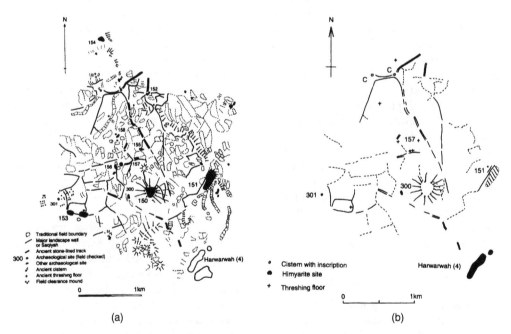

(a)   (b)

Figure 18.6 Dhamar, highlands of Yemen: (a) The Harwarwah landscape showing the very complex landscape evident within some 6 sq km of terrain (revised from Wilkinson et al. 1997). Solid lines represent trackways and other early alignments of probable Iron Age or Himyarite date. Site 151 is Iron Age, 150 Bronze Age and Harwarwah (4) Himyarite; (b) The same landscape but showing selected features that are associated with Himyarite sites or cisterns and therefore roughly 2,000 years old. Note the convergence of the trackways on the Himyarite site of Harwarwah.

accumulation of soils these can be seen to be ancient features in their own right. As in Upper Mesopotamia, it is within this intermediate zone that conditions are optimal for the survival of early sites. In this marginal zone later settlements are less common than in the moister regions, where settlement continuity over long periods of time appears to have resulted in preexisting sites being dismantled by later occupations. It is therefore within this marginal zone that sites usually provide coherent building plans and there are also remains of threshing floors, relict terrace fields, dams, cross-valley field walls, and other features.

Zone 5: the coastal zone

The small tidal range of Near Eastern coastal waters restricts the potential for the discovery of sites in intertidal locations. Nevertheless, following on from the pioneering work assembled by Masters and Flemming (1983), shallow underwater survey has now yielded impressive results of prehistoric occupation. Sites on the coast of Israel (Galili et al.1993) and Greece (Flemming 1983) indicate that the level of preservation is often considerable, and this zone itself has its own processes of taphonomy that encourage or discourage preservation (Flemming 1998). When investigated using innovative techniques of geoarchaeology and geophysical prospection, such landscapes can provide results that complement the record from adjacent drylands. As in coastal sites in northwest Europe, the level of preservation is often extremely good, and in future this zone will provide valuable control for the heavily modified archaeological record from adjacent drylands.

Discussion

By focusing upon the Middle East, an area endowed with often massive sites as well as a wide range of landscape features, this chapter has underemphasized the biological component of the archaeological landscape. On the other hand, in places such as northern Europe, which possess well-preserved vegetation records, one can recognize a distinctive school of landscape archaeology that emphasizes the ecological record (Birks et al. 1988). Thus, for Kristiansen (1998), a precondition for understanding the settlement history of a region is a knowledge of its vegetation history, a demand that is difficult to satisfy in much of the Middle East. In northwest Europe these conditions can be met, however, and at Thy in northwest Jutland, Kristiansen demonstrates the relationship through time between the opening up of the landscape on the one hand and settlement and burials on the other. Similar approaches have been taken in the Ystad project in southern Sweden (Berglund 1988: 242–5). Both projects demonstrate that different environmental and cultural zones present different possibilities (and limitations) for landscape archaeology, and because of such variations there must necessarily be many different approaches to landscape archaeology.

This chapter has adopted a broad-brush approach to landscapes because it is over large areas that landscape transformations are most recognizable. As with historical texts, faunal assemblages, and other raw data, the landscape must be critically examined to determine the completeness of the record. Such landscape transformations are not simply a function of time, because landscape features in the right circumstances can persist for remarkably long periods. Taphonomic processes are therefore fundamental to an understanding of the landscape record, and as stated by Schiffer (1987) and Boismier (1997), it is apparent that in some circumstances the operations of cultural transformation processes may themselves structure the archaeological record, or at least in the case of landscapes, its visibility. Hence the appearance of a zone of landscape visibility near the margin of cultivation in both northern Mesopotamia and Yemen is partly a result of a change in settlement structure and some degree of local decline during the later archaeological periods, as well as taphonomic factors.

One cannot, however, impose wholesale the principles of landscape taphonomy on all parts of the world, and in some areas there remains a certain ambiguity of interpretation. For example, in the Andes, massive sequences of terraced fields exemplify a classic landscape of attrition, where terrace construction may have largely destroyed what came before. On the other hand, it is possible to perceive the same landscape as one of survival. This is because in areas such as the Colca valley, Peru, large-scale abandonment of prehispanic terraces (Denevan 1987) has left a landscape of relict terraced fields. Owing to the potential instability of such terraces, such a system may then rapidly disappear as a result of the operation of rapid downslope geomorphic processes, thereby resulting in yet another phase of landscape transformation.

In the Near East the landscape of attrition represents the most problematic area of research, because very little analysis has yet been undertaken on the evolution of field systems. This is partly because many Near Eastern archaeologists are more interested in earlier phases of settlement than the later periods, during which coherent field systems are likely to survive. Therefore a future generation of Islamic and medieval archaeologists may hold the key to developments of the landscape history branch of the subject.

An additional problem in many Middle Eastern countries has been the limited availability of good maps with field boundaries on them. Fortunately, with the widespread availability of satellite images, which are particularly useful for field pattern recognition, this lacuna can now be closed. In addition to relict features that persist in the form of field boundaries, field scatters of pottery may remain from earlier periods. However, within the landscape of destruction, such scatters will also include artefact scatters derived from sedentary sites, which have been destroyed during earlier periods of land use. Such dispersed scatters are particularly characteristic of upland terraced areas such as Yemen, where field scatters from manuring can be difficult to distinguish from reworked settlement sites incorporated into more recent terraced fields.

To conclude, landscape archaeology in all its manifestations continues to provide a valuable but under-used tool for reconstructing ancient societies and economies. However, the record is complex and needs to be interpreted in terms of taphonomic processes, economic models (both formalist and substantivist), and social and symbolic systems. Cultural landscape processes interact with geoarchaeological systems to provide a distinct and unique set of interrelationships, which in future should not only bring the two subdisciplines closer together, but should also help geoarchaeology develop a more distinct manifesto. The taphonomic model described here is probably too rigid to be applied as it stands. Rather, a mosaic of taphonomic systems may represent the most realistic approach to many landscapes in future. But will the fragmentation of archaeology into subdisciplines also result in the balkanization of landscape archaeology? Fortunately, with the widespread adoption of GIS systems, and (in the near future) techniques of dynamic modeling, we may witness greater integration of methodologies, so that archaeologists will be able to work within a more uniform framework of analysis.

References

Adams, R. M. 1981. *Heartland of Cities*. Chicago: University of Chicago Press.

Alcock, S. E. 1993. *Graecia Capta: The Landscapes of Roman Greece*. Cambridge: Cambridge University Press.

Alcock, S. E, J. F. Cherry, and J. L. Davis 1994. "Intensive survey, agricultural practice and the classical landscape of Greece." In I. Morris (ed.), *Classical Greece: Ancient Histories and Modern Archaeologies*, pp. 137–70. Cambridge: Cambridge University Press.

Aston, M. 1985. *Interpreting the Landscape: Landscape Archaeology and Local History.* London: Routledge.

Avner, U. 1998 "Settlement agriculture and palaeoclimate in Uvda valley, southern Negev desert, sixth–third millennia BC." In A. Issar and N. Brown (eds.), *Water, Environment and Society in Times of Climatic Change*, pp. 147–202. Dordrecht: Kluwer.

Barker, G. W., O. H. Creighton, D. D. Gilbertson, et al. 1997. "The Wadi Faynan project, southern Jordan: a preliminary report on geomorphology and landscape archaeology." *Levant*, 29: 19–40.

Berglund, B. 1988. "The cultural landscape during 6,000 years in south Sweden – an interdisciplinary project." In H. H. Birks, H. J. B. Birks, P. E. Kaland, and D. Moe (eds.), *The Cultural Landscape: Past, Present and Future*, pp. 241–54. Cambridge: Cambridge University Press.

Bintliff, J. L., B. Davies, C. Gaffney, A. Snodgrass, and A. Waters 1992. "Trace metal accumulations in soils on and around ancient settlements in Greece." In P. Spoerry (ed.), *Geoprospection in the Archaeological Landscape*, pp. 9–24. Oxford: Oxbow Monograph 18.

Birks, H. H., H. J. B. Birks, P. E. Kaland, and D. Moe (eds.) 1988. *The Cultural Landscape: Past, Present and Future.* Cambridge: Cambridge University Press.

Bloch, M. 1952. *Les Caractères originaux de l'histoire rural français.* Paris: A. Colin.

Boismier, W. A. 1997. *Modelling the Effects of Tillage Processes on Artefact Distributions in the Ploughzone: A Simulation of Tillage-Induced Pattern Formation.* Oxford: British Archaeological Reports (British Series) 259.

Bowen, H. C. and P. J. Fowler (eds.) 1978. *Early Land Allotment.* Oxford: British Archaeological Reports (British Series) 48.

Bradford, J. (1980) [1957] *Ancient Landscapes Studies in Field Archaeology.* Westport, CT: Greenwood Press.

Caulfield, S. 1978. "Neolithic fields: the Irish evidence." In H. C. Bowen and P. J. Fowler (eds.), *Early Land Allotment*, pp. 137–44. Oxford: British Archaeological Reports (British Series) 48.

Chapman, J. 1997. "Places as timemarks: the social construction of prehistoric landscapes in eastern Hungary." In G. Nash (ed.), *Semiotics of Landscape: Archaeology of Mind*, pp. 31–45. Oxford: British Archaeological Reports (International Series) 661.

Cherry, J. F., J. L. Davis, and E. Mantzourani 1991. *Landscape Archaeology as Long-Term History: The Keos Survey.* Los Angeles: UCLA Institute of Archaeology.

Cole, S. W. and H. Gasche 1998. "Second and first millennium BC rivers in northern Babylonia." In H. Gasche and M. Tanret (eds.), *Changing Watercourses in Babylonia: Towards a Reconstruction of the Ancient Environment in Lower Mesopotamia*, pp. 1–64. Ghent: University of Ghent; Chicago: Oriental Institute.

Coles, J., and B. Coles 1989. *People of the Wetlands: Bogs, Bodies, and Lake Dwellers.* London: Thames and Hudson.

Costa, P. M. and T. J. Wilkinson 1987. "The hinterland of Sohar: archaeological surveys and excavations within the region of an Omani seafaring city." *Journal of Oman Studies*, 9: 1–238.

Crowther, D., C. French, and F. Pryor 1985 "Approaching the Fens the flexible way." In C. Haselgrove, M. Millett, and I. Smith (eds.), *Archaeology from the Ploughsoil: Studies in the Collection and Interpretation of Field Survey Data*, pp. 59–76. Sheffield: Department of Archaeology and Prehistory, University of Sheffield.

Dalfes, N., G. Kukla, and H. Weiss 1997. *Third Millennium* BC *Climate Change and Old World Collapse*. NATO ASI Series: Global Environmental Change, vol. 49. Berlin: Springer.

Danti, M. and R. L. Zettler 1998. "The evolution of the Tell es-Sweyhat (Syria) settlement system in the third millennium BC." *Bulletin of the Canadian Society for Mesopotamian Studies*, 33: 209–28.

Dar, S. 1986. *Landscape and Pattern*. Oxford: British Archaeological Reports (International Series) 308.

Dar, S. 1993. *Settlements and Cult Sites on Mount Hermon, Israel*. Oxford: British Archaeological Reports (International Series) 589.

de Maigret, A. 1990. *The Bronze Age Culture of Hawlan at-Tiyal and al-Hada (Republic of Yemen): A First General Report*. Rome: ISMEO.

Denevan, W. M. 1987. "Terrace abandonment in the Colca valley, Peru." In W. M. Denevan, K. Matthewson, and G. Knapp (eds.), *Pre-Hispanic Agricultural Fields in the Andean Region*, pp. 1–43. Oxford: British Archaeological Reports (International Series) 359.

Denevan, W. M. 1991. "Prehistoric roads and causeways of lowland tropical America." In C. D. Trombold (ed.), *Ancient Road Networks and Settlement Hierarchies in the New World*, pp. 230–42. Cambridge: Cambridge University Press.

Dodgshon, R. A. 1994. "Budgeting for survival: nutrient flow and traditional highland farming." In S. Foster and T. C. Smout (eds.), *The History of Soils and Field Systems*, pp. 83–93. Aberdeen: Scottish Cultural Press.

Dodinet, M., J. Leblanc, J.-P. Vallat, and F. Villeneuve 1990. "Le Paysage antique en Syrie: l'exemple de Damas." *Syria*, 67: 339–55.

Emanuelsson, U. 1988. "A model for describing the development of the cultural landscape." In H. H. Birks, H. J. B. Birks, P. E. Kaland, and D. Moe (eds.), *The Cultural Landscape: Past, Present and Future*, pp. 111–21. Cambridge: Cambridge University Press.

Everson, P. and T. Williamson (eds.) 1998. *The Archaeology of Landscape*. Manchester: Manchester University Press.

Fales, M. 1990. "The rural landscape of the Neo-Assyrian empire: a survey." *State Archives of Assyria, Bulletin*, 4 (2): 81–142.

Finkelstein, I. and Z. Lederman 1997. *Highlands of Many Cultures: The Southern Samaria Survey*. Report no. 14. Tel Aviv: Institute of Archaeology, Tel Aviv University.

Fleming, A. 1988. *The Dartmoor Reaves: Investigating Prehistoric Land Divisions*. London: Batsford.

Flemming, N. C. 1983. "Preliminary geomorphological survey of an early Neolithic submerged site in the Sporadhes, N. Aegean." In P. M. Masters and N. C. Flemming (eds.), *Quaternary Coastlines and Marine Archaeology*, pp. 233–68. London: Academic Press.

Flemming, N. C. 1998. "Archaeological evidence for vertical movement of the continental shelf during the Palaeolithic, Neolithic and Bronze Age periods." In I. Stewart and C. Vita-Finzi (eds.), *Coastal Tectonics*, pp. 129–46. London: Geological Society.

Fulford, M. G. 1990. "The landscape of Roman Britain: a review." *Landscape History*, 12: 25–31.

Fulford, M. G., T. Champion, and A. Long (eds.) 1997. *England's Coastal Heritage: A Survey for English Heritage and the RCHME*. London: English Heritage, Royal Commission on the Historical Monuments of England, Archaeological Report 15.

Gaffney, V. L., J. Bintliff, and B. Slapsak 1991. "Site formation process and the Hvar survey project, Yugoslavia." In A. J. Schofield (ed.), *Interpreting Artefact Scatters: Contributions to Ploughzone Archaeology*, pp. 59–77. Oxford: Oxbow Monograph no. 4.

Galili, Y., M. Weinstein-Evron, I. Hershkovitz, et al. 1993. "Atlil-Yam: a prehistoric site on the sea floor off the Israeli coast." *Journal of Field Archaeology*, 20: 133–57.

Gasche, H. and M. Tanret (eds.) 1998. *Changing Watercourses in Babylonia: Towards a Reconstruction of the Ancient Environment in Lower Mesopotamia.* Ghent: University of Ghent; Chicago: Oriental Institute.

Guy, M. and M. Passelac 1991. "Prospection aérienne et télédéction des structures de parcellaires." In J. Guilaine (ed.), *Pour une archéologie agraire*, pp. 103–29. Paris: A. Colin.

Hoskins, W. G. 1955. *The Making of the English Landscape.* London: Hodder and Stoughton.

Kelso, W. M. and R. Most (eds.) 1990. *Earth Patterns: Essays in Landscape Archaeology.* Charlottesville: University of Virginia Press.

Kennedy, D. 2001 "History in depth: surface survey and aerial archaeology." *Studies in the History and Archaeology of Jordan,* 7: 39–48.

Kennedy, D. and P. Freeman 1995. "Southern Hauran Survey 1992." *Levant,* 27: 39–73.

Killion, T. W. (ed.) 1992. *Gardens of Prehistory: The Archaeology of Settlement Agriculture in Greater Mesoamerica.* Tuscaloosa: University of Alabama Press.

Kristiansen, K. 1998. "The construction of a Bronze Age landscape: cosmology, economy and social organisation in Thy, northwestern Jutland." In B. Hänsel (ed.), *Mensch und Umwelt in der Bronzezeit Europas,* pp. 281–91. Kiel: Oetker-Voges Verlag.

Lloyd, J. 1991. "Conclusion: archaeological survey and the Roman landscape." In G. Barker and J. Lloyd (eds.), *Roman Landscapes: Archaeological Survey in the Mediterranean Region,* pp. 233–40. British School at Rome, Archaeological Monograph no. 2.

Masters, P. M. and N. C. Flemming (eds.) 1983. *Quaternary Coastlines and Marine Archaeology,* pp. 233–68. London: Academic Press.

Metheny, K. B. 1996. "Landscape archaeology." In B. Fagan (ed.), *The Oxford Companion to Archaeology,* pp. 324–77. Oxford: Oxford University Press.

Miller, N. 1997. "Sweyhat and Haji Ibrahim: some archaeobotanical samples from the 1991 and 1993 seasons." In R. L. Zettler (ed.), *Subsistence and Settlement in a Marginal Environment: Tell es-Sweyhat, 1989–1995 Preliminary Report,* pp. 95–122. Philadelphia: MASCA Research Papers 14.

Miller, N. F. and K. L. Gleason 1994. *The Archaeology of Garden and Field.* Philadelphia: University of Pennsylvania Press.

Northedge, A. 1990. "The racecourses at Samarra." *Bulletin of the School of Oriental and African Studies,* 53: 31–56.

Prickett, M. 1986. "Settlement during the early periods." In T. W. Beale (ed.), *Excavations at Tepe Yahya, Iran 1967–1975: The Early Periods,* pp. 215–46. Cambridge, MA: American Society for Prehistoric Research.

Purdy, B. 1988. *Wet-Site Archaeology.* Caldwell, NJ: Telford Press.

Riley, D. N. 1980. *Early Landscapes from the Air.* Sheffield: Sheffield University Press.

Rippon, S. 1991. "Early planned landscapes in southeast Essex." *Essex Archaeology and History,* 22: 46–60.

Rippon, S. 1997. *The Severn Estuary: Landscape Evolution and Wetland Reclamation.* Leicester: Leicester University Press.

Roberts, B. K. 1987. "Landscape archaeology." In J. M. Wagstaff (ed.), *Landscape and Culture: Geographical and Archaeological Perspectives,* pp. 77–95. Oxford: Blackwell.

Rodwell, W. 1978. "Relict landscapes in Essex." In H. C. Bowen and P. J. Fowler (eds.), *Early Land Allotment,* pp. 89–98. Oxford: British Archaeological Reports (British Series) 48.

Rossignol, J. 1992. "Concepts, methods and theory building: A landscape approach." In J. Rossignol and L. A. Wandsnider (eds.), *Space, Time and Archaeological Landscapes,* pp. 3–16. New York: Plenum.

Safrai, Z. 1994. *The Economy of Roman Palestine.* London: Routledge.

Schiffer, M. B. 1987. *Formation Processes of the Archaeological Record*. Albuquerque: University of New Mexico Press.

Smith, G. 1996. "Archaeology and environment of a Bronze Age cairn and prehistoric Romano-British field systems at Chysauster, Gulul, near Penwith, Cornwall." *Proceedings of the Prehistoric Society*, 62: 167–219.

Stein, M. A. 1921. *SerIndia*, 5 vols. Oxford: Clarendon Press.

Stone, E. C. and P. Zimansky 1994. "The Tell Abu Duwari Project, 1988–1990." *Journal of Field Archaeology*, 21: 437–55.

Stone, E. C. and P. Zimansky, in press. *The Anatomy of a Mesopotamian City: Survey and Soundings at Mashkan-Shapir*. Winona Lake, IN: Eisenbraun.

Tate, G. 1992. *Les Campagnes de la Syrie du nord*, vol. 1. Paris: Librairie Orientaliste Paul Geuthner.

Taylor, C. C. 1972. "The study of settlement pattern in pre-Saxon Britain." In P. J. Ucko, R. Tringham, and G. W. Dimbleby (eds.), *Man, Settlement and Urbanism*, pp. 109–14. London: Duckworth.

Taylor, C. C. 1983. *Village and Farmstead: A History of Rural Settlement in England*. London: George Philip.

Tchalenko, G. 1953. *Villages antiques de la Syrie du nord II*. Paris: Librairie Orientaliste Paul Geuthner.

Thomas, C. 1978. "Types and distributions of pre-Norman fields in Cornwall and Scilly." In H. C. Bowen and P. J. Fowler (eds.), *Early Land Allotment*, pp. 7–16. Oxford: British Archaeological Reports (British Series) 48.

Thomas, J. 1993. "The politics of vision and the archaeologies of landscape." In B. Bender (ed.), *Landscape: Politics and Perspectives*, pp. 19–48. Oxford: Berg.

Tilley, C. 1994. *A Phenomenology of Landscape*. Oxford: Berg.

Tsoar, H. and Y. Yekutieli 1993. "Geomorphological identification of ancient roads and paths on the loess of the northern Negev." *Israel Journal of Earth Sciences*, 41: 209–16.

Van Liere, W. J. 1958–9. "Ager Centuriatus of the Roman colonia of Emesa (Homs)." *Les Annales archéologiques de Syrie*, 8–9: 55–8.

Verhoeven, K. 1998. "Geomorphological research in the Mesopotamian floodplain." In H. Gasche and M. Tanret (eds.), *Changing Watercourses in Babylonia: Towards a Reconstruction of the Ancient Environment in Lower Mesopotamia*, pp. 159–245. Ghent: University of Ghent; Chicago: Oriental Institute.

Weber, J. A. 1997. "Faunal remains from Tell es-Sweyhat and Haji Ibrahim." In R. L. Zettler (ed.), *Subsistence and Settlement in a Marginal Environment: Tell es-Sweyhat, 1989–1995 Preliminary Report*, pp. 85–94. Philadelphia: MASCA Research Papers 14.

Wilkinson, T. J. 1994. "The structure and dynamics of dry farming states in Upper Mesopotamia." *Current Anthropology*, 35 (1): 483–520.

Wilkinson, T. J. and D. J. Tucker 1995. *Settlement Development in the North Jazira, Syria*. Warminster: Aris and Phillips.

Wilkinson, T. J., C. Edens, and M. Gibson 1997. "The archaeology of the Yemen high plains: a preliminary chronology." *Arabian Archaeology and Epigraphy*, 8: 99–142.

Williamson, T. 1987. "Early coaxial field systems on the East Anglian boulder clays." *Proceedings of the Prehistoric Society*, 53: 419–31.

Williamson, T. 1998. "Questions of preservation and destruction." In P. Everson and T. Williamson (eds.), *The Archaeology of Landscape*, pp. 1–24. Manchester: Manchester University Press.

Wirth, E. 1971. *Syrien, eine geographische Landeskunde*. Darmstadt: Wissenschaftliche Buchgesellschaft.

19

Archaeology and Art

Raymond Corbey, Robert Layton, and Jeremy Tanner

Archaeologists have approached the study of art from several directions, drawing their inspiration variously from evolutionary biology, anthropology, and art history. We examine the strengths and weaknesses of each of these approaches and hope to demonstrate the unique opportunities open to archaeology in the study of art, from its origins to the recent past.

What is Art?

The first problem facing archaeologists interested in studying the art of past societies is identifying their proper subject matter. What is art? The modern concept of art is a recent historical phenomenon. The word *art* once referred to any specialized skill or application of technical knowledge including, for example, the art of medicine, the art of rhetoric. Only in the eighteenth century did the term acquire its modern specialized reference to the "fine arts" of painting, sculpture, architecture, music, and gardening – all characterized by technical skill, imagination, and aesthetic expression (Kristeller 1990; Williams 1983, s.v. "aesthetics," "art"). This development was associated with important changes in the institutional frameworks for the production, appropriation, and consumption of art. Art, in particular painting, was increasingly produced as a commodity for a relatively anonymous market, rather than directly commissioned by patrons. This gave rise to the modern Romantic conception of the artist as an isolated individual expressing inner experience or feelings (Pears 1988; Wolff 1981: 9–25). Artefacts which had previously been encountered in specific practical contexts, as objects of ritual in churches, or political monuments in public spaces, were extracted from those contexts and displayed as autonomous, self-sufficient objects of disinterested aesthetic contemplation, in collections in elite country houses and later the public art galleries and museums sponsored by modern national states (Duncan and Wallach 1980; Abrams 1989).

Both art history and archaeology were invented as academic disciplines during the course of the eighteenth century as part and parcel of the same process, replacing amateur traditions of antiquarianism (Schnapp 1993). One key figure in this transformation was J. J. Winckelmann, who connected literary accounts of the development of sculpture from classical antiquity with the surviving remains of statues in Rome. By this means Winckelmann produced a systematic account of the development of the styles of ancient art as expressions of national character, determined by climatic environment and political organization.

The distinction between works of art, the proper object of aesthetic and art historical discourse, and mere artefacts (which could be treated in more narrowly archaeological terms) was articulated in terms of the level of technical skill, aesthetic sensibility, and individual (or "national" – Egyptian, Greek, Roman) artistic imagination embodied in a particular object (Potts 1982). Following the model of Winckelmann, Greek red figure and black figure pots (Figure 19.1), once looked on as mere artefacts, were elevated to the status of art objects when it was discovered that individual artists' hands could be recognized and even named (on the basis of signatures), and their changing style could be used as a proxy for the history of the (lost) paintings of classical antiquity, described in the works of ancient authors (Vickers 1987). Winckelmann's stylistic

Figure 19.1 Attic black-figure amphora, signed by Exekias, with scene of combat between Achilles and Penthesilea ca. 530 BC. Ht: 16.5 inches. British Museum GR 1836.2-24.12. Photo: Museum.

scheme, which passed from archaic beginnings through classical florescence to post-classical decline, became the model not only for the national histories of European art, but also for the description of the origins, development, and decay of world archaeological cultures (for example formative, classic, and post-classic Mesoamerican culture – Kubler 1970).

It is by no means clear that we can legitimately transfer modern Western concepts of art and artists, along with all their implications, to past cultures and societies. In ancient Greece the word often translated as art, *techne*, referred to any skilled application of knowledge in practice. Similarly, in ancient Egypt, there is no single word that refers to art or artist, but instead a range of terms each related to the particular materials that the artists/craftsmen in question use: *qstj*, worker in bone and ivory; *nbw*, gold-worker; *qd*, "former" or "shaper" for potter or brick-layer (Baines 1994; Drenkhahn 1995). Different researchers adopt different conceptual strategies to overcome this problem. We seek to replace the culturally relative concept of art, with a harder analytical (generally functional) concept – such as "visual communication" or "expressive-affective symbolism" (Layton 1981: 4–5; Tanner 1992) – of which the modern concept can be seen as a special limited case. Others admit the irretrievably relativist character of the concept *art*, and recognize that in writing about the history of art in China, for example, one is grouping together objects including terracotta sculptures, wall paintings, and ritual bronzes that would never have fallen under the same category for their original producers and users (Clunas 1997: 9–13). In the cases of the prehistoric societies with which archaeologists are most typically concerned, we can only guess how members may have conceptualized the objects and processes we now classify as art.

Visual communication implies the purposeful use of regular visual forms that are intended to communicate ideas, whether or not we can decode those messages. The definition of art as visual communication is relatively easy to apply cross-culturally, because it avoids having to determine whether other peoples' aesthetic criteria coincide with ours, or whether we and they share imaginative systems of metaphor and symbolism. This is especially difficult for prehistoric cultures, but it is always easy to read the wrong message into art produced in other cultures. The word *art* is sometimes used as a synonym for pictures conveying a message in our culture, as when advertising agencies talk about "doing the art work." But is an advertisement *art*? The same question can be asked of objects produced in the small-scale cultures anthropologists and archaeologists study. Visual forms such as technical drawings, photographs, or models produced for purely utilitarian purposes may be disqualified as art, because they lack the special qualities of form or imaginative content that sets art apart. Qualities of form, of rhythm, balance, and harmony can be detected in prehistoric art (e.g., bisons in the cave of Lascaux, which are about 16,000 years old: Figure 19.2). Qualities of imaginative content may also be apparent in imagery through which the entities represented in the art have deeper resonances, or stand for more general and profound ideas. Plaques from the former royal palace of the West African kings of Benin depict the king grasping a leopard in each hand; the ruler of civilization controls the ruler of the wild forest. Such visual imagery is harder to detect in prehistory, although one of the oldest known three-dimensional carvings appears to depict a lion-headed human (Hohlenstein-Stadel, Germany, about 30,000 years old: Figure 19.3). There is, however, a strong school of thought in anthropology that denies the usefulness of a semiotic model for studying art as a cultural phenomenon. This argument has been advanced by Forge (1967, 1970), O'Hanlon (1989), and Gell (1998). All three have worked in Papua New Guinea, focusing on predominantly non-figurative art, whereas

several exponents of a semiotic approach to art have worked in Australia (Munn 1973; Morphy 1991; Layton 1981). The preferred theoretical approach may therefore be dictated to some extent by the character of the cultural traditions studied. Gell, however, exemplifies his theory as much through the highly iconic and symbolic art of India as through decorative aspects of the arts of Oceania. He rejects use of a linguistic model in the analysis of art and dismisses aesthetics as a concept taken from Western art history.

In Gell's view art objects play an active part in social relationships. They extend their maker's or user's *agency*. Agency is the ability to act in particular ways, where more than one course of action is possible (Giddens 1984). Art objects have agency when they affect the response of those who see or use them. While the notion of art objects as agents has been used before (e.g., Layton 1981: 43, 85), the originality of Gell's approach lies in his refusal to treat art objects as vehicles for the expression of ideas. At his most extreme, he conceives of art objects as possessing the same kind of agency as land mines (Gell 1998: 21).

Perhaps the most ecumenical way to conceptualize art for the purposes of this survey, and the most appropriate to give a sense of both the range of objects and approaches archaeologists deploy, is to look at how the concept of art is used by archaeologists in actual practice.

Archaeological art as a field of study is too varied and has too fuzzy boundaries to admit a precise definition, but here, nevertheless, is a tentative delineation and identification of some prominent features. It concerns intentionally produced, repeated objects or patterns, which may be more or less sacred or profane, private or public. Such objects or patterns deliberately express, and communicate to others, beliefs and values, or affective meanings, which may be multiple, unstable, ambiguous, contradictory, and vary according to context and receiver. They may embody, contain, or depict

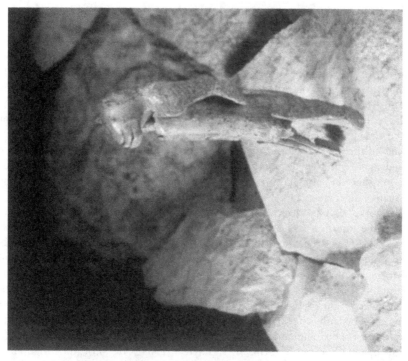

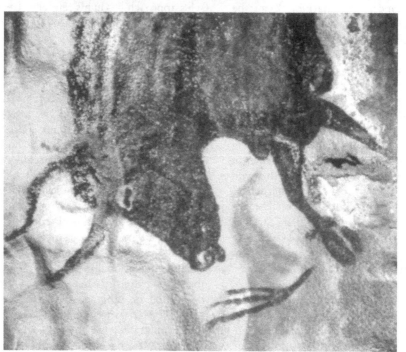

Figure 19.2 Aurochs in the Lascaux cave, Montignac, Southern France. Magdalenian. (Department of Archaeology, Leiden University.)

Figure 19.3 An Aurignacian statuette lion-human from the Hohlenstein-Stadel cave, Germany; 29.6 cms. Courtesy of Ulmer Museum, Ulm, Germany.

ancestors, spirits, or gods, either appeasing them, evoking them, or narrating their accomplishments. Such objects are often made with skill and imagination, and are often aesthetically pleasing to their makers.

One may think of the features highlighted in this description as family resemblances in the sense of Ludwig Wittgenstein. In the aphorisms 65 to 69 of his *Philosophical Investigations* Wittgenstein criticized the notion of essence as a set of features common to all cases. None of the features identified above, even intentionality, is "essential" in the sense of being necessarily shared by all members of the set. Like fibers in a thread, they overlap, but no one fiber runs through the whole thread. Wittgenstein elaborates upon the example of games, and what he says here holds for archaeological art too: there are board games, card games, ball games, Olympic games, and so on, and they are all games, but "if you look at them you will not see something that is common to all, but similarities, relationships, and a whole series of them at that . . . overlapping and criss-crossing" (Wittgenstein 1998). They crop up and disappear, like the various resemblances between members of a family such as build, facial features, eye color, gait, and temperament.

Every individual piece of art has blurred edges or fuzzy boundaries in another sense too, which adds to the complexities of interpreting art outlined above. Art is so intricately connected to local circumstances and suspended in webs of local meanings that we may draw our interpretive circles ever wider without reaching a point where it would be natural to stop. Obviously we cannot go on indefinitely when interpreting, for example, the meaning of the dwarves that frequently appear in Nilotic scenes picturing the flooded Nile, for centuries popular throughout the Roman Empire. Exactly where we stop is a decision taken for practical reasons, not least lack of data. The problems of interpretation encountered here are analogous to the "frame problem" as discussed in analytic philosophy and artificial intelligence (Haselager 1997) and the "hermeneutical circle" in hermeneutical philosophy (Gadamer 1989). Both have to do with the substantial role of (framing) circumstantial knowledge and presuppositions in human knowledge, interpretation, and communication.

Like anthropologists, archaeologists can draw upon various and often conflicting theoretical orientations, which make a world of difference to the sort of questions they pose and the answers they give. Furthermore, boundaries between disciplines are hard to draw. It is not unusual to come across archaeological researchers trained as art historians, philologists, ethnologists, biological anthropologists, geographers, palaeontologists, or in a combination of these disciplines, and it is very usual that expertise from various disciplines is drawn upon in any individual archaeological research project.

Publications on archaeological art (ranging from Upper Palaeolithic cave art through Olmec temples to terracotta grave gifts in Han China) may exclusively stress or combine the following types of analysis:

- *Iconographic:* the meaning of specific motifs, such as the artefacts associated with particular saints in Christian religious art.
- *Formal:* the style of a work of art, and the stylistic tradition it belongs to.
- *Semiotic:* the ways in which objects and patterns refer beyond themselves.
- *Functionalist:* the practical purpose the work of art served, for example as expressing and strengthening group identity, or appeasing spirits and thereby reducing anxiety.
- *Aesthetic:* how, why, and to whom it is attractive.
- *Structuralist:* the recurrent combinations of elements and the underlying structures they hint at.
- *Deconstructivist:* reacting against the rigidity of structuralist analysis, stressing the elusiveness of meaning and the subjectivity of the analyst.

- *Critical:* ways in which the art reflects, legitimizes, or criticizes power relations.
- *Hermeneutic:* interpreting the maker's intentions through empathy and contextual information.
- *Processual:* the contribution of art objects to the ways in which humans adapt to their environment.

How one conceptualizes art and where one draws the boundary between art and non-art is not merely a scholastic issue. It affects both the methods archaeologists use to interpret art and the status, as "knowledge," that can be attributed to such interpretations. Art as skill points towards artistic technologies and the artist as producer. Art as objectified meaning suggests iconographic and other methodologies to decode those meanings. Art as creative imagination might invite attempts to identify individual artists and their specific subjectivity. Art as visual communication highlights the social and relational character of art. Art as affective expression implies interest in the aesthetic and stylistic means by which affect is culturally shaped. Strongly relativist conceptions of art emphasize the present-oriented character of art interpretation, a mediation of the past for the present: the very idea of "art" interpretation involves relating to past objects in ways which may not have made sense for their original users, and indeed may not make sense to future readers of our interpretations. Every generation gets the Renaissance (or the Upper Palaeolithic) it deserves. Conversely, more robust "realist" conceptualizations of art may be associated with stronger claims that our interpretations and explanations of past art are at least adequate to the kinds of meanings such objects held in their past settings, and the social contexts which shaped the way they functioned and the form they took. Further, critical discussion of both interpretations and interpretive methodologies can produce cumulative progress in our knowledge and understanding of past art, interpretations which are not

just different from but also better than those of former scholars.

Anthropological Insights and Archaeological Method

Unlike anthropologists, archaeologists cannot observe directly how an art object was fabricated and used, nor can they ask its makers and users what it represents or what it was used for. Even anthropologists often find it difficult to learn about an item's meaning. There may be difficulties of translation, and deeper levels of meaning of the item may be inaccessible to native interlocutors who have not been fully initiated. Often objects or patterns are ambiguous, have different meanings to different people or generations, or no clear meaning at all. Archaeologists find it much more difficult, compared to anthropologists, and some consider it impossible, to reconstruct what meanings specific visual forms were intended to encode and communicate. Rock pitting which seems to be art may prove to be a by-product of some technical process (such as grinding axes or pounding fruit).

Archaeologists have the added problem that contextual data may be sparse, precise dating impossible. Several reindeer may be depicted next to each other on the wall of an Upper Palaeolithic cave in southern France, but it is rarely clear whether they were made at the same time by the same person, or are separated by weeks, years, centuries, or even several millennia. Clottes describes a puzzling case from the French cave of Cosquer. Two bison, painted in the same style, were directly dated. One was found to be more than 8,000 years older than the other. Did the same style persist for 8,000 years, or was one painted with charcoal left on the floor of the cave by other visitors 8,000 years previously (Clottes 1988: 115)? Even when there is some degree of cultural continuity between the makers of art and their present-day descendants, as in the case of Maya cloth or Aboriginal rock paintings, the extent to which meanings have changed in the course of time is difficult to ascertain. A wealth of information about the content of an ancient art tradition may still fail to elucidate the precise meaning of certain figures and scenes. Many thousands of spectacular "Celtic" art objects are now known from graves and sacred sites, richly decorated with human and animal figures and geometric patterns, and contextualized by systematic archaeological excavation. Nonetheless, we still know little about the myths these figures must have been associated with in their original cultural setting.

Archaeologists are therefore usually forced to refrain from delving deeply into the iconographic and cultural meanings of objects. Unlike anthropologists and art historians, archaeologists concentrate on reconstructing and explaining the fabrication of objects, the spatiotemporal distribution and variability of their motifs and styles, how they relate to ecology, and the like.

In recent years it has become popular to interpret much prehistoric rock art as the product of shamanism. The shaman is a figure who enters trance to communicate with the spirit world, and uses the knowledge or power he gains to cure illness or secure hunting success for his community. Whether shamanism is a unitary phenomenon, or an artefact of academic analysis, is debatable (Hultkrantz 1989; Vitebsky 1995). The South African archaeologist Lewis-Williams prompted the current popularity of shamanic interpretations through his work on the art of the Drakensberg Mountains. Lewis-Williams relied in part on highly opaque statements obtained from an indigenous survivor of a nineteenth-century massacre. He also found specific parallels between the iconography of the rock art and the ethnography of a wider region, including the depiction of figures wearing documented shamanic costume and performing dances resembling those described ethnographically.

Another inspiration for the current trend was Reichel-Dolmatoff's ethnography of shamanism among the Tucanoa of South America. Reichel-Dolmatoff described a range of simple geometric motifs in their art which Tucanoa say depict shapes seen in shamanic trance, and pointed to parallel "entoptic" shapes recorded in Western studies of drug-induced states of altered consciousness (Reichel-Dolmatoff 1978). A restudy of South African rock art reveals formally similar motifs, although no matching ethnography of entoptics (Lewis-Williams and Dowson 1988). Whitley's analysis of Coso rock art (southwest United States) identifies references to shamanic practices. Whitley (1992) has limited ethnographic evidence that a Californian rock shelter containing geometric paintings was a girls' initiation site. Since then, ancient rock art in Europe and Australia has been construed as the product of shamanism (Clottes and Lewis-Williams 1998; Chippindale et al. 2000).

There is no doubt that some recent hunter-gatherer rock art was inspired by trance experience and that such experiences were sometimes harnessed by shamans (Hann et al., in press; Reichel-Dolmatoff 1978). It is rare, however, for archaeologists both to propose a shamanic interpretation and ways of falsifying it (see, however, Francfort 1998; Dronfield 1996). Hedges (2000) and Quinlan (2000) have critically reviewed Whitley's use of Californian ethnography, while De Beaune (1998) has examined the recurrent fascination of Upper Palaeolithic archaeologists with the ethnography of shamanism.

The Earliest Art

Arguably, art is produced in all living human cultures, but by no other living species. The oldest secure dates for rock art come from the paintings in the French cave of Chauvet, where paintings of two rhino and a bison have been dated to ca. 30,000 BP. The Upper Palaeolithic cave art of France and Spain spans a continuous period from about 30,000 to 12,000 BP. The art of the Upper Palaeolithic was produced by anatomically modern humans. The skilled draftsmanship with which animals are portrayed is as fine as any art among recent small-scale societies. The number of species, that is, the "vocabulary" of animal subjects, is comparable to the number of species portrayed in recent Australian or southern African rock art. But we must not forget that the purpose and meaning of the art to those who painted or were intended to respond to it were specific to the cultures of the Solutriean or Magdalenian.

The geometric rock art of southern Australia may date from 30,000 BP or earlier. If so, this would be the oldest continuously practiced art tradition, persisting in the recent rock art of central Australia and contemporary commercial Aboriginal art. Both Australia and Europe are far from the regions of East and South Africa where modern humans are thought to have evolved. Fallen slabs bearing paintings excavated at Apollo 11 shelter in southern Namibia have been dated to between 19,000 and 26,000 years BP (Wendt 1974). This must have been long after the ancestors of indigenous Australians left Africa, and after the arrival of modern humans in Europe. Most southern African rock art was painted or engraved during the last few hundred years.

Before Art

If art originated before the appearance of modern humans, then it was first practiced by creatures who no longer exist and whose culture has no modern parallels. Modern art and language have many-layered structures and leave unmistakable material traces but, just as the first simple organisms exuded no durable shell or skeleton, the first expressions of art were probably ephemeral and simpler in structure. We may never know some, perhaps even much art from the past; decorated and gendered carrying nets, for example, or body tattoos and scarifications, performing and verbal art, or Neanderthal clothing.

Human culture may have been practiced for some time, perhaps a long time, before cultural behavior became sufficiently formalized and engrained in material artefacts to leave a recognizable trace. It is not acceptable, therefore, to consider all available fragmentary hints of expressive material as the beginnings of art. Early examples of apparently decorative or iconic artefacts may be chance products of natural weathering or, if deliberate, may have been the result of idiosyncratic play. Before the appearance of anatomically modern, Upper Palaeolithic humans, no undisputed art objects seem to be known. There have, however, been occasional finds of older, Neanderthal Middle Palaeolithic stones and bones with relatively systematically engraved lines of unclear significance which have been interpreted as non-utilitarian.

Evidence for the early use of ocher comes from the Howieson's Poort industry of South Africa, between 50,000 to 75,000 BP (Barham 1998; Klein 1995). Unfortunately, there is no indication of what it was used for. Even if it was used to color artefacts or the body, that is not necessarily a visual language in the modern sense. If color signified a simple unitary message such as "adult" or "sexually receptive" the use of ocher would have been no more complex than a non-human call system. Many species, including non-human primates, use a "call system," in which single cries signify "predator!", "my turf!", etc.

If one stresses aesthetics, a better, or at least a borderline, case of art before modern humans is provided by a tiny proportion of the billions of Acheulean handaxes produced in Africa and, subsequently, Eurasia from about 1.5 million to 35,000 years ago (if the Mousterian of Acheulean Tradition is included). An estimated 1 in 100, or perhaps even 1 per 50 (which is an enormous number, given the total amount of handaxes) shows up symmetry and regularity seemingly beyond practical requirements (Figure 19.4). Such specimens may have been very pleasing to their makers, and may have had additional functions and meanings, perhaps articulating clan or age group identity. One intriguing hypothesis is that, in addition to their other functions, they may have served in sexual selection, signaling the genetic fitness of their makers (Kohn and Mithen 1999). While this is difficult to verify, applying the explanatory force of evolutionary biology to such archaeological phenomena is extremely fruitful (cf: Shennan, ch. 1).

Highly regular handaxes are probably one of the earliest manifestations of an aesthetic sense, although it has been argued that bowerbird nests provide a non-human parallel (Miller 2000). Another family resemblance that is germane according to many (how difficult it is to avoid essentialism and live up to Witttgenstein's very point!) is linguistic or narrative meaning. There is no consensus, however, on the extent to which the makers of the handaxes – *Homo erectus*, *Homo heidelbergensis*, and *Homo neanderthalensis*, among others – were linguistic-

ally competent. It is clear that during the 1.5 million years during which Acheulean handaxes were made, major changes in cognitive, linguistic, and behavioral competences took place, but scholars disagree on the nature and the timing of these developments.

Art and Adaptation

For many art historians as well as cultural anthropologists, culture is not so much a mode of adaptation supplementing and interacting with genetics, but a means to transcend the limitations of biology. Art is deemed to testify to humankind's ability to rise above the struggle for survival and endow life with symbolic, moral, and religious meaning. Together with such (associated) features as religion and language, art is one of the last bastions of the presumably unique human soul, still resisting the evolu-

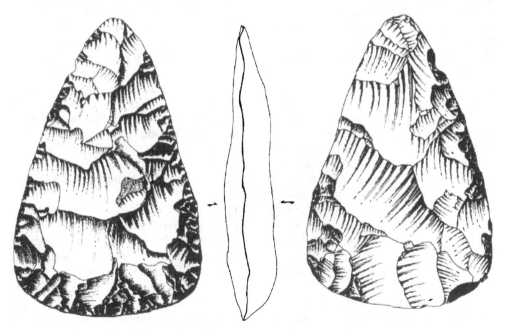

Figure 19.4 Very regular Middle Palaeolithic handaxe, Lailly, Vanne river valley, France. Mousterian. (From Deloze et al. 1994: fig. 126. Courtesy of J.-L. Locht.)

tionary approaches to culture which have been expanding over the past few decades.

That presupposition is challenged by evolutionary psychology and behavioral ecology, which stress the uniformity of all behaving organisms, including humans. Such natural history approaches have finally begun to spill over even into the study of art. There are now scholars who focus on the evolutionary backgrounds and functions of forms of art and aesthetic experience as one of many human cultural behaviors, intricately connected with genetic make-up, epigenetic development, and biological adaptation. Such scholars pose fresh questions about art. They typically go beyond culturally specific meanings in the search for human universals: species-wide inborn perceptual schemes and preferences, cognitive and motivational features underlying cultural variability and connected to the solving of adaptational problems faced by our early hunter-gatherer ancestors (e.g., Miller 2000).

An early contribution to this field compared phallic display by male baboons guarding their troop with the same feature in tribal statues, for example wooden ancestor figures functioning as village guardians in Dayak villages in Kalimantan, Indonesia (Eibl-Eibesfeldt 1978). The universal meaning of the facial configuration of eyes, nose, and mouth and the force of the direct gaze in animals, humans, and art objects was pointed out early on. Symmetry of face and body is found attractive by other humans (Grammer and Thornhill 1994). Symmetry and repetitive patterns in the natural environment draw the attention immediately, and probably influence the appearance and appreciation of similar features in art (Onians 1996). Art also has roles to play in human dealings with such universal features of existence as death, birth, sickness, and fertility, which to some extent makes it transcend culturally specific aspects in content and style.

Van Damme (1996, 2000) points to a preference in many cultures for such visual properties as symmetry and balance, clarity, shininess or brightness, novelty, and smooth-ness (which, in the case of human skin, is seen as an index of health). There is ethnographic evidence from West Africa which supports this claim (Boone 1993; Lawal 1993). Van Damme developed a transcultural evolutionary aesthetics attempting to explain universals and differences in aesthetic preference by drawing upon both universally human, neuropsychologically based tendencies and varying sociocultural ideals acquired through social formation. An inherited predisposition to respond affectively to such collective ideals, he hypothesizes, accounts for favorable responses to art forms which he construes as visual metaphors for these ideals. He argues that affective responses to collective ideals are adaptive, since they enhance various forms of cooperation that benefit individuals and others sharing their genes.

Along similar lines, Barrow (1995) argued that the tropical savannah habitats of early hominids correspond to the visual preferences of present-day children and adults across cultures, and are recreated in paintings and urban parks. Other authors focus instead on the function of art, myth, and ritual as repositories of knowledge useful for survival (e.g., Minc 1986), or a reinforcement of solidarity in groups and alliance networks. One refreshing aspect of natural history approaches to art is the downplaying of the linguistic, mythical, and narrative meanings of art that figure so largely in most other approaches.

Art and Communication

The linguist Bickerton (1996) has proposed an evolutionary stage characterized by a semantically rich but syntactically poor protolanguage, which he associates with *Homo erectus*. This might have constituted nothing more than a vast vocabulary of calls. Donald, a psychologist, on the other hand, stresses mimetic imitation as a flexible and creative, nonlinguistic (*sic*) mode of representation and communication (Donald

1991). This has to do with artistic competence, and imitation as another "germane" family resemblance. Mithen (1998) argues that simple language may have preceded fully modern humans: there may have been syntax, but its function may have been limited to regulating relationships within the social group.

For Mithen, the diagnostic feature of fully developed human language is its ability to link cognitive domains. This is an essential aspect of modeling reality, so as to explain and predict. On the other hand, as several authors have pointed out, language would need the capacity to refer to things and actions distant in time and space from the speaker. Transcending the "here and now," implying a release from proximity, was a necessary precondition for language to sustain social networks on the scale found among modern hunter-gatherers. These allow individual bands to hunt and gather on neighboring bands' territories and maintain various sorts of exchange relations with them. Mellars (1998) regards Upper Palaeolithic art (undoubtedly drawn from memory) as the best evidence for the cognitive skills that modern languages make possible.

Aitchison (1996) suggests two models for the origin of language. These can also be envisaged as possible origins for art as a cultural system. In one, language begins as a limited number of opposed signs based on a clear but simple structure. In the other, everyone is chattering away about all sorts of things, but there is very little mutual comprehension. The arbitrariness of sounds in spoken language seems to benefit from, indeed to depend on, tightly structured oppositions. This implies that language more probably required Aitchison's first scenario. The iconicity of art might, on the other hand, facilitate Aitchison's second scenario. She hypothesizes that a few small sparks of verbal communication were around for a long time, then the whole "language bonfire" suddenly caught fire. The archaeological evidence suggests something similar may have occurred with art.

D'Errico (1992) postulates symbolic meaning for personal ornaments and decorated artefacts from Châtelperronian sites in Western Europe such as Roc de Combe and Arcy-sur-Cure, along with perforated and ochered shells associated with 100,000-year-old burials of anatomically modern humans at Qafzeh. He also rightly points out that there is no ethnographic model for the initial development of symbolic communication in humans (see also d'Errico et al. 1998). We cannot assume Neanderthal necklaces relied on an expressive system of modern human complexity.

Structures, Signs, and Agents

Anthropologists traditionally distinguish between the meaning and function of sociocultural traits. The function of a custom has been defined as the contribution it makes to satisfying the individual's needs or to the organization of social relations (Malinowski 1922: 515–16; 1954: 202; Radcliffe-Brown 1952: 178–9). The study of symbolism investigates the meaning of elements of culture.

The theory of communication in art begins with structuralism. The structuralist theory of communication is concerned with the connection between a sound or picture and its meaning, i.e., with signification. The theory originated in the work of the French sociologist Emile Durkheim (1915) on Australian aboriginal religion. Durkheim considered aboriginal Australian communities had preserved the original form of human religion, which therefore showed how meaning in human culture had come about. He supposed the simplest, and therefore earliest, social structure would be one with two segments, i.e., moieties ("halves"). Moieties often have totemic emblems that form opposed pairs, such as eagle hawk (a hunting bird) and crow (a scavenging bird). As each community grew in size, the moieties subdivided into clans, which also had animal emblems. Celebration of the clan's totemic ancestor in ritual was a reaffirmation of the group's identity as a segment of society. The association of each clan with a particular animal emblem was arbitrary. It did not matter whether a particular clan had snake, possum, or kangaroo as its emblem. Clan x was only kangaroo because it was not possum or snake. Once the association was established within the collective consciousness, however, it seemed natural and unchangeable. Spencer and Gillen reported that people attached particular importance to the designs on sacred objects and body paintings used in ritual to represent clan totems. The geometric style of central Australian art was so simplified that to Durkheim the designs seemed arbitrary. Because they are arbitrary, they depend entirely on cultural convention; their meaning was determined by a "collective consciousness."

Ferdinand de Saussure is reported to have been influenced by Durkheim's ideas (Ardener 1971: xxxiv, quoting Doroszewski 1933; Barthes 1967: 100; Ricoeur 1976: 3). He developed Durkheim's model of clan totemism into a general theory of communication through signs. One of the crucial additions that Saussure made was to introduce the distinction between *language* and *speech*. Speech draws upon the vocabulary and grammar of the language to construct a limitless series of statements. Saussure saw language change as evolution in the system, rather than the result of changes introduced by individuals. Individual idiosyncrasies can have no meaning, because they are not part of the system. Individuals *use* the system, but it exists independently of them, and has its own dynamic.

Saussure's primary concern was with how ideas are related or juxtaposed to other ideas in the structure of the language. The American theorists Peirce and Morris, on the other hand, argued that signs can be classified according to the way they denote or *refer* to objects in the environment. An indexical sign points to what it refers to, like a finger post, just as "smoke 'means' fire" (or, in a well-known example, a warm cardigan "means" long winter walks; Barthes 1967:

43). An indexical sign has something in common with what it refers to: a sundial is an index of the time of day, a weathervane an index of wind direction (Peirce 1955: 102–3). Icons look like what they refer to, as in representational art, whereas symbols are arbitrarily associated with the objects they refer to, like the words of language. Morris argued that symbols reproduce the *structure* of what they refer to (rather than resembling it), as when a chemical formula such as $C + O_2 = CO_2$ models the reaction between carbon and oxygen (Morris 1938: 24). Gell's explanation for the capacity of art to extend its maker's agency by objectifying his/her mind (presented in the final sections of Gell 1998) is very similar. In our opinion, both signification and reference must be taken into account. Representational art is iconic, but what the subject matter *signifies* is specific to the cultural tradition within which it was produced.

Beyond a Language of Art

Looking for meaning can sometimes be misleading. The "Maroons" of Surinam and French Guiana are descendants of escaped slaves. Price and Price (1980) show that the motifs Maroon artists carve on bowls or weave into textiles are purely decorative. Many ethnographers hoped to find surviving elements of West African religion in their art. Maroons who denied any meaning in their art generally enjoyed only a short career as ethnographic informants. Writers assumed instead that the Maroons were unwilling to tell them, or even that they had forgotten the meaning of their own art, rather than accept what they were told at face value. But what does it mean, in terms of a theory of culture, to say people have forgotten what their own art means?

No one would deny that art and language have different capacities. Gell argues that art objects have a semantic value only when they function as graphic signs, i.e., as visual expressions of language (Gell 1998: 6).

Otherwise, art objects are better treated, in Gell's view, as what Pierce called indices or icons (Gell 1998: 13, 25). Indices can be read as an expression of human agency (Gell 1998: 14–15), while icons (as was explained above) look like what they refer to (Gell underestimates the conventional character of representational traditions). While Gell correctly argues that both indices and icons can function without the support of the kind of structural system that language depends upon, he does, however, accept there can be units and rules for combining artistic motifs within a stylistic (cultural) system; indeed, each culture *is* in his view a distinctive style (Gell 1998: ch. 8). This links his approach with that of art historians discussed below.

The notion of art as a visual language has also suffered from the deconstructivist or postmodernist critique of structuralism. Derrida (1976) is famous for this attack, although his argument derives in part from Wittgenstein's later theory of language. Derrida accepted Saussure's theory that meaning is arbitrary or conventional, but rejected the idea of a "collective consciousness." He also argued that the impossibility of exact translation between languages demonstrates there is no meaning that exists outside language. As he put it, there is no "transcendental signified." Knowledge is an artefact of the system's structure and as arbitrary as language itself. Derrida points out that terms like culture, rationality, and progress only make sense because they are opposed to other terms: nature, superstition, stagnation. The virtue of anthropology has been to call the familiar into question by showing that such oppositions are not as self-evident as they might seem (Derrida 1978: 282).

For Derrida, language is nothing more than a series of performances by speakers. As language changes, so it becomes impossible to recover the meanings that people intended in the past. Each performance leaves a "trace" of current usage. Thus the ancient Australian geometric art of Panaramittee includes many of the motifs familiar from the recent acrylic art of central Australia, but deploys those motifs in different ways and with different frequencies (Layton 1992: 189–90, 206–11).

The absence of "transcendental" meaning outside language has the consequence that it is only through practice that meaningful oppositions are established. A language is the outcome of practice through which the "trace" of opposed signs can be detected. Since no external constraints are imposed on this practice, meanings will constantly change, in random fashion (see Derrida 1976: 50–60). Thus, even where an art system exists today, and anthropologists can learn how to make sense of it, neither they nor members of the indigenous community can reread past works produced in that tradition in the way they would have been "read" at the time they were produced.

Derrida is clearly right to argue that language (or art) changes through use. A language can only exist because it is realized through peoples' performances. Texts record performances that may predate the current structure. Both Ricoeur and Eco have argued that, while there are many ways of reading a text, they are not all equally valid. Eco argues that any text directs the reader toward particular readings, even if these are open-ended, because its *style* locates the statement in the context of a certain discourse (Eco 1990: 45). A discourse is "the outline of a new way of being in the world" (Ricoeur 1991: 149), and a text is an invitation to see the world in a particular way. The chicken-and-egg problem (what came first, structure or performance?) has been resolved by Bourdieu (1984) and Giddens (1984) through the concepts of *habitus* and *structuration*. The structure generates performance, which recreates the structure. People are not just *users* of a system that exists independently of them in Durkheim's "collective consciousness"; they are also *agents* who both realize the structure and transform the system through the ways they harness it to their purposes. Meaning is negotiated. Derrida's mistake was to overlook reference.

In use, language or art is constantly used to refer to, and comment on, real-life situations familiar to the performer and his or her audience. Historic and prehistoric archaeology face very different problems in this regard. Much of Upper Palaeolithic cave art is highly iconic. We can often recognize the references paintings or engravings make to horses and bison, deer and ibex, and we can appreciate the subtle ways in which the complex forms of real animals are reduced to visions of simplicity. Ironically, however, the references are all that are left. The negotiated meanings were lost ten thousand or more years ago.

It is now appreciated that everyone has a slightly different interpretation of the meaningful behavior of those around them (that is, each has internalized their own *habitus*). It has become clear that interpersonal variation in interpretations varies considerably, although complete randomness or chaos is avoided (e.g., O'Hanlon 1989). In an oral tradition, legends are constantly retold, but there is no orthodox version. Everyone suits their telling to the time and place, the audience and their own skills as a narrator, but there is general consensus as to what constitutes a legitimate performance (for some examples of legends related to rock art, see Layton 1992: 40–5).

Anthropologists now see fieldwork, and subsequent writing, as a dialogue between themselves and members of the community they are seeking to understand. Archaeological "readings" of prehistoric art are an extreme use of power, because prehistoric people cannot respond to or challenge them. The archaeologist can only look to see what it was possible to do with an art tradition (the corpus of surviving performances) and cannot test what is not "grammatical," or whether references have been correctly identified.

Archaeology and Art History

The shared orientations, and the divergences, between art historical and archaeological approaches to art can best be understood in terms of the emphasis and the significance attributed to the relationship between "form" and "context." These differences are partly rooted in the different nature of the materials typically studied by art historians and archaeologists, also partly a result of disciplinary traditions, and finally partly a function of the differing relationships of art historians and archaeologists to the broader extra-academic art world.

Art historians and archaeologists share fundamental interpretive methods, such as style analysis and iconography. The iconographic protocols originally designed for modern Western art – connecting a motif such as the body of a man nailed to a cross, with a particular story found in a text, the crucifixion – can easily be transferred to the art of complex societies with writing systems more normally studied by archaeologists: the myths on Greek vases, or the historical narrative relief sculptures from Assyrian palaces. Even in the absence of texts, in prehistoric societies, closely analogous procedures may be followed. Although cultural meanings cannot be quite so precisely decoded, the contexts in which particular motifs are found, or indeed in which their viewers might have encountered the objects represented in particular motifs, may point towards the cultural connotations of those motifs (Morgan 1988).

The study of Mayan art is particularly instructive in this respect, since, with the decipherment of Mayan script – which plays a major role alongside figurative imagery on vase paintings and sculptures – Mayan art has changed from being "prehistoric" to "historic." On the one hand, there is considerable continuity in the basic methods of iconographical analysis used (see Kubler 1990: 201–340; Miller 1999 for "before and after" decipherment surveys). On the other hand, the availability of texts has permitted a much more nuanced cultural contextualization of Mayan art. The concept *u-ba(h)*, for example, signifying "his self/face/person," is used in such a way as to suggest that some representations on stelae were intended to be portraits of specific individuals (Stuart 1996; Houston and Stuart 1998). Awareness of such concepts allows analysts to achieve a much deeper and more precise understanding of the exact purposes underlying specific iconographic choices in Mayan rulers' strategies of self-presentation.

Both art historians and archaeologists also see style as a fundamental interpretive resource and object of explanation, but they differ in the way they place it in a broader social and cultural context. The critical tradition in art history, heir to Kant and Hegel through Winckelmann, distinguishes between "archaeological questions" – concerning brute facts of the material from which an object is made, physical aspects of its construction and placement – and "critical questions" which address style as the expression of the cultural freedom of the human mind. Style is held to articulate a relationship or attitude to the world and its objects, represented in art through the specific stylistic treatment of these objects or aspects of the world (landscape, people, artefacts) as represented in images (Podro 1982; Schapiro 1951). Congruent with the modern conception of art, the focus of art historians' style analysis is either the critical appreciation of a creative artist's individual inflection of inherited tradition (Baxandall 1985), and the personal attitudes expressed by that inflection, or an intuitive linking of shared patterns of stylistic expression to broader aspects of culture, indicating, for example, a period or group mentality or attitude (Panofsky 1939, 1951; Pollitt 1972).

Early twentieth-century cultural historical archaeology shared the concept of style as an expression of group identity and mentality. Since the 1960s, however, archaeologists' contextualizations of style have had a strongly sociological character, whether as a passive indicator of social processes or more recently as a marker consciously manipulated by culturally strategic agents. In either case, the features of style are connected to their context not by intuition or analogy, but

through causal or functional models. These link the specific stylistic features of the artefacts in question with social structure, by reconstructing the production systems which generated the artefacts, and the social systems that lie behind the objects and their social uses as revealed in the systematic patterning of their distribution in contexts of deposition (Davis 1990; Conkey 1990). The social functions being performed by style may be held by archaeologists to be recognizable even while the specific cultural meanings of prehistoric styles, in the absence of textual keys, may be thought to be archaeologically irrecoverable (Earle 1990). Although the costs of such a reduced emphasis on the cultural specifics of style seem rather high, especially from an art historical point of view, it does have considerable advantages in trying to generalize across contexts, and develop broad models of the relationship between style and social structure (see below), in contrast to art historians' emphasis on the particularities of single cultural traditions.

These differences of emphasis can, however, have far reaching practical entailments when the assumptions encoded in the modern concept of art – as autonomous objects of aesthetic contemplation, the imaginative expression of creative individuals – are extended to archaeological artefacts. This is well illustrated by the fate of Cycladic marble figurines in the twentieth century (Figure 19.5). Largely ignored when they were first discovered in the late nineteenth century, these objects became increasingly fashionable during the course of the twentieth century due to their apparent formal similarity to the modernist sculpture of Epstein and Brancusi. Reclassified from artefactual curiosity to work of art, celebrated as the first stirrings of the spirit of European abstraction by aesthetes (Renfrew 1991), and attributed to individual "masters" by art historian connoisseurs with close relations with collectors and dealers (Getz-Preziosi 1987), Cycladic "idols" became "must have" objects of aesthetic desire on the part of museums and collectors, fueling

Figure 19.5 Cycladic marble figurine, ca. 2500 BC. Ht: 76.8cm. British Museum GR 1971. 5–21.1. Photo: Museum

and the richer the textual resources available to them from that society, the nearer are the theories and methods commonly used to those of mainstream art historians. Perhaps the most conflict-ridden and stimulating fields are those of protohistoric societies – on the edge of history, with some but limited textual materials. In the interpretation of early Chinese ritual bronzes (see Whitfield 1993), Sarah Allan (1993) adopts a conventional iconographic methodology, interpreting the development of animal/monster motifs – the *taotie* (Figure 19.6) – as encodings of specific myths and beliefs of Shang religion. Robert Bagley (1993) denies the possibility of recovering such precise meanings on the basis of texts for the most part later than the bronzes in question, and explains the decoration in terms of the evolution of technologies of bronze casting and the characteristic design style to which they gave rise. Turning away from a focus on art production, Jessica Rawson (1993) explains the vessels' style and iconography in terms of their

an orgy of illicit excavation of early Bronze Age Cycladic cemeteries. This destroyed forever all the contextual information that might have allowed us to understand the social uses and cultural meanings of these fascinating images (Gill and Chippindale 1993). Correspondingly, while many art historians have quite close connections with the art market – providing attributions in their areas of expertise, authenticating works, writing catalogues for dealers' exhibitions and auctions – the relationship between archaeologists and the art antiquities market is one of generally undisguised hostility, and those who ignore the ethical standards upheld by most practitioners of the field, are looked on with some disdain (Tubb and Brodie 2001; Corbey 2000).

In practice, the more complex the society whose art archaeologists seek to understand,

Figure 19.6 Bronze ritual vessel, *hu*. Shang Dynasty, 1300–1100 BC. Ht: 29.8cm British Museum, OA 1983. 3-18.1. Photo: Museum.

consumption (ritual dining) and deposition (burials), as means by which attention might be differentially attached to vessels with different functions and status, and to the varying social ranking of their owners and users.

Art and the Evolution of Social Complexity

The art of the large majority of the societies, cultures, and artistic traditions known to modern researchers has been recovered archaeologically. Archaeological students of art are thus in a particularly strong position to explore fundamental questions about the relationship between art and the development of social complexity. Both cultural historical archaeology and processual archaeology recognized that development of sophisticated, specifically monumental, art traditions was both a good marker, and constitutive of the development of urbanism, states, and civilizations, although the mechanisms connecting art and society were left underexplored, and the qualitative aesthetic features of the art rather ignored (Childe 1950; Willey 1962; Renfrew 1972).

A more stylistically oriented interest in the relationship between social and political structure and the structure of systems of artistic representation goes back to Hegel's grand evolutionary scheme of the development of Western art. It has been revived in sociologically more sophisticated forms, incorporating contemporary research in perception and cognitive psychology, both in grand versions of the history of Western art (Witkin 1995), and more modest accounts exploring particular social, cultural, and artistic transitions (Baines 1985). Work in the "archaeology of contextual meaning" opposes such "totalizing" grand narratives, and questions the possibility of cross-cultural comparison (Hodder 1987, 1991: 121–55). It parallels traditional iconographic art history in emphasizing the social and cultural particularity of the contents of visual symbolism, which articulates systems of social relations or legitimates structures of domination (Taylor 1987; cf. Zanker 1988 for a classic example of such a study in Roman art and archaeology).

The most sophisticated of current studies seek to combine close analysis of particular cases with the development of generalizing models. Flannery (1999), for example, has explored the use made of art in the transition from chiefdoms to states. He suggests that while the cultural repertoire in each case is unique, there are close parallels in the ways that visual symbolism is used across cases of state formation – to break down old loyalties, symbolize the state's capacity for violence, and reconfigure ideologies to fit more closely the structure of the emergent state. Baines and Yoffee (2000) have developed a general model to explain the structure and function of art in early state-based civilizations. They argue that the development of the characteristic civilizational styles of Egypt and Mesopotamia are linked to an ideology of order which undergirded elite identity and legitimacy. The centralized control of labor-intensive production and ritualized consumption of a new order of highly stylized artefacts, materialized a new ideology of order and was instrumental in socializing members of the elite into their new roles and as an embodiment of a monopoly of symbolic legitimacy.

From an art historical or contextual archaeological view, such work might seem to abstract too much from the specifics of the visual forms used in particular cases, and the implications that these aesthetic features might have for the relative success of different visual strategies, or for the qualitative experience of relationships of power and solidarity particular to specific societies. In some degree it is a matter of intellectual taste, whether one emphasizes the detailed particularistic contextual analysis of the art of a single time and place, or prefers to develop generalizing models which abstract from cultural particulars. It should not be assumed, however, that the relationship between particularity and generalization is necessarily a zero sum game. Layton (1985, 2000), for example, has explored some of the commonalities of hunter-gatherer rock art traditions, shared by virtue of their common social structures and similar relation to their environment, and the differences, notably in style and iconography, which cut across different groups of hunter-gatherers – for example, the South African San Bushmen and Australian aborigines – according to their distinctive social organization (totemic clans versus bands with no totemic clans). Similarly, Blanton et al. (1996) have explored the different kinds of art work sponsored by differently organized early states in Mesoamerica. Their arguments suggest that "corporate" states, like classic Teotihuacan, ruled by relatively egalitarian elites, characteristically sponsor monumental architecture designed for large-scale celebration of communal rituals and iconography representing collective participation in such rituals. By contrast, "network states" like the early Olmec, characterized by highly individualistic power strategies and a single dominant ruler, also sponsor monumental art, but often of an exclusionary and hierarchical kind, whether palaces or princely burials for a ruler or monumental individualized portraits (Figure 19.7). This comparative

Figure 19.7 Olmec head, from La Venta Archaeological Park, originally San Lorenzo, Veracruz, Mexico, ca. 1150–1000 BC. Photo: Jeremy Tanner.

archaeology of art, whether internal to cultural traditions or across cultures, represents one of the most distinctive and promising areas of archaeological contribution to the understanding of art in the coming years.

Conclusion

We have discussed how archaeologists studying art have been able to draw upon the theories and methods of three neighboring disciplines: art history, social anthropology, and evolutionary biology. We have shown how the application of such ideas and methods presents particular problems for archaeology, but how archaeology has its own, distinctive contributions to make to each debate. With regard to evolutionary biology, archaeology has been able to extend the study of cognitive evolution to art, and cast some doubt on the reductionism of some evolutionary explanations. On the other hand, some of the hypotheses advanced for the role of art in human adaptation remain speculative. Archaeology has an incomparable advantage over the snapshot-like field studies of social anthropology, yet archaeologists cannot observe or interview the artists whose work they study. Although prehistoric archaeologists should resist attempting to recreate in much detail the worlds of intersubjective meaning unpacked by anthropologists' participant observation, archaeologists working on the art of historical periods are, with sufficiently helpful textual sources, better able to emulate anthropologists' interpretive approaches. Even when they lack such sources, archaeologists have considerably extended the range of comparative case material available, testing and refining Eurocentric theories about the historical trajectory of art traditions that accompany the growth of complex social systems, and developing generalizing models which go beyond the sometimes narrowly particularistic approaches of conventional art history.

References

Abrams, M. H. 1989. "Art as such: the sociology of modern aesthetics." In M. H. Abrams, *Doing Things With Texts: Essays in Criticism and Critical Theory*, pp. 135–58. New York: Norton.

Aitchison, J. 1996. *The Seeds of Speech: Language Origin and Evolution*. Cambridge: Cambridge University Press.

Allan, S. 1993. "Art and meaning." In R. Whitfield (ed.), *The Problem of Meaning in Early Chinese Ritual Bronzes*, pp. 9–33. London: Percival David Foundation.

Ardener, E. 1971. "Introductory essay." In E. Ardener (ed.), *Social Anthropology and Language*, pp. ix–cii. London: Tavistock.

Bagley, R. W. 1993. "Meaning and explanation." In R. Whitfield (ed.), *The Problem of Meaning in Early Chinese Ritual Bronzes*, pp. 34–55. London: Percival David Foundation.

Bahn, P. G. and J. Vertut 1988. *Images of the Ice Age*. London: Windward/W. H. Smith.

Baines, J. 1985. "Theories and universals of representation: Heinrich Schaefer and Egyptian art." *Art History*, 8: 1–25.

Baines, J. 1994. "On the status and purposes of ancient Egyptian art." *Cambridge Archaeological Journal*, 4 (1): 67–94.

Baines, J. and N. Yoffee 2000. "Order, legitimacy and wealth: setting the terms." In J. Richards and M. van Buren (eds.), *Order, Legitimacy and Wealth in Ancient States*, pp. 13–17. Cambridge: Cambridge University Press.

Barham, L. 1998. "Possible early pigment use in south-central Africa." *Current Anthropology*, 39: 703–10.

Barrow, J. D. 1995. *The Artful Universe*. Oxford: Clarendon Press.

Barthes, R. 1967. *Elements of Semiology*. Trans. A. Lavers and C. Smith. London: Cape.

Baxandall, M. 1985. *Patterns of Intention: On the Historical Explanation of Pictures*. New Haven, CT: Yale University Press.

Bickerton, D. 1996. *Language and Human Behaviour*. London: University College London Press.

Blanton, R. E., G. M. Feinmann, S. A. Kowalewski, and P. N. Peregrine 1996. "A dual processual theory of the evolution of Mesoamerican civilization." *Current Anthropology*, 37 (1): 1–14.

Boone, S. 1993. "Radiance from the waters: Mende feminine beauty." In R. Anderson and K. Field (eds.), *Art in Small-Scale Societies: Contemporary Readings*, pp. 303–8. Englewood Cliffs, NJ: Prentice-Hall.

Bourdieu, P. 1984. *Outline of a Theory of Practice*. Cambridge: Cambridge University Press.

Childe, V. G. 1950. "The urban revolution." *Town Planning Review*, 21: 3–17

Chippindale, C., B. Smith, and P. S. C. Taçon 2000. "Visions of dynamic power: archaic rock-paintings, altered states of consciousness and 'clever men' in Western Arnhem Land (NT), Australia." *Cambridge Archaeological Journal*, 19 (1): 63–101.

Clottes, J. 1988. "The 'Three Cs': fresh avenues towards European Palaeolithic art." In C. Chippindale and P. Taçon (eds.), *The Archaeology of Rock Art*, pp. 112–29. Cambridge: Cambridge University Press.

Clottes, J. and J. D. Lewis-Williams 1998. *Shamans of Prehistory: Trance and Magic in the Painted Caves*. New York: Harry Abrams.

Clunas, C. 1997. *Art in China*. Oxford: Oxford University Press.

Conkey, M. W. 1990. "Experimenting with style in archaeology: some historical and theoretical issues." In M. W. Conkey and C. A. Hastorf (eds.), *The Uses of Style in Archaeology*, pp. 5–17. Cambridge: Cambridge University Press.

Corbey, R. 2000. *Tribal Art Traffic: A Chronicle of Taste, Trade and Desire in Colonial and Post-Colonial Times*. Amsterdam: KIT Publishers/Royal Tropical Institute.

Davis, W. 1990. "Style and history in art history." In M. W. Conkey and C. A. Hastorf (eds.), *The Uses of Style in Archaeology*, pp. 18–31. Cambridge: Cambridge University Press.

De Beaune, S. 1998. "Chamanisme et préhistoire. Un feuilleton à épisodes." *L'Homme*, 147: 203–19.

Deloze V. et al. 1994. *Le Paléolithique moyen dans le Nord du Sénonais* (Yonne). Paris: Editions de la Maison des sciences de l'homme.

d'Errico, F. 1992. "Technology, motion, and the meaning of Epipalaeolithic art." *Current Anthropology*, 33: 185–201.

d'Errico, F., J. Zilhâo, M. Julien, D. Baffier, and J. Pelegrin 1998. "Neanderthal acculturation in Western Europe? A critical review of the evidence and its interpretation." *Current Anthropology*, 39 Supplement: S1–S44.

Derrida, J. 1976. *Of Grammatology*. Baltimore, MD: Johns Hopkins University Press.

Derrida, J. 1978. *Writing and Difference*. London: Routledge.

Donald, M. 1991. *Origins of the Modern Mind: Three Stages in the Evolution of Culture and Cognition*. Cambridge, MA: Harvard University Press.

Doroszewski, W. 1933. "Quelques remarques sur les rapports de la sociologie et de la linguistique: Durkheim et F. de Saussure." *Journal de Psychologie*, 30 (1): 82–91.

Drenkhahn, R. 1995. "Artists and artisans in pharaonic Egypt." In J. M. Sasson (ed.), *Civilizations of the Ancient Near East*, pp. 331–43. New York: Simon and Schuster.

Dronfield, J. 1996. "The vision thing: diagnosis of endogenous derivation in 'abstract' arts." *Current Anthropology*, 37: 373–91.

Duncan, C. and A. Wallach. 1980. "The universal survey museum." *Art History*, 3 (4): 448–69.

Durkheim, E. 1915. *The Elementary Forms of the Religious Life*. Trans. J. W. Swain. London: Allen and Unwin.

Earle, T. 1990. "Style and iconography as legitimation in complex chiefdoms." In M. W. Conkey and C. A. Hastorf (eds.), *The Uses of Style in Archaeology*, pp. 73–81. Cambridge: Cambridge University Press.

Eco, U. 1990. *The Limits of Interpretation*. Bloomington: Indiana University Press.

Eibl-Eibesfeldt, I. 1978. *Grundriss der Vergleichenden Verhaltensforschung* [Outline of comparative behavioral science], 5th edn. Munich: Piper.

Flannery, K. V. 1999. "Process and agency in early state formation." *Cambridge Archaeological Journal*, 9 (1): 3–21.

Forge, A. 1967. "The Abelam artist." In M. Freedman (ed.), *Social Organization: Essays Presented to Raymond Firth*, pp. 65–84. London: Cass.

Forge, A. 1970. "Learning to see in New Guinea." In P. Mayer (ed.), *Socialisation: The Approach from Social Anthropology*, pp. 269–91. London: Tavistock.

Francfort, H.-P. 1998. "Central Asian petroglyphs: between Indo-Iranian and shamanistic interpretations." In C. Chippindale and P. Taçon (eds.), *The Archaeology of Rock Art*, pp. 302–18. Cambridge: Cambridge University Press.

Gadamer, H.-G. 1989. *Truth and Method*, 2nd revd. edn. Revd. trans. J. Weinsheimer and D. G. Marshall. London: Sheed and Ward.

Gell, A. 1998. *Art and Agency: An Anthropological Theory*. Oxford: Oxford University Press.

Getz-Preziosi, P. 1987. *Sculptors of the Cyclades: Individual and Tradition in the 3rd Millennium* BC. Ann Arbor: Michigan University Press.

Giddens, A. 1984. *The Constitution of Society*. Cambridge: Polity Press.

Gill, D. W. J. and C. Chippindale 1993. "Material and intellectual consequences of esteem for Cycladic figures." *American Journal of Archaeology*, 97: 601–59.

Grammer, K. and R. Thornhill 1994. "Human (*Homo sapiens*) facial attractiveness and sexual selection: the role of symmetry and averageness." *Journal of Comparative Psychology*, 108: 233–42

Hann, D., J. Keyser, and P. Cash, in press. "Columbia Plateau rock art: a window to the spirit world." In D. Whitley (ed.), *Ethnography and North American Rock Art*. Walnut Creek, CA: Altamira Press.

Haselager, W. F. G. 1997. *Cognitive Science and Folk Psychology: The Right Frame of Mind*. London: Sage Publications.

Hedges, K. 2000. "Traversing the great gray middle ground: an examination of shamanistic interpretation of rock art." *American Indian Rock Art*, 28: 123–36.

Hodder, I. (ed.) 1987. *The Archaeology of Contextual Meanings*. Cambridge: Cambridge University Press.

Hodder, I. 1991. *Reading the Past: Current Approaches to Interpretation in Archaeology*, 2nd edn. Cambridge: Cambridge University Press.

Houston, S. and D. Stuart. 1998. "Personhood and portraiture in the classic period." *RES: Anthropology and Aesthetics*, 33: 73–101.

Hultkrantz, A. 1989. "The place of shamanism in the history of religions." In M. Hoppál and O. J. von Sadovszky (eds.), *Shamanism: Past and Present*, pp. 43–51. Los Angeles: Fullerton.

Klein, R. G. 1995. "Anatomy, behavior and modern human origins." *Journal of World Prehistory*, 9: 167–98.

Kohn, M. and S. Mithen 1999. "Handaxes: products of sexual selection?" *Antiquity*, 73 (281): 518.

Kristeller, P. O. 1990 [1951/2]. "The modern system of the arts." In P. O. Kristeller, *Renaissance Thought and the Arts*, pp. 163–227. Princeton, NJ: Princeton University Press.

Kubler, G. 1970. "Period, style and meaning in ancient American art." *New Literary History*, 1: 127–44.

Kubler, G. 1990 [1962]. *The Art and Architecture of Ancient America*. New Haven, CT: Yale University Press.

Lawal, B. 1993. "Some aspects of Yoruba aesthetics." In R. Anderson and K. Field (eds.), *Art in Small-Scale Societies: Contemporary Readings*, pp. 309–16. Englewood Cliffs, NJ: Prentice-Hall.

Layton, R. 1981. *The Anthropology of Art*. London: Granada.

Layton, R. 1985. "The cultural context of hunter-gatherer rock art." *Man* (n.s.), 20: 434–53.

Layton, R. 1992. *Australian Rock Art, A New Synthesis*. Cambridge: Cambridge University Press.

Layton, R. 2000. "Shamanism, totemism and rock art: les chamanes de la préhistoire in the context of rock art research." *Cambridge Archaeological Journal*, 10: 169–86.

Leroi-Gourhan, A. 1968. *The Art of Prehistoric Man in Western Europe*. London: Thames and Hudson.

Lewis-Williams, D. 1981. *Believing and Seeing: Symbolic Meanings in Southern San Rock Paintings*. London: Academic Press.

Lewis-Williams, D. and T. Dowson 1988. "The signs of all times: entoptic phenomena in Upper Palaeolithic rock art." *Current Anthropology*, 29 (2): 201–45.

Malinowski, B. 1922. *Argonauts of the Western Pacific: An Account of Native Enterprise and Adventure in the Archipelagoes of Melanesian New Guinea*. London: Routledge.

Malinowski, B. 1954. *Magic, Science and Religion*. New York: Doubleday.

Mellars, P. 1998. "Neanderthals, modern humans and the archaeological evidence for language." In N. G. Jablonski and L. Aiello (eds.), *The Origin and Diversification of Language*, pp. 89–115. San Francisco: Memoirs of the California Academy of Science.

Miller, G. 2000. *The Mating Mind*. New York: Doubleday.

Miller, M. E. 1999. *Maya Art and Architecture*. London: Thames and Hudson.

Minc, L. D. 1986. "Scarcity and survival: The role of oral tradition in mediating subsistence crises." *Journal of Anthropological Archaeology*, 5, 39–113.

Mithen, S. 1998. "A creative explosion? Theory of mind, language and the disembodied mind of the Upper Palaeolithic." In S. Mithen (ed.), *Creativity in Human Evolution and Prehistory*, pp. 165–91. London: Routledge.

Morgan, L. 1988. *The Miniature Wall-Paintings of Thera: A Study in Aegean Culture and Iconography*. Cambridge: Cambridge University Press.

Morphy, H. 1991. *Ancestral Connections*. Chicago: University of Chicago Press.

Morris, C. 1938. *Foundations of the Theory of Signs*. Chicago: University of Chicago Press.

Munn, N. 1973. *Walpiri Iconography*. Ithaca, NY: Cornell University Press.

O'Hanlon, M. 1989. *Reading the Skin: Adornment, Display and Society Among the Wahgi*. London: British Museum Publications.

Onians, J. 1996. "World art studies and the need for a new natural history of art." *Art Bulletin*, 78: 206–9.

Onians, J. 1999. *Classical Art and the Cultures of Greece and Rome*. New Haven, CT: Yale University Press.

Panofsky. E. 1939. "Introduction." In *Studies in Iconology: Humanistic Themes in the Art of the Renaissance*, pp. 3–27. Oxford: Oxford University Press.

Panofsky, E. 1951. *Gothic Architecture and Scholasticism*. New York: Meridian.

Pears, I. 1988. *The Discovery of Painting: The Growth of Interest In the Arts in England, 1680–1768*. New Haven, CT: Yale University Press.

Peirce, C. S. 1955. "Logic as semiotic: the theory of signs." In J. Buchler (ed.), *The Philosophy of Peirce: Selected Writings*, pp. 98–119. London: Kegan Paul.

Podro, M. 1982. *The Critical Historians of Art*. New Haven, CT: Yale University Press.

Pollitt, J. J. 1972. *Art and Experience in Classical Greece*. Cambridge: Cambridge University Press.

Potts, A. 1982. "Winckelmann's construction of history." *Art History*, 5 (4): 377–407.

Price, S. and R. Price 1980. "Exotica and community." *Caribbean Review*, 9 (4): 13–17, 47.

Quinlan, A. 2000. "The ventriloquist's dummy: a critical review of shamanism and rock art in Far Western North America." *Journal of California and Great Basin Anthropology*, 22: 92–108.

Radcliffe-Brown, A. R. 1952. *Structure and Function in Primitive Society*. London: Cohen and West.

Rawson, J. 1993. "Late Shang bronze design: meaning and purpose." In R. Whitfield (ed.), *The Problem of Meaning in Early Chinese Ritual Bronzes*, pp. 67–95. London: Percival David Foundation.

Reichel-Dolmatoff, G. 1978. *Beyond the Milky Way: Hallucinatory Imagery of the Tukano Indians*. Los Angeles: UCLA Latin American Center Publications.

Renfrew, C. 1972. *The Emergence of Civilization: The Cyclades and the Aegean in the Third Millennium BC*. London: Methuen.

Renfrew, C. 1991. *The Cycladic Spirit: Masterpieces from the Nicholas P. Goulandris Collection*. London: Thames and Hudson.

Ricoeur, P. 1976. *Interpretation Theory: Discourse and the Surplus Of Meaning*. Fort Worth: Texas Christian University Press.

Ricoeur, P. 1991. "The model of the text: meaningful action considered as a text." In P. Ricoeur, *From Text to Action: Essays in Hermeneutics*, vol. 2, pp. 144–67. Evanston, IL: Northwestern University Press.

Saussure, F. de 1959. *Course in General Linguistics*. Trans. C. Bally and A. Sechehaye. London: Owen.

Schapiro, M. 1951. "Style." In A. L. Kroeber (ed.), *Anthropology Today*, pp. 287–312. Chicago: University of Chicago Press.

Schnapp, A. 1993. *The Discovery of the Past: The Origins of Archaeology*. London: British Museum Press.

Stuart, D. 1996. "Kings of stone: a consideration of stelae in ancient Maya ritual and representation." *RES: Anthropology and Aesthetics*, 29/30: 148–71.

Tanner, J. J. 1992. "Art as expressive symbolism: civic portraits in classical Athens." *Cambridge Archaeological Journal*, 2 (2): 167–90.

Taylor, T. 1987. "Flying stags: icons and power in Thracian art." In I. Hodder (ed.), *The Archaeology of Contextual Meanings*, pp. 117–32. Cambridge: Cambridge University Press.

Tubb, K. and N. Brodie 2001. "From museum to mantlepiece: the antiquities trade in the United Kingdom." In R. Layton, P. Stone, and J. Thomas (eds.), *Destruction and Conservation of Cultural Property*, pp. 102–16. London: Routledge.

Van Damme, W. 1996. *Beauty in Context: Towards an Anthropological Approach to Aesthetics*. Leiden: Brill

Van Damme, W. 2000. "Universality and cultural particularity in visual aesthetics." In N. Roughley (ed.), *Being Humans: Anthropological Questions of Universality and Particularity in Transdisciplinary Perspectives*, pp. 258–83. Berlin: De Gruyter.

Vickers, M. 1987. "Values and simplicity: eighteenth-century taste and the study of Greek vases." *Past and Present*, 116: 98–137.

Vitebsky, P. 1995. *The Shaman: Voyages of the Soul*. London: Macmillan.

Wendt, W. E. 1974. "'Art mobilier' aus der Apollo-11 grotte in Südwest-Afrika." *Acta Praehistorica et Archaeologica*, 5: 1–42. A report was published in English in *South African Archaeological Bulletin*, 31 (1976): 5–11.

Whitfield, R. (ed.) 1993. *The Problem of Meaning in Early Chinese Ritual Bronzes*. London: Percival David Foundation.

Whitley, D. 1992. "Shamanism and rock art in Far Western North America." *Cambridge Archaeological Journal*, 2: 89–113.

Willey, G. 1962. "The early great style and the rise of precolumbian civilization." *American Anthropologist*, 64: 1–24.

Williams, R. 1983. *Keywords: A Vocabulary of Culture and Society*. London: Fontana.

Witkin, R. W. 1995. *Art and Social Structure*. Cambridge: Polity Press.

Wittgenstein, L. 1998 [1953]. *Philosophical Investigations/Philosophische Untersuchungen*. Trans. G. E. M. Anscombe, 2nd edn. Oxford : Blackwell.

Wolff, J. 1981. *The Social Production of Art*. London: Macmillan

Zanker, P. 1988. *The Power of Images in the Age of Augustus*. Ann Arbor: University of Michigan Press.

20

Putting Infinity Up On Trial: A Consideration of the Role of Scientific Thinking in Future Archaeologies

A. M. Pollard

Inside the museums infinity goes up on trial.

(Bob Dylan, *Visions of Johanna*, 1966)

There can be little doubt about the significance of the contribution made by scientific studies within archaeology over the last fifty years or so. Despite (or perhaps because of) this there has been a continuing but sporadic debate about the nature of academic archaeology itself. Some have contested the degree to which archaeology could or should be regarded as a scientific discipline. Others, less extreme, have debated the extent to which science has a role in archaeology, which often reduces to a discussion of the degree of coincidence between the goals of scientific and archaeological investigations. Cynically (but perhaps realistically), it might be noted that in many Higher Education funding systems there is a strong positive correlation between levels of funding and the "scientificness" of the discipline. It is therefore essential to appreciate that this is no sterile debate, but neither is it a contest for the soul of archaeology – real academic staff salaries and promotion prospects depend upon it!

"Let Us Compare Mythologies"[1]

Academic disciplines are generally classified using a divisive taxonomic procedure. Thus, "science" is broken down into "chemistry," "physics," etc., and "chemistry" is subdivided into "organic," "inorganic," and "physical." Endless further divisions emerge, although some recombination is allowed – biology and chemistry, for instance, can recombine to form biochemistry. Doubtless this taxonomy of knowledge is useful at some level or other, but it gives the impression of everything being discrete, self-contained, and highly ordered. I still do not fully appreciate the difference between chemical physics and physical chemistry! Is it purely for the convenience of librarians, who are programmed to classify all human knowledge using the Dewey system? The result is divisive in the other sense of the word, and militates against genuine interdisciplinarity in modern-day science. How much simpler was the Renaissance world, where everything could be included in the convenient catchall of "natural philosophy."

Disciplines such as archaeology do not fit this simple classificatory system. More than twenty-five years ago, when I began to consider for myself the postulate that archaeology was, indeed, a science, the route to the solution seemed obvious: just look at the respective definitions of "archaeology" and "science." If there is sufficient similarity between the two, then the case is proved – a typically "scientific" approach to the problem, of course! I might even have considered using Mahalanobis distance as the appropriate similarity metric, and produced a dendrogram, better known to biologists as a cladogram. Sadly, of course, the outcome of such an experiment is likely to be, at best, inconclusive. More significantly, it is methodologically flawed: such experiments can only ever confirm differences, not "prove" similarities. Nevertheless, it is amusing and perhaps instructive to carry out such an exercise.

At the risk of gross oversimplification, the following definitions are taken from the *Concise Oxford English Dictionary*:

Archaeology: the study of human history and prehistory through the excavation of sites and the analysis of physical remains.

This definition of archaeology could be excessively restrictive, since it apparently omits the study of landscapes, biological remains, etc. However, if we interpret "sites" to mean any part of a landscape impacted by human activity, and "physical remains" to encompass any material remains related to human activity (deliberately or not), then it will suffice. A related definition is:

Anthropology: (1) the study of mankind [*sic*], especially of its societies and customs; (2) the study of the structure and evolution of man [*sic*] as an animal.

The first part of this definition is usually considered to be *social anthropology*, while the second is *biological anthropology*. There is no universal dictionary definition of the following terms, but these are likely to be broadly acceptable:

Archaeological science: the application of the methods of the physical, chemical, biological, and engineering sciences to archaeology.

Archaeometry: originally conceived to describe the use of physical measurements in archaeology, but now more broadly taken as the application of the physical sciences to archaeology.

The original concept of the term *archaeometry* appears to have been modeled on the relationship between the terms *anthropology* and *anthropometry* (*OED*: "the scientific study of the measurements of the human body").

On these definitions, archaeometry is seen as a subdiscipline of archaeological science, which itself is but one aspect of archaeology. This convenient hierarchy is supported by the use of the phrase "the analysis of physical remains" in the definition of the latter, since it could be construed that science has a large and essential part to play in the analysis of physical remains. However, the relationship between archaeology and anthropology remains somewhat confused. It appears simplest to assume that archaeology provides a time-depth to anthropology. Given that anthropology is generally classified as a science and archaeology as a humanity, however, we appear to be heading towards a contradiction.

In the light of such impending difficulties, it is best to declare victory and move on! In the same dictionary, *science* is defined as follows:

(1) A branch of knowledge conducted on objective principles involving the systematized observation of and experiment with phenomena, especially concerned with the material and functions of the physical universe; (2a) systematic and formulated

knowledge, especially of a specified type or on a specified subject (e.g., political science); (b) the pursuit of this; (3) an organized body of knowledge on a subject (e.g., the science of philology); (4) skillful technique rather than strength or natural ability; (5) archaic knowledge of any kind.

Archaeology certainly conforms to some parts of this definition. It is "a branch of knowledge conducted on objective principles involving the systematized observation of and experiment with phenomena" (e.g., excavation and experimental archaeology, respectively), although it is not concerned only with the "material and function of the physical universe." It clearly consists of "systematic and formulated knowledge," ranging from excavation and recording methodologies to understandings of, for example, ceramic typologies, and presents "an organized body of knowledge" (e.g., the "grand historical narrative"). Definition (4) does not apply, although it might be taken by some as an allegory for the relationship between archaeological science and archaeology. The final phrase is a curious catchall, which could apply to almost any well-established academic discipline.

It could therefore be argued on these definitions that archaeology is itself a science, and that the term "archaeological science" is tautological. This, however, may be the result of using simple dictionary definitions, which are not particularly rigorous. The definition of science, for example, makes no explicit reference to process (beyond the phrase "on objective principles"), which for many is the essential characteristic of science. Chalmers (1976: 100) states simply that "science is a process without a subject." Whether naive inductivist, falsificationist, hypothetico-deductivist, or some other methodology, what actually counts is the process, usually involving hypothesis building, and testing this hypothesis against observation. Here, perhaps, we might note that this is in itself a very Bayesian process, in which a prior assumption about the world is modified in the

light of some new information, to produce an improved posterior understanding. On this measure, all academic thought processes are Bayesian sciences!

The postulate that archaeology is a science appears to hinge on the degree to which "objective principles" are followed. Most archaeologists would subscribe to the use of objective principles in the interpretation of material evidence, and even in the reconstruction of such intangible entities as belief systems and cognitive processes. If this is so, then the contention that archaeology is a science is proven, at least to the same degree as is the case for anthropology. This therefore lifts the contradiction presented by archaeology (a humanity) being the "past tense" of anthropology (a science), and is consistent with the view that archaeology is about understanding past human behavior (a science), rather than reconstructing a historical narrative (a humanity).

Whether any of this erudition matters, or makes any difference, is itself a debatable question. Perhaps it need not be debated seriously (it makes a good source of argument over a few beers in the pub when archaeologists gather). Which other discipline spends so much time on internecine warfare about the very nature of itself? If it resulted in universities worldwide relocating their Departments of Archaeology into Faculties of Science, and funding them as such, then perhaps it would be worthwhile. This, however, might then mark the end of archaeology as a broadly based interdisciplinary subject attractive to students from many academic backgrounds. The truth is, as usual, somewhere intermediate between the extremes. Archaeology is a "broad church," with room for all perspectives – indeed, needing and benefiting from all perspectives. Like all broad churches it occasionally exhibits internal strife, but it will survive as such providing the competencies of all of the components are respected and valued. Perhaps, therefore (despite the tautology), it is better to retain the term *archaeological science* to characterize those domains of archaeology in which the scientific process is explicitly used to increase our understanding of the human past.

Science Friction

The common criticisms of the shortcomings of the application of science to archaeology need only brief summary here (see, for example, Edmonds and Thomas 1990; Thomas 1990, 1991; Tite 1991; Renfrew 1992; Dunnell 1993; Ehrenreich 1995; Pollard 1995; Killick and Young 1997; and O'Connor 1998 for a range of views and responses). Perhaps the most fundamental is the allegation that scientific approaches ignore, misunderstand, or obscure the essential humanity of the discipline of archaeology – the fact that the subject of study is human behavior, in all its power, complexity, and irrationality. The most frequent criticism is that of "technological determinism," typified by titles in the literature which proclaim "A study of some pottery type or other using Neutron Activation Analysis/X-Ray Fluorescence/X-Ray Diffraction (or similar)." The reader may justifiably ask what is to be seen as the most important element of the study – the pottery type or the analytical technique used? And what is the question? Are we seeking some insight into technological development, or some understanding of the behavior of the potters, or is the pottery merely a proxy for social contact? Perhaps it is just a poor choice of title, but, unsurprisingly, studies of this kind are criticized for being techniques in search of a problem, or answers in search of a question. In fact, of course, such studies are often suspect not only because they are disarticulated from any meaningful archaeological question, but also because they follow a dubious model of the scientific process. Some archaeological scientific studies do not possess the necessary characteristic of refutability (i.e., they lack an answer to the essential question: "How would we know if we were wrong?"). They may justifiably be described

as "pseudoscience," or "scientism," by which I mean the application of scientific technology without the application of scientific methodology.

Much of this criticism has either been accepted as largely valid (the "fair cop" school of thought) and used as a basis for improvement, or has been contested, but mostly on a case-by-case basis. The debate has been substantially a one-sided critique of scientific methodologies as applied to archaeology, with the response being purely defensive. There has been little in the way of a counter-attack against the basic premise that the perspective of "traditional archaeology" is inalienably correct, and that any scientific approach which contradicts this position is therefore "wrong." There must be some scope for a debate along these lines, particularly in the area of one of the favorite taunts of theoretical archaeologists, the position of "environmental determinism" – the extent to which human behavior is dependent on environmental controls. This is essentially a debate about the degree to which the history of the human species can be regarded as conforming to the laws of the animal kingdom, or as something quite independent. Nor has substantial consideration been given to the possibility that the parent discipline of archaeology might sometimes itself benefit by adopting more generally a scientific methodology. One possible criticism of archaeology as a whole is a peculiar obsession with "uniqueness" (of site in particular, but also of artefact), resulting in difficulties when attempting to prioritize competing claims. Using an analogy from another area of science, the possible consequences of this dogma are discussed below.

Some Achievements of Archaeology as a Science

Perhaps the strongest justification for accepting scientific archaeology as a valid contribution to our understanding of the human past is provided by considering some of the major contributions over the past few decades. Early seminal contributions which still contain useful perspectives include Zeuner (1946) on geochronology, Biek (1963) on the contribution of microscopic analysis to the study of archaeological materials, and Brothwell and Higgs (1963), which provides the first compendium of scientific studies in archaeology. It is impossible here to review all the many aspects of these contributions (see, for example, Brothwell and Pollard 2001 for a recent overview), and so what follows is necessarily a personal selection.

Making a date

Conventionally, the strongest scientific contribution to archaeology is regarded as the provision of reliable chronologies, independent of conventional calendrical or typological dating. The most obvious contribution has been that of radiocarbon dating, a consideration of the history of which provides a microcosm for the role of science in archaeology. Taylor et al. (1992) and Taylor and Aitken (1997) give authoritative reviews of the history and contribution of radiocarbon dating to all of the historical sciences. Radiocarbon now provides the vast majority of all dates used in archaeology – the exception, of course, being in the period before the range of radiocarbon (conservatively taken as 35–40 ka BP). The initial development of radiocarbon was greeted with a predictable range of responses, from wild enthusiasm to complete rejection. The subsequent realization that radiocarbon dates required "calibrating" was taken by some as evidence of the complete futility of such an approach, but was hailed by others as "the second radiocarbon revolution" (see, for example, Renfrew 1970). For example, calibrated dates, being substantially earlier than uncalibrated dates by the third millennium BC, provided evidence of the impossibility of contact between the Megalith builders of Atlantic Europe and the "civilized" world of the Myceneans and the eastern Mediterra-

nean. Any scientific method which, at a stroke, demonstrates the independence of European prehistory and refutes the diffusionist hypothesis of *ex oriente lux* (e.g., Childe 1957) for the origins of European civilization deserves considerable credit. And yet radiocarbon is inherently no more than that: a method, a technique. Given a suitable organic sample it is likely that a reliable date can be produced. It is what is done with the date that actually counts – the way that it is used to test or refute a particular cultural hypothesis (is this an echo of the description of the scientific process itself?).

Perhaps this is the most instructive and interesting aspect of the story. After the "first radiocarbon revolution" (Libby's original announcement of the method), Renfrew proclaimed: "the prehistorian could hope to date his [sic] finds, both accurately and reliably, by a method that made no archaeological assumptions whatever . . . all that was needed was a couple of ounces of charcoal . . . and science would do the rest" (Renfrew 1976: 53). Twenty-five years later, this view has been turned on its head. By the late 1980s it had become clear that a single radiocarbon date, unless of the highest possible precision, is unlikely to resolve an archaeological event to much better than a century. A few laboratories, notably Queen's University Belfast and the University of Washington, Seattle, are capable of producing "high precision" dates, with a quoted counting error of around ± 20 years during the Holocene. Radiocarbon errors are conventionally given at the 1 standard deviation level, i.e., at 68 percent confidence as opposed to the more acceptable 2 s.d. level, corresponding to 95 percent confidence, so this figure should be doubled to provide a reliable estimate of the associated error. However, the majority of radiocarbon dates are obtained with quoted errors around ± 30–40 years, which corresponds to an uncalibrated error range of more than 120 years. With this counting error, once calibrated, it is highly unlikely that a single date will define an event in the Holocene to better than a century. In some cases this is useful, but increasingly it is not.

It is in the light of this realization that the next "radiocarbon revolution" has taken place, and one that relies explicitly on the associated archaeological evidence, rather than being independent of it. This involves the use of multiple radiocarbon dates (e.g., a series of dates linked by stratigraphic progression), and the subsequent application of Bayesian methods during calibration (Buck et al. 1996). This allows the "prior knowledge" such as that provided by the stratigraphy (e.g., layer A must be older than layer B, etc.) to be combined with the radiocarbon dates during the calibration process to constrain the resulting dates. The result is usually a series of dates with a narrower age range than would otherwise be the case, and it also allows "rogue dates" to be identified and eliminated on a transparent and systematic basis. The wheel has therefore turned full circle, from a dating technique which was lauded because of its independence of the archaeological evidence, to a process which uses all the available archaeological evidence to produce the highest possible chronological resolution. It is perhaps ironic that the single most significant scientific contribution to archaeology has only begun to deliver to its true potential by using the exceptionally powerful Bayesian process to combine other sources of information. Evidence, indeed, that "hard" physical science has to be tempered with "softer" sources of information (perhaps geological stratigraphy, but possibly also the typological sequence of brooches in an Anglo-Saxon cemetery) to provide the best chronological framework.

All built on a timber framework

Although radiocarbon dating now dominates the field of archaeological dating, it is not, to my mind, the most significant achievement of scientific archaeology. This position is occupied by dendrochronology: the study of the ring patterns in certain trees from temperate climates (e.g., Baillie 1995).

Deceptively simple in concept, the idea that a date, precise to a single year, or perhaps even to a season, can be provided by counting and measuring the annual growth rings in particular trees, is astonishing in practice. Ironically, again, it is worth remembering that the pioneer of dendrochronology, A. E. Douglass, did not actually set out to provide the most precise chronological tool in the world. He was in fact an astronomer, interested in sun spot cycles, who hit upon the idea that variations in the ring width of trees might be influenced by, and therefore record, these cycles. The result is an achievement of late twentieth-century science that might be ranked alongside the splitting of the atom and the decoding of the Human Genome. Not, admittedly, simply because it has provided archaeology with a dating tool of astonishing precision, but because of the wider services it is now providing to the environmental sciences. Clearly, radiocarbon dating (with or without Bayesian logic) could not have attained its current level of achievement without "dendrocalibration," now available for the last 10,000 years. This is made transparently clear if the challenges of Late-glacial calibration are considered. The step from the end of the dendrocalibration to the much more poorly defined coral or terrestrial varve calibration is currently the equivalent of leaping into a cold and dark abyss.

Even more significant than this, however, is the contribution of dendrochronology to the study of Holocene global change. The long tree-ring records, now constructed or under construction in many parts of the world, provide an unparalleled archive of climate change at, potentially, annual or sub-annual resolution, and with an undisputed annual chronology (Fritts 1976). This compares favorably with the (admittedly much) longer ice-core records from Greenland and Antarctica, which have less securely dated chronologies. Although the tops of the ice cores (corresponding to the Late-glacial and Holocene) are basically dated by layer counting, the errors associated with the age estimations down the cores are somewhat difficult to determine. They are undoubtedly of the order of several decades, if not a century or so, by the onset of the Holocene. Only ice cores can, as yet, provide detailed evidence of the cataclysmic climatic changes associated with the last deglaciation, but the rather less (as yet!) turbulent climatic events during the Holocene are best studied through detailed examination (morphological, physical, chemical, and isotopic) of humble tree rings. Moreover, tree rings provide the additional advantage of recording the climate in an environment which is potentially much more relevant to contemporary humans than that offered by the remote ice cores. That is providing, of course, the information obtained can be "translated" from the raw data (e.g., ring width variation, or changes in wood density) into something meaningful in climatological terms – mean summer temperature, annual summer rainfall or humidity, or something similar. Deriving this so-called "transfer function," which allows a proxy measurement to be converted into a climate variable, is not always easy.

The problem is one familiar to many scientists – the imprecise biological world impinging on the highly precise world of physical or chemical measurements. Living trees, being biological organisms, do not necessarily respond linearly to a single convenient measurable parameter such as Mean July Temperature. Nor, necessarily, do they respond linearly to multiple such parameters. They might respond linearly to one or more of the so-called "derived climate variables" such as the "number of frost-free days between April and September," or the "total number of sunshine hours during the peak growing season." These relationships can be determined from careful studies of modern trees, but the real situation is likely to be even more complex. Different species of trees behave differently. Some may be relatively simple, particularly if one climatic parameter such as rainfall exerts an overwhelming control over ring growth. In these cases, it is likely that the trees will be drought-sensitive, and the ring-width record will be an excellent proxy for annual rainfall, as appears to be the case in the American southwest (Kuniholm 2001). In more temperate regions, such as northwestern Europe, the situation is much less clearcut (apart from trees growing at the edge of their natural distribution, in which case there may still be a simple relationship between climate and vigor of growth). It is likely that more than one climatic variable will exert some control over growth. Indeed, it is conceivable that the dominant factor may change over time – at times of plentiful rainfall, for example, growth may be controlled by mean summer temperature, but if rainfall drops, then water supply may become the controlling factor irrespective of temperature (Aykroyd et al. 2001). Yet again, hard science (this time physical or chemical measurements made on tree rings) requires additional inputs (perhaps an understanding of tree physiology) to interpret the data in a meaningful fashion. I can't help feeling that a pattern is beginning to emerge here!

Despite the complexity, it still remains that tree rings (and, for earlier periods, but with less chronological precision, ice cores and other proxies such as coleopteran sequences) can provide information on how the climate has changed in the past. This fact is a much-used example when arguing with funding bodies about why they should allocate a proportion of their scarce resources to archaeological research. Who could have guessed that such valuable knowledge would result from grant proposals which appeared to want to piece together bits of old wood? (That age-old question which sinks without trace 80 percent of all grant applications – "What *exactly* is the model being tested?" – can be heard clearly, but fortunately the 1970s were a more innocent, or perhaps more adequately funded, period of Research Council history!) It is an excellent, perhaps even the best, example of how archaeology, when funded as a science, can provide information of immense value to the other historical sciences. It is probably the single most important source of information in what is likely to be one of the greatest scientific debates in the twenty-first century: to what extent has human activity changed the earth's climate system? The reluctant politician's favorite retreat – "How do we know that the recent sequence of warmest years on record is the result of human activity, and not part of the long-term natural variability?" – is gradually being closed off by studies of variability in the Holocene climatic record using data from tree rings, among other sources.

Ice, what ice?

But the loop has yet to close. Archaeology provided this information (either in some cases by providing the raw material – the wood itself – but perhaps more fundamentally, at least in the UK, by providing the impetus to construct long tree-ring chronologies), but it has yet to use it to its full extent. It is obvious that climate has changed substantially since the Last Glacial Maximum, but high precision studies (both chronologically and geographically) can provide much more detail than this. It appears that the *rate* of climate change has been astonishing in some parts of the world, at certain times. For example, around the northern north Atlantic, ice core estimates suggest that average temperatures fluctuated by more than 5° C on a timescale of 50–100 years during the last deglaciation, probably as a result of changes to ocean currents (Smith et al. 1997). This poses, for me, one of the most interesting questions in archaeology: how did human populations respond to such rapid rates of climatic change? Not only is it intrinsically interesting, but it also may provide an insight into what might happen if further weakening in the Atlantic warm water current results in rapid climatic cooling. The inappropriately named phenomenon of global warming may actually manifest itself as a reversion to Ice Age conditions around the north Atlantic. It is, of course, inherently unlikely that any detailed

knowledge of how Palaeolithic hunter-gatherers in Europe at the end of the last Ice Age responded to rapid climatic change will directly inform the response of *homo sapiens supermarketicus* to a similar phenomenon in the mid-twenty-first century. What might be useful, however, is some knowledge of the time lag between the various components of the system – how long does it take for deglaciation to occur once the ocean warms up, and how rapidly do continental European climate systems respond to these changes? Late-glacial archaeological evidence, combined with careful palaeoenvironmental reconstructions from terrestrial sequences along with the ice-core data, might just be able to answer these questions, providing sufficient well-resolved chronological and spatial evidence is available. But in order to answer such finely resolved questions of rates of change and sequential relationships between events we need the tightest possible chronological control. This can be provided by Bayesian-constrained calibration of radiocarbon sequences, which also allows combination with other sources of dating evidence, such as tephra, using techniques pioneered primarily for archaeology (e.g., Blockley 2002). Only once we have a highly textured model of how terrestrial conditions changed in response to rapid climatic change can we begin to look at how the human and other biota responded to this rather rapidly changing stage scenery.

This consideration of human response to rapid climate change brings me to a defense of "environmental determinism." This is now a derogatory term, used mostly by archaeologists of the postprocessual persuasion, who regard the view that human behavior is responsive to environmental change as antithetical to the existence of any form of social behavior. A Thatcherite denial of the existence of society, perhaps? It is clearly no such thing, as can be shown by a simple model set out in Figure 20.1. The horizontal axis represents increasing complexity in human society, perhaps ranging from family groups on the left to state-level societies on the right. It

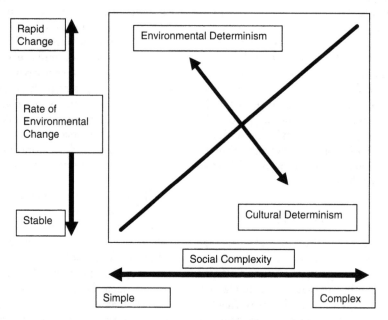

Figure 20.1 Simple model of relationship between complexity of society and rates of environmental change.

might equally represent increasing average size of human groups, ranging from a few dozen on the left to millions on the right. The vertical axis represents the rate of change of environmental conditions, ranging from completely stable at the bottom to rapidly changing at the top. At the bottom are stable environments such as those traditionally thought to exist during the Holocene (although this may turn out to be a fallacy), while the top represents rates of change now known to have been experienced during the last deglaciation. Inasmuch as, crudely speaking, environment is a (delayed) response to climate, then the vertical axis may be proxied by rate of climate change, measured by some simple parameter such as average temperature rise or increase in annual rainfall per decade. The domain of extreme environmental determinism lies in the top left-hand corner, where human societies organized in small groups are subjected to rapid change. The domain of the opposite paradigm ("cultural determinism"?) lies in the bottom right-

hand corner, where large complex societies exist in a stable environment. Clearly, because this model is based on rates of change rather than absolute values of environmental conditions, there are bound to be some anomalies. Some extreme environments, no matter how stable, are not conducive to supporting large complex societies – one thinks immediately of polar or desert environments. Figure 20.1 could perhaps be modified to take into account the "absolute value" of the environment, rather than just the rate of environmental change. Nevertheless, it is clear that environmental determinism is not completely inimical to cultural determinism – it is part of the same continuum. It is as unrealistic to suppose that the behavior of Late-glacial hunter-gatherers was not predominantly dictated by environmental factors (a nearby ice sheet several kilometers thick is a pretty substantial environmental factor!) as it is to believe that complex state-level societies cannot tolerate the impact of moderate rates of environment change.

It is interesting to muse further on the nature of the relationship between environmental stability and social complexity. It is tempting to assume that the development of complexity is predicated on the existence of climatic stability. After all, there is ample evidence that the city-state, with its associated agriculture, craft specialization, and hierarchical social structures, only appeared once the relative stability of the Holocene was well established. Perhaps so, but it is obviously not as simple as that. Stable environmental conditions, potentially conducive to agriculture, must have existed in more equatorial regions during the last glaciation, and certainly occurred during earlier interglacials. In both cases, humans were present, and so the availability of stable environmental conditions is not of itself sufficient to precipitate the development of complex societies. Clearly, there has to be a parallel condition of a stable environment and some development in human behavior before complexity appears. Is it simply controlled by population density – was it not until the Holocene that the population of the human species attained a high enough value to take advantage of the environmental stability? It is apparent that a better understanding of the precise timing and estimates of the rate of change of climatic parameters is necessary to answer some of the most fundamental questions in human prehistory.

Putting the magic back into your life

Moving away from chronology and the environment, one of the largest scientific inputs into archaeology has been the study of ancient materials and technologies (see, for example, Henderson 2000; Ciliberto and Spoto 2000). We now understand in great detail, for some parts of the world, the sequence of events which followed the realization that certain brightly colored earths, if treated with suitable magic, could yield malleable and ductile materials suitable for the manufacture of ornaments, weapons, and tools. Similar but different magic was also applied to soft clays to produce useful vessels for the storage, transport, and cooking of food. Even more marvelous is the magic which converts sand and ash into a material which can be molded, cast, or blown into clear or highly colored decorative vessels.

It is tempting from a twenty-first-century perspective to believe that, because we can explain how and when such magic occurred, it tells us something about the much more difficult question of why. An understanding of when and how is an essential prerequisite to addressing this more interesting question, but it contains no inherent explanation. From a post-industrial Western capitalist perspective, the question "Why?" is not really an issue. The answer is self-evident, and summarized by that watchword of Victorian imperialism: "progress." It is natural to assume that, because a sword made from tempered steel is a better killing tool than one made from uncarburized iron, this of itself is sufficient explanation. It assumes, of course, that this observation was inherently apparent to the ancient swordsmith, without the benefit of metallography and devices to measure Vickers hardness. It is a common layperson's fallacy to assume that ancient artisans were ignorant of the properties of the material upon which their livelihoods (and possibly their lives) depended. The reverse must be true: ancient technologists had a much better practical knowledge of the working properties of materials than the average archaeological scientist. I recall with some pleasure (at least in hindsight) the experience of showing the chemical analyses of some Chinese porcelain to an eminent working potter. He looked at them carefully for a while, and then pronounced quietly that they must be wrong. Why? Because they would not fire and mature at the correct temperature. He had, in his head, converted them from numbers on a page into an imaginary clay in his hands, and concluded that it couldn't possibly work. I protested, of course – how could results from the latest shiny whatever with additional flashing lights be wrong? Chastened, and tail between legs, I went away and concluded after some effort that he was in fact right. Never underestimate the practical knowledge of somebody who has spent a lifetime working with raw materials! They use a different paradigm and language, but a white coat is no substitute for experience.

We simply cannot presume that the concept of progress is in itself a sufficient explanation for the adoption of a new technology. In fact, the reverse is probably true: conservatism is the dominant force in many traditional technologies. So why adopt the earliest known metal tools when in all likelihood contemporary stone tools were much more effective at chopping down trees or skinning animals? The answer must involve something unquantifiable in a microscopic section or chemical analysis – availability, fashion, prestige, or magical symbols of patronage and power. Because these factors are non-quantifiable, they rarely occur in technical discussions of ancient technologies, and so the question "Why?" is rarely satisfactorily addressed. At least it leaves a substantial and fundamental question to be addressed by the upcoming generation of students of ancient technology, and there are several who have already taken up this challenge (e.g., Killick 2001). Yet again, however, the message is clear: scientific data alone are insufficient to answer the real question, and they need to be constrained by other information, this time derived from a study of human behavior, including the irrational (and even magical) bits.

"Light breaks where no sun shines"[2]

That other great twentieth-century contribution of science to archaeology is the study of biological remains from archaeological contexts, described as environmental archaeology in the case of macroscopic and microscopic remains (see, for example, Evans and O'Connor 1999 or Dincauze 2000). In addition to its many archaeological achievements, it has also successfully addressed some of the processual issues discussed above. It is generally much better integrated into archaeological thinking, and environmental archaeologists have appreciated the crucial role of human behavior in the creation of "death assemblages." There is still, occasionally, a tendency to resort to "the naming of parts" rather than reflecting on broader implications – a temptation reinforced (or, some would say, precipitated) by "the specialist appendix syndrome." The traditional archaeological report contains a whole series of appendices written by different specialists on a particular material (animal bone, human bone, small finds – usually broken down by material category, etc.), sometimes poorly digested and badly integrated into the overall narrative. Sometimes these appendices are conveniently bound into a separate volume, for ease of omission (this possibility is considerably facilitated if microfiche, insert disks, or even web-based archiving is employed). It is not, of course, easy to propose a simple mechanism which bypasses this syndrome, since the "expertization" of a particular category of material often draws on a lifetime of specialization on that material. Additionally, "specialists" are often jealously protective of their regional or material territoriality – in my view, a distinctly unhealthy and anti-scientific behavioral trait. Is it possible that such intense and exclusive specialization is counter-productive, and that the answer lies in training a generation of more flexible post-excavation researchers who can cover a whole range of materials?

The problem is compounded by the automatic assumption that every class of material needs expert study, no matter what the quality of the information, or the relevance of the data generated to the original research question(s) of the archaeological excavation. Good for the employment (if not necessarily the long-term career prospects) of archaeologists, but perhaps highlighting the need for better prioritization of objectives? More competent archaeologists than I have addressed this issue, and produced the concept of different levels of archiving and reporting, in which material which does not address the immediate research agenda is briefly recorded and then archived for future study, should that become worthwhile (English Heritage 1991). Perhaps this is, indeed, the best compromise, but for how long can several tons of material be stored in an accessible place? What happens when the key people have moved on, depriving the archive of anybody who actually knows what is there? And is the material really useful, particularly from a biomolecular perspective, after years of storage? Basically, archaeology is an exceedingly data-rich subject, and must therefore demand more prioritization of objectives, combined with a little more confidence in our own abilities to judge these priorities.

Such brief consideration of the macro- and microscopic study of biological remains in archaeology leads inevitably to a consideration of the achievements of the latest, most high-profile tool in the armory of the archaeological scientist: biomolecular archaeology. The achievements to date are, genuinely, many, and yet this is still undoubtedly the area with the greatest growth potential in archaeological science (see Brothwell and Pollard 2001: 295–358). The realization that molecular evidence is preserved in a whole range of increasingly unlikely loci has revolutionized the way in which archaeologists approach material evidence. It might even be the justification required for the immense expense associated with storing thousands of boxes of archived material. We have come to understand that "biomarkers" – chemical compounds which survive (or are created during) degradation and which uniquely identify the parent material – can be used to discern the original contents of ceramic vessels, often without any external evidence of their presence. Isotopic studies of the carbon, nitrogen, sulfur, and oxygen from identified compounds extracted from human and other animal tissue can elucidate diets, positions in foodwebs, and even health status and cultural parameters such as status and migratory behavior. And, of course,

there is the study of that most significant biomolecule of all, deoxyribonucleic acid (DNA). Since the first demonstration in the 1980s that fragments of DNA could be extracted from museum specimens of extinct animals such as the quagga, and the excitement of extracting tiny fragments of human DNA from mummified tissue, studies of ancient DNA (aDNA) have attracted a great deal of professional and media attention (Brown 2001). The search for the oldest DNA has frequently filled the pages of distinguished journals such as *Nature* over the past fifteen years, although some practitioners now suspect that much of this early work is invalid because the problems of contamination are greater than was previously thought. Nowhere is the problem more acute than in the search for the oldest surviving human DNA. The mathematics of the amplification process embodied in the polymerase chain reaction technique (PCR) mean that minute traces of human DNA from any source – the sweat of an archaeologist handling the bone, or a sneeze in a nearby laboratory – can give false positives.

It has, however, been clearly demonstrated, using rigorous protocols in which replicate samples of bone (or teeth) recovered under sterile conditions are analyzed in different laboratories (Hofreiter et al. 2001), that endogenous but highly fragmentary human DNA can be extracted from human mineralized tissue. The range of burial conditions which support such survival, however, appears to be rather restrictive, and theoretical simulations of the degradation process suggest that survival beyond the Holocene is likely to be very rare (Smith et al. 2001). So it is no small technical achievement to obtain DNA from our nearest but extinct cousins, the Neanderthals (Krings et al. 1997; Ovchinnikov et al. 2000). Potentially, this should be able to answer another of those great questions in archaeology: what happened to the Neanderthals? Were they just poorly adapted to a warmer Late-glacial world, and/or were they unable to compete with more adaptable humans, or were they one of *Homo sapiens*' early genocidal victims? Or, using the principle of uniformitarianism, and given a knowledge of modern human behavior in conflict situations, were they bred out of their own independent gene pool? On current DNA evidence, the answer is extinction with no gene transfer, but I for one can't help feeling that there is still more to be learnt in this most fascinating of areas.

In fact, it looks like the "aDNA experiment" has been technically a triumph, but intellectually, to date, somewhat disappointing. The potential for sexing fragmentary and juvenile remains (probably one of the most significant contributions aDNA can make to a study of the fossil human record) seems to be about as successful as tossing a coin (but much more expensive). The elucidation of familial relationships in contemporary burials, or in deriving relationships between successive generations, has had more success (however, the best case seems to be the temporally less remote case of the Romanov dynasty; Gill et al. 1994). One of the great hopes for (and justification of) aDNA studies of fossil remains, that of providing a chronology for the human evolutionary cladogram which is independent of the "molecular clock," has not to date yielded substantial results. This may simply be the result of not allowing sufficient time for a complicated technique to fully mature, and critical new data are just around the corner. It may, however, be a reflection of the fact that archaeology has lost control of its own research agenda. The capacity for DNA research effectively resides in biomedical laboratories, partly because of the expense of the equipment, but more significantly because of the levels of contamination control required. It therefore requires a supreme effort to make sure that archaeological relevance and expertise is fully incorporated into the research design.

From a different context, I am reminded of a meeting in the British Museum some time ago, at which the difficulties associated with obtaining high quality radiocarbon dates

were being discussed at length, largely by radiocarbon specialists. After some hours of intricate technical discussion, a patient but obviously irritated senior archaeologist stood up and said: "Archaeology is difficult, too!" Stunned silence descended – clearly this was an aspect which had been lost sight of in the welter of technical detail. The world of aDNA also needs to heed that same voice. We are in danger of repeating some of the mistakes of the last century, when paradigms typified by "XRF studies of a hundred irrelevant pots" or "Yet more lead isotope determinations from two mine sites in adjacent fields" were allowed to divert attention from questions of real archaeological significance. It need not and must not be that way again.

This is not intended to detract from the potential of carefully focused work using DNA in archaeology. Indeed, with emerging hindsight, it looks like the search for fragmentary aDNA may be but a distraction from the more significant action in the main theater: the study of modern population genetics, and resulting inferences about population movements and interactions in the past (e.g., Richards et al. 1998; Forster et al. 2001). To paraphrase a well-known saying, the present may be the key to the past.

A Peculiar Obsession: Drawing the Stripes on a Zebra

Having spent some time on musing on the sins of those scientists who have tried to make a contribution to the study of the human past, it is perhaps allowable to reverse the microscope and consider some of the sins of the parent. Archaeology is an unusual observational science, in that no experiment (i.e., excavation) can ever be satisfactorily repeated. If a site is excavated, then the evidence encapsulated in that site is destroyed forever, beyond what is recorded, whatever remains in the site archive, and that which is left in the ground. It is now common practice to leave as much as possible of the site untouched, for that very reason, but, inevitably, the cherries tend to get picked. The result is that the interpretation of the site team is inevitably the strongest voice when the story comes to be told. *Ergo*, nothing can ever be "checked," in the scientific sense of independent replication of an experiment. This has an interesting consequence for the career-track of archaeologists, since they are in many ways the only competent "judge and jury" for the quality of their own work. What is of concern here, however, is the dogma of "uniqueness" which follows from this situation, and the other consequences which flow from this dogma.

It is a generally unchallenged truth that every archaeological site is unique, and therefore when "threatened" (however that is interpreted), each site must be excavated, recorded, and/or preserved *in situ* (whatever is deemed most appropriate). At one level, of course, all of this is true. A Roman villa in the line of the new bypass around Warmington-on-Sea (or wherever) is, indeed, the only Roman villa on that particular spot, and is therefore, by definition, unique. It therefore demands whatever is necessary to record it in advance of destruction. The archaeological record is undeniably a finite (and fragile) resource. And yet, at a higher level of hierarchical thinking, the case is less self-evident. It may well be only one of a relatively substantial number of Roman villas to be found along the south coast of England, of which a large proportion may already have been excavated. What is it that we actually learn from an additional excavation, beyond, of course, the satisfaction of knowing that something has been salvaged from an otherwise lost site? There may, of course, be a perfectly rational and unarguable case for such a course of action, but sometimes it seems as if there is not.

My analogy is with zoology. Zebras exist in large numbers on the plains of southern Africa. It is well known that the pattern of stripes on each zebra is unique, and moreover that the pattern of stripes may be the expression of underlying genetic patterning, relating to the regional distribution of different herds. A few zoologists have spent significant amounts of time studying and publishing the implications of this variation in individual and group patterns. The majority of zoologists, however, do not devote substantial resources to recording the details of every pattern. It is widely understood that any attempt to do so would be pointless, and only serve to confirm that zebra are, indeed, large stripy animals with distinctive regional variation. Archaeology, on the other hand, has a tendency to record the pattern of stripes on each individual in infinite detail. Every new zebra is recorded to the same level of detail as the first, because each is deemed unique. Zoologists are generally content to record the existence of one or more zebra, perhaps of a particular subgroup if that is noteworthy, and not to get involved directly in the detail of the pattern of the stripes. Once identified as a zebra, what is more important is where it is found, and how it is interacting with its peers, environment, and other inhabitants of the plain. In other words, it is zebra behavior and ecology that are of genuine interest, not the detail of its pattern.

Does this help in a consideration of the archaeological dogma of uniqueness? Yes and no. The zoological analogy breaks down quite quickly when the time dimension is considered – a Roman villa site may not always have been a villa: it might have started life as an Iron Age farmstead, and ended as an Anglo-Saxon fortified settlement. In other words, the zebra may not always have been a zebra. Its history therefore becomes important, but even such transfigurations may follow a recognizable trajectory – possibly only noteworthy by deviation from the norm. This may not of itself detract from the observation that a zebra is a large stripy animal, with no further description being necessary. It poses the question: "Are some archaeologists too obsessed with detail?"

This somewhat silly excursion into interdisciplinarity is not intended to undermine one of the fundamental tenets of the resource, nor the efforts of the Heritage organizations in the various countries to preserve or record that cultural heritage. It is, however, intended to suggest that one of the consequences of the blind acceptance of the dogma of uniqueness is the inability to prioritize between competing demands on resources. If all sites are unique, and no piece of information about the past is more valuable than any other, then each has equal priority. To my mind, this effectively paralyzes substantial progress in a tough world in which funding is allocated according to the ability to demonstrate priorities, objectives, and achievement. I have attended meetings at which a group of very senior earth scientists have constructed a ten-year forward plan for the discipline, identifying the five major priority areas, and the key questions to be addressed within each area. Granted, every academic involved in the process accepts that it is a presentational exercise, aimed largely at politicians and civil servants in the Treasury, who demand to know (with, admittedly, some justification) what exactly they will get for their (meager) expenditure on research in the earth sciences. It is largely a device – part of playing the grand political game – but one generally accepted in many disciplines as being necessary.

On recounting the above story to a well-known professor of archaeology, he simply commented that it shows what a boring discipline earth sciences must be if you can predict what is going to happen over the next ten years! I have a deal of sympathy for this viewpoint, but I fear the consequences. I have often mused on what might be the outcome of a similar meeting of senior academic archaeologists. My guess is that they would spend most of the time arguing about definitions, and then go to great lengths to avoid putting down anything in writing which admits that some parts of archaeology are currently more "important" than others. I admire this respect for the academic freedom of others (a very humanities-orientated characteristic, in my experience), but, again, I fear the consequences. It is, of course, part of the charm of archaeology – anarchic, irreverent, populated by individualists (less so now than previously, of course!), and is partly why somebody like myself trained in physics was attracted to archaeology in the first place. But consequential too is the lack of a coherent voice at the "top table." Perhaps this is the real difference between archaeology and the other sciences. What sort of archaeology do we want?

Summary

My message is simply summarized:

- The time has come to stop arguing internally about the nature of archaeology, and to recognize that understanding the human past in all its complexity requires every and all inputs.
- Scientific data alone are rarely sufficient to answer questions about human behavior: the last fifty years show clearly that scientific measurements in archaeology, whatever the quality, can only contribute to the debate when embedded in a suitable framework of archaeological understanding.
- Archaeology is one of the most data-rich academic subjects, and therefore needs to think hard (and with self-confidence) about its own research priorities, and also how these priorities might articulate with those of the myriad of subjects which interface with archaeology.

Can you now list the five most important questions in archaeology for the next decade, in order of priority?

Acknowledgments

I would like to dedicate this essay to the memory of Leo Biek, formerly of English Heritage's Ancient Monuments Laboratory, and one of the unsung founders of archaeological sciences in the UK. I'm not sure he would have approved entirely of the contents, but I am sure he would have been amused by it, and it might have appealed to his penchant for the unconventional!

Notes

1 Cohen (1969).
2 Thomas (1934).

References

Aykroyd, R. G., D. Lucy, A. M. Pollard, A. H. C. Carter, and I. Robertson 2001. "Temporal variability in the strength of proxy-climate correlations." *Geophysical Research Letters*, 28: 1559–62.

Baillie, M. G. L. 1995. *A Slice Through Time: Dendrochronology and Precision Dating.* London: Batsford.

Biek, L. 1963. *Archaeology and the Microscope: The Scientific Examination of Archaeological Evidence.* London: Lutterworth.

Blockley, S. P. E. 2002. *Assessing the Timing of and Human Interaction with Late-Glacial Climate Change.* Unpublished PhD thesis, University of Bradford.

Brothwell, D. R. and E. S. Higgs (eds.) 1963. *Science in Archaeology: A Comprehensive Survey of Progress and Research.* London: Thames and Hudson.

Brothwell, D. R. and A. M. Pollard (eds.) 2001. *Handbook of Archaeological Sciences.* Chichester: Wiley.

Brown, T. A. 2001. "Ancient DNA." In D. R Brothwell and A. M. Pollard (eds.), *Handbook of Archaeological Sciences,* pp. 301–11. Chichester: Wiley.

Buck, C. E., W. G. Cavanagh, and C. D. Litton 1996. *The Bayesian Approach to Interpreting Archaeological Data.* Chichester: Wiley.

Chalmers, A. F. 1976. *What is this Thing Called Science?* St. Lucia: University of Queensland Press.

Childe, V. G. 1957. "Retrospect." *Antiquity,* 32: 69–74.

Ciliberto, E. and G. Spoto 2000. *Modern Analytical Methods in Art and Archaeology.* New York: Wiley.

Cohen, L. 1969. *Poems 1956–1968.* London: Jonathan Cape.

Dincauze, D. F. 2000. *Environmental Archaeology: Principles and Practice.* Cambridge: Cambridge University Press.

Dunnell, R. C. 1993. "Why archaeologists don't care about archaeometry." *Archaeomaterials,* 7: 161–5.

Edmonds, M. and J. Thomas 1990. "Science fiction: scientism and technism in archaeology." *Scottish Archaeological Review,* 7: 1–2.

Ehrenreich, R. M. 1995. "Archaeometry into archaeology." *Journal of Archaeological Method and Theory,* 2: 1–6.

English Heritage 1991. *Management of Archaeological Projects.* London: English Heritage.

Evans, J. G. and T. P. O'Connor 1999. *Environmental Archaeology: Principles and Methods.* Stroud: Sutton.

Forster, P., A. Torroni, C. Renfrew, and A. Rohl 2001. "Phylogenetic star contraction applied to Asian and Papuan mtDNA evolution." *Molecular Biology and Evolution*, 18: 1864–81.

Fritts, H. C. 1976. *Tree Rings and Climate*. London: Academic Press.

Gill, P., P. L. Ivanov, C. Kimpton et al. 1994. "Identification of the remains of the Romanov family by DNA analysis." *Nature Genetics*, 6: 130–5.

Henderson, J. 2000. *The Science and Archaeology of Materials*. London: Routledge.

Hofreiter, M., D. Serre, H. N. Poinar, M. Kuch, and S. Pääbo 2001. "Ancient DNA." *Nature Reviews Genetics*, 2: 353–9.

Killick, D. 2001. "Science, speculation and the origins of extractive metallurgy." In D. R Brothwell and A. M. Pollard (eds.), *Handbook of Archaeological Sciences*, pp. 301–11. Chichester: Wiley.

Killick, D. and S. M. M Young 1997. "Archaeology and archaeometry: from casual dating to a meaningful relationship?" *Antiquity*, 71: 518–24.

Krings, M., A. Stone, R. W. Schmitz et al. 1997. "Neandertal DNA sequences and the origin of modern humans." *Cell*, 90: 19–30.

Kuniholm, P. I. 2001. "Dendrochronology and other applications of tree-ring studies in archaeology." In D. R Brothwell and A. M. Pollard (eds.), *Handbook of Archaeological Sciences*, pp. 35–46. Chichester: Wiley.

O'Connor, T. P. 1998. "Environmental archaeology: a matter of definition." *Environmental Archaeology*, 2: 1–6.

Ovchinnikov, I. V., A. Götherström, G. P. Romanova et al. 2000. "Molecular analysis of Neanderthal DNA from the northern Caucasus." *Nature*, 404: 490–3.

Pollard, A. M. 1995. "Why teach Heisenberg to archaeologists?" *Antiquity*, 69: 242–7.

Renfrew, A. C. 1970. "The tree-ring calibration of radiocarbon: an archaeological evaluation." *Proceedings of the Prehistoric Society*, 36: 280–311.

Renfrew, A. C. 1976. *Before Civilization: The Radiocarbon Revolution and Prehistoric Europe*. Harmondsworth: Penguin Books.

Renfrew, A. C. 1992. "The identity and future of archaeological science." In A. M. Pollard (ed.), *New Developments in Archaeological Science*, pp. 285–93. *Proceedings of the British Academy*, 77. Oxford: Oxford University Press.

Richards, M. B., V. A. Macaulay, H. J. Bandelt, and B. C. Sykes 1998. "Phylogeography of mitochondrial DNA in western Europe." *Annals of Human Genetics*, 62: 241–60.

Smith, C. I., A. T. Chamberlain, M. S. Riley et al. 2001. "Not just old but old and cold?" *Nature*, 410: 771–2.

Smith, J. E., M. J. Risk, H. P. Schwarcz, and T. A. McConnaughey 1997. "Rapid climate change in the North Atlantic during the Younger Dryas recorded by deep-sea corals." *Nature*, 386: 818–20.

Taylor, R. E. and M. J. Aitken (eds.) 1997. *Chronometric Dating in Archaeology*. New York: Plenum Press.

Taylor, R. E., R. Kra, and A. Long (eds.) 1992. *Radiocarbon after Four Decades: An Interdisciplinary Perspective*. New York: Springer-Verlag.

Thomas, D. 1934. *18 Poems*. London: Fortune Press.

Thomas, J. 1990. "Silent running: the ills of environmental archaeology." *Scottish Archaeological Review*, 7: 2–7.

Thomas, J. 1991. "Science versus anti-science?" *Archaeological Review from Cambridge*, 10: 27–37.

Tite, M. S. 1991. "Archaeological science – past achievements and future prospects." *Archaeometry*, 31: 139–51.

Zeuner, F. E. 1946. *Dating the Past: An Introduction to Geochronology*. London: Methuen.

21

Experiencing Archaeological Fieldwork

John Bintliff

Is the past "knowable" or is its study just "do-able"? One and a half million witnesses from nowhere in particular have something to contribute... [1]

Archaeology is the study of past material culture and officially, at least, it exists and is widely funded because a better understanding of the past is argued to have value in the present, and indeed could help us plan a better future. However, if we take away the elements of entertainment and sheer curiosity which make most people fascinated by reenactments or virtual reality reconstructions of exotic past peoples, and ask more seriously whether archaeological results are *regularly* employed to make us rethink our own lives or help planners to make novel decisions, most archaeologists will quickly admit that our work does not change nor will change contemporary society.

That is not to say that *society* has not regularly dipped into archaeological literature to very selectively pull out bits of information to suit certain agendas – nineteenth-century nationalists and twentieth-century totalitarian states provide a continuous story of the *abuse* of archaeological publications to provide supposed scientific support for already-elaborated political agendas. The prehistorian Jacquetta Hawkes wittily remarked: "Every age has the Stonehenge it deserves – or desires" (Hawkes 1967).

Moreover, archaeologists have always tried to *make* themselves relevant by seizing the latest social trend in the hope of finding some reflection in the past, so that they *might* make some vital contribution to modern life. Current preoccupations in the more theoretical sectors of archaeology are focused, for example, on gender, cultural identity, and individualism – hardly surprising in an age when we are rethinking the role of women, restructuring the Western cultural tradition into multiculturalism, and finding ourselves subtely remolded by the propaganda of post-Fordist global capitalism (Harvey 1989) into believing that we are isolated, atomistic entrepreneurs rather than cooperative social animals.

As you can gather, I am pretty skeptical about the track record of the discipline of archaeology when it comes to changing the present or the future. By now you might be wondering if this essay is going to be a public requiem rather than a celebration of the subject! Thankfully, I hope by the conclusion of this chapter to have given you grounds for optimism, but only through a radical reinterpretation of what archaeologists *can* do – and in the process raising doubts whether during the thirty or so years of my academic career there hasn't been too much *thinking* in archaeology.

That is a cue to take you back to the time I began to study the subject, in the late 1960s. This was a very exciting moment in the development of the discipline, because revolutionaries such as the American Lewis Binford and my own teacher David Clarke, were creating the so-called New Archaeology: the discipline was going to become a hard science, and discover the underlying general laws that govern the development of human society in all times and places. With such a program, other academic communities (especially those highly regarded physicists) and the general public would have to take notice of the results of archaeological research! But it is now clear that archaeology once again was merely reflecting society – here the postwar confidence in science, technology, and social planning that typified the West up until the 1970s (Bintliff 1986).

The lofty aims of formulating what Binford called the "Laws of Cultural Process" and the parallel goals of Clarke to see how far the human past could be reduced to a series of mathematical equations, proved illusory. By the early 1980s archaeological thinkers were in any case becoming enamored of the very different intellectual movement called postmodernism. Among other things, this tradition casts heavy doubt on the credentials of science to find facts or truth, especially where it concerns human behavior, preferring to redirect our sympathies into the humanities, and our academic goals into the creation of literary texts. History as a kind of imaginative novel-writing reflecting the autobiography of its contemporary author should replace the archive-researcher claiming to compile statistics which will eventually add up to a full picture of the past.

Here we find ourselves in a strange situation: if all attempts to write summary stories about the past by archaeologists are essentially expressionist statements of modern-day individuals with their contemporary biasses and concerns, then what do all the bits of evidence that we dig up or record mean? As the historian Kuzminski humorously commented, in the postmodern (or to use the archaeological version, postprocessual) view, our empirical data from the past, cut loose from the possibility of reliable interpretation as factual history, become merely "one damn thing after another" (cited in Steinberg 1981: 463). Archaeology is therefore not about finding the "truth" but – to quote a leading postprocessualist – it is a form of "cultural product."

Between the 1950s and the current new millennium we seem to have passed from what was called "traditional archaeology" – a kind of archaeology concentrating on action, digging and putting back houses, and people doing everyday things – into the 1960s New Archaeology – with its emphasis on *thinking* about how all these things ought to be done – then on into postmodern archaeology – where we *think* about how we *think* about everything: more a kind of philosophy of life and textual criticism of archaeological writings than an attempt to convey the key trends of a past reality. Moreover, even these semi-fictional narratives about the past, which are all we can realistically hope to produce, are prone to *reinterpretation* in the mind of each and every reader.

But this story I have related is about academic archaeology and mainly in Western Europe and parts of North America. Moreover, to put it into context, David Harvey in his masterly deconstruction of postmodernism (1989) has demonstrated to my satisfaction that this intellectual movement is essentially an unthinking reflection of the ethos and practices of late capitalism (cf. Bintliff 1993). Once more, archaeological ideas are the froth of the age!

What, you might ask, has the general public made of the rapid conversion of history and archaeology into fiction and self-expression? What about the state archaeologists and heritage managers whose job it is to convince funders that the past is worth saving because it tells us something about our ancestors rather than ourselves? Actually, the public are unaware of the existence of postmodern archaeology, and the offices and field huts of professional public archaeologists are not the places to find manuals of philosophy and literary criticism, the *oeuvres* of Derrida and Foucault. By and large the archaeology that the general public wants and gets, whether it is Indiana Jones, *Time Team*, or the *Discovery* program, and the archaeology carried out by public archaeologists, has parted company with the thinking archaeology of the universities. Ironically, the more academic archaeologists have invested in thinking about their discipline, with the good intentions of making it more relevant to the world, the more remote their work has become.

Now let me make my own position clear. I agree that the big intellectual debates and the grand reconstructions in archaeology tell us more about the preoccupations of our own age than emerge as unavoidable interpretations from the actual evidence of the past. However, this is not to say that the froth of our age is not useful in defined ways. Thus, the desire to treat contemporary issues in our research often means we have to collect different kinds of data to previous researchers, so new kinds of evidence appear – even if the question at issue tends to drop out of interest after a few years. But this justification for theory reinforces its ephemeral nature, as an ever-changing set of stimuli driven by short-lived fads and leaving a lasting impression only in the creation of new and different data.

If archaeology exists to make progress in our understanding of the past – and if you do not accept this there can be no reason to continue with our work – then somehow that improvement in our picture of past societies must be found rather in that ever-larger mountain of empirical observations whose importance has been minimized by an over-privileging of theory during the last thirty years. Can we make something *real* and impressive out of the evidence archaeologists dig up, map, catalogue, and order, those

items of data Kuzminski called jokingly (and significantly in a critique of postmodern history), "one damn thing after another"?

Now, there are actually powerful but neglected reasons to elevate the importance of *practical* research in archaeology over *thinking* about the discipline, and if this is so, the most important people for the long-term results of our work are not ivory-tower philosopher-archaeologists but public professionals, and the excitement of fieldwork discovery which most grips the public is correctly focused on the genuine cutting-edge of the discipline.[2] They have it right and the universities have got it wrong!

This provocative inversion of our customary assumption that brilliant theorists are at the top of the pyramid of importance, with lowly laboratory experimenters at the bottom, was indeed a position argued for by the famous physicist Ernst Mach, in a very public debate with Max Planck shortly before World War I (Fuller 2000: ch. 2). For Planck, an elite of very brainy ideas-people set tasks for practical researchers and then told them what they had found, while, for Mach, the best science was democratic and arose from the physical skill and high craftsmanship of experimenters finding practical patterning in real-world, hands-on encounters with matter.

Apart from invoking Mach's challenging perspective, I would also like to shock you by pointing out that recent research in artificial intelligence (AI) (Preston 1992; Davidson 1995) gives even stronger grounds for putting practical empirical research at the top of the creative knowledge pyramid and demoting thinking about things to the bottom! When AI specialists started to design computer robots which would duplicate human beings, the natural assumption was that the difficult bit would be programming those gifts that separate us from the rest of the animal world – conversing about philosophy, playing chess, doing mathematics – *higher intelligence*. In fact, writing programs to do this has proved to be easier than expected. Already computer robots can fool some people in a neighboring room that they are talking with another human. Computers *can* beat chess grand masters, and unsolved mathematical problems are being resolved through high-speed computing.

Mysteriously, what proved extraordinarily difficult was in fact programming computer robots to do everyday human things – getting the cat to come out from under the bed, moving rapidly through an overgrown forest. It turns out that this so-called "peripheral intelligence" is much more *complex* than "higher intelligence" and has largely defied the ability of AI researchers to reduce it to logical programs. Indeed, robot designers have turned instead (this time with marked success) to a Darwinian process of building robots with lots of variable properties of uncertain purpose, merely copying or "breeding from" those designs which adapted best to the experimental challenges the machines were set. Current reasoning within the AI community is that whereas arguing about philosophy is a very recent human activity and has been of minimal survival value, hence gets no special support from the body, in contrast peripheral intelligence – finding our way about the physical *and* social world – has been a vital adaptive factor in higher ape and human evolution and hence exists as a very complex set of intuitive skills.

I have been a regular contributor to theory debates in archaeology, and yet I have become more and more aware that my most significant contribution to the discipline will be from my fieldwork and the ordering of my field data into reconstructed patterns of past processes and lifeways – a "thick description" of lost communities. Ideas indeed help me, but ultimately to get better data and look for new shapes and trends or discontinuities in the practical evidence.

This is the point where I shall enlist the aid of my almost one and a half million witnesses from nowhere in particular. I am a landscape archaeologist, specializing in surface archaeology. I am setting myself a seemingly tough task to demonstrate to you that this kind of practical fieldwork is more informative than

grand theory, since *we* do not even excavate, merely record and analyze those bits of underground settlements and other kinds of buried past human activity which modern farming plows up and brings to the surface. But, whereas I can knock up a reasonable theory paper in a few weeks of library work (to impress the intelligentsia at theory conferences), when it comes to my surface archaeology, let me tell you – my project in Boeotia, central Greece began in 1978; 27 years on, with my co-director Anthony Snodgrass, we are about to publish the first volume of its final publication and are *still* extracting additional subtleties of human activity from the incredibly complex evidence we obtained in the field. Not only is this hands-on encounter with the rich web of past activity-traces the most profitable environment for the production of lasting knowledge about earlier societies, but also I can sense that I am using my abilities to their fullest, from the *physical* associations that arise. Mach referred to this when he talked about psychophysics – the reinforcing pleasure we get from manipulation and probing of the physical world. My research involves walking, with teams of students, every field, hill, and valley in extensive landscapes, counting and taking a sample of all the ancient artefacts we see on the surface (usually small broken pieces of ceramic or potsherds). We get immense physical pleasure from moving across the land and enumerating by quality and quantity the contents of the soil surface in relation to the changing properties of the landscape. Recently, the American biologist E. O. Wilson (1984) and the University of Sussex astronomer John Barrow (1995) explained this pleasure in landscape with their Agrophilia and Biophilia hypotheses. Human beings receive chemical gratification which makes us feel good when we do things that have become inbuilt survival skills. We developed for millions of years as expert foragers in open landscapes; hence, we needed to note and explore the changing properties of the natural environment essential for obtaining food and avoiding dangers.

So here I am, field walking, using the best part of my intelligence – the peripheral part – to make intuitive and pleasurable contact with the landscape *and* those clues to how past peoples lived and worked there – can I find a "knowable" past that outshines the passing stories of theory? I shall take you now to one small sector of Greece – a mere 7 square kilometers out of the 50 or so we have walked over since the project began 22 years ago. Now here is a surprise: this area, consisting of two small valleys and an intervening low range of hills, contains only one small cluster of visible archaeological remains on the surface. In the north, beside one valley, once lay an important classical city – Thespiae. Its ruins are so scanty that only practiced eyes can spot them – a bank that marks a Late Roman fort, traces of brick pillars and a cut stone outline that are the remains of Roman baths and early Christian churches. In the mid-1980s we laid a giant grid across the whole valley to enclose the city – almost 600 squares over an area of 1.5 square kilometers (Bintliff and Snodgrass 1988a). The whole locality is fortunately intensively farmed, and pottery lies densely exposed, which in the downtown area of such Graeco-Roman towns can easily reach a quarter of a million pieces of surface pottery per hectare. We carefully counted the surface finds and noted the points where dense urban debris dropped off rapidly into levels typical of rural activity, thus defining the city at its maximum extent – some 95 hectares or almost 1 square kilometer. Empirical study from excavated towns suggests this would represent something like 12,000 inhabitants. From the millions of broken pots lying on the city surface we collected some 12,000 pieces and dated them, then symbolically put back the finds for each phase onto the grid of the city. The broad lines of Thespiae's history emerged clearly: a small village in early farming times – the Neolithic; then several adjacent hamlets in the Bronze Age; the classical Greek city began also as several small Iron Age hamlets that later exploded and merged into the giant

95-hectare town by 400 BC. In Roman times, however, economic and political decline had caused the town to shrink to 40 percent of its previous maximum, and in Late Antiquity a fort was built of ruined Greek monuments in a small part of this town against the rising threat from barbarian invasions. One part of this Late Roman town, which lay just outside the fort, later became a flourishing medieval village, and it could be that although the city disappeared in the troubled post-Roman Dark Ages, a group of peasant farmers remained at the site till the thirteenth century AD, getting more numerous as Byzantine civilization reintroduced peace and prosperity to Greece. It seems that in another troubled period, the fourteenth and fifteenth centuries AD, the villagers moved elsewhere for reasons of security, but they returned by the seventeenth century and now live on a hill overlooking the ancient city.

What about the rural hinterland, the countryside beyond the walls of ancient Thespiae city, where nearly all the wealth and support for those many thousands of inhabitants were derived? Let us pass out through the city wall and walk south into a 5-kilometer square area. In this block of landscape there is not a single standing monument, no visible archaeology, until you learn to spot the minor differences in shape, color, and texture that distinguish small pieces of ancient broken pottery from stones and clods of soil. Then, in fact, the entire surface is seen to be an enormous archaeological site. When every field had been walked, and a continuous count of surface artefact density made, we had recorded 1.37 million pieces of ancient pottery, some 2,500 potsherds per hectare – or in practical terms, with every step you saw another piece of pottery.

In some 13 places this carpet of pottery grew unusually dense to over 4,000 or 5,000 sherds a hectare, and these we made small study grids over, since they should represent rural farms or villages – the farms are usually a few hundred square meters, the villages 1–2 hectares in area. At first it seemed easy enough to collect the pottery from these rural "sites" and map them by period to show how large the country population was in comparison to the expansion and contraction of the city they belonged to. But our obsessive counting, mapping, and dating of pottery from both these dense spots and the carpet that covered all the rest of the landscape revealed all kinds of curious and difficult features, suggesting a far more elaborate set of past human behaviors at work. Firstly, if these highspots in the countryside with lots of pottery were places where rural farms and villages lay, how were we to account for the over a million bits of broken pot that filled all the rest of the countryside? Secondly, we also found four locations where there were small clusters of very beautiful fine pottery of classical date, but here the surface density was less than the average for the whole landscape.

I did not use elaborate thinking to understand the complexity which seemed to be emerging from our observations. Instead, I looked with more and more close attention to the features of the data we had collected – and it took more than ten years to tease apart the different kinds of past behavior we were picking up signals from (Bintliff and Howard 1999).

What do I now suggest we have found in the countryside of ancient Thespiae city? The story begins with very faint traces of a past human landscape whose evidence has 99 percent disappeared to erosion and plow destruction: all across the whole 5 square kilometers we found sporadic finds of prehistoric coarse pottery and stone tools – in twos and threes – and although the 17 identified, "official" rural sites were full of classical Greek and Roman pottery, half of them also gave us a similar handful of prehistoric finds. When I examined the sampling statistics of what these finds should mean, it probably suggests that there are up to 20,000 pieces of prehistoric pottery in this small area of landscape – but seemingly no prehistoric settlements! Empirical research suggests that even that reconstructed evidence is a small surviving proportion of the original

density of prehistoric artefacts across our landscape. The kind of rural life most plausibly giving rise to such vestigial data (Bintliff et al. 1999) is a period of some 4,000–5,000 years when the first farmers in this area lived in small farms, the life of which spanned a mere one or two generations before a new farm was built on fresh farmland nearby. Across this immense period eventually the entire countryside – all of it very fertile land – was at one time or another the location of a small family farm. Around 2000 BC with the later Bronze Age this evidence drops off and people nucleated into villages, four of which we found on the edges of the study area, but none within. Our countryside is reoccupied again at the time of the great expansion of the classical Greek city of Thespiae, and the people of that city-state, whether living within the walls or outside in its rural territory, have left us four kinds of behavior detectable in the patterns of the relevant pottery we found.

Firstly, the vast majority of the citizens of this city-state must have lived in the walled town with its 12,000 or so inhabitants – the density of farms and villages of classical date in its countryside represents a mere 25 percent of the total citizen body. No wonder that politics was so central to ancient Greek life! Secondly, among the rural sites with their abnormal amounts of surface pottery, most showed a strong classical Greek presence, and from the extent of the pottery scatter for just that period we can estimate whether they were family farms or small villages. Careful study of the type of pots being broken at these sites helps us fill out the picture of the kinds of everyday activities rural farmers carried out at these country estates – storage vessels, vessels for preparing food, finer tablewares, lamps, beehives, fragments of olive and wine presses. The third phenomenon was the most intriguing: over a million of all the pieces of pottery coating the countryside under study lay not on these rural sites but in between them, in the open fields, and 80 percent of it belonged only to the classical Greek period – the very time when the city itself reached unparalleled size. One explanation was erosion – could all this broken pot have been washed out and plowed away from the city itself and the 17 rural sites? Empirical geomorphological study shows this to be impossible. Could they represent generations of donkeys accidentally dropping loads in the fields, or farmers eating their lunch and smashing pottery in drunken moments? The extraordinary numbers and almost complete cover of the land surface rule this out.

Similar carpets of household debris have been found around ancient towns in the Middle East (Wilkinson 1989), and in recent history are comparable to the nightsoil of nineteenth-century West European cities collected and taken into the surrounding countryside – thus the origin is systematic collection of urban refuse for use as crop fertilizer in the farming lands around (Bintliff and Snodgrass 1988b; Snodgrass 1994, *contra* Alcock et al. 1994). Elsewhere, such intensive rubbish collection to aid crop production coincides with periods of high population in the towns concerned (Wilkinson 1989, 1994). What more likely period for such activity than the one phase when the town of Thespiae reached a vast extent? We can even raise the question as to whether the obsessive manuring activity of classical Greek times marks overpopulation and increasing soil decline from overcropping, suggesting one reason for the subsequent implosion of the city to 40 percent of its size by Roman times.

Finally, the fourth kind of classical activity in this landscape is represented by four small areas with a shortage of broken pottery but unusual numbers of very fine pottery. These are actually small rural family cemeteries, with special kinds of vessels deposited with the dead. These places are impoverished numerically because farmers of this period did not cultivate and spread manure across cemetery areas.

After this climax of population and land use in town and country, the subsequent Roman and early Christian eras show radical changes to everyday life. As I mentioned already, the city itself lost some three-fifths of its population. In the countryside the intensive manuring disappears, clearly because the number of mouths to feed had been so diminished. Also, in place of the small family farms and the villages of free citizens of classical Greek times we now find large villa estates and a few villages – which may well be those of dependent laborers working on those villas. Roman period travel guides and geographies tell us that Thespiae was a pretty flourishing place, but now this seems to reflect good times for big landowners rather than for peasants.

After the collapse of Roman power, in the Middle Ages, most people clustered into villages some kilometers apart in the landscape, and ancient cities were usually downgraded to such a status – Thespiae city suffers such a fate. In the rural area to its south, we did find another medieval hamlet, some 2 kilometers from the medieval village at the city itself, and this is dated to a time of revival when Byzantine civilization was at its peak. Not surprisingly, the needs of these two small nucleated settlements were easily met without intensive farming, and no carpet of rubbish is found of this date smeared over surrounding hills. During the following centuries of Crusader and Turkish occupations of our area, villages remained modest in size and few people sought life in the open countryside. When in the late nineteenth century AD a new political stability and global trade penetrated into our rustic area and the villages exploded again into several thousand inhabitants, the use of modern fertilizers, improved crops and stock, and a population still way below classical Greek levels, meant that domestic rubbish stayed on and around the villages themselves – where we later collected it so that my colleague Joanita Vroom (1998) could chart the impact of factory economies and wider trade on these traditional Greek villages.

I have just constructed a narrative for you, to account for the main trends in 9,000 years of landscape history in central Greece. In it, theoretical models have certainly played a part, *and* some of those have stemmed from the preoccupations of *our* age: our current heightened ecology awareness, a Marxist concern for class conflict reflecting my youth in the 1960s and 1970s. There are clear influences also from contingent factors in my own academic development: the centrality of landscape archaeology came from researching with Eric Higgs and his Palaeoeconomy group; my obsession with counting and measuring things to justify reconstructions shows the powerful influence of David Clarke and my early teaching years in a nuclear physics community at Bradford University.

And yet what really matters in my story from Boeotia is that vast mass of complex *evidence* we have taken 25 years to accumulate, order, and seek patterns from. Later scholars with other preoccupations will, I hope, be able to use these observations both to formulate new projects to enrich my data, and to test my reconstructions as to what these patterns of past human activity amount to on the grand scale of historical meaning. For each new generation of researchers, the rising mountain of elaborate evidence provides stronger grounds for favoring certain interpretations over others and increasingly constrains weak models, enabling the past reality to come gradually into sharper focus.[3]

The study of the past is therefore eminently "do-able." I have also argued to you that postmodern loss of nerve regarding the concept of progress in reconstructing past lifeways is not only part of the froth of the chattering academic classes. More importantly, it is also remote from the important constructive edge of practical discovery, where we see that the past is also "knowable" in ever better detail. I hope also that I have taken you back to the atmosphere which brought most archaeologists into their discipline: the excitement and uncertainty of physical encounters with the debris of lost communities; and shared with you the intense pleasure we get from the intuitive piecing together, from millions of fragments, of the original webs of human behavior over space and time that constitute the fabric of history.

Notes

1 This essay is an extended version of my Inaugural Address when taking up the Chair of Classical Archaeology at Leiden University, October 6, 2000.

2 A previous, funny, and trenchant call in this same direction can be found in Kent Flannery's classic paper "The Golden Marshalltown: A parable for the 1980s" (Flannery 1982).

3 The cumulative knowledge-base, founded on forward-looking improvements in data collection and simply more and more relevant observations, as well as backward-looking critiques of preceding analyses, means that in archaeology we constantly find that on each intellectual revisit of a significant phase of the past we need to apply more elaborate interpretations. As the great American historian W. H. McNeill argued in a keynote lecture: "I actually believe that historians' truths, like those of scientists, evolve across the generations, so that versions of the past acceptable today are superior in scope, range, and accuracy to versions available in earlier times" (McNeill 1986: 9; cf. Bintliff 1988: 6–12).

References

Alcock, S. E. et al. 1994. "Intensive survey, agricultural practice and the classical landscape of Greece." In I. Morris (ed.), *Classical Greece: Ancient Histories and Modern Archaeologies*, vol. 1, pp. 137–70. Cambridge: Cambridge University Press.

Barrow, J. D. 1995. *The Artful Universe*. Oxford: Oxford University Press.

Bintliff, J. L. 1986. "Archaeology at the interface: an historical perspective." In J. L. Bintliff and C. F. Gaffney (eds.), *Archaeology at the Interface: Studies in Archaeology's Relationships with History, Geography, Biology and Physical Science*, pp. 4–31. Oxford: British Archaeological Reports 4–31.

Bintliff, J. L. 1988. "A review of contemporary perspectives on the 'meaning' of the past." In J. L. Bintliff (ed.), *Extracting Meaning from the Past*, pp. 3–36. Oxbow Monograph 1. Oxford: Oxbow Books.

Bintliff, J. L. 1993. "Why Indiana Jones is smarter than the postprocessualists." *Norwegian Archaeological Review*, 26: 91–100.

Bintliff, J. L. and P. Howard 1999. "Studying needles in haystacks – surface survey and the rural landscape of central Greece in Roman times." *Pharos*, 7: 51–91.

Bintliff, J. L., P. Howard, and A. M. Snodgrass 1999. "The hidden landscape of prehistoric Greece." *Journal of Mediterranean Archaeology*, 12 (2): 139–68.

Bintliff, J. L. and A. M. Snodgrass 1988a. "Mediterranean survey and the city." *Antiquity*, 62: 57–71.

Bintliff, J. L. and A. M. Snodgrass 1988b. "Off-site pottery distributions: a regional and interregional perspective." *Current Anthropology*, 29: 506–13.

Davidson, C. 1995. "Robots: the next generation." *New Scientist*, January 14: 32–4.

Flannery, K. V. 1982. "The Golden Marshalltown: a parable for the archaeology of the 1980s." *American Anthropologist*, 84 (2): 265–78.

Fuller, S. 2000. *Thomas Kuhn: A Philosophical History For Our Times*. Chicago: University of Chicago Press.

Harvey, D. 1989. *The Condition of Postmodernity*. Oxford: Blackwell.

Hawkes, J. 1967. "God in the machine." *Antiquity*, 41: 174.

McNeill, W. H. 1986. "Mythistory, or truth, myth, history and historians." *American Historical Review*, 91: 1–10.

Preston, B. 1992. "An ethics of reasoning." *The Times Higher Educational Supplement*, July 24: 17.

Snodgrass, A. M. 1994. "Response: the archaeological aspect." In I. Morris (ed.), *Classical Greece: Ancient Histories and Modern Archaeologies*, pp. 197–200. Cambridge: Cambridge University Press.

Steinberg, J. 1981. "'Real Authentick History' or what philosophers of history can teach us." *Historical Journal*, 24: 453–74.

Vroom, J. 1998. "Early modern archaeology in central Greece: the contrast of artefact-rich and sherdless sites." *Journal of Mediterranean Archaeology*, 11 (2): 131–64.

Wilkinson, T. J. 1989. "Extensive sherd scatters and land-use intensity: some recent results." *Journal of Field Archaeology*, 16: 31–46.

Wilkinson, T. J. 1994. "The structure and dynamics of dry-farming states in upper Mesopotamia." *Current Anthropology*, 35: 483–520.

Wilson, E. O. 1984. *Biophilia*. Cambridge, MA: Harvard University Press.

Part IV
Archaeology and the Public

22

Public Archaeology:
A European Perspective

Timothy Darvill

Introduction

Do you remember when we were all explorers? A time when archaeologists boldly went all over the world to seek out new monuments and new civilizations? Whether it was Heinrich Schliemann at Troy, Sir Arthur Evans at Knossos, Giuseppe Fiorelli at Pompeii, or Howard Carter in the Valley of the Kings, archaeology was an enterprising, daredevil, intrepid, eccentric, and slightly perilous pursuit. This of course is how archaeologists are sometimes still perceived, and is an image occasionally promoted by archaeologists themselves, as Mortimer Wheeler's autobiography, subtitled "Adventures in Archaeology," emphasizes (Wheeler 1955). Filmmakers love the image too and have exaggerated it widely, from the comically camp Professor Ronald Crump played by Kenneth Williams in *Carry on Behind*, through to the ruggedly reliable Indiana Jones played by Harrison Ford. Television has also succeeded in capturing the essence of the pursuit from time to time: in Britain the series *Animal, Vegetable, Mineral?* was acclaimed in the 1950s, *Chronicle* in the 1960s and 1970s, *Down to Earth* in the 1980s, and in the 1990s *Time Team* and *Meet the Ancestors* drew very respectable viewing figures for weekly adventures.

Throughout the twentieth century, archaeology was, and remains, a very public endeavor. Almost uniquely in the sciences, the very process of finding out about the past is of public interest. But this interest is perhaps just one visible symptom of more deep-seated passions and concerns relating to identity, the sense of being, origins, tradition, and the cultural heritage; highly emotional responses to matters that bundled together are increasingly being referred to as the "historic environment."

Such concerns can also have darker and potentially more dangerous sides that, from time to time, reveal themselves in various forms of fanatical nationalism, what has become known as ethnic cleansing, and rapid shifts in political perspective. Historically speaking, few parts of Europe are immune from involvement in such matters in one way or another, and archaeology has often been implicated through the development of propaganda and the legitimation of constructed identities. Some of the better-studied examples include Nazi Germany (Arnold 1990), Ceausescu's Romania (Chippindale 1989: 416–17), and the transition from dictatorship to democracy in Albania (Miraj and Zeqo 1993). Ironically, as Olivier (1998) has pointed out with reference to the Vichy regime in France between

1940 and 1944, it is sometimes these moments of extremism that have created the foundations for archaeological traditions of thought that continue long after the regime itself has perished, leaving behind intellectual and practical tensions in the way the past is understood. Very similar patterns have been recognized by Kohl (1993) in Soviet Transcaucasia on the far southern borders of Europe, where religious differences in outlook between Christians and Muslims contribute another dimension to the issue.

Underpinning all these various interests in archaeology, good and bad, there exists a widely held understanding, in most parts of Europe backed by national legislation, that the very raw materials of archaeology – the sites, structures, monuments, deposits, and objects – are important, and have an existence that transcends the possessiveness of individuals. Moreover, public bodies from national governments, through regional authorities, and down to local councils, have assumed, or been given, responsibilities for many aspects of the archaeological heritage within their jurisdiction. And they spend significant sums of public money discharging those responsibilities. In consequence, the majority of practicing archaeologists are today employed either directly or indirectly in such work.

It was the recognition that archaeology potentially involves everyone in society that led American archaeologist Charles McGimsey III (1972) to coin the rather useful phrase "public archaeology" to refer to the way in which the discipline articulates itself with wider social, political, and economic issues. Accepting the principles behind the notion of public archaeology effectively abrogates the possibility of a "private archaeology," even though the application of private funds to archaeological research, the responsibilities born of legal ownership and title to objects and land, and the personal interests of some practitioners have sometimes been twisted to create that impression from time to time (cf. Pryor 1989).

Public archaeology has an exceedingly broad domain, and a number of key areas that are currently topical are addressed by other chapters in this book. Here the emphasis is on what in Britain, and some other parts of Europe, has become known as archaeological resource management or cultural resource management. This relatively new subdiscipline lies at the very heart of public archaeology because, in large measure, it is driven by public authorities spending public resources on, and diverting private resources towards, what it sees as the public good and in the public interest. Operationally, archaeological resource management may be defined as reconciling the many and varied demands placed upon archaeological remains by today's population within the context of prevailing legislation, agreed policies, and collectively endorsed ethical codes.

In this review I shall discuss a selection of five contemporary issues within archaeological resource management that serve to emphasize both the achievements and the tensions within the field. Inevitably, much of what follows is a personal perspective on fast-changing matters that can be seen in several different ways. Arrangements in Britain, and particularly in England, provide the starting point and lie at the center of much of this discussion, because this is what I am most familiar with and which is currently best documented in the archaeological literature. However, the five issues tackled here are of far wider relevance and find expression in different ways in many parts of Europe.

Defining and Recording the Field of Interest

Archaeology as a whole has never been a very tightly defined discipline in terms either of its scope of inquiry or the materials that are drawn upon and utilized. This is mainly because of its worldwide relevance and great chronological depth. Overlaps with related disciplines such as anthropology, history, and classics have been widely recognized for a long time and there has been much debate as to whether one is a subdiscipline of another, or vice versa. The problem of course is that these disciplines share similar targets, either in terms of the sources of evidence used or the problems being addressed. What to me is becoming more apparent, however, is that archaeology is no longer about writing history or prehistory: quite simply, archaeologists write archaeology. It is developing a distinctive discourse and becoming, as Gordon Childe (1947) predicted it would, a form of social science. But, uniquely, it is a social science whose methodologies span the arts and the sciences, whose perspectives are essentially humanistic, and whose investigations can, at one and the same time, deal with the actions of an individual that lasted only minutes, through to the accumulated behavior of successive communities spanning millennia. Such possibilities to explore the longest running participant-observed experiment in human existence ever carried out, would surely be the envy of the ancient philosophers and the desire of many modern social scientists. Yet instead of stimulating the core of our discipline, a great deal of effort is being devoted to exploring the periphery and attempting to redefine and reinvent the fundamentals (e.g., Barrett 1995).

Creating an archaeological discourse, stimulating the "archaeological imagination," depends on a relationship between archaeologists and the stuff of archaeology, the residues and remains that have come down to us from the past and that we can engage with. At the heart of archaeological resource management is the idea of a "resource," or at least the conceptualization of a resource as the things that represent the raw materials for archaeological inquiry, the stuff of archaeology (Darvill 1999a: 300–2). Defining what constitutes the archaeological resource is far from easy, and has both intellectual and practical dimensions.

What the archaeologist normally finds are hotspots or nodes where the evidence of the activities that took place is rich enough, or substantial enough, or well-preserved enough, to be visible, recognizable, and legible. This is the archaeological resource, but there is no neat embracing definition of it; it is effectively whatever archaeologists recognize as relevant to their work at any given point in time. The critical and extremely exciting shift that is taking place now, is a movement away from the oversimplistic notion of monuments and sites as the places where the past happened and where it exists to be discovered, towards the investigation of the social use of space at different scales in ways that are appropriate to the issues being studied. In this sense the intellectual or theoretical constitution of archaeological work drives and defines its practical application.

Since about 1960, the field of archaeology has broadened very considerably, with the development of new and exciting subdiscipline areas and fields of inquiry. Collectively, these have massive implications for archaeological resource management, because each new domain emphasizes particular aspects of the archaeological resource, which in some cases were previously considered outside the scope of archaeological interest. Many of these new subdiscipline areas developed first by taking the methodologies of archaeology – excavation, systematic survey, technical analysis – and applying them to new kinds of data, new problems, and new situations. Gradually, as the body of research develops, interpretive theory and appropriate philosophies and general theory are pulled down to provide better and more comprehensive intellectual frameworks. A small selection from the many new subdisciplines of archaeology illustrates the changing nature of the subject:

- Industrial archaeology focusing on structures and landscapes of the Industrial Revolution and afterwards (Buchanan 1972).

- Maritime archaeology dealing with remains that lie underwater and offshore is another important area of growth (Muckleroy 1978).
- Experimental archaeology dealing with the interpretation of archaeological material and the formation and decay processes behind what remains to be explored (Coles 1973).
- Buildings archaeology (Wood 1994).
- Gardens archaeology (Taylor 1983).
- Forensic archaeology (Hunter 1994; Hunter et al. 1996).
- Archaeology of military remains (Schofield 1998; Baker 1993).

Traditionalists may see some of these new adventures in archaeology as broadening the discipline too far, with a resulting dissipation of endeavor and resources away from core themes. But I think these trends actually emphasize the health and strength of the discipline: they show that archaeology is able to spawn, develop, and support new and diverse fields of inquiry. The focus of attention is the human past, whether it is the recent past or the ancient past; the material which forms the raw material for study is as much part of today's world as anything else that archaeologists deal with, and like many other elements of the archaeological resource it is under constant threat.

One of the biggest changes in the way archaeological materials are defined and handled is in the field of landscape archaeology (Darvill 1997b). Like many other areas of the discipline discussed above, landscape archaeology first found focus in essentially methodological developments (Aston and Rowley 1974; Taylor 1974) connected with the application to earlier periods of landscape history of the sort so well developed by W. G. Hoskins (1955). This provided an essentially diachronic, in many ways rather evolutionary, view of landscape change, in which the focus was on time-depth and the idea of a "palimpsest." Such interests still remain, but in recent decades landscape

archaeology relevant to archaeological resource management has developed in three distinct ways.

First, building on earlier traditions of landscape archaeology, is the recognition that it is not only palimpsests that are interesting, but synchronic patterns too. Here attention is given to the distribution of monuments and structures at a particular time-slice, or patterns of land use within specific time-space situations. Detailed recording and survey is the key to this approach, and in recent years a large number of very detailed pieces of work have been reported, for example in England for Bodmin Moor (Johnson and Rose 1994), the Fenland (Hall and Coles 1994), and the Essex coast (Wilkinson and Murphy 1995); in Scotland for Perthshire (RCAHMS 1990, 1994); in Ireland for the Neolithic of County Sligo (Bergh 1995); in the Gyomaendrod area of Hungary (Bökönyi 1992); for the Aegean Island of Keos in Greece (Cherry et al. 1991); and for many other areas too. In resource management terms the results of such intensive studies can provide the basis for the definition of what are sometimes called "relict cultural landscapes." These recognize the totality of the archaeology for a particular period, and delineate areas within it for appropriate, but varied, kinds of management. This has been pioneered in England (Darvill et al. 1993) and has already begun to find useful application in the examination of the Stonehenge landscape (Batchelor 1997).

A second area of development takes a slightly different approach to the delineation of specific blocks of landscape as being of archaeological or historic importance. This involves identifying and defining discrete units within the modern countryside that are of special interest because they embody links to particular historic traditions, or events, or associations. The result of such work is a set of designations or protected areas. In Wales, the Register of Landscapes of Outstanding Historic Interest (Cadw 1998) is a particularly fine example of such an approach. However, one problem with

such studies is that areas that are not designated are perceived as not being special, and
this does seem rather odd. In addition to
simple designation, however, some such
areas may be made into archaeological
parks. Méndez (1997) has suggested that
such parks may be considered as a group of
known sites integrated with meaningful surroundings, and complemented by services
and infrastructures to facilitate public access.

The third set of developments is perhaps
the most wide ranging and most exciting, as
it involves the application of general theory
relating to the social use of space, which is as
applicable for looking at the past as it is for
approaching the management of today's
countryside. In studies of past landscapes
innovative use has been made of theories of
social action and structuration (Darvill
1997a), hermeneutics (Thomas 1993), and
phenomenology (Tilley 1994); and such
work is not confined to the British Isles
(e.g., Chapman and Dolukhanov 1997;
Criado and Parcero 1997). All, however, embrace postmodernist reconceptualizations of
the idea of landscape as a socially constructed reality, that involve the embodiment
and communication of cosmologies, economic relations, power structures, and
order, in what might also be seen as a more
anthropological view of landscape (Ucko
and Layton 1999; Ashmore and Knapp
1999). In this thinking there is no such
thing as a "natural landscape," only sets of
spaces and things that have socially defined
meanings and values that are constantly
being contested and renegotiated; it is people
who define what is natural and in so doing
bring nature into the realm of the social.

In conceptualizing past landscapes as sets
of meanings and differentially valued spaces,
structures, and things, archaeology has
equipped itself, both intellectually and practically, with the means to contribute to larger
ongoing debates about the landscape present
and future (cf. Countryside Commission
1996). Instead of subdividing the landscape
into particular segments or blocks on the
basis of some special interest, there is in-

creasing emphasis on the integration of
archaeology with other environmental and
conservation disciplines, to create more holistic perspectives. This is closely bound up
with two trends. First is the integration of
archaeology into the green movement
(Macinnes and Wickham-Jones 1992;
Swain 1993). Second is the way in which
multidisciplinary consultancies and local
government departments have put archaeologists alongside their counterparts from
disciplines such as ecology, nature conservation, and countryside access, in order to provide advice to planners, land managers, and
the public.

In Britain the holistic approach to landscape study for management purposes is
being pursued through the recognition of
"landscape character" (Countryside Commission 1991: 3). A countryside character
map of England was published in 1996
(Countryside Commission et al. 1996) in
which 181 character areas were identified,
defined, and plotted. The definition of these
areas involved the consideration of many
separate layers of spatially referenced information, of which four were archaeological in
origin. Since 1996, more detailed work has
been undertaken in order to develop methodologies for assessing the historic dimensions of landscape character (Herring 1998;
Fairclough 1999), with the ultimate objective of being able to make stronger contributions about the conservation and
management of the countryside. The inclusion of archaeology in these considerations
means that, for the first time, archaeological
resource management is moving away from
dealing only with the physical remains of the
past, and is now involved in the perceptual
renegotiation of the present. Again, archaeology is developing a new form of social
relevance way beyond the explication of
historical narrative.

Underpinning all archaeological resource
management initiatives, whether they relate
to traditionally defined archaeological
monuments, known deposits, or holistically
conceived entire landscapes, is the need for

accessible and consistent records of what is known. The development of archaeological records on a European scale, especially since the widespread availability of computerized databases, has been phenomenal (Larsen 1992). With a constantly changing set of primary interests among archaeologists, what goes on the records becomes critical too. Most Western European countries now have some kind of National Monuments Record, and many have local records of various sorts. In retrospect it is sad that there was not more international collaboration at an early stage in the development of these systems. This would have avoided considerable duplication of effort in the technical side of record development, and would also have allowed greater compatibility of records and thus the possibility of looking at wider patterns. The dream of looking, for example, at the distribution of Neolithic passage graves across Europe is a long way off being attainable. The United Kingdom provides a microcosm of a series of wider problems.

Within the United Kingdom there are separate National Monuments Records covering England, Wales, and Scotland. Within England, each of the forty or so counties, and an increasing number of Unitary Authorities, has a separate local Sites and Monuments Record for its area of jurisdiction. A survey of England's archaeological resource in 1995 (Darvill and Fulton 1998) gives some impression of the scale of what has been achieved. It found that the National Monuments Record for England held about 284,000 separate retrievable records on its computerized index, with about 100,000 items awaiting input. At the same time, the 46 surveyed local Sites and Monuments Records (SMRs) held a combined total of about 657,619 retrievable records and a further 280,000 anticipated records. This gives an average density of 2.34 records per square kilometer in England. Analysis of these records showed that about half related to defined archaeological monuments, about a quarter to historic buildings, with the remainder relating to stray finds and miscellaneous items of various sorts (Darvill and Fulton 1998: 72). Chronologically speaking, about 17 percent of records were for prehistoric items, 9 percent Roman, 2 percent early medieval, 16 percent medieval, 36 percent post-medieval, and about 20 percent of uncertain date.

Behind these bold breakdowns it is widely recognized that there are major discrepancies in the quality and nature of the information held by these records (Baker 1999). Despite huge investment in the construction of archaeological records, there is a long way to go before they can be relied upon to provide solid data sets for management and research purposes. In many ways the records illustrate the distribution of archaeological activity, rather than anything approaching the original distribution of archaeological remains. In this regard it is sad to reflect that, in England certainly, there has been very little attempt to learn from the results of sampling programs carried out, for example, in east Hampshire (Shennan 1985) and east Berkshire (Ford 1987). These tried to model and understand patterns of archaeological deposits in the countryside. In some cases there is the very real question of whether what already exists should be put to one side and a replacement constructed from scratch. To what extent similar problems lie below the surface in other parts of Europe is not clear, although attempts to define Europe-wide core data standards are a welcome start to the harmonization of archaeological records (CoE 1993, 1995). In Ireland, the development of a National Monuments Record based upon the capture of data from a defined range of primary sources, validation through a program of fieldwork, and the use of a single recording system at national and local level, shows just what can be achieved and deserves wider recognition (Moore 1992).

One of the big issues raised by the compilation of sites and monuments records is quite simply: what is the most appropriate unit of record? And, more generally, what is a site? a monument? an ancient landscape? the historic environment? and any of the other terms that are used when referring to the "stuff" that archaeologists deal with. Traditionally, rather little attention has been given to this question of conceptualization, but increasingly archaeological resource management is developing its own body of theory and philosophical arguments in order to underpin some of the pragmatically constituted approaches favored in the past. In relation to archaeological records, one of the most exciting developments is the creation of so-called Event-Monument (EM) data structures.

The idea that archaeological activity can be considered as a series of "events" – an excavation, a survey, or a watching brief, for example – has been around since the late 1980s and was recognized as potentially relevant to the construction of local SMRs by Glenn Foard and others (cf. Foard 1997). Over the same period, research into the assessment of archaeological remains for England's Monuments Protection Programme began to explore the definition and constitution of archaeological entities that for more than a century have been known as "monuments" (Darvill 1987; Darvill et al. 1987; Startin 1993b). The two elements were brought together in a powerful and highly structured way during work connected with the development of Urban Archaeological Databases, especially the experimental work based on Cirencester (Darvill and Gerrard 1994). This involved the explicit recognition that positivist philosophies underpinned much work on the development of archaeological records and that, accordingly, it was appropriate to utilize the inductive–deductive distinctions inherent to positivist science and to allow the separation of observation from interpretation. Quite simply, archaeological operations such as excavations and surveys were conceptualized as observations of archaeological phenomena (i.e., inductive experiences), from which interpretations and generalizations are made (i.e., deductive descriptions).

Other areas in which general theory is being introduced to archaeological resource management include the problems of determining value and importance (see below); assessment and evaluation procedures (Champion et al. 1995); the introduction of a process-based system or management cycle to archaeological work (Darvill and Gerrard 1994: 171; Figure 22.1); and the social relevance of archaeological remains and the work of archaeology (Kristiansen 1993; Barrett 1995). In some respects the increased role of theory in archaeological resource management is a consequence of maturity, but it also relates to more widespread patterns of change in which the practitioners of archaeological resource management have gradually found themselves working in new and different organizational situations.

Repositioning, Sectorization, and the Impact of the European Union

In many parts of Europe the place of archaeology in organizational and institutional terms changed dramatically during the 1990s and will change still more in the future (Willems 1999; Willems et al. 1997). In almost all cases this has involved reduced direct involvement by governments or the state and greater participation by agencies and private companies. In England, the National Heritage Act 1983 created a new agency called the Historic Buildings and Monuments Commission for England (popularly known as English Heritage) to be responsible for the archaeological and built heritage. Its main three defined functions were to (1) secure the preservation of ancient monuments and historic buildings; (2) promote the preservation and enhance the character and appearance of conservation areas; and (3) promote the public's enjoyment of, and advance their knowledge of, ancient monuments and historic buildings and their preservation. Meanwhile, elsewhere within the United Kingdom,

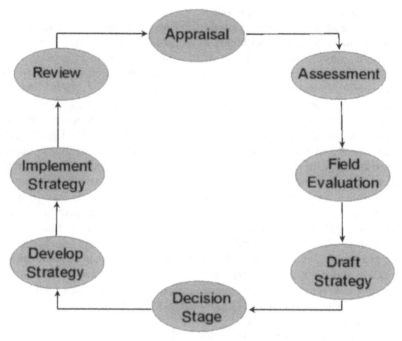

Figure 22.1 Schematic representation of the archaeological management cycle.

archaeology remained within the remits of government departments, for example Historic Scotland, Cadw in Wales, and the Department of the Environment in Northern Ireland. This created a strange, and sometimes confusing, mosaic of arrangements. Further afield in Europe, similar trends are evident, mainly in the way that state archaeological services such as the Rijksdienst voor het Oudheidkundig Bodemonderzoek (ROB) in Holland and the Riksantikvarieämbetet in Sweden lost their monopolies on carrying out archaeological work amid changes in the way that archaeological services are purchased.

The commercialization of archaeology, and with it the market-based practice of competitive tendering, has caused the separation of archaeological functions between, on the one hand, giving advice, setting briefs, and monitoring quality, and on the other actually carrying out the work. When first introduced, competitive tendering was highly controversial (Swain 1991), although the system settled quickly, and the main problem with it now is that it tends to depress prices at a time when archaeological organizations need substantial capitalization, new investment, and sufficient turnover to improve the working conditions and pay of those involved. My own experience as Chairman of the Directors of the Cotswold Archaeological Trust is that while archaeological work is highly valued in social terms, even to the extent that it is used constructively by other parties pursuing quite separate political agendas, it has yet to establish its true market value in terms of the contribution it makes to the development process, through enhancing the quality of life for the community at large.

Greater role specialization within archaeology, and the emergence of organizations with closely defined remits, have led to the definition within archaeological resource management of three clearly defined major role sets or groupings – known as the three C's:

Curators: organizations wholly or partly concerned with the long-term preservation, protection, conservation, and management of archaeological remains through the application of statutory or non-statutory powers and defined publicly accountable responsibilities. At the national level, curators are identified with archaeological officers in government departments and agencies. At a local and regional level, curators are mainly identified with the archaeological officers in county, district, borough, city, National Park, or unitary authorities.

Contractors: archaeological organizations which provide contracting services in archaeological fieldwork, analysis, research, and reporting. These are mainly constituted as units or trusts; some have defined operating areas, while others are free to work anywhere.

Consultants: individuals or organizations that provide archaeological advice, act as agents or representatives for others, and/ or who work as intermediaries in commissioning and monitoring archaeological work on behalf of clients.

To these can be added three further groups:

University-based archaeologists: groups of academics providing teaching, research, and consultancy services based in archaeology departments within higher or further education institutes.

Museum-based archaeologists: curators, keepers, researchers, conservators, and technicians of various sorts looking after, reporting, and presenting and interpreting to the public, collections of archaeological material and related research.

Independent archaeologists: individuals, local societies, or other bodies that voluntarily indulge a personal, collective, or institutional hobbyist or research interest in archaeology, which is driven by their own aspirations and curiosity.

In Britain, as now in many European countries, the vast majority of practicing archaeologists are employed in one or other of the first three groups. A very detailed survey to profile the archaeological profession in the UK, with a census date of March 1998, estimated that of the 4,500 or so archaeologists, about 34 percent worked as contractors or in other commercial organizations, 14 percent were curators based in local government, 15 percent worked for national heritage agencies, 3 percent were consultants, 15 percent worked in universities, and the remainder (29 percent) worked in museums, voluntary bodies, and a range of other organizations (Aitchison 1999: table 6). Of course, many have spoken out against increasing role definition among archaeologists, but on balance it seems to me that many of the arguments are tainted with desires for control, possession, and self-interest; within the emergent system there is scope at least for greater personal freedom, more inclusion of diverse interests, and the proper recognition of skills and achievement.

Traditionally, arrangements for the protection, conservation, and management of archaeological remains in particular, and the cultural heritage in general, have been matters for individual states to determine. Within the European Union this looks set to continue for the foreseeable future, although the trans-state movement of professional archaeologists is very likely to increase and raises questions about the recognition of qualifications and professional status (see below). Unlike its predecessor, the Treaty of Rome, the Maastricht Treaty (signed on February 7, 1992) deals with cultural issues (CEC 1992: 48–9: Title IX, Article 128). The emphasis is very much on cultural matters, important because they lie at the heart of the debate about European identity. The treaty provides the European Commission with powers to include such matters in their programs and opens the way for future initiatives; Directorate General X for culture, and Directorate XXII for education, already have archaeology within their remits, but far more is now possible. No Directives dealing solely with archaeology are currently proposed, although archaeology is included in the important and wide-ranging Directive dealing with Environmental Impact Assessment. This must surely be one of the greatest opportunities ever presented to archaeology, both in terms of enhancing its social relevance and exploring the past.

In technical terms, Environmental Impact Assessment is a multidisciplinary, and to some extent interdisciplinary, audit of the environmental resources and attributes of a specified area, the results of which are then related to the anticipated impacts on the environment of a proposed development and variations of it. The result is an Environmental Statement that forms the basis of discussions between interested parties and informs the decision-making process within the planning system. The idea of Environmental Impact Assessment has a long history in the United States of America (Wathern 1988; cf. Cleere and Fowler 1976), and was formally introduced to Europe as a selectively applied requirement by the European Commission in June 1985 (EC 1985). Archaeology is listed under the heading "material assets" and is one of a dozen or so topics that should be considered when carrying out an environmental assessment (EC 1985: Annex III.3). More important still, however, is the fact that topics are not considered in isolation, but rather there are opportunities to explore interrelationships too. This is the stuff that for decades archaeologists have dreamed about, yet now that it is here the subject is rarely discussed.

In Britain the original EU Directive was introduced as legislation in July 1988, with full details of procedures set out in a circular and advisory booklet (DoE 1988, 1989). Specific guidance and reviews of procedures relating to many of the subjects covered under the regulations have also appeared, including one volume of papers relating to archaeology (Ralston and Thomas 1993). Between 1988 and 1999 more than 2,000 Environmental Impact Assessments were undertaken in England, but studies suggest that less than half include archaeological components (Darvill and Russell 2002: 39). This is a tragedy, born I suspect of archaeologists' failure to become wholeheartedly involved with the wider environmental movement that has strongly supported and gained much from the process. On a Europe-wide scale the success of the first Directive has been such that in March 1997 the EU issued a revised Directive (EC 1997) that was implemented in the UK in April 1999. The changes in the revised regulations are fairly far-reaching but, ironically, archaeology is not explicitly cited in the revised European Directive (although it is assumed to be subsumed within "cultural heritage"), even though it is now itemized in the revised UK legislation, where the list of matters to be considered specifies "material assets, including the architectural and archaeological heritage." So the gauntlet is now on the floor, and it is for archaeologists to rise to the challenge and fully exploit this major new opportunity.

Alongside the "official" legislation that embodies archaeological principles at the international scale, there is an increasing flow of non-governmental international conventions and recommendations. Globally, the Convention Concerning the Protection of the World Cultural and Natural Heritage, the World Heritage Convention, is the most important. This is a UNESCO convention, adopted by the General Conference in Paris on November 16, 1972. Some twenty European states have ratified the convention; the UK government signed up to it in 1984. By 2001 there were 20 cultural and 2 natural World Heritage Sites within the UK (see DCMS 1998 for other nominations made). This compares with, for example, a total of 36 sites in Spain, 35 in Italy, 29 in the Federal Republic of Germany, 27 in France, 16 in Greece, 12 in Portugal, and 4 in Norway (WHC 2002).

Perhaps the most important international agreement for archaeology in Europe is the European Convention on the Protection of the Archaeological Heritage (Revised) (CoE 1992), opened for signature in Valletta, Malta, in January 1999 and generally known as the Malta Convention. This convention, and its implications for individual states, has been widely discussed (O'Keefe 1993; Trotzig 1993). It is wide ranging in its coverage and, despite the title, a little unconventional in its definitions. In setting out its scope, the convention stresses the value of the archaeological heritage as "a source of the European collective memory and as an instrument for historical and scientific study" (CoE 1992: Article 1.1). The idea of the collective memory is a particularly interesting one, which introduces an emotional commitment to archaeology, alongside the practical matter of it being an instrument for study. The definition of archaeological sites in the convention is also broad, including structures, constructions, groups of buildings, developed sites, movable objects, and monuments of other kinds, whether situated on land or under water (CoE 1992: Article 1.2–3). Emphasis is quite properly placed on the need to maintain proper inventories of recorded sites, and that this information is used in the planning process to ensure well-balanced strategies for the protection, conservation, and enhancement of sites of archaeological interest. Many things are covered by the convention, and some will provide challenges to individual states when they come to revise their domestic legislation.

The Malta Convention is complemented by a series of other agreements and recommendations, resulting from the work of various committees and groups of experts convened by the Council of Europe. These are becoming so numerous and specialized that most practicing archaeologists soon lose track of what is going on, even if they knew them all in the first place. Important recent additions to the mountainous pile of Euro-documents include the Convention for the Protection of the Architectural Heritage of Europe, adopted in 1985, and the Recommendation on the Integrated Conservation of Cultural Landscape Areas as part of land-scape policies, adopted in 1995. Together with others, these documents provide a robust framework at a European scale within which to situate approaches to archaeological resource management and, although daunting in their presentation and proliferation, are important in the way they externalize and communicate core ideals.

The doctrinal setting of much of what is contained in recent Council of Europe conventions and recommendations is contained in the Charter for the Protection and Management of the Archaeological Heritage, which was prepared by the International Committee on Archaeological Heritage Management and ratified by the General Assembly of its parent body, ICOMOS, in Lausanne in 1990 (ICAHM 1990; see Biörnstad 1989; Cleere 1993). This provides yet another variation in the way the archaeological heritage is defined, in this case taking an operational view in suggesting that it is "that part of the material heritage of which archaeological methods provide primary information." It then goes on to note that the archaeological heritage "comprises all vestiges of human existence and consists of places related to all manifestations of human activity, abandoned structures, and remains of all kinds (including subterranean and underwater sites), together with all the portable cultural material associated with them" (Article 1). This is probably the most wide-ranging and all-embracing view of the archaeological resource yet published, and might serve to endorse the fears of some that archaeologists are indeed intent on taking over the world. What is nice about it, however, is the way it sets the stage for exactly the kinds of development in thinking and practical approaches that I discussed above.

Taken as a whole, the international charters, conventions, recommendations, and agreements of various kinds introduce variety to the approaches taken to the identification, protection, conservation, and management of the archaeological heritage. Embedded in their carefully crafted articles and clauses is much that still needs to be taken apart and considered in relation to the everyday business of archaeology. Running through all these documents, however, is a series of principles and new philosophies on which there is a high degree of consensus.

New Philosophies and Principles

The philosophical basis of archaeological resource management is different from that of earlier incarnations of public archaeology, for example the "rescue" movement. Within archaeology itself the critical change has been from an essentially reactive response to other people's proposals, to a proactive, considered, structured, academically sound, and professionally presented strategy, that both prompts proposals and provides measured responses to them. At the heart of this is the idea that archaeological remains are a resource that has certain characteristics which shape the way it is used and our stewardship of it (Darvill 1993: 6–7). Not all archaeologists accept that archaeological materials can or should be treated in this way (Shanks and Tilley 1987; but cf. Hodder 1999: 170), but many such objections are based on attempts to reduce the differences between knowledge produced through the study of archaeology and the raw materials on which such studies are based. In practical terms, a lot of archaeological resource management is primarily concerned with the raw materials of archaeology, always recognizing that these provide the foundations upon which anyone can produce knowledge at any time. This is the political reality.

The objectives of archaeological resource management have rarely been made explicit, but may in broad terms be seen as being to:

- retain the rich diversity of archaeological remains that is known to exist in the countryside and in urban areas – the historic environment;
- facilitate the archaeological heritage in satisfying the demands made upon it by society as a whole;

- reconcile conflict and competition for the use of land containing archaeological remains.

These all relate to an evolving series of core principles and ideas that can be said to lie at the heart of modern archaeological resource management. The starting point, and one of the most fundamental principles, is that all archaeological sites and deposits are decaying to the extent that there will be less of them, and less within them, in the future than there is now. This in a sense reflects in archaeological terms the Second law of Thermodynamics: in the absence of a separate organizing force, things tend to drift in the direction of greater disorder or greater "entropy." Left alone, archaeological remains follow what can be conceived graphically as a natural decay trajectory (Darvill and Fulton 1998: 16–18). The majority of monuments, however, are subject to what might be termed accelerated decay; that is, changes to their shape, size, content, and archaeological integrity, as a result of destructive actions brought about through some kind of landuse change or development process. In the language of environmental economics, the perpetrators of such accelerated decay can be seen as "polluters." Throughout Europe, it is now a well-established principle that the "polluter pays" for the mitigation or rectification of damage done to the environment, whether this is the destruction of archaeological remains, chemical spillages, radiation leakage, or whatever. Most property developers find it rather irritating that they are castigated as polluters, because in their eyes they are actually trying to do something for the public good as well as make a living, and many are genuinely dedicated to improving the quality of life for those who will benefit from a development scheme. But equally they increasingly realize that progress, as they perceive it, has costs attached, and that not all of these can be reduced to simple monetary values.

The overarching philosophy guiding archaeological resource management over the last thirty years or so is what has been called the PARIS principle: the preference wherever possible, for Preserving Archaeological Remains In Situ (cf. Corfield et al. 1998). This is not always possible of course, and here a second philosophy comes into play, the READING principle, in which it is appropriate to Research and Excavate Archaeology Destroyed In Necessary Groundworks. Balancing these two principles involves the application of another principle: sustainability. The notion of sustainable development has been widely bandied about, and may be defined, in the words of the Brundtland Commission (cited in Clark 1993: 87), as development which "meets the needs and aspirations of the present generation without compromising the ability of future generations to satisfy their own needs."

However, despite the best intentions, sustainability has not yet adequately been translated into practical terms for archaeological resource management (English Heritage 1997); it remains another of the big challenges for archaeology in the early twenty-first century.

The underlying problem that has to be solved is that, unlike approaches to renewable resources, archaeology has to deal with non-renewable remains. This, as in the case for example of fossil fuels, seems to me to require a two-pronged attack. First, limiting consumption to acceptable levels in relation to the known supply. Second, getting the most out of what we choose to consume. A good example of what can be achieved is provided by the petrochemical industry. Here, during the late twentieth century, companies and governments invested heavily in oil prospection to safeguard supplies, while at the same time funding research into the radical redesign of the internal combustion engine in order to increase its efficiency. So, during the early decades of the twenty-first century, archaeology must focus attention on systematic survey and recording to establish the scale of the resource, while improving investiga-

tion methodology to ensure better returns from excavated deposits.

Pursuing these principles brings new intellectual and professional challenges to archaeologists, and raises a number of ethical and moral dilemmas. Foremost among these is the big issue of "who owns the past," but equally important are matters such as the treatment of human remains, the storage and disposal of finds, the illicit trade in illegally recovered antiquities, scoping and placing archaeological contracts, and the use of archaeological information for non-archaeological ends. These and other issues are increasingly being addressed and debated (Green 1984; Vitelli 1996), and while most have been in the background for some time, archaeologists are feeling increasingly uncomfortable as they are forced to confront them.

Equally worrying for many archaeologists is the fact that archaeology is only one of a wide range of environmental concerns held by society as a whole, and that these have to be balanced against other pressures arising from economic, political, and social needs. In the end, most land-use change and property development involve compromises by all parties. Although many see the process as a simple negotiation, great skill and diplomacy is needed in order to achieve the best result for a particular interest. Central to the debate are the matters of value and importance. The two are not the same, although sometimes confused, for while all archaeological deposits are valuable, some are more important than others.

I have argued elsewhere that value relates to broad socially defined perceptions of what is good, right, and acceptable (Darvill 1995). It applies not so much to individual sites or monuments, but rather to the resource as a whole. There are several alternative ways of perceiving value, most of which recognize a series of value-sets relating to archaeological remains. Lipe (1984) took a consumerist view based on types of value (economic, aesthetic, associative/symbolic, informational) within a range of contexts. In contrast, value-sets can be seen in historical context developing from medieval times through to a late twentieth-century preference for selectivity. Present-day society holds three interpenetrating value systems, or value gradients as they are sometimes known, in special regard: use value, option value, and existence value (Darvill 1995). John Carman (1996) in connection with the development of legislation and Martin Carver (1996) in relation to the formulation of management strategies have both explored these broad issues further and made good progress with defining the problems. Formal principles of accountancy and economics have also been applied to the determination of value for historic resources (Allison et al. 1996), and environmental economics are now playing an increasing role in the debate. Not all of these studies are based upon a sound understanding of the archaeological issues, and as the arguments unfold, there is a growing need for archaeologists to become more closely involved in the detail. Early contributions focused on the idea of environmental capital, and the classification of particular resources within a scheme that differentiated critical, constant, and tradable values. More recently it has been suggested that the focus should be moved from the things themselves to the idea of "environmental functions" and "services" that resources serve in relation to human well-being (CAG and LUC 1997). Here there is a big danger that some of the obvious and widespread functions that archaeological remains perform, such as a nice place to go for a Sunday afternoon picnic, will overshadow what I imagine most archaeologists would argue is the important service: the creation of new knowledge about the past.

The generality of value systems bear upon the specific question of what the importance of a particular site, monument, or deposit might be, but there is also the question of "importance for what?" Archaeological remains selected as being worthy of legal protection to form reservoirs for future research may not be the same group as would be selected for excavation now, or for the display of current understandings of the past to the general public. The matter of importance therefore relates to the aims and objectives of a ranking or discriminating operation. As such, the process of determining importance is a tool in formulating, justifying, and supporting particular arguments or actions. It is an area that, subconsciously perhaps, most archaeologists engage in every day, but making the process explicit has proved more complicated and increasingly controversial. Two main approaches to the systematic determination of importance are currently emerging within European archaeology (cf. Briuer and Mathers 1996 for the American situation).

First are the multi-judgment quantitative systems developed initially for the Monuments Protection Programme in England (Darvill et al. 1987; Startin 1993b, 1993c) but now widely applied to other situations. In this approach, defined monuments or deposits are individually measured against a series of criteria that represent dimensions of archaeological value: Survival/Condition, Period, Rarity, Fragility/Vulnerability, Diversity, Documentation, Group value, and Potential. How each criterion is applied depends upon the availability of carefully compiled resource assessments (monument class descriptions), defined research/management agendas, and the recognition of academically viable samples (Fairclough 1996; Olivier 1996; Startin 1993a). A similar system has been proposed for use in the Netherlands (Deeben et al. 1999), although here the criteria are structured into three sequentially applied groups: Perception (aesthetic value and historical value); Physical Quality (integrity and preservation); and Intrinsic Quality (rarity, research potential, group value, and representivity) (Figure 22.2).

A second approach is qualitative, and is based on the match between articulated research proposals current at any one time, and deposit legibility seen in terms of the potential of particular deposits to answer the

English Monuments Protection Programme criteria (Darvill et al. 1987)	Dutch archaeological site protection criteria (Deeben et al. 1999)
Characterization Period currency Rarity Diversity Period (representativity) **Discrimination** Survival Potential Diversity (features) Documentation (archaeological) Documentation (historical) Group value (clustering) Group value (association) Amenity value **Management Assessment** Fragility Vulnerability Condition General conservation value	**Perception** Aesthetic value Historical value **Physical Quality** Integrity Preservation **Intrinsic Quality** Rarity Research potential Group Value Representativity

Figure 22.2 Comparison of principal attributes identified in archaeological value systems.

research questions. Importance is seen in terms of the potential for knowledge and understanding. Drawing indirectly on earlier work by Groube (Groube and Bowden 1982) on rural resources in Dorset, this approach was developed into its present form during an urban assessment based on the City of York (Ove Arup et al. 1991: 3.10). Its potential in other urban areas is certainly very considerable, although it is reliant on the formulation of strong research agendas and the rigorous characterization of buried deposits.

Both approaches to importance assume that monuments are important until proven otherwise (cf. Schaafsma 1989) and rely on the careful, systematic, and even-handed assembly of data relating to all the items or areas to be considered. Smoothing out the biases in recorded data, insofar as this is possible given the history of investigations, is an important part of the process. Both schemes are also united in their need for strong, collectively agreed, and regularly up-

dated research agendas. A recent review of such research agendas found that the need for them is almost universally accepted, and that the process of creating and implementing such research agendas could be of fundamental importance in realigning and reequipping the discipline to face the challenges of the twenty-first century. A systematic scheme for the development of what is called a "research framework" has been proposed through the three-stage process of resource assessment, agenda definition, and strategy formulation (Olivier 1996). As in any academic discipline, however, there is always a danger that research agendas become either shopping lists or instruments of exclusion to legitimate a failure to support particular lines of inquiry. However, against this must be set the fact that the power of established research frameworks is only just beginning to be recognized and deserves to be explored further; one area of very great potential for future application is in the integration of archaeology with planning.

Planning and Archaeology

Integrating archaeological with spatial planning systems has been the aspiration of archaeologists since the 1960s, but it has been slow to happen. Two main approaches have emerged, both strong, and underpinned by legislation. In some states the environment is seen as a totality of which archaeology is one part. Denmark is one such case. Here, archaeology is included in the Protection of Nature Act 1992 (MoE 1993), which prohibits the alteration of ancient monuments and a protected area of 100 meters all around – in effect a cordon sanitaire. It applies automatically to all visible monuments, and to all other monuments if their existence has been notified to the owner. This latter category is extremely broad and can include, for example, stones and trees connected with popular beliefs, historical tradition, or folklore.

Elsewhere, by contrast, parallel control systems have emerged, one involving the protection of defined ancient monuments, the other concerned with the control of development. England is a case with such an arrangement. Here, since 1990, archaeological issues were firmly drawn into the town and country planning system through the publication of *PPG16 Archaeology and Planning* (DoE 1990) and *PPG15 Planning and the Historic Environment* (DoE 1994) to sit alongside the existing measures set out in the Ancient Monuments and Archaeological Areas Act 1979 (Wainwright 1993; Champion 1996). The parallel provision provides an extremely robust framework for managing archaeological remains, but although planning controls are superficially wide ranging, they do not cover all kinds of operation that are potentially damaging to archaeological deposits: agriculture and forestry remain two of the most difficult. Another problem is that, hitherto, planning in England has been highly local, the county being the largest unit for most practical purposes. Increasingly, however, there is pressure to develop a stronger regional and supraregional basis to spatial planning. The provisional identification of seven interstate planning areas within the European Union (Darvill 1997c) will, in due course, provide a still wider perspective on strategic planning, and mention has already been made of the pan-European development of Environmental Impact Assessment as a means of providing a consistent approach to development control for large and potentially harmful development proposals.

Both development control and Scheduled Monument Consent procedures need good quality information upon which to base sound judgments. The starting point is usually the national or local record of sites and monuments. In England these are not, at the time of writing at least, official records in the sense of being statutory, although they deserve to be made so. They have been the subject of much debate, however, especially in relation to their ownership, situation within local government departments, compilation and structure, and long-term curation (Burrow 1985; Baker 1999). While having good data sources physically near to where they are most used is undoubtedly very important, modern information technology means that the development and curation of archaeological records can be discoupled from the need to have them physically situated in the places where the data are accessed. This should allow economies of scale and the realization of benefits from having a concentration of experts responsible for regional or national archaeological data centers. Still more adventurous would be the integration of archaeological data servers with comparable facilities for other dimensions of the natural and built environments.

Getting high quality information in order to make decisions about the future of archaeological sites involves more than consulting existing records. Developers themselves are now expected to get involved in the process, through the commissioning of what are known as field evaluations.

Field evaluation is one of the success stories of archaeology in the 1990s, for the practice has become one of the most widely used and powerful tools available to those seeking to determine the presence/absence, nature, extent, and significance of archaeological deposits. A little of the background to field evaluation, and its origins in the idea of "trial trenching," has been presented elsewhere (Darvill et al. 1995: 6), as too an analysis of early approaches to the issues of sampling and the range of techniques deployed (Champion et al. 1995).

Since 1990 the number of field evaluations per year has risen steadily from about 500 in 1991 to more than 1,200 in 1999 (Figure 22.3). Because of the number of field evaluations being carried out every year, there have been suggestions that archaeology is in danger of getting bogged down by the kind of limited data sets that such work reveals. In fact, however, there is no evidence that the number of major excavation programs has decreased in recent years, and the advent of field evaluation should be seen as an addition to what is otherwise available, rather than a substitute for it. The criticism has also been

made more generally that planning-led or development-prompted archaeology stifles research because the process itself, rather than archaeological preferences, dictates where work is carried out and where resources are deployed. Against this must be set the argument that archaeologists tend to return time and time again to familiar territory and well-known sites, rather than branch out into new areas that might seem less attractive and less certain to yield results. One of the lessons from the motorway building program of the 1970s in Britain was that being forced to look in unpromising areas often opened up new interpretations and more balanced views of the distribution of sites (Fowler 1979). The development-prompted archaeology of the 1990s has had much the same effect again by introducing a randomizing element to the selection of archaeological samples for study. The important point here is that the balance of archaeological work is changing, and that some of that work cannot easily be judged on the basis of traditional approaches. What are needed are new approaches to the way that data are brought together and used. As

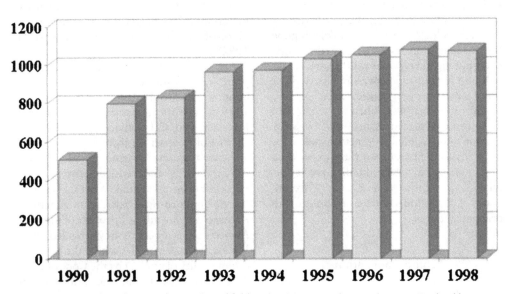

Figure 22.3   Bar chart showing the number of field evaluations carried out each year in England between 1990 and 1998. Data from the Archaeological Investigations Project.

Thomas (1997) explains, good research frameworks hold the key to this, but some progress has already been made by harnessing new technology, as in the case of Yates' (1999) study of Late Bronze Age fieldsystems in the upper Thames Valley.

One increasingly serious problem brought about by the increase in archaeological activity is the quantity of data being produced, and the matter of access to it. The possibility of drowning in data, especially repetitious data, has been recognized for some years (Thomas 1991), but solutions have been slow to arrive, despite various reviews and studies from the mid-1970s onwards (Frere 1975; Cunliffe 1982; Carver et al. 1992). No single approach is likely to solve all the problems. At a fundamental level, the creation of annual gazetteers of archaeological investigations published for England as supplements to the *British and Irish Archaeological Bibliography* provides a crucial starting point for providing an index to what is happening when and where. The data collected as part of assembling the gazetteers also allow periodic reviews of the state of what is happening (e.g., Darvill and Russell 2002). At an altogether different scale, the storing and making accessible of digital archives through the electronic sources gateway, provided by the Archaeological Data Service, offers hope for the long-term future of records laboriously put together by many different individuals and organizations over long periods of time, and at very considerable expense (Condron et al. 1999). Whether anyone will actually use these records, once the novelty of dipping into an online Internet site has worn off, remains to be seen; sadly, the experience of museums and libraries holding paper and microfiche archives of archaeological excavations is that hardly anyone resorts to the original material.

Professionalization

Archaeological resource management provides the main sphere of employment for archaeologists in many European countries, and for this reason alone it is hardly surprising that groups of archaeologists should band together to determine, endorse, and enforce professional standards. The first professional institute for archaeologists in Europe was founded in 1982 in Britain, as the Institute of Field Archaeologists (Addyman 1989; Darvill 1999b). Since its creation, the IFA has been concerned with the promotion and raising of professional standards. Its membership, which represents over one-third of all professional archaeologists in the UK, agrees to abide by the institute's Code of Conduct and other by-laws, and works to an agreed set of "standards" for archaeological projects. Five main levels of membership are available, reflecting successively higher levels of qualifications, training, and experience.

More recently, professional bodies have also been established in Ireland (Irish Association of Professional Archaeologists), Spain (Asociación Profesional de Arqueólogicos de España), and the Netherlands (Nederlandse Vereniging van Archeologen). Other countries in Europe will no doubt follow in due course. At the European scale these institutes and associations will have an increasingly important role to play in the interstate recognition of qualifications and competence (DTI 1992).

Although not attempting to function as a professional institute, the European Association of Archaeologists was established in 1994 to provide a pan-European context for archaeological activity and allow the sharing of experiences through publications and meetings (cf. Willems 1998a, 1998b). An exciting development for anyone interested in European archaeology that will one day no doubt rival the Society for American Archaeology, membership of the European Association is open to any archaeologist. Joining, however, carries with it the personal responsibility of abiding by the Code of Conduct (EAA 1997) and the Principles of Conduct for Archaeologists Involved in Contract Archaeological Work (EAA 1998).

As the European Union becomes politically powerful and more influential in the lives of its inhabitants, the need for a strong voice at the international level becomes increasingly important. This also lies behind the establishment in 1999 of the Europae Archaeologiae Consilium as a body to bring together the heads of national organizations charged by law with the management of the archaeological heritage.

At the same time as developments at the European scale serve to bind archaeology together, things are also happening at the local scale. Voluntary and amateur interest in archaeology has been one of the distinguishing features of archaeology in many countries, and as Riemer Knoop (1993) has argued, this is a tradition that deserves to be properly recognized, maintained, and indeed strengthened within the context of archaeological resource management. One of the most important ways in which this can happen is through the involvement of local communities in strategic planning, and most especially with the formulation of so-called Agenda 21 proposals to promote sustainable development. In the UK this process was begun in 1990 with the publication of *This Common Inheritance* (HMG 1990), and continued with *Sustainable Development: The UK Strategy* (HMG 1994). Both documents emphasize the way in which all sectors of society, individually or collectively, must work together, and Kate Clark (1993: 90) has argued that addressing questions of sustainable development could be the vehicle to integrate archaeological issues into the broader environmental movement. So far, however, little progress has been made in defining exactly what contribution archaeology can make and how it will work. Like the question of Environmental Impact Assessment raised above, there is great potential here, but achieving it will require a revolution in the way that archaeology and its place in the world is perceived by practitioners and the public alike.

Conclusion

Archaeological resource management in Europe has developed and changed remarkably quickly over the last twenty-five years or so, in part driven forward by broader social and political changes related to the expansion and strengthening of the EU and the breaking down of East–West barriers. Key moments in the evolution of archaeological resource management in the UK include the translation across the Atlantic of key principles and philosophies of conservation archaeology and cultural resource management; the transition from destruction-led rescue programs to problem-oriented research frameworks and the emergence of evaluation and assessment techniques; the integration of archaeological issues into countryside management; and the positioning of archaeological concerns for both development control and strategic planning within the town and country planning system. Alongside these changes there has also been the increasing professionalization of archaeology, its commercialization, and increasing role differentiation in the way it is carried out.

In one sense these things perhaps represent a maturing of the archaeological profession, and may be seen as inevitable. In another sense they continue to represent a series of challenges. Training, education, and continuing professional development are tasks that need substantial development in future. So, too, enhancing the quality and accessibility of records and archives. Archaeological data are hard-won and cannot be replicated in the conventional scientific sense; there is a huge responsibility on archaeologists to make the best of what they collect and to do it for the public good. Within Europe, after more than fifty years of dreaming, there is the opportunity now to study past human societies at a broad scale and without undue restrictions brought about by the constraints imposed through modern political boundaries. Throughout Europe, archaeology is considered a worthwhile subject to pursue. The reality is that more archaeology is being done in more places than ever before. Perhaps this makes it seem more familiar and less glamorous, but every foray into a hole in any city, town, village, hamlet, or piece of countryside is a journey into the unknown: in a sense we are still all explorers.

Acknowledgments

Preparing this chapter would not have been possible without the help and advice of many people, and I would especially like to thank Miles Russell, Bronwen Russell, Jeff Chartrand, Felipe Criado, Cecelia Åqvist, Alexander Smirnov, and others who have been pestered for information, for their forbearance in fulfilling what must at the time have seemed rather odd requests.

References

Addyman, P. V. 1989. "The role of the professional institution." In H. Cleere (ed.), *Archaeological Heritage Management in the Modern World. One World Archaeology*, 9: 302–7. London: Unwin Hyman.

Aitchison, K. 1999. *Profiling the Profession: A Survey of Archaeological Jobs in the UK*. York: Council for British Archaeology, English Heritage, and the Institute of Field Archaeologists.

Allison, G., S. Ball, P. Cheshire, A. Evans, and M. Stabler 1996. *The Value of Conservation?* London: English Heritage, Department of National Heritage, and the Royal Institution of Chartered Surveyors.

Arnold, B. 1990. "The past as propaganda: totalitarian archaeology in Nazi Germany." *Antiquity*, 64: 464–78.

Ashmore, W. and A. B. Knapp (eds.) 1999. *Archaeologies of Landscape*. Oxford: Blackwell.

Aston, M. and T. Rowley 1974. *Landscape Archaeology*. London: David and Charles.

Baker, D. 1999. *An Assessment of English Sites and Monuments Records*. Bedford: Historic Environment Conservation. Limited circulation printed report prepared for the Association of Local Government Archaeological Officers.

Baker, F. 1993. "The Berlin Wall: production, preservation and consumption of a 20th century monument." *Antiquity*, 67: 709–33.

Barrett, J. C. 1995. *Some Challenges in Contemporary Archaeology*. Oxbow Lecture 2. Oxford: Oxbow Books.

Batchelor, D. 1997. "Mapping the Stonehenge World Heritage Site." *Proceedings of the British Academy*, 92: 61–72.

Bergh, S. 1995. *Landscape of the Monuments: A Study of the Passage Tombs in the Cúil Irra Region, Co. Sligo, Ireland* (Arckeologiska undersökningar Skrifter nr 6). Stockholm: Riksantikvarieämbetet.

Biörnstad, M. 1989. "The ICOMOS International Committee on Archaeological Heritage Management (ICAHM)." In H. Cleere (ed.), *Archaeological Heritage Management in the Modern World. One World Archaeology*, 9: 70–8. London: Unwin Hyman.

Bökönyi, S. 1992. *Cultural and Landscape Changes in South-East Hungary I*. Budapest: Archaeolingua.

Briuer, F. L. and C. Mathers 1996. *Trends and Patterns in Cultural Resource Significance: An Historical Perspective and Annotated Bibliography*. Vicksburg: Center for Cultural Site Preservation Technology.

Buchanan, R. A. 1972. *Industrial Archaeology in Britain*. Harmondsworth: Penguin Books.

Burrow, I. (ed.) 1985. *County Archaeological Records: Progress and Potential*. Taunton: Association of County Archaeological Officers.

Cadw 1998. *Register of Landscapes of Outstanding Historical Interest in Wales*. Cardiff: Cadw in association with the Countryside Council for Wales and ICOMOS UK.

CAG and LUC [CAG Consultants and Land Use Consultants] 1997. *What Matters and Why. Environmental Capital: A New Approach*. Cheltenham: Countryside Commission. Limited circulation printed report prepared for the Countryside Commission, English Heritage, English Nature, and the Environmental Agency.

Carman, J. 1996. *Valuing Ancient Things: Archaeology and Law*. Leicester: Leicester University Press.

Carver, M. 1996. "On archaeological value." *Antiquity*, 70: 45–56.

Carver, M., H. Chapman, B. Cunliffe et al. 1992. *Archaeological Publication, Archives and Collections: Towards a National Policy*. London: Society of Antiquaries. Printed as a supplement to *British Archaeological News*, 7 (2): March 1992.

CEC [Council of the European Communities] 1992. *Treaty on European Union*. Luxembourg: Office of the Official Publications of the European Communities.

Champion, T. 1996. "Protecting the monuments: archaeological legislation from the 1882 Act to PPG16." In M. Hunter (ed.), *Preserving the Past: The Rise of Heritage in Modern Britain*, pp. 38–56. Stroud: Alan Sutton.

Champion, T., S. Shennan, and P. Cuming 1995. *Planning for the Past, Vol. 3: Decision-Making and Field Methods in Archaeological Evaluation*. Southampton: Southampton University and English Heritage.

Chapman, J. and P. Dolukhanov (eds.) 1997. *Landscapes in Flux: Central and Eastern Europe in Antiquity. Colloquia Pontica* 3. Oxford: Oxbow Books.

Cherry, J. F., J. L. Davis, and E. Mantzourani 1991. *Landscape Archaeology as Long-Term History: Northern Keos in the Cycladic Islands from Earliest Settlement Until Modern Times (Monumenta Archaeologica 16)*. Los Angeles: UCLA Institute of Archaeology.

Childe, V. G. 1947. "Archaeology as a social science." *University of London Institute of Archaeology Annual Report*, 3 (1946): 49–60.

Chippindale, C. 1989. "Editorial." *Antiquity*, 63: 411–20.

Clark, K. 1993. "Sustainable development and the historic environment." In H. Swain (ed.), *Rescuing the Historic Environment: Archaeology, the Green Movement and Conservation Strategies for the British Landscape*, pp. 87–90. Hertford: RESCUE.

Cleere, H. 1993. "Managing the archaeological heritage: special section." *Antiquity*, 67: 400–5. (Includes the text of the 1990 ICAHM Charter.)

Cleere, H. and P. Fowler 1976. "US archaeology through British eyes." *Antiquity*, 50: 230–2.

CoE [Council of Europe] 1992. *European Convention on the Protection of the Archaeological Heritage (revised)*. Strasbourg: Council of Europe. European Treaty Series 143.

CoE [Council of Europe] 1993. *Core Data Index to Historic Buildings and Monuments of the Architectural Heritage*. Strasbourg: Recommendation R(95)3 of the Committee of Ministers of the Council of Europe to member states.

Coles, J. 1973. *Archaeology by Experiment*. London: Hutchinson.

Condron, F., J. Richards, D. Robinson, and A. Wise 1999. *Strategies for Digital Data*. York: Archaeological Data Service. (Available on line at <http://ads.ahds.ac. uk/ptojects/strategies/ >.)

Corfield, M., P. Hinton, T. Nixon, and M. Pollard (eds.) 1998. *Preserving Archaeological Remains in Situ: Proceedings of the Conference of 1st–3rd April 1996*. London: Museum of London and Department of Archaeological Sciences, Bradford University.

Countryside Commission 1991. *Assessment and Conservation of Landscape Character: The Warwickshire Landscape Project Approach*. Cheltenham: Countryside Commission, CCP332.

Countryside Commission 1996. *Views from the Past – Historic Landscape Character in the English Countryside*. Cheltenham: Countryside Commission, CCW4.

Countryside Commission, English Heritage, and English Nature 1996. *The Character of England: Landscape, Wildlife and Natural Features*. Cheltenham: Countryside Commission, CCX 41.

Criado, F. and C. Parcero (eds.) 1997. *Landscape, Archaeology, Heritage*. Santiago de Compostela: Grupo de Investigación en Arqueología del Paisaje. *Trabojos en Arqueología del Paisaje* 2.

Cunliffe, B. 1982. *The Publication of Archaeological Excavations*. London: Council for British Archaeology and Department of the Environment. Limited circulation printed report.

Darvill, T. 1987. *Ancient Monuments in the Countryside: An Archaeological Management Review (Historic Buildings and Monuments Commission for England Archaeological Report 5)*. London: English Heritage.

Darvill, T. 1993. " 'Can nothing compare 2 U?" Resources and philosophies in archaeological resource management and beyond." In H. Swain (ed.), *Rescuing the Historic Environment: Archaeology, the Green Movement and Conservation Strategies for the British Landscape*, pp. 5–8. Hertford: RESCUE.

Darvill, T. 1995. "Value systems in archaeology." In M. A. Cooper, A. Firth, J. Carman, and D. Wheatley (eds.), *Managing Archaeology*, pp. 40–50. London: Routledge.

Darvill, T. 1997a. "Ever increasing circles: the sacred geographies of Stonehenge and its landscape." *Proceedings of the British Academy*, 92: 167–202.

Darvill, T. 1997b. "Landscapes and the archaeologist." In K. Barker and T. Darvill (eds.), *Making English Landscapes*, pp. 40–50. Oxford: Oxbow Books. *Bournemouth University School of Conservation Sciences Occasional Paper 3*, pp. 70–91.

Darvill, T. 1997c. "Archaeology and Europe: an update." *The Archaeologist*, 29: 15–17.

Darvill, T. 1999a. "Reeling in the years: the past in the present." In J. Hunter and I. Ralston (eds.), *The Archaeology of Britain*, pp. 297–315. London: Routledge.

Darvill, T. 1999b. "The IFA: what it means to be a member of a professional body." In J. Beavis and A. Hunt (eds.), *Communicating Archaeology*, pp. 35–48. Oxford: Oxbow Books. *Bournemouth University School of Conservation Sciences Occasional Paper 4*.

Darvill, T., S. Burrow, and D. A. Wildgust 1995. *Planning for the Past, Vol. 2: An Assessment of Archaeological Assessments, 1982–91*. Bournemouth and London: Bournemouth University and English Heritage.

Darvill, T. and A. Fulton 1998. *MARS: The Monuments at Risk Survey of England 1995. Main Report*. London and Bournemouth: English Heritage and Bournemouth University.

Darvill, T. and C. Gerrard 1994. *Cirencester: Town and Landscape*. Cirencester: Cotswold Archaeological Trust.

Darvill, T., C. Gerrard, C. and B. Startin 1993. "Identifying and protecting historic landscapes." *Antiquity*, 67: 563–74.

Darvill, T. and B. Russell 2002. *Archaeology after PPG16: Archaeological Investigations in England 1990–99*. Bournemouth and London: Bournemouth University and English Heritage. *Bournemouth University School of Conservation Sciences Research Report 10*.

Darvill, T., A. Saunders, and B. Startin 1987. "A question of national importance: approaches to the evaluation of ancient monuments for the Monuments Protection Programme in England." *Antiquity*, 61: 393–408.

DCMS [Department of Culture, Media, and Sport] 1988. *UNESCO World Heritage Sites: Consultation Paper on a New UK Tentative List of Future Nominations.* London: DCMS. Limited circulation printed report.

Deeben, J., B. J. Groenewoudt, D. P. Hallawas, and W. J. H. Willems 1999. "Proposals for a practical system of significance evaluation in archaeological heritage management." *European Journal of Archaeology*, 2 (2): 177–98.

DoE [Department of the Environment] 1988. *Environmental Assessment.* London: Department of the Environment. Circular 15/88.

DoE [Department of the Environment] 1989. *Environmental Assessment: A Guide to the Procedures.* London: HMSO.

DoE [Department of the Environment] 1990. *Planning Policy Guidance: Archaeology and Planning.* London: HMSO. PPG16.

DoE [Department of the Environment] 1994. *Planning Policy Guidance: Planning and the Historic Environment.* London: HMSO. PPG15.

DTI [Department of Trade and Industry] 1992. *The Single Market: Europe – Open For Professionals.* London: Department of Trade and Industry.

EAA [European Association of Archaeologists] 1997. "The EAA Code of Practice." *European Archaeologist*, 8: 7–8.

EAA [European Association of Archaeologists] 1998. "Principles of conduct for archaeologists involved in contract archaeological work." *European Archaeologist*, 10: 2–3.

EC [European Commission] 1985. "Council Directive 85/337/EEC on the assessment of the effects of certain public and private projects on the environment." *Official Journal of the European Communities*, L 175/40–8.

EC [European Commission] 1997. "Council Directive 97/11/EC of 3 March 1997 amending Directive 85/337/EEC on the assessment of the effects of certain public and private projects on the environment." *Official Journal of the European Communities*, L 73/5–15.

English Heritage 1997. *Sustaining the Historic Environment: New Perspectives on the Future.* London: English Heritage.

Fairclough, G. 1996. *The Monuments Protection Programme 1986–96 in Retrospect.* London: English Heritage.

Fairclough, G. 1999. *Historic Landscape Characterization.* London: English Heritage. Limited circulation printed report containing papers from a seminar held on December 11, 1998.

Foard, G. 1997. "What is a site event?" *SMR News*, 3: 4 (internet: <http://www.rchme. gov.uk/smrnews3.html#event>).

Ford, S. 1987. *East Berkshire Archaeological Survey.* Reading: Department of Highways and Planning, Berkshire County Council.

Fowler, P. J. 1979. "Archaeology and the M4 and M5 motorways, 1965–78." *Archaeological Journal*, 136: 12–26.

Frere, S. S. 1975. *Principles of Publication in Rescue Archaeology.* London: Department of the Environment.

Green, E. L. (ed.) 1984. *Ethics and Values in Archaeology.* New York: Free Press.

Groube, L. M. and M. C. B. Bowden 1982. *The Archaeology of Rural Dorset: Past, Present and Future.* Dorchester: Dorset Natural History and Archaeological Society. Monograph 4.

Hall, D., and J. Coles 1994. *Fenland Survey: An Essay in Landscape and Persistence.* London: English Heritage. *English Heritage Archaeological Report 1.*

Herring, P. 1998 *Cornwall's Historic Landscape: Presenting a Method of Historic Landscape Character Assessment*. Truro: Cornwall Archaeological Unit and English Heritage.

HMG [Her Majesty's Government] 1990. *The Common Inheritance*. London: HMSO. Command Paper 1200.

HMG [Her Majesty's Government] 1994. *Sustainable Development: The UK Strategy*. London: HMSO. Command Paper 2426.

Hodder, I. 1999. *The Archaeological Process: An Introduction*. Oxford: Blackwell.

Hoskins, W. G. 1955. *The Making of the English Landscape*. London: Hodder and Stoughton.

Hunter, J. 1994. "Forensic archaeology in Britain." *Antiquity*, 68: 758–69.

Hunter, J. and I. Ralston (eds.) 1993. *Archaeological Resource Management in the UK: An Introduction*. Stroud and Birmingham: Alan Sutton and Institute of Field Archaeologists.

Hunter, J., C. Roberts, and A. Martin (eds.) 1996. *Studies in Crime: An Introduction to Forensic Archaeology*. London: Batsford.

ICAHM [International Committee for Archaeological Heritage Management] 1990. "Charter for the protection and management of the archaeological heritage." London: ICOMOS.

Johnson, N. and P. Rose 1994. *Bodmin Moor: An Archaeological Survey, Vol. 1: The Human Landscape to c. 1800*. London: English Heritage, RCHME and Cornwall Archaeological Unit. *Historic Buildings and Monuments Commission for England Archaeological Report* 24.

Knoop, R. 1993. "Public awareness and archaeology: a task for the voluntary sector." *Antiquity*, 67: 439–45.

Kohl, P. L. 1993. "Nationalism, politics, and the practice of archaeology in Soviet Transcaucasia." *Journal of European Archaeology*, 1 (2): 181–8.

Kristiansen, K. 1993. "The strength of the past and its great might: an essay on the use of the past." *Journal of European Archaeology*, 1: 3–32.

Larsen, C. U. (ed.) 1992. *Sites and Monuments: National Archaeological Records*. København: National Museum of Denmark, DKC.

Lipe, W. D. 1984. "Value and meaning in cultural resources." In H. Cleere (ed.), *Approaches to the Archaeological Heritage*, pp. 1–11. Cambridge: Cambridge University Press.

McGimsey, C. R., III 1972. *Public Archaeology*. New York: Seminar Press.

Macinnes, L. and C. R. Wickham-Jones (eds.) 1992. *All Natural Things: Archaeology and the Green Debate*. Oxbow Monograph 21. Oxford: Oxbow Books.

Méndez, M. G. 1997. "Landscape archaeology as a narrative for designating archaeological parks." In F. Criado and C. Parcero (eds.), *Landscape, Archaeology, Heritage*, pp. 47–51. Santiago de Compostela: Grupo de Investigación en Arqueología del Paisaje. Trabojos en Arqueología del Paisaje 2.

Miraj, L. and M. Zeqo 1993. "Conceptual changes in Albanian archaeology." *Antiquity*, 67: 123–5.

MoE [Ministry of the Environment] 1993. *Protection of Natura Act. Act No. 9 of 3 January 1992*. Copenhagen: National Forest and Nature Agency, Ministry of the Environment, Denmark.

Moore, M. 1992. "The National Monuments Branch of the Office of Public Works." In C. U. Larsen (ed.), *Sites and Monuments: National Archaeological Records*, pp. 223–8. København: National Museum of Denmark, DKC.

Muckleroy, K. 1978. *Maritime Archaeology*. Cambridge: Cambridge University Press.

O'Keefe, P. J. 1993. "The European Convention on the Protection of the Archaeological Heritage." *Antiquity*, 67: 406–13.

Olivier, A. 1996. *Frameworks for Our Past: A Review of Research Frameworks, Strategies and Perceptions*. London: English Heritage.

Olivier, L. 1998. "L'archéologie française et le Régime de Vichy (1940–1944)." *European Journal of Archaeology*, 1 (2): 241–64.

Ove Arup and Partners and York University 1991. *York Development and Archaeology Study*. York: Ove Arup and Partners and York University for English Heritage and York City Council.

Pryor, F. 1989. " 'Look what we've found": a case study in public archaeology." *Antiquity*, 63: 51–61.

Ralston, I. and R. Thomas (eds.) 1993. *Environmental Assessment and Archaeology*. Birmingham: Institute of Field Archaeologists. *IFA Occasional Paper 5*.

RCAHMS [Royal Commission on the Ancient and Historical Monuments of Scotland] 1990. *North-East Perth: An Archaeological Landscape*. Edinburgh: HMSO.

RCAHMS [Royal Commission on the Ancient and Historical Monuments of Scotland] 1994. *South-East Perth: An Archaeological Landscape*. Edinburgh: HMSO.

Schaafsma, C. F. 1989. "Significant until proven otherwise: problems versus representative samples." In H. Cleere (ed.), *Archaeological Heritage Management in the Modern World*. London: Unwin Hyman. *One World Archaeology*, 9: 38–51.

Schofield, J. (ed.) 1998. *Monuments of War: The Evaluation, Recording and Management of Twentieth-Century Military Sites*. London: English Heritage.

Shanks, M. and C. Tilley 1987. *Social Theory and Archaeology*. Cambridge: Polity Press.

Shennan, S. 1985. *Experiments in the Collection and Analysis of Archaeological Survey Data: The East Hampshire Survey*. Sheffield: University of Sheffield Department of Archaeology and Prehistory.

Startin, B. 1993a. "Preservation and the viable sample." *Antiquity*, 67: 421–6.

Startin, B. 1993b. "The Monuments Protection Programme: protecting what, how, and for whom?" In M. A. Cooper, A. Firth, J. Carman, and D. Wheatley (eds.), *Managing Archaeology*, pp. 40–50. London: Routledge.

Startin, B. 1993c. "Assessment of field remains." In J. Hunter and I. Ralston, (eds.), *Archaeological Resource Management in the UK: An Introduction*, pp. 184–96. Stroud and Birmingham: Alan Sutton and Institute of Field Archaeologists.

Swain, H. 1991. *Competitive Tendering in Archaeology: Papers Presented at a One Day Conference in June 1990*. Hertford: Standing Conference of Archaeological Unit Managers and RESCUE.

Swain, H. (ed.) 1993. *Rescuing the Historic Environment: Archaeology, the Green Movement and Conservation Strategies for the British Landscape*. Hertford: RESCUE.

Taylor, C. 1974. "Total archaeology." In A. Rogers and T. Rowley (eds.), *Landscapes and Documents*, pp. 15–26. Bury St. Edmunds: Standing Conference on Local History.

Taylor, C. 1983. *The Archaeology of Gardens*. Princes Risborough: Shire Archaeology.

Thomas, J. 1993. "The politics of vision and the archaeologies of landscape." In B. Bender (ed.), *Landscape: Politics and Perspectives*, pp. 19–48. Oxford: Berg.

Thomas, R. 1991. "Drowning in data? – publication and rescue archaeology in the 1990s." *Antiquity*, 65: 822–88.

Thomas, R. 1997. "Research frameworks – what are they and why do we need them?" *The Archaeologist*, 29: 10–11.

Tilly, C. 1994. *A Phenomenology of Landscape*. Oxford: Berg.

Trotzig, G. 1993. "The new European Convention II." *Antiquity*, 67: 414–15.

Ucko, P. J. and R. Layton 1999. *The Archaeology and Anthropology of Landscape*. London: Routledge. *One World Archaeology 30*.

Vitelli, K. D. (ed.) 1996. *Archaeological Ethics*. Walnut Creek, CA: Altamira Press.

Wainwright, G. J. 1993. "The management of change: archaeology and planning." *Antiquity*, 67: 416–21.

Wathern, P. (ed.) 1988. *Environmental Impact Assessment*. London: Unwin Hyman.

WHC [World Heritage Committee] 2002. "The World Heritage List." WWW page at <http://whc.unesco.org/heritage.htm>. Accessed 8/11/02.

Wheeler, Sir M. 1955. *Still Digging: Adventures in Archaeology*. London: Michael Joseph.

Wilkinson, T. J. and P. L. Murphy 1995. *The Archaeology of the Essex Coast, Vol. 1: The Hullbridge Survey*. Chelmsford: East Anglian Archaeology. *Report* 71.

Willems, W. J. H. 1998a. "Archaeology and heritage management in Europe: trends and developments." *European Journal of Archaeology*, 1 (3): 293–311.

Willems, W. J. H. 1998b. "European Association of Archaeologists: new venture for collaboration and exchange." *Society for American Archaeology Bulletin*, 16 (3): 9.

Willems, W. J. H. 1999. *The Future of European Archaeology*. Oxbow Lecture 3. Oxford: Oxbow Books.

Willems, W. J. H., H. Kar, and D. P. Hallewas (eds.) 1997. *Archaeological Heritage Management in the Netherlands*. Amersfoort: Rijksdienst voor het Oudheidkundig Bodemonderzoek.

Wood, J. (ed.) 1994. *Buildings Archaeology*. Oxford: Oxbow Books.

Yates, D. T. 1999. "Bronze Age field systems in the Thames Valley." *Oxford Journal of Archaeology*, 18 (2): 157–70.

23

Persistent Dilemmas in American Cultural Resource Management

Joseph A. Tainter

Wherever public archaeology develops anew, practitioners debate how to accomplish it. This happened in the United States in the 1970s and 1980s, and in Europe in the 1990s. In North America, cultural resource management (CRM) has produced its second generation of practitioners and this question is now rarely discussed. Today, American cultural resource managers seem unconcerned with the epistemology of a now-mature field. Yet human institutions are rarely static, and American CRM has changed substantially in recent years. Few practitioners are aware that the field is now far from its origins. The changes have produced some favorable results, including programs of public interpretation and improving relations with American Indians. As American CRM has grown, though, it has ceased discourse about the key concept of conservation for the future. In the area of conservation, CRM has developed into a technical field, in which regulations are often applied by rote.

This chapter addresses two audiences: American cultural resource managers and practitioners of public archaeology elsewhere. For an American audience I intend to resurrect philosophical issues that once filled our literature. For public archaeologists elsewhere I offer a comparative perspective on the dilemmas that universally confront this field. The terms vary but the conflicts are universal: quality vs. expediency, diversity vs. consensus, flexibility vs. rigidity, rationality vs. regulation.

This chapter concerns the issues of discovery, evaluation, and preservation in North American CRM. Many topics are not discussed, and readers seeking comprehensive coverage should look elsewhere (e.g., Johnson and Schene 1987; Mathers et al. 2005). There is much to CRM in the US: state programs (e.g., Arkansas); federal agencies that hold and manage land (e.g., National Park Service, Forest Service, Bureau of Land Management, Department of Defense); agencies that affect land but don't control it (such as the Natural Resources Conservation Service); agencies established exclusively for historic resources (the National Register of Historic Places and the Advisory Council on Historic Preservation); *ad hoc* entities (National Conference of State Historic Preservation Officers); private efforts (e.g., National Trust for Historic Preservation); research programs (e.g., National Center for Preservation Technology and Training or the Midwestern Archeological Center); private consultants; programs of public involvement (notably the Forest Service's Passport in Time); and programs of relations with Native Americans, to list a few elements.

These programs exist to manage the remains of the past, use them to best advantage, and preserve them for the future. Yet the simplicity of stating these goals obscures great uncertainty and effort in the development of theory and methods. The early development of theory and methods for American CRM yielded a florescence of literature that remains the best the field has produced. Yet while the topics raised in that literature remain unresolved (e.g., Zeidler 1995; Briuer and Mathers 1996; Mathers et al. 2005), we have largely abandoned their discussion. By examining how these topics arose I will show why they remain critical, and why they should be returned to the center of discussion.

Development of American Cultural Resource Management

American CRM arose from the merger of two discrete efforts. In the nineteenth century private groups formed to preserve disappearing remnants of American history. Their initial efforts concerned buildings valued for their association with historical events or persons. By the late nineteenth century, preservation efforts expanded beyond "associative" value to include cultural and artistic qualities (Hosmer 1965: 261, 263).

While architectural preservation began in the private sector, the federal government concerned itself with prehistoric antiquities, which were little known but stirred public imagination. The government initially owned most of the land in the western states, from which individuals could select homesteads. By the end of the nineteenth century the best agricultural lands had been selected, but in this largely arid region the government still held much land containing many archaeological sites. In the southwest, architectural sites were found, fueling legends of

buried Spanish or Aztec treasure. Even without such legends the mystery of these sites, such as those on remote cliffs, produced an aura of discovery (Figure 23.1).

The government took early but contentious steps to preserve such sites. In 1896 the Supreme Court ruled that a law permitting condemnation for public use could be used to protect archaeological sites only if they were nationally valuable (Fowler 1974: 1469–73). The 1906 Antiquities Act protected archaeological sites on federal land and authorized the establishment of national monuments.

In the early twentieth century architectural and archaeological preservation progressed largely separately. John D. Rockefeller funded the restoration of colonial Williamsburg (Hosmer 1981). In the 1920s and 1930s a formal preservation effort emerged in the federal government. National Park Service Chief Historian Verne Chatelain undertook the task of establishing standards for selecting historic properties (Hosmer 1981: 565). These standards focused on "Sites . . . from which the broad aspects of prehistoric and historic American life can be presented . . . Sites . . . associated with the life of some great American . . . [or] sites . . . associated with some sudden or dramatic incident in American history" (Schneider 1935: 3–4). In these selection criteria, and in the contemporaneous Historic Sites Act (1935), the government began to formalize programs to preserve historic and prehistoric sites. The Great Depression of the 1930s found the federal government employing masses of laborers to excavate archaeological sites in such areas as the Tennessee River Basin (Lyon 1996), and architects to measure historic buildings (Hosmer 1987: 9).

World War II caused this progress to be suspended (King et al. 1977), and initiative returned to the private sector (Hosmer 1987: 10–11). The National Council for Historic Sites and Buildings formed to lobby Congress for a National Trust for Historic Preservation. The selection standards that it

Figure 23.1 Exploring the ruins of the American southwest (Holmes 1878: plate 35).

issued merged, for the first time, associative, architectural, and archaeological value (Finley 1965: 74; Mulloy 1976: 13; Hosmer 1981: 813–63). The National Historic Preservation Act of 1966 established the National Register of Historic Places, to list properties important in American history, archaeology, or architecture. Listing in or eligibility for this register determines whether a site merits federal consideration. An executive order of 1971 (EO 11593) directed federal agencies to consider the effects of their activities on historic properties listed in or eligible for the National Register. From this order developed both today's federal CRM program and a great outpouring of literature.

Although CRM has expanded in multiple directions, from public involvement to Native American relations, its foundations lie in the concerns of scholarship. Since World War II there has been massive land development across North America. The archaeological record of North America was being lost, and archaeologists urged legislation to save it. CRM arose to ensure the future of archaeological research (McGimsey 1972), and this remains a key responsibility.

Archaeological management arose *de novo*. From the early 1970s through the mid-1980s the field's intellectual founders debated and established CRM's early directions. In this period the giants of the field generated intellectual ferment that we seem unable to reproduce today. The topics addressed in this literature were those of any emerging field: Of what entities does the field consist, and how may we best find or recognize them? What are the important things to know? How do we distinguish that which is worth preserving, or even worth noting, from that which is not? These topics serve to organize this chapter. They are presented under the headings (a) units and techniques of identification, (b) regional research, and (c) selection criteria.

Establishing Units and Techniques of Identification

Archaeology is rich in potential data. A single locus may yield thousands of objects in dozens of categories. While CRM was established to protect a heritage thought to be rare, our work consists also of managing abundance. The first step in managing both rare and abundant phenomena is to determine the units that are of interest and how they may be found.

The US National Register of Historic Places recognizes districts, sites, buildings, structures, and objects (Title 36, *Code of Federal Regulations*, Part 60.4). Archaeologists usually concentrate on sites. Yet the term has various meanings. In European urban archaeology a site is a location within a city where one may excavate, while in North America any occupation locus (including a city) is a site.

Regardless of whether CRM *should* be site-oriented (rather than artefact-oriented (Ebert 1992) or landscape-oriented (Sullivan et al. 1999: 509)), regulation specifies that it *must* be. Deciding what to label a site is critical, for all else flows from this: entering the locus in an electronic database, evaluating it for National Register eligibility, and deciding whether to manage it. The simple act of *not* labeling cultural remains a site, consigns them forever to managerial and intellectual oblivion. Cultural remains not labeled sites are usually not entered into electronic databases. They can never be employed in studies of distributions or land use. Archaeologists who bestow the label "site" wield great influence.

The meaning of "site" has long remained implicit. One knew a site when one saw it, and the meaning was commonly understood. CRM, based on legal mandates, requires that concepts be explicit, or at least consistent. Implicit site conceptions no longer suffice.

The response has not been CRM's finest hour. A plethora of site definitions has appeared, most of them flawed. Some are arbitrary, others confuse identification and evaluation, while the worst suppress valuable data (Tainter 1979, 1983, 1998; Sullivan et al. 1999). A survey in the early 1980s (Tainter 1983) revealed seven types of site definitions. These emerged among only ten respondents, suggesting the prevalent lack of standardization. The seven types of definitions (and their problems) are as follows (Tainter 1983: 131).

1 *Behavioral.* A site is any intentionally used location. This gives no guidance on how to identify sites, and borders on tautology.

2 *Arbitrary.* A site meets certain criteria, usually material density, or density modified by artefact diversity and the presence of features. Such definitions are easily operationalized: if a site is any locus displaying at least five artefacts per square meter (a common definition in the US southwest), identification is a simple matter of counting. Manifestations failing to meet the threshold may go unrecorded, or be recorded in categories that merit no further consideration. One problem is that the cut-off is always set too high: by definition alone important remains are excluded (Tainter 1998; Sullivan et al. 1999). The designation becomes *de facto* an evaluation, which should logically be a separate step, and which legally must be.

3 *Inclusive.* Everything is a site, including isolated manifestations. While this relieves the investigator of having to think, it will never have credibility with land managers, who believe that archaeologists already record too much. More subtly, archaeology as a social science concerns itself with intentional or patterned behavior. To record as a site every lost or discarded bit of human debris is both to merge too much variety into a single term, and to lose the ability to distinguish the patterned from the accidental.

4 *Research potential.* Archaeological sites are those concentrations whose potential information cannot be exhausted during field recording. This deliberately blurs discovery and evaluation. Clusters of items not qualifying as sites, it is assumed, will never have value beyond what the recorder perceives. It is difficult to say whether the primary problem is

ignorance or arrogance: the investigator assumes that she or he alone knows what future archaeologists will wish to study.

5 *Research objectives.* The definition of site varies with research objectives: whatever is not of interest to one's research is not a site. Aside from the absurd prospect of hunter-gatherer researchers not considering Teotihuacán a site, this approach fails to provide for management of the spectrum of cultural remains.

6 *Content.* A site contains a prescribed list of remains. Here again the investigator is relieved of having to think, and future archaeologists are denied the chance to study anything but what we consider important.

7 *Density.* The stringency of a site definition varies with the richness of the record. Where remains are abundant only the most salient loci are acknowledged. Conversely, if one studies desert hunter-gatherers, one considers most of the little they left behind. All hope of consistency is abandoned.

Thus stood the profession's thinking on a fundamental concept in the early 1980s. A more recent assessment (Zeidler 1995) suggests that the situation has hardly improved since. We seem unable to delineate one of the most fundamental CRM concepts. This forces agencies to impose their own definitions, which tend to be formal or arbitrary. The problems of such definitions then become institutionalized, and the archaeological record selected for management becomes systematically distorted.

Once (or if) we define the entities we seek to manage, it is a matter of practicality that we find them reliably and economically. Discovery techniques are central to CRM and were prominent in its early literature.

Early archaeology in any region tends to concentrate on the most salient sites – those that are large, deep, old, or with rich artefact assemblages (Tainter 1998). Early methods of locating sites were correspondingly coarse-grained. Into the 1970s it was common in the United States to locate sites by interviewing collectors, by motorcar, or even from the air. Two developments ended these methods. The first was the interest in settlement patterns, which emerged as a research focus from the 1950s through the 1970s. The second was CRM. To satisfy laws requiring evaluation for management, sites must be found. This institutionalized the systematic, pedestrian survey common today.

The primary uncertainty in survey archaeology is the level of intensity (Zeidler 1995). Survey intensity increases with decreasing distance between surveyors and subsurface sampling. There is no such thing as a "complete" archaeological survey. With more intense inspection more cultural remains can always be found (e.g., Judge 1981: 129; Zeidler 1995: 73; Sullivan et al. 1999: 507). Archaeology is labor intensive. Increasing the intensity of survey causes the cost to rise almost linearly. Those who fund CRM prefer minimal expenditures, so surveys tend to be just intensive enough to satisfy reviewers. The costliness of survey has spawned literature on sampling (e.g., Mueller 1974, 1975) and predictive modeling (e.g., Cordell and Green 1984; Judge and Sebastian 1988). Sampling is useful to estimate frequencies, but is not useful to locate or estimate the frequency of remains that are rare or in unusual locations. Sampling and modeling involve a trade-off between economies gained and information foregone.

Establishing Regional Research

CRM acquired critics early on (King 1971, 1981; Tainter 1987: 217). Land managers, businesses, and legislators had difficulty discerning the goals of CRM (e.g., Muniz 1988). Archaeologists disagreed about which sites merited study or preservation. There were inconsistencies in fieldwork and reporting, and perceptions that some practitioners produced substandard work. Moreover, after many years and expenditure of

large sums, it was difficult to point to significant advances in knowledge (King 1981), although many sites had been saved.

The challenge was to design CRM so that it would be less obstructive, more efficient, and more productive. The solution frequently urged is the *regional research design* (e.g., McMillan et al. 1977; Raab and Klinger 1977; Goodyear et al. 1978; Aten 1980; Davis 1980, 1982; Nickens 1980; Wendorf 1980; Tainter 1987). The philosophy of such a design is that the value of an individual site cannot be assessed in isolation. The region is the context for individual sites. Regions have prehistories, and professionals know the problems and gaps in those prehistories, and questions to be resolved. A regional research design would begin by synthesizing a region's prehistory. It would then identify gaps in knowledge and important problems to resolve. Sites that have the highest value are those that contribute to resolving the identified gaps in knowledge. Specifying uniform questions enforces minimum commonality in field methods, analysis, and reporting. Progress is gauged by reducing knowledge gaps.

Regional research designs are widely accepted, and their use is recommended by the US National Park Service. Generally, they are commissioned by states, although designed for smaller areas. Programs have been recommended to expand research designs to address problems that are national or international in scope (e.g., King 1981), but the profession has mostly been indifferent to these.

Establishing Selection Criteria

Organizations such as the Society for the Preservation of New England Antiquities, established to save things thought to be disappearing, soon recognized that they faced embarrassment both of riches, in the things meriting preservation, and of resources (Hosmer 1965). Selection standards were needed so that funds were reserved for the most worthy properties. Yet to identify those properties is a vexing problem. A historical evaluation is often in effect forever. "What is a significant historical property?" is a question that has no permanent reply, but a thoughtless answer can cause lasting harm (Tainter and Lucas 1983).

The US National Register of Historic Places lists as eligible (significant) properties, districts, sites, buildings, structures, or objects that possess integrity and:

(a) that are associated with events that have made a significant contribution to the broad patterns of our history; or

(b) that are associated with the lives of persons significant in our past; or

(c) that embody the distinctive characteristics of a type, period, or method of construction, or that represent the work of a master, or that possess high artistic value, or that represent a significant and distinguishable entity whose components may lack individual distinction; or

(d) that have yielded, or may be likely to yield, information important in prehistory or history. (Title 36, *Code of Federal Regulations*, Part 60.4)

Archaeological sites have generally been evaluated under criterion (d). To be eligible for the National Register is to merit management and protection under federal law. Briuer and Mathers (1996) have categorized much literature on archaeological significance. They organized discussions of significance into 21 categories. Some of these concern selection criteria, while others discuss the significance dilemma in practice. These categories lack much in common, which reflects the rigor we have brought to the matter (Table 23.1).

There is little commonality to significance evaluations. Selection criteria may rank even below site definitions among the accomplishments of CRM. Notwithstanding this diversity, how to select sites meriting preservation remains unresolved. As with site definitions, this diversity invites standardized approaches that suppress innovation.

Persistent Dilemmas: Cultural Resource Management Today

Archaeology of the late twentieth century was diverse. Our theorists proffer many frameworks to interpret the past (Cordell 1994). Future archaeologists will undoubtedly consider this a hallmark of our time. They will evaluate whether our introspection was productive, and whether we indulged too little or too much. They will judge CRM as well, and note that the initial creativity in delimiting this field was exhausted by the late 1980s. The 1970s and much of the 1980s witnessed exciting debates on the practice of CRM (e.g., Glassow 1977; King 1971; King et al. 1977; Lipe 1974; Lynott 1980; McMillan et al. 1977; Moratto and Kelly 1978; Raab and Klinger 1977; Schiffer and Gumerman 1977; Sharrock and Grayson 1979; Tainter 1979, 1983; Tainter and Lucas 1983). Since then such discussions, with rare and ineffective exceptions (e.g., Leone and Potter 1992), have disappeared (Figure 23.2).

Discussions of selection criteria, for example, have clustered in two modes: 1976–80 and 1982–7 (Figure 23.3). The literature on this topic declined thereafter (with a secondary florescence, about 1990, on historic site significance). As the professional debate waned, governmental pronouncements on significance grew (Briuer and Mathers 1996: 7, 9). Written by officials who seek to do good, these documents sometimes create new waves of consternation even as they try to soothe others (e.g., Parker and King 1990). New officials strive to correct the problems introduced by previous officials.

One might suppose from this quietude that the uncertainties of CRM were satisfactorily resolved. Regrettably this is not so: much malpractice remains in CRM, and our closure of the literature was premature. The

Table 23.1 Discussions of archaeological significance (abstracted from Briuer and Mathers 1996: 42–4).

Discussion category	Discussion content
1 Significance as dynamic and/or relative	Significance is in the eye of the beholder, and thus can vary between individuals and change through time (e.g., Tainter and Lucas 1983; Tainter 1987).
2 General categories	Reduce CRM to manageable categories such as historical, social, or monetary value.
3 Explicit criteria	Use criteria to evaluate sites such as "integrity" or "clarity" (e.g., Glassow 1977).
4 Significance vs. non-significance	Argue that some sites are insignificant, rather than showing that others are significant.
5 Need for representative samples	Archaeologists should ensure that preservation efforts include the variety of cultural remains characterizing a region.
6 Redundancy	Well-represented types don't require further examples.
7 Regional research designs	Sites are significant if they help to address a regional research design.
8 Problem orientation	Significant sites can contribute data toward a research problem.
9 Is CRM research?	Do we manage sites to preserve opportunities for research or because legally required?
10 Archaeological preserves	Preserve areas with a variety of cultural resources (e.g., Lipe 1974).
11 Active planning and mitigation	Anticipate threats and take action beforehand.
12 Public involvement	Spend more time teaching the public about cultural resources values.
13 Ethnic	Sites may have value in the history or cosmology of ethnic groups.
14 Interdisciplinary	Base evaluations on a range of sciences.
15 Innovative strategies	We need new theoretical and/or methodological strategies.
16 Holistic evaluations	Move beyond "representativeness" toward expansive evaluations using geographical information systems, landscape-level analysis, networks of related features, and regional contexts (e.g., Briuer et al. 1990; Hardesty 1990; McManamon 1990).
17 Non-intrusive field methods	Conduct evaluations so as not to degrade sites.
18 Data-supported discussions	Base evaluations on data rather than theory.
19 Multi-phase investigations	Conduct repeated investigations to evaluate significance.
20 Adequacy of the National Register	The eligibility criteria of the National Register are either too broad, too narrow, or just right.
21 Federal guidance	Guidance to implement laws and regulations.

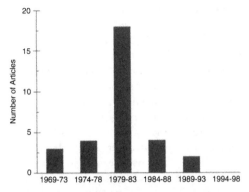

Figure 23.2 Discussions of how to practice cultural resource management in *American Antiquity*, 1969–98.

problems of units and techniques of identification, regional research, and selection criteria continue to confound much that we do. In the absence of prominent debate, CRM has become a discipline of technicians (Tainter 1998), who apply regulations by rote, and who understand poorly the implications of this practice.

Evaluating Units and Techniques of Identification

The goal of conservation is to minimize the difference between what we have today and what we pass on. American CRM fails on this criterion, for it passes to the future one segment of the archaeological record and suppresses the rest. Cultural resource management in at least the US is guided by what I have called the "National Geographic" approach (Tainter 1998). This is the notion that importance or significance lies primarily in sites that are superlative – exceptionally large, or deep, or old, or possessed of a rich material assemblage – the kind of site featured in *National Geographic* magazine. It is unsurprising that many of us hold this view, for it is implicit in how students are taught and professionals trained. When children are introduced to archaeology it is through accounts of such sites as Troy and Tutankhamun's tomb. At an early age we are taught to equate archaeology with the examination of such places. Even at university,

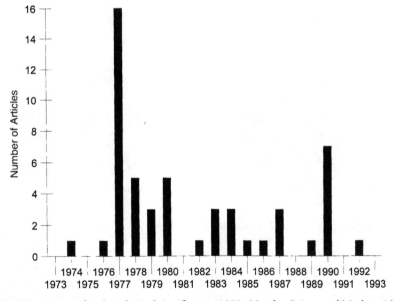

Figure 23.3 Discussions of archaeological significance, 1973–93 (after Briuer and Mathers 1996: fig. 3).

students are taught initially by accounts of similarly conspicuous sites.

CRM reveals the results of this training: the larger, deeper, older, or richer a site, the more likely it will be considered worthy of study or preservation. Conversely, the shallower, smaller, or more impoverished a site, the less most American archaeologists are likely to consider it further (Figure 23.4). The overriding but unstated criterion for valuing a site in American CRM is its *salience* (Tainter 1998). Artefacts occur ubiquitously (Ebert 1992), so that they are often seen as background noise. Salient sites are those that stand out most clearly from their backgrounds. Obvious examples include tells, barrows, mounds, the large pueblos of the southwestern US, or sites with deep, stratified deposits. Sites that are well known, either within the profession or among the public, are always salient (e.g., Fagan 1997). It is common to human perception to respond to clear signals amid a disordered world. Unfortunately, American cultural resource managers have given little thought to the implications of this bias.

The problem with most site definitions is that they exclude too much. The archae-ological record is a continuum of patterns, from those that are highly salient to those that are ephemeral (Plog 1983; Tainter and Plog 1994). The latter may consist of light scatters of undiagnostic artefacts, such as plainware pottery or stone tool manufacturing debris. Superficially they show little content, structure, or analytical redundancy. They are routinely dismissed in CRM (Tainter 1998; Sullivan et al. 1999). Yet in one study in northwestern New Mexico, 95 percent of the archaeological record consisted of occurrences so ephemeral that they would not usually be recorded as sites (Plog et al. 1978). We should wonder how well we can preserve or write prehistory relying on an unrepresentative sample of 5 percent of the archaeological record.

Site definitions that emphasize salient remains bias what we record and exclude much of past behavioral systems. Alan Sullivan, for example, examined small, surficial sites in the area of the Grand Canyon in Arizona. Few cultural resource managers regard such remains as worth their attention (Tainter 1979, 1983, 1998), but Sullivan's findings illustrate what such an attitude may cause us to lose. In the conventional

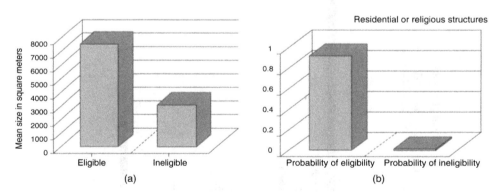

Figure 23.4 Implicit criteria for the National Register evaluation of archaeological sites in northern New Mexico. The charts are based on all Anasazi sites from the period AD 400–1600 in the data files of the Archaeological Records Management Section, New Mexico Historic Preservation Division (data provided courtesy of Scott Geister and Timothy Seaman). (a) Mean sizes of sites or components determined to be eligible or ineligible for the National Register of Historic Places. The mean size of all sites is 5,312 square meters. (b) The presence of residential or religious structures produces a probability of eligibility of 0.921 and a probability of ineligibility of 0.015.

view, southwesterners depended substantially on maize agriculture from about AD 500. Maize is commonly found in Puebloan sites and figures prominently today in ritual life. Yet in the small sites that Sullivan investigated, maize is barely represented in pollen profiles (Sullivan 1996: 154). The predominant pollen types are of undomesticated species processed at these locations.

These sites suggest a different view of Puebloan subsistence and of the importance of maize. Excavations in Puebloan-era sites have focused on pueblos, which range in size up to 3,000 rooms. Sullivan shows that to focus on these alone is to bias prehistory. Pueblos are where food was *consumed*, while the ephemeral sites are where food was *produced* (Sullivan 1996: 154). Each type yields by itself an incomplete view of Puebloan subsistence. To study or manage only the salient part of the Puebloan archaeological record is clearly an error.

In the case of foragers, alarmingly little of the archaeological record they produce is noteworthy to managers. In one study, Binford (1976) found that Nunamiut Eskimo foraging produces an archaeological record averaging little more than one item per trip. Most site definitions exclude isolated items, so this entire aspect of Nunamiut land use would be invisible to managers and researchers (Sullivan et al. 1999: 499–500). Recognizing the nature of hunter-gatherer archaeology, Thomas (1971, 1972, 1973) employed the full spectrum of the Great Basin archaeological record when he set out to test whether Steward's (1938) account of historic Shoshone subsistence was valid for the prehistoric period. The archaeological remains he studied ranged from winter villages to isolated artefacts. He was able to confirm Steward's description *only* because he considered the *full* archaeological record.

In part through site definitions, CRM excludes a great deal of the archaeological record. Our focus on salient sites limits our ability to fulfill much of what we preserve sites for – future research. This bias limits the

record that we pass to future archaeologists, and their ability to correct our errors. Numerically and fiscally, CRM dominates American archaeology. Because of this, cultural resource managers *shape* and *produce* the archaeological record. What they choose to recognize *becomes* the archaeological record.

To understand human use of a region we cannot limit ourselves only to salient sites. The record consists of sites and artefacts scattered across and under a landscape (Sullivan et al. 1999). Of course, the less salient or more elusive the cultural remains we seek, the more we must pay to find them. There is much literature on economizing in survey by sampling and predictive modeling. There are two general approaches to finding elusive things: by increasing the brute intensity of the search, which I call the *industrial* approach to archaeological survey, or by increasing the information content of the search, which I label the *post-industrial* approach.

The industrial approach to survey finds elusive cultural remains by raw power – by shortening inter-surveyor distances, shovel testing, increasing sample percentage, using mechanical equipment to locate buried deposits, and reinspecting areas. Industrial survey offers the highest certainty, but is labor intensive. It has forced cultural resource managers to try to economize.

Post-industrial survey finds elusive things by greater application of knowledge – by deploying such methods as predictive and geomorphic modeling to ascertain beforehand where cultural remains may be. The approach is to replace energy with information. Ideally this involves theoretical understanding of how people practicing different economic patterns use a landscape, combined with extrapolation from known distributions (e.g., Cordell and Green 1984). Post-industrial survey has the advantage that when we do find ephemeral remains we may understand them better, having modeled their distribution beforehand (e.g., Thomas 1971, 1972, 1973). Post-industrial survey is meant to cost less, but to increase its certainty we have spawned subdisciplines that concern sampling, modeling, and statistics. Each of these subdisciplines has its own specialists, training, literature, and debates, and each drives up the cost of post-industrial survey. The disadvantage of this approach is that survey coverage of less than 100 percent is less certain. It requires that we accept some risk.

I have presented the industrial and post-industrial approaches to survey as ideals. In practice they blend into and complement each other. Neither is inherently superior, both will always be necessary, and most of us practice a combination of each. The challenge is that if we accept the point that non-salient archaeological remains merit consideration, we are confronted with the expense of finding them. This dilemma persists whether the survey method is industrial or post-industrial. It is the timeless conundrum of price vs. quality.

Evaluating Regional Research

Kenneth Boulding once observed that all predictions are that nothing changes (Allen et al. 1999: 421). His point was that we always assume that the constraints governing conditions today will continue. If this is not so, the prediction fails. Designing regional research is a prediction of what future archaeologists will wish to learn. The matter is complicated by the fact that our predictions are based not just on science, but on the sociology and politics of science.

The public, and many scientists, think of science as the domain of lone adventurers – Darwin with his finches, Mendel with his peas, or Schliemann at Troy. This view reflects how many scientific fields did emerge in the nineteenth century. Pedagogy reflects this image: students are taught science as breakthroughs by persistent individuals. These breakthroughs are made by patient, unbiased inquiry, and they are cumulative: each increment to knowledge builds on those

before. The view of science as rational, linear, and cumulative is the foundation of regional research designs (Tainter 1987). Research designs are based on the best cumulative knowledge of the past, and direct research to provide continued knowledge accumulation.

The problem is that regional research designs are based on an outmoded view of science, and on an epistemology that is naive. Scientific knowledge is a social production. The era of the naturalist who could single-handedly establish a field has been transformed into the era of disciplines, subdisciplines, specialties, invisible colleges, and multidisciplinary teams. Research is a social activity, carried out in scientific communities (Blissett 1972: 92). Scientific knowledge is the consensus of a practicing community of specialists (Barnes 1982; Blissett 1972; Kuhn 1970, 1977; Lucas 1975; Polanyi 1958; Ziman 1968), factually based but socially derived.

The members of a scientific community are united by education, apprenticeship, ethical standards, shared goals, communication, and consensus in professional judgment (Kuhn 1970: 177–8; 1977: 296). A scientist is socialized to the values of a group. As in any community this socialization is implicit: the values appear natural and proper. The socialization process defines membership. It delimits the subject matter, specifications for research, and standards of procedure, and specifies the material that may be studied. Most importantly for designing regional research, a scientific consensus specifies the range of problems that merit investigation (Barnes 1982: 7, 114; Blissett 1972: 94; Kuhn 1970: 5, 7, 11, 25–7, 103, 109; Polanyi 1958: 217, 219; Ziman 1968; for extended discussion see Tainter 1987: 219–22).

Beyond its formative era, any scientific field functions as a social system. It exists through mechanisms that select for and perpetuate its consensus. These mechanisms range from subtle selection and training, to peer pressure, to political manipulation and hierarchical power (Blissett 1972; Blume 1974: 64–5, 78; Kuhn 1970: 5; Raab 1984: 83; Ziman 1968: 64–5, 78-9, 132, 147). Science must be so or there would be no standards of observation and inference: each investigator would, like a nineteenth-century naturalist, have to build a field anew. A social consensus is fundamental to science.

This is not to suggest that knowledge does not accumulate, or that scientific disciplines do not improve their accounts of the subject matter. Scientific disciplines tend to become more rigorous and complex, to demand higher standards of analysis and documentation, and to produce models of increasing sophistication (Tainter 1988: 112–15). The difficulty is that science presents itself as exclusively progressive. Regional research designs are based on this posture, and so ignore the fact that disciplines undergo revolutions in which previous lines of inquiry may be dropped (Kuhn 1970). To base our approach to regional research on a view of science that is incomplete, and thus misleading, is to do a disservice to future archaeologists. The fundamental problem is basing preservation decisions on the assumption that future research will be no more than an extrapolation of the present. Based on this assumption, we allow sites to be destroyed merely because they do not fit within *contemporary* research interests, ignoring the certainty that *future* research concerns will differ.

The social and political nature of science deserves prominent discussion, for American archaeology has a peculiar structure. In 1976 Michael Schiffer queried 195 American archaeologists about the state of method and theory (Schiffer 1978). Among 94 respondents, over 100 topical specialties were listed and 137 research issues were identified. The respondents recommended 150 scholars to write articles for a volume on method and theory, but the top 11 won 31 percent of nominations. Three universities were recognized as dominant in method and theory. Although this survey has not been repeated, there is no doubt that archae-

ology remains similarly diverse today (Cordell 1994: 150).

Marlan Blissett once characterized disciplines by their power structures and degree of theoretical consensus (Blissett 1972: 107–9). Based on Schiffer and Cordell, archaeology would be categorized within Blissett's framework as a *scientific plurality* (Tainter 1987: 222–3). This is a field with low theoretical consensus and few decision-makers. Thus, the challenge for managers is to design regional research programs that are acceptable to most practitioners and responsible to the future. This challenge is almost Solomonic, yet to ignore it as we do is to contravene the principle of conservation by privileging the present over the future.

Recognizing that regional research designs are a transient political process, their development should be based on the following considerations.

1   The theoretical diversity of archaeology must be accommodated without degrading archaeology's acceptability to the public and to those who fund CRM.
2   The regional research design must find a balance between consensus and freedom of inquiry. It must allow for innovation while avoiding short-lived fads and idiosyncrasies.
3   The design must institutionalize flexibility and innovation, so that promising new approaches or ideas can be accommodated (at least within the constraints of the previous point).
4   The design must recognize that long-term, irrevocable decisions cannot be based on short-term political considerations.

These are formidable requirements, and CRM has yet to face them. They suggest that any regional research design will constantly be in flux and require regular revision. Most importantly, since scientific priorities and politics change, a regional research design can never be used to *exclude* a site from study or preservation.

Evaluating Selection Criteria

Cultural resource managers approach the problem of significance or importance with the assumption that this quality is *intrinsic.* A site either possesses or lacks significance. It is treated as an attribute or dimension of a site, to be recorded on a form just as one records area and contents. Preservation regulations encourage this view. The eligibility criteria of the National Register of Historic Places state, for example, that "The quality of significance . . . *is present in* districts, sites, buildings, structures, and objects" (Title 36, *Code of Federal Regulations*, Part 60.4; emphasis added).

This view of significance originates in the empiricist–positivist tradition of Western philosophy (Tainter and Lucas 1983; Tainter 1987). This tradition holds that knowledge and meaning derive from sensory experiences. All knowledge claims must either be based directly in sensory experience, or refer to other knowledge that is so based. Since all meaning and knowledge come from sensory experience, the source of both rests *in* the observed phenomenon. The qualities of physical phenomena that give rise to knowledge are intrinsic and the knowledge to be derived immutable. The common view of archaeological significance, as intrinsic to a site and immutable, arises from this deep-seated tradition of thought (Ayer 1962, 1972; Carnap 1967; Hill and Evans 1972; Hume 1961; Kolakowski 1972; Lakatos 1968; Locke 1950; Quine 1963; Tainter and Lucas 1983: 711–12).

Empiricist–positivist thought is open to serious question. It requires the notion that we can view the world free from socialization, education, training, theoretical orientation, and personal bias. It implies that scientific views and language need never change. If knowledge cannot transcend immediate sensory experience, there is no basis for generalization. More basically, social science has shown that meaning is not tied inflexibly to phenomena, but is assigned by the human mind based on the factors that the empiricist–positivist view ignores: socialization, education, training, and the like (Feyerabend 1962; Hanson 1958; Hill and Evans 1972; Kuhn 1970; Tainter and Lucas 1983: 713–14).

Rejection of a significance concept based on empiricist–positivist thought questions much of our approach to CRM. If significance is not inherent and immutable, then it is assigned. It will vary between individuals and change over time. Our conception of significance suffers the same flaw as our approach to regional research: neither accommodates variation and change. Many sites will never be *permanently* significant or insignificant (Tainter and Lucas 1983: 714–15; Tainter 1987: 219). Mark Lynott (1980) observed this at Bear Creek Shelter in central Texas. Considered insignificant in 1947, reevaluation in the middle 1970s resulted in it being considered eligible for the National Register of Historic Places. If the significance we assign to a site can change, then to use significance evaluations to decide whether to protect a site is clearly inappropriate. We fail again to fulfill our obligations to the future.

Final Remarks

These pages hint at the topics that American cultural resource managers must continue to debate, and why it is alarming that they no longer do. There are many reasons to practice archaeological management, but it was established to protect scientific data for the future and continues to have this purpose. How best to do this is an enduring question.

Funding agencies and land managers always prefer CRM programs that are as inexpensive as possible, involving rigid research designs, high site-definition thresholds, unintensive survey, and evaluation of sites on salient characteristics. Such programs, which are commonly practiced, actually suppress valuable data (Sullivan et al. 1999) and contravene the principle of conservation. Yet the converse – flexible research designs, site definitions sensitive to low-density remains, intensive surveys, and accepting transience in selection criteria – greatly increases the cost of management. The challenge is to debate the value of current savings vs. passing to the future a sample of archaeological remains as undistorted as we can make it.

While archaeology continues its introspection, CRM persists in its long-standing tendency to divorce itself from the rest of the field. As theoretical archaeology acknowledges uncertainty, and so positions itself squarely in contemporary thought, CRM denies uncertainty and so presents itself as an anachronism. The contrast with CRM's beginnings could not be more stark. In those days, scholar-managers debated questions that lie at the core of science and of Western philosophy. Today, American CRM is a technical field, in which irrevocable decisions are made without critical thought. The era of scholar-managers has passed.

This might be acceptable if CRM faced no uncertainties. There are clearly many uncertainties. In the areas raised, we provide for the future little better today than we did in the 1970s. What has changed is that we no longer talk about it. We will always face uncertainty in preparing for the future. The questions raised here will never yield to definitive answers, so they are not offered. The point is more subtle: we will serve future archaeology better if we practice CRM in a spirit of humility, acknowledging uncertainty, than if we callously assume that today's answers will always suffice.

Acknowledgments

I am pleased to express my appreciation to Tim Darvill and Hester Davis for recommending that I write this chapter, to John Bintliff for the invitation to do so, and to John and two anonymous reviewers for comments on the first version. The data used to develop Figure 23.4 were provided by Scott Geister and Timothy Seaman of the Archaeological Records Management Section, New Mexico Historic Preservation Division.

References

Allen, T. F. H., J. A. Tainter, and T. W. Hoekstra 1999. "Supply-side sustainability." *Systems Research and Behavioral Science*, 16: 403–27.

Aten, L. E. 1980. "Historic preservation planning." *American Society for Conservation Proceedings*, 7: 1–4.

Ayer, A. J. 1962. *The Foundations of Empirical Knowledge*. London: Macmillan.

Ayer, A. J. 1972. *Language, Truth, and Logic*. Harmondsworth: Penguin Books.

Barnes, B. 1982. *T. S. Kuhn and Social Science*. New York: Columbia University Press.

Binford, L. R. 1976. "Forty-seven trips: a case study in the character of some formation processes of the archaeological record." In E. S. Hall (ed.), *Contributions to Anthropology: The Interior Peoples of Northern Alaska*, pp. 299–351. *Archaeological Survey of Canada Paper*, 49.

Blissett, M. 1972. *Politics in Science*. Boston: Little, Brown.

Blume, S. S. 1974. *Toward a Political Sociology of Science*. New York: Free Press.

Briuer, F. L. and C. Mathers 1996. *Trends and Patterns in Cultural Resource Significance: An Historical Perspective and Annotated Bibliography*. Vicksburg: US Army Corps of Engineers, Waterways Experiment Station.

Briuer, F. L., G. I. Williams, and W. F. Limp 1990. "Geographic information systems: a tool for evaluating historic archaeological sites." *Mississippi Archaeology*, 25: 43–63.

Carnap, R. 1967. *The Logical Structure of the World*. Trans. R. A. George. Berkeley: University of California Press.

Cordell, L. S. 1994. "The nature of explanation in archaeology: a position statement." In G. J. Gumerman and M. Gell-Mann (eds.), *Understanding Complexity in the Prehistoric Southwest*, pp. 149–62. Reading: Santa Fe Institute, *Studies in the Sciences of Complexity*, Proceedings Volume 16. Addison-Wesley.

Cordell, L. S. and D. F. Green (eds.) 1984. *Theory and Model Building: Refining Survey Strategies for Locating Prehistoric Heritage Resources*. USDA Forest Service, Southwestern Region, *Cultural Resources Management Report 5*.

Davis, H. A. 1980. "A state plan for archeology in Arkansas." *American Society for Conservation Archaeology Proceedings*, 7: 11–15.

Davis, H. A. 1982. "A state plan for the conservation of archeological resources in Arkansas." *Arkansas Archeological Survey Research Series*, 21.

Dunnell, R. C. 1984. "The ethics of archaeological significance decisions." In E. L. Green (ed.), *Ethics and Values in Archaeology*, pp. 62–74. New York: Free Press.

Ebert, J. I. 1992. *Distributional Archaeology*. Albuquerque: University of New Mexico Press.

Fagan, B. M. (ed.) 1997. *Eyewitness to Discovery*. New York: Oxford University Press.

Feyerabend, P. F. 1962. "Explanation, reduction, and empiricism." In H. Feigl and G. Maxwell (eds.), *Minnesota Studies in the Philosophy of Science*, Vol. 3, pp. 28–97. Minneapolis: University of Minnesota Press.

Finley, D. E. 1965. *History of the National Trust for Historic Preservation, 1947–1963*. Washington, DC: National Trust for Historic Preservation.

Fowler, J. M. 1974. "Protection of the cultural environment in federal law." In E. L. Dolgin and T. G. P. Guilbert (eds.), *Federal Environmental Law*, pp. 1466–1517. St. Paul, MN: West Publishing.

Glassow, M. A. 1977. "Issues in evaluating the significance of archaeological resources." *American Antiquity*, 42: 413–20.

Goodyear, A. C., L. M. Raab, and T. C. Klinger 1978. "The status of archaeological research design in cultural resource management." *American Antiquity*, 43: 159–73.

Hanson, N. R. 1958. *Patterns of Discovery*. Cambridge: Cambridge University Press.

Hardesty, D. L. 1990. "Evaluating significance in historical mining districts." *Historical Archaeology*, 24: 42–51.

Hill, J. N. and R. K. Evans 1972. "A model for classification and typology." In D. L. Clarke (ed.), *Models in Archaeology*, pp. 231–74. London: Methuen.

Holmes, W. H. 1878. "Report on the ancient ruins of southwestern Colorado examined during the summers of 1875 and 1876." In *Tenth Annual Report of the United States Geological and Geographical Survey of the Territories, Embracing Colorado and Parts of Adjacent Territories, Being a Report of Progress for the Year 1876*, by F. V. Hayden. Washington, DC: US Government Printing Office.

Hosmer, C. B., Jr. 1965. *Presence of the Past: A History of the Preservation Movement in the United States Before Williamsburg*. New York: Putnam.

Hosmer, C. B., Jr. 1981. *Preservation Comes of Age: From Williamsburg to the National Trust, 1926–1949*. Charlottesville: University Press of Virginia.

Hosmer, C. B., Jr. 1987. "Preservation – a historical perspective." In R. W. Johnson and M. G. Schene (eds.), *Cultural Resources Management*, pp. 5–20. Malabar: Krieger Publishing.

Hume, D. 1961 [1739]. *A Treatise of Human Nature*. New York: Dolphin.

Johnson, R. W. and M. G. Schene (eds.) 1987. *Cultural Resources Management*. Malabar: Krieger Publishing.

Judge, W. J. 1981. "Transect sampling in Chaco Canyon – evaluation of a survey technique." In A. C. Hayes, D. M. Brugge, and W. J. Judge (eds.), *Archeological Surveys of Chaco Canyon, New Mexico*, pp. 107–37. US Department of the Interior, National Park Service, *Publications in Archeology* 18A.

Judge, W. J. and L. Sebastian (eds.) 1988. *Quantifying the Present and Predicting the Past: Theory, Method, and Application of Archaeological Predictive Modeling*. Denver: US Department of the Interior, Bureau of Land Management.

King, T. F. 1971. "A conflict of values in American archaeology." *American Antiquity*, 36: 255–62.

King, T. F. 1981. "The NART: a plan to direct archaeology toward more relevant goals in modern life." *Early Man*, 3 (4): 35–7.

King, T. F., P. P. Hickman, and G. Berg 1977. *Anthropology in Historic Preservation: Caring for Culture's Clutter*. New York: Academic Press.

Kolakowski, L. 1972. *Positivist Philosophy*. Harmondsworth: Pelican Books.

Kuhn, T. G. 1970. *The Structure of Scientific Revolutions*, 2nd edn. Chicago: University of Chicago Press.

Kuhn, T. G. 1977. *The Essential Tension: Selected Studies in Scientific Tradition and Change*. Chicago: University of Chicago Press.

Lakatos, I. 1968. "Changes in the problem of inductive logic." In I. Lakatos (ed.), *The Problem of Inductive Logic*, pp. 315–417. Amsterdam: North-Holland.

Leone, M. P. and P. B. Potter, Jr. 1992. "Legitimation and the classification of archaeological sites." *American Antiquity*, 57: 137–45.

Lipe, W. D. 1974. "A conservation model for American archaeology." *The Kiva*, 39: 213–45.

Locke, J. 1950 [1690]. *An Essay Concerning Human Understanding*. Oxford: Oxford University Press.

Lucas, G. J. 1975. *The Nature of Scientific Explanation*. Unpublished PhD thesis, School of Humanities, Melbourne: Flinders University of South Australia.

Lynott, M. J. 1980. "The dynamics of significance: an example from central Texas." *American Antiquity*, 45: 117–20.

Lyon, E. A. 1996. *A New Deal for Southeastern Archaeology*. Tuscaloosa: University of Alabama Press.

McGimsey, C. R. 1972. *Public Archaeology*. New York: Seminar Press.

McManamon, F. P. 1990. "A regional perspective on assessing the significance of historic period sites." *Historical Archaeology*, 24: 14–22.

McMillan, B., M. Grady, and W. Lipe 1977. "Cultural resource management." In C. R. McGimsey III and H. A. Davis (eds.), *The Management of Archeological Resources: The Airlie House Report*, pp. 25–63. Washington, DC: Society for American Archaeology.

Mathers, C., T. Darvill, and B. Little (eds.) 2005. *Heritage of Value Archaeology of Reknown: Reshaping Archaeological Assessment and Significance*. Gainesville, FL: University Press of Florida.

Moratto, M. J. and R. E. Kelly 1978. "Optimizing strategies for evaluating archaeological significance." In M. B. Schiffer (ed.), *Advances in Archaeological Method and Theory*, Vol. 1, pp. 1–30. New York: Academic Press.

Mueller, J. W. 1974. "The uses of sampling in archaeological survey." *Memoirs of the Society for American Archaeology*, 28.

Mueller, J. W. (ed.) 1975. *Sampling in Archaeology*. Tucson: University of Arizona Press.

Mulloy, E. D. 1976. *The History of the National Trust for Historic Preservation, 1963–1973*. Washington, DC: Preservation Press.

Muniz, S. 1988. "What forest managers need to do a better job of managing cultural resources." In J. A. Tainter and R. H. Hamre (eds.), *Tools to Manage the Past: Research Priorities for Cultural Resources Management in the Southwest*, pp. 4–5. USDA Forest Service, Rocky Mountain Forest and Range Experiment Station, *General Technical Report* RM-164.

Nickens, P. R. 1980. "Regional research design in cultural resource management: problems and prospects." *Southwestern Lore*, 46 (3): 23–30.

Parker, P. and T. King 1990. "Guidelines for evaluating and documenting traditional cultural properties." *National Register Bulletin*, 38.

Plog, F. 1983. "Political and economic alliances on the Colorado plateaus, AD 400–1450." In F. Wendorf and A. E. Close (eds.), *Advances in World Archaeology*, Vol. 2, pp. 289–330. New York: Academic Press.

Plog, S., F. Plog, and W. Wait 1978. "Decision making in modern surveys." In M. B. Schiffer (ed.), *Advances in Archaeological Method and Theory*, Vol. 1, pp. 383–421. New York: Academic Press.

Polanyi, M. 1958. *Personal Knowledge: Towards a Post-Critical Philosophy*. Chicago: University of Chicago Press.

Quine, W. V. O. 1963. *From a Logical Point of View: 9 Logico-Philosophical Essays*. New York: Harper and Row.

Raab, M. L. 1984. "Toward an understanding of the ethics and values of research design in archaeology." In E. L. Green (ed.), *Ethics and Values in Archaeology*, pp. 75–88. Glencoe, IL: Free Press.

Raab, M. L. and T. C. Klinger 1977. "A critical appraisal of 'significance' in contract archaeology." *American Antiquity*, 42: 629–34.

Schiffer, M. B. 1978. "Taking the pulse of method and theory in American archaeology." *American Antiquity*, 42: 629–34.

Schiffer, M. B. and G. J. Gumerman 1977. "Assessing significance." In M. B. Schiffer and G. J. Gumerman (eds.), *Conservation Archaeology: A Guide for Cultural Resource Management Studies*, pp. 239–47. New York: Academic Press.

Schneider, J. T. 1935. *Report to the Secretary of the Interior on the Preservation of Historic Sites and Buildings*. Washington, DC: US Department of the Interior, Washington.

Sharrock, F. W. and D. K. Grayson 1979. " 'Significance' in contract archaeology." *American Antiquity*, 44: 327–8.

Steward, J. H. 1938. "Basin-Plateau aboriginal sociopolitical groups." *Bureau of American Ethnology Bulletin*, 120.

Sullivan, A. P., III 1996. "Risk, anthropogenic environments, and Western Anasazi subsistence." In J. A. Tainter and B. B. Tainter (eds.), *Evolving Complexity and Environmental Risk in the Prehistoric Southwest*, pp. 145–67. Santa Fe Institute, *Studies in the Sciences of Complexity*, Proceedings Volume 24. Reading: Addison-Wesley.

Sullivan, A. P., III, J. A. Tainter, and D. L. Hardesty 1999. "Historical science, heritage resources, and ecosystem management." In R. C. Szaro, N. C. Johnson, W. T. Sexton, and A. J. Malk (eds.), *Ecological Stewardship: A Common Reference for Ecosystem Management*, Vol. 2, pp. 493–515. Oxford: Elsevier Science.

Tainter, J. A. 1979. "The Mountainair lithic scatters: settlement patterns and significance evaluation of low density surface sites." *Journal of Field Archaeology*, 6: 463–9.

Tainter, J. A. 1983. "Settlement behavior and the archaeological record: concepts for the definition of 'archaeological site.' " *Contract Abstracts and CRM Archaeology*, 3: 130–3.

Tainter, J. A. 1987. "The politics of regional research in conservation archaeology." *American Archeology*, 6: 217–27.

Tainter, J. A. 1988. *The Collapse of Complex Societies*. Cambridge: Cambridge University Press.

Tainter, J. A. 1998. "Surface archaeology: perceptions, values, and potential." In A. P. Sullivan III (ed.), *Surface Archaeology*, pp. 169–79. Albuquerque: University of New Mexico Press.

Tainter, J. A. and G. J. Lucas 1983. "Epistemology of the significance concept." *American Antiquity*, 48: 707–19.

Tainter, J. A. and F. Plog 1994. "Strong and weak patterning in Southwestern prehistory: the formation of Puebloan archaeology." In G. J. Gumerman (ed.), *Themes in Southwest Prehistory*, pp. 165–81. Santa Fe: School of American Research Press.

Thomas, D. H. 1971. "Prehistoric Subsistence-Settlement Patterns of the Reese River Valley, Central Nevada." PhD dissertation, University of California, Davis. Ann Arbor: University Microfilms.

Thomas, D. H. 1972. "A computer simulation model of Great Basin Shoshonean subsistence and settlement patterns." In D. L. Clarke (ed.), *Models in Archaeology*, pp. 671–704. London: Methuen.

Thomas, D. H. 1973. "An empirical test for Steward's model of Great Basin settlement patterns." *American Antiquity*, 38: 155–76.

Wendorf, F. (ed.) 1980. "Report of the Fort Burgwin Conference on national archaeological policies." *Journal of Field Archaeology*, 7: 248–53.

Zeidler, J. A. 1995. *Archaeological Inventory Survey Standards and Cost-Estimation Guidelines for the Department of Defense*. US Army Corps of Engineers, Construction Engineering Research Laboratories. USACERL Special Report 96/40, Vol. 1.

Ziman, J. M. 1968. *Public Knowledge: An Essay Concerning the Social Dimension of Science*. Cambridge: Cambridge University Press.

24

Museum Studies

Linda Ellis

Introduction

People have collected items of cultural or natural history probably as long as we have expressed an interest in preserving cultural memory, in understanding the world around us or, at the very least, in placating curiosity for exotica. Moreover, the *collecting instinct* appears throughout humankind and has even been the subject of Freudian psychoanalysis (Muensterberger 1994; Elsner and Cardinal 1994). In China, Japan, Europe, Iran, and Iraq the initiative for much collecting of art and antiquities for more than two millennia has been through the efforts of private individuals, ecclesiastical institutions, and royal houses (Alsop 1982; Bazin 1967; Beurdeley 1966). The first documented public art galleries were the collections of the Greek temples, which displayed both statues of historical persons and signed paintings of the best artists. The most celebrated schools of Greek painting were organized into *pinakothekai* (from paintings on wooden planks, *pinas*), visited by both locals and tourists, the oldest mention of which was at the Acropolis of Athens in the fifth century BC (Bazin 1987: 13–14). The word *museum* derives from the *Mouseion* – a research institution, founded by Ptolemy in Alexandria, with salaried scholars, natural science collections, and

educational lectures – which operated from the third century BC to the third century AD (Bazin 1987: 16). The oldest museum still in existence is the Shō sō-in at Nara, Japan, which has continuously operated from its establishment in the eighth century AD to the present (Bazin 1987: 28, 29, 34–5). But in Europe, it was not until the founding of the first publicly accessible museum, the Ashmolean at Oxford, in 1687, that the institution, as we recognize it today, appeared in Western culture.

At the close of the twentieth century, museums have become important educational institutions worldwide – from the African continent (Nzewunwa 1994) to the Pacific Islands (Foanaota 1994). Furthermore, many First Peoples are telling their own histories through both government-sponsored institutions in collaboration with indigenous groups (e.g., the National Museum of the American Indian, Washington DC; Head-Smashed-In Buffalo Jump, Alberta) and the financially independent museums on Native American reservations throughout the US. Museums, in fact, have become ever more numerous throughout the world, with some 16,000 in the US alone, demonstrating their endurance, popularity, and their many useful roles and future potential. The museum is so firmly entrenched in contemporary society that we now rely on the institution of the museum for the preservation of our collective memory.

During the past twenty years I have been working in and with (and learning from) the entire spectrum of museums in the US and many other nations, and since 1987 I have been educating both prospective and experienced museum professionals, and advising museums both in the US and overseas. From this perspective of practical experience, I have selected some issues in museums which have received significant examination over the past decade, but all of which, despite their disparity, intersect with *knowledge* – its creation, collection, loss, dissemination, preservation, and costs. This chapter reflects the opinions of the author, as requested by the volume editor, and thus the reader is encouraged to follow up on the citations provided for expanded debate and alternative opinions. Furthermore, I have the daunting role of providing the only substantive essay on museums for this volume on archaeology and I obviously cannot do justice to this vast subject. Nevertheless, for the foreseeable future, the broader issues below will continue to be fundamental for discussion among museum professionals and students in any university degree program in museum studies.

Defining and Theorizing the Museum

The traditional definition of a museum, found in most standard treatises, is changing as both the institution and its profession evolve. The standard eight criteria usually attributed to a museum are as follows:

A *non-profit*, *educational* institution, which is *open to the public* and located in a *permanent structure*, and whose work is devoted to the *collection*, *study*, *preservation*, and *exhibition* of the world's cultural and natural heritage.

Study, *preservation*, and *education* are probably the only criteria with which no one

would disagree. However, not all museums maintain research collections (e.g., children's museums, science education centers), and not all collecting institutions develop exhibits (e.g., some herbaria, archives, archaeological repositories). Other aspects of the definition are changing as well, especially from a financial perspective (Weisbrod 1998). Museums throughout the world are finding it more difficult to rely on the economic inconsistencies of the "patron state" (Robison et al. 1994). Therefore, fundraising has become a highly specialized profession and museum shops have become major commercial enterprises – and even the subject of study (Fliedl et al. 1997). Thus, many tax issues are contentiously debated among non-profit organizations, the business community, and the US government (Fullerton 1991).

Furthermore, museums have reached far beyond the confines of their permanent buildings. Museums have developed a wide variety of outreach programs, from packing objects in suitcases and traveling trunks for public schools and hospitals, to using the railways to bring museum exhibits to remote communities – *Artrain USA* is a welcome sight for communities with populations varying from just 300 to 3 million throughout the US. The concept of the "virtual museum" has arrived and both the World Wide Web and other "new media" not only bring exhibits and services to audiences round the globe, but also will change the way we relate to our public, and vice versa (Thomas and Mintz 1998). But while the Internet and the WWW have provided museums with the technological wherewithal to make collections, exhibits, and knowledge accessible anywhere in the world, there is still too much economic disparity, with many countries and regions lacking the necessary infrastructure to effect technological accessibility. Computers are not yet a panacea while so much basic economic development remains undone.

However, if we maintain the broadest possible definition of a museum to be inclusive rather than exclusive, we may perhaps more appropriately refer to a museum as a family of educational institutions, from aquaria to zoos, including historical societies, non-profit art galleries, archives, historic houses, historical sites and districts, herbaria, arboreta, archaeological repositories, botanical gardens, planetaria, science centers, children's museums, heritage interpretation centers, natural parks and preserves, as well as the standard bearers of the name – a view of museums similar to that of UNESCO's International Council of Museums. All of these non-profit institutions have one thing in common: the creation and dissemination of knowledge – via the preservation of the physical evidence and/or by the exhibition medium – from which people of all ages and abilities may learn, through informal (i.e., voluntary or non-classroom) education.

Moving from the museum as institution to the work practiced therein, we need to distinguish between *academic discipline* and *professional practice* on the one hand, and *museology*, *museum studies*, and (eventually) *new museology* on the other. A museum must have some basis in one or more academic disciplines – archaeology, history, art, natural sciences, etc. – which is reflected in the curatorial research required for the development of the collections, content of exhibits, educational programs, and publications. The day-to-day operation of the museum falls into the domain of professional practice: administration, financial planning and development, exhibition design, educational and public programming, collections management, and conservation. Finally, we need to define *museology* – the study of museums, their origins, history, evolution, and roles in society, culture, the economy, and politics – vs. *museum studies* – the analysis of internal museum functions, operations, organization, and professional practices.

Over the past fifteen years a number of provocative and timely publications have appeared which have examined how museums order their universe of space,

time, and collections; how museums create and control culture and knowledge; how they have participated in the maintenance and reproduction of socioeconomic class relations; and how they have developed with and benefited from colonialism and the growth of the capitalist system (Lumley 1988; Vergo 1989; Pearce 1992; Bennett 1995; Macdonald and Fyfe 1996). The now semi-established phrase *new museology* (Vergo 1989) focuses on the museum as an "object" of sociocultural study from the perspective of the late twentieth century, and examines museums as artefacts of Western capitalist society, which can and should be evaluated as any social–political–economic institution in any culture. The work of artist/curator Fred Wilson serves as an exemplar and is illustrative of the general trend in the field of cultural studies. Wilson's exhibitions focus on ironic juxtapositions of objects from art, history, and archaeology in order to reveal latent biases based on class, race, and gender relations, not only in museums but also pervasive throughout society (Corrin 1994). In this postcolonial, postmodern era, we have become, essentially, anthropologists and sociologists examining ourselves, and the questions raised below reveal our cultural paradigms, the nature of museums and their ideological foundations.

Cultural criticism of museums has evolved from a number of assumptions which had never been sufficiently addressed heretofore. How and why did the idea of a museum originate? What is the social-psychological meaning of space inside the museum and the organization of its collections? Why are museums important and to whom? Are museums creating culture as well as knowledge and, if so, for whom and for what purposes? What is the relationship between museums and the nation-state? How do museums perpetuate class-based society? Criticism of museums has focused on every museum function, including (1) object acquisition (how objects are acquired and from whom, what are the original sources of objects), (2) research (how decisions are made on what will be collected and exhibited), (3) exhibition and interpretation (whose culture will be represented and where, whose voice is being heard in the exhibit text), (4) visitor studies (who is/is not visiting the museum, are all *publics* being served equally, do museums understand their visitors and their needs), (5) finances and management (how do sources of funds affect decision-making, how do governments control their nations' museums).

For the archaeological readership, some of these questions might be translated as follows: Why is there a preference for exhibiting the best examples of ancient "art"? Why do museums select cultural objects from mostly the upper classes of the ancient world? Why is the archaeology of literate societies (Greece, Rome, Near East, China) usually collected by and displayed in art museums, whereas that of colonized areas (Americas, Australia, Africa) is often displayed in natural history museums? What does it say about our ideas of value that certain archaeological objects are often exhibited on a pedestal and isolated under sterilized vitrines? Whose opinion is being represented in the exhibitions of non-Western cultures? How were those perfect Greek and Native American pots acquired by the museum or by their former owners? Who has the right to own the past? Did anyone give permission? Did anyone even ask? These are abstruse questions on the interrelationships of power and authority with no black-and-white answers, but they are very important to ask and both the museum and archaeological professions will be judged by the forthrightness and humanity of their responses.

Moving from academic criticism of museums to the practical world of museum operation, I have heard consternation among museum colleagues over the term *new museology*, which in many respects is also justified. Unfortunately, *new* automatically implies *antiquated* or redundant; and museum employees, never mind the legions of volunteers upon whom we depend, sense that their years of good service to society, contributions to the profession, and innovations in museums are being ignored. Furthermore, as a workplace 52 weeks per year, museums must address many long-term issues: providing educational services to underfunded public school systems; maintaining vigilance over the inevitable deterioration of unique collections; competing with numerous other social service, cultural, scientific, and health organizations for the same pot of philanthropic funds; fighting politicians (who control public funding) on censorship issues; preparing facilities in earthquake, flood, and fire zones; and dealing with legal compliance issues ranging from hazardous waste to tax liability. Finally, too little recognition is accorded those museum employees and community volunteers around the world who commit acts of unparalleled heroism to protect museums and their collections in times of war, revolution, and natural disaster (Varshavskii and Rest 1985; Caygill 1992; Saunders 1992; Al-Radi 1992; Belmarić 1992; Tribolet 1967).

Critical evaluation through academic journals and books is necessary for the development of one's discipline; however, the perceived reproach of someone else's workplace can be misunderstood and at the very least needs to be accompanied by constructive, low-cost solutions. The very act of publication is a political and powerful privilege and most museum employees (with the exception of those at larger institutions) have little access to these avenues. Rather, the *culture* of museum work is that collegial communication and the process of "publication" takes place through oral tradition, and not necessarily through the print medium. In fact, most of the innovations in all aspects of museum operation are transmitted via annual meetings of associations of museum employees, professional workshops, and colleague networks, where information is freely given without insistence on acknowledgment – a civility which is rare among other professions. Thus, I would encourage critics of museums to hear the voices of the "other" and to provide realistic solutions through collegial dialogue at regional and national meetings of museum associations.

Without a doubt, the analysis of museums is timely and the ideas and questions raised are very much needed for a healthy reexamination of the profession and improvement in museum services. After all, *new museology* is really about *asking*, rather than dictating – *asking* the community to participate in museum life, *asking* cultural groups for their advice on exhibitions and knowledge about collections, and *asking* more questions about provenience and ownership.

Knowledge Workers and Knowledge Organizations

Robert Janes (1997), Director of the Glenbow Museum (Calgary), has referred to museums as *knowledge organizations* and their employees as *knowledge workers*. As much as schools, universities, and libraries, museums are also in the business of knowledge, not only its creation and dissemination, but also its preservation via the physical evidence (i.e., the object). The more prominent of the knowledge workers, the *curator* (or *keeper* in the UK), is an academic subject specialist upon whom the museum, its director, and governing board can rely, firstly, to make cogent and reliable decisions on the growth and evolution of the museum's collections; secondly, to be able to identify, classify, and interpret the collections; and thirdly, to formulate both the content of individual exhibits and the long-range planning for exhibitions. While the creation of knowledge has traditionally been the responsibility of the curator, in actuality, however, most employees of the museum are knowledge workers: from registrars tracking and documenting information, conservators preserving information, exhibits and graphics staff designing information, public

relations and fundraising staff marketing information, educators translating curatorial information, to volunteer docents (guides) explaining information.

In the act of creating knowledge, the curator relies upon both *research* and *connoisseurship*, again two terms which are not always clearly differentiated. *Research* refers to the methodological processes used to reveal facts or information which were hitherto unknown (i.e., a contribution to and a furtherance of knowledge). *Connoisseurship* involves a mature, intellectual judgment about an object or collection based on years of continuous analysis of relevant objects of study and the accumulated experience of examining such objects, so that they can be accurately identified, attributed, and understood in their appropriate context. A connoisseur is capable of undertaking research; the researcher, however, may in time develop a certain degree of connoisseurship. Connoisseurship in art history and art museums has been critiqued as a subjective process that is the result of socialization and enculturation within class-based society, rather than a purely aesthetic response to art (Bourdieu 1979; Bourdieu and Darbel 1990; Price 1989). I would advocate a broader definition of connoisseurship, moving beyond aesthetics, referring more to academic expertise in all museums regardless of discipline, and encompassing not only the breadth and depth of knowledge necessary to make connections among objects, knowledge, and society, but also, most importantly, to communicate that story to the public.

Knowledge, pedagogy, and illiteracy

University- and museum-based scholars again face a great divide by way of the *publics* that they serve and also in the methods of presentation of their subject matter. Museums open their doors to people from all walks of life, including adults, families, schoolchildren, senior citizens, immigrants, tourists, and local residents, all of whom come from many socioeconomic backgrounds and educational levels. The presentation of knowledge to the general public in a museum setting requires recognition of and respect for the variety that exists in humanity. The responsibility to communicate as much knowledge as is feasible is truly a daunting pedagogical task, especially to offset deficiencies in underfunded public educational systems. For archaeology in museums, the pedagogical issues are compounded by the disinformation emanating from the media (Stone 1989) – especially with respect to the relationship of dinosaurs to *Homo sapiens* – as well as the generally poor knowledge of historical chronology and geography. But in their very role of creators and disseminators of knowledge, museums also have the opportunity to be agents of social change, especially in the eradication of illiteracy.

If the truth were told, the presentation of knowledge in museums largely depends on the outcome of numerous battles between objects and words competing in the war over finite gallery space and for visitors' very limited attention span. During the eighteenth and nineteenth centuries it was common practice for museums of all academic disciplines to attempt to show the entirety of their collections and, in so doing, objects were often mounted vertically ceiling to floor, across the entire wall, revealing little or no white space and no room for didactic labeling. In the absence of any pedagogical research, nineteenth-century museums were considered "civilizing" influences – the act of simply gazing at objects was thought to educate the viewer and therefore showing more objects would accomplish this task better. However, since the early decades of the twentieth century, museums have developed remarkably efficient ways of presenting *knowledge*, rather than just objects in space, and to make that knowledge accessible to the many publics who visit the museum. Thus, museums have produced over sixty years of sound and pioneering research in the fields of visitor psychology, informal education, and especially the pedagogy of reading (Melton 1996; Melton et al. 1996; Berry and Mayer 1989; Miles et al. 1988; Hooper-Greenhill 1991; Hein 1998; Serrell 1997; Blais 1995).

One might be tempted to ask, how can illiteracy be addressed in institutions so dependent on the written word? Many museums internationally have assumed a role as agents of social change, and combating illiteracy – the ultimate barrier to knowledge accessibility – is a major issue where museums, as creators and disseminators of knowledge, can have an impact. Illiteracy, in the strictest sense, includes those persons who cannot read and write at all and those who learned a writing system but still have difficulties in reading – both situations having arisen usually because of lack of access to education, recent immigration, socioeconomic pressures to terminate education too early, or due to undiagnosed or neglected learning disabilities. In a wider sense, "illiteracy" also includes the more pervasive problem of insufficient knowledge of basic subjects ("math literacy," "science literacy," "cultural literacy") deemed important in contemporary industrialized society. Museum professionals in Canada have been at the forefront of innovative, no-nonsense, applied research in museum pedagogy that may not be as well known as it should be. Canadian museums have confronted and discussed such difficult issues, and for a long time have been developing and implementing experimental educational and multicultural programs, for both urban and rural populations, incorporating effective exhibition techniques, and forming alliances with other social service organizations (Dubinsky 1990).

Illiteracy is both an urban and a rural problem, but statistically illiteracy is higher in rural areas, which also have the highest rate of unemployment and the least access to knowledge. On a larger scale, and particularly germane to this volume, are the benefits, to archaeology and ultimately to museums, which accrue from improving relations with rural populations. Both field and museum researchers need to develop more proactive programs of inclusion. It has been amply demonstrated that all people, if given an opportunity, have a genuine interest in the past, and much effort to present archaeology to the public has already been made (cf. Smardz and Smith 2000; Jameson 1997). However, including rural populations in fieldwork in a productive way, and providing education about local cultural heritage through museum outreach, especially through literacy programs, may contribute to a much needed support base for archaeology as a profession, for preservation of unexcavated sites, and for protection of standing monuments. This is certainly not inexpensive, nor is the only issue involved looting or vandalism, but given the many threats against archaeological sites – as well as the Western attitudes and malpractices which gave rise to the repatriation movement among First Peoples – the loss of knowledge by maintaining the current status quo will continue to rise.

The taphonomy of knowledge

The processes of *information loss* and *gain* throughout the production–use–discard cycle of objects, the history of objects upon removal from their cultural context, and the human behavior associated with ownership, have a direct impact on research, connoisseurship, accuracy, and precision in the production and presentation of knowledge by museums. The general public relies on the museum, as a knowledge organization, for the authenticity of objects on display, for the accuracy of the information presented in text, and for the integrity of the museum in the level of precision embedded in that information. The terms *accuracy* and *precision* refer, respectively, to the veracity of information ("Yangshao is one of the Neolithic cultures of China") vs. the reproducibility of the information ("The

age of the materials in this Yangshao grave is 4000 BC ± 300 years, based on both thermoluminescence and carbon-14 dating methods"). Accuracy and precision do become important issues for museums when we use interpolation or extrapolation in the restoration of objects or the reconstruction of environments or events – all of which are acts of interpretation. The public rarely questions, or is able to evaluate, the *accuracy* of information provided in exhibits, but quite interestingly ordinary museum visitors of any age group spontaneously, and often, ask questions that relate to *precision* (How do you know that? How can you be so sure?). For archaeologists and curators alike, objects can pose problems of attribution, taxonomy, and interpretation. Many objects surviving from the past and acquired by a museum may not be readily identifiable with respect to their history, function, and provenience. Since there is always a close association between what an object is thought to be and how it is then interpreted, museums of any academic domain need to be vigilant of what I would term the *taphonomy of knowledge*.

The archaeological term *taphonomy* is used here in a different context, but not incongruous with its original application, in order to remind ourselves of our responsibility in the creation of knowledge. In archaeology, taphonomy refers to the processes and agents responsible for deterioration, change, and loss in the archaeological record prior to excavation and the effects of these chemical, biological, and physical changes and loss of information on subsequent analysis, interpretation, reconstruction, and theory about human cultural development. In museums, we have a situation not unlike that met in field archaeology – how has the object itself survived? – but with two additional, and important, factors: which object will be selected for survival and what implications does this have for the taphonomy of knowledge?

The taphonomy of knowledge for any object or specimen in any museum – whether history, natural sciences, arts, or culture – is going to depend on all the selection *agents* and selection *processes* before and after acquisition, and these will dictate what knowledge will be created and any subsequent interpretation for the general public. For archaeological objects deriving from scientific excavations, both selection agents and selection processes intercede not only in the burial environment, but also at the point of archaeological site discovery and excavation. Which site (if there are multiple choices) will eventually be chosen by the archaeologist? Once decided, how much money there is available for excavation (among many other factors) will determine what percentage of the site can be excavated. In the process of excavation, which of the finds will be taken back to the laboratory and/or museum? Selection processes and agents affecting objects *not* deriving from scientific fieldwork reflect how these objects were "brought to light" in the first place and afterwards from the decisions unique to each individual owner. Did looters, middlemen, or dealers tamper with the object in order to increase its selling price? Which objects were chosen by private collectors, how and which objects were disposed of by their owners, and which objects eventually make their way to a museum by way of gift? On the museum side, the selection processes and agents reflect decisions made by the curator and museum management. Since not all objects available are pertinent or useful to the museum's mission, which objects offered for donation will be accepted by the museum? If the museum has an acquisitions fund, which of the objects available on the open market will be selected for purchase? For objects already in the museum's collection, which objects will be chosen to support the storyline of the exhibit (while others remain in storage)? If objects relevant to the exhibit exist in the collections of other museums or private individuals (and pending funding!), which objects will the curator decide to borrow for the exhibition and why?

How an object survives "life after excavation" will also determine what *information* about that object will have deteriorated, changed, disappeared, or will have been reconstructed or even invented. Survival of information, like survival of the object itself, is dependent not only on deterioration by chemical and biological agents above ground, but also on human taphonomic agents – responsible vs. neglectful owners (Sax 1999), the fate of owners and their collections in war (Simpson 1997) – or taphonomic processes introduced by humans – on-site cleaning and packaging of archaeological finds, museum conservation (intervention and arrest of chemical or biological deterioration), restoration (repair and reconstruction), and preservation (passive methods of preventative care) – any one of which could have been conducted with varying degrees of success depending on the collections' care expertise and analytical technology available at the time.

At any point along the journey for survival, information about an object can be added, lost, changed, reconstructed, or even invented as a result of deterioration, human decisions, selection processes, or other factors. These taphonomic processes and agents at work – changing in one way or another both object and information – leave the curator in a quagmire as to retrieval of information and how much can be known about an object. Curators learn to deal with what they have, communicating to the public only what is the best available information. Therefore, we return to our two earlier concepts of accuracy and precision. While both are clear objectives of any researcher or connoisseur, we must accept the fact, that in our struggle for accuracy and precision of information, we will never achieve completion of knowledge – the taphonomic processes and their magnitude simply will not allow that. For all its detractors, the museum's responsibilities in the acquisition, understanding, and interpretation of objects – as imperfect and culturally embedded a process as *any* human endeavor – are an enormous challenge, based on what little has survived, but more regretfully on what must have been lost.

Red herrings

As in any good detective story, the museum world is rife with red herrings – those false-hoods, misleading information, investigative dead-ends, and numerous other ways which detract from the path to knowledge. High market prices for antiquities, art, fossils, and historical materials have led not only to looting of sites and theft from museums, but also to fraud. Even though the public finds the topic of fakes quite entertaining, especially when told by the former director of the Metropolitan Museum of Art (Met) (Hoving 1996), the effects of forgeries of art, archaeological, historical, ethnographic, and palaeontological objects are considerably more ominous. Both individual owners and museums, equally and often, fall victim to the deliberate falsification of authenticity. Because archaeological objects worthy of museum display are a finite resource and rare commodity, and because the knowledge base will always be incomplete, the production and marketing of archaeological forgeries has been rampant throughout Europe and in many other countries ever since people expressed an academic and commercial interest in the past. Museums, with all of their academic resources, have made some serious mistakes in acquisitions, such as the Etruscan terra-cotta warriors who were for a long time the logo of the Met in New York City (von Bothmer and Noble 1961; Jeppson 1970) and the yet unresolved (and very expensive!) saga of the Greek *kouros* at the J. Paul Getty Museum in California (Margolis 1989; Hoving 1996: 279–310). Nevertheless, and to their credit, museums have even turned their acquired fakes into exhibits, the most comprehensive of which was the exhibit *Fake?* at the British Museum in 1990 (Jones 1990) and which is notable for the clarity and comprehensiveness of information presented for public education.

The contamination of the knowledge base can occur in abstruse ways completely unbeknownst to both the archaeological and museum communities. For three decades, Oscar Muscarella (2000), an archaeologist and curator at the Metropolitan Museum of Art, has investigated how an archaeological culture, or provenience, was invented, then slowly and methodically infiltrated Near Eastern archaeology. This was not a case of a cunning character producing fake objects (that would be too simple). Rather, this is a dangerous case of inaccurate "knowledge" presented with remarkable "precision," as a result of too much reliance on the presumed veracity of published opinion and successive layers of reproduced misinformation. Unclear provenience, muddled research, faux connoisseurship, and antiquities-dealing all contributed to an illusion of knowledge. Unfortunately, only regional specialists would probably appreciate the depth of detail presented. However, Muscarella's work is important reading for all museum curators and archaeologists alike who, it is guaranteed, will find and start to question analogies in their own areas of expertise.

Excavating the museum

In a conversation with the late Professor Cyril Stanley Smith of MIT in 1979, he told me that the best thing archaeologists could do was excavate their own museums. This idea raises two issues worth commenting on and relates specifically to archaeology: the research neglect of museum collections and the repatriation movement. Firstly, there is a justifiable tendency among most archaeologists to focus their energies on surveying, excavation, and analysis. Once the field campaigns are finished and the results published, archaeologists then set their sights on other projects. The awful truth about archaeology is the curious *neglecting instinct* towards these accumulated field collections that ensues after publication. Furthermore, as salvage or rescue archaeology (including cultural resource management (CRM) in the

US) has escalated in the West since the 1970s, these collections remain not only unstudied for the most part, and therefore no longer contributing to knowledge, but also abide in oftentimes abysmal storage conditions in various types of governmental repositories (Ford 1984).

It is a tacit but erroneous assumption in archaeology that both types of field collections – either from systematic or salvage excavations – are thought to have outlived their usefulness as a source for more information once they are retrieved and published. In fact, nothing could be further from the truth. This is not meant to be unfairly critical to archaeologists (as an archaeologist myself, I have been conducting research in Romania for over twenty years). But, as in any culture, we learn the rules for career success from those who teach us. While we are graduate students, we observe our professors driven by university hiring policies and tenure decisions, which, together with the archaeological profession itself, place more value on *new* and *newsworthy*, scientifically conducted excavations, as opposed to the reanalysis of museum collections with the aid of rapid advances in analytical technology.

The second issue mentioned above – the idea of "excavating" a museum – was considerably more prophetic than anyone at that time could have ever imagined, for, in the decade to follow, the repatriation movement would bring a confusing period of urgency in museums and in the field of archaeology, especially in the United States. At once, both university archaeologists and museum employees were taken aback by the thought of repatriating the enormity of their stored collections. With the passage of repatriation legislation in 1990, archaeologists and museums in the US finally realized the lost opportunities for the retrieval of information from older collections and the prospects for expansion of knowledge.

Ironically, repatriation may have served academia well in one aspect, by encouraging archaeologists to consider on a more consistent basis what many art museum curators have known for a long time (Young 1967, 1973; England and van Zeist 1985): that analytical technology from the physical and biological sciences can be used in a non-destructive or minimally destructive way to extract new and often surprising information from long-forgotten museum collections (cf. Cantwell et al. 1981). It is ironic that analysis of archaeological finds via archaeometry (or archaeological science), while having a long tradition in archaeology, is hardly ever done once the collections go to storage. Furthermore, when materials from current excavations are submitted for analysis, the results are often an appendix to, and not well integrated in, the published archaeological report, or are published separately in specialized scientific journals (e.g. *Archaeometry, Journal of Archaeological Science*).

The scientific neglect and lack of analysis of stored field collections also has a negative impact on how archaeology is taught at colleges and universities: Firstly, field archaeologists seldom use museum collections in their teaching, preferring convenient 35 mm slides rather than providing students with hands-on experience with objects. Secondly, students of archaeology are generally not encouraged by their professors to do museum-based research as a complement to field research. Thirdly, archaeology is generally organized within the social sciences, whose undergraduate students both enter and exit universities usually with an inadequate education in, or fear of, the physical or biological sciences (propagating even more the lack of integration of archaeological and archaeometric results). Therefore, it should be made clear to students anticipating a career in archaeology that (1) a basic understanding of DNA research, radiometric and optical dating methods, trace element and isotopic methods of chemical analysis, and scanning electron microscopy, for example, will prove to be absolutely necessary for implementation of any new archaeological field program; and (2) the worldwide plundering of archaeological sites will require the "reexcavation" and scientific analysis of collections in museum storage.

Collecting Objects, Losing Knowledge

Patrimony and "patrimoney"

Museums with archaeological materials acquired their collections usually in any one of the following ways: through donations of objects by private individuals, as designated repositories for the results of archaeological excavations, or by purchase from dealers or auction houses. Each one of these acquisition methods has the potential to raise serious ethical and legal issues, depending on the location of the museum, who conducted the archaeological excavation (if any was conducted at all), and the origin and authenticity of the objects. It is perhaps safe to say that, *if* an object was legitimately excavated from public land, with the requisite permissions, by a recognized archaeologist, in a country which was not colonized in the past 500 years, and excavated while that country enjoyed a democratically elected government, and *if* this object was then promptly donated to a museum in that same country, *then* the museum could probably expect to keep that object. If acquisition of an archaeological object does not meet all of these criteria, then at some point in the future, questions could be raised. Obviously, most museum collections of archaeological objects throughout the world do not have such a straightforward provenience or genealogy of ownership.

In nations where there is a history of substantial private collecting of art and antiquities, and a tradition of philanthropy, donation of objects to museums is commonplace, for reasons ranging from personal recognition to reduction in tax liability. For an individual to own an antiquity, that object would probably have to have been purchased through any number of venues: antiquities dealers, public auctions, or (quite literally)

off the street. However, if one traces back these purchases, it is only logical that an antiquity had to have come from some archaeological site, and herein lies an ugly truth which no one in the art market and very few in the museum world find comfortable discussing. Looting – which includes clandestine excavation during peacetime, rampant theft during civil unrest or natural disaster, and wartime pillage – has been a well documented activity since antiquity (Treue 1960) and is still one of the main channels by which archaeological objects end up in private hands and eventually get donated or sold to museums (Renfrew 2000; Chamberlin 1983; Simpson 1997). It is sometimes surprising to be made aware of the wide variety of individuals who participate in looting in one way or another – it is not just army conscripts, the peasantry, or local get-rich-quick middlemen, but equally guilty are high-ranking military officers, misguided scholars, missionary clergymen, auction house employees, licensed dealers, and titled individuals from the aristocracy (D'Arcy 1993; Nicholas 1994; Watson 1997). These activities may be more or less organized, from individual initiative, to local gangs, facilitation by organized crime, or as a government directive in wartime.

A thief cannot transfer rights of ownership (*title*), no matter how many sales or gift transactions have transpired since the original theft, and regardless of the innocence and ignorance of the buyer – although statutes of limitations may limit property claims. Moreover, when a museum acquires an object either as a gift from a donor or through purchase on the antiquities market, the museum will inherit any preexisting problems with the transfer of title, as well as being a participant, if only indirectly, in the web of looting. However, the unspoken assumption among art and antiquities collectors is that the more times an object has exchanged hands, psychologically the more "sanitized" that ownership becomes in the minds of the participants, hence the continued social prestige attached to the collecting of antiquities and the accolades accorded upon their donation to museums. The irony here is that, even with sales receipts and generations of well documented chains of ownership, neither individuals nor museums have clear title to those antiquities which did *not* come from scientific excavations and for which permission was not received. Many museums – e.g., Harvard University's museums (Peabody Museum of Archaeology and Ethnology, Fogg Art Museum, Busch-Reisinger Museum, Dumbarton Oaks Collection), University of Pennsylvania University Museum, and numerous others – do self-police through strict policies of not accepting antiquities without clear provenience and the requisite permissions (Bator 1988: n. 144). However, other museums still rely on donations by private collectors and on the antiquities market to expand their collections, and in so doing become part of the looting "food chain." A few representatives of the various parties to antiquities collecting have engaged in some dialogue (Messenger 1989), but the vast financial interests may just be too powerful for the business to change significantly (Watson 1997).

In order to prevent and prosecute theft and illegal trafficking in cultural patrimony, three levels of international agreements and/or legislation exist: the UNESCO Convention on the Means of Prohibiting and Preventing the Illicit Import, Export and Transfer of Ownership of Cultural Property (1970), bilateral agreements between nations (such as those between the US and other nations to return specific classes of archaeological materials which were illegally exported), and some form of national cultural protection legislation which most countries have enacted for their own patrimony. However, legislation is one issue; law enforcement is quite another. David Lowenthal (1994: 109) has stated: "So numerous and powerful are looters of Mexico's 30 million burial sites that they have their own unions and government lobby." In Africa – which has not received as much press – it is not just

the archaeological sites that are looted, but the museums themselves are also at an enormous, if not greater, exposure to theft (ICOM 1995; Schmidt and McIntosh 1996). Even with the experience of nearly 100 years of antiquities legislation in the US and despite a few, well publicized successes (Smith and Ehrenhard 1991) and laudable efforts to strengthen cooperation between archaeologists and law enforcement professionals (Hutt, Jones, and McAllister 1992), it is apparent that no government initiative anywhere in the world can be remotely effective in curbing looting if the psychological and economic roots of the problem are not addressed.

Firstly, the psychological background to both collecting and looting phenomena is in dire need of research, and yet may prove to be critical to eliminating their contribution to the theft of finite archaeological resources. The passion to own a piece of the past is omnipotent and much social prestige is bestowed on the "great" collectors and "great" donors (e.g., Currelly 1956). These underlying attitudes in Western society must change fundamentally so that one major reason for the antiquities market can be eliminated. Ironically, the rural poor, upon whom the antiquities market relies as a source for objects, are often hypocritically maligned or ignored by the West. However, we must be able to explain the attitudes of looters and behavior patterns among the rural poor, which are far from uniform. The *huaqueros* (looters) of Central and South America, as well as similar operators from the poorest parts of Italy, Africa, and Asia, believe that what is on *their* land was left to *them* by *their* ancestors – an obviously destructive, yet very powerful logic. Yet I have observed during my own work in Romania that the rural population, no stranger to difficult politico-economic circumstances, often take a genuine pride in their past, many among whom voluntarily relinquish, to archaeologists or authorities, archaeological finds plowed up on their land (including hoards of Roman silver coins) or simply leave archaeological sites alone. Many Romanian archaeologists have a tradition of building relationships in the village community most directly affected by the proposed archaeological excavation; living and communicating with village families; working closely with the local schoolteachers, headmasters, and local authorities; employing rural youth during the summer; and giving due credit in their publications to those in the rural community who discover and turn over any finds. Therefore, it is imperative to study and explain variations in and origins of rural attitudes and for the archaeological profession to develop programs of inclusion where possible.

Secondly, and more importantly, is the glaring economic disparity, on the one hand, between the art-consuming regions (e.g., North America, Western Europe, Japan) and the art-source regions (e.g., Central America, Andean South America, circum-Mediterranean, Africa), and on the other hand, between the urban elites and the rural poor in many archaeologically fertile countries. Rural poverty, in combination with the lack of public education about the local cultural heritage, are the real underpinnings in the looting of antiquities. A tragic irony is that the illicit art and antiquities market is second only to the illegal drug trade, and archaeologically rich nations with low GNPs are not only forfeiting economic benefits but are also losing their cultural heritage in the process. It is for this reason that John Merryman (1995) has argued for a "licit" international trade in art and antiquities to discourage looting and to bring some profit to those nations most adversely affected. Issues of cultural commodification aside, will the economic benefits of "licit" trade trickle down to the economically underprivileged or remain in the overseas bank accounts of government officials? The implications of a concerted effort by art-source nations to supply objects to Western markets are complicated (Coggins 1995) and, with unknown results, should we even risk the gamble of turning patrimony into, dare it be said, "patrimoney"? However,

unless these issues are resolved – and these would need more complex solutions which no government to date has been willing to address – the loss of an irreplaceable archaeological database, the feeding frenzy on the Western antiquities market, and the resulting destruction of knowledge will continue to cost us all.

Who owns the past?

Many museums share one issue in common with archaeologists. We are both being forced to reevaluate what it means to "possess" something – especially to "own" the past – even though such possession may have been in the pursuit of knowledge. Property ownership by individuals is a sanctified tenet of Western cultural and legal traditions, and as such has been assumed to be both legally correct and morally right. It took the issue of *domestic repatriation* to First Peoples in the United States, Canada, Australia, and New Zealand to force us to examine our own cultural values (through museums, exhibitions, language, and possession) as we have studied those of others (Hubert 1992). While a detailed discussion of the relationship between colonialism and museums would be too lengthy here and is eloquently described by others (e.g., Cole 1985; Hinsley 1981; Specht and MacLulich 2000), it is important to bear in mind that museums today, and probably for the next century or more, will have to confront and resolve serious issues of cultural property ownership and repatriation.

Repatriation, however, is both a broader, humanitarian issue as well as a legal, intellectual issue. Australian museums decided to work directly with aboriginal groups in the collection, documentation, interpretation, care, and display of indigenous objects, and the results are a model of intercultural collaboration (e.g., Baillie 1998; see especially Specht and MacLulich 2000). Other nations have adopted a legislative approach, and ironically, legal solutions have been so inconsistent as to perpetuate some of the very problems they were designed to resolve. Nowhere is this more apparent than in the way the US (Pace 1992; Pinkerton 1992; Price 1991) and Canada (Edgar and Paterson 1995) have handled repatriation claims of their respective First Nations. In the US, rather predictably, the strictly legal route was taken with the enactment of federal legislation: the Native American Graves Protection and Repatriation Act (NAGPRA) in 1990. NAGPRA laid out specific rules, with ambiguous terminology, for a two-stage mass inventorying of all archaeological and ethnographic materials, identification of cultural affiliation, and notification of closest living descendant groups for repatriation – all within five years. NAGPRA affected any museum that had received direct or indirect federal grant money at any time in the past (basically almost all museums with relevant collections), with the exception of the Smithsonian Institution, which had negotiated a similar but separate repatriation agreement. While it is too soon to know the long-term impact of NAGPRA, some signs as to future trends are emerging. Introducing human rights philosophy in the resolution of cultural patrimony issues was a long-overdue idea; however, resorting to the law has not completely satisfied any of the parties and repatriation has become a cumbersome and underfunded bureaucratic process. Although the museums have not been emptied out (as some had feared), and responses from Native Americans to huge museum inventory lists have been mixed, archaeological excavation on US territory may see its days numbered unless archaeologists receive permission from, or collaborate in some way with, Native Americans (Swidler et al. 1997), otherwise archaeology will have to focus on non-indigenous populations or be reduced to mere salvage operations on construction projects.

With respect to international repatriation, claims for cultural patrimony can be analyzed only on a case-by-case basis (Greenfield 1996), with results that run the spectrum from irreconcilable differences to

the effective use of diplomacy, three examples of which will demonstrate the point. In the UK, the most infamous example is the claim of the Greek government for the Parthenon ("Elgin") Marbles at the British Museum (Merryman 1985; Hitchens 1998). In this instance, over 200 years of contentious debate have produced a legal and diplomatic impasse and establishes itself as a textbook case of how *not* to handle international repatriation claims. The second example is the claim of the Turkish government for the "Lydian Hoard" at the Metropolitan Museum of Art, which unfortunately tried to cover up the exact origins ("East Greek") of the ancient silver objects, with obvious results (Lowenthal 1988, 1993). Turkey had found a successful legal avenue to repatriation by filing suit in *state* court, where the property is located, and this has now become a standard *modus operandi* for several foreign governments with repatriation claims against American dealers and museums (Byrne-Sutton 1992; Church 1993). The last example is that of the fate of the once privately owned Teotihuacán Murals, which were mysteriously bequeathed to the predominantly city-financed Fine Arts Museums of San Francisco in 1972. This complicated story has been published (Seligman 1989), but suffice it to say that the FAMSF was put into a legal no-win situation. According to Mexican law, the murals belonged to Mexico; according to San Francisco municipal laws, city property could not be given away without something of comparable value in return. Since the laws were irreconcilable, FAMSF decided to initiate its own diplomatic negotiations directly with Mexico and eventually both sides worked out a mutually agreed-upon arrangement of shared custodianship.

Fear and Remembrance of Knowledge

On a concluding note, we might also mention the censorship, unparalleled in frequency within the span of a single decade since 1989, of so many prominent museum exhibitions in the US (Dubin 1999). We should not be surprised by the political censorship experienced by museums, anywhere in the world, and the extent of fear governments have about museums and their stores of knowledge – whether it be the Third Reich's infamous *Entartete Kunst Austellung* (Degenerate Art Exhibition) (Barron et al. 1991; Petropoulos 1996) or the Smithsonian's reevaluation of the dropping of the atomic bombs on Japan (Harwit 1996; Nobile 1995). But during the dark decades of twentieth-century totalitarianism, we also saw the early Soviet government build 542 museums in just 15 years (1921–36) and the construction of over 2,000 local culture-history museums (*Heimatmuseen*) in Germany between the two world wars (Bazin 1967: 269; Roth 1990). There is no incongruity with the condemnation of "politically incorrect" museum objects or exhibits simultaneously with the undertaking of massive museum building programs. State structures both fear and admire the evidence of a people's memory, and thus have a compelling reason not only to control existing museums but also to build new "historical" monuments and new museums, in order, it seems, to select knowledge and revise memory, rather than (unsuccessfully) erase them entirely.

The not-so-future shock is that some students of archaeology being educated in universities today may very well find themselves working for museums of twentieth-century history, especially since, as should surprise no one, Auschwitz is fast becoming an archaeological site. Before its construction, curators and designers from the Holocaust Memorial Museum in Washington, DC, were sent to the area of the Warsaw Ghetto to consult with local archaeologists whose techniques were the only means available for retrieval of evidence (now conveniently built over) and the preservation of knowledge (Linenthal 1995). For this and many other reasons, museums are first and foremost about remembering our humanity (and all too often the lack of it), as well as for understanding the natural and celestial worlds that allow us to exist. The *idea* of a museum has traveled a somewhat circuitous, and occasionally maladroit, path since Athens and Alexandria – but now remains an idea that our collective memory cannot afford to be without.

References

Al-Radi, S. M. S. 1992. "The Gulf War and its aftermath on the cultural heritage of Iraq." In P. B. Vandiver, J. R. Druzik, G. S. Wheeler, and I. C. Freestone (eds.), *Materials Issues in Art and Archaeology III* (Materials Research Society Symposium Proceedings, vol. 267), pp. 121–3. Pittsburgh: Materials Research Society.

Alsop, J. W. 1982. *The Rare Art Traditions: The History of Art Collecting and Its Linked Phenomena* (Bollingen Series 35). New York: Harper and Row/Princeton University Press.

Baillie, A. (compiler) 1998. *Taking the Time: Museums and Galleries, Cultural Protocols and Communities*. Fortitude Valley, Queensland: Museums Australia.

Barron, S. et al. 1991. *"Degenerate Art": The Fate of the Avant-Garde in Nazi Germany*. Los Angeles: Los Angeles County Museum of Art/New York: Harry N. Abrams.

Bator, P. M. 1988. *The International Trade in Art*. Chicago: University of Chicago Press.

Bazin, G. 1967. *The Museum Age*. New York: Universe Books.

Belmarić, J. 1992. "Croatian monuments as targets, 1991/92." In P. B. Vandiver, J. R. Druzik, G. S. Wheeler, and I. C. Freestone (eds.), *Materials Issues in Art and Archaeology III* (Materials Research Society Symposium Proceedings, vol. 267), pp. 127–40. Pittsburgh: Materials Research Society.

Blais, A. (ed.) 1995. *Text in the Exhibition Medium*. Québec: Société des musées québécois and Musée de la civilisation.

Bennett, T. 1995. *The Birth of the Museum: History, Theory, Politics*. London: Routledge.

Berry, N. and S. Mayer (eds.) 1989. *Museum Education: History, Theory, and Practice*. Reston, VA: National Art Education Association.

Beurdeley, M. 1966. *The Chinese Collector through the Centuries, from the Han to the Twentieth Century*. Rutland, VT: C. E. Tuttle.

Bourdieu, P. 1979. *La Distinction: critique sociale du jugement*. Paris: Editions de Minuit.

Bourdieu, P. and A. Darbel 1990. *The Love of Art: European Art Museums and their Public*. Stanford, CA: Stanford University Press.

Byrne-Sutton, Q. 1992. "The Goldberg case: a confirmation of the difficulty in acquiring good title to valuable stolen cultural objects." *International Journal of Cultural Property*, 1 (1): 151–68.

Cantwell, A.-M., J. B. Griffin, and N. A. Rothschild (eds.) 1981. *The Research Potential of Anthropological Museum Collections* (Annals of the New York Academy of Sciences, vol. 376). New York: New York Academy of Sciences.

Caygill, M. L. 1992. "The protection of national treasures at the British Museum during the First and Second World Wars" [with appendix: *Air Raid Precautions in Museums, Picture Galleries and Libraries* (1939) London: Trustees of the British Museum]. In P. B. Vandiver, J. R. Druzik, G. S. Wheeler, and I. C. Freestone (eds.), *Materials Issues in Art and Archaeology III* (Materials Research Society Symposium Proceedings, vol. 267), pp. 29–99. Pittsburgh: Materials Research Society.

Chamberlin, R. 1983. *Loot! The Heritage of Plunder*. London: Thames and Hudson.

Church, J. 1993. "Evolving US case law on cultural property disputes." *International Journal of Cultural Property*, 2 (1): 47–71.

Coggins, C. 1995. "A licit international traffic in ancient art: let there be light!" *International Journal of Cultural Property*, 4 (1): 61–79.

Cole, D. 1985. *Captured Heritage: The Scramble for Northwest Coast Artifacts*. Seattle: University of Washington Press.

Corrin, L. G. (ed.) 1994. *Mining the Museum: An Installation by Fred Wilson*. Baltimore: The Contemporary/New York: New Press.

Currelly, C. T. 1956. *I Brought the Ages Home*. Toronto: Ryerson Press.

D'Arcy, D. 1993. "The Sevso melodrama: who did what and to whom." *Art Newspaper*, 31: 14–16, 38.

Dubin, S. C. 1999. *Displays of Power: Controversy in the American Museum from the Enola Gay to Sensation*. New York: New York University Press.

Dubinsky, L. (ed.) 1990. *Literacy and the Museum: Making the Connections*. Ottawa: Canadian Museums Association.

Edgar, D. N. and R. K. Paterson (eds.) 1995. *Material Culture in Flux: Law and Policy of Repatriation of Cultural Property* (University of British Columbia Law Review, special issue). Vancouver: UBC Law Review Society.

Elsner, J. and R. Cardinal (eds.) 1994. *The Cultures of Collecting*. Cambridge, MA: Harvard University Press.

England, P. A. and L. van Zeist (eds.) 1985. *Application of Science in Examination of Works of Art*. Boston: Museum of Fine Arts.

Fliedl, G., U. Giersch, M. Sturm, and R. Zendron (eds.) 1997. *Wa(h)re Kunst. Der Museum-shop als Wunderkammer: Theoretische Objekte, Fakes und Souvenirs*. Frankfurt: Anabas.

Foanaota, L. 1994. "Archaeology and museum work in the Solomon Islands." In P. Gathercole and D. Lowenthal (eds.), *The Politics of the Past*, pp. 224–32. London: Routledge.

Ford, R. 1984. "Ethics and the museum archaeologist." In E. Green (ed.), *Ethics and Values in Archaeology*, pp. 133–42. New York: Free Press.

Fullerton, D. 1991. "Tax policy toward art museums." In M. Feldstein (ed.), *The Economics of Art Museums*, pp. 195–235. Chicago: University of Chicago Press.

Greenfield, J. 1996. *The Return of Cultural Treasures*, 2nd edn. Cambridge: Cambridge University Press.

Harwit, M. 1996. *An Exhibit Denied: Lobbying the History of Enola Gay*. New York: Copernicus.

Hein, G. 1998. *Learning in the Museum*. London: Routledge.

Hinsley, C. M., Jr. 1981. *Savages and Scientists: The Smithsonian Institution and the Development of American Anthropology 1846–1910*. Washington, DC: Smithsonian Institution Press.

Hitchens, C. 1998. *The Elgin Marbles: Should They Be Returned to Greece?* London: Verso.

Hooper-Greenhill, E. 1991. *Museum and Gallery Education*. Leicester: Leicester University Press.

Hoving, T. 1996. *False Impressions: The Hunt for Big-Time Art Fakes*. New York: Simon and Schuster.

Hubert, J. 1992. "Dry bones or living ancestors? Conflicting perceptions of life, death and the universe." *International Journal of Cultural Property*, 1 (1): 105–27.

Hutt, S., E. W. Jones, and M. E. McAllister 1992. *Archeological Resource Protection*. Washington, DC: National Trust for Historic Preservation.

ICOM 1995. *Illicit Traffic of Cultural Property in Africa*. Paris: International Council of Museums, UNESCO.

Jameson, J. H., Jr. (ed.) 1997. *Presenting Archaeology to the Public: Digging for Truths*. Walnut Creek, CA: AltaMira Press.

Janes, R. R. 1997. *Museums and the Paradox of Change: A Case Study in Urgent Adaptation*, 2nd edn. Calgary, Alberta: Glenbow Museum and University of Calgary Press.

Jeppson, L. 1970. *The Fabulous Frauds: Fascinating Tales of Great Art Forgeries*. New York: Weybright and Talley.

Jones, M. 1990. *Fake? The Art of Deception*. London: British Museum Publications.

Linenthal, E. T. 1995. *Preserving Memory: The Struggle to Create America's Holocaust Museum*. New York: Viking Penguin.

Lowenthal, C. 1988. "Republic of Turkey v. Metropolitan Museum of Art." *IFAR Reports*, 9 (7–8): 9–10. International Foundation for Art Research, New York.

Lowenthal, C. 1993. "Met returns silver to Turkey." *IFAR Reports*, 14 (10): 3–4. International Foundation for Art Research, New York.

Lowenthal, D. 1994. "Conclusion: Archaeologists and others." In P. Gathercole and D. Lowenthal (eds.), *The Politics of the Past*, pp. 302–14. London: Routledge.

Lumley, R. (ed.) 1988. *The Museum Time-Machine: Putting Cultures on Display*. London: Routledge.

Macdonald, S. and G. Fyfe (eds.) 1996. *Theorizing Museums*. Oxford: Blackwell and *Sociological Review*.

Margolis, S. V. 1989. "Authenticating ancient marble sculpture." *Scientific American*, 246 (6): 104–10.

Melton, A. 1996 [1935]. *Problems of Installation in Museums of Art*. Washington, DC: American Association of Museums.

Melton, A., N. G. Feldman, and C. W. Mason 1996 [1935]. *Measuring Museum Based Learning: Experimental Studies of the Education of Children in a Museum of Science*. Washington, DC: American Association of Museums.

Merryman, J. H. 1985. "Thinking about the Elgin Marbles." *Michigan Law Review*, 83: 1880–1923.

Merryman, J. H. 1995. "A licit international trade in cultural objects." *International Journal of Cultural Property*, 4 (1): 13–60.

Messenger, P. M. (ed.) 1989. *The Ethics of Collecting Cultural Property: Whose Culture? Whose Property?* Albuquerque: University of New Mexico Press.

Miles, R. S. et al. 1988. *The Design of Educational Exhibits*, 2nd edn. London: Unwin Hyman.

Muensterberger, W. 1994. *Collecting: An Unruly Passion. Psychological Perspectives.* Princeton, NJ: Princeton University Press.

Muscarella, O. 2000. *The Lie Became Great: The Forgery of Ancient Near Eastern Cultures.* Groningen: Styx.

Nicholas, L. H. 1994. *The Rape of Europa: The Fate of Europe's Treasures in the Third Reich and the Second World War.* New York: Knopf.

Nobile, P. 1995. *Judgment at the Smithsonian – The Bombing of Hiroshima and Nagasaki: The Uncensored Script of the Smithsonian's Fiftieth Anniversary Exhibit of the Enola Gay.* New York: Marlowe.

Nzewunwa, N. 1994. "Cultural education in West Africa: archaeological perspectives." In P. Gathercole and D. Lowenthal (eds.), *The Politics of the Past*, pp. 189–202. London: Routledge.

Pace, J. A. (ed.) 1992. *Symposium: The Native American Graves Protection and Repatriation Act of 1990 and State Repatriation-Related Legislation* (Arizona State Law Journal, vol. 24, no. 1). Tempe: College of Law, Arizona State University.

Pearce, S. 1992. *Museums, Objects, and Collections.* Washington, DC: Smithsonian Institution Press.

Petropoulos, J. 1996. *Art as Politics in the Third Reich.* Chapel Hill: University of North Carolina Press.

Pinkerton, L. 1992. "The Native American Graves Protection and Repatriation Act: an introduction." *International Journal of Cultural Property*, 1 (2): 297–305.

Price, H. M. 1991. *Disputing the Dead: US Law on Aboriginal Remains and Grave Goods.* Columbia: University of Missouri Press.

Price, S. 1989. *Primitive Art in Civilized Places.* Chicago: University of Chicago Press.

Renfrew, C. 2000. *Loot, Legitimacy and Ownership.* London: Duckworth.

Robison, O., R. Freeman, and C. A. Riley, II (eds.) 1994. *The Arts in the World Economy: Public Policy and Private Philanthropy for a Global Cultural Community.* Hanover, NH: University Press of New England.

Roth, M. 1990. *Heimatmuseum: zur Geschichte einer deutschen Institution.* Berlin: Mann.

Saunders, D. 1992. "The National Gallery at war." In P. B. Vandiver, J. R. Druzik, G. S. Wheeler, and I. C. Freestone (eds.), *Materials Issues in Art and Archaeology III* (Materials Research Society Symposium Proceedings, vol. 267), pp. 101–10. Pittsburgh: Materials Research Society.

Sax, J. L. 1999. *Playing Darts with a Rembrandt: Public and Private Rights in Cultural Treasures.* Ann Arbor: University of Michigan Press.

Schmidt, P. R. and R. J. McIntosh (eds.) 1996. *Plundering Africa's Past.* Bloomington: Indiana University Press/London: James Currey.

Seligman, T. K. 1989. "The murals of Teotihuacán: a case study of negotiated restitution." In P. M. Messenger (ed.), *The Ethics of Collecting Cultural Property: Whose Culture? Whose Property?* pp. 73–84. Albuquerque: University of New Mexico Press.

Serrell, B. 1997. *Exhibit Labels – An Interpretive Approach.* Walnut Creek, CA: AltaMira Press.

Sherman, D. and I. Rogoff (eds.) 1994. *Museum Culture*. Minneapolis: University of Minnesota Press.

Simpson, E. (ed.) 1997. *The Spoils of War: World War II and its Aftermath: The Loss, Reappearance and Recovery of Cultural Property*. New York: Abrams and the Bard Graduate Center for Studies of the Decorative Arts.

Smardz, K. and S. J. Smith (eds.) 2000. *The Archaeology Education Handbook: Sharing the Past with Kids*. Walnut Creek, CA: Altamira Press.

Smith, G. S. and J. E. Ehrenhard (eds.) 1991. *Protecting the Past*. Boca Raton, FL: CRC Press.

Specht, J. and C. MacLulich 2000. "Changes and challenges: the Australian museum and indigenous communities." In P. M. McManus (ed.), *Archaeological Displays and the Public: Museology and Interpretations*, 2nd edn., pp. 39–63. London: Archetype Publications.

Stone, P. G. 1989. "Interpretations and uses of the past in modern Britain and Europe. Why are people interested in the past? Do the experts know or care? A plea for further study." In R. Layton (ed.), *Who Needs the Past? Indigenous Values and Archaeology*, pp. 195–206. London: Unwin Hyman.

Swidler, N. et al. (eds.) 1997. *Native Americans and Archaeologists: Stepping Stones to Common Ground*. Walnut Creek, CA: Altamira Press/London: Sage Publications.

Thomas, S. and A. Mintz 1998. *Virtual and the Real: Media in the Museum*. Washington, DC: American Association of Museums.

Treue, W. 1960. *Art Plunder: The Fate of Works of Art in War and Unrest*. New York: John Day.

Tribolet, H. W. 1967. *Florence Rises from the Flood: The Full Picture Story of the November 1966 Flood as Dramatically Reported in National Geographic*. Chicago: Lakeside Press.

Varshavskii, S. P. and B. Rest 1985. *The Ordeal of the Hermitage: The Siege of Leningrad, 1941–44*. Leningrad: Aurora Art Publishers.

Vergo, P. (ed.) 1989. *The New Museology*. London: Reaktion Books.

von Bothmer, D. and J. V. Noble 1961. *An Inquiry into the Forgery of the Etruscan Terracotta Warriors in the Metropolitan Museum of Art* (Papers, no. 11). New York: Metropolitan Museum of Art.

Watson, P. 1997. *Sotheby's: Inside Story*. London: Bloomsbury/New York: Random House.

Weisbrod, B. A. (ed.) 1998. *To Profit or Not to Profit: The Commercial Transformation of the Nonprofit Sector*. Cambridge: Cambridge University Press.

Young, W. J. (ed.) 1967. *Application of Science in Examination of Works of Art*. Boston: Museum of Fine Arts.

25
Relating Anthropology and Archaeology

Michael Rowlands

Introduction

Anthropology and archaeology share a common origin in Victorian preoccupations with the evolution of civilization (Stocking 1987). They developed as academic subjects during the later part of the nineteenth century, as various strands of thought about human biological and social evolution were drawn together, to form a consistent and coherent framework to measure the progress of civilization from the primitive to the modern. Whether separated by space or time the material vestiges of a human past, like so many fossil cultural relics, were assembled in elaborate typologies of evolutionary progress. Artefacts and evidence of technical skills were significant elements of all such schemes and by 1890, the date of the publication of Sir James Frazer's *Golden Bough*, ethnographic and archaeological materials were being displayed together in museums. As objects, the things preserved in museum displays were seen as the products of "alien cultures" separated by time and space from the "modern world." Artefacts were viewed as survivals wrenched from the past, separated from us by time and space. There was little to distinguish between archaeological objects discovered through excavating relic sites, and ethnographic artefacts collected from geographically remote yet living "primitive societies." The way "we" related to our "primitive others" was through a form of linear thinking, that emphasized a message of conservative evolutionism culminating in the triumph of the modern world.

In the Anglo-American traditions of anthropology in the twentieth century, a shift towards a more behaviorist orientation rejected evolutionary studies of the past as "conjectural history" lacking any empirical foundation. In the period from 1920 to 1960 the ethnographic study of material culture, associated with outmoded ideas of evolutionary progress, was relegated as the task of the museum interested only in questions of technology and primitive art. Archaeology, meanwhile, went through its own fieldwork revolution, emphasizing excavation as an independent technique for studying regional developments in human cultures. The approach placed greater emphasis on establishing localized historical development, rather than large-scale evolutionary generalizations. Anthropology and archaeology also diverged in the kinds of societies they were thought to be studying. From the 1920s, the development of anthropology in Europe and North America, now inseparable from the development of colonialism, became affiliated to the study of non-Western societies, or those "peoples without history" to use

Eric Wolf's felicitous phrase (Wolf 1982). Anthropologists studied the functioning of "primitive societies" precisely because they had abandoned any hope of being able to study the past through distilling a nugget of historical truth from myth or oral tradition. Lévi-Strauss, for example, strongly suspected that most written scholarly history was in fact myth, and Sahlins was concerned to show that in Hawaii myth only became history as origin myths got mixed up in oral tradition with real historical events (Lévi-Strauss 1966: 245–69; Sahlins 1985: 58). For the structuralists, history as mythology was a mode of philosophizing and for functionalists it acted as an "origin charter" to legitimize the present.

Meanwhile, archaeology continued to develop as a skilled practice in the excavation of the remote pasts of historically rich (i.e., civilized) societies. Research on the origins of food production, urbanism, or the earliest metallurgy assumed that such questions would contribute to our understanding of either the development of "Western civilization" or civilization in general, while the archaeology of anthropologically rich areas (e.g., Africa, Oceania, and Melanesia) remained relatively neglected until the late 1960s. Even today, studying the "clash of civilizations" legitimates a political understanding of the West as a destiny finally achieved in the "end of history" (Huntington 1996; Fukuyama 1992). Lévi-Strauss (1966) defined this historical project as the contrast between "hot" and "cold" societies (alluding to the richness or poverty of a perception of events in different societies). But it was also supported by retaining the nineteenth-century separation of the "primitive" from the modern in time and space; a division of labor that came to increasingly justify the differences in approach and methodology of archaeology and anthropology (cf. Fabian 1982). If archaeology studied the remote pasts of historically rich societies through excavation and artefact comparison, anthropologists studied "the primitive" by rejecting the time dimension and embarking on a

quest for the meaning of cultures remote in space – and therefore time – from each other.

It may seem paradoxical that my aim in this chapter should be to suggest that a convergence is now taking place between these two disciplines. I think a case can be made, as long as we recognize that both subjects are going through profound reevaluations of their aims. Archaeology is finally shriving itself of what remains of its nineteenth-century origins and revising its relationship to the pasts of "societies," both hot and cold. A postmodern anthropology, on the other hand, has rediscovered an interest in material culture, in museums and in the study of the past. We can never assume anything contrived or deliberately intended in such affinities, but rather assume that they are to be found in styles of argument and discourses in circulation at any particular time. I would argue that such an epistemic character can be traced in archaeology and anthropology at present, in two linking themes. Firstly, a consensus has emerged that the relationships between past and present are inseparable and mutually constitutive – that how we live in the present and are able to think about our pasts is shaped by structures of consciousness that are inherited and to varying degrees internalized and understood from the past. While some may see the past as nothing other than projections of concerns of the present, others cogently express the view that the unintended consequences of past practices have material effects for later generations, which can be exposed and liberated through critical judgment. Secondly, while language and linguistic models have dominated Western social theory, there is a growing recognition that a focus on material and visual culture allows us to reflect on subject–object relations in novel and distinct ways. In a short review it is not possible to study cases in any detail, so what follows has more the character of an outline of recent trends, which demonstrate the emergence of a more united field of study around these two themes.

Material Culture and Language

The rejection by Radcliffe-Brown of material culture as a form of study which could not be carried out in the field was symptomatic of the turn to language as the primary medium for the investigation of cross-cultural differences and similarities in anthropology (Radcliffe-Brown 1922). The consequences of the radical nature of this rejection of studies of art and material culture for the subject began to be recognized by the early 1970s. From the very beginning, Lévi-Strauss had argued that anthropology was not limited to the study of language *tout court*, but should be developing a language of things. Formal analysis of artefacts to isolate underlying grammars or codes to account for their form appears in volume 1 of *Structural Anthropology*, as does his advocacy that only a cross-cultural comparative approach would allow us to understand particular cultural forms within a wider setting of regional mythic and material transformations. A number of structuralist studies of material form appeared in the 1970s which aimed at isolating underlying grammars of stylistic form. Munn's (1973) study of Walbiri iconography showed that circles and ellipses could be given different meanings in the contexts of mythic descriptions of Dream Time events in Australian aboriginal culture. Her aim was to show how a small range of shapes could be used to generate a wide range of semantic codes. Carried out in conjunction with Anthony Forge's study of Abelam art of the Sepik, Francis Korn (1978) conducted a separate formal stylistic analysis of the art, and subsequently compared her findings to those of Forge (1979) in order to establish the differences between visual- and language-based codes. There were other attempts to relate formal visual codes to their social context, very much following in the tradition of Lévi-Strauss' original seminal analysis of Bororo settlement patterns in *Structural Anthropology*. Bourdieu's (1977) influential study of the Kabyle house showed how it was organized according to a set of structural oppositions such as cooked–raw, fire–water, high–low, light–shade, male–female, etc., forming a set of codes that he argued were basic to Berber culture in more general terms.

Structuralism was enormously influential in reestablishing material culture and art as serious areas of study in anthropology and in a short period this had a significant impact in archaeology and art history (cf. Hodder 1982). The identification of systematic and recurrent rules of transformation, linking materials and social practices in generating the real worlds inhabited by people, followed similar principles to those established in structural linguistics. While the idea that there is a language of things has proved to be influential, such studies have been criticized for the excessive formalism of the approach, which in turn has been related to the tendency to reduce basically aesthetic questions to the rigor of linguistic rules. Morphy's book *Ancestral Connections* (1991) effectively counters this criticism by demonstrating that such rules in a body of aboriginal art are effectively only realized and given form through the actions of particular artists enacting mythic representations. But the basic question remains that while analogies between the structures of language and things in the sense that both are assumed to communicate has been very beneficial, it remains unclear how things communicate in ways different from language; things say or communicate precisely that which cannot be communicated in words. The aesthetic response, that it is only in the performance that things can be fully experienced, has in turn been emphasized in anthropology recently (e.g., Feld 1982), but this also turns attention away from objects to cultural performance and the experiences of actors and audiences. An alternative development can be found in studies that detect material patterns in artefacts that are simply not communicated in words or other forms of nonverbal discourse. MacKenzie's (1991) study of netbags in the New Guinea Highlands develops this point in ways that have direct archaeological implications, in the sense that she recognizes spatial and other variations in styles of netbags, but interprets them as belonging to a silent discourse about the complementary roles of males and females in reproductive life. Gell (1998) has also been concerned with recognizing the distinctiveness of material form as a means of communication in contrast to language. He argues that any distinctive artwork relates to a wider stylistic canon which pervades the material culture of an area, and which has a reality regardless of other social or linguistic differences. He analyzes in detail a set of Marquesan artefacts to demonstrate that they relate to each other through a complex set of transformational rules, that can all be traced to a single structuring principle, which, he argues, is characteristic of cultural patterns in the Marquesas in general.

Anthropologists since the 1970s, through the impact of structuralism, have attempted to apply a similar framework of decoding rules of transformation to the meanings of objects (cf. Munn 1986; Faris 1972). The attempt to demonstrate that material culture formed a system of communication and meaning was also developed by postprocessual archaeology, as part of a critique of positivist approaches in the subject (Hodder 1986). The role of ethnoarchaeology in many ways converged with developments in the anthropology of art, in stressing that objects could also be treated as meaningful systems of communication. The question was perhaps more about what kind of communication takes place through things in contrast to language. The fact that artefacts do not necessarily communicate and certainly not in the same way as language, developed as part of the critique of excessive formalism of structuralist methods in anthropology. For some, this meant the rediscovery of the work of art historians such as Panofsky and Langer, whose work on iconology emphasized the difference between language and image (cf. Berger 1972: 19–33; Pinney 1997). To interpret visually,

they had argued, was completely unlike hearing the spoken sentence, since the impact of an image depended on seeing it all at once rather than as a sequence of sounds that make sense only in linear time (cf. Mitchell 1986; Forge 1979). Objects have value because of their visibility as images, or their materiality as things, and not necessarily because they mean something or communicate a message. The argument that materiality gives access to a different sort of knowledge, now generally repressed in Western social science, can be seen as one of those "voices of silence" that characterize alternative discourses in Western twentieth-century thought (Ginzburg 1983; Jay 1988). But the present trend is to emphasize a more forceful distinction between objects and texts and to elaborate the importance of the former in a world increasingly dominated by theories of materiality.

Materiality

The structuralist phase both revived material culture studies and yet at the same time opposed them to the dominance of linguistic models in standard anthropological theory and practice. Various developments towards an autonomous theory of material culture have since been presented, on the basis of a fundamental assumption that materiality itself is not open to language-based rules. Morphy's (1991) study of Yolngu (Australian aboriginal) art emphasizes that the meaning of images is created within frameworks of social action, that relate to generative rule-based structures but are not determined by them. What Yolngu art means, depends in any particular situation on the intentions of the individuals and groups involved, and how they internalize the meanings available to them. Restriction on what these might be, then separate young from old and men from women, creating a system of knowledge that encodes and orders the way it can be acquired. The influence of Giddens and Bourdieu in this part of his work is fairly clear and a similar influence can be found in archaeology at this time (Barrett 1994).

One of the most influential theories in recent material culture studies has been derived from theories of objectification (cf. Miller 1987, 1995). It has its source in Hegel and the questioning of both Descartes' separation of the thinking mind or subject from the material world of things or objects, and Kant's distinction of the material and the real. The idea that the book of nature is written in the language of mathematics alone, and all other impressions of the material world are illusory, confirmed the idea that material reality should be understood as a mechanical nature that could not be reduced to linguistic or visual principles. While the tendency in Western philosophy has been to stress the active subject in determining the meaning of passive objects, it is equally inadequate to simply invert the relationship and end up with a rather moribund objectivism. Bourdieu, in particular, argued in *Outline of a Theory of Practice* that the relationship has to be seen more dialectically, not only in terms of active subjects internalizing and externalizing inherited rules and structures, but also in the process changing and transforming their effects. Cultural identity is simultaneously embodied in persons and objectified in things and institutions that can take on a "thing-like" appearance. Things can have effects on people and to that extent may be deemed as active, in contrast to the bias towards seeing all matter as inert. Some of the weaknesses in these approaches lie certainly in their inability to develop a theory of materiality, in favor of ideas about what people do with objects, essentially as a theory of culture rather than material culture (Van Beek 1996). Miller, in his book *Material Culture and Mass Consumption*, was primarily concerned with the mutual constitution of subject and object, and further claims that he is developing a theory of culture that will transcend limited symbolic approaches in which "values and social relations . . . are created in the act by which cultural forms come into being" (Miller 1995: 277). He focuses on the place of material culture in this process of objectification and specifically chooses modern mass consumption as the key arena in the constitution of culture and society. There are strong parallels in these ideas with those of Strathern in *Gender of the Gift* (1988), published about the same time as a call to dissolve the imposition of Western biased subject/object relations as universally significant. More radically, Strathern challenged the assumption of subjects as integral individuals that, as a historical feature of the development of capitalism, would also be found in a gift economy in Melanesia, where persons and things may instead be aspects of each other. Where reification in a commodity economy makes a person appear as a thing, personification in a gift economy makes things appear as persons. The Western/non-Western contrast she constructs has been criticized for exaggerating a sense of difference, and the reality is perhaps that elements of both are found in all social situations (e.g., Thomas 1991; Carrier 1996). Nevertheless the idea that persons and things are partly interchangeable was also based on the idea that the nature of exchange in gift economies is rooted in the belief that things shared properties of the person who made them, and therefore were not alienable in exchange (Weiner 1992). Instead, they were associated with the personhood of the owner, with clan histories and ancestral connections, and it is gaining the possession of these aspects of the person that is the object of exchange. In his classic work on the gift, Mauss had described this spirit of the gift as a mystical quality that compelled its eventual return, and argued that control over its circulation allowed the emergence of rank and political hierarchies. Miller's argument relates this general thesis to commodity consumption, where things are definitely alienable, but he is concerned to show that people turn them into meaningful (in part inalienable) possessions through the action of buying and consuming goods. Commodities become goods when embodied and absorbed into the construction of social identities. His argument on shopping, for example, is not that provisioning the home just involves economic calculation, but that the act embodies otherwise alienable commodities with personal motives such as love and self-sacrifice, that gives them "gift-like" properties in their consumption. As the dominant cultural forms of modernity, the commodity and consumption emerge as the arena in which "people have to struggle towards control over the definition of themselves and their values" (Miller 1995: 277; 1998).

There may be some who would doubt whether a concentration alone on ideas and values (in particular, normative values) is sufficient to generate these differences in social relations, but as a theory of culture, objectification focuses on material culture as the form of this mediation. The message is that culture – and in particular material culture – is the essential element in the definition of human nature and the dominant force in history. A weakness of the approach lies in the unclear way in which the materiality of objectification is approached. Objects are cultural forms and are the outcomes of a dialectical process of self-constitution. But why this form, style, or object rather than another remains a bit of a mystery. Tilley (1999) has argued that a theory of metaphor, suitably modified to relate to material culture, could bridge this gap. Metaphors are usually a form of language that helps us to grasp the vague and the unknowable, by relating them to some more comprehensible, concrete idea. Tilly argues that material metaphors operate in a similar manner to linguistic metaphors, but through a process of material condensation rather than linear thought. Body metaphors, house metaphors, textile metaphors, are the sort of categories of materiality that help us grasp more abstract issues, such as the relationship between fertility and growth or domesticity and kinship, by material exchanges of gifts or as clothing or house decoration. More significant are the cases where material metaphors appear to be the only mechanism

by which such abstract ideas can be articulated and grasped. The power of saints' relics or the healing powers of medicines are the sort of examples which fail to respond to anthropological questions, such as what do they mean or on what is their efficacy based. But, again, the only way we can see this as a general theory of material culture is to locate metaphor as a mode of thought, and in particular as a cognitive principle universal to the human mind. In which case the reasons why cognition chooses to operate materially rather than linguistically may have more to do with the dominance of visual cognition in certain aspects of mental ordering, rather than a particular propensity for material culture to operate in this way.

The approaches discussed so far assume that human intentionality is the basis for self-constitution through material culture. Another view would assert instead that it is the very physicality of objects that allows them to carry certain forms of signification that transcend whatever intentions or constructions humans may impose upon them (cf. Gell 1998). Gell, in his *Art and Agency*, is concerned with the creative ability of material objects to externalize agency and entrap subjects into relations with each other. The approach is cognitive in focusing on pattern and object analysis as a way of understanding how these are apprehended by thinking subjects. The Freudian theme "when the fetish comes to life" connotes materiality as an independent force, evoked as forgetfulness or repression, but it can also be generalized to a wider sense of fetishism describing objects taking on a life of their own. For Marx, the phantom-like quality of the commodity form lay in its immaterial power to dominate every waking moment of the desiring human. But this does not mean that objects are not, nor ever can be, genuinely magical or sensuous simply in their own right. The sense of the self being overwhelmed by the sensuous qualities of things, and the need to maintain proper boundaries between persons and things, resonate with issues of difference and inequality and in particular those dealing with unacceptable forms of heterogeneity. It is not insignificant that the majority of these discussions take for granted the primacy of embodied experience as the basis of materiality. To be a social being is, from this perspective, seen to be more a matter of recognizing that objects, including the human body, can be charged with powers in a diversity of historical moments and contexts, that channel human passions and energies in ways that they neither intended, nor necessarily recognize, as being in their best interests (cf. Speyer 1999). Endowing objects with "social lives" is merely another attempt to universalize the social as uniquely human (Appadurai 1986).

The work that has emerged out of a critique of science and nature, as found in several influential publications by Latour (1993, 1999), is concerned with materiality as part of the constitution of networks in which persons and things animate, constrain, and work in relation to each other. Latour argues that, since Durkheim, objects have presented only a surface for the projection of our social needs and interests. This emphasis on the "social" has meant that objects count only as mere receptacles for human categories (Latour 1993: 52). Instead, persons and things dissolve into each other through their mutual interaction in agency, while the boundaries between the social and the material dissolve. That subjects and objects are essentially hybrids with no boundaries is also the view of Harraway (1991), who declares herself to be cyborg (part organism, part machine), since it is no longer possible to separate the self from all the technical and material entanglements that surround and form the person. What appears to be emerging as a general consensus is that mind, body, and objects cannot be considered separate from each other. Warnier (2000), for example, develops a praxeology of human action to describe the performative aspect of self-making, and Ingold in various publications has also emphasized the rhythmic movements of embodied action as the essential basis of

making both persons and things, rather than them being the products of mental schemas (Ingold 2000).

I have argued that theorizing materiality has developed well beyond the linguistic models of the structuralist paradigm and, in the process, may begin to form a common discourse in both anthropology and archaeology. If it is only archaeology that can claim material culture to be its unique source of evidence, anthropology has a long tradition of keeping material and linguistic models in creative tension as modes of interpreting human cultures. There is still some way to go, however, before either subject can justifiably claim to have developed an autonomous theory of materiality that in some sense is not reducible to linguistic, cognitive, or agency forms of social theory. This may direct us instead to the contribution of both disciplines to theories of what they hold empirically in common.

Memory, Artefacts, and Cultural Transmission

One of these is certainly time, but in the social sense of perceived or acted time in the shaping of social relationships, rather than linear or chronologically defined time. We are all born into preconstituted worlds of artefacts that convey to us ideas of familiarity or ways of doing things, and which are effectively the inheritance of past generations. What are deemed to be appropriate implements to prepare, cook, or eat food or as socially adequate forms of dress are not self-inventions, but are transmitted cultural forms and dispositions that are adopted unquestioningly. The value of Bourdieu's concept of *habitus* for us here is that it allows us to conceive of such dispositions as preconstituted culture, rather than involving some kind of active remembering or learning as basic knowledge acquisition. Time in this sense as experience is objectified as sets of embodied material practices that shape our everyday lives and social interactions.

Durability may therefore constitute the valued relationship between objects and embodied time. Monuments, buildings, and ruins have the obvious merit of time literally being inscribed on the surface of things. What Nora (1991) has called places of memory share in common this "dreamlike" effect, of convincing us that reality retains this iridescent quality of an enchanted, timeless world regardless of all the evidence to the contrary. Collective and individual biographies are part of the daily experience of living in or with such objects and places; a comforting reminder that things "will always be the same" regardless of the superficialities of change. The destruction of such material environments in war and sometimes in forms of cultural genocide equally has the effect of brutally disenchanting one of such illusions and fragmenting the unity of place and self. Reproducing images of continuity through physical form are central to the production of memory, not only as a visual experience of continuity of form, but through the act of renewing buildings and environments, or in acts such as buying domestic furniture or shopping that emphasize a comfortable sense of always making a similar choice. Many of these features characterize the themes of memory and nostalgia in the Western experience; so it is salutary to reinforce the point that rupture and mobility can be the experience of others. In contrast to the Western preoccupation with a sort of passive remembering, Kuchler (1997) describes how sacrificial economies such as described in her study of mortuary rituals in New Ireland direct memory towards ensuring the reproduction of social relations in the future.

Archaeology provides us with one of the most important sources of evidence of how continuities in material form are maintained over long periods of time, sometimes in spite of other changes in language, religion, and political economy. Continuities in forms of land use, in technologies of building and materials, in the composition of household space, can be the basis for understanding processes of cultural reproduction that archaeologists do have a significant skill in identifying. Concepts such as archaeological cultures or culture areas may be conceptually blunt tools for recognizing the outcomes of these material practices, yet there can be no denial that the recognition of long-term continuities of cultural form has been and remains perhaps the most significant independent contribution archaeology makes to the understanding of human social identity. Duration, in which time is literally inscribed as age, preserves both personal and collective memories by the form of buildings and monuments or the patina on antique objects. But this predominantly Western relationship between representation and memory, familiar in the form of durable artefacts and monuments, has been contrasted by Kuchler with ritualized practices that literally destroy objects so that they can be renewed as part of regenerating social relationships in the future (Kuchler 1987, 1992). This reworking of memory in ritualized form relates the renewal of a material form to knowledge as a resource to be renewed, in contrast to the Western concern with the reproduction of memory (Rowlands 1993). This example also serves to question the ethnocentric bias in assuming that mental representations are simply objectified as material objects. Hoskins' work on personal life histories in Sumba, Indonesia is a significant development away from the assumption that objects are simply *aides-mémoire* for eliciting a speech narrative. Instead, she found that personal identities could only be articulated elusively through talking about objects such as a betel bag, a drum, or a spindle whorl, as things which contain and preserve memories and personal experiences (Hoskins 1998). While words may fail us, things in the home and the personal possessions we habitually use and carry with us may speak volumes about life histories and identities.

In anthropology, work on memory has been part of a wider interest in understanding how personal identities are embedded in the circulation and making of things (cf. Myers 2001). Appadurai (1986) has shown how the meaning of things changes as objects circulate, are exchanged and consumed in different social contexts. Of crucial importance for him was the need to break away from the unilineal implications of the term *commoditization* as an inevitable and increasingly global condition of capitalism. Instead of juxtaposing the Marxian notion of exchange versus use value, he argued that attention should rather be directed towards the varying commodity potential of all things. Whether things are in turn more "commodity-like" or "gift-like" at a particular stage depends on their social history and their cultural biography (Appadurai 1986: 34). This concern with flow and flexibility in social identities was part of a renewed interest in material culture in the 1980s, as the collapse of belief in various unilineal metanarratives led to a fascination with objects as a more secure starting point for understanding the varying ways people mapped their social networks through the circulation of things. Appadurai, for example, developed further his ideas on the politics of value by claiming that it was always in the interest of those in power to freeze the flow of commodities (Appadurai 1986: 57). Finally, Thomas (1991), working on the theme of inalienable wealth derived from the debate between Weiner (1992) and Strathern (1988), argues that gift/commodity distinctions did not apply in any absolute sense from the beginning of European contact in the Pacific, and were always a matter of negotiation rather than absolute categorization. A significant issue raised by this discussion has been the recognition that objects are far more problematic than the simple gift versus commodity dichotomy makes them out to be. When Strathern, writing on the way New Guinea Highlanders first "saw" Europeans, describes the wealth they brought with them not as objects but as images, we have to recognize that the ethnocentrism of our understanding of the "social life of things" remains tied to a particular ontological dimension. The idea that "tournaments of value" in contact situations may

have been aesthetic and visual rather than a desire to participate in ostentatious consumption, suggests that memory and visual value may be a more important matter in past societies as well.

Who Needs the Long Term?

So far I have emphasized the conceptual links between archaeology and anthropology; in particular, those that show most promise in developing common theory. A shared focus on material culture is evidently the basis to this, and in particular I have stressed that this is as an alternative (but not exclusive) approach to the dominance of language in our current understanding of human sociality. But the question remains: why do we need archaeological knowledge to pursue this goal?

Contemporary material culture studies tend to reproduce the synchronic bias of social anthropology, in the sense that even where an interest in the past is claimed, the focus is on present projections onto the past rather than understanding the past in itself. This can obviously create further unnecessary dichotomies between subjective and objective understandings of the past, but nevertheless much of contemporary theorizing in archaeology, it can be argued, is derivative and is being done by archaeologists who are implicitly abandoning the study of the past *per se*. This is not to say that it is not interesting to extend contemporary debates to archaeological case studies, particularly where the latter genuinely represent modes of life that extend our understanding of the human condition. But it is not an answer to the anthropologists asking why they should be interested in the study of archaeological pasts, when the claim is no more than the extension of a theme that has already been explored and potentially better understood in contemporary settings.

The answer which stresses a connection between past and present, on the lines of George Santayana's well-known quote that "he who knows the past controls the future," has gone through some rough treatment in recent years, in particular by archaeologists who might be thought to have a vested interest in defending its principle. Those who argue that the past is a matter of a reading by the present are most prone to deny any kind of causality, in favor of the construction of the former by the latter. Even though this still allows for a certain resistance or evasion by the materiality of the past to any particular construction being imposed upon it, nevertheless the past is devalued by comparison to the historicity of "grand narratives" that linked the present to the past as a mediation of the future. Anthropologists, anxious still to avoid charges of evolutionism, have tended to concentrate on the knowledge that people in the present have of historical events and processes, rather than on the substantive nature of their historical effect (for an exemplary discussion, see Gell 1992; and for exceptions, see Thomas 1989; Schneider and Rapp 1995). This is a pity since, while the former entails important issues, the tendency to reduce the past to the "view that past events have no bearing on a social situation or a cultural order unless they are perceived and imagined by the actors involved" is really an excessive reaction to a positivist account of socially objective history. That temporality should be seen as constitutive of, rather than marginal to, social systems has been part of a reorientation of anthropology in the last ten years (cf. Sahlins 1985; Thomas 1989; Gell 1992). The view that the past is motivated by the present does not mean that matters are necessarily improved by simply encompassing the usual anthropological preoccupations with a narrative history to give them some context. Nor does it deepen the anthropological project if we limit the notion of history to perceptions of actors experiencing it, nor by collapsing agency into modernist ideas of individual action.

However, the argument that archaeology provides evidence of longer-term historical processes to contextualize contemporary anthropological concerns is still open to critical evaluation (cf. Kristiansen and Rowlands 1998). Because of a lack of contemporary relevance, understanding the long-term prehistory of a region remains something that many anthropologists acknowledge but do not themselves conceptually engage with. Partly this is because of the different frameworks in use for explaining social transformations. The refinement of Sahlins' concept of structural history would be one achievement of such a project, if the excessive culturalism of his notion of transformation could be related to prior conditions of political and economic change. These include indigenous ideas of transformation and not simply the imposition of Western categories. We might recall the earlier-cited ideas of Strathern concerning "first contacts" in Melanesia, where contact with "whites" in the New Guinea Highlands was more like the appearance of an image in a ceremonial context rather than an historical event (Strathern 1990). The fact that people bring different cultural dispositions and historicities to their encounters in the same historical process (in this case European contact) still allows us to understand them as different responses to common processes which have affected us all. The notion of social transformation retains its value to describe this larger sense of historical process, which entangles mutual experiences of what we share in common with the consequences of long-term change that may set us apart. Understanding these historical effects requires both a knowledge of the local settings in which, for example, culture invests a person with an identity, and how these interact with other things, such as biological reproduction, power, and economic processes.

One area where we can see increasing convergence between anthropology and archaeology concerns the understanding of the entities within which comparisons of social transformations can be understood. Classifications of society, whether of the neo-evolutionary kind (band, tribe, chiefdom, state) or the functionalist type (state/stateless), have not only been subject to critique but, we now realize, were the product of the strong center/periphery ideologies that maintained colonial and Cold War senses of separate worlds, which have now largely dissolved. Regional analysis or even a return to questions of what constitutes a cultural area seem likely, therefore, to be the more appropriate units within which detailed ethnographic and archaeological field research will be conducted in future. Examples of such an approach would be Kirch and Sahlins' (1992) work in Hawaai, Knauft's (1993) synthesis of the coastal societies of Melanesia, or Vansina's (1990) synthesis of the development of the forest societies of equatorial Africa. Perhaps the key idea ought to be how people establish a sense of identity through tracing continuities in a sense of belonging that is not necessarily coterminous with recent, particularly colonial, definitions of cultural boundaries consistent with that of the nation-state. Recently, this idea has been realized principally through a focus on landscape, which has developed as a key intellectual contact between archaeology and anthropology (see Chapters 17, 18, 27, this volume).

For some, the most exciting convergence has been the redefinition of cultural evolution within the field of cognition and social transmission. The debate as to whether cultural phenomena are "learned" or "innate" has been resolved into various positions that claim to reconcile the two. Some, like Sperber (2001), emphasize the genetically specified mechanisms in the brain that structure various inputs. Hence, the contents of these inputs from the organism's external environment are less important than the filtering mechanisms in the brain that give them meaning. Others, such as Ingold, would claim that no such determination exists and if such a thing as culture exists, it is as the result of emergent properties from a total system of relations set up "by the presence of the organism in its environment" (Ingold 2001). Critics of the determinism of evolutionary approaches, which in this latest cognivitist model is comprised by sets of

instructions in the forms of genes passed down through the generations, emphasize instead the need to take account of the total environment, which is the product of developmental processes rather than genetic endowment.

Postcolonial and Indigenous Archaeology and Anthropology

Changes in the relationship between archaeology and anthropology since the nineteenth century have largely been in response to wider changes in the perception of the importance of the knowledge they produce. One of these changes is what passes at present under the term of globalization. We see this as a growing tendency for the devolution of metropolitan power from the West to the rest of the world (Friedman 1994). The apparent decline of the nation-state has also encouraged regional devolution, attended by the pursuit of the cultural resources needed to preserve autochthonous identities. And in academic terms, there has been a decline in the obvious superiority of Western knowledge and a feeling that much of its social content has been rendered obsolete. The certainties of an objective, scientifically based knowledge have been disrupted by the recognition that all knowledge is authorized by power relations, and that other areas of the developed world now have alternative claims based on their own traditions. The natives are answering back, and the ethnographic description of "their cultures" as a timeless present separate from our own is no longer acceptable. The influence of postmodernist writers such as Foucault and Lyotard exposed the Western power/knowledge bias in anthropological and archaeological writings, and showed instead that history is now being made by contending cultural projects. Clifford talked of this conceptual shift as "tectonic" in its implications; the loss of certainty meant that cultural analysis was now enmeshed in global movements of difference and power which link all societies in a common historical process (Clifford and Marcus 1986: introduction).

Yet, in what constituted itself as a postmodern anthropology, it became too easy to simply assume an extension from Western postmodernist debates to postcolonial issues in the rest of the world, on the assumption that "they" would still follow metropolitan aspirations. Controversies over the recognition of cultural difference, particularly in the challenges made to multiculturalism, are indicative of conflicts in the future (Taylor 1994). The movement of immigrants from the former colonized periphery to metropolitan centers shows, for example, that to claim citizenship based on the right to maintain cultural difference exposes them to the dangers of being enclaved and made suitable for deportation at any convenient moment. It is precisely the claim to share in what we all hold in common as humanity that gives ethnic minorities rights to citizenship in multicultural societies, while allowing them as minorities to retain other distinctive features of their cultural identity (cf. Kuper 1999: 243). This has for some times encouraged anthropologists to see the past as an impure mishmash of influences, in which case a nineteenth-century diffusionism may not have been too far off the mark. "All cultures are the result of a mishmash, borrowings, mixtures that have occurred, though at different rates, ever since the beginning of time" (Lévi-Strauss 1985). We remain unsure, therefore, what claims to alternative knowledges will be; in particular, how indigenous knowledges will develop as alternatives to Western universal paradigms, and how such competing claims to separate cultural pasts will be evaluated, against the fact that refugees and immigrants and diaspora communities seem to manage quite well in pursuing syncretic cultural projects, adapting to, and claiming aspects of, a dominant culture as part of their identities, while not forgetting their origins.

However, we can already detect certain broad strands in global cultural politics to which anthropology and archaeology will

need to respond. Globalization as an economic process developed over much the same period as decolonization and the formation of new nation-states in the former colonial peripheries. The last decade has seen the transformation of what was seen as a gradual devolution of a centralized center-periphery system into a more fragmentary system of multiple centers and semi-peripheries. Terms such as First World and Third World now seem strangely out of touch with current realities, to which terms such as North and South appear more appropriate. Postcolonial authoritarian states that were legitimized through their client relations with either the US or the Soviet Union in the contexts of the Cold War, are now fragile and under pressure to change and become more representative of populations within their territories. Older established states equally face tensions in their relations with ethnic and other minorities, and in the present contexts of local access to media and communications technology, cannot indulge in well tried methods of violent suppression. In Europe, what Verena Stolcke has termed the rise of cultural fundamentalism, has shocked the Western liberal orders of representative democracies, by the capacities for essentialized (i.e., culture serving as a racial ideology) identities to reappear and justify ethnic exclusion (Stolcke 1995). Indigenous social movements in North America, Australia, and Africa also witness the power to rediscover precolonial identities in the present, as part of the process of resisting state power or combatting the global interests of transnational companies. Land claims and access to mineral resources increasingly depend on assertions of cultural rights, based either on treaties and agreements that have been ignored or suppressed during colonial occupation, or by establishing ownership of land, sacred sites, and natural resources by reasserting their traditional use.

These trends raise questions as to the kinds of knowledge that archaeology and anthropology will be expected to provide. These are quite pragmatic issues of how knowledge and policy combine in the shape of research grants and funding for academic posts. But they also raise questions about the adequacy of the Western-derived knowledges that may be taught as having universal applications. Ann Salmond (1995), for example, writing on Maori intellectual property, asks significant questions about academic teaching: whether European-derived anthropology/ archaeology is capable of dealing with the complexities of bicultural knowledges and whether courses in anthropology in her university should not in future be taught jointly by European and Maori anthropologists/ archaeologists. It may well be the case that the relativization of knowledges is an inevitable feature of these trends. If we can accept the juxtaposition of local knowledges, there is also no reason to privilege one over the other, and anthropology may no longer be the international yardstick by which the adequacy of such statements is to be judged. This has led to heated debates between indigenous activists and anthropologists/archaeologists on the lines of who has the right to speak for whom (cf. Keesing 1987). On the one hand, there is the academic appeal to standards of evaluation and verification of knowledge; on the other hand, there is the indigenous argument that only those of original descent can have direct access to their own culture, although they may need access to the technical skills required to make this possible.

Some of the more hostile debates recently have focused on questions of representation and possession of material culture in museums. The "Into the Heart of Africa" exhibition at the Royal Ontario Museum in Toronto caused much debate among museum practitioners on the dangers of using overly sophisticated narratives to represent the impact of colonialism in Africa, which could and were taken instead by visitors as evidence of support for colonial rule. The exhibition of Maori treasures from New Zealand in 1984 raised seminal questions about whether curators had the right to display their collections of indigenous materials,

without consultation with representatives of the original owners of cultural heritage as to how the artefacts should be displayed. The sensitivity of questions of cultural property and ownership will increase with the growth of localized identities, as a response to increasingly globalized cultural identities. We can already see that anthropologists and archaeologists in Africa, Oceania, and America are far more conversant with each other's work on an empirical first-hand level than is usual for their colleagues working in Europe. It simply makes the development of the disciplines as Western products a feature of a certain period, when colonial rule defined a strong metropolitan superiority to European schools of thought, which will increasingly become untenable.

Conclusion

Relating anthropology and archaeology will always have a special purpose for those who are interested in seeing how others negotiate a sense of past. Many anthropologists remain rather skeptical of such endeavors, and while they claim greater concern for temporality in their work, this does not necessarily imply any great interest in archaeology, as a rigorous means of providing an independent source of evidence outside the memory and oral traditions of living informants. Archaeologists, on the other hand, are wary of being overly dependent on anthropology, as an apparently obvious source of relevant theory for non- or precapitalist societies that are supposed to have existed in the past. The burden of ethnographic parallels and the distortions these have introduced into archaeological theorizing have led to a backlash, which tends to emphasize the singularity of archaeological pasts by comparison to anything encountered in the recent present, affected as they have been by several hundred years of European presence, if not active interference. It would be unfortunate, however, if this reifies once again a present/ past separation of social forms, as if the anthropologists studying the more fine-grained patterns of how people build their social lives can have no interest for the broader regional and temporal interests of the archaeologist. Certainly, one solution is to stress the historicity of both, and bias our understanding away from temporal dichotomies such as modern–tradition and look more closely at the historical emergence of communities and peoples. The archaeology of colonialism is one such instance where the traditional distinctions of anthropological and archaeological subject matter can be seen as the outcome of common historical processes.

One of the purposes of this review has been to show how changes have taken place in the kinds of knowledge produced by archaeologists and anthropologists in the last hundred years or so. I have argued that we are witnessing another major change at present that will lead to greater convergence of interests. The focus is more on how local people in their own historically given circumstances create identities on the basis of the cultural resources available to them. Devolution and regionalism are taking on much greater priority as a means of binding people to a sense of place in a globalizing world, where flows of capital, information, and people seem to dissolve ties and create a hyperreal world of momentary attachments. People struggle to sustain their sense of identity in these circumstances, and the growth of ethnic and regional "ties that bind" is witness to this. Claims to heritage resources and property that were formerly deemed to be "traditional" and museological, are now prominent features of UNESCO and other organizations involved in setting the criteria for defining the role of "community" in economic and political development.

In other words, shifts and changes in knowledge are not features of fashion but respond to changing political circumstances. One of these is the tendency for history to repeat itself, as a return to the holistic concerns of nineteenth-century archaeology and anthropology involving questions of cultural origins and difference and what maintains our sense of common humanity in an increasingly interlinked world. If much of the twentieth century has been a matter of dealing with the fragments of social worlds disrupted and cast adrift by the momentous changes of the growth of global capitalism, perhaps the future holds the promise of a return to a more unifying and cohesive sense of what it is that holds our cultural worlds together.

References

Appadurai, A. 1986. *The Social Life of Things*. Cambridge: Cambridge University Press.

Asad, T. 1979. *Anthropology and the Colonial Encounter*. New York: Ithaca Press.

Barrett, J.1994. *Fragments from Antiquity*. Oxford: Blackwell.

Berger, J. 1972. *Ways of Seeing*. Harmondsworth: Penguin Books

Binford, L. 1972. *An Archaeological Perspective*. New York: Seminar Press.

Bourdieu, P. 1977. *Outline of a Theory of Practice*. Cambridge: Cambridge University Press.

Carrier, J. 1996. *Gifts and Commodities*. London: Routledge.

Clifford, J. and G. Marcus (eds.) 1986. *Writing Culture*. Berkeley: University of California Press.

Fabian, J. 1982. *Time and the Other*. New York: Columbia University Press.

Faris, J. 1972. *Nuba Personal Art*. London: Duckworth.

Feld, S. 1982. *Sound and Sentiment*. Philadelphia: University of Pennsylvania Press.

Forge, A. 1979. "Learning to see in New Guinea." In P. Mayer (ed.), *Socialization: The View From Social Anthropology*, pp. 269–92. London: Tavistock Institute.

Friedman, J. 1994. *Cultural Identity and Global Process*. London: Sage.

Fukuyama, F. 1992. *The End of History*. New York: Free Press.

Garlake, P. 1995. *The Hunter's Vision: The Prehistoric Rock Art of Zimbabwe*. London: British Museum Press.

Gell, A. 1992. *The Anthropology of Time*. Oxford: Berg.

Gell, A. 1998. *Art and Agency*. Oxford: Clarendon Press.

Ginzburg, C. 1983. "Clues: Morelli, Freud and Sherlock Holmes." In U. Eco and T. Seboek (eds.), *The Sign of Three: Dupin, Holmes and Peirce*, pp. 81–118. Bloomington: Indiana University Press.

Harraway, D. 1991. *Simians, Cyborgs and Women: The Reinvention of Nature*. London: Free Association Press.

Herle, A. and S. Rouse 1998. *Cambridge and the Torres Straits Expedition*. Cambridge: Cambridge University Press.

Hodder, I. (ed.) 1982. *Symbolic and Structural Archaeology*. Cambridge: Cambridge University Press.

Hodder, I. 1986. *Reading the Past: Current Approaches to Interpretation in Archaeology*. Cambridge: Cambridge University Press.

Hoskins, J. 1998. *Biographical Objects*. London: Routledge.

Huntington, S. 1996. *The Clash of Civilizations and the Remaking of a New World Order*. New York: Simon and Schuster.

Ingold, T. 2000. "Making culture and weaving the world." In P. Graves-Brown (ed.), *Matter, Materiality and Modern Culture*, pp. 50–68. London: Routledge.

Ingold, T. 2001. "From the transmission of representation to the education of attention." In H. Whitehouse (ed.), *The Debated Mind*, pp. 113–53. Oxford: Berg.

Jay, M. 1988. "Scopic regimes of modernity." In H. Foster (ed.), *Vision and Visuality*, pp. 3–26. Seattle: Bay Press.

Keesing, R. 1987. "Anthropology as an interpretive quest." *Current Anthropology*, 28: 161–76.

Kirch, P. and M. Sahlins 1992. *Anahulu*. Chicago: University of Chicago Press.

Knauft, B. 1993. *South Coast New Guinea Cultures*. Cambridge: Cambridge University Press.

Kopytoff, I. 1986. "The cultural biography of things: commoditization as a process." In A. Appadurai (ed.), *The Social Lives of Things*, pp. 64–91. Cambridge: Cambridge University Press.

Korn, F. 1978. "The formal analysis of visual systems as exemplified by a study of Abelam paintings." In M. Greenhalgh and V. Megaw (eds.), *Art in Society*, pp. 161–75. London: Duckworth.

Kristiansen, K. and M. Rowlands 1998. *Social Transformations in Archaeology*. London: Routledge.

Kuchler, S. 1987. "Malangan: art and memory in a melanesian society." *Man*, 22 (2): 238–55.

Kuchler, S. 1992. "Making skins: Malangan and the idiom of kinship in northern New Ireland." In J. Coote and A. Shelton (eds.), *Anthropology, Art and Aesthetics*, pp. 94–112. Oxford: Clarendon Press.

Kuchler, S. 1997. "Sacrificial economy and its objects." *Journal of Material Culture*, 2 (1): 39–61.

Kuper, A. 1999. *Culture: The Anthropologist's Account*. Cambridge, MA: Harvard University Press.

Latour, B. 1993. *We Have Never Been Modern*. Harlow: Prentice-Hall.

Latour, B. 1999. *Pandora's Hope*. Cambridge, MA: Harvard University Press.

Leach, E. 1961. *Rethinking Anthropology*. London: Athlone Press.

Lévi-Strauss, C. 1966. *Structural Anthropology*. Harmondsworth: Penguin Books.

Lévi-Strauss, C. 1966. *The Savage Mind*. London: Weidenfeld.

Lévi-Strauss, C. 1985. *View from Afar*. Oxford: Blackwell.

Lewis Williams, J. 1981. *Believing and Seeing: Symbolic Meanings in San Rock Art*. London: Academic Press.

Mackenzie, M. 1991. *Androgynous Objects: String Bags and Gender in Central New Guinea*. Melbourne: Harwood Academic Press.

Marx, K. 1970. *The German Ideology*. London: Lawrence and Wishart.

Miller, D. 1987. *Material Culture and Mass Consumption*. Oxford: Blackwell.

Miller, D. 1995. *Acknowledging Consumption*. London: Routledge.

Miller, D. 1998. *A Theory of Shopping*. Cambridge: Polity Press.

Mitchell, W. J. T. 1986. *Iconology: Image, Text, Ideology*. Chicago: University of Chicago Press.

Morphy, H. 1991. *Ancestral Connections*. Chicago: University of Chicago Press.

Munn, N. 1973. *Walbiri Iconography*. Chicago: University of Chicago Press.

Munn, N. 1986. *Fame of Gawa*. Durham, NC: Duke University Press.

Myers, F. 2001. *The Empire of Things*. Santa Fe: University of Texas Press.

Nora, P. 1991. *Les Lieux de mémoire*. Paris: Seuil.

Pinney, C. 1997. *Camera Indica*. London: Reaktion Books.

Price, S. 1989. *Primitive Art in Civilized Places*. Chicago: University of Chicago Press.

Radcliffe-Brown, A. 1922. *The Andaman Islanders*. Cambridge: Cambridge University Press.

Radcliffe-Brown, A. 1952. *Structure and Function in Primitive Society*. London: Cohen and West.

Rowlands, M. J. 1993. "The role of memory in the transmission of culture." *World Archaeology*, 25 (2): 141–51.

Sahlins, M. 1985. *Islands in History*. Chicago: University of Chicago Press.

Salmond, A. 1995. "Self and other in contemporary anthropology." In R. Fardon (ed.), *Counterworks: Managing the Diversity of Knowledge*, pp. 23–49. London: Routledge.

Schildkrout, E. and C. Keim 1998. *The Scramble for Art in Central Africa*. Cambridge: Cambridge University Press.

Schneider, A. and R. Rapp 1995. *Articulating Hidden Histories*. Los Angeles: University of California Press.

Sinclair, P. 1993. "Urban trajectories on the Zimbabwean plateau." In T. Shaw, P. Sinclair, B. Andah, and A. Okpoko (eds.), *The Archaeology of Africa*, pp. 705–31. London: Routledge.

Sperber, D. 2001. "Mental modularity and cultural diversity." In H. Whitehouse (ed.), *The Debated Mind*, pp. 23–56. Oxford: Berg.

Speyer, P. 1999. *Border Fetishisms*. London: Routledge.

Stahl, A. 1993. "Concepts of time and approaches to analogical reasoning in historical perspective." *American Antiquity*, 58: 235–60.

Stocking, G. 1987. *Victorian Anthropology*. New York: Free Press.

Stolcke, V. 1995. "Talking culture: new boundaries, new relations of exclusion in Europe." *Current Anthropology*, 36 (1): 1–24.

Strathern, M. 1988. *The Gender of the Gift*. Cambridge: Cambridge University Press.

Strathern, M. 1990. "Artefacts of history: events and the interpretation of images." In J. Siikall (ed.), *Culture and History in the Pacific*, pp. 25–41. Helsinki: Finnish Anthropological Society.

Taylor, C. 1994. *Multiculturalism*. Princeton, NJ: Princeton University Press.

Thomas, N. 1989. *Out of Time*. Ann Arbor: University of Michigan Press.

Thomas, N. 1991. *Entangled Objects*. Cambridge, MA: Harvard University Press.

Tilley, C. 1999. *Metaphor and Material Culture*. Oxford: Blackwell.

Ucko, P. 1969. "Ethnography and the archaeological interpretation of funerary remains." *World Archaeology*, 1 (2): 262–80.

Van Beek, G. 1996. "On materiality." *Etnofoor*, 1: 5–25.

Vansina, J. 1990. *Paths in the Rainforest*. London: James Currey.

Warnier, J.-P. 2001. "A praxeological approach to subjectivation in a material world." *Journal of Material Culture*, 6 (1): 5–25.

Weiner, A. 1992. *Inalienable Possessions*. Berkeley: University of California Press.

Wolf, E. 1982. *Europe and the People Without History*. Berkeley: University of California Press.

26

Archaeology and Politics

Michael Shanks

The Politics Of Archaeology: Some Scenarios

Controversy, 1986 in Southampton UK – what stand should be taken on the participation of archaeologists from South Africa in one of the largest international gatherings of the discipline? South African archaeologists are excluded from the conference on the grounds of sanctions against apartheid. Arguments erupt over academic freedom. The World Archaeological Congress becomes its own organization after being expelled from the UISPP (the *Union Internationale des Sciences Pre-et Protohistoriques*). It claims to represent fairly the interests of archaeologists from postcolonial societies and declares its aim of diminishing the influence of archaeological models and organizations centered upon Europe.

For months I acted as a traditional academic would, arguing that academic freedom was more important than anything else, and I claimed to myself and others that one could be totally against apartheid while at the same time doing nothing about it in the sphere of academia. Shockingly, it took many months for me to realize what a patronizing stance I was adopting. (Ucko 1987: 4)

In 1985 in a culmination of weeks of violent tension and after experience of previous

years, police use force in preventing "travelers" – itinerant people – from attending the midsummer solstice at Stonehenge. One of the most visited and iconic of archaeological sites in the world, the monument is indeed suffering tremendous erosion from visitors. The official reason for the expulsion: to protect the prehistoric monument.

The police have spent over £5 million policing Stonehenge. The government have passed a Public Order Act and a Criminal Justice Act. The police can now arrest two or more people "unlawfully proceeding in a given direction," and can create "exclusion zones" to prevent confrontation. The antagonism towards the traveler is not surprising. At the end of the day England's landscape is a proprietorial palimpsest. The travelers own no land or houses, and pay no direct taxes. (Bender 1998: 130)

In 1990 the US government recognizes, after a long campaign by pressure groups, the right of Native American groups to claim back the archaeological remains of their societies held in academic collections – the Native American Graves Protection and Repatriation Act. (http://www.uiowa.edu/~anthro/reburial/repat.htm)

In 1992, members of the Department of Archaeology at the University of Zagreb publish a booklet which outlines the political program of systematic destruction of archaeological sites in Croatia, part of the former Yugoslav republic. (Department of Archaeology, Zagreb 1992; Chapman 1994)

In 1994 a final session of the World Archaeological Congress in New Delhi erupts in hostile argument. Dispute still continues over the history of the site of Ayodya, archaeological evidence being cited for and against the presence of a Hindu temple pre-existing to the Muslim mosque, which has been demolished by Hindu fundamentalists. (Rao 1994; Colley 1995)

The Politics of Archaeology: Academic Contexts of Dispute

These are just a few examples of what may be called the politics of archaeology. No archaeologist since the 1990s remains unaware of the connection their work may have with political interests, though many may wish to deny it and maintain ideas of academic neutrality.

A context of this awareness and concern for archaeology's political role is the spread and acknowledgment of the relevance of what is usually called *critical theory*.

It is appropriate to mention David Clarke's classic essay of 1973, "Archaeology: the loss of innocence," which appeared in the journal *Antiquity*. Drawing attention to the development of what he called a critical self-consciousness in the discipline, the essay described a new archaeology pulled out of its introspective focus on its subject matter to consider its shape and place in the humanities and sciences. Elsewhere, Clarke (1972) had sketched the shape of a discipline radically different to the archaeology accepted in the 1950s. The very character of archaeology was under question by a new generation, typified by Clarke himself. They argued that the quiet common sense of a traditional archaeology concerned with writing descriptive historical narrative must give way to a sophisticated and professional academic pro-

cess of theory construction and testing. This was the loss of innocence of Clarke's essay – archaeology was to take its place as one of the social sciences, with a critical attitude of doubt and suspicion about its goals and practices. Questions were raised concerning the status of archaeological practices and claims to know the past.

Clarke was, of course, one of the proponents of the New Archaeology, with his own views developed in dialogue with the new scientific geography (Clarke 1968). A powerful case was being articulated for archaeology being an anthropological science, rather than a "handmaiden to history" (Trigger 1989a: 312–18; Watson et al. 1984). The interest of the new archaeologists in radical debate about the very character of their subject was not isolated. A wave of theory building and disciplinary critique was rolling through the social sciences and humanities. Clarke was right to associate both with a reflexive self-consciousness about academic aims and methods. I see this as an essential context for an interest in the politics of disciplines.

From the beginning, there was an uneasy, if often unvoiced, tension between the two fundamental elements of this "paradigm shift" (Meltzer 1979) in archaeology – the emphasis upon a solid scientific grounding of archaeological knowledge, and an enthusiasm for theoretical critique and reflexive self-consciousness. The first tended towards an isolationist view of knowledge – value-free science as a force independent of its social and cultural context. The second encouraged a connection between academics and the location of their work – standing back and considering how social and cultural forces may impinge upon the construction of knowledge (as in Trigger's *History of Archaeological Thought*, 1989a). And indeed this tension is evident in Clarke's own work, though he is often now simply associated with "new" archaeological science: he was very conscious of archaeology as a disciplinary community (that essay with which I began this section) and explicitly acknowledged the preconceptions held by every archaeologist and which tied them to their cultural milieu (consider figure 1.1 in Clarke 1972).

So it is clear that many new archaeologists were dissatisfied. They found fault with the way archaeological knowledge and practice were being justified, with the view of archaeology as one of the humanities, its knowledge founded upon the academic status and reputations of its practitioners rather than the objective (read neutral and scientific) merit of their work. This is the significance of the turn to positivist social science so clear in new and processual archaeology. Science is seen as a neutral independent force in the service of truth claims, and archaeology, to be a respectable and responsible academic practice, should be scientific (Shanks and Tilley 1992: ch. 2; Binford 1987). This is one answer to the question of the relation of intellectual work to society – science is a neutral and detached commentary on society and culture, an independent tool for various political purposes.

On the other hand, intellectual critique and theory building have long been associated with left-wing thought and *intimately tied* to a program of social change. This connection between academic theory and political practice is encapsulated in Marx's eleventh thesis on Feuerbach, that philosophers had so far interpreted the world whereas the point was to change it (Marx 1970: 123). In this position it is not conceived possible or appropriate to separate the practices which make up science, academic claims to knowledge, and society. Theory building has here focused upon the nature of the relationships between academic work, disciplines, society, and culture (Lampeter Archaeology Workshop 1997).

A factor in the explosion of the discussion of theory in the social sciences and humanities since the 1960s is certainly the emergence of the new left (Gombin 1975). This was, and still is for some, a broad and multifaceted concern with rational responses to the failure of socialist programs in Eastern Europe and the Soviet Union, particularly after the Soviet invasion of Hungary in 1956. The appetite for rethinking and reconstructing ways of thinking about culture and society was sustained through the radical student politics of the 1960s, and the expansion of universities and the higher education sector seen across the developed world in the second half of the twentieth century. The role of the academic as cultural critic has been subject to extraordinary inspection. The fundamental question is whether academics can stand back detached from their subject matter and their place in society.

Clarke claimed that the self-consciousness emerging in archaeology was a critical one and I certainly see the new archaeology, as well as further changes in archaeological thinking, as programs of critique. Indeed, changes in archaeological thought in the last three decades can easily be interpreted as cycles involving critique, formalization of a position, then further critique (consider culture history brought under critique by new archaeology, this formalized as processual, followed by postprocessual standpoints).

Theory building in the social sciences and humanities more generally has incorporated a broad field often termed *critical theory*. This has both a particular and more general reference. The first is to the branch of Western Marxian thought which developed in the 1920s and after, as an intellectual expansion of Marxian thought into areas of culture and consciousness (Anderson 1976). It is frequently associated with the work of members and associates of the Frankfurt School of Social Research, and with debates around their work which still carry on. Familiar names here are Adorno, Horkheimer, Marcuse, Benjamin, and Habermas (Held 1980; Geuss 1981). The second more general and often unspecific use of the term *critical theory* refers to a restructuring of the social sciences and humanities around various agendas and debates focused upon continental, particularly French, philosophy (Culler 1982; Dews 1987). Names which may be mentioned are Derrida, Foucault, and Baudrillard. The broad reference of the term comes from its use in literary studies to refer to theories of criticism. Here critical theory is commonly connected with post-structuralism, cultural commentary on post-modernity, new feminism, and a wide range of postcolonial cultural thought.

This is not the place to review critical theory, to which there are many introductions (Calhoun 1995 is relevant to this chapter). It is important nevertheless to draw clear attention to three elements of critique which are central to our understanding of the politics of archaeology and how it has become the issue it now is.

The first is the wide-ranging concern in critical theory with the sociology of knowledge. This can be traced back to Kant's critiques and includes work in phenomenology after Husserl and Schutz. Notably it centers upon those who have considered the social context of the construction of scientific knowledge (Fuller 1993, 1997): from Mannheim through Thomas Kuhn to contemporary constructivist thought (Schwandt 1994). The latter emphasizes the inseparability of social location and claims to truth, upholding the argument that there is no truth in and of itself, beyond society, culture, and history.

The second element of critical theory I wish to emphasize is feminist critique (Andermahr et al. 1997). A broad range of sometimes contradictory work has raised awareness of the gendered bias of the construction of knowledge and the production of culture. This has involved both criticism of the sociology of disciplines (for example, the systematic inequalities rooted in gender which lead to disproportionate success accruing to male academics and professionals) and the inherent gender bias of some systems of knowledge.

The third, and more specific, aspect of critical theory is a critique of anthropology (Marcus and Fisher 1986; Clifford and Marcus 1986; Clifford 1988, 1997). This may be seen as self-consciousness and questioning of the role of anthropological science in a world after the dissolution of the old Western European empires. Here the inter-

ests of the discipline of anthropology, archaeology included, have been traced to the colonial expansion of newly industrialized nation-states in the eighteenth and nineteenth centuries, encounters with Western Enlightenment's cultural Other, and an assimilation of "other" people, theorized as "exotic," into objects of scientific and academic study (Fabian 1983; Herzfeld 1987).

Critical theory has thus raised the following questions:

- how academic and scientific disciplines may be subject to systematic bias;
- how this bias may be rooted in conceptions of gender and ethnocentric views of other cultures;
- how the history of disciplines is not necessarily a story of the neutral progress of knowledge of an independent object of interest.

In all there is serious doubt that academics can inhabit an ivory tower of intellectual freedom from society, history, and culture.

In accounts of the history of archaeological thought it is not usual to connect critique and science in this way. I think, however, that it is necessary to do so to account for a set of tensions in current archaeology and at the heart of the concern about the politics of the discipline.

One tension is between innocence and skepticism. Innocence refers to the fascination with the act of discovering lost times in the immediacy of the physical encounter with ruins and remains. This is not just the innocence of the freshman undergraduate drawn to archaeology by the fascination of discovering the past. It is a cultural tourism of times gone by, great discoveries of lost civilizations, investigations of great themes in human history, from hominid origins through to the relics of industrialization. Perhaps not always innocent, it is certainly, in my view, naive in its belief in a direct route from the discovery of archaeological finds through to knowledge of the past. This innocence and naivety may be contrasted with the skepticism, implicit in what I have written about critique, that knowledge is ever value free.

There are those in archaeology and other humanities and social sciences uneasy with disciplinary change, the questioning or critique of orthodoxy, the renegotiation of disciplinary boundaries, the recycling of ideas, the necessity of learning new techniques and skills, and the doubts raised by theorizing how disciplines construct knowledge (Flannery 1982). In contrast are those who embrace all this, fervently pursuing Clarke's critical self-consciousness. This tension is between the stability represented by self-contained scientific neutrality and the commitment of the cultural politician, locating knowledge in different political agendas (consider Yoffee and Sherratt 1993 and Hodder's 1994 response).

Other related tensions, often unvoiced, are between the university academic who believes in academic neutrality, those authoring in a public media sector (writers, television producers, educators, movie makers), and professional workers in cultural resource management who manage the material remains of the past. These are classic tensions between the research oriented academic and the popular author, between the interested amateur and the professional. At the heart of these tensions is the question of to what extent archaeological knowledge can stand on its own, to what extent the remains of the past should be directed at an amateur public, serviced by responsible, neutral professionals.

This review of the explicit theory building around the history and shape of disciplines can help account for the disputes about academic neutrality, about the role and responsibility of professionals, about the independence of archaeologists from broader cultural issues such as religion, spirituality, ownership and rights to the past.

To develop a deeper understanding as a basis for attempting some resolution of these problems like academic neutrality, I will introduce some of the cultural changes of the last thirty years, associated with ideas of a cultural shift to postmodernity.

Archaeology and the Politics of Postmodernity

It is clear that archaeology and anthropology are central to the cultural development of the advanced capitalist nation-states of the nineteenth century. Political revolution (Britain in the seventeenth century, France and the United States at the end of the eighteenth) accompanied the forging of a new form of political unity through the industrial nation-state (Hobsbawm 1990). A crucial factor in ideas of national identity was the imperialist and colonial experience of travel and other cultures (Pratt 1992). I have already made mention of the role of anthropology in confronting the industrial West with its alternative. Archaeology provided material evidence of folk roots of the new state polities. This has been one of the main cultural successes of archaeology – to provide the new nation-states of the eighteenth and nineteenth centuries with histories and origin stories rooted in the material remains of the past (Díaz-Andreu and Champion 1996). Myths of ancestry were articulated in new national narratives, stories of belonging and common community. Both archaeology and anthropology provided specific symbols and evidences used to create exclusive and homogeneous conceptions of identity rooted in national traditions, conceptions of race, ethnicity, and language. Many archaeologies around the world perform a role of providing material correlates for stories and myths of identity and belonging (Trigger 1984; Kohl and Fawcett 1995; Olivier and Coudart 1995; Meskell 1998).

Conceptions of modern identity are still dependent upon the idea of the nation-state and upon the formation of nation-states in the nineteenth century, but recent history clearly shows their instability. They often have no obvious cultural justification in geography, history, race, or ethnicity.

Nation-states are social constructions (Anderson 1991; Bhabha 1990). Growing out of the demise of old empires, nation-states have frequently been connected with Enlightenment notions of human rights and rational government (democracy and representation), relying on these to unify people around a common story of their national identity. Such unified history and culture has always failed to cope with diversity. The distinction between nation and nation-state has frequently collapsed into contention, with ideas of self-determination and freedom, identity and unity colliding with the suppression of diversity, and relying on domination and exclusion that override a genuine egalitarian pluralism (Chatterjee 1993).

This is a modernist tension between Enlightenment ideas of popular will and sovereignty, universal human rights, and locally circumscribed nation-states, each independent of similar polities on the basis of cultural identity and history (Turner 1990).

The tension has shifted emphasis in recent decades. Nation-states now have less power and agency, which is in stark contrast to the ever-increasing influence of structures and movements of corporate and transnational capital. In a period of rapid decolonization after World War II this globalization is about the transformation of imperial power into supranational operations of capital, communications, and culture. This postcolonial world is one of societies, including new nation-states, that have escaped the control of the empires and ideological blocs of Western and Eastern Europe. An ideological unity is engineered through mass culture – a predominantly American culture. And the integrated resources of the global economy lie behind it (Curti and Chambers 1996; Featherstone et al. 1995; Featherstone 1990; Spybey 1996).

But with international capital, global telecommunications, and world military order, the nation-state continues to be a major structural feature of this postmodern scene. The postcolonial state is heavily and ironic-ally dependent upon notions of the state and nation developed in Europe, and so too it is dependent upon the same sorts of ideological constructions of national identity developed through history, archaeology, and anthropology (Hobsbawm and Ranger 1983). Hence a key tension or contradiction in globalization is between the fluid free market between nations, epitomized in multinational and corporate capital and based upon ideologies of the free individual operating beyond boundaries of any individual polity, and ideologies of difference, ideologies of local identity. Here the nation, nation-state, and nationalism remain potent.

And here archaeology remains a vital cultural factor, in the context too of ideas of heritage. For the crucial cultural issue is that of the ways local communities engage with these processes of globalization. And the ways they do, compare with the ways colonized communities dealt with imperial colonial powers; the interpenetration of local and global cultural forces is a feature of modernity since at least the nineteenth century. It is not simply a one-way process of influence, control, dissemination, and hegemony, with an American Western homogenized culture taking over and supplanting local identity. It is not just top-down dominance, but a complex interplay of hegemony, domination, and empowerment. A key issue is the way external and internal forces interact to produce, reproduce, and disseminate global culture within local communities. To be asked, is to what extent the global is being transformed by peripheral communities; to what extent, by appropriating strategies of representation, organization, and social change through access to global systems, are local communities and interest groups empowering themselves and influencing global systems.

Here then is a broad context for some of those issues on the archaeological agenda already illustrated. There is the part archaeology plays in the construction of national and cultural identities (Rowlands 1994). A key is an encounter with materiality and regional focus, the ruins of a local past, setting the homogenization of processes like nationalism, colonization, and imperialism against the peculiarities of history and geography. This is about the relation between local pasts and those global methods, frameworks, and master narratives which may suppress under a disciplinary and cultural uniformity the rich pluralism and multicultural tapestry of peoples and histories.

The Grounds of Dispute

This politics of archaeology can also be seen as a series of debates or disputes. Let me clarify.

The perceived importance of the material past has led to a tangle of issues surrounding preservation and conservation. This has been a significant area of legislative effort in heritage management. What should be preserved for posterity? It is fundamentally about value: what of the material past is valued most and on what grounds? (Carman 1996).

Questions of what should be preserved, how and for whom, lead immediately to questions of ownership and access. The repatriation of cultural goods and valuables also comes under this heading: should museum collections be dispersed to their places of origin and their supposed cultural owners, or are there grounds other than provenance upon which ownership may be decided?

There are disputes about academic neutrality. Can the academic archaeologist stand back from the past and present, claiming scholarly neutrality?

Closely connected is a question of pluralism (correlating with the issue of diversity and multiculturalism introduced in the previous section). Can there be multiple and commensurable claims on the material past? If not, who is to decide whose interests are to be heeded?

This issue of pluralism is also about authority. For example, do the claims and views of an amateur carry the same weight as those of an academic? More generally this is a question of who should represent the past. Is it only the professional academic claiming scientific authority?

The authority and role of the academic, professional, or intellectual may be argued to depend upon notions of neutrality. Professional independence may be associated with freedom from politics and therefore authority. But religion and spirituality hold competing claims on authority. So is archaeological science to be considered only a body of theory, in contrast to the fundamental spiritual truths of a religion?

On these issues of science, religion, and identity, it matters what is said of the past, the precise way in which it is reconstructed or told. Clearly, there are disputes about what happened in the past, but disputes which go beyond mere academic interest are clear candidates for the political in archaeology. Did the expansion of the Third Reich find precedent in the prehistoric and, according to some, archaeologically attested expansion of Aryan peoples in prehistory? Many have argued this is an incorrect reading of prehistory.

The growth of archaeology as a profession working in universities and government organizations, and tied to significant bodies of conservation legislation, has led to professional associations such as the Institute of Field Archaeologists in Britain and the Society for American Archaeology in the USA. They have developed codes of practice frequently and explicitly based upon ideas of professional ethics. How should a field archaeologist deal with different demands of clients? How should a field archaeologist be trained? What are the rights of archaeological workers? Some of these are obvious political issues. Others may appear more to do with professional practice, though I am going to contest this distinction below.

Some have argued that there is a marked disparity in the distribution of influence and authority in the world archaeological community, with archaeologists from the First World effectively exporting their theories, practices and frameworks abroad.

In all these areas of debate and dispute it is common to find that the politics of the discipline is held to be separate from its science, and from the past itself. Politics is seen as referring to what is done with the past. If the political is identified in archaeological thought, it is frequently seen as a source of undesirable bias or prejudice, at best to do with the *application* of knowledge to a social, cultural, or political issue. The political is seen as to do with the *context* of scientific study.

Under this view I identify as follows the key concerns of conventional academic politics:

- *Sovereignty, legality, and border disputes:* Over what intellectual territory does archaeological science hold sway? What is considered right and wrong in archaeological practice? What are the terms under which archaeology and other academic or cultural practices may encroach upon each other's territory?
- *Policing the boundaries of the discipline:* how to maintain archaeology's integrity in the face of competing claims on its sphere of influence
- *The rights, competencies, and role of the academic, intellectual, professional, or "scientist":* what makes an archaeological scientist a good practitioner in the discipline.

Archaeological Community

I now wish to build on this commentary about the organization of groups of archaeological workers and approach the topic of archaeology and politics in a different way.

I do not see the politics of the discipline as about its social and cultural *context* at all. Instead, I am going to consider what may be termed the political economy of the discipline of archaeology. In focusing upon archaeological communities, I will argue that archaeology is best seen as a mode of cultural

or scientific production rather than scientific discovery. It is not useful to think of the politics of archaeology being about the *application* or *context* of archaeological knowledge.

The Archaeological Site of Dispute: Legislating Difference

Let me begin with a simple question: What happens on an archaeological site?

Let me explain the question with an example. At the moment, I am part of a large international project excavating a protohistoric settlement in Sicily and surveying its region (http://www.stanford.edu/~mshanks). Several universities, government organizations, groups, and individuals are involved from Sicily itself, Northern Europe, and the United States. There is a broad research design and some individual areas of interest, for example in regional economic organization, in the cultural groups interacting in the mid-first millennium BC. We rely on different sources of funding. Sometimes the different interests work together efficiently, sometimes not, as we debate method, management structures, our different agendas. Is a traditional archaeological approach to culture history really compatible with the aims of others to study the negotiation of cultural identity? Is an ethnography of the project, locating its interests in a broader intellectual community and landscape, to be pursued, or should the site and the past be the focus?

These debates worked themselves out through the use of trowels and picks (the trowel the favorite tool of the stratigraphic aficionado), surveying instruments (the total station and GIS an ideal for detailed contextual information record), terminologies (orthodox Greek words for finds or more neutral terms?), lines of authority (who, ultimately, is to reconcile different interests?), rights of access (who can have access to material and information?), issues at the local superintendency of antiquities (conservation of the finds, permissions, negotiations with the forestry commission over the use of earth-moving machinery), arrivals at the local airport (organizing transport), photography (digital and conventional, of what and of whom; are the diggers themselves legitimate subjects for record?), recording systems (the design of a database which could encompass different approaches to the site and its finds), phone lines (ISDN lines and portable cellular phones offering remote access), the intellectual boundaries of the project (how far should our critical self-consciousness go?).

Where is the science in such a project? Do science and archaeology refer tightly to the work on site, shifting earth, bagging materials, processing them in a lab and on computer screen? Is the ethnography of a project, studying its participants and accounting for their interests not part of archaeology, something to do with the context of the archaeological study of the past? And if so, what of the rest? Everything from permissions to funding to relations with the Sicilian town which so hospitably receives our interests. Is the task of organizing efficient earth moving simply the *context* of doing the science of discovery?

I refer back now to that orthodox and basic insistence on the distinction between science and non-science, seen here in various forms. This is politics – the permissions, the interest of the local minister of culture, the different local interest groups. This is heritage and identity – ideas of a Sicilian prehistory to be found in a conventional designation of culture historical archaeology, the Elimi culture of the mid-first millennium BC. These are the objects of archaeological inquiry – finds and deposits.

I wish to take issue with these distinctions, with this sort of insistence upon distinguishing the scientific from the spiritual from the political from the personal. It is, I believe, part of a desire to keep science and society or politics apart, this notion of archaeology and its context. And with this desire I connect a radical separation of the technical and

the social, the professional from the political, the past from the present.

These distinctions are about value, it might be noted (Shanks 1992: 99–101). A potsherd may invoke an interest in ceramic petrology which is considered quite separate from the value the piece may have to the art market, or to a local antiquarian in a town in Sicily, or to a school child interested in its images of waterbirds. But the different interests are not commensurable, for archaeologists alone are held to speak for the remains of the past, representing them in gaining reliable knowledge of the past.

And the introduction here of value reminds us that these distinctions are often about separating archaeology's proper practice from distractions or irrelevant matters. What really matters, under this view, is that the project pulled through the summer, in spite of the political/cultural/logistical/practical *difficulties*. I do not see these as trivial interests or values, irrelevancies distracting us from the real past, from archaeological methods, ideas, and narratives. Instead, I insist that without what is normally kept separate from the field science, there could be no field science. Workers need to be transported and fed. Permissions are needed. And, as is commonplace to any researcher, research simply would not happen without the grant applications and awards. All this experience that is a field project is the *concrete life of science*.

Building Archaeological Communities: The Professional Answer

What holds this project together? It is a question of archaeology's political economy – what makes a project work? This is a classic question of political philosophy – the nature of social order.

The conventional answer is that this order arises from the subject itself, the *discipline* of archaeology. Order lies in the disciplinary paradigms and practices. It is not that order of this sort arises from a common interest in the material past. For this would bring incompatible and potentially conflicting practices together – treasure hunting art collector with dispassionate scientist. Instead of interest, the very term *discipline* communicates the order and unity. Discipline includes accredited methods, systems of qualification for practitioners and codification of archaeology's object. There are systems of entry and rules of belonging to the discipline. Discipline is thus also partly a moral order of duties and responsibilities, according to which one may be an archaeologist.

Power and normative behavior are closely associated in disciplines. Borders are policed to ensure the quality of what is taken for normal, accredited, practice and belief. Cranks and charlatans need to be kept out. Respectability needs to be ensured. When there is doubt, for example in contentious issues, there are systems of arbitration and appeal. These are located in a public sphere of disciplinary members, the community of archaeology. Reference may be made to peers of professionals or particular authorities for arbitration or judgment. Of course, general debate also takes place in this same public sphere, through the systems of peer review and publication. The public sphere of a discipline is usually held in great value, considered to be the fundamental basis of the rational establishment and progress of knowledge. I also hope it is clear how notions of academic collegiality and freedom of speech fit into such a sketch of disciplinary community.

Building Archaeological Communities: The Question of Constitution

However, I propose that this conventional answer to the question of social order in archaeology – discipline – does not adequately answer the question of what holds everything together in a field project such as ours in Sicily. For there are still emphasized the boundaries between what is archaeological and what is not, and for our purposes here, the distinction between matters appropriate to science and those appropriate to politics, between science and its context or application.

In this political economy of archaeology let me now introduce the concept of constitution. A constitution may lie behind the establishment of social or political order. A constitution determines who shall be a social subject, a social agent, and empowered member of a society; it governs the distribution of competencies in a community, decides the rights and duties of subjects. Forms of representation are central to constitutional arrangements, according to which it is decided who may speak and for whom. In legal terms this is also a matter of the reliability of different kinds of speech and witnessing, being about to whom we listen and pay heed.

Again, the archaeological constitution is to do with the discipline and its regulation. Archaeologists are the empowered subjects, representing, or speaking on behalf of, usually, the past, through its testimony, the remains of the past. Archaeologists are obliged to do this fairly and without avoidable bias.

An immediate constitutional question is that of the strength or validity of the arrangement. What makes people believe in archaeology? What makes the archaeological constitution robust? Confidence may reside in the guarantees of quality built into the discipline as a profession – the systems of qualification and regulation. But these can only claim to guarantee a certain kind of relationship with the past on the part of archaeologists. This relationship is one that is argued to deliver the most secure knowledge of the past; it is built on epistemological links related to the reality of the past. It seems to me that we believe in archaeology because we believe that the past happened and that its evidence or testimony, the real and material remains of past times, may be fairly represented by an archaeologist working under this particular discipline.

I am going to question some of the assumptions made in this archaeological constitution, particularly the *legal* arrangement between the past, its material remains, and their fair representation by archaeologists.

A Historical Interlude: Modernity and the Political Economy of Natural Science

Archaeology shares its constitution with many other academic disciplines. Like other political constitutions, it took its present form some time ago as part of the Enlightenment's reassessment of people's place in the world.

To illustrate and explain how science and politics come together and diverge, let me introduce Robert Boyle, seventeenth-century chemist and natural philosopher, an acknowledged father of modern science. He conducted experiments on air, vacuums, combustion, and respiration, developed a new theory of matter, and researched various chemical elements. Steven Shapin and Simon Schaffer have written about his arguments for the empirical method in science, the method that is the basis of all modern scientific inquiry, archaeology included (Shapin and Shaffer 1985; Shapin 1994; I rely heavily on the reading of Bruno Latour 1993: 13–43).

Boyle was critical of the science, or rather "natural philosophy," of his time. And instead of grounding his criticisms and new ideas in the traditional way, in logic, mathematics, or rhetoric, Boyle argued that scientific experimentation, based upon direct experience, is the best way of acquiring factual knowledge of the world. A bird suffocates in a vacuum pump in a scientist's laboratory. This is witnessed by the scientist and his gentlemen associates. It is held to display the existence of air. How is the fact to be disseminated and believed?

Boyle modeled his answer to this issue of reliability on a legal and religious system of witnessing: witnesses gathered at the scene of the event can attest to the existence of a fact, the matter of fact, even indeed if they do not know its true nature (air essential to respiration). Boyle and his colleagues abandoned the certainties of apodeictic reasoning through logic and mathematics in favor of direct experience, the testimony of witnesses, and opinion.

Juridical witnessing carries the danger of insecure testimony. But Boyle's witnesses are not the fickle masses; they are gentlemen – independent of the state, credible, and trustworthy. So experimental philosophy emerged partly through the purposeful reallocation of the conventions, codes, and values of gentlemanly conduct and conversation into the domain of natural philosophy.

There is a crucial difference to the practice of courts: the nature and agency of the events, their significance, and the witnesses. In experimental science, trials were now to deal with affairs concerning the behavior of inert materials and bodies – the world of natural phenomena. These are not of the human world, but they are endowed with meaning and indeed "will" – through affecting laboratory instruments before trustworthy witnesses.

This is also the problem of the relationship between direct experience and its report or representation. Proper science is seen as a culture which rejects reliance upon authority and others and seeks direct experience. But not everyone has a vacuum pump in the seventeenth century, a piece of laboratory equipment perhaps as advanced as a fusion reactor of today. And the juridical model of credibility and argument has a new mechanism for winning the support of one's peers – the marshaling of the opinion of as many trustworthy "gentlemen" as possible, whether this opinion is expressed directly, or through footnotes in a scientific paper.

The broader argument here is that in securing knowledge we rely upon others. This reliance is a moral relationship of trust; crucial to knowledge is knowing who or what to trust – knowledge of things depends upon knowledge of others. Hence Boyle's translation of gentlemanly conduct into scientific practice. What we know of the chemistry of air, or atoms, or indeed the past *irreducibly* contains what we know of the people who speak for and about these things (just as what we know about people irreducibly depends upon what they say about the world). Essential, therefore, to the spread of science is machinery, the laboratory instruments capable of inscribing the witnessing, trust in the freedom of action and virtue of gentlemanly conduct, and a network or community of science ensuring the consistency of instrumentation and communication between its members.

Central to this experimental life is the conduct of the experimenter. For Boyle is not only creating a scientific discourse. He is creating a political discourse from which politics is to be excluded. Gentlemen proclaim the right to have an independent opinion, in a closed space, the laboratory, over which the state has no control. Reliability thus hinges on freedom – political freedom. This involves an absolute dichotomy between science as the production of knowledge of facts, and politics, the realm of state and sovereign.

Nevertheless, the empirical method is based upon a juridical and indeed political metaphor of representation, agency, and competency. Machines and instruments in the laboratory or in the field produce costly and hard to reproduce facts, witnessed by only a few, and yet these facts are taken to be nature as it is, directly experienced, believed ultimately by the majority. The witnesses are believed to be reliable, fairly *representing* the facts to others. The key term uniting science and politics is *representation*. Consider two fundamental and homologous questions of science and politics. Who is speaking when the scientist speaks? Who speaks when the political representative speaks? It is proposed that this homology makes it possible to speak of the conjoined invention of scientific facts and modern citizenship, dependent as it is upon

representation and in democracy, trust in the virtue of the political will of the majority.

This intimate connection between inquiry and politics is denied or found problematical, as I have tried to argue in the case of archaeological field science. It is as if the stability of knowledge of things requires the implicit relations of trust and issues of representation to become invisible, the politics of inquiry to be a problem or embarrassment. For Bruno Latour, Boyle's arguments are archetypical of this parallel strategy or structure of modernity. On the one hand is the creation of extraordinary *hybrids* or translations, like Boyle's joining of law court, moral virtue, the accoutrement of scientific laboratory, the facts of nature and its underlying reality – all in an experimental method which, of course, has been extraordinarily successful. On the other hand, such hybrids are often fervently denied, being based upon a partitioning of experience and practice. Latour (1993: 5–8, 35–7) calls this the modern critical stance: a radical separation of science, society, politics, and religion, the human world of people and culture divorced from the natural world of things.

Let me summarize and pull together the main points of this digression into the history of science:

- Scientific credibility, rooted in empirical and experimental method, has a moral history as well as an epistemological structure.
- The history of modern science is not about the emergence of "proper" scientific practice out of prescientific superstition. This is not just the case of Boyle. Historical studies have repeatedly shown how the progress of science does not depend upon some force of truth operating in favor of better science; it is not about the achievement of closer epistemological approximations to truth or reality (Fuller 1997).
- We are encouraged to see scientific disciplines as communities and moral

orders inseparable from the construction of knowledge. We should be suspicious of the sort of splits I have claimed are endemic to the politics of a discipline like archaeology: the separation, for example, of method from political significance or context.

- We are encouraged to consider science as an irreducible hybrid of heterogeneous cultural and natural elements. The corollary is that society, too, is so composed. Concepts applicable to both are representation and constitution.

- This all points towards scientific knowledge being understood as a social achievement. This is a performative model of reasoning and the building of knowledge.

Heterogeneous Social Engineering and Political Ecology

This digression was to illustrate the relevance of the concept of constitution in an analysis of the politics of the discipline of archaeology. What I have described as archaeology's current constitution is only one limited schema of apportioning rights, responsibilities, competencies, agencies, and pertinences. For this is what constitutions do. And more: as a mode of constructing knowledge of the past, archaeology is rooted in a metaphysics of reality, past, present, subject, subjectivity, object, objectivity. For every constitution determines who counts, who, or what, is subject to the will, desire, scrutiny, and use of its social agents. And on what basis: for example, complex notions of subjectivity and objectivity, or personal bias and distanced fair-mindedness, are considered important for judging the words and actions of one who is representing another.

This constitutional issue involves the past itself, which is represented, in its remains, by the archaeologist and is deemed subject to their competency and responsibility as an accredited member of the archaeological profession or community. Let me deal a little

further with this political issue of representation.

Representation may be more or less direct. The strongest position in this political economy is often considered to be one where the role of representation is apparently minimized or absent, where emphasis is thrown upon the past itself. The ideal is thus to let the past speak for itself, an ideal found in those calls for a return to simple field practice, calls which regret the arrival of Clarke's critical self-consciousness. This throws suspicion on the activity of interpretation, on the representative, and refers us to the grounds upon which adequate representation may be considered to have been made. Whom do we believe when they talk of the ruined past? The matter is sharpened by the difficulty, indeed frequent unfeasibility, of corroborating witnesses, of questioning again the represented interest, the ruined past, because the past is partly or wholly destroyed in its excavation, in the act of questioning. We cannot pose the question again, reexcavate a site, so we must assess the trustworthiness of the archaeologist, the representative. Professional accreditation becomes all the more important.

It should be noted that such a disciplinary constitution involves apportioning rights to inanimate objects – the remains of the past. We are not used to thinking in terms of such political *rights*. Nor are we used to crediting agency to such things as instruments of examination and measurement like laboratory equipment, yet this is the implication of histories such as that of Boyle and the early days of the Royal Society. Seeing archaeology in terms of its constitution reconnects archaeologists and the past that is their interest. Anthropological and historical studies of science have shown again and again how it is so little about abstract method or epistemology. Every practicing scientist knows the importance of the committees, institutions, and funding agencies. Alongside Latour's familiar critical stance of science and its objects radically separated from a context of society, history, religion, and metaphysics, we find *networks* of fundamentally *political* connection running through archaeological and other scientific projects. Like Boyle, they may connect laboratories with field locations, with instruments, with new insights into real homologies between scientific and cultural practice. I am picking up here that point above, about the hybridity of Boyle's scientific innovation. The hybridity of these networks of association, these social orders, makes my argument less about political economy and more an *ecology* of practices and knowledge. For the systems of translation that are archaeology may connect a trowel with a computer database, with a debate about cultural ethnicity, with a community's aspiration to tap the affluence of a tourist trade, all as I described in our field project in Sicily. The political is not just about people, rights, and relationships; it is about things, too. This is the main thrust of Latour's fascinating history of modernity, *We Have Never Been Modern* (1993).

So a discipline like archaeology is, I propose, a hybrid process of *heterogeneous engineering*, to borrow a phrase from the sociologist of technology John Law (1987). Archaeology may connect all sorts of heterogeneous things, ideas, aspirations, values, communities, subcultures, and contexts (Shanks 1992). The things left of the past are translated through the cultural and political interests of the present. As Bruno Latour (1993: 4) puts it: "it becomes impossible to understand brain peptides without hooking them up with a scientific community, instruments, practices – all impedimenta that bear very little resemblance to rules of method, theories and neurons."

Archaeology as Cultural Production

So how am I proposing to think of the politics of archaeology? It is an ecology of mobilizing resources, managing, organizing, persuading. Archaeology is a *hybrid* practice and I think this is more useful and indeed more correct than seeing archaeology as beginning with method and an epistemological relationship between past and present.

So archaeologists do not happen upon or discover the past that may then become contentious or subject to some political wrangle. Archaeology is a process in which archaeologists, like many others, take up and make something of what is left of the past. Archaeology may be seen as a mode of cultural production (McGuire and Shanks 1996).

I also note here, and not without some irony, the profound relevance of management studies to such political ecology. We are becoming used to discussions of the profession of archaeology and its management of the past (for example, Cooper et al. 1995; McManamon and Hatton 2000). Some focus on archaeology's politics. Most sustain the paradox of a scientific neutrality or expertise connected to the cultural hybridity that I have been concerned with in this chapter. But think again of matters such as organizing projects, information flow, harnessing the creative energies of flexible teams of people, designing intelligent and reflexive record and accounting systems. Hybridity and heterogeneous engineering is the subject of the best of management thinking (consider, out of a vast selection, Peters 1992, 1999). It is about political mobilization.

Constituting New Communities

I end by drawing out some implications.

Archaeology precipitates political issues in which many archaeologists feel helpless or at a loss for words, other than those which assert their expertise in representing an image of what may have happened in the past. I see this as a political impasse that can be avoided. Archaeologists should wise-up and not expect to disconnect archaeological method, however scientific we want it to be, from everything that allows it to happen the way it does. So, ultimately, there can be no escape from politics behind a stand for neutrality or correct scientific answer. The corollary is that there is no knowledge for its own sake and archaeologists should maintain a deep skepticism towards all claims to knowledge, whatever their disciplinary origin. This gives to the archaeologist a responsibility for his or her actions far wider than assumed at present.

The hybrid unity I have described as the typical archaeological project makes archaeology comparable and commensurable with other social practices Archaeologists are in the same social and cultural milieu as those others who take up and work with the material remains of the past. Albeit under different *constitutional arrangements* – this is the difference, and simultaneously the grounds for comparing and connecting archaeology with other interests in the material past. So the boundaries of the discipline are arbitrary, though justifiable (on the grounds of archaeology's constitution). The accredited norms of the discipline should be constantly reviewed.

My argument implies a crucial difference in the definition of archaeological community: who is held to belong, how one may join, and on what grounds. It is not now something definitively legislated by professional associations, though they may wish to have the monopoly. It is not just about adherence to a common method. Community is formed in the construction of cultural works. So our critical attention is drawn to the mechanisms of community building in academic and professional discourse. I note the key issues of freedom of access, pluralism, and borders.

For me, what David Clarke's critical self-consciousness did was to blow archaeology apart, spreading it through a shifting disciplinary and cultural space. What is the archaeological project in these postcolonial times? In political terms I suggest we could do worse than look to the building of new communities, with a commitment to unceasing and open experiment around our assumptions, methods, media, and our ultimate aim of understanding the past in the present.

References

Andermahr, S., T. Lovell, and C. Wolkowitz 1997. *A Concise Glossary of Feminist Theory*. London: Arnold.

Anderson, B. 1991. *Imagined Communities: Reflections on the Origin and Spread of Nationalism*, 2nd edn. London: Verso.

Anderson, P. 1976. *Considerations on Western Marxism*. London: Verso.

Atkinson, J. A., I. Banks, and J. O'Sullivan 1996. *Nationalism and Archaeology*. Glasgow: Cruithne Press.

Bender, B. 1998. *Stonehenge: Making Space*. Oxford: Berg.

Bhabha, H. (ed.) 1990. *Nation and Narration*. London: Routledge.

Binford, L. 1987. "Data, relativism and archaeological science." *Man*, 22: 391–404.

Bond, G. C. and A. Gilliam (eds.) 1994. *Social Construction of the Past: Representation as Power*. London: Routledge.

Calhoun, C. 1995. *Critical Social Theory*. Oxford: Blackwell.

Carman, J. 1996. *Valuing Ancient Things: Archaeology and Law*. London: Leicester University Press/Cassell.

Chapman, J. 1994. "Destruction of a common heritage: the archaeology of war in Croatia, Bosnia and Herzegovina." *Antiquity*, 68: 120–6.

Chatterjee, P. 1993. *The Nation and its Fragments: Colonial and Postcolonial Histories*. Princeton, NJ: Princeton University Press.

Clark, G. 1983. *The Identity of Man*. London: Methuen.

Clarke, D. 1968. *Analytical Archaeology*, 1st edn. London: Methuen.

Clarke, D. 1972. "Models and paradigms in contemporary archaeology." In D. L. Clarke (ed.), *Models in Archaeology*. London: Methuen.

Clarke, D. 1973. "Archaeology: the loss of innocence." *Antiquity*, 47: 6–18.

Clifford, J. 1988. *The Predicament of Culture: Twentieth Century Ethnography, Literature and Art*. Cambridge MA: Harvard University Press.

Clifford, J. 1997. *Routes: Travel and Translation in the Late Twentieth Century*. Cambridge, MA: Harvard University Press.

Clifford, J. and G. Marcus (eds.) 1986. *Writing Culture: The Poetics and Politics of Ethnography*. Berkeley: University of California Press.

Colley, S. 1995. "What happened at WAC-3." *Antiquity*, 69: 15–18.

Cooper, M., A. Firth, J. Carman, and D. Wheatley (eds.) 1995. *Managing Archaeology*. London: Routledge.

Culler, J. 1982. *On Deconstruction: Theory and Criticism after Structuralism*. London: Routledge and Kegan Paul.

Curti, L. and I. Chambers (eds.) 1996. *The Post-Colonial Question: Common Skies, Divided Horizons*. London: Routledge.

Denzin, N. 1997. *Interpretive Ethnography: Ethnographic Practices for the 21st Century*. London: Sage.

Dews, P. 1987. *Logics of Disintegration: Poststructuralist Thought and the Claims of Critical Theory*. London: Verso.

Díaz-Andreu, M. and T. Champion (eds.) 1996. *Nationalism and Archaeology in Europe*. London: University College London Press.

Fabian, J. 1983. *Time and the Other: How Anthropology Makes its Object*. New York: Columbia University Press.

Featherstone, M. (ed.) 1990. *Global Culture: Nationalism, Globalization and Modernity*. London: Sage.

Featherstone, M., S. Lash, and R. Robertson (eds.) 1995. *Global Modernities*. London: Sage.

Flannery, K. 1982. "The golden Marshalltown: a parable for the archaeology of the 1980s." *American Anthropologist*, 84: 265–78.

Fuller, S. 1993. *Philosophy of Science and its Discontents*, 2nd edn. New York: Guilford Press.

Fuller, S. 1997. *Science*. Buckingham: Open University Press.

Gathercole, P. and D. Lowenthal (eds.) 1989. *The Politics of the Past*. London: Unwin Hyman.

Gero, J. M. and M. W. Conkey (eds.) 1991. *Engendering Archaeology: Women and Prehistory*. Oxford: Blackwell.

Geuss, R. 1981. *The Idea of Critical Theory: Habermas and the Frankfurt School*. Cambridge: Cambridge University Press.

Gombin, R. 1975. *The Origins of Modern Leftism*. Harmondsworth: Penguin Books.

Graves-Brown, P., S. Jones, and C. Gamble (eds.) 1996. *Cultural Identity and Archaeology: The Construction of European Communities*. London: Routledge.

Hassan, F. 1995. "Truth, morality and politics in archaeology: the WAC-3 Ayodya case study." *Papers from the Institute of Archaeology*, 6.

Held, D. 1980. *Introduction to Critical Theory: Horkheimer to Habermas*. London: Hutchinson.

Herzfeld, M. 1987. *Anthropology Through the Looking Glass: Critical Ethnography in the Margins of Europe*. Cambridge: Cambridge University Press.

Hobsbawm, E. 1990. *Nations and Nationalism Since 1780*. Cambridge: Cambridge University Press.

Hobsbawm, E. and T. Ranger (eds.) 1983. *The Invention of Tradition*. Cambridge: Cambridge University Press.

Hodder, I. 1994. "Digging up the foundations." *Times Higher Education Supplement*: 22.

Kohl, P. L. and C. Fawcett (eds.) 1995. *Nationalism, Politics and the Practice of Archaeology*. Cambridge: Cambridge University Press.

Lampeter Archaeology Workshop 1997. "Relativism, objectivity and the politics of the past." *Archaeological Dialogues*, 4: 164–75.

Latour, B. 1987. *Science in Action: How to Follow Scientists and Engineers Through Society*. Milton Keynes: Open University Press.

Latour, B. 1993. *We Have Never Been Modern*. London: Harvester Wheatsheaf.

Law, J. 1987. "Technology and heterogeneous engineering: the case of Portuguese expansion." In W. E. Bijker, T. P. Hughes, and T. Pinch (eds.), *The Social Construction of Technological Systems*, pp. 111–34. Cambridge, MA: MIT Press.

Layton, R. (ed.) 1989a. *Conflict in the Archaeology of Living Traditions*. London: Unwin Hyman.

Layton, R. (ed.) 1989b. *Who Needs the Past? Indigenous Values and Archaeology*. London: Unwin Hyman.

Leitch, V. 1983. *Deconstructive Criticism*. London: Hutchinson.

Leone, M. and R. Preucel 1992. "Archaeology in a democratic society: a critical theory perspective." In L. Wandsneider (ed.), *Quandaries and Quests: Visions of Archeology's Future*, pp. 115–35. Carbondale: University of Southern Illinois Press.

Leone, M. and P. Shackel 1987. "Toward a critical archaeology." *Current Anthropology*, 28: 283–302.

Leone, M. P., P. R. Mullins, M. C. Creveling et al. 1995. "Can an African-American historical archaeology be an alternative voice?" In I. Hodder, M. Shanks, A. Alexandri, V. Buchli, J. Carman, J. Last, and G. Lucas (eds.), *Interpreting Archaeology: Finding Meaning in the Past*, pp. 110–30. London: Routledge.

McGuire, R. and M. Shanks 1996. "The craft of archaeology." *American Antiquity*, 61: 75–88.

McManamon, F. and A. Hatton (eds.) 2000. *Cultural Resource Management in Contemporary Society: Perspectives on Managing and Presenting the Past*. London: Routledge.

Marcus, G. E. and M. Fisher (eds.) 1986. *Anthropology as Culture Critique: An Experimental Moment in the Human Sciences*. Chicago: University of Chicago Press.

Marx, K. 1970. "Theses on Feuerbach." In K. Marx and F. Engels (eds.), *The German Ideology*, pp. 121–3. London: Lawrence and Wishart.

Meltzer, D. 1979. "Paradigms and the nature of change in American archaeology." *American Antiquity*, 44: 644–57.

Meskell, L. (ed.) 1998. *Archaeology Under Fire: Nationalism, Politics and Heritage in the Eastern Mediterranean and Middle East*. London: Routledge.

Miller, D., M. Rowlands, and C. Tilley (eds.) 1989. *Domination and Resistance*. London: Unwin Hyman.

Olivier, L. and A. Coudart 1995. "French tradition and the central place of history in the human sciences: preamble to a dialogue between Robinson Crusoe and his Man Friday." In P. Ucko (ed.), *Theory in Archaeology: A World Perspective*, pp. 363–81. London: Routledge.

Pearson, M. and M. Shanks 2000. *Theatre/Archaeology*. London: Routledge.

Peters, T. 1992. *Liberation Management: Necessary Disorganization for the Nanosecond Nineties*. New York: Fawcett Columbine.

Peters, T. 1999. *The Circle of Innovation*. New York: Vintage.

Pratt, M. L. 1992. *Imperial Eyes: Travel Writing and Transculturation*. London: Routledge.

Rao, N. 1994. "Interpreting silences: symbol and history in the case of Ram Janmabhoomi/ Babri Masjid." In G. C. Bond and A. Gilliam (eds.), *Social Construction of the Past: Representation as Power*, pp. 154–64. London: Routledge.

Renfrew, C. 1989. "Comments on 'Archaeology into the 1990s.' " *Norwegian Archaeological Review*, 22: 33–41.

Rowlands, M. 1994. "The politics of identity in archaeology." In G. Bond and A. Gilliam (eds.), *Social Construction of the Past: Representation as Power*, pp. 129–43. London: Routledge.

Schmidt, P. R. and T. C. Patterson (eds.) 1995. *Making Alternative Histories: The Practice of Archaeology and History in Non-Western Settings*. Santa Fe: School of American Research Press.

Schwandt, T. 1994. "Constructivist, interpretivist approaches to human inquiry." In N. K. Denzin and Y. S. Lincoln (eds.), *Handbook of Qualitative Research*, pp. 62–79. London: Sage.

Shanks, M. 1992. *Experiencing the Past: On the Character of Archaeology*. London: Routledge.

Shanks, M. and C. Tilley 1987. *Social Theory and Archaeology*. Cambridge: Polity Press.

Shanks, M. and C. Tilley 1989. "Archaeology into the 1990s." *Norwegian Archaeological Review*, 22: 1–12.

Shanks, M. and C. Tilley 1992. *Reconstructing Archaeology: Theory and Practice*, 2nd edn. New Studies in Archaeology. London: Routledge.

Shapin, S. 1994. *A Social History of Truth: Civility and Science in Seventeenth Century England*. Chicago: University of Chicago Press.

Shapin, S. and S. Schaffer 1985. *Leviathan and the Air Pump: Hobbes, Boyle and the Experimental Life*. Princeton, NJ: Princeton University Press.

Shennan, S. (ed.) 1989. *Archaeological Approaches to Cultural Identity*. London: Unwin Hyman.

Spybey, T. 1996. *Globalization and World Society*. Oxford: Blackwell.

Trigger, B. 1984. "Alternative archaeologies: nationalist, colonialist, imperialist." *Man*, 19: 355–70.

Trigger, B. 1989a. *A History of Archaeological Thought*. Cambridge: Cambridge University Press.

Trigger, B. 1989b. "Hyperrelativism, responsibility and the social sciences." *Canadian Review of Sociology and Anthropology*, 26: 776–97.

Tunbridge, J. E. and G. J. Ashworth 1996. *Dissonant Heritage: The Management of the Past as a Resource in Conflict*. Chichester: Wiley.

Turner, B. (ed.) 1990. *Theories of Modernity and Postmodernity*. London: Sage.

Ucko, P. 1987. *Academic Freedom and Apartheid: The Story of the World Archaeological Congress*. London: Duckworth.

Ucko, P. J. (ed.) 1995. *Theory in Archaeology: A World Perspective*. London: Routledge.

Watson, P., S. LeBlanc, and C. Redman 1984. *Archaeological Explanation: The Scientific Method in Archaeology*, 2nd edn. New York: Columbia University Press.

Yoffee, N. and A. Sherratt (eds.) 1993. *Archaeological Theory: Who Sets the Agenda?* Cambridge: Cambridge University Press.

Further Reading

Many works on the politics of archaeology have appeared in Routledge's One World Archaeology series (previously published by Unwin Hyman), and edited by Peter Ucko. These gather many short papers (of varying quality) delivered at the World Archaeological Congress meetings. Relevant volumes coming from the first 1986 gathering mentioned in this chapter include those edited by Miller et al. (1989), Gathercole and Lowenthal (1989), Layton (1989a, 1989b), and Shennan (1989). Another later book has been edited by Bond and Gilliam (1994). These review issues such as the importance of local pasts to contemporary notions of identity, and different interests in the archaeological past which sometimes deviate significantly from the academic. A broad theoretical survey dealing with contexts for this world archaeology program has been edited by Ucko (1995).

Most work on the management of archaeology radically separates it from the politics of the discipline, preferring to stress that archaeology should be a professional, and so independent, practice. Nevertheless, Tunbridge and Ashworth (1996) have written an excellent general study of the political implications of heritage management. For the particular issue of the return or repatriation of artefacts, see Greenfield (1996).

Various works by Grahame Clark through his career display a clear awareness of the cultural politics, or rather implications of archaeology from a distinctive and principled stand. See the chapter "Prehistory and today" in his *Archaeology and Society* (originally 1939), then late works such as *The Identity of Man* (1983), for example.

Peter Ucko's (1989) account of the events surrounding WAC 1986 is invaluable as a case study in academic politics and its confusions. He deals with academic freedom and the role of the academic in society, as well as the personal politics of academic institutions. For another more abstract treatment of the same issue, and equally controversial, see the chapter on the politics of theory in *Social Theory and Archaeology*, my book written with Tilley (1987). This was followed by a programmatic statement in the journal *Norwegian Archaeological Review* (Shanks and Tilley 1989), with a discussion which includes a clear argument for neutrality and science from Colin Renfrew (1989). My understanding of the way disciplines work was changed enormously through encounter with the work of Bruno Latour; see especially his *Science in Action* (1987). He is at the forefront of studies of science which focus on the micropolitics of the construction of knowledge.

For critical theory and archaeology one should definitely examine Mark Leone's pioneering and well-conceived position in American historical archaeology (Leone 1987; Leone and Preucel 1992).

The debate about relativism, science, and value freedom and whether it is feasible to have different, perhaps contradictory and incommensurable accounts of the past, is reviewed in an article by the Lampeter Archaeology Workshop, and in the ensuing, sometimes heated, debate in the journal *Archaeological Dialogues* (1997). Different positions can be found articulated by Trigger (1989b) and Binford (1987). The issue of alternative pasts (to those constructed in mainstream academia) is also tackled by Schmidt and Patterson's edited volume (1995), and in the Annapolis project (Leone et al. 1995). For a more academic treatment of the question of archaeology's agendas, see the collection edited by Yoffee and Sherratt (1993).

Nationalism and archaeology has received a great deal of attention since the 1980s. Edited books are by Atkinson et al. (1996), Kohl and Fawcett (1995) and Díaz-Andreu and Champion (1996): these include a diverse range of views illustrating many of the positions outlined in this chapter. Meskell's edited collection (1998) is particularly interesting, with its explicit political focus.

27

Archaeology and Green Issues

Martin Bell

Changing Agendas in Archaeology and Society

The green movement places particular emphasis on the environment, conservation, the value of diversity, and the need for sustainable development. Although diverse, even anarchic in some political manifestations, it is given unity by concern for key issues: global warming; pollution; extinctions; deforestation; soil erosion; nuclear issues; and most recently the possible negative effects of genetically modified organisms. Green concerns originated with the testing of nuclear weapons (1945–60s), disillusionment fostered by the Vietnam War (1964–75), and growing awareness of pollution pioneered by Rachel Carson's *Silent Spring* (1962). These concerns challenged the view, accepted since the eighteenth-century Enlightenment, of the value of science and technology and the march of progress.

Green concerns are about current and future trends. However, understanding them requires knowledge of what has happened in the past. Here, archaeological science and environmental archaeology can contribute to green issues. For other writers, greenness in archaeology has a humanistic hue. Meskell (1995) connects earth religion, the mother goddess, growing environmental movements, and ecofeminism, showing that all draw on the archaeological record to suggest the existence of a former utopian, greener and sexually more equal past. For Pitts (1992) and Greeves (1992), green archaeology is just as much about empathy with the landscape and respect for the differences between people, as it is about specific environmental concerns. The two strands of thought, scientific and humanistic, are strongly linked: "the green archaeologist has an important role to play in highlighting threats to the information base from which the story of humanity must needs be written" (Pitts 1992: 212).

Postmodernism, the One World concept, and green issues lie in the same arena of political and social concerns. Postmodernism in archaeology stimulated the development of postprocessual archaeology (Shanks and Tilley 1987; Chs. 6 and 26, this volume). The concept of One World, an archaeology respecting diversity and racial equality, inspired the first World Archaeological Congress in 1986 (Ucko 1987). Within archaeology, postmodern/One World perspectives, which have dominated theoretical debate since the 1980s, have neglected green concerns. Social and environmental perspectives became separated or even opposed (Thomas 1990; O'Connor 1991), at variance with their perception in contemporary society. Can an opposition of culture and nature at a theoretical, institutional, and legislative level be intellectually justified? Does this enhance or damage our ability to protect the past for the benefit of the future?

Green archaeologies are interdisciplinary, not respecting subject boundaries which are anachronistic to present concerns. Within archaeology, the influence of green concerns can be measured in two ways. Firstly, what has archaeology contributed to the wider environmental science agenda? This is timedepth for the study of people–environment relationships. Secondly, specific to archaeology, through the development of a conservation ethos. Until the early 1980s, the emphasis was on the destruction of heritage – American "salvage archaeology," British "rescue archaeology" (Rahtz 1974). There subsequently arose greater emphasis on Environmental Impact Assessment. The USA Natural Environmental Policy Act of 1969 pioneered the analysis of federal activities that affected human health and environment, including the historical, cultural, and natural heritage. Environmental Impact Assessment likewise became central to planning policy in European Union countries and formed Principle 17 in the declaration of the United Nations Rio conference (1992). Increasingly in the USA the benefits of development are balanced against calculation of the losses to "nature's services" (Daily 1997): pest control, insect pollination, fisheries, climate, vegetation, flood control, cycling of matter, atmospheric composition, genetic library and soil retention, formation and fertility (Mooney and Ehrlich 1997).

The growth of a conservationist ethos in archaeology from around 1980 reflects a quiet revolution. This hardly figures in the theoretical literature, but dominates the activities of field archaeologists. It may influence archaeology's future just as much as postmodern perspectives.

In this chapter, space precludes full details of the work of various relevant organizations, but further information is given as World Wide Web resources in the list of references. This chapter is written from a British and European perspective and that area provides the most detailed examples; however, where possible, reference is made to evidence from other parts of the world.

Ecology, Archaeology, and Environmental Change

The term *ecology* was first used by Ernst Haeckel in 1873 and since the 1960s has entered public consciousness as the intellectual underpinning of the green movement. Ecology is defined as "scientific study of the interactions that determine the distribution and abundance of organisms" (Krebs 1985). Recognition of the interconnectedness of species challenges the human mastery of nature, long dominant in Judaeo-Christian Western thought.

Ecological concepts underpin environmental archaeology (see Chapters 17 and 18, this volume), an approach taking off from the 1940s with the work of Iversen (1973), who identified anthropogenic influence in Holocene vegetation sequences. Ecological perspectives were emphasized following World War II by Steward in the USA and Clark in Britain. This led to interdisciplinary projects involving natural scientists on agricultural origins at Jarmo, Iraq (1947–55) and Tehuacan Valley, Mexico (1960–8).

Many pioneering environmental archaeologists began with an interest in the documentation of environmental change, and later in their careers became committed to the nature conservation implications of their studies. Godwin from the 1940s founded British vegetation history (Godwin 1975), later emphasizing the conservation importance of the Fenland (Godwin 1978) and peat bogs in general (Godwin 1981). Similarly Mitchell, pioneering Irish palaeobotany from the 1940s, increasingly stressed conservation perspectives (Mitchell 1986, 1990). G. W. Dimbleby was trained in botany and ecology and initially researched in forestry, where he demonstrated in the 1950s that buried soils under barrows (burial mounds) in heathland contained evidence of former deciduous woodland (Dimbleby 1962, 1978). This challenged the prevailing policy of coniferous afforestation of these areas; deciduous afforestation would restore some of the fertility lost following prehistoric clearance. Dimbleby attained an archaeology chair at London University in 1964 and was a signatory of the *Blueprint For Survival* (Goldsmith et al. 1972). This document played a significant role in raising awareness in the UK of green concerns. It was naturally focused on contemporary concerns, but drew on anthropology and the past to demonstrate alternatives to the profligate exploitation of environmental resources.

The 1960s saw the development of New (or processual) Archaeology. Reacting against the particularism of earlier cultural historical approaches, it adopted an explicitly scientific position within a neo-evolutionary tradition (Trigger 1989), seeking regularities in human societies. External causes of cultural change, such as environmental change, or population factors, were emphasized. Binford emphasized ecology, drawing on his background in forestry and wildlife conservation. Systems ecology could lead to the development of explanatory theory in archaeology (Binford 1983). Systems theory was similarly part of the new analytical archaeology advocated by David Clarke (1968) in Britain.

Karl Butzer, since 1959 based in America, worked on Quaternary geography and chronology (Butzer 1964), and pioneered geoarchaeology, also drawing on Clarke's systems theory approach for human palaeoecology (Butzer 1982). His work has increasingly focused on the contribution of people to environmental change (Butzer 1981) and the implications for environmental concerns, leading to the proposition that archaeology should be a key player in interdisciplinary research on people's impact on ecosystems (Butzer 1996).

Palaeoenvironmental studies by these pioneers and others made it increasingly clear that in many parts of the world natural ecosystems are rare; human impact is ubiquitous. Hence the increasing scale and early date of human impact identified in successive syntheses by Thomas (1956), Goudie (1981), and Simmons (1989, 1993a). The scale of human agency is evident even where, before European contact, agriculture was not practiced, such as California (Blackburn and Anderson 1993) and Australia (Bridgewater and Hooy 1995). Tropical rainforest environments, previously regarded as untouched, contain evidence of clearance, as noted by Dimbleby (1965) in Nigeria and Butzer (1996) in Peten (Guatemala). Similarly, there is considerable evidence of human impact on Polynesian islands, even on Henderson Island, which was not settled at the time of European contact, but had been previously (Kirch and Hunt 1997).

Long histories of human impact were one challenge to "classical" ecology, which had emphasized climax, stability, and balance within ecosystems. This approach was to some extent atemporal, as Dimbleby (1965) argued. New approaches in ecology stress contingency and multiple pathways rather than a single definable succession. For Worster (1990), ecology today is the study of disturbance, disharmony, and chaos. This is a seminal development for archaeologists. McGlade (1995) sees human agency as more than a "pathology" in the environment, but rather as one of a range of disturbance factors alongside fauna, storms, floods, disease, volcanism, etc. None operate on a constant and even timescale; they are episodic processes, those most influential often being of high magnitude and low frequency. Central to this is the concept of pulse stability: long periods over which an ecosystem may remain relatively unchanged, separated by short-term pulses of change. The emphasis here is on contingency and the role of chance events (Gould 1987; Bintliff 1999). Such events will frequently be unrepresented in the relatively short snap-shots of most scientific research.

The effects of storms and floods were always evident in the tropics and subtropics, but were insufficiently considered by those working in temperate climates. Recent extreme events, arguably more frequent consequent on global warming, have highlighted their ecological effects. Examples are the hurricane in England on October 16, 1987 which felled 15 million trees, and the even larger-scale storm centered on France which devastated European forests on Boxing Day 1999. Past events of this kind may prove difficult to distinguish in pollen diagrams from anthropogenic effects, particularly because they created opportunities for human exploitation (Brown 1997). The elm decline ca. 5000 radiocarbon years BP in northwest Europe was long attributed to Neolithic activity (perhaps fodder gathering), dominating thinking about the Mesolithic–Neolithic transition from around 1960 to 1993. Now that a precise timescale for the decline has been established (Peglar 1993), disease has become the favored cause; indeed, the beetle vector of Dutch Elm Disease is known from contemporary horizons (Girling 1988). Farmers may unwittingly have assisted the spread of disease, and forest openings which it created would certainly have attracted people. Faunal factors may be similarly significant. Coles and Orme (1983) show that European beavers can affect the extension of wetland habitats and create openings within woodland.

What must be overcome is a twentieth-century perception of people as external to the environment, a view Ingold (1993) symbolizes with the image of the world from outer space. By linguistic definition we do not live on or off the environment, but within it, from the experiential center of our own environmental perception. Archaeologists investigate cultural landscapes comprising landforms, soils, and plant and animal communities modified by human agency and forming part of a socially constructed land-scape of settlements, fields, tracks, tombs, managed woodland, etc. Understanding requires an integrated scientific and social perspective in which the palaeoenvironmental and the phenomenological (Tilley 1994) are equally important. People change the world and thereby set up new conditions for social action (Gosden 1994). The integration of nature and culture is further highlighted by the significance of natural places in aboriginal Dream Time legend (Flood 1983), which similarly became attached to geological materials such as Jadeite axes or Stonehenge bluestones in prehistory, or the incorporation of natural places such as rock outcrops into prehistoric ritual and funerary monuments and landscapes (Bender et al. 1997; Bradley 1998). All of these serve to erode the perennial nature–culture distinction.

Just as changing perspectives in ecology have archaeological implications, so the application of more sophisticated social theory through postprocessual archaeology requires a rethink of human–environment relationships (McGlade 1995). Archaeological interest in the environment was initially based on Darwinian adaptation, underlying the bioarchaeological approach of Clark (1972), the palaeoeconomic approach of Higgs (1972), and the processual approach of Clarke and Binford, which assumed that societies were to some extent determined by their environmental context. Trigger (1989: 322) has argued that New Archaeology treated people as passive victims of forces outside understanding and control. The mathematically based catastrophe theory of social change (Renfrew 1978) attracted particular attention among a generation preoccupied by the threat of nuclear war.

There remains within archaeology a deterministic strand of thought, given new impetus by greater chronological precision. In tree ring sequences, Baillie (1995) has identified periods of much-reduced tree growth, some of which occur at the same time from California to Northern Ireland and are apparently contemporary with acid peaks in Greenland icecaps. These phenomena he associates with volcanic episodes, or possibly comet impact (Baillie 1999). Such a view might be described as a new catastrophism, since Baillie correlates these episodes with dramatic social change, famine, civilization collapse, etc. Baillie (1995: 160) makes his position clear: "archaeologists and historians have allowed determinism to go out of fashion and have given people a possibly false impression of being somehow in control." That view has significant implications for archaeology and associated green issues. Is environmental policy then of little more value than arranging the deck chairs on the *Titanic*? Baillie (1999: 215) is more positive: "it behooves us to assess the risks seriously and to begin the long haul of doing something about mitigation." The existence of sudden and global environmental changes (however caused) *is* of immense scientific importance, but we need not necessarily assume that these changes offer a simple explanation for past cultural change.

While profound social changes can result from environmental perturbations, most deterministic reasoning neglects the range of issues required for a convincing case. Rarely will the perception of an environmental problem have presented past communities with a single possible solution. More generally, it would offer a range of possible strategies for risk buffering (Hardesty 1977; Halstead and O'Shea 1989): abandon area; greater mobility; food storage; diversification; trade; alliances; population reduction (e.g., infanticide); warfare; altering the environment by burning, draining, irrigation, etc. This shifts the question of how societies are shaped by environmental change towards more challenging and (for current environmental concerns) more relevant questions of how people cope with environmental change in diverse temporal, geographical, and social contexts. Here, archaeology, with anthropology, investigates, even celebrates, the diversity of human existence and environmental

relationships, which cannot be imagined if we restrict our horizons to the narrow experience of our own time and place.

The Past and Lessons for the Future

Timescales

Decisions on current environmental issues are frequently made on the basis of data of alarmingly short duration. Frequently, scientific instrumental measurements are only available for a period of one to four decades, for instance concerning soil erosion. Extreme tidal events are recorded for around a century and basic instrumental weather information in Britain commences in AD 1659. The palaeoenvironmental record provides a longer perspective to which archaeology contributes through dated palaeoenvironmental sequences, and information on how those changes interacted with past human communities.

Research questions to which archaeology can contribute, figure prominently in the international research agenda evolving from the Environment and Development Conference at Rio in 1992 and the subsequent Kyoto conference of 1997. Climate change, sustainable development, and biodiversity moved center stage. Governments concerned by global warming formulated the Framework Convention on Climate Change, aiming to stabilize greenhouse gas emissions at levels that would prevent anthropogenic interference with the climate system. The Intergovernmental Panel on Climate Change (IGPC) sought to pool expert international opinion. Agenda 21, an international environmental action plan, was agreed.

Current preoccupations with global warming make the effects of natural climatic changes on past human communities of particular interest. Examples include the rapid climate change at the end of the last glaciation (Lowe and Walker 1996); evidence of climatic deterioration in the first millennium BC (Barber et al. 1994; Van Geel et al. 1996);

and the Little Ice Age from AD 1550–1850 (Grove 1988). In the following section we deal with environmental changes where human activity was a possible cause; for more detail, see Bell and Walker (1992) and Roberts (1998).

Extinctions and biodiversity

The genetic library of biodiversity is essential to the development of pharmaceuticals and new crops for areas where people are inadequately fed (Myers 1997). Understanding of biodiversity changes requires a historical perspective from the palaeoecological record (Brown and Caseldine 1999), in particular investigating links between past extinctions and human activity. People have been accused of causing megafaunal extinctions at the end of the Pleistocene (Martin and Klein 1984), although the limited evidence of kill sites must now be evaluated against growing evidence for rapid climate changes (Lowe and Walker 1996). Evidence for Holocene extinctions following human activity is stronger, particularly with endemic taxa which had evolved in remote islands; for example, Mediterranean island megafauna which became extinct in prehistory (Davis 1987), giant flightless birds after human arrival in Madagascar and New Zealand, or the extinction of the Dodo following European discovery of Mauritius (Bell and Walker 1992). The Pacific islands provided a laboratory for the theory of island biogeography (MacArthur and Wilson 1967), but its implicit assumption was that the plants and animals encountered at European contact reflected the natural biodiversity. On that basis were formulated relationships between island size and taxonomic diversity. It is now clear that most Polynesian islands suffered significant reduction in biodiversity during the Polynesian period. In Hawaii half the endemic bird fauna became extinct due to deforestation, which also extinguished many land snail species (Kirch and Hunt 1997).

In Britain a steady loss of taxa during the Holocene resulted mainly from hunting pressure and deforestation, including the aurochs (Bronze Age), beaver (twelfth century) and boar (sixteenth century). Beetles suffered local extinctions in Britain as a result of habitat changes such as deforestation, drainage, etc. (Buckland and Dinnin 1993), and though few mollusks became extinct, many have reduced and patchy distributions as a result of habitat loss by clearance for agriculture, etc. (Kerney 1999). What is unclear for these invertebrates is whether range reductions occurred gradually with deforestation through prehistory or accelerated due to drastic environmental changes in the post-Medieval period.

In contrast, there is growing recognition that native cultural practices have played an important part in the maintenance of biodiversity (Mitchell 1995); for instance, native peoples in California (Blackburn and Anderson 1993) and Amazonia (McNeely and Keeton 1995). The role of indigenous peoples in sustainable development was enshrined as Principle 22 in the Rio Declaration of 1992.

Deforestation and soil erosion

Easter Island offers a valuable case study of the effects of deforestation on a closed system (Bahn and Flenley 1992). Pollen analysis shows that the island was once forested with wine palms. Clearance followed Polynesian colonization, leading ultimately to the present totally treeless landscape. Thus the inhabitants could no longer build boats, or move the giant statues which are a manifestation of the most sophisticated Neolithic society known. Bahn and Flenley contend that deforestation caused social collapse, warfare, and the toppling of all the once-majestic statues. Easter Island provides lessons "of fundamental importance to every person alive today and even more to our descendants" (Bahn and Flenley 1992: 9). Issues of timescale are central to this question. Polynesian communities were clearly responsible for deforestation; what is less clear is the reason for social collapse – endemic environmental impact or tensions introduced by contacts with Europeans, who recorded a society in the process of self-destruction. This is not the only context in which Pacific societies, whose popular image is one of harmony with nature, were responsible for environmental degradation (Gosden and Webb 1994; Kirch 1983; Spriggs 1997).

Some 17 percent of the earth's surface has suffered humanly induced soil degradation since 1945 (Daily et al. 1997). A sustainability strategy for soil resources requires an understanding of erosion rates in the medium to long term in order to establish whether average annual soil loss exceeds the rate of soil formation. Soil erosion is a particular issue in the US where, in the Dust Bowl of 1934, 300 million tonnes of soil and sediment were blown away in a four-day storm. Until the 1980s, there was a view in Britain that erosion was a minor problem. Chalk and limestone soils were not thought to suffer erosion until evidence for past erosion began to emerge, followed by evidence for major episodic erosion in the same landscapes today (Bell and Boardman 1992). Severe current erosion is in autumn-sown fields where the soil is exposed during peak rainfall. Plant macrofossils likewise show autumn sowing during the Bronze Age to Romano-British periods, when some of the most severe early erosion took place.

Landscape acidification and pollution history

There is convincing evidence for the progressive acidification of lakes and upland soils, the latter process contributing to the death of conifer forests. Government strategies target coal-fired power stations and other pollutants feeding acid precipitation. Landscape acidification is not a new problem; in many upland areas it has been a progressive process through the later Holocene, resulting in soil leaching, podsolization, and the extension of blanket peat. There is also similar evidence from preceding interglacials (Birks

1986). Upland acidification is thus manifestly natural, but in the Holocene occurs much more widely as a result of anthropogenic deforestation. This is documented even in West European high rainfall areas, where we expect such processes to be largely naturally induced, such as the west of Ireland (O'Connell 1994) and the Norwegian coast (Kaland 1986). On the other hand, diatom assemblages, sensitive indicators of lake acidity, show dramatic acidification in the last 200 years, correlating with increased fossil fuel usage (Battarbee 1984; Mannion 1991). Thus the palaeoenvironmental record puts a current problem in a much longer perspective and supports current energy policy which aims to reduce acid emissions.

Significant metal pollution, especially lead, emanates from smelting and mining, and the histories of these activities can be traced in the palaeoenvironmental record. Metal levels in river sediments correlate with mining histories in their catchments (Macklin et al. 1985; Allen and Rae 1987). Metal levels in peats offer precise records of metallurgical activities (Mighall and Chambers 1993). In classical times lead use for water supply and utensils led to such high lead levels in bone that adverse health effects are postulated (Aufderheide et al. 1992). Classical pollution also produced a hemispheric effect with enhanced lead and copper levels in a Greenland ice core, correlated with intensive metal production in the Graeco-Roman period ca. 400 BC–AD 400 (Hong et al. 1994, 1996). Evidence for significant lead and other trace metal pollution has also been found as a "habitation effect" in the soils of ancient Greek towns and ordinary farms of the classical Greek period (Bintliff et al. 1990).

However, following industrialization, pollution occurs on a far greater scale. Lead deposition in Greenland during the ca. 800 years of classical civilization was roughly 15 percent of deposition in the last 70 years since leaded petrol appeared. Modern Inuit and sea mammals in Greenland have greatly enhanced mercury and lead in their bodies compared to the fifteenth century AD Qila-kitsoq mummies (Hansen et al. 1991). The fact that these people and sea mammals are 2,000 km away from sources of concentrated pollution, underlines the value of a time-depth perspective and the imperative of global rather than national solutions to problems of environmental pollution.

Gardens of Eden?

While they are appealing, ideas of a golden age before population explosions, cities, and industries, where Gardens of Eden existed in which people were in harmony with their environment, clash with the reality sketched in the preceding section. The Eden concept represents an imagined "past as a foreign country" (Lowenthal 1985). Furthermore, people's statements about the environment may diverge from their actions (Simmons 1993b). Societies respecting the natural world may, nonetheless, be responsible for significant environmental impact, e.g., the effects on vegetation of burning by Australian aboriginal communities (Jones 1969). In the Americas the assumption has been that an alien agricultural system introduced from Europe was environmentally harmful by comparison with systems developed indigenously over a long period. However, in Mexico, pre-Columbian agriculture produced soil erosion as damaging as Spanish forms of land use (O'Hara et al. 1993; Butzer 1996).

Is the natural state of affairs, then, the uncaring dominance of nature by people? Will environments eventually heal themselves as, presumably, they did in the past? We cannot ignore the vastly greater scale of human environmental manipulation in the post-Medieval period. It is therefore critical to achieve a precise understanding of the timescales of past environmentally destructive practices. We also need to understand better how these changes were perceived. Were environmentally destructive practices normal or aberrant behavior?

Nature Conservation and Archaeology

Archaeologists sometimes seem semi-detached members of the conservation lobby, leading Greeves (1990) to question whether archaeology has yet moved from the "egg collecting" to the "bird watching" phase. Archaeologists' vested interest in disturbance, however, has shifted in favor of preservation rather than rescue (see also Chapter 22, this volume). Common ground between archaeological and nature conservation interests is reflected in conference proceedings (Lambrick 1985; Macinnes and Wickham-Jones 1992; Cox et al. 1995). Archaeological sites which have escaped disturbance for millennia often contain plant and animal communities of biological interest. Ravensmose, Denmark, for example, is a small bog basin in an agricultural landscape protected as a nature reserve. It is also the findspot of the Gundestrup Cauldron, one of the most remarkable Iron Age artworks (Figure 27.1).

However, the archaeological resource is finite. Once destroyed it is unable to regenerate; conversely, many nature reserves are on regenerated land such as abandoned peat cuttings or quarries. Excavation is destructive of the archaeological record, whereas ditch digging, or the creation of wet hollows by machine-dug "scrapes," can be essential to the survival of endangered species in nature reserves. Biological resources can be audited by site survey. Archaeological evaluation is possible using non-destructive geophysical techniques, but also often requires some excavation. Protected archaeological sites tend to be spatially restricted, so they are easier to avoid in development proposals than the spatially less easily defined habitats of animals and birds. However, in reality the boundaries of a site's interest are often much more complex. Landscape context is important and palaeoenvironmental sequences are frequently off-site and without protection and spatially extensive.

Figure 27.1 The bog at Ravensmose, Jutland, Denmark: at the spot marked by the stone the Iron Age Gundestrup Cauldron was found.

There are significant national contrasts in the integration between nature conservation and archaeology (Cleere 1989). Denmark possesses a particularly well-integrated strategy in which ancient monuments, wildlife, and landscapes are all protected under the Conservation of Nature Act, reflecting the context of archaeological sites within the almost wholly humanly created landscape of Denmark (Kristiansen 1989) in which 5 percent is designated for conservation. Norway is similar (Solli 2000). In the USA the emphasis has been for federal agencies and other developers to carry out environmental assessments, including archaeological aspects, of the effects of development proposals (O'Donnell 1995; McManamon 2000).

In countries where archaeological conservation has historically focused on the mainly cultural aspects, the extent of both habitat destruction and sites has tended to be greater, as argued by Reichstein (1984) for Germany. England emerges as having a schizoid tendency as between arts and environmental emphases. At present, nature conservation does not come under the same government department and it is not surprising that the two are less effectively linked than is the case in the devolved regions of Scotland and Wales, as reflected in Scotland by support for publication of a conference on integration (Macinnes and Wickham-Jones 1992) and in Wales by strategies for the registration of historic landscapes of special conservation importance (e.g., Rippon 1996).

Above national provision there is an increasingly important international tier. The worldwide Ramsar convention on wetland conservation is aimed particularly at bird conservation, although many of the sites will also be of archaeological importance. At a European Union level there is increasing emphasis on environmental regu-

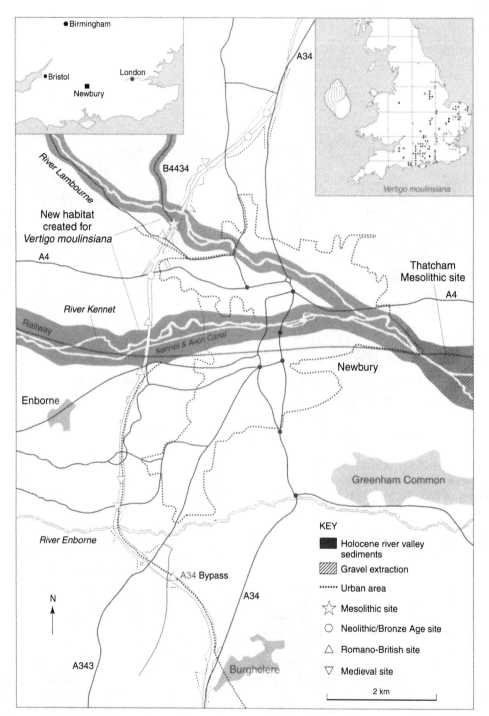

Figure 27.2 Archaeology and nature conservation around Newbury, UK: the route of the Newbury bypass A34T, and associated archaeology and Holocene sediments (after Birbeck 2000). The diagram also shows the location of Greenham Common. The insert compares the past and present distributions of *Vertigo moulinsiana* (after Kerney 1999): solid circles are records after 1965, open circles are records pre-1965, and crosses are sub-fossil records.

lations. The Habitats Directive creates special areas of conservation, which in the UK are expected to comprise 340 sites occupying 1.7 million ha (McCarthy 1999). UNESCO designates World Heritage sites on the basis of either cultural or natural significance, or a combination of the two (Prott 1992). There seems to be growing recognition of the need to link nature and culture in the development of effective conservation strategies (von Droste et al. 1995).

Wetland conservation

Many of the most successful integrated conservation strategies have been in wetland contexts (Cox et al. 1995). Raising watertables preserves the habitat of wetland biota and ensures the preservation of wood and other organics, including palaeoenvironmental resources. Shapwick Heath in Somerset (Brunning 1999) has a preserved section of the Neolithic Sweet Track within its nature reserve. Similar schemes are found in Denmark (Fischer 1999) and Ireland (Raftery 1996). A particularly ambitious scheme concerns the Federsee in Germany (Schlichtherle and Strobel 1999).

More problematic in Britain are Holocene (10,000 BP to present) palaeoenvironmental sequences which, if they lack significant archaeological sites, are not protected by English Heritage. If they lack living taxa of conservation importance, they have a low conservation priority with English Nature. The most recent sequences have special value because they can be compared with historical and instrumental records of environmental change, particularly climate change. Lowland mires are especially endangered; only 5 percent of those existing in Britain in 1850 now remain (Buckland and Dinnin 1992).

Thorne and Hatfield Moors are a striking example of a peat bog with an unparalleled beetle record (16 species now extinct in Britain) and an important dendrochronological sequence. This area was milled for peat extraction on a vast scale, but during 2002 agreement was reached to end peat cutting and restore the remaining raised mire for nature conservation.

Issues of transport infrastructure: English examples

Motorway developments are increasingly contested by green groups concerned about vehicle pollution and habitat loss. In England during the 1990s it was proposed to dig a deep cutting through Twyford Down, a site with designations for Special Scientific Interest, Scheduled Ancient Monuments, and an Area of Outstanding Natural Beauty. Despite temporary occupations of the site, construction went ahead, preceded by some archaeological excavation.

This was followed by a more considerable battle over a bypass for the town of Newbury (Figure 27.2). The Newbury area contains one of the richest concentrations of hunter-gatherer Mesolithic sites (10,000–5000 BP) in lowland Britain, of which the most famous is Thatcham (Wymer 1962). These sites are stratified in the peats, tufas, and alluvial deposits of the River Kennet, but neither English Nature nor English Heritage regarded the conservation of these sediments as a priority. English Nature was concerned about the present-day wetland overlying the Holocene sequence, a key species being *Vertigo moulinsiana*, a mollusk listed in the European Community Habitats and Species Directive (Drake 1999). Eventually, plant communities containing the mollusks were moved to a newly created wetland habitat nearby (Stebbings and Kileen 1998).

The strategy at Newbury developed by Wessex Archaeology involved a careful evaluation of the route, including fieldwalking, test pits, coring, etc., which identified ten sites (Birbeck 2000). Two were of regional or national importance, and the road was modified to preserve them *in situ*. Sites of lesser importance were subject to strategic excavation in advance of destruction.

Although the conservation of Holocene sediment sequences did not receive emphasis at Newbury, the Channel Tunnel provides an example where effective scientific recording of Holocene sediment sequences and archaeological sites was carried out when total conservation was not possible. An "archaeological style" rescue excavation of the geological sediment sequence spanned the last 13,000 years, and provided, from a molluskan and botanical perspective, the most important case study of the ecological history of any area of English chalk (Preece and Bridgland 1998).

Habitat and species history

Effective conservation requires historical information on habitat history on diverse timescales. Many heathland reserves rely on traditional grazing, burning, etc. for their maintenance, otherwise they can suffer scrub invasion, or like the Drenthe Plateau in the Netherlands, turn from heath to grassland (Bottema 1988).

Botanical evidence from chalk grassland at Overton Down, Wiltshire emphasizes the value of data on a decadal timescale. In 1960 the reserve was selected for the long-term Experimental Earthwork Project (Bell et al. 1996) – thus the botany has been monitored at regular intervals. What this has documented is a reduction of species diversity and the loss of calcium loving plants, which now survive only in the chalk-rich disturbed environment of the Experimental Earthwork itself, being lost elsewhere following changes in grassland type resulting from a reduction in sheep and an increase in cattle grazing. Thus an archaeological experiment to study changes to earthworks over a timescale of 0–128 years has fortuitously revealed recent botanical changes, with implications for the management strategy in this nature reserve.

Longer-term palaeoenvironmental information may be central to an understanding of what is being conserved, as in the case of ancient woodlands (which English Nature defines as having existed since AD 1600). Many such contain what Rackham (1980) describes as ancient woodland indicators,

(e.g., the rare small-leaved lime), supposedly marking unbroken woodland history on that site back to the time of the wildwood (Rackham 1982), albeit modified and managed. Sidlings Copse, Oxfordshire has 43 such indicators, and a pollen sequence offering an opportunity to test the theory (Day 1993). It was established that the area had been largely cleared in the Bronze Age and was totally open in Romano-British times. The existing botanically rich woodland is the result of regeneration, probably following the designation of the area as a legal forest in the eleventh century. The botanical richness of this site reflects a combination of a prolonged (ca. 1000 years) history as woodland, geological diversity, and management by coppicing (P. Dark, pers. comm.). The new knowledge about the site's history alters, but does not diminish, the significance of this Site of Special Scientific Interest.

Introductions and reintroductions

Robinson (1985) mentions weeds such as the corn cockle (*Agrostemma githago*) which have become rare in Britain following changes in arable agriculture through the twentieth century. This example was, however, only introduced to Britain within the last two millennia. Without ruling out conservation measures, the message here is that some recent introductions, during particular climatic and land-use regimes, may be unsustainable in the context of environmental fluctuations which are both naturally and humanly induced.

In attempting to enhance the biodiversity of an area the palaeoenvironmental record provides a guide to sustainability. In Britain the Sea Eagle was successfully reintroduced (Love 1983). As for proposals to reintroduce the beaver in Scotland, the palaeoenvironmental record and a recent archaeologically based study of modern European beaver populations in France (Coles 2000) assist evaluation of the likely ecological effects.

Green development

Green developments enhance the natural value of landscapes by the digging of lakes, the flooding of wetland, or managed retreat in coastal areas. The American airbase at Greenham Common, England was closed with the end of the Cold War and is now being restored to heathland. Ground disturbance on a colossal scale includes excavation of a substantial area of gravel and Holocene sediments, with slight evidence of Mesolithic activity, in the neighboring Kennet Valley.

The dilemmas of green development can be illustrated from the Gwent Levels wetlands, Wales (Bell 1995), and on a large scale. Regeneration of Cardiff docks created a barrier across Cardiff Bay that permanently flooded an area of intertidal mudflats in order to create a waterfront. Conservationists were alarmed by the implications for bird populations, but the issue was resolved by creating lagoons as alternative feeding grounds. Three possible sites with deep Holocene sediment sequences all contained significant archaeological evidence. Eventually it was decided that the only suitable site was the most archaeologically sensitive, adjacent to the greatest concentration of intertidal prehistoric archaeology identified in Britain (Figures 27.3 and 27.4), and with a palaeoenvironmental sequence spanning the last 6,000 years (Bell et al. 2000). The concentration extended into the proposed nature reserve area. The solution was shallow embanked lagoons which only penetrated prehistoric levels in small areas and were designed to do as little damage as possible to a buried, at least partly Romano-British, landscape of ditches and banks revealed during the assessment (Locock 1997).

In the Netherlands, prehistoric environmental data help recreate lost natural landscapes (Louwe Kooijmans 1995; Bottema 1988). Flevoland was reclaimed from the sea between 1957 and 1968, and includes bird reserves and a recreated wildwood in which roam elk, deer, reindeer, European bison, and Przewalski horse – a curious menagerie, most of which have been extinct in the Netherlands since the late glacial or early Holocene. Clearly, such recreations are not without academic controversy. In some Dutch recreated "wildwoods" open woodlands allow higher grazing levels than indicated by the palaeoenvironmental record. That is an issue because, in addition to their role in the enhancement of biodiversity, such sites present palaeoenvironmental research to the public. A less controversial achievement is the archaeological museum at Aarhus, Denmark where, in the surrounding park, woodland has been created representing the successive vegetational stages found in Holocene pollen diagrams.

Wider Access and Openness

In many ways archaeology may appear as undemocratic and conservative. The way heritage is presented appeals mainly to the middle classes, and the types of sites selected for preservation are remote from the interests of ethnic minorities. However, a recent MORI (2000) poll showed that 96 percent of the sampled population think that the heritage is important for teaching us about our past. Regional and class differences in perception of the heritage were marked and 50 percent of blacks and Asians felt that English Heritage is relevant. Even so, 75 percent of black people and 61 percent of Asians felt that their heritage was inadequately represented. For some of these, just as for *some* of the constituent peoples of Britain, particularly the Welsh or Scots, castles, stately homes, and industrial monuments may represent symbols of repression. Pryor (1990) proposed that making archaeology greener included achieving a broader base beyond a minority and elitist subject. Since that was written, archaeology has become a significant presence in British television schedules (see Chapter 22, this volume). A unifying theme of popular programs such as *Time Team* and *Meet the Ancestors* is that a knowledge of the past is within the grasp of

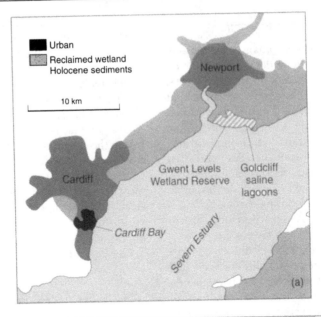

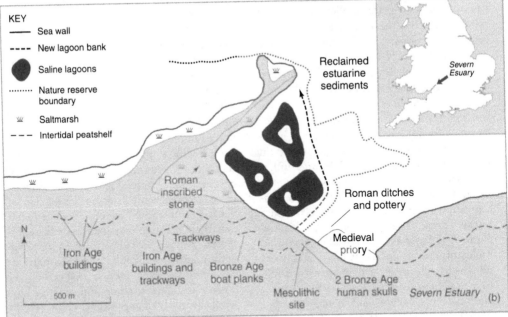

Figure 27.3   The Gwent Levels Wetland Reserve, Goldcliff, South Wales: (a) the Severn Estuary showing Cardiff Bay, the Gwent Levels Reserve, and Goldcliff; (b) intertidal archaeological sites and their relationship to the saline lagoons and nature reserve.

the person in the street and all sorts of people have something to contribute. Millions of people watch these programs, but there is little evidence that archaeologists have mobilized this growth in public interest in conservation debates.

Figure 27.4   View of the saline lagoons after completion. The photograph is from the northern corner of the saline lagoons area marked with a triangle on Figure 27.3(b). The original seabank is on the right and in the distance. A new bank associated with the saline lagoons is to the left. Photo: Edward Sacre.

At an academic level, Hodder (1999) has argued for an archaeology which is self-critical (reflexive) and multivocal, acknowledging the validity of multiple approaches to, and interpretations of, the past. Team members with very different backgrounds – arts and sciences – contribute different perspectives to projects in the way that Hodder (1996) has particularly promoted in relation to the Çatalhöyük project.

I do not see this as implying the extreme relativist position, that all interpretations are of equal value. Multiple interpretations have a right to appear on the agenda regardless of the scientific authority of their advocates. Thereafter, their value is established by rigorous interdisciplinary debate, allowing some interpretations to be provisionally accepted, others provisionally rejected. Following Adams (1988), facts are now generally understood as compelling interpretive statements which are accepted pending further critical inquiry.

Multivocality will inevitably lead to a more contested past and greater challenges to the academic authority of the professional archaeologist. In the US since 1990, archaeologists must consult with native communities before conducting excavations which might reveal human bones or sacred artefacts (McManamon 2000). In Australia, aboriginal communities increasingly participate

in a range of heritage and natural history management decisions (Bridgewater and Hooy 1995).

In Britain, heritage organizations are beginning to encounter groups with very different perspectives on the past, as the following example concerning prehistoric henges illustrates. In 1998–9 a timber circle was discovered in the intertidal zone at Holme-next-the-Sea, Norfolk (Figure 27.5), within which was a large inverted treestump (Brennard and Taylor 2000). English Heritage wished to excavate and remove this "seahenge" to prevent destruction by coastal erosion. Some local people and those described in the press as "demonstrators ranging from Druids to environmental protestors" (Davison 1999) argued the site should not be touched.

Green protesters attached significance to the site being of wood and manifestly ritual. Past respect for trees was contrasting with wholesale destruction during road developments, etc., as noted above. The protestors had an undeniable point, given the importance that archaeologists have long attached to context and the enhanced significance this has recently acquired with the development of a phenomenological perspective (Tilley 1994). However, balanced against this was the site's rapid ongoing destruction by coastal erosion. Excavation

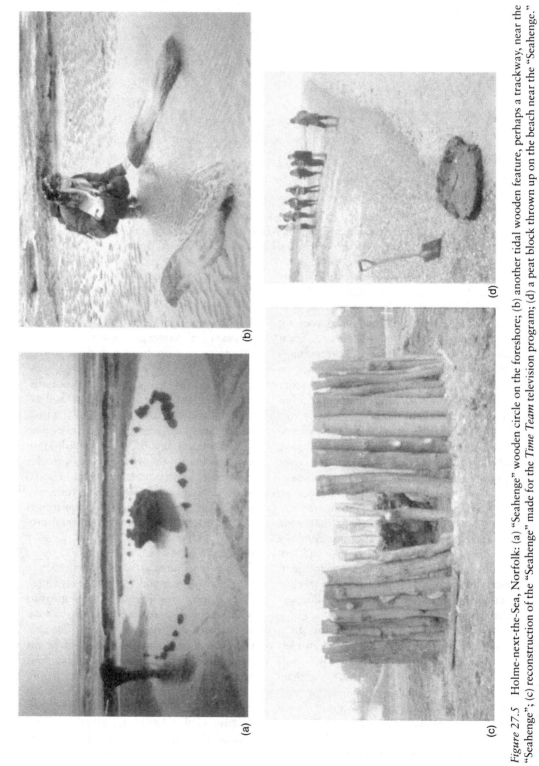

Figure 27.5   Holme-next-the-Sea, Norfolk: (a) "Seahenge" wooden circle on the foreshore; (b) another tidal wooden feature, perhaps a trackway, near the "Seahenge"; (c) reconstruction of the "Seahenge" made for the *Time Team* television program; (d) a peat block thrown up on the beach near the "Seahenge."

eventually went ahead with significant information gain about this enigmatic site, including a date of 2049 BC from dendrochronology (Bayliss et al. 1999). Excavation should eventually establish the original environmental context of the site – whether saltmarsh or freshwater wetland – and thus test a controversial statement justifying its rescue excavation, namely that originally the site lay 3–30 miles inland (*Time Team* 2000). We will certainly learn about prehistoric use of this wetland and more on prehistoric coastal change, aiding the development of more effective nature conservation strategies.

Conclusions

I have argued that green perspectives have contributed to a quiet revolution in archaeology, from rescue/salvage towards conservation. There is increasing recognition that palaeoenvironmental resources provide valuable time-depth for current environmental concerns. We have outlined the convergent trajectories of archaeology and nature conservation.

As regards the future, governments need to establish frameworks which are more favorable to integration and are designed to remove social exclusion. Local communities are likely then to engage as actively with the conservation of the archaeological heritage as they have in nature conservation issues. More effective integration involves archaeologists learning to understand and empathize more with the interests and concerns of nature conservation. Arguably some knowledge of nature conservation should be part of every archaeology degree.

Acknowledgments

This chapter is dedicated to the memory of Professor G. W. Dimbleby, who inspired the writer's interest in this and many other topics and died when it was being finished. I am grateful to Professor John Bintliff for his patience. I thank him, my colleague Dr. Petra Dark, and two referees for valued comments on an earlier draft.

References

Adams, R. M. 1988. "Introductory remarks: spatial and temporal contexts." In J. L. Bintliff, D. A. Davidson, and E. G. Grant (eds.), *Conceptual Issues in Environmental Archaeology*, pp. 1–15. Edinburgh: Edinburgh University Press.

Allen, J. R. L. and J. E. Rae 1987. "Late Flandrian shoreline oscillations in the Severn Estuary: a geomorphological and stratigraphical reconnaissance." *Philosophical Transactions of the Royal Society of London*, B315: 185–230.

Aufderheide, A. C. et al. 1992. "Lead exposure in Italy: 800 BC–700 AD." *International Journal of Anthropology*, 7: 9–15.

Bahn, P. and J. Flenley 1992. *Easter Island, Earth Island*. London: Thames and Hudson.

Baillie, M. 1995. *A Slice Through Time: Dendrochronology and Precision Dating*. London: Routledge.

Baillie, M. 1999. *Exodus to Arthur*. London: Batsford.

Barber, K. E., F. M. Chambers, D. Maddy, R. Stoneman, and J. S. Brew 1994. "A sensitive high-resolution record of late Holocene climatic change from a raised bog in northern England." *The Holocene*, 4: 198–205.

Battarbee, R. W. 1984. "Diatom analysis and the acidification of lakes." *Philosophical Transactions of the Royal Society of London*, B305: 451–77.

Bayliss, A., C. Groves, G. McCormac et al. 1999. "Precise dating of the Norfolk timber circle." *Nature*, 402: 479.

Bell, M. 1995. "Archaeology and nature conservation in the Severn Estuary, England and Wales." In M. Cox, V. Straker, and D. Taylor (eds.), *Wetlands: Archaeology and Nature Conservation*, pp. 49–61. London: Her Majesty's Stationery Office.

Bell, M. and J. Boardman (eds.) 1992. *Past and Present Soil Erosion*. Oxbow Monograph 22. Oxford: Oxbow.

Bell, M., A. Caseldine, and H. Neumann 2000. *Prehistoric Intertidal Archaeology in the Welsh Severn Estuary*. York: CBA Research Report 120.

Bell, M., P. J. Fowler, and S. W. Hillson 1996. *The Experimental Earthwork Project 1960–1992*. York: CBA Research Report 100.

Bell, M. and J. C. Walker 1992. *Late Quaternary Environmental Change*. Harlow: Longman.

Bender, B., S. Hamilton, and C. Tilley 1997. "Leskernick: stone worlds; alternative narratives; nested landscapes." *Proceedings of the Prehistoric Society*, 63: 147–78.

Binford, L. R. 1983. *In Pursuit of the Past*. London: Thames and Hudson.

Bintliff, J. L. (ed.) 1999. *Structure and Contingency in the Evolution of Life: Human Evolution and Human History*. London: Cassell.

Bintliff, J. L., B. Davies, C. Gaffney et al. 1990. "Trace metal accumulation in soils on and around ancient settlements in Greece." In S. Bottema, G. Entjes-Nieborg, and W. van Zeist (eds.), *Man's Role in the Shaping of the Eastern Mediterranean Landscape*, pp. 159–72. Rotterdam: Balkema Press.

Birbeck, V. 2000. *Archaeological Investigations on the A34 Newbury Bypass, Berkshire/Hampshire, 1991–7*. Salisbury: Wessex Archaeology.

Birks, H. J. B. 1986. "Late Quaternary biotic changes in terrestrial and lacustrine environments, with particular reference to northwest Europe." In B. E. Berglund (ed.), *Handbook of Holocene Palaeoecology and Palaeohydrology*, pp. 3–65. Chichester: John Wiley.

Blackburn, T. C. and K. Anderson (eds.) 1993. *Before the Wilderness: Environmental Management By Native Californians*. Menlo Park, CA: Ballena Press.

Bottema, S. 1988 "Back to nature: objectives of nature management in view of archaeological research." In H. van Bierma, O. H. Harsema, and W. van Zeist (eds.), *Archeologie en Landschap*, pp. 185–206. Groningen: Biologisch-Archeologisch Instituut Rijkuniversiteit Groningen.

Bradley, R. 1998. "Ruined buildings, ruined stones: enclosures, tombs and natural places in the Neolithic of southwest England." *World Archaeology*, 30: 13–22.

Brennard, M. and M. Taylor 2000. "Seahenge." *Current Archaeology*, 167: 417–24.

Bridgewater, P. and T. Hooy 1995. "Outstanding cultural landscapes in Australia, New Zealand and the Pacific: the footprints of man in the wilderness." In B. von Droste, H. Plachter, and M. Rossler (eds.), *Cultural Landscapes of Universal Value*, pp. 162–9. Stuttgart: Fischer.

Brown, A. J. and C. Caseldine 1999. "Biodiversity from palaeoecological data." *Journal of Biogeography*, 26 (1): 3–5.

Brown, T. 1997. "Clearances and clearings: deforestation in Mesolithic/Neolithic Britain." *Oxford Journal of Archaeology*, 16 (2): 133–46.

Brunning, R. 1999. "The *in situ* preservation of the Sweet Track." In B. Coles, J. Coles, and M. Schou Jorgensen (eds.), *Bog Bodies, Sacred Sites and Wetland Archaeology*, pp. 33–8. Exeter: Wetland Archaeology Research Project.

Buckland, P. et al. 1994. "Conserving the Holocene record: a challenge for geomorphology, archaeology and biological conservation." In D. O'Halloran et al. (eds.), *Geological Landscape Conservation*, pp. 201–4. London: Geological Society.

Buckland, P. C. and M. H. Dinnin 1992. "Peatlands and floodplains: the loss of a major palaeontological resource." In C. Stevens, J. E. Gordon, and M. G. Macklin (eds.), *Conserving our Landscape*, pp. 145–9. Crewe: Joint Nature Conservation Committee.

Buckland, P. C. and M. A. Dinnin 1993. "Holocene woodlands: the fossil insect evidence." In K. J. Kirby and C. M. Drake (eds.), *Dead Wood Matters: The Ecology and Conservation of Saproxylic Invertebrates in Britain*, pp. 6–20. Peterborough: English Nature.

Butzer, K. W. 1964. *Environment and Archaeology: An Introduction to Pleistocene Geography*. Chicago: Aldine Press.

Butzer, K. W. 1981. "Rise and fall of Axum, Ethiopia: a geo-archaeological interpretation." *American Antiquity*, 46: 471–95.

Butzer, K. W. 1982. *Archaeology as Human Ecology*. Cambridge: Cambridge University Press.

Butzer, K. W. 1996. "Ecology in the long view: settlement histories." *Journal of Field Archaeology*, 23 (2): 141–50.

Carson, R. 1962. *Silent Spring*. Harmondsworth: Penguin Books.

Çatalhöyük: http://www.catal.arch.cam.ac.uk

Clark, J. G. D. 1972. *Star Carr: A Case Study in Bioarchaeology*. Reading, MA: Addison-Wesley Modular Publications 10.

Clarke, D. L. 1968. *Analytical Archaeology*. London: Methuen.

Cleere, H. 1989. *Archaeological Heritage Management in the Modern World*. London: Unwin Hyman.

Coles, B. 2000. "Beaver territories: the resource potential for humans." In G. Bailey, R. Charles, and N. Winder (eds.), *Human Ecodynamics*, pp. 80–9. Oxford: Oxbow.

Coles, J. and B. Orme 1983. "*Homo sapiens* or *Castor fiber?*" *Antiquity*, 57: 95–102.

Cox, M., V. Straker, and D. Taylor (eds.) 1995. *Wetlands: Archaeology and Nature Conservation*. London: Her Majesty's Stationery Office.

Daily, G. (ed.) 1997. *Nature's Services: Societal Dependence on Natural Ecosystems*. Washington, DC: Island Press.

Daily, G., P. A. Matson, and P. M. Vitousek 1997. "Ecosystem services supplied by the soil." In G. Daily (ed.), *Nature's Services: Societal Dependence on Natural Ecosystems*, pp. 113–32. Washington, DC: Island Press.

Davis, S. J. M. 1987. *The Archaeology of Animals*. London: Batsford.

Davison, J. 1999. "Seahenge move defeats protestors." *Independent*, July 17, 1999: 6.

Day, P. 1993. "Woodland origin and 'ancient woodland indicators': a case study from Sidlings Copse, Oxfordshire, UK." *The Holocene*, 3: 45–53.

Dimbleby, G. 1962. *The Development of British Heathlands and Their Soils*. Oxford: Forestry Memoirs 23.

Dimbleby, G. 1965. *Environmental Studies and Archaeology*. Inaugural lecture May 18, 1965, Institute of Archaeology, London University.

Dimbleby, G. 1978. *Plants and Archaeology*. London: Paladin.

Drake, C. M. 1999. "A review of the status, distribution and habitat requirements of *Vertigo moulinsiana* in England." *Journal of Conchology*, 36: 63–79.

English Heritage: http://www.english-heritage.org.uk

English Nature: http://www.english-nature.org.uk

Fischer, A. 1999. "Stone Age Åmose: stored in museums and preserved in the living bog." In B. Coles, J. Coles, and M. Schou Jorgensen (eds.), *Bog Bodies, Sacred Sites and Wetland Archaeology*, pp. 85–92. Exeter: Wetland Archaeology Research Project.

Flood, J. 1983. *Archaeology of the Dreamtime: The Study of Prehistoric Australia and Its People*. Sydney: Collins Australia.

Girling, M. A. 1988. "The bark beetle *Scolytus scolytus* (Fabricius) and the possible role of elm disease in the early Neolithic." In M. Jones (ed.), *Archaeology and the Flora of the British Isles*, pp. 34–8. Oxford University Committee for Archaeology Monograph 14.

Godwin, H. 1975. *History of the British Flora*. Cambridge: Cambridge University Press.

Godwin, H. 1978. *Fenland: Its Ancient Past and Uncertain Future*. Cambridge: Cambridge University Press.

Godwin, H. 1981. *The Archives of the Peat Bogs*. Cambridge: Cambridge University Press.

Goldsmith, E., R. Allen, M. Allaby, J. Davoll, and S. Lawrence 1972. *A Blueprint for Survival*. Harmondsworth: Penguin Books.

Gosden, C. 1994. *Social Being and Time*. Oxford: Blackwell.

Gosden, C. and J. Webb 1994. "The creation of a Papua New Guinean landscape: archaeological and geomorphological evidence." *Journal of Field Archaeology*, 21: 29–51.

Goudie, A. 1981. *The Human Impact: Man's Role in Environmental Change*. Oxford: Blackwell.

Gould, S. J. 1987. *Time's Arrow, Time's Cycle*. Harmondsworth: Penguin Books.

Greeves, T. 1990. "Archaeology and the Green Movement: a case for *perestroika*." *Antiquity*, 63: 659–65.

Greeves, T. 1992. "Reclaiming the land." In L. Macinnes and C. R. Wickham-Jones (eds.), *All Natural Things: Archaeology and the Green Debate*, pp. 14–21. Oxford: Oxbow.

Grove, J. M. 1988. *The Little Ice Age*. London: Methuen.

Halstead, P. and J. O'Shea (eds.) 1989. *Bad Year Economics: Cultural Responses to Risk and Uncertainty*. Cambridge: Cambridge University Press.

Hansen, J. P. H., J. Meldgaard, and J. Nordqvist 1991. *The Greenland Mummies*. London: British Museum Publications.

Hardesty, D. L. 1977. *Ecological Anthropology*. New York: John Wiley.

Higgs, E. S. (ed.) 1972. *Papers in Economic Prehistory*. Cambridge: Cambridge University Press.

Hodder, I. 1996. *On the Surface: Çatalhöyük 1993–95*. London: British Institute of Archaeology at Ankara.

Hodder, I. 1999. *The Archaeological Process*. Oxford: Blackwell.

Hong, S., J.-P. Candelone, C. C. Patterson, and C. F. Boutron 1994. "Greenland ice evidence of hemispheric lead pollution two millennia ago by Greek and Roman civilisations." *Science*, 265: 1841–3.

Hong, S., J.-P. Candelone, C. C. Patterson, and C. F. Boutron 1996. "History of ancient copper smelting pollution during Roman and Medieval times recorded in Greenland ice." *Science*, 272: 246–52.

Ingold, T. 1993. "Globes and spheres : the topology of environmentalism." In K. Milton (ed.), *Environmentalism: The View From Anthropology*, pp. 31–42. London: Routledge.

Iversen, J. 1973. "The development of Denmark's nature since the last glacial." *Danmarks Geologiske Undersogelse*, V Raekke, 7C: 1–126.

Jones, R. 1969. "Firestick farming." *Australian Natural History*, September: 224–8.

Kaland, P. E. 1986. "The origin and management of Norwegian coastal heaths as reflected by pollen analysis." In K. E. Behre (ed.), *Anthropogenic Indicators in Pollen Diagrams*, pp. 19–36. Rotterdam: Balkema.

Kerney, M. 1999. *Atlas of the Land and Freshwater Molluscs of Britain and Ireland*. Colchester: Harley Books.

Kirch, P. V. 1983. "Man's role in modifying tropical and subtropical ecosystems." *Archaeology in Oceania*, 18: 26–31.

Kirch, P. V. and T. L. Hunt 1997. *Historical Ecology in the Pacific Islands: Prehistoric Environmental Landscape Change.* New Haven, CT: Yale University Press.

Krebs, C. J. 1985. *Ecology: The Experimental Analysis of Distribution and Abundance,* 3rd edn. New York: Harper and Row.

Kristiansen, K. 1989. "Perspectives on the archaeological heritage: history and future." In H. Cleere (ed.), *Archaeological Heritage Management in the Modern World,* pp. 21–36. London: Unwin Hyman.

Lambrick, G. 1985. *Archaeology and Nature Conservation.* Oxford: Oxford University, Department for Continuing Education.

Locock, M. 1997. "Gwent Levels Wetland Reserve, Hill Farm, Goldcliff: excavation 1997." *Archaeology in the Severn Estuary,* 8: 55–65.

Louwe Kooijmans, L. P. L. 1995. "Prehistory or paradise?" In M. Cox, V. Straker, and D. Taylor (eds.), *Wetlands: Archaeology and Nature Conservation,* pp. 3–17. London: Her Majesty's Stationery Office.

Love, J. A. 1983. *The Return of the Sea Eagle.* Cambridge: Cambridge University Press.

Lowe, J. and M. J. C. Walker 1996. *Reconstructing Quaternary Environments,* 2nd edn. Harlow: Longmans.

Lowenthal, D. 1985. *The Past is a Foreign Country.* Cambridge: Cambridge University Press.

MacArthur, R. H. and E. O. Wilson 1967. *The Theory of Island Biogeography.* Princeton, NJ: Princeton University Press.

McCarthy, M. 1999. "Wildlife sites to be made inviolate." *Independent,* June 21, 1999: 8.

McGlade, J. 1995. "Archaeology and the ecodynamics of human-modified landscapes." *Antiquity,* 69: 113–32.

Macinnes, L. and C. R. Wickham-Jones 1992. *All Natural Things: Archaeology and the Green Debate.* Oxbow Monograph 21. Oxford: Oxbow.

Macklin, M., S. B. Bradley, and C. O. Hunt 1985. "Early mining in Britain: the stratigraphic implications of metals in alluvial sediments." In N. G. R. Fieller, D. Gilbertson, and N. Ralph (eds.), *Palaeoenvironmental Investigations: Research Design, Methods and Data Analysis,* pp. 45–54. Oxford: British Archaeological Reports 258.

McNeely, J. A. and M. S. Keeton 1995. "The interaction between biological and cultural diversity." In B. von Droste, H. Plachter, and M. Rossler (eds.), *Cultural Landscapes of Universal Value,* pp. 25–38. Stuttgart: Fischer.

McManamon, F. P. 2000. "The protection of archaeological resources in the United States: reconciling preservation with contemporary society." In F. P. McManamon and A. Hutton (eds.), *Cultural Resource Management in Contemporary Society,* pp. 40–54. London: Routledge.

Mannion, A. M. 1991. *Global Environmental Change.* Harlow: Longman.

Martin, P. S. and R. G. Klein 1984. *Quaternary Extinctions.* Tucson: University of Arizona Press.

Meskell, L. 1995. "Goddesses, Gimbutas and New Age archaeology." *Antiquity,* 69: 74–86.

Mighall, T. M. and F. M. Chambers 1993. "The environmental impact of prehistoric mining at Copa Hill, Cymystwyth, Wales." *The Holocene,* 3 (3): 260–4.

Mitchell, F. 1986. *Reading the Irish Landscape.* Dublin: Country House.

Mitchell, F. 1990. *The Way That I Followed.* Dublin: Country House.

Mitchell, N. J. 1995. "Cultural landscapes in the US." In B. von Droste, H. Plachter, and M. Rossler (eds.), *Cultural Landscapes of Universal Value,* pp. 234–51. Stuttgart: Fischer Verlag.

Mooney, H. A. and P. R. Ehrlich 1997. "Ecosystem services: a fragmentary history." In G. C. Daily (ed.), *Nature's Services: Societal Dependence on Natural Ecosystems*, pp. 11–19. Washington, DC: Island Press.

MORI 2000. *Attitudes Towards the Heritage*. London: English Heritage.

Myers, N. 1997. "Biodiversity's genetic library." In G. C. Daily (ed.), *Nature's Services: Societal Dependence on Natural Ecosystems*, pp. 255–73. Washington, DC: Island Press.

O'Connell, M. 1994. *Connemara: Vegetation and Landuse Since the Last Ice Age*. Dublin: Office of Public Works.

O'Connor, T. P. 1991. "Science, evidential archaeology and the new scholasticism." *Scottish Archaeological Review*, 8: 1–7.

O'Donnell, P. M. 1995. "Cultural landscapes in North America: an overview of status in the United States of America." In B. von Droste, H. Plachter, and M. Rossler (eds.), *Cultural Landscapes of Universal Value*, pp. 210–33. Stuttgart: Fischer Verlag.

O'Hara, S. L., F. A. Street-Perrott, and T. P. Burt 1993. "Accelerated soil erosion around a Mexican highland lake caused by prehistoric agriculture." *Nature*, 362: 48–51.

Peglar, S. M. 1993. "The mid Holocene *Ulmus* decline at Diss Mere, Norfolk, UK: a year-by-year pollen stratigraphy from annual laminations." *The Holocene*, 3: 1–13.

Pitts, M. 1992. "Manifesto for a green archaeology." In L. Macinnes and C. R. Wickham-Jones (eds.), *All Natural Things: Archaeology and the Green Debate*, pp. 203–13. Oxford: Oxbow.

Preece, R. C. and D. R. Bridgland 1998. *Late Quaternary Environmental Change in Northwest Europe: Excavations at Holywell Coombe, Southeast England*. London: Chapman and Hall.

Prott, L. V. 1992. "A common heritage: the World Heritage Convention." In L. Macinnes and C. R. Wickham-Jones (eds.), *All Natural Things: Archaeology and the Green Debate*, pp. 65–88. Oxford: Oxbow.

Pryor, F. 1990. "The reluctant greening of archaeology." *Antiquity*, 64: 147–50.

Rackham, O. 1980. *Ancient Woodland*. London: Arnold.

Rackham, O. 1982. "The Avon Gorge and Leigh Woods." In M. Bell and S. Limbrey (eds.), *Archaeological Aspects of Woodland Ecology*, pp. 171–6. Oxford: British Archaeological Reports IS 146.

Raftery, B. 1996. *Trackway Excavations in the Mountdillon Bogs, Co Longford 1985–1991*. Dublin: Irish Archaeological Wetland Unit Transactions 3, Department of Archaeology, University College.

Rahtz, P. A. (ed.) 1974. *Rescue Archaeology*. Harmondsworth: Penguin Books.

Reichstein, J. 1984. "Federal Republic of Germany." In H. Cleere (ed.), *Archaeological Heritage Management in the Modern World*, pp. 37–47. London: Unwin Hyman.

Renfrew, C. 1978. "Trajectory, discontinuity and morphogenesis." *American Antiquity*, 43: 203–22.

Rio Summit on Environment and Development: http://www.igc.apc.org/habitat/agenda21/rio-dec.html

Rippon, S. 1996. *Gwent Levels: The Evolution of a Wetland Landscape*. York: Council for British Archaeology Research Report 105.

Roberts, N. 1998. *The Holocene*, 2nd edn. Oxford: Blackwell.

Robinson, M. A. 1985. "Nature conservation and environmental archaeology." In G. Lambrick (ed.), *Archaeology and Nature Conservation*, pp. 11–17. Oxford: Department for Continuing Education, Oxford University.

Schlichtherle, H. and M. Strobel 1999. *Archaeology and Protection of Nature in the Federsee Bog*. Stuttgart: Landesdenkmalamt Baden-Wurttemberg.

Shanks, M. and C. Tilley 1987. *Social Theory and Archaeology*. Cambridge: Polity Press.

Simmons, I. G. 1989. *Changing the Face of the Earth*. Oxford: Blackwell.

Simmons, I. G. 1993a. *Environmental History: A Concise Introduction*. Oxford: Blackwell.

Simmons, I. G. 1993b. *Interpreting Nature*. London: Routledge.

Solli, B. 2000. "Protection of the environment and the role of archaeology." In F. P. McManamon and A. Hatton (eds.), *Cultural Resource Management in Contemporary Society*, pp. 93–8. London: Routledge.

Spriggs, M. 1997. "Landscape catastrophe and landscape enhancement: are either or both true in the Pacific?" In P. V. Kirch and T. L. Hunt (eds.), *Historical Ecology in the Pacific Islands*, pp. 80–104. New Haven, CT: Yale University Press.

Stebbings, R. E. and I. J. Killeen 1998. "Translocation of habitat for the snail *Vertigo moulinsiana* in England." In I. J. Killeen, M. Seddon, and A. M. Holmes (eds.), *Molluscan Conservation: A Strategy For the 21st Century*, pp. 191–204. *Journal of Conchology Special Publication*, 2.

Thomas, J. 1990. "Silent running: the ills of environmental archaeology." *Scottish Archaeological Review*, 7: 2–7.

Thomas, W. H. (ed.) 1956. *Man's Role in Changing the Face of the Earth*. Chicago: University of Chicago Press.

Tilley, C. 1994. *A Phenomenology of Landscape*. Oxford: Berg.

Time Team 2000. "The Seahenge controversy." http://www.channel4.com/nextstep/timeteam

Trigger, B. G. 1989. *A History of Archaeological Thought*. Cambridge: Cambridge University Press.

Ucko, P. 1987. *Academic Freedom and Apartheid*. London: Duckworth.

Van Geel, B., J. Buurman, and H. T. Waterbolk 1996. "Archaeological and palaeoecological indications of an abrupt climate change in the Netherlands and evidence of climatological teleconnections around 2650 BP." *Journal of Quaternary Science*, 11 (6): 45.

von Droste, B., H. Plachter, and M. Rossler (eds.) 1995. *Cultural Landscapes of Universal Value*. Stuttgart: Fischer Verlag.

Whitehouse, N. J., M. H. Dinnin, and R. A. Lindsay 1998. "Conflicts between palaeoecology, archaeology and nature conservation: the Humberhead Peatlands SSSI." In M. Jones and I. D. Rotherham (eds.), *Landscapes: Perception, Recognition and Management: Reconciling the Impossible?*, pp. 70–8. Sheffield: Wildtrack Publishing.

World Heritage Sites (UNESCO): http://www.unesco.org/whc/welcome.html

Worster, D. 1990. "The ecology of order and chaos." *Environmental History Review*, 14: 1–18.

Wymer, J. J. 1962. "Excavations at the Maglemosian site at Thatcham, Berkshire, England." *Proceedings of the Prehistoric Society*, 28: 329–70.

Index

Owing to the immense range of references to people, places, and things or concepts in this volume, the index is confined to topics where some discussion occurs beyond mere citation.

Aarhus 521
Abbasid empire 131
aborigines, Australian 314, 317, 367, 475–6, 512, 523
Abu Duwari (Maschkan Shapir) 345–6
Abu Hureyra 299–300
accelerator mass spectrometry (AMS) 199, 218, 300
access analysis 104, 145
accuracy of information 460
Acheulean tradition 208, 365
acidification 515
Adams, R. M. 340, 345, 523
adaptation (culture as) 4, 10, 315–16
aerial photography 336, 338
African diaspora, African-American archaeology 277–80
Afro-Asiatic language family 58–9, 61
agency (human), agency theory 3, 9–11, 15, 21, 24–5, 34, 49, 77, 81, 98, 143, 145–6, 150–1, 159, 174ff., 186–7, 189–90, 199, 202, 265, 316, 323, 326, 358–9, 369, 477–8, 482, 495, 502
agrophilia, biophilia hypotheses 400
Aitchison, J. 367
Albarella, U. 305
Albigensian crusade 182, 184–5
Aldington, R. 314–15
Alexander the Great 257
Alexandria 155
al-Hamdani 340
Allan, S. 372

Allison, P. M. 115
Altertumswissenschaft 259, 264
amateur archaeology 427, 496
American Antiquity 443
Amerindian language family 55, 62–3, 68
Analytical Archaeology 3–5, 7, 17, 95
Anasazi sites 444
ancestor cult 115, 134, 148
ancient Greece 83, 187ff., 400ff.
ancient woodlands 520
Anderson, B. 146
Andes 352
Andrén, A. 262
Angkor 129–30, 136
animal butchery 293
Annales School 156, 174ff., 185, 189, 191–2, 198, 202
Anthropogeographie 313
anthropology *see* ethnography
antiquities market 372, 457, 461–2, 464–6
apartheid 489
Apollo 11 cave 364
Appadurai, A. 115, 479–81; *see also* social life of things
appropriate technology 156
Arabs 257
Arawakan language family 54
Archaeological Institute of America (AIA) 260, 267
archaeological record, formation of 79–80, 115, 293, 295, 300, 304, 335–6, 341, 351, 390, 460–1

The Archaeology of Communities 145ff., 150
archaeometry xviii, 381, 463
Archaic era (Greek) 188, 257
architecture and archaeology 84, 145
Arnold, B. 83
artificial intelligence (AI) 399–400
Arwill-Nordbladh, E. 85
Aryan 55
Ascher, R. 278
Ashmore, W. 274, 314, 325
Assiros 303
astroarchaeology 238
astronomy 219
Athens 257–8
attractors 187, 192
attributes, functional 8
Augustus 190
Australia 42, 62–3, 79, 202, 212, 215–16, 221, 314, 359, 364, 369, 466
Australopithecines 207, 294–5
Austronesian (Oceanic) language family 54–61, 64–6, 68
axes, prehistoric, also handaxes 161, 163, 208, 364–5
Ayodya 491
Aztecs *see* Nahuas/Aztecs

Baber, Z. 175
Baghdad 126–9, 131
Bagley, R. 372
Bahn, P. 253–4, 298, 514
Baillie, M. 199, 220, 512–13
Baines, J. 373
Baker, V. 279–81
band–tribe–chiefdom–state 240, 482
Bantu, language, people 57–8, 60, 62, 220
Barrett, J. C. 33, 158, 175, 177–8, 185
Barrow, J. 366, 400
Barth, F. 10–12
Bates, M. 321
battleship curves 4, 6
Bauplan 10, 13
Bayesian analysis 382, 385, 387
Bear Creek Shelter 448
Beazley, J. 260
beetles 519
Beijing 131, 136
Bell, S. 325
Bellwood, P. 57
Bender, B. 318–19, 325
Benin 359
Berbers 29, 60, 475
Bernal, M. 265
Bible (and archaeology), Biblical Archaeology 53

Bickerton, D. 366
Bijker, W. E. 158, 303
Binford, L. R. 4–5, 7, 94–6, 100, 264, 273, 296–7, 398, 445, 511
Bintliff, J. L. 198–9, 262–3, 340, 511, 515
biodiversity 514
Biqa valley 349
Black Athena 265
Black Death *see* plague
Blanton, R. 374
Blisset, M. 447
Bloch, M. 334
Blueprint for Survival 511
boar *see* pig
Boardman, J. 263, 304
Boas, F. 312
boats 161
Boeotia 176–7, 263, 400
Bonnichsen, R. 216
Bororo 122–3
Boulding, K. 446
Bourdieu, P., habitus theory of 10, 29, 146, 190, 249, 369–70, 475, 477, 479
Boyd, R. 8–10
Boyle, R. 500–1, 503
Bradford, J. 334, 336
Bradford University 404
Brain, C. K. 295–6
Brandt, R. 264
Braudel, F. 49, 115, 176, 186, 192, 238; *see also Annales* School
Brijder, H. 263
Britain, prehistoric 134, 334, 337
Briuer, F. L. 441–3
Bronze Age, the 82, 85, 160, 164, 219, 257, 259, 262–3, 301, 303
Brown, C. H. 64
Brown, F. 208
Brück, J. 32
Brunet, M. 207
Brunhes/Matuyama boundary 209
Buchanan, A. 168
Bull, G. 301
Bullen, A. and Bullen, R. 279–81
burial, archaeology of 83–4, 87, 144, 211
Butler, J. 27–8, 33
Butzer, K. 313, 321, 511
Byzantine empire 190, 257

c and n transforms 336, 351; *see also* Schiffer
C14 dating *see* radiocarbon dating
calibration of radiocarbon 384–5
Calvert, M. 159
Canada 459
Cann, R. 43, 45

Canuto, M. A. 145
Capetian dynasty 182–3
capitalism 99, 104–5, 182, 280–2, 398, 456, 477, 481, 494
carbon and nitrogen isotopes 218, 306
Carman, J. 422
Carneiro, R. 106
Carson, R. 509
Carver, M. 422
castles 93, 100ff.
Catal Huyuk 115, 523
catastrophe theory 187, 512
Cathar heresy 182, 184–5
cattle 44, 301ff., 304–5
Cavalli-Sforza, L. L. 40, 46–7, 65
Celtic art 363
censorship 467
center–periphery 483–4
ceramics 277, 280–1, 389, 391, 401ff.
cereals 44, 292–3, 300
Chalcatongo de Hidalgo 241
Chalcolithic Spain 189
Champion, T. 93
Ch'ang-an 129
Channel Tunnel 520
chaos theory *see* complexity theory
Chapman, J. 340
Chapman, R. 144
Charlemagne 258
Charter for the Protection and Management of the Archaeological Heritage 419
Chauvet cave 363
Childe, V. G. 4, 162, 164–5, 273, 311, 411
childhood 87
China 131, 133, 281, 316, 318
Chinese archaeology 274, 358, 372
Chinese cities 123, 125, 129, 131
Chinese metallurgy 165, 372
Chisholm, J. S. 9
Chisholm, M. 316
Christianity 190, 258
cinema and archaeology 409
city-state, archaeology and history of 176, 187–8, 265, 389, 401ff.
Civil Rights Movement 277
cladistics 17
Clark, G. 311–12, 508, 512
Clarke, D. L. 4–7, 9, 11–12, 14–15, 17, 95–6, 398, 404, 491–2, 494, 504
classical archaeology 253ff.
classical philology *see* classics
classics 253ff., 258–60, 264, 266–7
classification (artefact) 5–6, 9
Clifford, J. 483
climatic change 312, 385–9
Clottes, J. 362

The Cloud People 240
Clovis, culture, horizon 62
Clunas, C. 358
coastal archaeology 337–8, 351, 412
coastal resources 298–9, 304
Cockburn, C. 159
cognitive maps 244
coinage 161
Colca valley 352
collecting instinct 454
Collingwood, R. G. 95
colonialism 235–7, 239, 248, 259, 275, 282, 327, 466, 473, 485–6, 493–4
colonization of the New World 48, 216ff., 306
commercialization of archaeology 416, 455
community study 144ff., 188
complexity theory, chaos-complexity 15, 17, 74ff., 186ff., 190–1, 192
Conference on Historic Site Archaeology 276
Conkey, M. W. 75, 84, 96
connoisseurship 458
Constantine the Great 190, 257
Constantinople 131–2, 190
consumer choice studies 280
consumerism 281, 477
contingency 150, 185–6, 188, 190–2, 511
Conway-Morris, S. 186, 192
Coppack, G. 97
core–periphery theory 240, 495
corporate community 188
cosmology, cosmovision 123, 125, 242–4
Cosquer cave 362
Coulson, C. 106
Crawford, O. G. S. 334
critical self-consciousness 491–2, 494, 504
Critical Theory, Frankfurt School 23, 491–3
Croatia 491
Croce, B. 273–4
crop rotation 305
Crosby, C. A. 280
cult, archaeology of 149, 243–4, 335
cultural fundamentalism 484
cultural production, archaeology as 503
cultural resource management (CRM), cultural heritage 3, 79, 168, 237–8, 255, 394, 398–9, 409ff., 435ff., 455, 494–5
culturalism xxii, 388
culture (archaeological) 5, 9, 11, 53, 125, 142, 313, 358, 480
culture history (archaeology as) 4–5, 7–8, 11, 16, 262, 313, 371, 373, 492, 511

curator, keeper, in museum   458
Cycladic culture   371–2

Da-Du   123–4
Daic, language family   59
dairying   304, 306; *see also* secondary
    products revolution
Daniel, G.   53
Dar, S.   349
Dart, R.   294–5
Darwin, C.; neo-Darwinian synthesis;
    Darwinian archaeology   3, 7, 39–40, 54,
    65, 106, 120, 125, 134, 155, 157, 161–2,
    165, 187, 255, 315, 326, 365, 374, 400,
    473, 512
dating, archaeological   197ff., 206ff., 215,
    384ff.
David, N.   115
Davis, N. Z.   97
Davis, S.   305
Dawkins, R.   7–8
Dayaks   366
de Grummond, N.   256
decay trajectory, archaeological remains
    and   420
decolonization   239–40
deconstruction   361, 369
deep-sea cores   206, 210
Deetz, J.   274, 278–80
Deir el Medina   120
Deloria, V.   235–6
democracy   261
demography   13, 389, 402ff.
dendrochronology   200, 217, 219–20, 385–6,
    512, 519
Denmark   424, 517
deposit legibility   422
D'Errico, F.   367
Derrida, J.   369
Descartes, R.   24–5, 28
diachronism   144
Diamond, J.   57, 162
Diaz-Andreu, M.   78
diet   306; *see also* food and archaeology
diffusion (cultural)   4, 6, 9, 100, 484
Dilthey, W.   24
Dimbleby, G. W.   510–11
Diocletian   131, 191
direct historical approach   237
disciplinarity   498
disease   40, 45, 306; *see also* plague
dissipative structures   189–90
Djeitun   113
Dmanisi   209
DNA analysis   39, 41–8, 65, 206, 210, 212,
    305ff., 391ff.

dog   306
Dogon   123
Domesday Book   188
domestication of plants and animals, origin *see*
    farming
Donald, M.   366
Donaldson, J. W.   54
Dordogne   298
Dorfstaat model   187–8
Douglas, M.   14
Douglass, A. E.   385
dress codes   82, 84, 87, 105
Dudd, S. N.   306
Dunbar, R.   188
Durham, England   177–8
Durkheim, E.   98, 367, 369
d'Urville, D.   55
Dyson, S.   260–2

Easter Island   514–15
eclecticism   xviii
Eco, U.   369
ecological crisis   129, 150, 176, 322, 403
ecology; human ecology; ecology and
    archaeology   311ff., 404, 413, 510ff.; *see
    also* Green movement
ecosystem   511
edge of chaos   187, 189, 190
Edgerton, D.   160
education   79
Egypt, archaeology, history, and culture   53,
    315–16, 320, 322–3, 358
Eibl-Eibesfeldt, I.   366
electron spin resonance (ESR)   207
Elgin Marbles   467
Elichmann, J.   54
elm decline   512
Elvin, M.   132–3
embodied thinking   318, 479
emergence   190–1
Emesa (Homs)   349
empires   131, 133
employment, archaeological   417
Enghoff, I. B.   304
English Heritage   79, 415, 519, 523
Enlightenment, the   23–4, 31, 39, 100, 324,
    493, 495, 509
environment, physical *see* ecology
environmental determinism   383, 387–8
Environmental Impact Assessment   418, 424,
    510
environmental movement *see* Green
    movement
epistemology   435
erosion   515
Eskimo   294

Essentialism   75
ethnicity   47–8, 142, 261, 278–81
ethnography or anthropology and
    archaeology   3, 11, 16, 53, 77, 80, 84,
    93, 95, 102, 105, 115, 133–4, 143, 147,
    157, 159–60, 165, 192, 235ff., 259, 273,
    275, 277, 313, 359, 362, 369–70, 374,
    381–2, 413, 473ff., 491, 493–4, 498
Etruscan Places   314
eugenics   40–1
Europae Archaeologiae Consilium   427
European Association of Archaeologists   426
European global colonization   273, 275, 306
European Union, European Commission, and
    archaeology   417ff., 424, 427, 510
Europeanness   258–9, 265, 282, 374
événements; short-term history   176–7, 184
Event–Monument (EM) data structures   415
Evershed, R.   306
evolution *see* Darwin
evolutionary pyschology   366
exhibitions, museum   238, 455, 468, 485
exogamy, human   47–8
experimental archaeology   412
Experimental Earthwork Project   520
extinctions, faunal   514
extreme events, environmental   512

Fairbanks, C.   278
Fairclough, G.   104
fakes of antiquities   462
farming (origins of)   39–42, 44–5, 49, 55,
    57–9, 79, 106, 164, 198, 217ff., 220, 294,
    299ff., 300ff., 312–13
faunal and floral analysis   105, 206, 218,
    291ff., 334, 336
feminism   75–8, 80, 87, 93, 96–7, 159, 397,
    493
feudalism   104–5, 167, 179–81, 185, 188
field evaluations   425
field systems, ancient   148, 337ff., 341, 345,
    349–51
fieldwork, archaeological   397ff., 501
figured vase painting   260, 358
Fine Arts Museums of San Francisco   467
Finlay, R.   97
Finley, M.   167, 262
fire, origins of human use   210
Flannery, K.   313, 373, 404
Flenley, J.   514
Fleure, H. J.   311–12
flotation *see* sieving
food and archaeology   84, 87, 105
Forde, D.   311
Foster, L.   279–81
Foucault, M.   24, 27, 255

founder effect   10, 12, 48
Fox, Sir C.   311
Foxhall, L.   181
Framework Convention on Climate Change
    513
France   178ff.
Franciscan monasteries   120
Frank, A. G.   283
Frankfurt School *see* Critical Theory
Freud, S.   478
Friedman, J.   483
Fulani   115
Fuller, S.   399

Gadamer, H.-G.   22–5, 32, 34
Gamble, C.   162–3
game theory   14–15
Gardens of Eden model   516
garum   304
Gasche, H.   345
gazelle   299
Geddes, P.   312
Geertz, C.   313
Gell, A.   359, 368–9, 476, 478
gender   27, 75ff., 143, 156, 159
genetics (and archaeology)   39–51, 65–6,
    212
geoarchaeology   336, 339ff.
Geographical Information Systems (GIS)
    352
geography   491
Germany   259, 261
Gero, J. M.   79, 94, 96
Gerstenberger, J.   44
Giddens, A., structuration theory of   10, 21,
    94–5, 98, 99, 104–6, 143, 158, 174–5,
    177, 185, 189, 190, 369, 413
Gidney, L.   304–5
Gilchrist, R.   82–3, 97
Gilij, F. S.   54
Gilmour, J. C.   317
Ginzburg, C.   247
global colonization, human   45, 198, 208–9,
    211, 297
global warming   387, 513
globalization   63, 273, 282, 284, 325, 483–4,
    495
glottochronology   52, 55, 59
goat   300
Godwin, H.   510
Goldcliff   521
Gombrich, E.   316–17
Gomolava   301
Gordon, R. B.   168
Gould, S. J.   10, 134, 186, 192, 511
Grand Canyon   444

grave protection and repatriation 237; *see also* Native American **Graves** Protection and Repatriation Act
Graves, P. 305
Grays Thurrock 338
Greece 176, 187–9, 257, 259, 265, 358, 400ff., 454
Greek and Roman science 166ff.
Green, R. 56
Green movement 327, 413, 509ff.
Greenberg, J. 62
Greenham Common 521
Griaule, M. 123
Grimes Graves 301–4, 306
Groube, L. 423
Guam 118–19
Guilá Naquitz cave 300
Gwent Levels 521

habitation effect 515
habitus *see* Bourdieu, P.
Hallowell, I. 198
hallucinogens 246–8
Hamilton, W. 259
Hangchow 131
Harraway, D. 479
Harrington, J. C. 276
Harris, D. 313
Harvey, D. 398
Hausa, language 57
Hawkes, J. 178, 314, 397
Heer, O. 294
Hegel, G. W. F. 373
Heidegger, M. 23–7, 32, 135, 158
Hellenistic era 257, 260
Herculaneum 259
heritage industry, cultural heritage *see* cultural resource management
hermeneutics xxiii, 21–5, 34, 361–2, 413
Heslop, D. 305
heterarchy 104
Higgs, E. S. 298, 312, 404, 512
higher intelligence 399
Hillman, G. 300
Himyarite state 340, 350–1
historical archaeology, text-aided archaeology 272, 274–6, 372
History 273–4, 276
History of Technology 158
Hodder, I. 12, 22, 28–30, 32–4, 94, 164, 263, 265, 273, 475–6, 523
Hohlenstein-Stadel 359–60
Holmes, L. 281
Holocene sediments 519–21
Holt-Jensen, A. 312
Homo erectus 207, 209, 211, 215, 366

Homo habilis, rudolfensis, ergaster 207, 295
Hopewell Interaction Sphere 16
Hoskins, J. 480
Hoskins, W. G. 334, 412
Hosler, D. 166
house studies, household studies 110, 123, 141–3, 179, 265
Howieson's Poort industry 364
human ecology xxii
Human Genome Project 39, 41
human impact 511
human origins 40–3, 45, 198, 206–7
humanistic archaeology xxiii, 492, 509
humanistic geography 32
hunter-gatherer societies 83, 135, 159, 163, 208, 294, 297, 299, 367, 374, 387–8, 439, 445
Huntington, E. 313
Husserl, E. 23–5
hypothetico-deductive reasoning 29

Ice Man, the 34, 175
ice-cores 219–20, 385, 387
iconography, painting, art 240–8, 258–62, 264, 266, 357ff., 454, 457, 475–6; *see also* landscape painting
ideal type 256
identity 142, 145–7, 409, 477, 480, 483–4, 486, 494–5
illiteracy 459
imagined communities 146
imperialism 241, 259, 265–6, 275, 327, 494
incastellamento 181
indigenous peoples, archaeology of 235–7, 239, 241, 249, 275
individual, the active *see* agency
Indo-European languages, peoples 54, 56–8, 60–1, 68
inductive reasoning 29
industrial archaeology 167–9, 411
industrial model, in survey 445–6
Industrial Revolution 168, 275
information system (culture as) 6, 10
Ingold, T. 147, 157, 160, 198, 316, 479, 483
Institute of Field Archaeologists 426
Instituto Nacional de Antropologia e Historia (INAH) 238–9, 249
interdisciplinarity (and archaeology) 49
Intergovernmental Panel on Climate Change 513
International Labor Organization 236
intersubjectivity 239, 319
Iron Age, the 82–3, 148, 160, 164, 187, 257, 262–3
Iroquois 58
Isaac, G. 296

Isbell, W. 146
island biogeography 514
Italy 188, 190, 259
Iversen, J. 510

jaguar imagery 244–6
James, S. 253–4, 267
Jameson, M. 263
Jamestown 276
Janes, R. 458
Jardine, L. 97, 99
Jarman, M. 301
Jazira, the 347
Johnson, Dr. 27
Johnson, H. 22
Johnson, M. 253–5
Jones, C. 31
Jones, G. 303
Jones, Sir William 53–4
Journal of Material Culture 99
Justinian 257

Karg, S. 305
Karlsson, H. 32
Keane, W. 111
Kennedy, P. 133
Kidder 4
kinship studies 44, 48
Kirk, W. 321
Kirsten, E. 187
Kitchen, K. 219
Klasies River Mouth 297
Klein, R. 297
Knapp, B. 314, 317
knowledge 420, 455–6, 458–9, 467–8,
    484–6, 493ff., 497–9, 501, 503–4
Kohl, P. 410
Konigsberg, earls of 44
Korn, F. 475
Kossinna, G. 4, 311
Kreuz, A. 304
Krings, M. 43
Kristiansen, K. 351
Kroeber, 4
Kropotkin, Prince P. 318
Kuchler, S. 480
Kuhn, T. 261, 446–7
Kuiseb River villages 295–6

Ladurie, E. Le Roy 178ff., 188
Lake Mungo site 43
Lamarckism 125–6
landscape archaeology 147, 150, 313ff., 334,
    400ff., 412, 483
landscape architecture 325
landscape character areas 412–13

landscape painting 316ff., 324
Landschaftskunde 318, 321
language *see* linguistics; language games
language games xix
language, origins of 41, 210, 366ff.
Lapita tradition 221
Lascaux 359–60
late Antiquity 191, 257
Latham, R. G. 55
Latour, B. 158–9, 479, 500–3, 508
Launceston Castle 305
Law, J. 503
Lawrence, D. H. 314
laws of cultural process 398
Layton, R. 328, 370, 374
Le Play, P. 312
lead pollution 220, 221, 515–16
Leakey, L. 208
Lechtman, H. 166
Legge, A. 301–2, 306
legislation and archaeology 410
Leicester 305
Leonard, R. D. 162
Leone, M. 277, 280, 508
Lévi-Strauss, C. 122, 474–5, 484
Lewis-Williams, D. 363
Lewontin, R. 10
lexicostatistics 55, 62
Libby, W. F. 197
Lincoln, UK 304
Lindebjerg 303
linguistic turn, in theory 99, 474, 476
linguistics 9, 17, 28, 41, 48–9, 52ff.
Linienbandkeramik 16
Linnaeus, C. 207
Lipe, W. 421
lipid analysis 306, 391
literacy 272, 274–5
literary criticism 266, 492
lithic studies 136, 160, 163–4, 202, 209, 211,
    213–14, 221, 291, 295
loanwords 63–5
locational geography 334
loess 209
logical positivism *see* positivism
London 155
long-term history; *longue durée* 176–7, 179,
    187, 238, 323
longue durée, *see* long-term history
looting, of antiquities 464, 466
Lorrain, C. 316–17
Lowenthal, D. 465
Lydian Hoard, the 467
Lyman, R. L. 5
Lynott, M. 448
Lyotard, F. 23

Maastricht Treaty 417
Macedonia 257
Mach, E. 399–400
MacKenzie, M. 475
Magdalenian culture 84
Maitland, F. 273
maize 46, 218, 300, 445
Makapansgat 295–6
Malone, P. M. 168
Malta 181
Malta Convention 419
Malthusian cycles, agro-demographic 176–7,
    182, 184–5, 403
Management cycle, archaeological 416
management studies, and archaeology 503,
    508
man-the-hunter, model 75
manuring, agricultural 340, 347, 352, 403
Maori 485
maritime archaeology *see* coastal archaeology
Markov systems 5–6, 15
Maroons 368
Marquesas 476
marriage 98
Marx, K. 161, 478, 492
Marxism 21, 105, 135, 162–3, 404, 481, 492
Mary Rose, the 200
masculinist theory 76, 105
Mashantucket Pequot Reservation Museum
    249
material culture, active role of 77, 85–7, 99,
    111–12, 115, 133, 279, 476–7
Mathers, C. 441–3
Mauss, M. 477
Maya 146, 237, 370–1
McGimsey III, C. 410
McGlade, J. 187, 511
McNeill, W. 404
Medieval era, the 83, 167, 178ff., 188, 258,
    304
medium-term history; *moyenne durée* 176–7,
    181, 185, 187
megalithic monuments 144
meme theory 7–8
memory 177, 181, 184–5, 315, 340, 419,
    454–5, 468, 480
Méndez, M. G. 413
mentalités, history of 176, 323, 371
Merleau-Ponty, M. 317
Merryman, J. 466
Meskell, L. 32, 76, 509
Mesoamerican archaeology 235ff., 275, 374
Mesolithic 163–4, 299, 306
Mesopotamian plains 345–7, 351
metalworking 85, 160, 164–6, 169, 389–90
metaphor 478

Mexico 53, 165–6, 237ff., 250, 300
Miao-Yao, language family 60–1
micropredators *see* disease
middle-range theory xxii, 94, 321
migration (and archaeology) 4, 10, 39, 41,
    45–9, 52, 54, 57, 63, 79, 392
military technology 161
Millar, F. 190
Miller, D. 99, 477–8
Miller, N. 349
Minoans 220, 257
Mitchell, F. 510
Mithen, S. 367
Mithun, M. 58
Mitochondrial Eve 41, 43–6
Mixtec/Nuu Savi 238, 241
mode de vie, genre de vie 179, 181, 186–7,
    311
modern humans, origins of 79, 163, 210ff.,
    213–14
modern-world archaeology 168, 272ff.,
    282
modernism, modernization 272, 282
molecular clock 44–6, 305, 392
molluscan studies 518–19
Mongols 123, 127, 133
Montaillou 178ff., 185
Monte Alban 238–9, 243, 244–5, 247, 250
Monuments Protection Programme,
    England 422
Morgan, L. H. 161–2
Morkin, cemetery 84
Morphy, H. 475–6
Morris, C. 368
Morris, S. 265
Moser, S. 79
motorway developments 519
Mouseion 454
moyenne durée, see medium-term history
multi-regionalism model 43, 211–12, 213
multi-scalar approach 282–4
multivocality 523
Munn, N. 475
Munyimba, Ghana 121–2
Muscarella, O. 462
museums, museum studies 78, 238–9, 249,
    260, 371, 417, 454ff., 473, 485
mutation 15
mutualism 282–3
Mycenaean Greece 189
myth 236

nahualism 244–7
Nahuas/Aztecs 237
Nahuatl 241
Naipaul, V. S. 319–20

narratives   143, 157, 162, 239, 242, 373,
   496
nation-state   182, 184, 190, 493–5
National Geographic   443
nationalism   3–4, 9, 48, 53, 66, 238, 240, 259,
   265, 325, 397, 409, 455, 508
national monuments records *see* records,
   national archaeological
National Museum of the American
   Indian   249
National Register of Historic Places,
   US   437–8, 441, 444, 448
Native American Graves Protection and
   Repatriation Act (NAGPRA)   237, 467,
   489; *see also* repatriation movement
nature conservation   517ff., 525
nature–culture distinction   512
nature's services   510
Nazis   40, 53, 468, 496
Neanderthals   43, 163, 210–14, 297, 364,
   391
Near Eastern archaeology   334, 336, 339–41,
   352, 403
Neaverson, P.   168
negative–positive feedback systems   5
Neiman, F. D.   15–16
Neolithic   163–4, 213, 257, 265, 294, 301,
   303, 306
Netherlands, the   148, 423, 522
Nettle, D.   17
Nevett, L.   83
New Archaeology   xx, 3–5, 7, 10–11, 16, 21,
   29, 34, 53, 93–5, 102, 110, 126, 130,
   141–2, 151, 162, 169, 174, 187, 202, 240,
   262, 264, 266, 313, 335–6, 341, 362, 373,
   398, 404, 491–2, 511
new catastrophism   512
New Guinea   475, 481–2
New Mexico   444
new museology   456–8
Newbury   518–20
Newcastle-upon-Tyne   305
Nichols, J.   62
non-linearity   187, 191
Nora, P.   480
normal science   261
North and South American Indians   236–8,
   249, 435, 454, 467, 523
Norton, C. E.   260
Nunamiut Eskimo   445
Nuttgens, P.   314

Oakley, K.   163, 201
Oaxaca   235, 238ff., 243, 247, 250
Odum, E. P.   312
Oetzi, the Ice Man *see* Ice Man

off-site archaeology   334–5, 339, 347, 401–2,
   444–5
Ohalo   218
Ojibwa   198
Oldowan tradition   208
Olduvai Gorge   208–9, 295–7
Olivier, L.   409
Olmecs   244, 374
Olsen, B.   22
Olympia   260
One World Archaeology   507
Onians, J.   366
optimal foraging theory   7, 316
orbital tuning   201
Orientalism   258, 325
Ormrod, S.   159
Oseberg   85
Osteodontokeratic industry   295
Other, the   473, 493
Otto, J. S.   279–81
Out of Africa model   41, 43, 211
oxygen isotope stages   210

Paca, W.   277
palaeomagnetism   206, 209
Palaeolithic era   82, 160, 203
Palmer, M.   168
Pama-Nyungan, language family   63
Panaramittee   369
Papua   64, 359
PARIS principle   421
Paris School   263
Parker-Pearson, M.   82
Parkhill, J.   45
Parting Ways   279–80
Paterson, L.   182
Pawley, A.   56
Payne, S.   301
paysage   320
Peake, H.   312
Peirce, C. S.   368–9
Penwith   339
people without history   248, 276–8, 284,
   473
Pequot people   249
Perea, A.   169
performative politics   104–5
peripheral intelligence   400–1
The Personality of Britain   311
phenomenology   xxii, 3, 21, 23, 25, 31–3,
   250, 314, 317ff., 322, 334–5, 340, 413,
   512, 523
Pictet, A.   55
pig   301, 305
Piltdown Man   294
Pitt Rivers, A.   161

Pitts, M. 509
plague 45, 185
Planck, M. 399
plantation archaeology 277, 279
Pliny, the Younger 200
Plog, S. and Plog, F. 444
Po valley 257
politics, especially archaeology as, archaeology
and xviii, 7, 47, 75ff., 96, 142–3, 235ff.,
240, 244, 247, 263, 272ff., 279, 284, 313,
315, 362, 397, 409–10, 413, 415, 420–1,
427, 447, 457, 459, 468, 489ff., 522
pollution, metal 515–16; *see also* lead
pollution
Polynesian: language, peoples 66, 514–15
Pompeii 115, 200, 220, 259
positivism; logical positivism 23, 31, 53, 92,
94, 98, 236, 240, 324, 335, 341, 415, 448,
492
post-industrial model, in survey 445–6
post-industrialism, post-Fordism 325, 397
post-medieval archaeology 272ff.
Post-Medieval Ceramic Research Group
276–7
Post-Processual archaeology xx, 7, 76, 95,
99, 110, 141, 158, 164, 168–9, 174, 187,
192, 202, 242, 256, 263–6, 334, 341, 387,
398, 476, 492, 509, 512
postcolonialism 236, 239, 249, 456, 484,
495, 504
postmodernism xviii, xxiii, 76, 93–4, 106,
112, 146, 158, 186, 236, 239, 264, 266,
313ff., 324–5, 327, 369, 398, 404, 413,
456, 474, 483–4, 494, 509
postpositivism *see* postmodernism
poststructuralism *see* postmodernism
potassium–argon dating (K/Ar) 206
poverty, archaeology and 278ff., 281ff., 324,
466
PPG16 424
precision of information 460
predictive modeling, prediction 192, 440
prehistory 202, 253, 256, 259, 261–2,
264–5, 274, 276, 283, 358–9, 370, 402
Price, B. J. 240
Price, S. and Price, R. 368
primate studies 116ff., 136, 206–7
problème histoire 189–90
Processual archaeology *see* New Archaeology
progress, human 4, 39, 101, 157, 160,
389–90, 404, 509
Provence 182, 184
proxemics 118
Pryor, F. 522
public, archaeology and the 458ff.
pueblo, Pueblo culture 120, 445

punctuated-equilibrium theory 186ff.,
191–2; *see also* Gould, S. J.

Qasr Ibrim 306
queer theory 76
Quinlan, T. 327

race 41, 47, 280–1
Rackham, O. 520
Radcliffe-Brown, A. 475
radio, archaeology of 156
Radiocarbon 203
radiocarbon dating 94, 197, 199, 200–1,
203, 213–17, 219, 300, 384–5
radiometric dating techniques 198–9, 202
Rappaport, R. 313, 321
rates of change 199, 212, 388
Rathje, W. 142, 151
Ravensmose 516–17
Rawson, J. 372
READING principle 421
realism 362
records, national archaeological,
archaeological archives 414ff., 426
reflexivity 282, 284, 523
Rega, E. 84
regional research design 440, 446–7
regional studies 240, 311ff., 336, 440, 483
Reichel-Dolmatoff, G. 363
relativism xviii, 362, 485, 508, 523
religion *see* cult, archaeology of
Renaissance 258
Renfrew, C. 57, 65, 69, 95–6, 144, 187,
262–3, 384, 512
repatriation movement, of indigenous
antiquities and human remains 237,
463, 466–7, 496
rescue movement 420, 462, 508
research agendas 423
retrogressive analysis 337
Reynolds, T. S. 159
Richards, M. P. 306
Richerson, P. 8
Ricoeur, P. 24, 369
Rift Valley, Great 206–8
Rippon, S. 338
risk-buffering 513
Roberts, B. 323, 337
rock-art 314, 321, 363–4, 374
Rodwell, W. 338
Roland, L. 159
Roman Empire 155, 190–1, 258, 266, 304,
316, 361
Romantic Movement 258, 324–5
Rome, city of 131–2, 136–7, 190, 257
Rorty, R. 106

Rosen, S. 164
Rosenau, P. M. 324
Rosenberg, M. 10
Rossignal, J. 335
Royal Ontario Museum 485
Ruhlen, M. 57
Rushforth, S. 9
Ruskin, J. 325

Sahlins, M. 474, 482
Said, E. 258, 325
Salmond, A. 485
Samarra 129, 131
sampling 440
San, people 113
Sanders, W. T. 240
Sanskrit 53, 54
Sant Cassia, P. 181, 185
Santayana, G. 481
Santiago Apoala 242
Santorini/Thera 220
Sarich, V. 42, 45
satellite imagery 336, 352
Sauer, C. O. 321
Saussure, F. de 175, 368–9
Saxe, A. 144
Scandinavian school of landscape studies 336
scavenging model 297
Schaffer, S. 500
Schick, K. D. 161
Schiffer, M. 106, 156–7, 162, 168, 336, 351, 447
schlepp effect 297
Schöningen 210, 297
Schulting, R.
Schumacher, E. F. 156
science (archaeology as) xviii, xxii, 92, 130, 237, 239, 260–1, 263–4, 291, 313, 322, 324, 327, 335, 380ff., 398, 446–7, 463, 491, 496–9, 503, 509
science, critiques of 76–7, 237, 239, 325, 327, 383, 398, 446–8, 483, 500–2
scientific plurality 447
sea-level fluctuations 298–9
seahenge 523–4
seasonality 298–9
secondary products revolution 164, 301–2
sedentism 116, 133
self-constitution of material culture 478
self-organized criticality 15
Selkirk, A. 95
Selvaggio, M. M. 297
serpent imagery 244, 246–7
settlement archaeology 144–5, 147
sex, sexuality 75–7, 80–2, 86–7
sexual selection 13

Shackleton, N. 210
shamans 244, 247, 363
Shamsi-Addad, King 220
Shanks, M. 21, 284
Shapin, S. 500
Shapwick Heath 517
Sharer, R. J. 274
shell-middens 294
Sherratt, A. 164, 220
Sherratt, S. 220
shipwrecks 200, 219
Sicily 497–8
Sidlings Copse 520
sieving, flotation of archaeological deposits 293
sites, archaeological 438ff.
slavery, archaeology of 277–80
Smith, C. S. 462
Smith, G. 339
Smith, L. T. 239
Snodgrass, A. 253, 262–7, 400
social constructivism 75–7, 79–81, 85, 87–8, 146–7, 155, 158–9, 168–9, 315, 324, 328, 413, 446, 448, 458, 493, 495, 502
social evolutionism 157, 236, 240, 242, 373, 389, 473, 482
social life of things 479, 481
Society of American Archaeology 237
Society for Historical Archaeology 275
Society for Post-Medieval Archaeology 277
sociology 98, 174–5
Sofaer-Derevenski, J. 82
Sohar 342–3
Sontag, S. 22
sorghum 305
South, S. 276
South Africa 489
South Etruria Survey 312
South Shields 305
Southern Samaria survey 349
Soviet 53
Soviet Transcaucasia 410
spatial archaeology 110
Spector, J. 75, 97
Spencer, H. 161
Sperber, D. 12, 483
Stalsberg, A. 84
Star Carr 312
state, origins of 106, 240–2, 373
Stathern, M. 477, 481–2
Staudenmaier, J. 159–60
Steenstrup, J. 293
Stein, M. A. 342
Steinhardt, N. S. 123
Stellmoor 298
Steward, J. 312–13

Stolcke, V. 484
Stonehenge 178, 397, 412, 445, 489
Stoneking, M. 43
Stringer, C. 211
structuralism 11, 21, 361, 367, 369, 474–6
structuration theory *see* Giddens, A.
Sturdy, D. 298
style (artefact) 5, 8–9, 15, 17, 21, 371
Sullivan, A. 444–5
surface artefact survey, regional survey
    262–3, 312, 335–7, 341, 345, 349–50,
    400ff., 440, 445
sustainability, archaeological 421, 427
Swadesh, M. 55
Swiss lake villages 294
Switzerland 305
symbolism 12, 29, 86, 105, 142, 147, 198,
    213, 277, 314, 336, 358–9, 367, 373
systems theory 96, 143–4, 169, 262, 313,
    511

Tainter, J. 133
tanning 304
Tanret, M. 345
taphonomy *see* archaeological record
taphonomy of knowledge 460
Tate, G. 345
Taung 294
Taylor, C. 31, 337, 341
Taylor, T. 165
Taylor, W. 273–4
Tchalenko, G. 345
technology 155ff., 198, 389–90
Technology and Culture 157, 158, 159
teeth 298
television, archaeology and 409, 522–3
Tell es-Sweyhat 347–9
tells 340–1, 347
Teotihuacan 127
Teotihaucan Murals 467
Tepe Yahya project 344
territoriality, site catchment 144–5, 298, 312,
    340–1
Terry, J. 159
textuality 92, 99, 369, 398
Thatcher, M. 98, 387
Thebes, Greece 177, 312
thermodynamics 189, 420
thermoluminescence dating (TL) 215
Thespiae 401ff.
thick description 192, 400
Thomas, D. H. 445
Thomas, J. 303, 312
Thorne and Hatfield Moors 519
Three Age System 161
Thy project 351

Tilley, C. 22, 28, 32–3, 134, 284, 319, 335,
    340, 478, 512
timeless history 188
timescales 45, 48, 192, 197, 513; *see also*
    Annales School
Tiszapolgar-Basatanya, cemetery 82
Toth, N. 161
Toubert, P. 181
tourism 53, 238–9
Treherne, P. 33
Trigger, B. 259, 491, 512
Tringham, R. 143
Tuan, Y.-F. 318
Tucanoa people 363
Turner, B. 93–4
Twyford Down 519
Tylor, E. 161–2
Tylor, W. 273–4

Ubeidiya 209
Ucko, P. 328, 489, 508
Underwater archaeology *see* coastal
    archaeology
uniqueness of archaeological record 383,
    393–4, 485
United Kingdom 311, 410ff.
United Nations 236
United Nations Rio Conference 510, 513–14
Unites States, archaeology of 237, 276–7,
    435ff., 454ff., 523
university 259, 463, 492, 494
Upper Palaeolithic 203, 213–15, 298, 363,
    370
urbanism 110, 116, 126–7, 131ff., 136, 164,
    198, 283, 304, 373, 401ff.
urnfields 148–9

value, archaeological; archaeological
    evaluation 412, 421ff., 437, 441ff., 448,
    496, 498
van Boxhorn, M. 53, 63
van Damme, W. 366
van der Leeuw, S. 187
van der Veen 304
van Driem, G. 53, 60, 69
van Gogh 317, 319
van Reeland, A. 54
Vandkilde, H. 165
Vansina, J. 10
Vavilov, N. 40
Vernant, J.-P. 263
Vichy regime 409
Vidal de la Blache 311
Viking era 84–5
villa, Roman 393, 403
visibility research 78ff.

Vix, burial   83
volcanic ash–tephra chronology   207–8, 219–20
Voldtofte   303
Voltaire, F.   53, 59
Vroom, J.   403

Wadi Kubbaniya   299–300
Walbiri   475
Wallerstein, I.   240
Wang Cheng ideal   123–4
war, militarism   240, 243
Warsaae, J. J. A.   294
Waterbolk, H. T.   200–1
waterpower   160, 167
Weber, M.   256
Wells, L.   345
Werlen, B.   322
Wessex Archaeology   519
Western civilization, culture   256, 258, 262, 264, 267, 358–9, 373, 397–8, 448, 460, 465, 474, 476–7, 480, 482, 484–5, 495, 510
wetlands and wetland archaeology   338, 517, 519
Wheeler, Sir Mortimer   93, 95, 409
White, Hayden   157
White, Lynn, Jr.   167, 409
Whitley, D.   363
who owns the past   421, 457, 466, 496, 499
Wichmann, S.   64
Wilk, R.   142, 151
Williams, T.   155
Williamson, T.   337–9
Wilson, A.   42, 45

Wilson, E. O.   400
Wilson, F.   456
Winckelmann, J. J.   258–9, 357–8
Wittgenstein, L.   xviii, xix, xxiii, 361, 365, 369
Wolf, E.   248, 284, 474; *see also* people without history
women's movement *see* feminism
Wonderful Life   186
Woodland period   15–16
World Archaeological Congress   237, 490–1, 509
World Heritage Convention   418
World Heritage Sites   519
world systems theory   240
World Wide Web   455, 510
Worsaae, J. J. A.   294
Wotton, W.   54–5
Wounded Knee   235
writing, writing systems   164, 240, 242

Y chromosome   41, 47
Yaeger, J.   145–6
Yemen, archaeology of   340, 350
Yoffee, N.   373
Yolngu   476
York, UK   423
Ystad project   351

Zaachila   250
Zanker, P.   190, 373
Zapatista uprising   238
Zapotec/Beni Zaa   238, 241
zebras and their stripes   393
zones of survival and destruction   337ff.

CPSIA information can be obtained
at www.ICGtesting.com
Printed in the USA
LVHW050403290720
661630LV00015B/127